T0213896

Lecture Notes in Computer Science　　8909

Commenced Publication in 1973
Founding and Former Series Editors:
Gerhard Goos, Juris Hartmanis, and Jan van Leeuwen

More information about this series at http://www.springer.com/series/7410

Kyung-Hyune Rhee · Jeong Hyun Yi (Eds.)

Information Security Applications

15th International Workshop, WISA 2014
Jeju Island, Korea, August 25–27, 2014
Revised Selected Papers

 Springer

Editors
Kyung-Hyune Rhee
Pukyong National University
Busan
Korea, Republic of (South Korea)

Jeong Hyun Yi
School of Computer Science
  and Engineering
Soongsil University
Seoul
Korea, Republic of (South Korea)

ISSN 0302-9743   ISSN 1611-3349   (electronic)
Lecture Notes in Computer Science
ISBN 978-3-319-15086-4   ISBN 978-3-319-15087-1   (eBook)
DOI 10.1007/978-3-319-15087-1

Library of Congress Control Number: 2014960251

LNCS Sublibrary: SL4 – Security and Cryptology

Springer Cham Heidelberg New York Dordrecht London
© Springer International Publishing Switzerland 2015

Printed on acid-free paper

Springer International Publishing AG Switzerland is part of Springer Science+Business Media
(www.springer.com)

Preface

The 15th International Workshop on Information Security Applications (WISA 2014) was held at Ocean Suites Jeju Hotel, Jeju Island, Korea, during August 25–27, 2014. The workshop was hosted by Korea Institute of Information Security and Cryptology (KIISC) and sponsored by the Ministry of Science, ICT and Future Planning (MSIP). Also it was co-sponsored by Korea Internet and Security Agency (KISA), Electronics and Telecommunications Research Institute (ETRI), National Security Research Institute (NSRI), AhnLab, Korea Information Certificate Authority (KICA), REDBC, and UNET systems. The excellent arrangement was led by the WISA 2014 General Chair, Prof. Heekuck Oh and Organizing Chair, Prof. Jin Kwak.

This year WISA 2014 provided an open forum for exchanging and sharing of ongoing hot issues and results of research, development, and applications on information security areas. The Program Committee prepared a meaningful program including keynote speech from Prof. Gail-Joon Ahn of Arizona State University, USA, and an invited talk from Mr. Patrick Youn of Symantec, Korea. The workshop had roughly six tracks such as System Security (Track 1), Network Security (Track 2), Hardware Security (Track 3), Applied Cryptography including Cryptography (Track 4), Vulnerability Analysis (Track 5), and Critical Infrastructure Security and Policy (Track 6). We received 69 paper submissions from 10 countries, covering all areas of information security, more precisely, 20 submissions for Track 1, 15 submissions for Track 2, 6 submissions for Track 3, 16 submissions for Track 4, 4 submissions for Track 5, 8 submissions for Track 6. We would like to thank all authors who submitted papers. Each paper was reviewed by at least three reviewers. External reviewers as well as Program Committee members contributed to the reviewing process from their particular areas of expertise. The reviewing and active discussions were provided by a web-based system, EDAS. Through the system, we could check the amount of similarity between the submitted papers and the already published papers to prevent plagiarism and self-plagiarism.

Following the severe reviewing processes, 31 outstanding papers from 8 countries were accepted for publication in this volume of Information Security Applications. More precisely, they were 6 papers for Track 1, 5 papers for Track 2, 5 papers for Track 3, 6 papers for Track 4, 4 papers for Track 5, and 5 papers for Track 6.

Many people contributed to the success of WISA 2014. We would like to express our deepest appreciation to each of the WISA Organizing and Program Committee members as well as paper contributors. Without their dedication and professionalism, WISA 2014 could not be made.

August 2014

Kyung-Hyune Rhee
Jeong Hyun Yi

Organization

General Chair

Heekuck Oh   Hanyang University, Korea

Organizing Committee Chair

Jin Kwak   Soonchunhyang University, Korea

Organizing Committee

Hyo Beom Ahn	Kongju National University, Korea
Jongsung Kim	Kookmin University, Korea
Changhoon Lee	SeoulTech, Korea
Donghoon Lee	Korea University, Korea
Im-young Lee	Soonchunhyang University, Korea
Kyungho Lee	Korea University, Korea
Namje Park	Jeju National University, Korea
Changho Seo	Kongju National University, Korea
Jungtaek Seo	National Security Research Institute, Korea
Taeshik Shon	Ajou University, Korea
Kyungho Son	Korea Internet and Security Agency, Korea
Sangsoo Yeo	Mokwon University, Korea

Program Committee Co-chairs

Kyung-Hyune Rhee	Pukyong National University, Korea
Jeong Hyun Yi	Soongsil University, Korea

Program Committee

Gail-Joon Ahn	Arizona State University, USA
Man Ho Au	University of Wollongong, Australia
Padro Carles	Nanyang Technological University, Singapore
Sang Kil Cha	Carnegie Mellon University, USA
Seong-je Cho	Dankook University, Korea
Dooho Choi	ETRI, Korea
Hyoung-Kee Choi	Sungkyunkwan University, Korea
Byung-Gon Chun	Intel, USA
Dieter Gollmann	Technische Universität Hamburg-Harburg, Germany

Dong-Guk Han	Kookmin University, Korea
Jinguang Han	Nanjing University of Finance and Economics, China
Swee-Huay Heng	Multimedia University, Malaysia
Seokhie Hong	Korea University, Korea
Eul Gyu Im	Hanyang University, Korea
Seung-Hun Jin	ETRI, Korea
Namhi Kang	Duksung Women's University, Korea
Daeyoub Kim	University of Suwon, Korea
Ho Won Kim	Pusan National University, Korea
Huy Kang Kim	Korea University, Korea
Hyoungshick Kim	Sungkyunkwan University, Korea
Jeong Nyeo Kim	ETRI, Korea
Jong Kim	POSTECH, Korea
Seungjoo Kim	Korea University, Korea
Yongdae Kim	KAIST, Korea
Taekyoung Kwon	Yonsei University, Korea
Jin Wook Lee	Samsung Electronics, Korea
KyungHee Lee	Samsung Electronics, Korea
Mun-Kyu Lee	Inha University, Korea
Sangjin Lee	Korea University, Korea
Zhen Ling	Southeast University, China
John Chi Shing Lui	Chinese University of Hong Kong, Hong Kong
Di Ma	University of Michigan-Dearborn, USA
Yutaka Miyake	KDDI R&D Laboratories Inc., Japan
Kirill Morozov	Kyushu University, Japan
Collin Mulliner	Northeastern University, USA
Daehun Nyang	Inha University, Korea
Susan Pancho-Festin	University of the Philippines, Philippines
Raphael Phan	Multimedia University, Malaysia
Christina Poepper	Ruhr University Bochum, Germany
Junghwan Rhee	NEC Laboratories America, USA
Kouichi Sakurai	Kyushu University, Japan
Seungwon Shin	KAIST, Korea
Kiwook Sohn	The Attached Institute of ETRI, Korea
Tzong-Chen WU	National Taiwan University of Science and Technology, Taiwan
Chao Yang	Texas A&M University, USA
Chung-Huang Yang	National Kaohsiung Normal University, Taiwan
Yanjiang Yang	Institute for Infocomm Research, Singapore
Dae Hyun Yum	Myongji University, Korea
Xuehui Zhang	Oracle, USA
Yunlei Zhao	Fudan University, China

External Reviewers

Byungha Choi	Dankook University, Korea
Naixuan Guo	Southeast University, China
Woo Yeon Lee	Seoul National University, Korea
Minkyu Park	KonKuk University, Korea
Wun-She Yap	Universiti Tunku Abdul Rahman, Malaysia
Wei Chuen Yau	Multimedia University, Malaysia
Youngho Park	Pukyong National University, Korea
Chul Sur	Busan University of Foreign Studies, Korea

Contents

Applied Cryptography

Network Security

Cryptography

Hardware Security

Critical Infrastructure Security and Policy

Malware Detection

ADAM: Automated Detection and Attribution of Malicious Webpages

Ahmed E. Kosba[1], Aziz Mohaisen[2]([⊠]), Andrew West[2], Trevor Tonn[3], and Huy Kang Kim[4]

[1] University of Maryland at College Park, College Park, USA
[2] Verisign Labs, Reston, USA
amohaisen@verisign.com
[3] Amazon.com, Washington DC, USA
[4] Korea University, Seoul, South Korea

Abstract. Malicious webpages are a prevalent and severe threat in the Internet security landscape. This fact has motivated numerous static and dynamic techniques to alleviate such threat. Building on this existing literature, this work introduces the design and evaluation of ADAM, a system that uses machine-learning over network metadata derived from the sandboxed execution of webpage content. ADAM aims at detecting malicious webpages and identifying the type of vulnerability using simple set of features as well. Machine-trained models are not novel in this problem space. Instead, it is the dynamic network artifacts (and their subsequent feature representations) collected during rendering that are the greatest contribution of this work. Using a real-world operational dataset that includes different type of malice behavior, our results show that dynamic cheap network artifacts can be used effectively to detect most types of vulnerabilities achieving an accuracy reaching 96 %. The system was also able to identify the type of a detected vulnerability with high accuracy achieving an exact match in 91 % of the cases. We identify the main vulnerabilities that require improvement, and suggest directions to extend this work to practical contexts.

1 Introduction

The ever increasing online and web threats call for efficient malware analysis, detection, and classification algorithms. To this end, antivirus vendors and intelligence providers strived to develop analysis techniques that use dynamic, static, or hybrid—which use both—techniques for understanding web malware. While static techniques are computationally efficient, they often have the drawback of low accuracy, whereas dynamic techniques come at higher cost and provide higher accuracy. Certain functionalities, such as deep analysis of dynamic features, are more costly than gathering of indicators and labeling of individual pieces of malware. Systems that are costly utilizing dynamic features should be augmented with intelligent techniques for better scalability. Such techniques include machine learning-based components utilizing light-weight features, such

© Springer International Publishing Switzerland 2015
K.-H. Rhee and J.H. Yi (Eds.): WISA 2014, LNCS 8909, pp. 3–16, 2015.
DOI: 10.1007/978-3-319-15087-1_1

as network metadata, for finding the label and type of a given website without using the computationally heavy components. In addressing this problem, we introduce ADAM, an automated detection and attribution of malicious webpages that is inspired by the need for efficient techniques to complement dynamic web malware analysis.

The motivation of this work is twofold. First, iDetermine, a proprietary status quo system for detecting malicious webpages using dynamic analysis is a computationally expensive one. While iDetermine is the basis for our ground-truth and network metadata used for creating features for webpages, it also does a great quantity of other analysis to arrive at accurate labels (*e.g.*, packet inspection, system calls). We envision our efforts could integrate as a tiered classifier that enables greater scalability with minimal performance impact. Second, existing literature on webpage classification [7,17,18,23,24] provided promising accuracy. Because these approaches rely primarily on static features, we hypothesize that metadata from network dynamics might improve it as well.

There are multiple challenges that ADAM tries to address. First, webpages face different types of vulnerabilities: exploit kits, defacement, malicious redirections, code injections, and server-side backdoors – all with different signatures. This malice may not even be the fault of a webpage owner (*e.g.*, advertisement networks). Moreover, the distribution of behavior is highly imbalanced, with our dataset having $40\times$ more benign objects than malicious ones. Despite these challenges, our approach is currently broadly capable of 96 % accuracy, with injection attacks and server-side backdoors being identified as areas for performance improvement and future attention. The system is also capable of identifying the types of detected vulnerabilities with exact match in 91 % of the cases, with a difference of 1 and 2 labels in 6 % and 3 % of the cases respectively.

Contribution. The contributions of this paper are: (1) Presenting a system that identifies whether a webapge is malicious or not based on simple dynamic network artifacts collected in sandboxed environments, in addition to (2) Evaluating the system using a real dataset that contains multiple variants of malicious activity.

Organization. The rest of this paper is organized as follows: Sect. 2 discusses the background and related work. Section 3 presents some details on iDetermine system, which generates the data we use in ADAM and the ground truth, while Sect. 4 presents the architecture of the ADAM system. Section 5 presents the evaluation of ADAM and discusses the results, and finally Sect. 6 presents the conclusions and sheds some light on future work.

2   Related Work

There has been a large body of work in the literature on the problem at hand, although differing from our work in various aspects, including features richness, quality of labels, and their context. Most closely related to our work are the works in [7,17,18,23,24], although differing in using static analysis-related features in reaching conclusions on a webpage. On the other hand, ADAM relies on utilizing simple features extracted from the dynamic execution of a webpage and loading its contents in a sandboxed environment, with the goal of incorporating that as a tiered classifier in iDetermine.

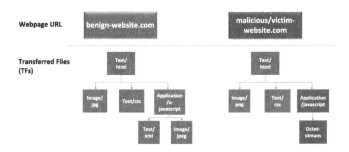

Fig. 1. Two examples of transferred file trees

Related to our work, but using structural properties of URLs in order to predict malice are the works in [10,17,25] for email spam, and in [6,19] for phishing detection. Additionally, using domain registration information and behavior for malware domain classification was explored in [14,17]. Related to that is the work on using machine learning techniques to infer domains behavior based on DNS traces. Bilge et al. proposed Exposure [5], a system to detect malware domains based on DNS query patterns on a local recursive server. Antonakakis et al. [2] functions similarly but analyzes global DNS resolution patterns and subsequently creates a reputation system for DNS atop this logic [1]. Gu et al. [11–13] studied several botnet detection systems utilizing the same tools of DNS monitoring. Dynamic malware analysis and sandboxed execution of malware were heavily studied in the literature, including surveys in [8,9]. Bailey et al. [3] and Bayer et al. [4] have focused on behavior-based event counts. Feature development has since advanced such that malware families can now be reliably identified [16] and dynamic analysis can be deployed on end hosts [15]. Finally, network signature generation for malicious webpages is explored in [21,22] for drive-by-download detection.

3   iDetermine

iDetermine is a system for classification of webpage URLs. It crawls websites using an orchestrated and virtualized web browser. For each analyzed URL, the system maintains records of each HTTP request-response made while rendering that page. The system applies static and dynamic analysis techniques to inspect each object retrieved while visiting the URL, and monitors any changes that happen to the underlying system to decide whether the retrieved object is malicious or not. We call these objects transferred files (TFs). If any of the retrieved objects was found malicious, iDetermine labels the object based on the type of malice uncovered. The system may label a malicious TF with one or more of the following:

Injection. Occurs when a website is compromised, allowing an attacker to add arbitrary HTML and javascript to the legitimate content of the site with the purpose of invisibly referencing malicious content aimed at silently harming visitors.
Exploit. Implies that an exploit code for a vulnerability in the browser or browser helper was found. Exploit code are the heart of drive-by downloads.
Exploit Kit. A collection of exploits bundled together and usually sold in black market. These kits increase the probability that the browsers of the visiting users are successfully exploited.
Obfuscation. A TF contains obfuscated code with known malicious activity behavior.
Defacement. Occurs when an attacker hacks into a website and replaces some content indicating that the site has been hacked into.
Redirection. A TF redirects to a known malicious content.
Malicious executable or archive. This means that either an executable or an archive file, e.g. zip, rar, jar, that contains malicious code of some sort was detected to be downloaded by visiting the webpage.
Server side backdoor. A TF shows symptoms of being a known server-side backdoor script, like the C99 PHP Shell. Such files allow remote attackers to control various aspects of the server.

The processing of the data of each URL by iDetermine results in a tree-like structure (see Fig. 1) where each node represents a TF. Each node stores basic file attributes and network information (*e.g.*, HTTP response code, IP address, and Autonomous System (AS) number). These nodes also contain classification data from iDetermine's deep analysis and we use this as ground-truth in training/evaluating our approach.

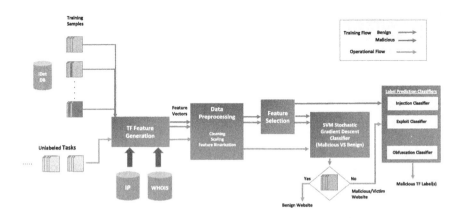

Fig. 2. The workflow for classifying URLs based on TFs

4 ADAM: System Structure and Overview

Design goals. There are two basic end goals for the proposed system. The main goal is to identify whether a webpage is malicious or not based on the basic metadata maintained by iDetermine, without the requirement to compute any complex and expensive features. If the webpage is classified as malicious, the system also aims at identifying which type of malice this webpage has.

Design. The layout of the system is outlined in Fig. 2. The figure shows the flow of both the training data and the operational data. The system is trained by labeled webpages, in which each individual TF is labeled whether it is benign (green), or malicious (red). The system uses the basic meta-data stored in the system, in addition to a set of simple features generated based on those attributes. This generation is handled by the feature generation module which uses IP and WHOIS databases to acquire information about the IP address and the domain name of the associated TF. After the feature generation stage, the data is preprocessed, and some features may be filtered using a feature selection module, before the data is sent to the classification modules. Then, a two-stage classification procedure is trained based on the preprocessed data.

In the operational mode, for an unlabeled webpage, the system transforms each TF into a feature vector as done by the feature generation module in the training phase, and then the features are pre-processed and filtered based on the feature selection results from the training phase. The TF is then labeled with the label most close to it in the vector space based on a highly accurate ground truth. To this end, in the following two subsections, we provide more details on the generated features, the preprocessing stage, and then we discuss the classification procedure needed to achieve the above two goals.

4.1 Features Used for Classification

To achieve the design goals, ADAM relies on a rich set of features, and uses nearly 40 basic features for the classification process. The features fall in the following categories:

- BASIC META-DATA FEATURES: This represents the simple meta-data attributes stored originally by iDetermine, such as the HTTP header information, which includes HTTP method, response code, Is Zipped, .. etc. The meta-data also includes the AS number, and the result of running the libmagic command on the TF file which gives information about the type of the retrieved file.
- URI-BASED FEATURES: These are the features derived from the URI associated with a TF. This includes some basic lexical statistics, e.g. URI components lengths (hostname, path and query), dot count, slash count, special characters ratio and the average path segment length. This also includes binary features to indicate whether the URI contains an explicit IP, or an explicit port number. Furthermore, the features include the top-level domain name in addition to the token words that appear in the different URI components for which we use a bag-of-words representation.

– TF Tree-based features: These are the features we extract from the TF-tree to capture the relationship between different TFs that belong to a single webpage. The TF-tree features capture Parent-child host/IP diversity; TF depth; number of children and the child-parent type relationship.
– Domain Name-based features: These features are derived from the domain name of the URI of the TF. This includes: the registrar's id and age information, e.g. creation data and expiration date.
– IP-based features: These are a set of features derived from the IP address associated with the TF. This includes the Geo-Location features: country, city and region, in addition to the domain/organization for which the IP is registered. Furthermore, we consider two IP prefixes (/24 and /28) as features to detect networks with malicious activity, instead of considering each IP individually.

It should be noted that the iDetermine system does process and store additional data that could be useful in the classification task. For example, payload and content-based features derived from Javascript as in [7,24], or flow information features as in [24] can be extracted and utilized. However, we do not integrate these features in order to maintain a content-agnostic and scalable classifier.

4.2 Preprocessing and Feature Selection

After the feature values for each category are inferred, a preprocessing stage is needed before forwarding this data to the classifiers for training and testing purposes. The preprocessing is done based on the feature type. For numeric features, such as the lexical counts, proper scaling is applied to keep the values between 0 and 1. For categorical features such as the top-level domain name or AS number, we apply feature binarization, in which a binary feature is introduced per each possible value, since the feature cannot be encoded numerically due to the absence of order between the values. This approach has been employed before, such as in [17]. This certainly will result in high-dimensional feature vectors that require a scalable classifier suitable for high dimensionality vectors.

Due to the high dimensional feature vectors, it could be beneficial to reduce the dimensionality through a feature selection technique. Therefore, in our experiments, we study the effect of reducing the dimensionality through a chi-square metric.

4.3 Classification

After preprocessing the data, we train a two-stage classification model to detect whether a webpage is malicious, and to identify the type of malice if needed.

The first classification stage includes a binary classifier that is trained with all the TFs from benign and malicious samples. We use an SVM classification algorithm based on Stochastic Gradient Descent using L1-norm for this stage. In the second stage, we build another binary classifier for each type of vulnerability.

Each classifier in the second stage is trained using the malicious TF data only, e.g. the injection classifier is trained by the data containing (injection TFs versus No injection but malicious TFs).

The reason we employ this two-stage model is due to the limitations of other possible approaches. For example, a multi-class classifier will not capture the observation that some TFs are labeled with more than one label. Additionally, we found that using multiple binary classifiers directly in a single stage, where each classifier is trained for only one type of attack—versus all the other benign and remaining malicious TFs—will lead to lower accuracy and a higher training time. The low accuracy in this case is due to the higher possibility of false positives because of using multiple classifiers at once. Therefore, we propose this two-stage model to filter out the malicious TFs first using a global classifier, then identify the type of malice separately.

In the operational phase, whenever a webpage is analyzed during operation, the data of each TF retrieved while visiting the URL are used to predict whether it is malicious or not. A URL is labeled as benign if all of its retrieved TFs were classified as benign by the classification algorithm. Then, the type of malice is identified through the second stage if the TF was labeled as malicious.

5 Evaluation

We present the evaluation and analysis of the proposed system. We give an overview and description of the dataset with the evaluation procedure and metrics. Then, we introduce the performance of the binary classification mechanism and malice label prediction, followed by the effect of feature selection on the system accuracy.

5.1 Dataset Description and Statistics

The dataset we consider for evaluation consists of 20k webpages, 10k each of "malicious" and "benign" types. These URLs were randomly selected from iDetermine's operational history of Internet-scale crawling. As mentioned earlier, iDetermine labels the webpages using sophisticated static and dynamic analysis techniques, and hence we consider such labels as our ground truth labels. Analyzing the URLs of the dataset yields 800k benign TFs and 20k malicious TFs. Each webpage contains about 40 TFs on average. A histogram of the number of TFs per webpage is provided in Fig. 3. For the malicious webpages, a histogram of the percentage of the number of malicious TFs per each malicious webpage is shown in Fig. 4. The figure shows that for most malicious webpages, less than 10 % of the retrieved TFs are malicious. This confirms the intuition we have for building the classifiers based on individual TFs.

The iDetermine system labels each malicious TF according to any type of malice it uncovered. Note that a malicious TF may be labeled with more than one label at the same time. That is a reason a classifier was built for each malice type in the label prediction module. The distribution of vulnerabilities among the malicious TFs can be illustrated in detail through Fig. 5.

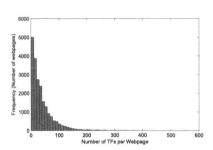

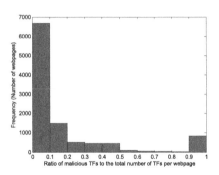

Fig. 3. A histogram of TFs per web-page

Fig. 4. Malicious TFs per malicious webpages

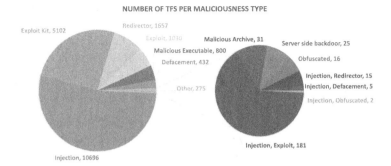

Fig. 5. Distribution of malice among the TFs

5.2   Evaluation Procedure and Metrics

A prototype of the system was built using Python 2.7, and Scitkit-learn [20] was used for data processing and classification. The evaluation of the system was conducted using 10-fold cross-validation, in which the webpages dataset were divided into 10 distinct partitions, nine of which are used for the training stage while the remaining partition is used as the testing data. For consistency, the dataset was partitioned randomly in a way that guarantees that the distribution of number of TFs per webpage (shown before in Fig. 3) is roughly maintained, so that the total number of TFs per partition is almost the same, since the TFs are the main classification data units the system works on.

The performance metrics will be provided at both the TF and the webpage granularity, with more focus on the latter since this is the end system goal. Recall that a webpage is labeled as malicious **if any** of its TFs was labeled by the classifier as malicious. The metrics considered for the evaluation are mainly the false positives rate, which describes the ratio of the benign objects that were labeled as malicious, and the false negatives rate which describes the ratio of the malicious objects that were labeled as benign. We also measure the effectiveness of the detection system through the F1-score, which is calculated based on the harmonic mean of precision and recall. Precision refers to the fraction of the objects that the system labeled as malicious that turned out to be truly malicious, while recall is the ratio of the truly malicious objects that the system was able to label malicious.

5.3   Binary Classification Performance

We start by describing the results of the first classification stage, which aims to identify whether a webpage is malicious or benign, only. Table 1 enumerates the performance metrics at both TF and webpage granularity, showing an overall result of 7.6 % FN rate and 6.3 % FP rate for the webpage results. The reason for having a 14.7 % FN rate on the TF-level is that simple metadata may not be indicative for all types of TF malice behavior. Additionally, compared to previous literature, the TF results are consistent with respect to the fact that our TF records dataset is highly imbalanced. Literature studies showed that as the data gets highly imbalanced, the accuracy degrades, e.g. 25 % FN rate at a ratio of 100:1 of benign to malicious URLs [18].

To better understand how well the detection mechanism performed, Fig. 7 shows the detection rate per each vulnerability/attack type at the TF-level, which describes the ratio of the TFs labeled as malicious successfully. Note that the "injection" and "server side backdoor cases" were most detrimental to overall performance. This is made clear in Table 2 which provides overall performance without those problematic instances, resulting in 2.5 % FP rate and 4.8 % FN rate overall.

Table 1. Binary classification results

	Prec.	Recall	F-score	FP	FN
TF-level	0.390	0.852	0.530	0.0314	0.147
page-level	**0.935**	**0.924**	**0.930**	**0.063**	**0.076**

Table 2. Binary classification w/o "injection"

	Prec.	Recall	F-score	FP	FN
TF-level	0.527	0.873	0.657	0.0153	0.126
page-level	**0.948**	**0.951**	**0.949**	**0.0257**	**0.048**

5.4   Label Prediction Performance

After a TF is labeled as malicious by the system, the system labels it according to the type of attack/malice it carries by the label prediction module described earlier in Sect. 4. In this section, the results of this module are presented. The main metric we used for the evaluation of the label prediction is the number of different labels between the ground truth and the predicted ones. As an example for illustration, if the ground truth is {Injection}, and the system labeled the malicious TF as {Injection, Exploit}, then this is considered a difference of one. If the predicted label was only {Exploit}, this is considered a difference of two, since two changes are necessary to make the prediction correct. Figure 6 illustrates the CDF of the label difference metric. As the figure clearly shows, the median of the difference in label predictions is zero. In fact in more than 90 % of the cases,

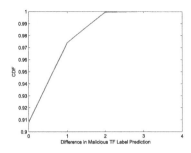

Fig. 6. The CDF of the difference in malice label predictions

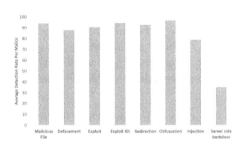

Fig. 7. Detection rate per TF vulnerability type for various malice types

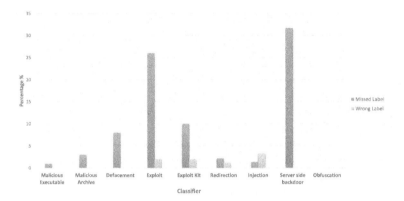

Fig. 8. Performance of individual label prediction classifiers

there was no difference between the predicted labels and the ground truth, and in only about 3 % of the cases there was a difference of two labels.

Furthermore, to evaluate the capability of each individual label prediction classifier. Figure 8 shows the performance of each classifier, by providing two quantities: the rate of miss-label, which indicates the ratio of the cases where a classifier was not able to detect a TF that has the type of attack it's concerned with, and the rate of wrong-label which is the ratio of the cases where the classifier gave a positive detection, while the TF does not include such type of malice. As the figure indicates, with respect to the miss-label rate, the server side backdoor classifier had the highest miss-label rate, which could be directly due to the few samples of server side backdoors that the dataset has (recall Fig. 5). Then, it can be observed the both the exploit and exploit kit classifiers have high miss-label rates as well, which suggests that new exploit attacks that the system did not specifically learn about may not be directly easy for the system to infer. With respect to the wrong-label rate, one interesting observation is that the injection classifier had the highest wrong-label rate. This could be because most of the malicious TFs in the dataset are Injection attacks (recall Fig. 5),

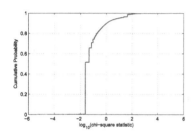

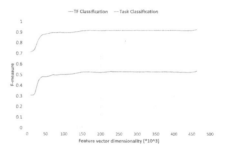

Fig. 9. The CDF of the feature scores. Note the vertical jump in the curve, indicating that half of the features are equally important.

Fig. 10. The effect of the number of features on detection accuracy. The detection accuracy gets stable after using only 50 % of the features.

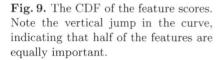

Table 3. Distribution of generated features

Feature category	Number of features
Meta-data based	18850
URL-based	378740
TF tree-based	157
Domain name-based	419
IP-based	65153

which could have resulted tendency towards labeling malicious TFs as injection due to the imbalanced training dataset.

5.5 Feature Selection Results

Due to the number of categorical features we have, high dimensional vectors result due to feature binarization. This can have a negative effect on the scalability of the system. Additionally, not all features after expansion/binarization can be directly useful in identifying whether a webpage is malicious or not. In this subsection, we provide some observations on feature selection results.

With respect to the chi-square score calculated for each feature by the feature selection module, it can be observed that the feature scores considerably vary, ranging from 10^{-5} to 10^5. To illustrate the distribution of the feature scores, Fig. 9 provides the CDF of the logarithm of all feature scores over the dataset. The main observation in this figure is that roughly the lowest 50 % of the features have the same score (Note the vertical jump after -2). This may suggest that half of the features may not be very important for the classification. This can be confirmed next by studying the effect of the number of features used for classification on the detection accuracy of the system. From another perspective, Fig. 10 illustrates the effect of the number of used features on the F1-score.

The features are selected based on their scores; when n is the number of features used, the top n features according to the scoring criteria are used. The figures shows the performance increases rapidly till it reaches some point, beyond which the F-score almost gets stable. This is consistent with the score CDF figure provided before.

It is also interesting to identify how important each feature category is. Since many of the features we use are categorical (and hence binarized), it may not be very helpful to solely identify the best feature or group of features, because this would be very specific to the dataset, and may be affected by the distribution of the malice types in the dataset. It could be more useful to see the histogram of the feature scores among the different feature categories that we employ in our classification process. Figure 11 illustrates the histogram of the logarithm of the feature scores among each feature category, while Table 3 shows the number of features generated per each feature category. As shown in the figure, each category has a percentage of its features with feature scores more than -2 (i.e. falling in the top 50 % features), providing a motivation for employing all these features for the classification process.

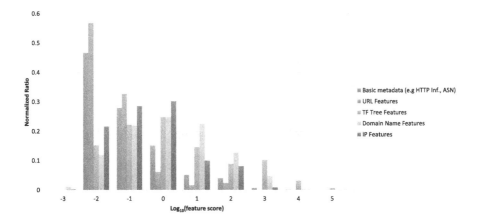

Fig. 11. Histograms of feature scores among feature categories

6   Conclusion and Future Work

This paper presented ADAM a system that uses machine learning over simple network artifacts that are inferred during dynamic webpage execution. ADAM's goal is to detect whether a webpage is malicious or not, and to identify the type of malice if the webpage was found malicious. Under cross-validation and a dataset that spans different types of attack behavior, the system was able to detect malicious webpages with an accuracy of 93 % identifying injection and derver-side backdoor vulnerabilities as the main areas requiring detection improvement. Excluding injection samples from the dataset has resulted in an accuracy reaching 96 %. Additionally, the malice labeling module was able to detect the label(s) of malicious TFs exactly in about 91 % of the cases, with a difference of one and two labels in 6 % and 3 % of the cases respectively.

Several directions can be explored to extend this work. Since many of the features have a dynamic nature over time, e.g., IP addresses, an adaptive mechanism will be needed to capture such dynamic changes. Furthermore, more studies could be done to enhance the accuracy of the model presented in this paper in order to better detect injection and server side backdoor attacks, in addition to identify exploit attacks.

References

1. Antonakakis, M., Perdisci, R., Dagon, D., Lee, W., Feamster, N.: Building a dynamic reputation system for DNS. In: USENIX Security (2010)
2. Antonakakis, M., Perdisci, R., Lee, W., Vasiloglou II, N., Dagon, D.: Detecting malware domains at the upper DNS hierarchy. In: USENIX Security Symposium (2011)
3. Bailey, M., Oberheide, J., Andersen, J., Mao, Z.M., Jahanian, F., Nazario, J.: Automated classification and analysis of internet malware. In: Kruegel, C., Lippmann, R., Clark, A. (eds.) RAID 2007. LNCS, vol. 4637, pp. 178–197. Springer, Heidelberg (2007)
4. Bayer, U., Comparetti, P.M., Hlauschek, C., Krügel, C., Kirda, E.: Scalable, behavior-based malware clustering. In: NDSS (2009)
5. Bilge, L., Kirda, E., Kruegel, C., Balduzzi, M.: EXPOSURE: finding malicious domains using passive DNS analysis. In: NDSS (2011)
6. Blum, A., Wardman, B., Solorio, T., Warner, G.: Lexical feature based phishing URL detection using online learning. In: AISec (2010)
7. Canali, D., Cova, M., Vigna, G., Kruegel, C.: Prophiler: a fast filter for the large-scale detection of malicious web pages. In: Proceedings of the World Wide Web (WWW) (2011)
8. Chang, J., Venkatasubramanian, K.K., West, A.G., Lee, I.: Analyzing and defending against web-based malware. ACM Comput. Surv. **45**(4), 49 (2013)
9. Egele, M., Scholte, T., Kirda, E., Kruegel, C.: A survey on automated dynamic malware-analysis techniques and tools. ACM Comput. Surv. **44**(2), 296–296 (2008)
10. Felegyhazi, M., Kreibich, C., Paxson, V.: On the potential of proactive domain blacklisting. In: LEET (2010)
11. Gu, G., Perdisci, R., Zhang, J., Lee, W.: BotMiner: clustering analysis of network traffic for protocol and structure independent botnet detection. In: USENIX Security (2008)
12. Gu, G., Porris, P., Yegneswaran, V., Fong, M., Lee, W.: Bothunter: detecting malware infection through IDS-driven dialog correlation. In: USENIX Security (2007)
13. Gu, G., Zhang, J., Lee, W.: BotSniffer: detecting botnet command and control channels in network traffic. In: NDSS (2008)
14. Hao, S., Thomas, M., Paxson, V., Feamster, N., Kreibich, C., Grier, C., Hollenbeck, S.: Understanding the domain registration behavior of spammers. In: IMC (2013)
15. Kolbitsch, C., Comparetti, P.M., Kruegel, C., Kirda, E., Zhou, X., Wang, X.: Effective and efficient malware detection at the end host. In: USENIX Security Symposium (2009)

16. Kong. D., Yan, G.: Discriminant malware distance learning on structural information for automated malware classification. In: KDD (2013)
17. Ma, J., Saul, L.K., Savage, S., Voelker, G.M.: Beyond blacklists: learning to detect malicious web sites from suspicious URLs. In: KDD (2009)
18. Ma, J., Saul, J.L.K., Savage, S., Voelker, G.M.: Learning to detect malicious URLs. ACM Trans. Intell. Syst. Technol. 2(3), 30:1–30:24 (2011)
19. McGrath, D.K, Gupta, M.: Behind phishing: an examination of phisher modi operandi. In: LEET (2008)
20. Pedregosa, F., Varoquaux, G., Gramfort, A., Michel, V., Thirion, B., Grisel, O., Blondel, M., Prettenhofer, P., Weiss, R., Dubourg, V., et al.: Scikit-learn: machine learning in python. J. Mach. Learn. Res. 12, 2825–2830 (2011)
21. Provos, N., Mavrommatis, P., Rajab, M.A., Monrose, F.: All your iFRAMEs point to us. In: USENIX Security (2008)
22. Provos, N., McNamee, D., Mavrommatis, P., Wang, K., Modadugu, N., et al.: The ghost in the browser analysis of web-based malware. In: HotBots (2007)
23. Thomas, K., Grier, C., Ma, J., Paxson, V., Song, D.: Design and evaluation of a real-time url spam filtering service. In: IEEE Security and Privacy (2011)
24. Xu, L., Zhan, Z., Xu, S., Ye, K.: Cross-layer detection of malicious websites. In CODASPY (2013)
25. Yen, T.-F., Oprea, A., Onarlioglu, K., Leetham, T., Robertson, W., Juels, A., Kirda, E.: Beehive: large-scale log analysis for detecting suspicious activity in enterprise networks. In: ACSAC (2013)

Detection of Heap-Spraying Attacks Using String Trace Graph

Jaehyeok Song, Jonghyuk Song, and Jong Kim[✉]

Department of CSE, POSTECH, Pohang, Republic of Korea
{the13,freestar,jkim}@postech.ac.kr

Abstract. Heap-spraying is an attack technique that exploits memory corruptions in web browsers. A realtime detection of heap-spraying is difficult because of dynamic nature of JavaScript and monitoring overheads. In this paper, we propose a runtime detector of heap-spraying attacks in web browsers. We build a *string trace graph* by tracing all string objects and string operations in JavaScript. The graph is used for detecting abnormal behaviors of JavaScript. We detect heap-spraying attacks with low false positive rate and overheads.

1 Introduction

In recent years, a drive-by-download attack becomes one of the most common methods to spread malware. Attackers tempt a victim to visit a website that contains a malicious code. The malicious code exploits vulnerabilities of a web browser to compromise a victim's computer. Compromised computers are used as components of botnets and conduct various attacks, such as spamming and distributed denial-of-service attack (DDoS). Various techniques are used in order to load shellcode into the memory and execute it.

Heap-spraying is the most common technique to compromise web browsers. Heap-spraying increases the possibility of successful attacks because attackers do not need to know exact heap addresses. Heap-spraying is carried out in two phases. The first phase is building a code block that contains a large chunk of CPU instructions. The code block consists of two parts: NOP-sled and shellcode. NOP-sled contains meaningless CPU instructions that induce execution to a malicious shellcode. In the second phase, the malicious code makes many copies of the code block. Heap-spraying tries to insert the code block as many as possible to increase the possibility of the attack. Therefore, heap-spraying technique uses a large amount of memory. In the real world, malicious JavaScript that uses heap-spraying usually allocates more than 100 MB of memory. In addition, heap-spraying should use only string objects of JavaScript to build the code block. The string object is the only object that controls each byte of memory, so heap-spraying uses JavaScript string objects.

In this paper, we propose a heap-spraying detection method based on a string trace graph. Our method builds a graph by tracing all string operations in JavaScript. We propose three features from a string trace graph and train

© Springer International Publishing Switzerland 2015
K.-H. Rhee and J.H. Yi (Eds.): WISA 2014, LNCS 8909, pp. 17–26, 2015.
DOI: 10.1007/978-3-319-15087-1_2

classifiers using the features to classify heap-spraying codes. We evaluate our method by using real-world data and evaluation results show that our method has low false positive and overheads.

We organize the remainder of this paper as follows. In Sect. 2, we introduce previous heap-spraying detection methods and malicious JavaScript detection methods. Section 3 explains background knowledge to understand our method. In Sect. 4, we explain our detection method in detail. In Sect. 5, we describe evaluation results. Finally, Sect. 6 concludes the paper and presents future work.

2   Related Work

2.1   Heap-Spraying Detection

Previous studies [6,13,14] have proposed to detect heap-spraying by finding sequences of x86 instructions. The heap blocks used in a typical heap-spraying attack contain a shellcode and the remainder of the heap block contains NOP-sleds. Previous studies focus on identifying large chunks of NOP-sleds. Nozzle [14] disassembles given a heap object with possible x86 instructions by building a control flow graph (CFG). However, Ding et al. [9] proved that Nozzle is broken by manipulating heap behaviors. Nozzle has too high overhead because it scans the contents of all allocated heap memory. We propose a method that has lower overhead than Nozzle because we do not check the contents of the memory. We simply check whether a memory is allocated and also get the size of allocated memory.

Several researches [6,12,16] have proposed to detect executable codes in payloads of network packets, but they have high false positives.

2.2   Malicious JavaScript Detection

There are researches to detect other malicious JavaScript codes, such as obfuscation, exploit or fingerprint. A number of server-side approaches [7,10] have been proposed to identify malicious code on the web. These approaches extract features of each webpage in run-time using an emulated browser. Cova et al. [7] propose a method to detect malicious JavaScript codes, but it takes too much time to analyze each page (about 10 s per page). In addition, the server-side approaches always suffer from IP based filtering and also have a lot of false positives.

A proxy approach [15] also has been proposed. It detects obfuscation and exploit code by dynamic and static analysis in the emulated environment at proxy level.

Zozzle [8] uses nearly-static approach to detect malicious JavaScript. When a JavaScript engine evaluates a source code, Zozzle analyzes the source code statically. Similar to our method, Zozzle uses a machine learning technique to classify malicious JavaScript. Zozzle trains the name of variables and functions as a feature but an attacker simply changes a variable name in source code or uses a JavaScript optimization compiler [2] to avoid Zozzle.

3 Background

3.1 A String Object in JavaScript

In JavaScript, a string object has unique characteristics distinguished from other languages. First, a value of string is immutable. This means that once a string is initialized, the value of the string will not be changed. Every string operation create a new string variable instead of modifying the original value [10].

```
<SCRIPT language="text/javascript">
1   var shellcode = unescape("%u4343%u4343%...");
2   var nopsled = unescape("%u0D0D%u0D0D");
3
4   while (nopsled.length<0x40000) {
5       nopsled += nopsled;
6   }
7   var nopsled = nopsled.substring(0,0x40000 - shellcode.length);
8
9   spray = new Array();
10  for (i=0; i<200; i++) {
11      spray[i] = nopsled + shellcode;
12  }
</SCRIPT>
```

Fig. 1. An example code of a typical heap-spraying in JavaScript

Second, a string is the only object to manipulate a memory in JavaScript. To succeed code injection attack, an attacker has to load a malicious code on the memory. Since the code consists of a sequence of CPU instructions, each byte of the code has to be accessible. In JavaScript, a string object is the only candidate to have that functionality among user controllable objects.

From the above characteristics, we can know that attackers exploit string objects in JavaScript to manipulate the memory.

3.2 Heap-Spraying

There are two types in code injection attacks which are stack-based and heap-based. Stack-based attacks are on the decline because numerous methods have been introduced to prevent the stack-based attacks. Therefore, attackers mainly

```
<SCRIPT language="text/javascript">
1   var x = "foo";
2   var y = "bar";
3   var z = "hello world";
4
5   var a = x + y + " " + z;
6   // a has "foobar hello world"
7
8   for(var i=0;i<5;i++) document.write(a.substring(0,5));
9   // "foobafoobafoobafoobafooba" is printed on a page
</SCRIPT>
```

Fig. 2. An example code to explain the string trace graph

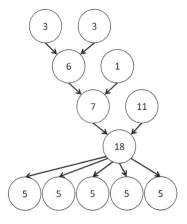

Fig. 3. An example graph of string trace graph

use heap-based attack to compromise victims. Heap-based attack is more difficult than stack-based attack because the addresses in heap memory are unpredictable. To overcome this trouble, attackers should adopt several strategies such as heap-spraying.

Figure 1 is an example code of a heap-spraying in JavaScript. Lines 1–2 indicates that allocating shellcode and NOP-sled into strings. Lines 4–7 build NOP-sleds to spray. In the first while loop, the NOP-sled is expanded by concatenating itself. When the NOP-sled is expanded, the NOP-sled is sliced to fit into the size of heap memory chunk. Although the NOP-sled size is different from a target of browsers and platforms, it has large size of memory than the memory page size, typically from 128 kB to 524 kB. Lines 9–12 codes are responsible for combining the NOP-sled with the shellcode. In this step, the code makes many copies for the effectiveness of the attack.

In our observation of heap-spraying analysis, we found out three features of heap-spraying. First, NOP-sled is generated from the small number of short strings because an exploit should be performed in a short time. If the exploit takes long time, a victim stops navigating the site.

Second, heap-spraying uses abnormally long strings. Attackers insert NOP-sleds as much as possible to increase the possibility that a jump instruction lands on the NOP sled. If a jump instruction lands on the NOP-sled, the execution is reached to a shellcode. Therefore, heap-spraying needs a large size of the NOP-sled string to increase effectiveness of the attack.

Third, heap-spraying makes many copies of a block that contains NOP-sleds and a shellcode. Increasing the number of the block that contains the attack codes is another way to increase the probability of the attack. Therefore, the block is copied the hundreds of times.

4   Heap-Spraying Detection Based on a String Trace Graph

We detect heap-spraying based on a string trace graph. We trace all string operations in JavaScript, such as concatenation, replacement and substring. Therefore, we can get an execution history of string operations by generating a string trace graph.

A string trace graph $\mathcal{G}$ consists of nodes $\mathcal{V}$ and directed edges $\mathcal{E}$. Each node $\mathcal{V}$ represents a string object and it has a length of the string as an attribute. There are two node types which are a leaf node $\mathcal{V}_{Leaf}$ and an internal node $\mathcal{V}_{Internal}$. A leaf node $\mathcal{V}_{Leaf}$ has no incoming edges but an internal node $\mathcal{V}_{Internal}$ has incoming edges. Initial strings are represented as leaf nodes and output strings of string operations are represented as internal nodes. Directed edges represent execution flows of string operations.

Figures 2 and 3 show how we create graphs from JavaScript codes. Each node represents a string object and the number means the length of the string. Each edge represents a flow of a string operation. By analyzing the graph in Fig. 3, we can know that there are four initial strings and a string operation is performed repeatedly in the last part of the graph.

4.1   Features

We propose three features to detect heap-spraying attacks: ratio of leaf nodes, length of a string and degree of the nodes. First, our method uses a ratio of leaf nodes as a feature to detect heap-spraying. A ratio of leaf nodes $LeafR_{\mathcal{G}}$ of a string trace graph $\mathcal{G}$ is computed as follows.

$$LeafR_{\mathcal{G}} = \frac{n_{leaf_{\mathcal{G}}}}{(n_{leaf_{\mathcal{G}}} + n_{internal_{\mathcal{G}}})}, \tag{1}$$

where $n_{leaf_{\mathcal{G}}}$ is the number of leaf nodes in $\mathcal{G}$ and $n_{internal_{\mathcal{G}}}$ is the number of internal nodes in $\mathcal{G}$. Heap-spraying has a few leaf nodes because it begins from

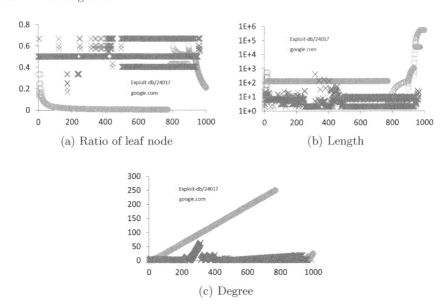

(a) Ratio of leaf node

(b) Length

(c) Degree

Fig. 4. Comparison of the features for google.com and a published exploit 24017 in exploit-db.com. x axis for the number of generated strings and y axis for each feature.

a small number of initial strings. In general, JavaScript codes in the normal websites have a lot of initial strings to represent texts.

Second, our method uses the length of strings to detect heap-spraying. Heap-spraying exploits long strings because it makes many NOP-sleds to increase possibility of the attack. Each node of the string trace graph contains the length of string objects, so we can detect abnormally long strings.

Third features is the degree of a node that is the number of outgoing edges of the node. The degree of a node represents how many string operations are performed with the node. Heap-spraying performs string operations many times to copy an object that contains NOP-sleds and a shellcode to increase the possibility of attacks. If string operations are performed many times, there is a node having an unusually larger number of outgoing edges. If there is a nodes that has a larger degree than a threshold, our method decides that there is a heap-spraying attack.

We train well-known classification algorithms with these three features. The trained classification algorithms classify whether a JavaScript contains heap-spraying codes.

5   Evaluation

We implement our method on JavaScriptCore (JSC) which is a default JavaScript engine of an open-source web engine Webkit [5]. The release version that we modify is r128399. We modify JavaScript String class to trace every constructor and destructor. Our code is written in 600 lines of code.

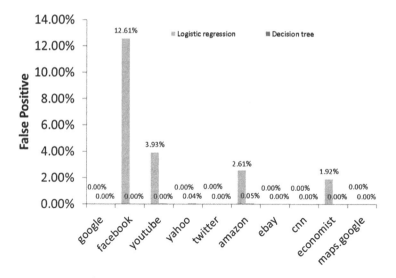

Fig. 5. Comparison of false positive rate for 10 benign web sites

We begin our evaluation by measuring the effects of each three feature mentioned in Sect. 4.1. Figure 4 shows the results on a benign website (google.com) and a site that contains a published heap-spraying attack code. Figure 4(a) shows the ratio of leaf nodes. The ratio of leaf nodes in the heap-spraying is much lower than that of the benign. In general, normal websites contain many initial strings to represent text but a heap-spraying code only uses a few initial strings for setting up attack blocks. Figure 4(b) shows the result of the length feature. The length of strings in the heap-spraying is much longer than that of benign because the heap-spraying uses abnormally long strings to increase the possibility of the attack. Figure 4(c) shows the result of the degree feature. The maximum degree of benign is 80 but the degree of heap-spraying is much higher than that. From this result, we can know that the heap-spraying code performs string operations much more than a benign website.

Overall, three features are very useful to distinguish between a malicious site that contains a heap-spraying code and a benign site.

5.1 False Positive Rate and False Negative Rate

In this section, we compute false positive rate and false negative rate. We crawl the front pages of Alexa top 500 sites [1] as a benign data set. We set up a malicious data set with 50 web sites in malwaredomainlist.com [4] and a published heap-spraying sample in exploit-db.com [3].

Weka [11] is used for classifications. We use 66 % of our data set for training and the remainder is used for validation. Four classifiers are trained: decision tree, logistic regression, naive Bayes and SVM. Table 1 shows the results of the four

Table 1. False positive and false negative of classifiers trained by four algorithms; decision tree, logistic regression, Naive Bayes and SVM.

Algorithms	False positive rate (%)	False negative rate (%)
Decision tree	0.00	0.00
Logistic regression	0.03	0.98
Naive Bayes	4.00	0.67
SVM	18.50	0.00

Table 2. Benign web sites that we used in experiments

Sites	Document (kB)	JavaScript (kB)
google.com	98	787
facebook.com	80	389
youtube.com	99	352
yahoo.com	316	651
twitter.com	52	306
amazon.com	227	316
ebay.com	75	272
cnn.com	110	1232
economist.com	150	610
maps.google.com	205	797

classifiers. Decision tree and logistic regression classifiers achieve outstanding performance. The others also have low false positive rate and false negative rate.

To examine the results of false positive rate in detail, we select the results of 10 popular sites (Table 2) that are classified with two classifiers which are decision tree and logistic regression. We visit not only the front page but also up to 20 internal pages of the sites. Figure 5 shows the result. Overall, logistic regression performs with low false positive rates and decision tree performs with almost zero false positive rates. In facebook.com case, logistic regression has the highest false positive rate because facebook.com has many copy operations. False positives are mainly caused from some benign sites implemented with obfuscated codes or many string operations.

5.2 Performance

We evaluate the time overhead and the memory usage on the 10 sites (Table 2). When we measure the performance, we except network and rendering overheads by executing only JSC with Webkit. The total memory usage is calculated by counting the number of objects. We conduct the evaluation with decision tree and logistic regression because these two algorithms have the low false positive rate and false negative in Sect. 5.1.

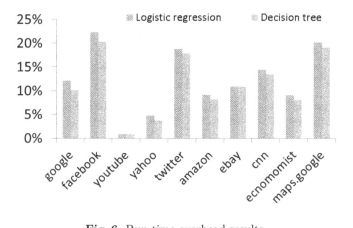

Fig. 6. Run-time overhead results

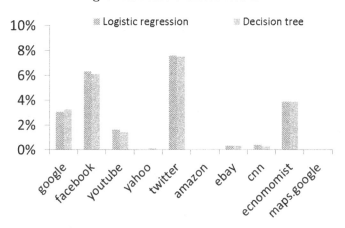

Fig. 7. Memory usage overhead results

Figure 6 shows the results of run-time overhead. Decision tree takes more time about 11 % and logistic regression takes more time about 12 %. Figure 7 shows the results of memory usages. On average, our method uses approximately 2.3 % additional memory. In facebook.com and twitter.com, we consume more time and memory because they have more string operations than other sites. Google Map site uses a lot of memory, so the additional memory usage is relatively too small for the existing memory usage.

6   Conclusions and Future Work

This paper proposed a heap-spraying detection method based on a string trace graph. We build a graph by tracing all string operations in JavaScript. Our method is executed in a client browser and checks every web page that a user visits. Evaluation results show that the proposed method have low false positive rates and low overheads. As the future work, we plan to apply the string trace graph for detection of other malicious JavaScript techniques, such as obfuscation. Obfuscation uses a lot of string operations to evaluate string as JavaScript code. String operations in obfuscation will reveal their pattern by string trace graphs.

Acknowledgements. This work was supported by ICT R&D program of MSIP/IITP. [14-824-09-013, Resilient Cyber-Physical Systems Research].

References

1. Alexa top 500 global sites. http://www.alexa.com/topsites
2. Closure compiler. https://developers.google.com/closure/compiler/
3. Exploit database. http://exploit-db.com
4. Malware domain list. http://malwaredomainlist.com
5. The webkit open source project. http://www.webkit.org/
6. Akritidis, P., Markatos, E.P., Polychronakis, M., Anagnostakis, K.: STRIDE: Polymorphic sled detection through instruction sequence analysis. In: Sasaki, R., Qing, S., Okamoto, E., Yoshiura, H. (eds.) Security and Privacy in the Age of Ubiquitous Computing. IFIP, vol. 181, pp. 375–391. Springer, New York (2005)
7. Cova, M., Kruegel, C., Vigna, G.: Detection and analysis of drive-by-download attacks and malicious javascript code. In: Proceedings of the 19th International Conference on World Wide Web, pp. 281–290. ACM (2010)
8. Curtsinger, C., Livshits, B., Zorn, B., Seifert, C.: Zozzle: low-overhead mostly static javascript malware detection. In: Proceedings of the Usenix Security Symposium (2011)
9. Ding, Y., Wei, T., Wang, T., Liang, Z., Zou. W.: Heap taichi: exploiting memory allocation granularity in heap-spraying attacks. In: Proceedings of the 26th Annual Computer Security Applications Conference, pp. 327–336. ACM (2010)
10. Egele, M., Wurzinger, P., Kruegel, C., Kirda, E.: Defending browsers against drive-by downloads: mitigating heap-spraying code injection attacks. In: Flegel, U., Bruschi, D. (eds.) DIMVA 2009. LNCS, vol. 5587, pp. 88–106. Springer, Heidelberg (2009)
11. Hall, M., Frank, E., Holmes, G., Pfahringer, B., Reutemann, P., Witten, I.H.: The weka data mining software: an update. ACM SIGKDD Explor. Newslett. **11**(1), 10–18 (2009)
12. Polychronakis, M., Anagnostakis, K.G., Markatos, E.P.: Network-level polymorphic shellcode detection using emulation. In: Büschkes, R., Laskov, P. (eds.) DIMVA 2006. LNCS, vol. 4064, pp. 54–63. Springer, Heidelberg (2006)
13. Polychronakis, M., Anagnostakis, K.G., Markatos, E.P.: Emulation-based detection of non-self-contained polymorphic shellcode. In: Kruegel, C., Lippmann, R., Clark, A. (eds.) RAID 2007. LNCS, vol. 4637, pp. 87–106. Springer, Heidelberg (2007)
14. Ratanaworabhan, P., Livshits, V.B., Zorn, B.G.: Nozzle: a defense against heap-spraying code injection attacks. In: USENIX Security Symposium, pp. 169–186 (2009)
15. Rieck, K., Krueger, T., Dewald, A.: Cujo: efficient detection and prevention of drive-by-download attacks. In: Proceedings of the 26th Annual Computer Security Applications Conference, pp. 31–39. ACM (2010)
16. Toth, T., Kruegel, C.: Accurate buffer overflow detection via abstract pay load execution. In: Wespi, A., Vigna, G., Deri, L. (eds.) RAID 2002. LNCS, vol. 2516, pp. 274–291. Springer, Heidelberg (2002)

A Simple Yet Efficient Approach to Combat Transaction Malleability in Bitcoin

Ubaidullah Rajput, Fizza Abbas, Rasheed Hussain, Hasoo Eun,
and Heekuck Oh$^{(\boxtimes)}$

Department of Computer Science and Engineering,
Hanyang University, Seoul, South Korea
{ubaidullah,hkok}@hanyang.ac.kr

Abstract. Bitcoin has emerged as a popular crypto currency. It was introduced in 2008 by Satoshi Nakamoto (A pseudonym). The reasons for its popularity include its decentralized nature, double spending prevention, smart strategy to counter inflation and providing a certain degree of anonymity. In February 2014, Bitcoin community was shocked to know that a Japan based company named Mt. Gox who, were dealing 70 percent of Bitcoin transactions that time, announced that they were hit by a bug in the Bitcoin protocol named as Transaction Malleability. The company lost hundreds of millions of dollars worth bitcoin. Soon after this, another company SilkRoad 2 also claimed to have affected by same issue. To date there is little research literature available on this recent issue and it is hard to grasp this problem. The purpose of writing this paper is twofold. We discuss Transaction Malleability in detail with respect to the structure of Bitcoin transactions in order to make reader properly understands what Transaction Malleability is and how it works. We also propose a mechanism to counter this issue.

Keywords: Bitcoin · Transaction malleability · Cryptocurrency

1 Introduction

Bitcoin is a decentralized cryptocurrency which was introduced in 2008 by Satoshi Nakamoto, an unknown author of the paper [1]. It is still a mystery that who is Satoshi Nakamoto and where is he from[1]. Bitcoin has gained significant popularity among other crypto currencies and many crypto currencies have emerged copying Bitcoin in principal such as Litecoin and Namecoin (just to name a few). Its current market value is just above 562 US dollars as of 25th May 2014(as by CoinDesk)[2]. Although one of the major criticisms over Bitcoin is that its value is very unstable. Despite this, its current market capitalization is over 5 Billion US dollars and no other crypto currency has achieved this high mark. The popularity of Bitcoin lies mostly in its distributed nature and certain

---

[1] Many theories have been presented but none has been proved to be correct.

[2] CoinDesk is a famous Bitcoin trading website (www.coindesk.com).

© Springer International Publishing Switzerland 2015
K.-H. Rhee and J.H. Yi (Eds.): WISA 2014, LNCS 8909, pp. 27–37, 2015.
DOI: 10.1007/978-3-319-15087-1_3

level of anonymity. It has an efficient mechanism to prevent double spending as well as inflation. More precisely it is not controlled by a central authority or by any government but by Bitcoin community itself. This is the reason, that it is computationally infeasible for someone to take control of the system or introduce inflation by creating large number of Bitcoins. It is controlled by Bitcoin users who are called Miners. Miners perform mining to verify Bitcoin transactions and get newly generated bitcoins in reward. This is how the new bitcoins are generated [1,3]. Another advantage of decentralization is that the Bitcoin payments are transferred directly between two exchanging parties and therefore the parties are not required to trust any intermediate authority. As discussed above, the Bitcoin provides a certain level of pseudo anonymity [2]. This is due to the fact that in the Bitcoin system, the users' accounts, that keep bitcoins, are identified by hash of public keys generated by users themselves. With different software available free of cost online, this is just the matter of a single click. Thus, so it is very hard to relate someone with an alpha-numeric string identifier.

In February 2014, one of the leading Bitcoin exchanges named as Mt. Gox, announced that their Bitcoin wallets (accounts that are holding bitcoins) were hacked and filed lawsuit for bank ruptsy [4]. The Japan based company put blame on a known Bitcoin bug "Transaction Malleability" to be the cause of the theft of their bitcoins. Similar incident happened with Silk Road 2 which was a black market and trading in Bitcoins. They claimed that their wallets are also hacked and they have lost millions of US dollars worth bitcoin. They also put the responsibility of the hack on the Bitcoin bug Transaction Malleability.

This paper proposes a robust strategy to combat the Bitcoin malleability issue. We first provide an in-depth study of Bitcoin transactions and then explain how a transaction can be made malleable. In the end, we present our simple yet efficient approach to counter this issue. The rest of the paper is organized as follows. In Sect. 2 we briefly describe the Bitcoin structure. In Sect. 3 we explain a Bitcoin Transaction. Section 4 explains Transaction Malleability in detail. Possible solutions of this issue will be addressed in Sect. 5, while we conclude the paper in Sect. 6.

2 Structure of Bitcoin

Bitcoin is a peer to peer network in which the participants of the network jointly act as a central server that control the Bitcoin and makes it sure that the overall network works correctly. As we know that in a peer to peer network, Sybil attacks are possible and providing fairness is one very important issue. The Bitcoin network overcomes this challenge by ensuring that an honest majority of users (therefore, an honest majority of computing power running the network) is in control. Due to this, it is computationally infeasible for an attacker to create enough fake nodes on the network to defeat the honest majority of the participants and compromise the system. In the world of digital currencies the main problem is double spending. If by calling digital money we mean string of bits then anyone can spend them twice or more. This is not a problem in a centrally governed money system, such as a bank, where it keeps a record of all transactions being made and therefore a seller can confirm that a cheque, which has been issued by a buyer has not been already utilized.

Bitcoin overcomes this challenge by maintaining a public ledger. By the public ledger we mean an online available record of all the transactions made in the Bitcoin system from the very beginning. This ledger is called Block Chain [6]. We can consider block chain as a trusted ledger where anyone who has access of Internet can access it. It is actually a database that is shared by all the nodes participating in the system. This ledger is maintained by Bitcoin participants, also known as miners. Once a transaction is made, it is collected in a block. After a certain time the block, which is containing all those transactions made during that time, is processed. Blocks in the block chain forms a chain where every block contains the hash of the previous block. Each block comes after the previous block chronologically and it is guaranteed due to the hash of previous blocks it contain. A modification of a block, once it has been confirmed for some times (usually an hour) on to the block chain, is impractical. This is due to the fact that the modification of subsequent blocks will also be necessary which is computationally infeasible for an adversary. This is due to the proof of work [1]. Simply, proof of work is a mathematical problem which is hard to compute and takes some time depending on how tough it is. It is generated different for each block. The miners who are validating transactions need to find the solution of it. After spending computational power needed to solve a block, the miner who successfully finds the solution announces it on to the network and get newly generated bitcoins in reward. Therefore, any transaction will be considered valid if it has been posted on to this ledger after verification by miners. In the Bitcoin protocol one party, who is sending Bitcoins to other, requires the Bitcoin address of the other party.

A Bitcoin address is an alphanumeric identifier consists of 27–34 characters. It begins with the number 1 or 3 and represents the destination for a Bitcoin payment. Addresses can be generated by any user of Bitcoin without any cost.

For just the basic understanding, consider that a user Y is going to transfer money to user X, then he creates a transaction Ty which will be like "Y is transferring b amount of Bitcoin money to address of X, where b amount was obtained by Y in a previous transaction Tz". The user X can then spend these b bitcoins by creating another transaction Tx by referring Ty in same manner. In fact the actual implementation of a transaction is much more complex than this. The next section will explain a Bitcoin transaction and various (but not all) of its components which are related to our study.

3   Bitcoin Transaction

In this section we will go through the details of a Bitcoin transaction. It is worth mentioning that we cover only the main aspects of a transaction related to our study and not all the details.

As we learned that Bitcoin crypto currency system consists of addresses and transactions between those addresses. A Bitcoin address is actually a hash of the

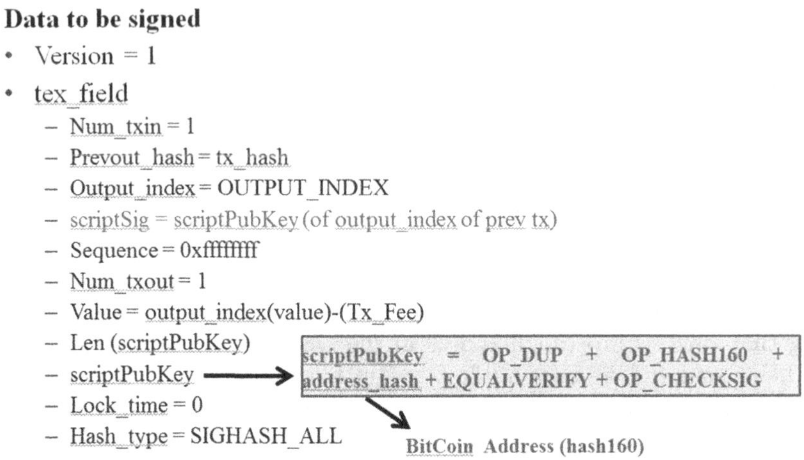

Data to be signed

- Version = 1
- tex_field
  - Num_txin = 1
  - Prevout_hash = tx_hash
  - Output_index = OUTPUT_INDEX
  - scriptSig = scriptPubKey (of output_index of prev tx)
  - Sequence = 0xffffffff
  - Num_txout = 1
  - Value = output_index(value)-(Tx_Fee)
  - Len (scriptPubKey)
  - scriptPubKey ⟶   scriptPubKey = OP_DUP + OP_HASH160 + address_hash + EQUALVERIFY + OP_CHECKSIG
  - Lock_time = 0
  - Hash_type = SIGHASH_ALL   BitCoin Address (hash160)

Fig. 1. Data in intermediate transaction

public key. A Bitcoin transaction is a script which is signed and broadcast on to the network and various transactions are collected in a block after a certain time period. A transaction is written in Bitcoin scripting language. For the sake of understanding we can divide a transaction in input, output and verification sections. An input contains actually a reference to an output in some other transaction. There can be multiple inputs enlisted in a transaction. These multiple inputs refer to transaction outputs containing unspent (if it's a valid transaction) bitcoins. Therefore, the input of a transaction is the sum of all these unspent bitcoins. The input section also contains the hash(es) of the previous transaction(s) which contained in the referenced outputs. It also contains the scriptSig, which is first half of a script. This scriptSig contains two things. One is the signed data and other is the public key. We will shortly explain the term "signed data". The public key belongs to the creator of this transaction and it proves that the creator of this transaction is indeed the owner of bitcoins mentioned in referenced outputs in input section and can spend them. It is worth mentioning that the hashed value of this public key is the Bitcoin address containing the bitcoins to be redeemed[3]. Along with the signature (hence the private key) and the public key, the creator of the transaction proves that he is the real owner of the Bitcoin address containing the coins which are being spent. The output section, on the other hand, contains instructions for sending bitcoins. It contains one or more outputs which share all the bitcoins in referenced inputs. One noticeable thing is that all the bitcoins in input must be spent. Therefore, if the combined value of referenced bitcoins is 75 and the creator of the transaction wants to send only 50 bitcoins of it, then he will create one more output containing an

---

[3] In fact it is not simply the hash, but the results of a series of steps performed on public ECDSA key to get the private key. For a demonstration please visit www.gobittest.appspot.com/Address.

address of himself to which he will send the "change" of 25 bitcoins. This output section contains the scriptPubKey which is the second half of the script. This script contains hash of the receiver's address and the instructions to send the data contains in the scriptSig on to the execution stack. Simply, we can say that scriptPubKey actually is a script which governs that how the values in scriptSig will be manipulated on verification. The signed data is actually the signature containing the inputs, outputs and value of bitcoins being transferred and puts in the middle of the transaction. Therefore, once signed, these values cannot be changed. The third section of transaction is related to its verification. The input scriptSig and output scriptPubKey are evaluated where scriptPubKey uses the values on the stack of scriptSig. If it returns true then it is a valid transaction [7]. It is interesting to note that by this scripting very complex scenarios can be made for the redeemers of this transaction. Scenarios include that more than one user use their keys to redeem the transaction or may use password to redeem it instead of a key. In Figs. 1, 2 and 3 we show a typical structure of a Bitcoin transaction. Figure 1 shows "Data to be signed" which is intermediate transaction containing all values that will be hashed and signed to be used as scriptSig in final transaction. Figure 2 shows the signing of intermediate transaction, while Fig. 3 shows the final transaction whose hash will serve as transaction id.

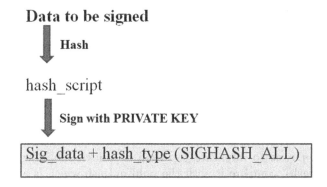

$$scriptSig = len(sig\_data) + sig\_data + len(pubkey) + pubkey$$

Fig. 2. Signing of intermediate transaction

We now look more into an script as it plays the fundamental role in the Bitcoin transaction malleability. A script in the bitcoin is essentially a series of instructions in a transaction that describe how the bitcoins containing in this transaction will be redeemed. It tells the conditions which the spender must fulfills. A standard Bitcoin transaction requires the spender to provide two things; the public key, that hashes to the address mentioned in the output field of some previous transaction containing unspent bitcoins and the signature, that ensures that the spender has the corresponding private key. A transaction will be considered valid if the top stack item return true and nothing returns failure on

Final Transaction

- Version = 1
- tex_field
  - Num_txin = 1
  - Prevout_hash = tx_hash
  - Output_index = OUTPUT_INDEX
  - Len (scriptSig)
  - scriptSig
  - scriptSigHAsh = scriptPubKey (of output_index of prev tx)
  - Sequence = 0xffffffff
  - Num_txout = 1
  - Value = output_index(value)-(Tx_Fee)
  - Len (scriptPubKey)
  - scriptPubKey
  - Lock_time = 0

Fig. 3. Final transaction showing scriptSig

evaluation of script. The commands or functions use in a script are called Script words. Certain words are used to push byte data on to the stack; some are used for flow control, some for bitwise logic operation, arithmetic operations and some for crypto operations like taking hash or for checking the signature. Below is the standard transaction script which is used to transfer bitcoins to a public key hash address.

scriptPubKey: OP_DUP OP_HASH160 <pubKeyHash> OP_EQUALVERIFY OP_CHECKSIG
scriptSig:<sig> <pubkey>

The first script typically means to duplicate top item of stack (public key), take hash of it (pubkey hash), compare it with the pubKeyHash which is also presented in the script and verify it. On returning true the script is considered to be valid. scriptSig is containing the signature as well as the public key. Another important thing related to "words" is that they are represented by hex codes in a raw transaction, for example, 76 is the hex code for "OP_DUP", A9 is the hex code for "OP_HASH160" and so on. The "raw transaction API" was to give developers or very sophisticated end users the access to transaction creation and broadcast. Thus, it let a company for example, to create its own software for exchanging bitcoins in the way their business operate. Finally, a transaction is identified by its hash. This, as we will see, is a very important characteristic of Bitcoin protocol. Once a raw transaction is written and dispatched on to the network it will be identified on block chain by its hash. The procedure is simple. Once you have written a complete transaction mentioning all the inputs, outputs, scriptSig and scriptPubKey etc., take the hash of the final transaction and that will be its transaction identifier or simply transaction id.

4   Transaction Malleability

In this section we explain what transaction malleability is and how it works. Although this transaction malleability was present in the system and identified first in 2011, until recently it was not considered to be a very serious issue. Before going through the details of it, we first report two of the incidents which shocked the Bitcoin community and made transaction malleability a hot issue.

Mt. Gox was a Bitcoin exchange that is based in Tokyo, Japan. It was established in 2010 and was dealing with almost 70 percent of the entire Bitcoin transactions. In February 2014 this company suspended their trading and closed its web site and filed for bankruptcy protection [8]. As it was working as a Bitcoin exchange, people used to deposit other currencies like US dollar in exchange of bitcoins. Now an attacker would request a transfer of bitcoins, then intercept that transaction from Mt. Gox and replaced that transaction with a modified one with a different hash. Because the modified transaction was still containing all the valid addresses and public key address, it would get verified by the network and bitcoins would transferred to the attacker's account. On the other hand because its id had been changed, the attacker would complain the company that he has not received the intended bitcoins and hence the company resent the amount of bitcoins. Mt. Gox later announced that they were affected by this bug in Bitcoin software and lost around 850 000 bitcoins. Although later they said that they recovered some of them. Total loss was more than 450 million US dollars. Bitcoin developers said this was a known bug and Mt. Gox had to make their exchange transaction software in accordance with this bug. Similar case was reported with another Bitcoin trading place known as Silk Road whose wallets lost over 4000 bitcoins with around 2.7 Million US dollar worth.

To understand this issue, we must understand that when the hash of some data is produced, even a slight change in data will change the hash entirely. We know that the transaction id is the hash of whole transaction. If we are able to change some of the details in transaction, the resultant hash will be completely different. Thus, So we can define transaction malleability is an attack in which an attacker can change the unique transaction id by manipulating the transaction which results in a different hash id while all the other details of the transaction are intact. Now the question is what an attacker can change in a signed and hashed transaction?

As we have discussed earlier that a transaction includes components like receiver's address, amount, inputs etc. To protect this data, hash of certain part is calculated and signed and this will be kept in scriptSig as a part of final transaction. Note that this signature is only a part of the transaction and not the complete final transaction is signed because it is not logically possible for a signature to sign itself. This introduces two ways of inducing malleability [9].

First is related to the signature. The Bitcoin uses ECDSA signature. For every ECDSA signature (r, s), the signature $(r, -s(mod\ N))$ is also a valid signature for the same message. Hence if a attacker intercepts the transaction and change the sign of s in signature pair (because this signature is itself not signed), takes the hash again then the resultant hash (hence the transaction id) will be completely different. Secondly each signature here has only one DER encoded ASN.1 octet representation, but openssl which is used in Bitcoin network, does not enforce it unless the signature is too much ill-formed [9]. This mean that if an attacker pads the signature with 0x000... or 0xFF.... then the signature will be accepted and will be resulted in a completely different hash.

The other problem is related to scriptSig. As we know that scriptSig is not itself signed in a transaction. Because it is a script, so one can add data on to the stack and then can use word like OP_DROP to leave the stack as before. By adding any values to it will result in a completely different hash and thus a different transaction id.More precisely, as scripts are in hex format, one can change the hex of op codes in such a way that two different op code work in similar manner. For example PUSHDATA 48 means push two bytes of data while OP_PUSHDATA2 means next two bytes. These are doing exactly same thing so it will not change the functionality of the transaction but two transactions with different op code will be having completely different hashes (or transaction ids).

This is what happened to Mt. Gox. Although the expected transaction ids of their transactions were not appearing on block chain, they were being executed and their clients (the attackers) were getting bitcoins. Attackers were claiming that they were actually not receiving transaction and Mt. Gox software was resending payments. Until they know what happened, it was already too late.

By now, we only know about one solution which has been presented in literature [10]. The authors propose that tx id should be made by taking hash of intermediate transaction without input scripts. This will be the hash without scriptSig. Note that script in intermediate transaction contains scriptPubKey of input transactions that contains information about how these transaction were redeemed by the previous owner. We argue that this is important information and eliminating this can result in ill-functionality of some of Bitcoin uses. Therefore, it is not a feasible solution. Let suppose X can utilize an unspent transaction by proving either of two condition c1 or c2 such that if c1 or c2 are true only then the transaction will be accepted. X provides either of one condition and broadcast her transaction which is added to block chain. Suppose Y and Z are two parties in some contract which says that "Y will get b bitcoins if X proved c1 and Z will get b bitcoins if X had proved c2". Now because there is no scriptSig present which can tell about this dispute therefore, Y and Z cannot get provable information about what X had proved. Furthermore, we argue that this change is too much for a protocol like Bitcoin as it has been at this stage of its development. The developers of Bitcoin will be hesitate to adopt it and hence a solution is required which is within acceptable range for the developers of this crypto currency.

5   Proposed Solution to the Transaction Malleability

A hash is of fixed length. This is why a malleable transaction has the same size hash. The fact that, it serves as a reference for each new transaction which try to redeems the inputs in it. Therefore, a new scheme for modifying the way a

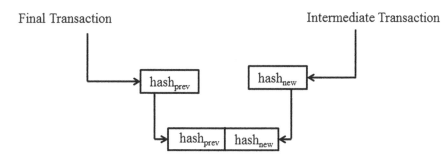

Fig. 4. The new structure of transaction id

transaction id is calculated, will not be welcomed in Bitcoin. Hence the solution to this problem should be in compliance of the current protocol. In the Sect. 3 we discussed how we can write a raw transaction. The idea of our solution is to use the hash which was calculated at the end of first part (hash_script in Fig. 2). Note that the values of this hash cannot be modified and thus any change to scriptSig will not modify this hash. We suggest that this hash should be appended to the hash of final transaction as shown in Fig. 4. This will serve us well because:

1. By doing this, we are only slightly modifying the current protocol for only the identification purpose of the transaction. In other words, because our new transaction id has two fixed length segments, miners will always take the first part of the transaction to verify it as they were doing before. Similarly other transactions that are referencing this transaction will also refer to the first part of it.
2. A sender who tries to find her transaction on to the block chain, will look for the second part of it and will eventually find it. We demonstrate our approach in the following way.

5.1   Attacker Scenario 1

Suppose our new transaction id is now in the form of hash$_{prev}$ | hash$_{new}$. hash$_{prev}$ is the hash calculated in existing protocol while hash$_{new}$ is the hash of intermediate raw transaction. Once it is broadcasted on to the network and if an attacker intercepts it and modifies it by transaction malleability issue as shown in Fig. 5, it will change the hash$_{prev}$ part of this id, but he cannot alter the hash$_{new}$ part of the transaction. Let's suppose he succeeded in sending this to block chain before actual legal transaction. Note that the modified transaction now in form of hash$_{prev}$'| hash$_{new}$. When a miner takes this transaction for verification he takes only hash$_{prev}$' part and verifies the transaction. All the funds will be transferred from sender to receiver (attacker). Now if the sender wish to confirm that his transaction has actually redeemed, he searches it with second part of this id which is hash$_{new}$. Because this part has not been altered by the attacker hence it will be verified by miners, therefore, the sender will be able to confirm that his transaction has been successfully verified.

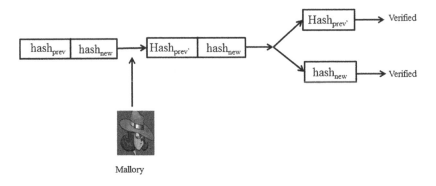

Fig. 5. Showing attack Scenario 1

5.2 Attacker Scenario 2

Suppose an attacker tries to change the $hash_{new}$ of the transaction as shown in Fig. 6. All the information in the intermediate transaction is verifiable and hence miners will discard it on verification. We know that $hash_{new}$ is formed by taking the hash of transaction at end of intermediate part of the transaction creation (intermediate transaction).

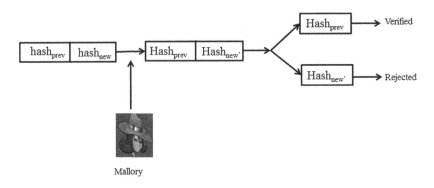

Fig. 6. Showing attack Scenario 2

This will not add any extra burden on miners as they already validate the values which are present in the intermediate transaction, hence they will validate the $hash_{new}$ in this process. Once approved this $hash_{new}$ will be validated as tx-id and a user will be able to search transactions with it. Due to the presence of $hash_{prev}$ not only all the current validations will be performed as they are being performed but also it will prevent from scenarios like we discussed earlier regarding contracts. The information will be verified as before.

6   Conclusion

Transaction malleability is an important issue for Bitcoin community. Millions of dollars' worth bitcoins were stolen due to this bug in the crypto currency. We presented a thorough study of Bitcoin transaction and explained the mechanism of tweaking it to make a different transaction id. We showed that how can we counter this problem by simply adding the hash of intermediate transaction to the current id. We analyzed our approach by presenting similar attack scenarios which have been used recently, to make transactions malleable. We conclude that our approach is very practical and can be used with the existing protocol of Bitcoin.

References

1. Nakamoto, S.: Bitcoin: A Peer-to-Peer Electronic Cash System, Consulted 1 (2008)
2. Androulaki, E., Karame, G.O., Roeschlin, M., Scherer, T., Capkun, S.: Evaluating user privacy in bitcoin. In: Sadeghi, A.-R. (ed.) FC 2013. LNCS, vol. 7859, pp. 34–51. Springer, Heidelberg (2013)
3. Meiklejohn, S., Pomarole, M., Jordan, G., Levchenko, K., McCoy, D., Voelker, G.M., Savage, S.: A fistful of bitcoins: characterizing payments among men with no names. In: ACM Conference on Internet Measurement, pp. 127–140 (2013)
4. Mt. Gox files for bankruptcy, hit with lawsuit. http://www.reuters.com/article/2014/02/28/us-bitcoin-mtgox-bankruptcy-idUSBREA1R0FX20140228
5. Mt. Gox files for bankruptcy, hit with lawsuit. http://www.forbes.com/sites/andygreenberg/2014/02/13/silk-road-2-0-hacked-using-bitcoin-bug-all-its-funds-stolen/
6. Blockchain.info: Bitcoin Block Explorer. https://blockchain.info/
7. Transactions. https://en.bitcoin.it/wiki/Transactions
8. TMt. Gox. Mtgox press release announcing the stop of withdrawls (2014). http://www.mtgox.com/press_release_20140210.html
9. Transaction Malleability. http://en.bitcoin.it/wiki/Transaction_Malleability
10. Nandrychowicz, M., Dziembowski, S., Malinowski, D., Mazurek, L.: Fair Two-Party Computations via the BitCoin Deposits. IACR Cryptology ePrint Archive (2013)

Mobile Security

Before Unrooting your Android Phone, Patching up Permission System First!

Zhongwen Zhang[1,2,3](✉)

[1] Data Assurance and Communication Security Research Center, Beijing, China
[2] State Key Laboratory of Information Security,
Institute of Information Engineering, CAS, Beijing, China
[3] University of Chinese Academy of Sciences, Beijing, China
zwzhang@lois.cn

Abstract. A common attack goal on Android phones is to steal private data, which is primarily protected by permission system. Therefore, permission system is more vulnerable to attackers, especially when a phone is rooted (which is common nowadays). On rooted phones, malware is able to run with root privilege. Three weak points of permission system have been identified, which can be used to carry out various permission escalation attacks by malware with root privilege. Unrooting a phone can make malware lose root privilege, but it cannot solve the security issues caused by these attacks. In this paper, we present a scheme that aims at patching up the three weak points of permission system. We expect that the scheme is used in the scenario where a user wants to unroot his phone and get his phone under protection. The scheme can apply to any version of Android system. In order to facilitate the scheme's deployment, we develop an app to automatically do the patching work. Moreover, the evaluation result shows that the scheme is small-footprint and only introduces 1.8 % overhead.

Keywords: Android · Permission system · Patch · Unroot

1 Introduction

Nowadays, stealing private data becomes a common attack goal on Android phones. Users' private data could be leaked out by abusing privacy-related system resources, such as various sensors (*Camera, Microphone, etc.*), sensitive data (*SMS, Contact, etc.*), and important communication modules (*3G, Wifi, etc.*). These resources are mainly protected by Android permission system, which enforces that only applications (apps) gained corresponding permissions can access system resources.

This work is supported by National Natural Science Foundation of China grant 70890084/G021102 and 61003274, Strategy Pilot Project of Chinese Academy of Sciences sub-project XDA06010702, and National High Technology Research and Development Program of China (863 Program, No. 2013AA01A214 and 2012AA013104).

© Springer International Publishing Switzerland 2015
K.-H. Rhee and J.H. Yi (Eds.): WISA 2014, LNCS 8909, pp. 41–54, 2015.
DOI: 10.1007/978-3-319-15087-1_4

Besides permissions, gaining root privilege is another way to access resources. According to [15], 23 % Android phones had been rooted at least once in China mainland by the first half of 2012. On rooted phones, malware is able to run with root privilege. With root privilege, malware can bypass permission check and directly read/write private data, such as SMS database files, Contact database files. We denote this kind of attacks as bypassing attack. Besides bypassing attack, various permission escalation attacks can be carried out with root privilege. According to [19], permission system has three weak points (see Sect. 2.2), which can be used to escalate permissions. Therefore, it is necessary to address the security issues towards permission system caused by malware with root privilege.

It is thought that updating the Android system may solve the security issues brought by rooting. However, updating to a higher Android version does not work. First, in most cases, after a phone is rooted, it cannot be updated to a new version anymore, since its *system* partition has been changed. Second, even if a rooted phone is updated, the escalated permissions and malicious apps still exist. That is because updating does not affect users' data (e.g., settings, installed apps).

To mitigate the security issues brought by root exploits, SEAndroid [17] is merged into Android Open Source Project (AOSP) since Android version 4.3 and enforced since version 4.4. Although SEAndroid can block attacks exploiting root privilege, it has a rather limited enforcement range. According to Google's survey [11], the phones shipped with version 4.3 and 4.4 each accounts for 8.5 % of the total at the beginning of May, 2014. That a phone shipped with 4.3 version of Android does not mean that the SEAndroid is enforced. So, nearly 90 % of the Android phones in the wild are however not protected by SEAndroid. So, most rooted phones in the wild face difficulties to get protection.

Another option to confront the root-exploiting attacks is making malware lose root privilege. This is usually carried out by unrooting a phone. Nowadays, users are motivated to unroot their phones, as the security threats on rooted phones become more and more serious. YaJin Zhou et al.'s work [20] reveals that 36.7 % malware leveraged root privilege to fully compromise the Android security. Unrooting a phone can block the bypassing attack, since without root privilege malware cannot access system resources files anymore. However, unrooting a phone cannot solve the security issues caused by the weak points (see Sect. 2.2) of permission system [19].

In this paper, we present a scheme that aims at patching up the three weak points of permission system and makes malware lose the escalated permissions. We expect the scheme is used in the scenario that a user wants to get permission system be patched and then unroot his phone. After a phone is patched up, it must be unrooted. Otherwise, the patches may be tampered by malware with root privilege. To make the scheme easy to deploy, we develop an app named PUapp (**P**atch and **U**nroot) to patch the permission system and unroot the phone. Unlike SEAndroid, the scheme applies to any Android versions and does not need to flash a ROM to a phone.

We encounter two main challenges in this work. First, to make our scheme easy to deploy, we only want to update the code files of permission system instead of flashing a ROM. All code files of Android framework (preserved in */system/framework*) are dependent on each other. How to make the code files of our scheme meet the dependance needs is a challenge. Second, permission system is frequently used, since whenever a resource access occurs, permission system will be called. Therefore, the patch-up scheme should not induce much overhead. How to make the patch-up scheme secure and lightweight is another challenge.

The scheme provides two-level guarantee for loading apps' permissions trustily. In the first level, the scheme guarantees permissions loaded from a metadata file (*packages.xml*) are creditable. When the *packages.xml* file does not exist, the second level guarantee can recover non-system and system apps' permissions in a trusted manner. We implement the scheme with a modification of less than 380 lines of code (LOC). The evaluation result shows that the scheme does not affect the boot-up time; the memory consumption increases less than 1 %; and the overall overhead increases 1.8 %. The main contributions of this paper are listed as follows:

- We offer a patching scheme towards permission system that can be used when users want to unroot their phones. The scheme mainly aims at confronting the security issues brought by the three weak points of permission system.
- We analyze the security and usability of the scheme, and evaluate the scheme in the aspects of start-up time, memory consumption, and benchmark. The result indicates that the scheme is lightweight, small-footprint, and easy to deploy.

The remainders of this paper are organized as follows: Sect. 2 gives a more detailed problem statement as a background knowledge; Sect. 3 describes the scheme design; Sect. 4 describes how to patch up permission system; Sects. 5 and 6 evaluate the effectiveness and efficacy of the scheme; Sect. 7 describes the related work and our conclusion is shown in Sect. 8.

2   Background

2.1   Problem Statement

Nowadays, people like to root their Android phones to, e.g., uninstall the pre-installed apps, flash third party ROMs, backup their phones and so on. The website [13] lists 10 reasons attracting users to root their phones. According to [15], 23 % Android phones had been rooted at least once in China mainland by the first half of 2012.

Rooting a phone is putting a *"su"* binary file into the */system/bin* or */system/xbin* directory. People usually use rootkit tools to root their phones. During the rooting process, the rootkit tool first exploits Linux vulnerabilities [7] to temporarily get the root privilege. The Linux vulnerabilities could be: *ASHMEM*,

Exploid, Gingerbeak, Levitator, Mempodroid, RageAgainstTheCage, Wunderbar, ZergRush, and *Zimperlich.* Then, the tool sets the *s* attribute to the *"su"* binary file. With the *s* attribute, the *"su"* binary file could run with root privilege. By executing the *su* command, attackers could let some peace of malicious code running with root privilege.

We assume attackers' goal is to steal users' private data, which is a common attack goal on Android phones. As Android mainly relies on permission system to protect the critical system resources from being abused, permission system is more vulnerable to suffer attacks. Therefore, we mainly focus on the attacks and defences towards permission system.

Getting root privilege will put permission system in a vulnerable position. With root privilege, permission system can be bypassed. In bypassing attacks, malware fully depend on root privilege. When malware lose root privilege, the bypassing attack can be blocked. Unrooting a phone can make malware lose root privilege, which is to remove the added *"su"* binary file from the phone. Without the *"su"* file, malware cannot execute the *su* command. As a result, they will lose root privilege. For the bypassing attacks, without root privilege, malware cannot directly access system resources anymore.

Problem Statement. However, just unrooting a phone is insufficient to defend other root-exploiting attacks towards permission system [19]. Those rooted phones in the wild also are lack of support from vendors. In addition, SEAndroid is limited to versions and somehow to vendors. Motivated by these observations, we aim at providing a scheme that patches up permission system and does not depend on Android versions.

2.2   Weak Points of Permission System

According to [19], the three weak points of permission system can be summarized as follows.

WP1: The protection to the packages.xml file is fragile. The heart of permission system is a system service named *PackageManager* Service (PMS). PMS maintains a *package setting info* for each app and preserves the info into a metadata file named *packages.xml.* The *package setting info* of an app contains the app's granted permissions, certification, UID, path, timestamp, etc. Each app's *package setting info* is denoted as a <package> node in the *packages.xml* file. Adding permissions into an app's <package> node can escalate the app's permission.

Normally, the *packages.xml* file belongs to the system user, and other users cannot access it due to the Linux user-based access control. However, the Linux user-based access control is invalid for the *super user.* As long as a malware has got root privilege and turned into a *super user*, it can tamper the file to add any permission to itself and even other apps.

What is more, permission system exploits the file to optimize the signature verification process to shorten boot time. Android allows different apps to share the same UID and enforces them to be signed by the same certificate.

By tampering the certificate info (preserved in the <package> node), malware can bypass the signature verification process and share UID with other apps.

WP2: Re-installation lacks of rigorous argument. All the installed apps, including system and non-system apps, will be reinstalled at system boot time. For a non-system app, if its <package> node exists, the app's permission will be obtained from the node. If its <package> node is removed, the app is actually regarded as being uninstalled; PMS still reinstalls the app and directly grant permissions declared in the app's *AndroidManifest.xml* file (manifest file) to the app. This is actually the same as installing a new app without users' approval. Taking advantage of this design, malware can escalate permissions by removing its <package> node and making PMS install a malicious version of it (e.g., permission-thirsty version). Lack of users' approval is a weak point when <package> node is removed at system boot time.

WP3: The system app identity authentication is loose. System apps play a more important role than non-system apps. However, there is no special requirement for the system apps' certificate. The system apps also apply to the self-signed certificate mechanism, which makes system apps can be replaced by a malicious one. The malicious one does not need to be signed by the same certificate as the target one.

Moreover, different from non-system apps, system apps can directly get full permissions applied in their manifest files. This advantage also attracts malware to disguise as a system app. Permission system treats apps in the */system/app* directory as system apps. As long as a malware is put in the */system/app* directory, no matter what kinds of certificate the malware has, it can be successfully installed into a phone as a system app.

Exploring the three weak points, attackers could carry out various permission escalation attacks. Exploring the escalated permission, attackers can steal various private data.

3   Scheme

We present a scheme to patch up the weak points of permission system and unroot a phone. To make the scheme easy to deploy, we developed an app (PUapp) to carry out the patching and unrooting functionality. When users want to unroot their phones, they just need to install the PUapp and do not need to flash a ROM or update the whole Android system.

3.1   Scheme Design

Aiming at patching up the three weak points of permission system mentioned above, we propose a scheme to enhance the security of permission system. The scheme should protect the integrity of the *packages.xml* file, recover the permissions of non-system apps in a trusted manner, and enhance the identity authentication of system apps.

Protecting the Integrity of the packages.xml File. The *package setting info* is kept in both internal memory and the *packages.xml* file. The two copies are synchronized by PMS. If one is tampered, the other one will be affected. Lacking of effective protection to the *packages.xml* file will lead to permission escalation attacks. To avoid the file been tampered, we propose a protection by slightly adjusting the file existing time on disk, which does not incur much modification.

The *packages.xml* file is only loaded one time at system boot time. There is no need to keep the file on disk all the time. To prevent the file from being tampered, we remove the file from disk immediately after it has been successfully loaded into memory. However, the *packages.xml* file is still needed at the next system boot time (e.g., to recovery each app's UID). Therefore, we should re-generate the file. To do this, we write the permission info kept in memory into the *packages.xml* file after all apps have been shut down by calling a method (*writeLPw*) provide by PMS. In this way, malware have no chance to tamper the *packages.xml* file on disk. As the memory space of permission system is protected by process isolation mechanism, malware cannot tamper the info through memory, either.

We modify the *PackageManagerService.java* file and the *ShutdownThread. java* file to achieve the above goal.

Recovering Permissions of Non-system App. Regarding the second weak points, we introduce users to participate in recovering non-system apps' permission when an app's <package> node is deleted from the *packages.xml* file. It is because that any assistant file is un-trustable on rooted phones.

When an app's <package> node is missing, we let permission system not load this app into memory at system boot time. Instead, we let the user re-grant the app's permission and then install this app with the permissions granted by the user after system is booted up. Moreover, our scheme allows users to selectively grant the necessary permissions to an app and leave the others un-granted. In addition, the scheme allows those un-granted permissions can be dynamically granted at runtime when needed.

The operation interface is provided by the PUapp, too. This design also needs to modify the *PackageManagerService.java* file and the *PackageParser.java* file to add an API to support the selectively permission granting way.

Enhancing Identity Authentication of System App. Regarding the third weak points, we let system apps' identity be verified by certificate instead of directory.

Instead of using more strong identity authentication, permission system regards apps in the */system/app* directory as system apps. As long as a malware is put in the */system/app* directory, no matter what kinds of certificate the malware has, it can be successfully installed into a phone as a system app. The identity authentication of system apps is too loose, which is the main cause of the attack. Thus, we let system apps' identity be verified by certificate instead of directory, which needs to modify the *collectCertificates* method of the *PackageParser* class (*PackageParser.java* file).

As the integrity of the *packages.xml* file can be guaranteed, the optimization to signature verification will not be exploited to escalate permission anymore. Considering the lightweight requirement, we still keep the optimization in our scheme. The code of all the modifications are less than 380 LOC, which indicates that our approach has a small footprint. Moreover, keeping the optimization mechanism also minimizes the performance loss.

3.2 Scheme Workflow

Based on the above design, we provide two levels of guarantees for permission system. In the first level, our scheme ensures the permissions loaded from the *packages.xml* file are credible. When the file fails to be generated (e.g., in case of battery died), the second level protection can load non-system and system apps' permissions in a trusted manner. The framework is shown as Fig. 1. We take one running circle to elaborate how the scheme works. When a phone is booted, PMS first checks whether the *packages.xml* file is correctly generated. If yes, PMS loads the info preserved in the *packages.xml* file into memory (arrow 1), and then deletes the file from disk. The following boot-up steps are not changed till the phone is booted up. When the user wants to shut the phone down, the shutdown thread will be called (arrow 7). Next, the thread will call PMS (arrow 8) to synchronize the *package setting info* from memory to disk to regenerate the *packages.xml* file (arrow 9).

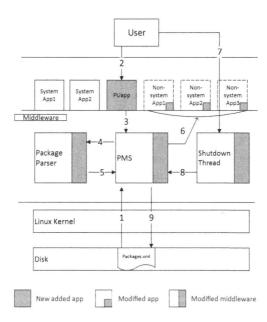

Fig. 1. The workflow of the scheme

Exceptions like battery died or system crash may cause the re-generating step fails. In this case, PMS re-grants permissions to system and non-system apps in different ways. For system apps, we let PMS use enhanced signature verification to verify their signatures and load the legal ones into system with full permissions requested in the manifest file. For non-system apps, PMS does not load any non-system app at system boot time except the PUapp (see Fig. 1). After the phone is booted up, we let the user re-grant the non-system apps' permissions via the PUapp (arrow 2). When the re-granting process is done, PUapp passes the permission granting result to PMS via IPC (arrow 3). PMS passes the result to the *PackageParser.java* file (arrow 4). The *PackageParser.java* file **removes** the un-granted permissions and returns the result to PMS (arrow 5). Then PMS grants the permissions following user's command to each app and installs them into system one by one (arrow 6). In case of emergency, users can skip the permission re-granting step and only use system apps. The shutdown step in this case is the same as described earlier (arrow 7–9).

4   Patching Permission System and Unrooting a Phone

We let the PUapp do the patch-and-unroot work as well. The source code of permission system are compiled into a file named *services.jar*, which is located in the */system/framework* directory. Patching permission system is updating the original *services.jar* file to the one containing our scheme code. To update the code file, we need to overcome three issues.

The first issue is how to get the legal certificates. As the legal certificates will be used to verify the system apps' identity, we should collect the certificates beforehand. There are two ways to get them. The first one is to ask the vendors. This way should seek for vendors' support, which is definitely trusted. The other way is to get the certificate from a phone with the same model of the target one and is not rooted before. Normally, phones with the same model shipped with the same system image, and the system apps are signed by the same certificates. The certificate of system apps are preserved in the *packages.xml* file. This file can be dumped from some phones (even not rooted) to a PC using the *adb pull* command. To make the certificates more trustable, we can obtain them from several phones with the same model, and compare them with each other. If all the certificates are the same, they can be trusted. The more phones we get, the more the certificates coming from unrooted phones are trusted. In the extreme case that none of them are the same, or the file cannot be dumped out, we may ask the vendor.

The second issue is optimization. In the real world, most vendors such as Samsung, Sony, HTC optimize the *jar* file to the *odex* file in their factory image. The optimization is hardware-related, and only the same *odex* file running on the same version of phone is allowed. Therefore, we provide *jar* format code file, and we let the PUapp optimize the *jar* format file to the *odex* format file on the target phone.

The third issue is dependency. During the system boot time, the Dalvik Virtual Machine (DVM) will load all Java classes into memory to create the runtime for Android system. In this process, the DVM verifies the *services.odex* files' dependencies with other *odex* files according to a 20-bytes feature code. The feature code is preserved in both the header field of the *services.odex* file and the dependency field of other *odex* files. The verification is to compare whether the feature code coming from the two parts is the same.

To overcome the dependency issue, we extract the feature code from the original *services.odex* file and use it to replace the feature code of the *services.odex* file provide by us. After analyzing the *odex* file's construction, we find that the feature code has a 20-bytes length and has a 52-bytes offset from the file header. To obtain the feature code, we use the *dd* command: *dd if=ori_services.odex of=our_services.odex bs=1 count=20 skip=52 seek=52*. The whole command means reading 20 bytes (feature code) from the original *service.odex* file, and writing the 20 bytes (feature code) to the file we provide. Both reading and writing should skip 52 bytes from the header.

After the patching step is done, the next step is unrooting the phone. To unroot the phone, we let the PUapp delete the *"su"* binary file. Moreover, the *packages.xml* should be deleted as well, because the file may be tampered before. Deleting the file will initiate a selectively permission granting process. If there are no attacks and exceptions, this process only need to be done for just one time.

We carry out a demo experiment on a Galaxy Nexus phone running 4.1.2 code version. This phone supports AOSP and runs *odex* version of code files.

5   Analysis

5.1   Security Analysis

Permissions Can Be Obtained in a Trusted Manner. Permissions can be obtained from the *packages.xml* file or the manifest file. The two ways are both properly protected. The *packages.xml* file cannot be tampered by malware, since the file do not exist when malware is running. The permissions got from the *packages.xml* file is trusted. When permission system needs to recover permissions from the manifest file, our scheme can make sure that the system and non-system apps' permissions are trustily recovered. For system apps, the enhanced identity authentication can guarantee that only apps with legal certificate are loaded into memory. For non-system ones, their permissions are selectively granted by users, which ensures that only permissions approved by users can be loaded into memory and be written into the *packages.xml* file.

Attacks Exploiting the packages.xml File Can Be Blocked. As the *packages.xml* file is unavailable to apps, it cannot be tampered by malware. Therefore, attacks exploiting the file can be defended by our scheme. However, attacks like battery exhausting may cause the *packages.xml* file cannot be successfully generated, which has the same effect as deleting apps' <package> node. Our scheme can combat this case as well. When the *packages.xml* file does not exist,

PMS will grant permissions under users command rather than automatically grant full permissions to non-system apps. Besides, users will be suggested to grant the most necessary permissions to apps and dynamically grant others when needed. Malware cannot get permissions without users' approval. Therefore, these attacks can be defended as well.

Malware Cannot Disguise as System Apps Anymore. Permission system treats system and non-system apps differently when updating their permissions. The granted permissions of system apps are not restricted by the *packages.xml* file. Even without tampering the *packages.xml* file, malware can also launch attack by disguising as a system app. Our scheme can combat this attack as well.

Malware cannot bypass the signature verification process as the *packages.xml* file cannot be tampered, and they cannot get the **private** key of a legal certificate, either. As our scheme enforces that only apps signed by legal certificate will be installed as system apps, malware staying in the */system/app* directory but not signed by legal certificate cannot be installed. Therefore, the attacks cannot be launched.

5.2 Usability Analysis

Our scheme introduces users' participation, therefore, the user experience should be considered. Involving users in recovering permissions is because any assistant file is un-trustable on rooted phones.

Users can use the PUapp to selectively re-grant permissions to non-system apps. Unlike the all-or-nothing decision way, users can only grant the permissions for running basic functions smoothly and temporarily deny others. For example, an e-book or a desktop app does not require the INTERNET permission, denying which will not affect usability.

Those temporarily denied permissions can be granted when needed. When users want to use the functionalities that require un-granted permissions, a dialog will be toasted and asks users whether or not to grant the permission this time. If users do want to use the permission-required function, they can dynamically grant the permission for one time. Every time the app wants to launch the function, it must be confirmed by the user. If users want to grant the permission permanently, they can grant the needed one using PUapp while still keep others not granted.

It should be mentioned that we do not handle the security exceptions when a permission is denied. One reason is that handling the security exceptions requires modifying other part of Android system, which will make the scheme complicated and difficult to deploy.

When a user wants to patch up permission system and unroot his phone, all he need is to install the PUapp. Also, we let the patch and unroot function be available by touching one button. The whole scheme is contained in a *services.jar* file. When a user touches the button, the PUapp will update the original code file to the one we provide, and then his phone will be patched and unrooted automatically. The PUapp is simple and easy to use.

6 Performance Evaluation

We tested our prototype system's performance in the following three aspects on the same Galaxy Nexus phone.

6.1 Start-Up Time Evaluation

Our scheme modifies the execution flow of permission system in the following ways: (1) adding several logical judgments; (2) preventing permission system from generating the *packages.xml* file during runtime; (3) loading non-system apps conditionally. The modification affects system start-up time. We test the modification influence in the following ways.

The system start-up time is affected by the number of installed apps. In order to exclude the impact of app number, we only install the same 52 system apps both in Android with and without patches. Then we respectively reboot each system for 53 times on the condition that the *packages.xml* file is correctly loaded. Therefore, the added logic flow is executed. The average boot time of Android with patches is 17481.48387 ms, which is about 3 % (0.5 s) shorter than that without one's 18031.41509 ms. The test result is shown as Fig. 2.

According to our test results, even though our scheme modifies the permission system, it has a merely invisible effect on start-up time. It is because that although we add some execution logic, we cut the I/O consumption by not writing the *packages.xml* file into disk, which reduces the start up time.

We did not install non-system apps, which does not affect the above result. Moreover, we can infer from the above results that without the *packages.xml* file, the start-up time of Android with patches will be much shorter than that without, as our scheme will not load non-system apps while the other does.

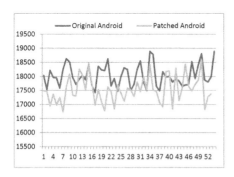

Fig. 2. Boot time comparison result

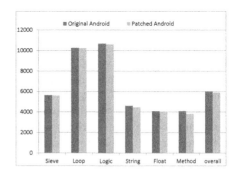

Fig. 3. Benchmark comparison result

6.2   Memory Consumption Evaluation

The scheme adds some APIs for selectively granting permission and reinforces the verification of system apps' identity. Both of them transfer information through memory, which affects memory consumption. In our enhancement, that transferring un-granted permission info through memory is the only memory-consuming protection newly added.

We tested the memory consumption of the *copy* and the *add* operation using *mem-benchmark*, whose result shows the memory consumption of *copy* operation increases by 1 %, while the *add* operation increases by 0.5 %. The result shows that although we add patches to permission system, the increase of memory consumption is invisible.

6.3   System Benchmark Evaluation

Combining the above analysis, we know that the scheme has an impact on performance of disk, memory, and CPU etc. To understand the impact of using our scheme to the whole performance of Android system, we tested its benchmark.

We use *CaffeineMark3.0* Performance Metrics tool, which measures the speed of Java programs and marks the scores by the number of Java instructions executed per second, to measure the performance of Android system with our enhancement. Figure 3 shows the benchmark comparison results of the original Android and Android with our enhancement.

As can be seen from Fig. 3, the *logic* and *method* terms have a slight decrease, which is expected because we have added some logic and new APIs. The *string* term also has a slight performance lose, which can be regarded as a side effect of our patching work. The overall performance loss is 1.8 %, which indicates that our scheme is quite lightweight.

7   Related Work

7.1   Enhancement Towards Permission System

Permission system, as the most important security system on Android, has drawn much attention these years. Attacks [2,3,6,12], detection tools [1,4,8–10], as well as many security enhancement solutions towards permission system have been proposed.

Some framework security extension solutions [5,14,16,21] enforces runtime permission control to restrict apps' permissions at runtime, but these works do not consider the problem system faced under the condition that malwares get root privilege. Although these works can control apps' permissions at runtime, all of them rely on policy database file and they lack protection measures to the file. When malwares get root privilege, the policy file can be easily tampered or deleted. Once the policy file is tampered or lost, the solution loses its effectiveness.

7.2 SEAndroid

To mitigate security issues brought by root exploits, SEAndroid is merged into AOSP since version 4.3 and enforced since version 4.4.

Although SEAndroid can mitigate the security issues brought by root exploits, it has a rather limited range of deployment. Nearly 90 % of the Android phones in the wild are however not protected by SEAndroid. It may take a long period of time before SEAndroid can be widely deployed in the wild. During this period of time, many users cannot be protected by SEAndroid.

Besides the distribution range limitation, SEAndroid has weakness as well. Pau Oliva shows three weaknesses of SEAndroid and gives out 4 ways to bypass SEAndroid [18]. We did an experiment, in which we change SEAndroid from enforce mode to permissive mode via PC terminals. The same principle could be applied to apps. The experiment shows that SEAndroid can indeed be bypassed.

8 Conclusion

Many rooted phones in the wild are not protected by SEAndroid or cannot get support from vendors. Even users are motivated to unroot their phones, the security risk caused by weak points of permission system still exists. In this paper, we present a scheme that patches up the week points of permission system. This scheme does not need to flash a ROM or update the whole Android system. The scheme applies to any Android version and is easy to deploy. The evaluation result shows the scheme is also lightweight.

References

1. Au, K.W.Y., Zhou, Y.F., Huang, Z., Lie, D.: Pscout: analyzing the android permission specification. In: ACM CCS (2012)
2. Bugiel, S., Davi, L., Dmitrienko, A., Fischer, T., Sadeghi, A.R., Shastry, B.: Towards taming privilege-escalation attacks on android. In: 19th NDSS (2012)
3. Chan, P.P., Hui, L.C., Yiu, S.: A privilege escalation vulnerability checking system for android applications. In: ICCT. IEEE (2011)
4. Chin, E., Felt, A.P., Greenwood, K., Wagner, D.: Analyzing inter-application communication in android. In: 9th MobiSys (2011)
5. Conti, M., Nguyen, V.T.N., Crispo, B.: CRePE: context-related policy enforcement for android. In: Burmester, M., Tsudik, G., Magliveras, S., Ilić, I. (eds.) ISC 2010. LNCS, vol. 6531, pp. 331–345. Springer, Heidelberg (2011)
6. Davi, L., Dmitrienko, A., Sadeghi, A.-R., Winandy, M.: Privilege escalation attacks on android. In: Burmester, M., Tsudik, G., Magliveras, S., Ilić, I. (eds.) ISC 2010. LNCS, vol. 6531, pp. 346–360. Springer, Heidelberg (2011)
7. Duo Security: X-ray for Android. http://www.xray.io/ (2012)
8. Enck, W., Ongtang, M., McDaniel, P.: On lightweight mobile phone application certification. In: 16th ACM CCS, pp. 235–245. ACM (2009)
9. Felt, A.P., Chin, E., Hanna, S., Song, D., Wagner, D.: Android permissions demystified. In: 18th ACM CCS, pp. 627–638. ACM (2011)

10. Fuchs, A.P., Chaudhuri, A., Foster, J.S.: Scandroid: automated security certification of android applications. Manuscript, University of Maryland (2009)
11. Google: Dashboards. http://developer.android.com/about/dashboards/index. html?utm_source=ausdroid.net#Platform (2014). Accessed Mar 2014
12. Hardy, N.: The confused deputy: (or why capabilities might have been invented). ACM SIGOPS Oper. Syst. Rev. **22**(4), 36–38 (1988)
13. LifeHacker: Top 10 reasons to root your android phone. http://lifehacker.com/ top-10-reasons-to-root-your-android-phone-1079161983 (2013). Accessed 10 Aug 2013
14. Nauman, M., Khan, S., Zhang, X.: Apex: extending android permission model and enforcement with user-defined runtime constraints. In: 5th ACM CCS (2010)
15. NetQin: 2012 moblie phone security report. http://cn.nq.com/neirong/2012shang. pdf (2012)
16. Ongtang, M., McLaughlin, S., Enck, W., McDaniel, P.: Semantically rich application-centric security in android. Secur. Commun. Netw. **5**(6), 658–673 (2012)
17. Smalley, S., Craig, R.: Security Enhanced (SE) Android: Bringing Flexible MAC to Android. In: NDSS (2013)
18. viaForensics: Defeating seandroid defcon 21 presentation. https://viaforensics. com/mobile-security/implementing-seandroid-defcon-21-presentation.html (2013). Accessed 3 Aug 2013
19. Zhang, Z., Wang, Y., Jing, J., Wang, Q., Lei, L.: Once root always a threat: analyzing the security threats of android permission system. In: Susilo, W., Mu, Y. (eds.) ACISP 2014. LNCS, vol. 8544, pp. 354–369. Springer, Heidelberg (2014)
20. Zhou, Y., Jiang, X.: Dissecting android malware: characterization and evolution. In: Security and Privacy (SP), pp. 95–109. IEEE (2012)
21. Zhou, Y., Zhang, X., Jiang, X., Freeh, V.W.: Taming information-stealing smartphone applications (on Android). In: McCune, J.M., Balacheff, B., Perrig, A., Sadeghi, A.-R., Sasse, A., Beres, Y. (eds.) Trust 2011. LNCS, vol. 6740, pp. 93–107. Springer, Heidelberg (2011)

I've Got Your Number:

Harvesting Users' Personal Data via Contacts Sync for the KakaoTalk Messenger

Eunhyun Kim[1], Kyungwon Park[1], Hyoungshick Kim[1], and Jaeseung Song[2]($\boxtimes$)

[1] Department of Computer Science and Engineering,
Sungkyunkwan University, Seoul, Korea
[2] Department of Computer and Information Security, Sejong University, Seoul, Korea
jssong@sejong.ac.kr

Abstract. Instant messaging (IM) is increasingly popular among not only Internet but also smartphone users. In this paper, we analyze the security issue of an IM application, KakaoTalk, which is the most widely used in South Korea, with a focus on automated friends registration based on contacts sync. We demonstrate that there are multiple ways of collecting victims' personal information such as their names, phone numbers and photos, which can be potentially misused for a variety of cyber criminal activities. Our experimental results show that a user's personal data can be obtained automatically (0.26 s on average), and a large portion of KakaoTalk users (around 73 %) uses their real names as display names. Finally, we suggest reasonable countermeasures to mitigate the discovered attacks, which have been confirmed and patched by the developers.

Keywords: Automated friends registration · Contacts sync · Enumeration attack · Information leakage · Security · Privacy · Smartphone · KakaoTalk

1 Introduction

Instant messaging (IM) has become a popular communication service for people who want to stay in touch with their family, friends and business colleagues since there is no cost (or low cost) to use IM services other than an Internet data plan that most users already have for their smartphones or PCs. However, IM services (e.g., WhatsApp, iMessage and Skype) have become the target of continuous cyber attacks such as spam, phishing and the misuse of personal data due to their growing popularity. For example, spammers might want to create rogue user accounts to effectively share their advertisements with IM users.

In this paper, we particularly focus on the discussion of security concerns raised by the automated friend registration (or recommendation) feature used by default for KakaoTalk (http://www.kakao.com/talk/en) which is the most widely used IM service in South Korea. Once this feature is enabled, the newly

© Springer International Publishing Switzerland 2015
K.-H. Rhee and J.H. Yi (Eds.): WISA 2014, LNCS 8909, pp. 55–67, 2015.
DOI: 10.1007/978-3-319-15087-1_5

added phone numbers from the address book in a user's mobile phone are periodically uploaded to the KakaoTalk server in order to maintain the list of the user's friends up to date by automatically registering friends based on their KakaoTalk accounts associated to the added phone numbers. This automatic process is based on the intuition that address book contacts in a mobile phone might be the people that the phone owner wants to communicate with.

This automated friend registration feature with phone numbers sufficiently convenient for an easy way to manage IM friends. However, we argue here that this feature leak critical information about IM users even if KakaoTalk is trying to prevent it. An adversary can attempt to collect victims' personal data such as their KakaoTalk accounts, names, phone numbers and even photos via the contacts sync for KakaoTalk messenger. This is because KakaoTalk accounts can be collected with only the phone numbers associated them. The collected KakaoTalk accounts (and their personal information) might be used for a variety of cyber criminal activities such as spam, phishing and rogue accounts — it can be beneficial for spammers to collect active phone numbers with the phone owners' real names; similar problems can arise if automated friend recommendation services based on users' personal data (e.g., a unique identifier such as phone numbers) are used.

Schrittwieser et al. [5] reported a similar security flaw named *enumeration* in several smartphone messaging applications (e.g., WhatsApp, Viber and Tango). We here extend their work by presenting new *enumeration* attacks that targeted the KakaoTalk service which already have some countermeasures unlike the other applications such as WhatsApp. Surely, if the contacts export function is explicitly provided, it is not difficult to implement an efficient *enumeration* attack. KakaoTalk originally allowed users to export their friends' information into a text file, but this function was recently removed for security reasons. In this paper, we show that users' names and phone numbers can still be obtained without the contacts export function by automatically generating a specific sequence of touch events and examining the heap memory that is used for the KakaoTalk process. Our key contributions can be summarized as follows:

- First, we introduce new *enumeration* attacks that targeted KakaoTalk and examine their feasibility and efficiency in practice. We collected more than 50,000 users' personal data and analyzed the data. The best attack method takes 0.26 s on average to obtain the information about a user's name and phone number.
- Second, we show the impacts of these attacks by analyzing the collected user profile information. Our experimental results show that 36,817 out of 50,567 samples 72.8 %) look like users' *real* names.
- Third, we suggest reasonable countermeasures to mitigate such *enumeration* attacks, which have been confirmed and patched by the developers.

The rest of this paper is organized as follows. In Sect. 2, we explain how the automated friend registration process in KakaoTalk works to provide a better understanding of *enumeration* attacks. Then we present the three *enumeration*

attacks that targeted KakaoTalk to collect KakaoTalk user's personal data in
Sect. 3. In Sect. 4, we introduce the implementations for *enumeration* attacks
and evaluate their feasibility and efficiency by conducting experiments in the
real-world environment. We present a discussion on countermeasures to mitigate
enumeration attacks and ethics in Sect. 5. Related work is discussed in Sect. 6.
Finally, we conclude in Sect. 7.

2   Automated Friends Registration in KakaoTalk

KakaoTalk is the most widely used free IM in South Korea — it currently has
over 145 million registered users worldwide, including 93 % of smartphone users
in South Korea [3]. The KakaoTalk service was originally developed as a mobile
application (similar to WhatsApp) for smartphones such as Android and iOS
devices, but the PC and Mac versions of KakaoTalk applications were also
recently released.

To encourage a user to find and add other users as his/her KakaoTalk friends,
there are three ways: (1) searching for a user by KakaoTalk ID, (2) using a
quick response (QR) code and (3) automatic syncing address book contacts
with the corresponding KakaoTalk accounts. When a user wants to add a specific
KakaoTalk user as a KakaoTalk friend, the user's KakaoTalk ID or the related
QR code can be used. However, the most popular way is to use the automated
friends registration option. In fact, this feature is turned on by default and can
be disabled for only those who do not want to use this.

Once the automatic sync feature is enabled, the contacts in the phone owner's
address book are added to the list of her KakaoTalk friends without manual inter-
vention if the phone number of them are associated with KakaoTalk accounts.
This process is shown in Fig. 1. The newly added phone numbers (step 1) from
the address book are uploaded to the KakaoTalk server (step 2); the KakaoTalk
server tries to find the KakaoTalk accounts with the phone numbers matched
to the received phone numbers from the phone owner's KakaoTalk application
and returns those to the KakaoTalk applications running on the requested user's
devices such as smartphone and PCs (step 3) to update the list of her KakaoTalk
friends with new friends (step 4). This automatic process is based on the intuition that address book contacts in a mobile phone might be the people that the
phone owner wants to communicate with.

Interestingly, the KakaoTalk service does not provide the newly added friends'
original display names, which are registered to the KakaoTalk server, via the
automated friends registration process. Therefore, their names are displayed on
the KakaoTalk application as the contact names in the address book rather than
their original display names which are kept confidential. We surmise that this
naming policy has been established to protect users' personal data from *enumeration* attacks which attempt to collect the KakaoTalk users' names and phone
numbers with enumerated the (possibly) entire phone number range. Since the
display names are not synced, the owner of a phone number cannot be identified
even when there exits a KakaoTalk account associated with the phone number.

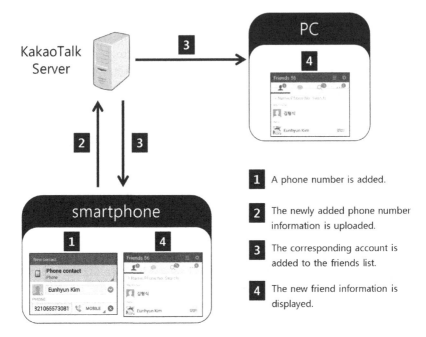

Fig. 1. The process of automated friends registration in KakaoTalk

Therefore, in designing a new *enumeration* attack against KakaoTalk, the main hurdle we had to overcome was to obtain the information about KakaoTalk accounts' original display names without any knowledge about the account holders. We will discuss the details of the proposed *enumeration* attacks in the next sections.

3 Enumeration Attacks via Contacts Sync

To conduct an *enumeration* attack via contacts sync, an attacker generates a range of phone numbers in a valid format and adds the generated phone numbers into the attacker's address book to collect valid phone numbers with their (display) names via the automated friends registration feature in KakaoTalk. The collected information might be effectively used for spam and phishing attacks. To make matters worse, victims do not find that their personal data were leaked by an *enumeration* attack since users can be added without their explicit consents in KakaoTalk.

In this paper, we introduce the following three *enumeration* attacks and discuss their advantages and disadvantages:

– **Use of the export function in KakaoTalk:** an attacker saves the added KakaoTalk users' personal data as a file and/or exports it to email.

- **Use of Optical Character Recognition (OCR) software:** an attacker uses OCR software to extract users' display names.
- **Use of a debugging tool:** an attacker uses a debugging tool to extract users' display names from the memory of a running KakaoTalk application.

3.1 Use of the Export Function in KakaoTalk

The KakaoTalk application allows a user to save the user's friend list as a text file and export the file via email as well. This feature is particularly useful if a user acquires a new device for the KakaoTalk service since the user can restore her KakaoTalk friends from the backup file. The first *enumeration* attack is to simply use this feature.

As described in Sect. 2, the KakaoTalk service uses the contact names in the address book as the names displayed on the KakaoTalk application rather than their original display names. Therefore, if an attacker exports the list of friends obtained by an *enumeration* attack into a file, the attacker can obtain those numbers with the unwanted *pseudo* names arbitrarily assigned by the attacker instead of their original display names in KakaoTalk. Figure 2(a) shows an example of the exported phone numbers with the arbitrary name of '*'.

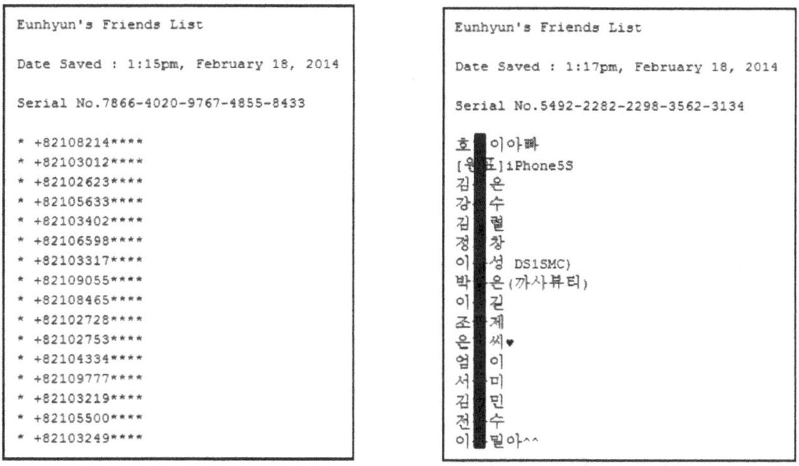

```
Eunhyun's Friends List

Date Saved : 1:15pm, February 18, 2014

Serial No.7866-4020-9767-4855-8433

*  +82108214****
*  +82103012****
*  +82102623****
*  +82105633****
*  +82103402****
*  +82106598****
*  +82103317****
*  +82109055****
*  +82108465****
*  +82102728****
*  +82102753****
*  +82104334****
*  +82109777****
*  +82103219****
*  +82105500****
*  +82103249****
```

```
Eunhyun's Friends List

Date Saved : 1:17pm, February 18, 2014

Serial No.5492-2282-2298-3562-3134

호█이아빠
[위█王]1Phone5S
김█은
강█수
김█렬
경█창
이█성 DS1SMC)
박█은(까사뷰티)
이█깁
조█제
은█씨♥
엄█이
서█미
김█민
전█수
이█필아ㅅㅅ
```

(a) Exported phone numbers   (b) Exported original display names

Fig. 2. Examples of exported contacts information by using the export feature

However, we found that when a KakaoTalk friend's phone number is removed from the address book, the friend's display name on the KakaoTalk application is changed to his/her original name by default via contacts sync. That is, when the friend's phone numbers are removed from the address book, an attacker can export the list of friends' original display names although their phone numbers are removed. Figure 2(b) shows an example of the list of KakaoTalk friends' original display names alone in the exported file.

Therefore, the following *enumeration* attack against KakaoTalk can be implemented by repeatedly exporting the friends list two times:

Step 1. A range of phone numbers in a valid format is generated and added into the address book.

Step 2. By using the export feature, the list of KakaoTalk friends' phone numbers is exported (see Fig. 2(a)).

Step 3. The added phone numbers are removed from the address book.

Step 4. The registered friends' display names on the KakaoTalk application are changed to their original names via contacts sync.

Step 5. By using the export feature, the list of KakaoTalk friends' original display names is exported (see Fig. 2(b)).

Step 6. The combination of these two lists of phone numbers and their KakaoTalk names is stored as the output of the attack.

As a countermeasure against *enumeration* attacks, however, the KakaoTalk service removes the last four-digits of each friend's phone number by masking them with a sequence of asterisk ('****') characters so that the user's private phone number is possibly protected (see Fig. 2(a)). At first glance, this seems secure and reasonable, in reality can do little or nothing to actually achieve improved security.

A simple trick can be used to successfully bypass this defensive mechanism. When a range of phone numbers is generated, an attacker can generate the phone numbers having the same last four-digits but (uniquely) different remaining digits. For example, the attacker can collect active numbers with '3333' as the last four-digits by generating phone numbers from '+82-10-0000-3333' to '+82-10-9999-3333' and entering those number into the attacker's address book. Although the information about '3333' is hidden since the last four-digits are masked, the attacker can easily recover this information by replacing '****' with '3333'.

3.2 Use of OCR Software

Although an efficient *enumeration* attack can be implemented by using the export feature, KakaoTalk recently removed this feature for security reasons (e.g., to prevent *enumeration* attacks).

Without the export feature, however, we can still collect KakaoTalk users' names and phone numbers by using another *enumeration* attack. We found that a victim's original display name can be shown by a specific sequence of user interactions.

When a user is blocked, the user's original name is displayed in the list of blocked friends. This vulnerability was discovered by generating possible user actions in a brute force manner. Figure 3 shows an example of this situation. We can see that a user's display name of '*' is replaced with 'Eunhyun Kim' when her account is blocked.

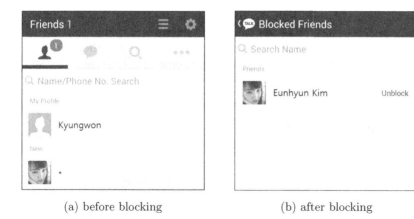

(a) before blocking   (b) after blocking

Fig. 3. An example of the displayed user name in the list of blocked friends

In the second *enumeration* attack, our main idea is to extract a user's original display name using OCR software after blocking the user. The *enumeration* attack can be implemented as follows:

Step 1. A phone number in a valid format is generated and added into the address book.

Step 2. The list of friends is synchronized with the added phone number for the automated friends registration.

Step 3. After the synchronization, it is checked whether the new KakaoTalk friend (associated with the added phone number) is added. This test can be easily implemented by checking the color of the pixel at the specified location in the captured image of the friends list. If a new user is added into the list of friends, the tested pixel should be yellow.

Step 4. If there exists a new friend, the friend is blocked in sequence to find his/her original display name.

Step 5. The screen of blocked friends is captured.

Step 6. The victim's display name is extracted from the captured image by using OCR software.

Step 7. The combination of the entered phone number and the recognized display name is stored as the output of the attack.

Step 8. This process is repeated with another phone number over and over, until there is no new phone number.

3.3   Use of a Debugging Tool

The KakaoTalk service allows a user to change their friends' display names on the user's KakaoTalk application according to the user's needs and preferences. This implies that a text object (i.e., TextView) should be used in the application to handle the display name of the friend's name in a flexible manner.

The third *enumeration* attack is based on the use of this feature. An attacker can retrieve the text of the object handling a victim's display name by using a debugging tool to track memory allocation of the object since there exist several debugging tools (e.g., DDMS: Dalvik Debug Monitor Server) which enable us to capture a snapshot of the volatile memory used by an Android application.

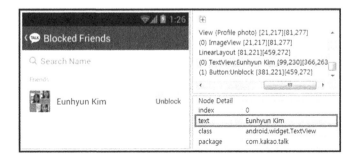

Fig. 4. An example of the victim's name in a memory dump

In the memory dump for the KakaoTalk application, the application's objects (e.g., text, image, list and etc.) and their properties can be retrieved. Figure 4 shows that a blocked friend's display name can be accessed from the associated TextView object. In the memory dump of the blocked friends layout, the text property of this object includes a blocked friend's original display name (highlighted in a red box).

This *enumeration* attack can be implemented in a similar way as the 'use of OCR software' except that a debugging tool is used to directly retrieve the victim's display instead of using OCR software. Instead of using OCR software, a debugging tool is used to directly retrieve the victim's display name.

4   Experiments

In this section, we describe the *enumeration* attacks described in Sect. 3 to show their feasibility against the KakaoTalk's countermeasures and evaluate their performance in a real-world setting.

4.1   Implementation

For the *enumeration* attack using the export function, we used a Google Nexus S (with a 1 GHz CPU and 512 MB RAM) running the Android 4.1.1 Jelly Bean. In Android, the contacts in the address book can simply be modified by sending an intent from the attacker's application.

For the other *enumeration* attacks, however, we additionally used a Windows PC (with an Intel core i5 CPU and 4 GB RAM) running the 64-bit Windows 7, equipped with a non-congested 100 Mbit/s WiFi connection to a LAN that was connected to the Internet via a Gigabit-speed link. The Windows PC was needed to use OCR software or a debugging tool.

For the *enumeration* attack using OCR, we used the OCR service provided by NAVER lab (http://t.lab.naver.com/ocr/) since most KakaoTalk users' display names are written in Korean and NAVER lab's OCR service supports Korean with a high accuracy. To improve the accuracy of text recognition in the OCR service, we increased the resolution of the captured image and cropped the image to remove unnecessary image area (e.g., the blank space).

For the *enumeration* attack using a debugging tool, we used a debugging tool called DDMS, which is commonly used for debugging a process, to track the thread and heap information on the KakaoTalk application.

4.2 Attack Results

With these implementations, we tested the sequentially generated 101,000 phone-like numbers and collected 50,567 KakaoTalk user data (about 50.1 %) in an automatic manner. When we conducted these experiments, the KakaoTalk server did not prevent us from synchronizing these numbers and blocking them in sequence. However, our intention is not to collect users' private data but test the feasibility of the attacks. We discuss the ethics in Sect. 5.

We analyzed the performance of the above three attack implementations by measuring the number of KakaoTalk users collected during a time period by each attack implementation (Table 1).

Table 1. Performance of *enumeration* attacks

	Export	OCR	Debugging
Time	0.26 s	51.07 s	32.56 s
Accuracy	1.00	0.32	1.00

Unsurprisingly, the 'use of the export function' (**Export**) outperformed the other *enumeration* attacks in terms of speed. In this attack, the average time required for a user's data is about 0.26 s. However, KakaoTalk recently removed the export feature for security reasons. Hence, this attack is no longer available.

In this situation, a more obvious recommendation would be to use the debugging tool (**Debugging**) since this approach does not rely on the KakaoTalk's export feature and is significantly better than the 'use of OCR software' (**OCR**) in terms of speed and reliability; when we use the 'use of a debugging tool', the average time required for a user's data is about 32.56 s — this enable us to collect around 2,654 KakaoTalk users' personal data within a day — while the average time required for a user's data is about 51.07 s when we use the 'use of OCR software'.

Finally, we analyze how many KakaoTalk users set real names as their display names in user profiles. When we manually checked the collected 50,567 KakaoTalk user data, we found 36,817 (72.8 %) users set real names as their display names. This implies that serious invasions of privacy might be raised since the collected users' personal data (e.g., phone numbers, status messages and profile pictures) can be effectively associated with their real identities. Probably, this private data can be used to design sophisticated spam and phishing attacks.

5   Discussion

In this section we discuss about potential countermeasures and ethical issues. First, we suggest the three reasonable countermeasures to mitigate *enumeration* attacks in different aspects. We also address the ethical issues in this section since we collected user information without permissions.

5.1   Countermeasures

We describe several potential mechanisms to mitigate the leakage of private information in KakaoTalk. Since these methods are tackling different aspects of the system design, instead of recommending a single approach, we discuss potential countermeasures without any preferences.

- **Detecting anomalous behaviors:** An *enumeration* attack blindly tries to collect user information by automatically sending a lot of queries to a server, which are totally different from normal users' behaviors — in general, the activities generated by an *enumeration* attack would be periodically repeated. Wang et al. [7] already introduced a system to detect automated activities in an online social network using server-side event models. They found that automated bots have shown significantly different behaviors (e.g., sending too many friend requests and spam) from human users during a session. Therefore, we can also build a similar system to detect the queries used in an enumeration attack with a server-side model.
- **Minimizing information leakage:** According to our experiments (see Sect. 4 for details), when the automated friends registration is processed, the KakaoTalk server tries to synchronize friends' personal data stored on the server-side database with the local database of a KakaoTalk application running on a user's (i.e., attacker's) device. This might be helpful for some users, but is not necessarily required to complete the automated friends registration process. We suggest that the KakaoTalk service should not provide any personal information (such as display name, profile picture and etc.) about new friends right after new friends are added via automated friends registration. For usability, instead, some user data (e.g., profile picture) can be synchronized after verifying that they actually know each other (e.g., after having a first chat).

– **Changing the registration policy:** Unlike other social network services (e.g., Facebook and LinkedIn) and IMs (e.g., Skype), KakaoTalk users can add their friends without their consents. If a user simply adds a phone number together with the corresponding contact name, the KakaoTalk service automatically adds the contact as the phone owner's KakaoTalk friend. This is a very convenient feature and helps KakaoTalk increase the number of users for a short-period. However, as we described in this paper, this feature now can be used for *enumeration* attacks. Therefore, in order to mitigate this type of vulnerabilities, KakaoTalk should consider changing the current friend registration mechanism to an invitation-based one.

5.2   Ethical Issues

The main motivation of our experiments is not to obtain personal information data or to use collected data for commercial or illegal purpose. We conduct research work in order to discover vulnerabilities from a popular smartphone IM and develop reasonable countermeasures to mitigate the discovered vulnerabilities. Therefore, we reported the discovered design flaws to the KakaoTalk developers, who acknowledged these flaws, patched them and released an updated version.

Soon after we reported the discovered vulnerabilities, KakaoTalk has released the patch fixing the vulnerabilities. We again tested the updated KakaoTalk and confirmed that a user's real name is not revealed anymore by the proposed attacks in this paper. However, we have found a side-effect from the patch that still revealing the user's real profile name. This is mainly because the patch has not been analyzed enough to guarantee the correct fixing the vulnerabilities.

In summary, our motivation is to open and discuss the vulnerabilities about *enumeration attacks* in the automated friends registration process. The countermeasures for our attacks are suggested in the above subsection.

6   Related Work

Schrittwieser et al. [5] analyzed the security of popular IM applications (e.g., WhatsApp, Viber and Tango) and particularly introduced an *enumeration* attack to collect active phone numbers. They showed the feasibility of the attack by collecting 21,095 valid phone numbers that are using the WhatsApp application within less than 2.5 h. We extend this work by introducing several *enumeration* attacks targeting KakaoTalk, which is widely used in South Korea.

A similar problem related to *enumeration* attack was already reported in social networks. Balduzzi et al. [1] showed the feasibility of an *enumeration* attack that automatically queries about e-mail addresses to collect a list of valid e-mail addresses by uploading them to the friend-finder feature of Facebook. Based on the return value of Facebook, they were able to determine the status of an email address. They tested about 10.4 million e-mail addresses and identified more than 1.2 million user profiles associated with these addresses.

Gross et al. [2] showed that user profiles in online social networks can be misused in ways that present an abuse of personal privacy. They observed that 77.7 % of users were stalked because of the disclosure of their profiles. Wanying Luo et al. [4] presented a group-key based social network service such that users' real identities can be revealed to only authorized group members who own a valid group key.

Smale et al. [6] analyzed online users' profile names (or display names) by categorizing them into several types: name, activity, advertisement, opinion, feeling and etc. According to their observations, about 42.4 % of users in an IM service used their real names as profile names (i.e., name: about 32.4 % and a modification of name: about 10 %).

7   Conclusion

This paper examines the security issues (i.e., three enumeration attacks) that arise in an IM service named KakaoTalk, which is the most widely used in South Korea and suggests potential countermeasures that have been designed to mitigate them. Our test results show that KakaoTalk users' personal data (such as phone numbers, display names and profile pictures) can effectively be collected in an automatic manner. Since a large number of KakaoTalk users (about 73 %) are using their real name as display names, serious invasions of privacy might be raised by the discovered *enumeration* attacks.

Although, we currently limited our attack experiments in KakaoTalk alone, we believe this type of attacks can also be applicable to other social networks and IM applications. For future work, we are planning to extend the proposed techniques (i.e., enumeration attacks and countermeasures) to other social network and IM applications.

Acknowledgements. This research was partly supported by the MSIP (Ministry of Science, ICT & Future Planning), Korea, under the ITRC (Information Technology Research Center) support program (NIPA-2014-H0301-14-1010) supervised by the NIPA (National IT Industry Promotion Agency) and is funded in part by the ICT R&D program (2014-044-072-003, 'Development of Cyber Quarantine System using SDN Techniques') of MSIP/IITP.

References

1. Balduzzi, M., Platzer, C., Holz, T., Kirda, E., Balzarotti, D., Kruegel, C.: Abusing social networks for automated user profiling. In: Jha, S., Sommer, R., Kreibich, C. (eds.) RAID 2010. LNCS, vol. 6307, pp. 422–441. Springer, Heidelberg (2010)
2. Gross, R., Acquisti, A.: Information revelation and privacy in online social networks. In: Proceedings of the 2005 ACM Workshop on Privacy in the Electronic Society, pp. 71–80. ACM (2005)
3. Khan, J.: KakaoTalk Launches Official Mac App. (2014). http://tropicalpost.com/kakaotalk-launches-official-mac-app/

4. Luo, W., Xie, Q., Hengartner, U.: Facecloak: an architecture for user privacy on social networking sites. In: International Conference on Computational Science and Engineering, CSE 2009, vol. 3, pp. 26–33. IEEE (2009)
5. Schrittwieser, S., Frühwirt, P., Kieseberg, P., Leithner, M., Mulazzani, M., Huber, M., Weippl, E.: Guess who's texting you? evaluating the security of smartphone messaging applications. In: NDSS 2012: Proceedings of the 19th Annual Network & Distributed System Security Symposium (2012)
6. Smale, S., Greenberg, S.: Broadcasting information via display names in instant messaging. In: Proceedings of the 2005 International ACM SIGGROUP Conference on Supporting Group Work, pp. 89–98. ACM (2005)
7. Wang, G., Konolige, T., Wilson, C., Wang, X., Zheng, H., Zhao, B.Y.: You are how you click: clickstream analysis for sybil detection. In: Proceedings of the 22nd USENIX Conference on Security, SEC 2013, pp. 241–256 (2013)

Analyzing Unnecessary Permissions Requested by Android Apps Based on Users' Opinions

Jina Kang[1], Daehyun Kim[1], Hyoungshick Kim[1], and Jun Ho Huh[2(✉)]

[1] Department of Computer Science and Engineering,
Sungkyunkwan University, Seoul, Korea
[2] Honeywell ACS Labs, Golden Valley, USA
etpfest@gmail.com

Abstract. Many existing mobile apps request for unnecessary permissions knowing that users often ignore permission warning messages. We conducted an online user study to investigate how users feel about permissions being requested by both free and paid Android apps. Results show that users tend to feel that free Android apps request for more unnecessary permissions compared to paid apps. Users also felt that older apps (those that are previously released and have gone through several updates) request for more unnecessary permissions than those that are newly released. Based on that observation, we surmise that many developers initially publish apps that require a small set of permissions (so that users are not discouraged from installing an app), and gradually add more permissions to their apps through updates.

Keywords: Permission · Android · Smartphones · Usable security

1 Introduction

When a user tries to install a mobile application (or an app) from `Google Play` (marketplace for Android apps), a list of *permissions* required by that app is shown to the user before initiating the installation process. Android asks the user if she or he wishes to continue installing the app and grant those permissions to that app. Most casual users, however, are not too interested in those permissions. Recent studies [5–7] have shown that the majority of users tend to ignore permission warning messages at installations time. Warning messages pop up on the screen when users have already decided to install an app; at that stage, users probably just want to continue with the installation without being interrupted [2,7]. Even for users who pay careful attention to permissions being requested, permission descriptions are often confusing and are hard to understand.

This is a big concern because more and more apps are increasingly asking for access to sensitive information on your phone to function properly. Facebook Messenger, for instance, asks to "record audit with the microphone (at any time without your confirmation)", "access the phone's call logs", "read data about

© Springer International Publishing Switzerland 2015
K.-H. Rhee and J.H. Yi (Eds.): WISA 2014, LNCS 8909, pp. 68–79, 2015.
DOI: 10.1007/978-3-319-15087-1_6

contacts stored on the phone", etc. In fact, a study shows that 96 % of iOS apps require email permissions, 92 % require address book, 84 % require location permissions, 52 % require camera permissions, and 32 % require calendar permissions [8]. Companies like Facebook, Twitter and Linkedin with huge userbase have recently figured out how to generate strong revenue through mobile advertisements (e.g., through sponsored ads and posts). To enhance the relevance and success of their ads (i.e., targeted ads), such companies will try to gather as much personal data as possible and the worst is yet to come in terms of apps requesting for unnecessary permissions.

As an extension of recent studies on permissions, we investigate how end-users feel about the level of permissions being requested by popular Android apps, asking which permissions seem unnecessary or necessary for an app to function properly. Users gave their opinions on the necessity of requested permissions; e.g., 'Angry Birds' (a free popular Android game) requiring a permission to read phone state and identity information is questionable. In many cases, such assessments for excessive permissions will be subjective. To strengthen the analysis, we gathered 234 popular Android apps from `Google Play` and conducted a user study with 125 participants, asking each participant to give their opinions on permissions being requested by all 234 apps. As mentioned above, since permission warnings are typically ignored by the majority of users [5–7], it is integral to identify unnecessary permissions and remove them (or highlight them) to follow the least privilege principle [9]. This study might be the cornerstone of identifying such unnecessary permissions in apps. Our key contributions can be summarized as follows:

– We identified the lists of permissions that are frequently considered by users as unnecessary or incomprehensible. About 24 % of the permissions we tested with were frequently considered as unnecessary. More permissions from the `PERSONAL_INFO`, `LOCATION`, and `MESSAGES` permission groups were considered to be unnecessary than those from the other groups. Some permissions were totally incomprehensible even for security experts. Many permissions defined by developers (e.g., `com.skt.aom.permission.AOM_RECEIVE`) were not well defined.
– We showed that users are more concerned with the permissions in free Android apps than with those in paid apps. Free apps tend to ask for more permissions that would allow them to collect sensitive personal information (e.g., 'Read your contact data'), implying that free apps rely more on the collection of personal data.
– We found that the numbers of unnecessary permissions in older apps (that have gone through several updates) are significantly greater than those in newly released apps. We surmise that many developers initially publish apps with a small set of permissions, but, through updates, incrementally add more unnecessary permissions.
– We observed that users with more awareness of permissions were more sensitive and careful about unnecessary permissions. This might be an evidence that security education can help users identify unnecessary permissions and make better decisions.

We believe those observations can help build more effective and reliable permission models for the Android platform. For example, permissions that are frequently considered as unnecessary can be highlighted to inform users about potentially dangerous permissions.

2   Related Work

The Android permission system limits access to sensitive data (SMS, contacts, calendar), resources (battery or log files) and system interfaces (Internet connection, GPS, GSM). To invoke sensitive APIs, users should grant the relevant permissions for an app at install time. Even though Android 4.3 provides a hidden feature called "App Ops", which allows users to selectively revoke unnecessary permissions on a per-app basis, users are still relied upon to determine the permissions that should not be granted.

Many researches have been concerned with understanding permissions used in Android. Kelley et al. [7] showed that most users cannot understand permission screens. Felt et al. [5] showed that Android permissions fail to clearly inform the majority of users about their privileges. To that end, Kelley et al. [6] suggested the use of a new design called 'privacy checklist' to display (potential) privacy risks of using an app, and showed that the proposed display does significantly affect users' app selection decisions compared with the current interface.

Felt et al. [4] surveyed 100 paid and 856 free apps to identify the most frequently used dangerous permissions (i.e., which generate permission warning notification) and showed that there was a significant gap between the free and paid apps in the frequency of dangerous permissions being requested; for example, 14 % of free apps ask for the INTERNET permission, but only 4 % of paid apps ask for the same permission. This disparity supports the hypothesis in [1] where free apps may frequently ask for the INTERNET permission in order to load advertisements. We extend their work by considering the relationship between the apps and the permissions. Unlike ours, Felt et al. [4] used a fixed set of common permissions categorized as Normal, Dangerous and Signature by Google but some apps even use Dangerous permissions legitimately.

One of the most important challenges for a better permission system is to develop automated tools to detect overprivileged and (potentially) malicious apps. Stowaway [3] was designed to detect overprivileged Android apps by checking whether an app asks for more permissions than what is needed. Felt et al. [3] found that about one-third of 940 Android apps are considered overprivileged. Vidas et al. [11] proposed a static analysis tool for finding the actual (minimum) set of permissions that an app uses to behave correctly.

3   User Study

3.1   Study Design

Our study was designed to answer the following research questions:

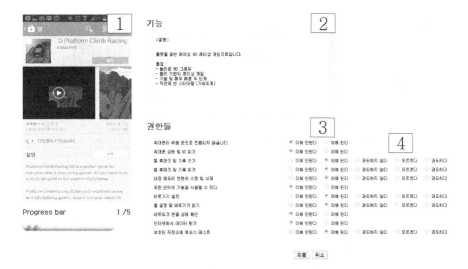

Fig. 1. An example of survey questions: (1) a randomly chosen app's screenshot (captured from `Google play`) was shown in the leftmost window; (2) the description of the app (obtained from `Google play`) was presented in the middle-upper window; (3) questions about comprehensibility of the permissions requested by the app were displayed with using two scales (incomprehensible–comprehensible) radio buttons in the middle-bottom window; and (4) when clicking the 'comprehensible' button for a permission, another question about excessiveness of the permission was displayed with using a three scales (not excessive–maybe–excessive) radio button in the rightmost window.

- **RQ1.** What are the most frequently reported unnecessary or incomprehensible permissions in Android apps?
- **RQ2.** Do free apps demand more unnecessary permissions than paid apps?
- **RQ3.** Does the number of unnecessary permissions requested by an app significantly increase over time?
- **RQ4.** Are users with more awareness of permissions also more sensitive toward unnecessary permissions being requested?

Answers to those research questions will help us understand more clearly how smartphone users behave when they install apps, and help them make better decisions by identifying unnecessary permissions requested by apps.

We conducted an online user study to examine the level of Android users' understanding and concerns about the permissions requested by apps. The survey could be accessed in an anonymous way by both PC and mobile users.

A pilot study was first conducted with four subjects (who were familiar with Android) to identify issues with the study and to get a sense of how well the questions and user interfaces were designed. Final modifications were made on the questionnaire based on the observations from the pilot study. Here is an overview of study design:

1. First, we gathered the participants' consent and asked them to complete a background questionnaire to obtain demographic information (gender, age,

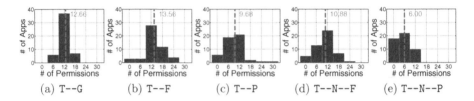

Fig. 2. Histograms of the number of permissions for the apps in each of the five categories (`Top Grossing`, `Top Free`, `Top Paid`, `Top New Free`, and `Top New Paid`) in `Google Play`. The red dotted lines represent the mean of the number of permissions over the all apps in each category (Color figure online).

job, and Android version) and data to assess their familiarity with Android permissions. To assess familiarity with Android permissions, we asked the following two questions: (Q1) Do you know what permissions mean when installing Android apps? and (Q2) Do you pay attention to permission information when downloading an app?.

2. Second, we provided an example (training) survey to increase participants' familiarity with our survey procedure. It was designed to help participants learn how to complete the tasks: given an app, participants were asked to read the description of the app and then carefully select incomprehensible or unnecessary permissions from the list of permissions requested by that app.

3. Third, in the real study, participants were asked to complete the same set of tasks for five randomly selected apps (see an example in Fig. 1). An app was randomly selected from each of the following five categories in `Google Play`: `Top Grossing`, `Top Free`, `Top Paid`, `Top New Free`, and `Top New Paid`.

3.2 Android Apps Used in Our Survey

We downloaded the top 50 Android apps from each of the five categories (`Top Grossing`, `Top Free`, `Top Paid`, `Top New Free`, and `Top New Paid`) in the Korean `Google Play` store. Some categories were not mutually exclusive though. For example, 10 apps from the `Top Grossing` category were also shown in `Top Free` and `Top Paid` categories. Consequently, we compiled a total of 73 permissions from 234 popular Android apps. Those permissions represent only a portion of all Android permissions, but are the most frequently used ones.

Histograms in Fig. 2 show the distributions of the number of permissions required all the apps in each category. From those histograms, we can see that `Top Free` and `Top Grossing` have relatively more permissions than the other categories.

3.3 Demographics

We recruited participants who own a smartphone by posting fliers about our study on bulletin boards in a university. We clarified the academic motivations behind this study to encourage participants to pay more attention to our study.

Table 1. The demographics of the participants

Gender	
Male	72.73%
Female	27.27%
Age group	
18–29	97.98%
30–49	2.02%
Highest level of education completed	
High school	85.86%
College/University	14.14%
Smartphone platforms	
Android	95.96%
iOS	4.04%
Do you know what permission means when installing apps?	
Yes	56.57%
Maybe	28.28%
No	15.15%
Have you paid attention to permission at install time?	
Yes	25.00%
Maybe	28.57%
No	43.43%

Participants also received a $2 honorarium for completion of the user study after investigating the validity of their responses.

During a week period, 125 participated in the survey, and 99 respondents (out of that 125) correctly completed the questionnaire. The majority of the respondents were male (72.73 %) and were in the age group of 18–29 (97.98 %). 56.57 % said that they are aware of permissions, while only 25 % of them actually paid attention to permissions during app installation (See Table 1).

4   Study Results and Discussion

This section analyses the results collected from the user study, and discusses the participants' levels of concerns with Android permissions with respect to their necessity and comprehensibility.

4.1   Incomprehensible Permissions

We first present the list of permissions that were frequently mentioned by participants to be *incomprehensible* (see Table 2). In order to identify those permissions,

Table 2. The list of frequently mentioned incomprehensible permissions. The number inside the parentheses in each type indicates the number of permissions included in the type.

Type	Permission
Android (3)	– Allows an application to call killBackgroundProcesses(String)
	– Allows an application to read from external storage
	– Allows an application to perform I/O operations over NFC
Google (1)	– Use the authentication credentials of an account
Third-party (1)	– `com.skt.aom.permission.AOM_RECEIVE`

we used "yes" or "no" type of questions, asking whether a participant thinks a permission is incomprehensible.

In general, a permission can be considered incomprehensible when "yes" responses are more likely to occur than "no" responses. After counting the numbers of "yes" and "no" responses, respectively, for each permission, the binomial exact test (one-tailed) was used to test whether the number of "yes" responses was significantly greater than the number of "no" responses (i.e., the expected probability of the "yes" response is significantly greater than 0.5).

From the study results, only 5 of 73 permissions (about 6.8 %) were frequently identified as incomprehensible permissions. Table 2 shows those incomprehensible permissions. We observed that all of those permissions contained a technical terminology or a jargon (e.g., 'NFC' or 'killBackgroundProcesses') that a casual user may not know. Three Android-defined permissions were also included in that list (see the number inside the parentheses in the 'Android' type). This shows that even some of the official, Android-defined permissions were not well understood.

Our results were quite different from a previous study [7], which showed that the majority of permissions were not well understood by Android users. Contrastingly, only about 6.8 % were seen as incomprehensible permissions in our study. The different demographics in the two studies may have caused that: Sect. 3.3 shows that our sample of users, on average, are younger (97.98 % of them were aged between 18 and 29) and have higher education (all participants were university students) than those who have participated in the previous study [7].

4.2 Unnecessary Permissions

In this section, we present the list of permissions that were frequently mentioned by participants to be *unnecessary*.

To ask whether a permission seems unnecessary for a given app, only those who understood the meaning of a permission were sequentially asked to respond to a question about the necessity of that permission. A three-point Likert scale ranging from 0 ("disagree") to 2 ("agree") was used to answer that question. A permission is considered unnecessary when "agree" responses occur more

Table 3. The list of frequently mentioned excessive permissions. The number inside the parentheses in each category indicates the number of permissions included in the category.

Category	Permission
`system tool` (2)	– Allows an application to call killBackgroundProcesses(String)
	– Changing the general settings of the system
`phone call` (1)	– Reroute outgoing calls
`personal information` (5)	– Allows an application to read the user's contacts data
	– Allows an application to read the user's call log
	– Allows an application to write (but not read) the user's call log
	– Allows an application to write (but not read) the user's calendar data
	– Allows an application to read the user's calendar data
`location` (3)	– Allows an application to access precise location from location sources such as GPS, cell towers, and Wi-Fi
	– Allows an application to create mock location providers for testing
	– Allows an application to access extra location provider commands
`message` (1)	– Allows an application to read SMS messages

than "disagree" responses. After counting the numbers of "agree", "neutral" and "disagree" responses for each permission, the one-tailed t-test was used to test whether the mean score was significantly greater than 1.0, which indicates the neutrality level.

From the results, 12 of 73 permissions (about 16.4 %) were frequently identified as unnecessary permissions (see Table 3). To analyze the characteristics of those permissions, we also looked at their category information defined by Google (see more details in http://developer.android.com/reference/android/Manifest. permission_group.html). We observed that participants were particularly concerned about the permissions that would allow apps to access personal data such as contacts, call logs, calendar, or locations. For example, 5 of 11 personal data permissions (about 45.45 %) were frequently mentioned as unnecessary, and 3 of 4 location permissions (75 %) were considered as unnecessary. On the other hand, participants considered only 2 of 26 permissions (about 7.69 %) in system tools as unnecessary. Moreover, participants were not too concerned with the permissions that would give apps direct access to hardware components like audio or camera. Such a lack of concern could have serious security and privacy implications as discussed in several previous studies (e.g., [10,12]). For instance, a malicious app that has requested for the camera permission could silently take pictures or record videos of private moments and transfer them over the air.

4.3   Comparing Free Apps and Paid Apps

This section analyses participants' responses to permissions in *free* apps compared with those in *paid* apps. We divided the apps into free (Top Free and Top New Free) and paid (Top Paid and Top New Paid) apps and analysed the differences in the required level of unnecessary permissions as opinionated by the participants – if the score is high for an app, that app can be considered risky in terms of the number of unnecessary permissions that it has.

From the study results, the mean score for the free apps was 5.9495 with the standard deviation of 6.4231 while the mean score for the paid apps was 4.3939 with the standard deviation 5.9085. We statistically tested the difference between free and paid apps using unpaired one-tailed t-test ($P \leq 0.05$) and obtained the P-value of 0.0063. From that test result, we can state with statistical significance that the mean score for free apps is higher than the mean score for paid apps, indicating that free apps (Top Free and Top New Free) request for more unnecessary permissions and tend to be riskier than paid apps (Top Paid and Top New Paid).

4.4   Comparing Top Apps and Top New Apps

This section analyzes participants' responses to excessive permissions in *top* apps compared with those in *top new* apps. To demonstrate this, we divided the apps into top (Top Free and Top Paid) and top new (Top New Free and Top New Paid) apps and analysed their differences in the number of excessive permissions.

From the study results, the mean score for the top apps was 6.5455 with the standard deviation of 7.4244 while the mean score for the top new apps was 3.7980 with the standard deviation of 4.2973. We statistically tested the difference between top and top new apps using unpaired one-tailed t-test ($P \leq 0.05$) and obtained a very small P-value ($\ll 0.0001$). From that test result, we can state with statistical significance that the mean score for top apps is significantly higher than the mean score for top new apps, indicating that top apps request for more unnecessary permissions and turned out to be riskier than the newly released apps.

This observation is interesting since it indicates that the developers might deliberately include less permissions in the initial version of an app – to make it look safer to use – but could be gradually adding more permissions through updates. In depth study of a randomly selected sample of apps (that requested a large number of permissions) reinforced that observation: for example, an app designed to allow home screen customization requested for unnecessary permissions like 'Allows an app to access precise location from location sources such as GPS, cell towers, and Wi-Fi', 'Allows an application to read SMS messages' and 'Allows access to the Gmail content provider' when it pushed out updates that did not have noticeable new features.

If a small number of extra permissions are requested incrementally through each update it would be harder for users to notice it, even if Google Play informs users about newly requested permissions. It might also be true that this trend is due to developers adding more features to their apps through updates and requiring more permissions as a result.

4.5   In Depth Analysis of Free Apps

It is our intuition that most free apps would heavily rely on mobile advertisements to generate revenue, and for such a reason, they tend to request more unnecessary permissions than the paid apps (to analyse personal data and enhance advertisement relevance). In this section, we study the number of free apps that have mobile advertisements and request for unnecessary permissions. We use static analysis tools and manual validation for this analysis.

We studied with 76 different free apps. To count the number of free apps that have in-app advertisements, we used three advertisement detectors (Lookout Ad Network Detector, TrustGo Ad Detector, and AppBrain Ad Detector), which cover most popular advertisement networks such as AdMob, TapJoy, Cauly and InMobi. From our observations, 29 of 76 free apps (about 38.16 %) had in-app advertisements. In particular, many free game apps (e.g., Bouncing Ball and Psychological Test) used advertisement networks. Among the remaining 47 apps, 10 apps requested for permissions to access personal data, and at least 6 apps requested for unnecessary permissions that seemed irrelevant to their core functions.

4.6   Effects of Users' Interests in Permissions

From the demographics in Sect. 3.1, we found that 56.57 % of participants answered 'Yes' to the question 'Do you know what permission means when installing apps?'. To check whether those who answered 'Yes' are more sensitive toward unnecessary permissions (than those who answered 'Maybe' or 'No'), we divided participants' responses according to their answers ('Yes': 56.57 %, 'Maybe': 28.28 %, 'No': 15.15 %) and analysed the differences in how they perceived excessiveness of permissions.

As mentioned before, each participant evaluated the excessiveness of every permission in each of five randomly selected apps using a three-point Likert scale, ranging from 0 ("disagree") to 2 ("agree"). Based on the sum of a participant's ratings for all the permissions in five apps, those who answered 'Yes' scored the highest with 5.7500 on average (standard deviation: 4.9036). The mean score for those who answered 'Maybe' is 3.8214 (standard deviation: 3.7718) and 3.4667 (standard deviation: 3.6227) for those who answered 'No'.

Unpaired one-tailed t-tests ($P \leq 0.05$) were used to compare their answers in a statistical manner. From these results (Yes vs Maybe: 0.0357, Yes vs No: 0.0486, Maybe vs No: 0.3836), we can see that there were significant gaps between participants who answered 'Yes', 'Maybe', and 'No' except for the case of 'Maybe' and 'No'. On the basis of those testing results, we surmise that subjects who are more aware of the meaning of permissions are more picky and careful when it comes to reading permission requests of apps. That finding, to some extent, can support the claims about how security education can help users identify permissions that seem unnecessary given the functions of an app, and make better decisions about upon installing it.

We ran similar tests on the question 'Have you paid attention to permission at install time?' but did not find any statistically significant differences among the participants.

5   Limitations

Our study has three limitations that are worth mentioning. First, we analyzed only 73 permissions from 234 popular apps rather than the full list of Google-defined permissions (145 Android-defined permissions).

Second, in the user studies, we asked the participants for their opinions on the necessity of the permissions based on the description of app features and functions. Fully understanding app functions and accurately selecting unnecessary permissions by just reading app descriptions could have been difficult for some participants.

Third, all of our participants are from a single pool of users. Finding an online survey tool (e.g., Amazon's Mechanical Turk in the U.S.) and surveying a random pool of participants in Korea was not easy. To that end, we conducted an online survey within an university campus, and, as a result, all of the participants were university students. That could have affected the results for identifying incomprehensible permissions. We originally expected that many participants would have low level of understanding of permissions and their terms, but the results showed that only about 7 % of the participants struggled with the terms of permissions. Participants' education level and age have probably affected that.

6   Conclusion

We studied how participants feel and think about Android permissions in terms of how 'unnecessary' and/or 'incomprehensible' they might be. We studied 73 permissions in total, where 12 of them have been frequently opinionated by the participants to be unnecessary: such permissions can leak personal/sensitive information about users and may even cause damages to the mobile devices.

Not surprisingly, free apps tend to ask for more permissions, where those permissions often lead to collection of personal information. Free apps heavily rely on advertisements as their primary monetization means, and that is one reason why we suspect that those apps ask for more permissions. We rated participants' answers based on a simple Likert scale to measure how much free apps and paid apps rely on unnecessary permissions. Free apps scored higher to indicate that they require more number of permissions that are frequently opinionated by users as unnecessary. From just the perspective of the permissions that an app has, those free apps seem to be relatively more dangerous and risky than paid apps. On those lines, our study shows that users are more concerned with permissions requested by free apps since they clearly ask for more permissions.

Interestingly, newly released apps (whether they are paid or free) tend to have much smaller number of permissions than those that have been released some time ago and have gone through several updates. It seems that the developers are putting a small number of permissions in their first releases (newly released apps), but gradually adding more permissions as they release more updates. Hence, users should be aware that the permissions they allow on a newly installed app might look completely different after installing a few updates on it.

Acknowledgements. This research was partly supported by the MSIP (Ministry of Science, ICT & Future Planning), Korea, under the ITRC (Information Technology Research Center) support program (NIPA-2014-H0301-14-1010) supervised by the NIPA (National IT Industry Promotion Agency) and is funded in part by the ICT R&D program (2014-044-072-003, 'Development of Cyber Quarantine System using SDN Techniques') of MSIP/IITP.

References

1. Barrera, D., Kayacik, H.G., van Oorschot, P.C., Somayaji, A.: A methodology for empirical analysis of permission-based security models and its application to android. In: Proceedings of the 17th ACM Conference on Computer and Communications Security (CCS) (2010)
2. Egelman, S., Tsai, J., Cranor, L.F., Acquisti, A.: Timing is everything?: the effects of timing and placement of online privacy indicators. In: Proceedings of the 27th ACM Conference on Human Factors in Computing Systems (2009)
3. Felt, A.P., Chin, E., Hanna, S., Song, D., Wagner, D.: Android permissions demystified. In: Proceedings of the 18th ACM Conference on Computer and Communications Security (CCS) (2011)
4. Felt, A.P., Greenwood, K., Wagner, D.: The effectiveness of application permissions. In: Proceedings of the 2nd USENIX Conference on Web Application Development (WebApps) (2011)
5. Felt, A.P., Ha, E., Egelman, S., Haney, A., Chin, E., Wagner, D.: Android permissions: user attention, comprehension, and behavior. In: Proceedings of the 8th Symposium on Usable Privacy and Security (SOUPS) (2012)
6. Kelley, P.G., Cranor, L.F., Sadeh, N.: Privacy as part of the app decision-making process. In: Proceedings of the 31st ACM Conference on Human Factors in Computing Systems (2013)
7. Kelley, P.G., Consolvo, S., Cranor, L.F., Jung, J., Sadeh, N., Wetherall, D.: A conundrum of permissions: installing applications on an android smartphone. In: Blyth, J., Dietrich, S., Camp, L.J. (eds.) FC 2012. LNCS, vol. 7398, pp. 68–79. Springer, Heidelberg (2012)
8. Leyden, J.: The TRUTH about LEAKY, STALKING, SPYING smartphone applications. The Register (2014)
9. Saltzer, J.H., Schroeder, M.D.: The protection of information in computer systems. Proc. IEEE **63**(9), 1278–1308 (1975)
10. Schlegel, R., Zhang, K., Zhou, X., Intwala, M., Kapadia, A., Wang, X.: Soundcomber: a stealthy and context-aware sound trojan for smartphones. In: Proceedings of the 18th Network and Distributed System Security Symposium (NDSS) (2011)
11. Vidas, T., Christin, N., Cranor, L.: Curbing android permission creep. In: Proceedings of the 5th Workshop on Web 2.0 Security and Privacy (W2SP) (2011)
12. Xu, N., Zhang, F., Luo, Y., Jia, W., Xuan, D., Teng, J.: Stealthy video capturer: a new video-based spyware in 3G smartphones. In: Proceedings of the 2nd ACM Conference on Wireless Network Security (WiSec) (2009)

Vulnerability Analysis

Reconstructing and Visualizing Evidence of Artifact from Firefox SessionStorage

Shinichi Matsumoto[1,2]($\boxtimes$), Yuya Onitsuka[2], Junpei Kawamoto[2], and Kouichi Sakurai[2]

[1] Institute of Systems, Information Technologies and Nanotechnologies, 2-1-22, Momochihama, Fukuoka, Japan
smatsumoto@isit.or.jp

[2] Department of Informatics, Faculty of Information Science and Electrical Engineering, Kyushu University, Fukuoka, Japan
onitsuka@bie.inf.kyushu-u.ac.jp, kawamoto@inf.kyushu-u.ac.jp, sakurai@csce.kyushu-u.ac.jp

Abstract. Importance of digital forensics is expected to increase in the future. Many of researches on digital forensics are targeted to persistent memory. These researches concerns about the extraction of evidence directly or via filesystem. On the other hand, there is a movement to employ the Web browser supports HTML5 as software platform. In this situation, it is considered that the forensics techniques for extracting evidences from HTML5 browser is important.

In this paper, we experimented to retrieve the artifacts left by Web-Storage feature for the Web browser for personal computer from the file system. In addition, we implemented a tool that constructs and visualizes the evidence from the artifacts.

Keywords: Computer forensics · Mobile forensics · Web browser · Privacy

1 Introduction

1.1 Background

PC and other digital devices that can connect to network into commodity goods. However, users who don't have enough information literacy has utilized these devices on a daily basis. Various activities that have been performed in the real world so far, are now come through the network that they connect by a terminal.

As a result, criminal acts have also moved to the network. Therefore, to investigate these acts, research of evidence on the network or on computer terminal has become essential. These activities of investigation of evidence focus not only on criminal acts, but also corporate governances and litigation of business [1]. With regard to these evidence investigation, the following three points are cited considering the characteristics of digital data.

The first author's work is supported by JSPS KAKENHI Grant Number 26330169.

K.-H. Rhee and J.H. Yi (Eds.): WISA 2014, LNCS 8909, pp. 83–94, 2015.
DOI: 10.1007/978-3-319-15087-1_7

Table 1. Relationship between mobile terminal platform and web technologies

Platform	Dedicated Apps. Support	Web Apps. Support
Android	✓(Dalvik bytecode)	✓
iPhone (iOS)	✓(Objective-C)	✓
WindowsPhone	✓(CLR)	✓
Tizen	✓(C++)	✓
Firefox OS	Not Supported	✓
Ubuntu OS	✓(Qt & Javascript)	✓
Sailfish OS	✓(C++ & Qt)	✓
Chrome OS	Not Supported	✓

- Retrieve data as an evidence.
- Find and summarize the relationship between the data.
- Certify that the data has not been tampered.

In order to keep the effectiveness of evidence acquired in the survey process, it is necessary to pay attention to the above. It is possible that for this purpose, to take advantage of a number of tools, including those from open source that can be used free of charge.

1.2   Motivation

With the spread of HTML5, Web browser is becoming the platform to running applications.

These applications expand the functionality and improve the usability of the terminals. It can be regarded as comparable to native applications, in the viewpoint of the operating speed and usability.

These applications are described in languages relevant to Web technology and aims at high portability and development efficiency. Mobile platforms encompass execution environment which can run both styles of application.

Furthermore, some of software platforms are based on the Web browser supporting HTML5 as an application execution environment. Table 1 summarizes the software platforms from the viewpoint of the application execution environment. It includes platforms that have not been released.

1.3   Related Works

Forensic research on Web browsers is well developed especially for private browsing mode and portable browsers. Private mode of Web browsers is provided for privacy against the network and privacy against local machines. The former one prevents identification of the user over the network. On the other hand, the later one prevent leaving the evidence on the terminal (local machine). Portable Web browser is the browser that is primarily designed to be installed on a removable disk (e.g. USB flash drive). These browsers can be used if the user does not want to leave the evidences of a browsing activity on personal computer terminal primarily.

Donny [2] examined private mode of Web browsers mainly with memory forensic techniques. As the experimental result shown, in all private mode and portable browsers, evidences are left. Left evidences are residuals of Web browsing history, e-mail address, browsed pictures. In addition, for some browsers, browsed movie is acquired from main memory. Furthermore, Aditya [3], Mulazzani [4] and Aggarwal [5] also used memory forensics techniques as well, and their experiments show these evidences are left is private mode of browsers.

Amari reported on forensics techniques from the viewpoint of memory forensics [6]. On the other hand, in terms of anti-forensics or privacy protection, there is a study [7]. In the position of forensics that targets featured phones, Willassen [8] discussed about the acquisition of evidence left by featured phone. He has acquired the evidence from the flash memory in the feature phone. In addition, [9] and [10] is discussing on this theme.

1.4   Challenging Issues

We carried out the experiment to acquire the artifact left by WebStorage that is a part of HTML5 standard. This acquisition is performed via file system and not from Web user interface and/or APIs of Web framework. Reading the data handled by HTML via Web user interface and/or Web framework API means reading the data via Web browser framework. In this case, it is difficult to ensure the admissibility of evidence. In order to ensure the admissibility, it is necessary to retrieve the evidence via side channel. In this research, we try to retrieve it via file system.

Furthermore, size of retrieved artifact may be become quite large. Therefore, find fragments of evidence from the artifact, and correlate these fragments to construct new evidence may be humanly impossible. This task is hard to perform if there is no automated assistance by computer. However to automate this, it is necessary to elucidate the structure of the artifact. Therefore, it is necessary to analyze the encoding format and data structure of artifacts. Then, based on its results, we have to design/implement the tool for evidence structuring/visualization.

1.5   Contributions and Result

This research is about the forensics experiment related to HTML5 that is still under standardization process. HTML5 runtime is expected to be the foundation of mobile devices, especially smartphones. These devices From the native nature of the devices, these devices have aggregate information related to the behavior of user. Therefore, retrieve the evidence of user behavior from the foundation layer of these devices is very effective in forensics.

In this paper, we experimented the acquisition of the evidence of artifact left by HTML5 sessionStorage from file system. This is intended to be acquire the artifact of Web browser from the lower layer of the system. Especially, it is important that acquisition is performed with not mediated by the Web browser framework.

Furthermore, we investigated the format of this artifact. In the result, it is found that the artifact is encoded as JSON. Furthermore, we investigated the structure of this artifact and found it records the user's Web browsing history. URL of browsed page and its referrer page is recorded according to the browsing order. In Addition, it was found that artifact recording the additional information of Web pages. At the same time with the investigation, it is found that the size of the artifact can be enormous. Therefore, analyze the artifact and retrieve some evidence from it by human will be difficult. Since forensics work need some manually task, it is necessary to work cooperative with automation tool. Therefore, we designed and implemented the tool that visualize and correlate the evidences from the artifact.

By using this tool, it makes that a forensics investigation of artifacts left by HTML5 Web browser more realistic.

1.6   Comparison with Existing Work

Donny [2] and Aditya [3], Mulazzani [4] have investigated the artifact left by Web browsers. They examined especially on private browsing mode of Web browsers and verified that privacy can be acquired from artifacts. Forensics analysis on artifact of Web browser is also discussed by Satvat [11], Murio [12] and Junghoon [13].

However, these studies do not address the evidence left by APIs added in the HTML5 standard. In contrast to these, in this research, we focus on retrieving the evidence left by HTML5 related APIs. From the viewpoint of memory forensics, basics of its technique is described in Kristine [6]. In addition, memory forensics on Windows machine is discussed bu Runn [14]. Compared to them, our study aims at extraction of evidence from the file system.

2   Overview of Digital Forensics

Subjects of digital forensics is spreading rapidly in response to the transforming in IT. Nowadays, devices handle digital data, such as networks, cloud system, information appliances, and mobile devices are included in this target.

2.1   Applications of Digital Forensics

Digital forensics investigation is included not just those related to the criminal case, also related to civil litigation. In addition, forensics investigation involving patents and disputes between companies, diplomatic international dispute has also gathering attention in recent years. Uses of digital forensics is widely spreading as follows [1].

Criminal Investigations. The term "digital forensics" is told in this context primarily. Its main objective is to find and retrieve the electronic evidences left by the criminal act and conserve these evidences validity.

Civil Litigation. This application of digital forensics is called "eDiscovery", and its market is spreading rapidly. eDiscovery is defined as "refers to any process in which electronic data in sought, located, secured, and searched with the intent of using it as evidence in a civil or criminal legal case".

Intelligence. This application field is called "DOMEX (Document and Media Exploitation)" especially. Modern governments and terrorists are utilizing digital devices. DOMEX is "the collection and exploitation of captured equipment, documents, and media to generate actionable intelligence [15]".

2.2   Mobile Forensics

Mobile forensics, or mobile device forensics is the techniques to investigate on portable device to retrieve the evidence left on it. In generally, investigation is targeting on the cellular phone and smartphones, etc. Because the user is always carrying the device, it aggregates various private information of users. Examples of such private information are, phone book, e-mails, photos and music files. In addition, mobile device is consist of many sensors, such as microphone, camera, acceleration sensor, barometer and GPS antenna. These can also capture private information.

There are many literatures on mobile device forensics. Most of those are targeting feature phones still often [8–10]. In addition, Report by SANS [16] is targeting not only cellular phone but also MP3 players. However, literature on forensics that targets smartphones has been increasing [17,18].

When considering digital forensics that targets smartphones, Web browser framework is not negligible. This frameworks is located at the core of the smartphone platform, and many services are implemented thereon.

Especially, Web framework provided in the smartphone platform has been utilized as the execution engine of the HTML5 standard currently under development. Analyzing the artifact left by Web browser supports HTML5 will occupy important place in the mobile forensics.

2.3   About Web Browser Anti-forensics

For the progress of the research on digital forensics, research on countermeasure against it is also progressing. The countermeasure techniques, called anti-forensics, has many definitions [1]. Harris [19] defines it as "consider anti-forensics to be any attempts to compromise the availability or usefulness of evidence to the forensics process".

Of course, anti-forensics that targets cellular and/or smartphone have been studied. Azadegan [20] designed and developed the tool to disrupt the connection between smartphone and forensics device. From the standpoint of anti-forensics on Web browser, it is important to make hard or impossible to analyze or retrieve the artifact of Web browser. Anti-forensics techniques for making evidence unavailable is classified into four categories by Harris [19]. These categories are "Destroying","Hiding", "Eliminating source" and "Counterfeiting".

3   HTML5 as a Application Development Language

3.1   Abstract of HTML5

Currently, standardization process of HTML5 [21] as the latest version of HTML, is in progress by the W3C and the W3C. It is expected to be modified in many ways to the previous edition [22]. HTML5 has been developed to improve the appearance and usability for Web browser user, and to improve the expressiveness for Web page developers. In addition, HTML5 has been developed to improve the perfection as an application description language. For this reason, many API definitions has been added in HTML5.

3.2   WebStorage

The cookie [23] is a technique that is defined for the purpose of having to maintain information about any status set by the server primarily. In addition, Local Shared Object, is called "flash cookie" is the another method to record some information in client side [24,25]. In some ways, flash cookie is more useful than cookie. e.g. it never expire. However, this property may cause problems in terms of privacy.

WebStorage [26] is one of the API newly defined in HTML5 standard. It is another method to store data in the client side. There are characteristics of WebStorage below.

Storage Capacity. Storage capacity of Cookie is 4 KB, but capacity of WebStorage is up to at least 5 MB. Enlarged storage capacity can increase the amount of data that can handle in client, and thus increasing the flexibility for application developer.

Expiration Time. Cookie has a limited lifetime and when the cookie expires, it is deleted. In contrast with it, WebStorage can retain the data until deleted explicitly.

Data Transmission. Cookie is sent over the network when the client interact with server every time. On the other hand, WebStorage must not sent over network. It lessen the burden of network bandwidth and is preferred from the viewpoint of security.

Store Format. WebStorage is maintained by key-value pair. This is similar to NoSQL style database.

WebStorage is classified as localStorage and sessionStorage, these are defined for different purpose.

3.3   LocalStorage and SessionStorage

LocalStorage is one of the kind of WebStorage and the mechanism to store some data in Web browser side. As described in the previous section, localStorage is isolated based on the concept of Web origin [27].

LlocalStorage can be shared between another tabs and/or windows if even have the same Web origin. Furthermore, contents of localStorage is kept after browser has been closed and retained until deleted explicitly.

On the other hand, sessionStorage is the another kind of WebStorage. However, unlike local storage, session storage is not shared between different windows and tabs even if have the same origin. Furthermore, sessionStorage is kept until session. Therefore, when the session is finished, the session storage space will be removed and inaccessible.

3.4 HTML5 and Mobile Devices

As discussed in 3.1, HTML5 has been developed to improve the perfection as an application description language. Especially, it is expected that it will be used as the foundation of mobile platform. Some mobile platforms equip only Web browser framework as the foundation of application execution platform. These platforms have in view to take advantage of the portability and development efficiency of HTML. The potential of HTML5 as a mobile platform is discussed by Juntunen [28].

4 Investigation Result and Proposal Method

Our goal is the realization of a mobile forensics that targets smartphone, but in this paper, we carried out experiments and tool development with Web browser for personal computer. We examined with Firefox 26.0 for Windows and browse dozens of pages. After that, extract the artifact file of sessionStorage before it has been deleted.

4.1 Artifact Format of Web Browser

Example of artifact by Firefox is shown in Fig. 1. As is apparent in this figure, artifacts left by Firefox browser is text data and it is encoded in JSON format. In this JSON format artifact, "key indicating URL of the page" indicates the

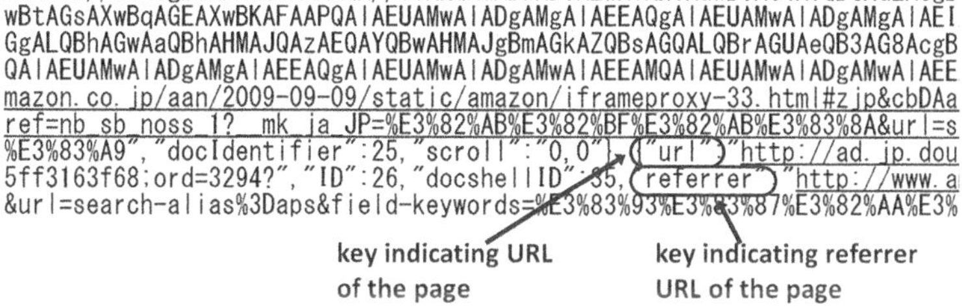

Fig. 1. Artifact example

URL of the Web page browsed. In Addition, "key indicating referrer URL of the page" indicates the referrer of Web page. The referrer, to present the Web page visit before making a transition to the Web page.

As a result we analyzed that the structure of artifact as in tree structure. Tree structure of evidence is constructed as Fig. 2. In this format, [windows] and [_closedWindows] nodes describes the Web browser windows, respectively. These nodes have [tabs], [_closedTabs] nodes as subsidiary and These nodes may have multiple [entries] nodes. [entries] node describes web page browsed respectively and these have subsidiary nodes [url], [title], [ID], [referrer], etc. [url] node describes the URL of the Web page. [title] node describes the title of the Web page. [referrer] node describes the URL to link the original Web page. In addition, [children] contain the information about the pop-up page kicked by parent window. If there are multiple [entries] nodes as subsidiary of a [tabs] node, it means that this session includes multiple tabs.

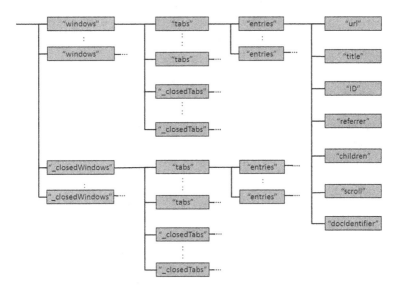

Fig. 2. Structure of artifact

It is specified that sessionStorage is deleted when the browsing has been finished. However, as the result of our examination, we confirmed that the artifact of sessionStorage is deleted when the browser is launched, not browser is finished. It is thought to be in order to allow the recovery of the last tab, as a function of the browser.

4.2   Location of Artifact

Location of the artifact of Web browser is depend on the Web browser implementation. As a result of survey, Table 2 summarize the location of WebStorage of major Web browsers.

Table 2. Stored location of WebStorage

Browser	Version	Stored Path
Internet Explorer	8 or later	N/A
Mozilla Firefox	3.6 or later	`<usershome>\AppData\Roaming\Mozilla\` `Firefox\Profiles\<profileFolder>`
Google Chrome	8 or later	`<usershome>\AppData\Local\Google\` `Chrome\UserData\Default`
Opera	11 or later	`<usershome>\AppData\Roaming\` `Opera␣Software\Opera␣Stable`
Safari	5 or later	`<usershome>\AppData\` `Local\Apple␣Computer\Safari`

4.3   Our Proposal Method

In this section, we describe the design and implementation of tool that retrieve the evidences from the artifact left by Web browser (Firefox browser) and visualize it.

We assume to investigate the evidence from the artifact of sessionStorage left by criminal act. Artifact of sessionStorage is accumulating the history that user browsed. But it has a large amount of information (page display size and window size, etc.). These are not related to the investigation. Therefore, we must extract the information that need to be investigated. It is expected to take huge time as human task, and we propose the tool that process the structuration and visualization of evidence semi-automatically.

In this method, we examined on the artifact of Firefox's sessionStorage. About Firefox, if more than one window is open, until all of those windows are closed is considered as period of the same session. Therefore, the browsing history within its period is accumulated in the sessionStorage. By using this property, it is possible to retrieve the evidence not only on the window that is closed at the end, also on the window or tab that has been closed during the same session may be obtained from artifacts file of sessionStorage. Furthermore, Firefox keep the artifact of the last session as backup. From these properties, it is possible to obtain the evidence about session.

From these properties, we can retrieve the evidence about sessions on the closed browser and evidence about previous session.

4.4   Design and Implementation

Processing procedure of this tool is described as bellow.

1. Copy the artifact file of sessionStorage to another path and launch the tool to load its file.
2. Parse artifact file to JSON objects and extract "entries" that denotes Web page browsed.
3. Classify each "entries"node to root entry(has no "referrer" node immediately below) and not root entry(has "referrer" node immediately below).

4. Inspect [url] node that immediately below of node root entry, and search the "referrer" that has [url] node same to former node.
5. If search succeed, trace to search for the "entries" node with URL as a key.
6. If search failed, finish to trace, and print the traced "entries" and value of its subsidially node [url], [title], [ID], [docshellID], [referrer].
7. In addition, represent the distance from root as the number of "*".
8. Move to the next root node, and start the search.
9. When process to all root has been finished, exit.

In this process, we treat just Web page browsed directly. It means we do not treat popped-up page opened by other page.

4.5   Evaluation

We examined on the tool implemented. We used to browse with the Web browser Firefox 26.0. When move between pages, we record the URL of the page move source and the URL of the page move destination. After reading dozens of pages, retrieve the artifact of sessionStoarge.

Result of examination indicates, we found that mismatch between the value of [referrer] and [URL]. The reason for this is that wen keyword searching, when loading the page, referrer of the page viewed has been changed. It is observed only when using a specific search site.

5   Conclusion

In this research, we examined the artifact of Web browsers. For four Web browsers (Google Chrome, Mozilla Firefox, Apple Safari and Opera browser), we located the path of artifact that is left by sessionStorage function.

Furthermore, we examined the format of the artifact, and we revealed that it is encoded as JSON format. Based on these results, we have designed and implemented a tool that structures the evidence of artifact and visualize its result. Which makes it possible to extract the evidence necessary to investigate digital forensics from data fragment left by sessionStorage and present the findings to the investigator.

From the viewpoint of anti-forensics, it must be prevented to locate the artifact file and to be analyzed. Especially later is more important. To prevent the contents of the artifact file to be analyzed and achieve the anti-forensics, it is necessary to revise the implementation of Web browser. According to the classification by Harris [19], adopt "Destroying" or "Eliminating source" for anti-forensics methods of Web browser running is difficult. Adoption of these methods would be to impair the normal function of the Web browser. Therefore other methods, "hiding" and/or "Counterfeiting" would be effective as anti-forensics techniques. In particular, it is expected "Hiding" of artifacts fileusing any encryption technology to be effective.

5.1   Future Work

In this research, we examined on Firefox browser and another Web browsers, MS Internet Explorer, Google Chrome, etc. is not examined sufficiently. We must examine other Web browsers and carry out implementation of the tool using the same verification and evaluation. In addition, the artifact by localStorage must be examined and correlation between the evidence left by WebStorage from file system and other evidence.

As a part of this effort, we are studying about the memory forensics in WebStorage if Web browsers on Windows [29]. In addition, to apply to mobile forensics on the results of this study, it is necessary to survey the browser of the mobile OS and on iPhone and Android.

References

1. Sammons, J.: The Basics of Digital Forensics. Elsevier, Waltham (2012)
2. Ohana, D.J., Shashidhar, N.: Do private and portable web browsers leave incriminating evidence? A forensic analysis of residual artifacts from private and portable web browsing sessions. In: Security and Privacy Workshop (SPW), pp. 135–142, May 2013
3. Mahendrakar, A., Irving, J., Patel, S.: Forensic Analysis of Private Browsing Artifacts, pp. 197–202. IEEE, New York (2011)
4. Mulazzani, M.: New challenges in digital forensics: online storage and anonymous communication. Ph.D. thesis, Vienna University of Technology (2014)
5. Aggarwal, G., Bursztein, E., Jackson, C., Boneh, D.: An analysis of private browsing modes in modern browsers. In: USENIX Security Symposium, pp. 79–94 (2010)
6. Amari, K.: Techniques and tools for recovering and analyzing data from volatile memory (2009). http://www.sans.org/reading-room/whitepapers/forensics/tech niques-tools-recovering-analyzing-data-volatile-memory-33049
7. Waksman, A., Sethumadhavan, S.: Silencing hardware backdoors. In: Proceedings of the 2011 IEEE Symposium on Security and Privacy, SP '11, pp. 49–63 (2011)
8. Willassen, S.: Forensic analysis of mobile phone internal memory. In: Pollitt, M., Shenoi, S. (eds.) Advances in Digital Forensics. IFIP—The International Federation for Information Processing, vol. 194, pp. 191–204. Springer, Berlin (2005). doi:10.1007/0-387-31163-7_16
9. Jansen, W., Ayers, R.: Guidelines on Cell Phone Forensics. NIST Special Publication 800-101, Gaithersburg, Maryland (2007)
10. Ahmed, R., Dharaskar, R.V.: Mobile forensics: an overview, tools, future trends and challenges from law enforcement perspective. In: 6th International Conference on E-Governance, ICEG, Emerging Technologies in E-Government, M-Government, pp. 312–23 (2008)
11. Satvat, K., Forshaw, M., Hao, F., Toreini, E.: On the privacy of private browsing—a forensic approach. In: Garcia-Alfaro, J., Lioudakis, G., Cuppens-Boulahia, N., Foley, S., Fitzgerald, W.M. (eds.) DPM 2013 and SETOP 2013. LNCS, vol. 8247, pp. 380–389. Springer, Heidelberg (2014)
12. Tito, M.: Forensic analysis of the firefox 3 internet history and recovery of deleted sqlite records. Digit. Invest. Int. J. Digit. Forensics Incident Response Arch. 5, 93–103 (2009)

13. Oh, J., Lee, S., Lee, S.: Advanced evidence collection and analysis of web browser activity. Digit. Invest. Int. J. Digit. Forensics Incident Response Arch. **8**, S62–S70 (2011)
14. Ruff, N.: Windows memory forensics. J. Comput. Virol. **4**(2), 83–100 (2008)
15. U.S. Army.: 2009 army posture statement (2009). http://www.army.mil/aps/09/ information_papers/document_media_exploitation.html
16. Martin, A.: Mobile device forensics (2008). http://www.sans.org/reading-room/ whitepapers/forensics/mobile-device-forensics-32888
17. Hoog, A., Strzempka, K.: iPhone and iOS Forensics: Investigation, Analysis and Mobile Security for Apple iPhone, iPad and iOS Devices. Syngress, Waltham (2011)
18. Hoog, A.: Android Forensics: Investigation, Analysis and Mobile Security for Google Android. Syngress, Waltham (2007)
19. Harris, R.: Arriving at an anti-forensics consensus: examining how to define and control the anti-forensics problem. Digit. Invest. **3**, 44–49 (2006)
20. Azadegan, S., Yu, W., Liu, H., Sistani, M., Acharya, S.: Novel anti-forensics approaches for smart phones. In: IEEE 2012 45th Hawaii International Conference on System Science (HICSS), pp. 5424–5431 (2012)
21. Berjon, R., Faulkner, S., Leithead, T., Navara, E.D., O'Connor, E., Pfeiffer, S., Hickson, I.: HTML5 a vocabulary and associated APIs for HTML and XHTML W3C candidate recommendation. http://www.w3.org/TR/2013/CR-html5-20130806/. Accessed 6 Aug 2013
22. Pieters, S.: Differences from HTML4 (2013). http://www.w3.org/TR/2013/ WD-html5-diff-20130528/
23. Barth, A.: HTTP State Management Mechanism RFC6265 (2011)
24. Soltani, A., Canty, S., Mayo, Q., Thomas, L., Hoofnagle, C.J.: Flash cookies and privacy (2009). http://ssrn.com/abstract=1446862
25. Ayenson, M.D., Wambach, D.J., Soltani, A., Good, N., Hoofnagle, C.J.: Flash cookies and privacy II: now with HTML5 and Etag respawning (2011). http:// ssrn.com/abstract=1898390
26. Hickson, I.: Web Storage, July 2013. http://www.w3.org/TR/2013/REC-web storage-20130730/
27. Barth, A.: The web origin concept (2011). http://tools.ietf.org/html/rfc4627
28. Juntunen, A., Jalonen, E., Luukkainen, S.: Html 5 in mobile devices-drivers and restraints. In: IEEE 2013 46th Hawaii International Conference on System Sciences (HICSS), pp. 1053–1062 (2013)
29. Matsumoto, S., Sakurai, K.: Acquisition of evidence of webstorage in html5 web browsers from memory image. In: AsiaJCIS 2014, Sept 2014

Analyzing Security of Korean USIM-Based PKI Certificate Service

Shinjo Park[1]($\boxtimes$), Suwan Park[1], Insu Yun[2], Dongkwan Kim[3], and Yongdae Kim[1,3]

[1] Graduate School of Information Security, KAIST, Daejeon, South Korea
peremen@kaist.ac.kr
[2] Department of Computer Science, KAIST, Daejeon, South Korea
[3] Department of Electrical Engineering, KAIST, Daejeon, South Korea

Abstract. This paper analyzes security of Korean USIM-based PKI certificate service. Korean PKI certificate consists of public key and password encrypted private key on disk. Due to insufficient security provided by single password, Korean mobile operators introduced USIM-based PKI system. We found several vulnerabilities inside the system, including private key's RSA prime number leakage during certificate installation. We also suggest possible improvments on designing secure authentication system (Preliminary work of this paper was published previously [1]. This work was responsibly disclosed to the vendor and associated government organizations.).

1 Introduction

PKI certificates are used in several places, including nationwide identification service in several countries. One of the implementation is smartcard-based PKI. PKI certificate on smartcard based national ID card is secure due to card operating system with access control, interfaces to block access of private key and only provides interfaces for signing functionality, but card reader infrastructure costs a lot initially. Korean implementation chose public and encrypted private key on disk, and this caused problem later since it created single point of failure on certificate encryption password and OS security. Most users set certificate password as what they use in other web sites. When malware steals them, attacker can easily decrypt certificate by that password. To mitigate private key leakage program, Korea introduced USIM-based PKI service.

Advancement of mobile technology enabled certifiate storage in USIM card. USIM card is a smartcard conforming to ISO/IEC 7816 with telecom functions. Unlike traditional smartcard, mobile phone already has the reader built-in. Wide penetration of mobile phone enabled USIM-based certificate service in some countries, including Estonia, Finland, and Korea. Estonia started mobile PKI service in 2007 [2], aiming 300,000 users (about 25 percent of population) by 2017 [3]. All Korean mobile operators started commercial USIM-based PKI service in July 2014. They were certified by KISA (Korea Internet and Security Agency) before starting service [4]. Korean PKI service was originally developed

© Springer International Publishing Switzerland 2015
K.-H. Rhee and J.H. Yi (Eds.): WISA 2014, LNCS 8909, pp. 95–106, 2015.
DOI: 10.1007/978-3-319-15087-1_8

for authentication in online banking, but it is now widely used in about 800 sites for the purpose of financial transactions, government services, foreign trading, etc.

In this paper, we analyze the security of commercial implementation of Korean USIM-based certificate service, and find design and implementation flaws. By intercepting PKI certificate installation, attacker can eavesdrop RSA private key in both PC and mobile phone. Other implementation flaws such as not validating SSL certificate, inappropriate debugging message, ineffective code obfuscation makes current implementation more vulnerable.

Section 2 introduces existing work related to USIM-based PKI service in Estonia. In Sect. 3, we present preliminaries of USIM-based PKI system including system overview and possible attack models. Our security analysis is presented in Sect. 4. Section 5 details possible attack scenarios. Discussion and conclusion is in Sects. 6 and 7.

2   Related Work

Formal security analysis for Estonian Mobile ID has been presented by Peeter Laud et al. [5] Prerequisites of Estonian Mobile ID are mobile ID enabled USIM card and activation of the card using smartcard based Estonian ID card. Mobile ID could be used for both identification and signing, with two separate PIN numbers for each purpose. During identification and digital sign process, message set by institution and control code generated by combination of the nonce values of institution and certifiate management authority are shown in both user and USIM application. It provides verification of current action and visual indicator of channel security. Messages between network operator and USIM are based on SMS, and encrypted using a symmetric key. They used protocol analyzer ProVerif, with formal language based on π-calculus. The paper also presents scenarios when each components are controlled by adversary, and provides possible protocol modification on each scenario. In general, despite some weaknesses, Estonian Mobile ID is equal or more secure than smartcard based authentication.

3   Preliminaries

Unlike typical PKI implementation where private key is stored in secure storage, Korean nationwide PKI service chose certificate storage based on files in disk. Certificate of multiple users $(U_A, U_B, \cdots)$ could be stored in one storage. Certificate of U_i contains public key PK_{U_i} and encrypted private key $E_P(SK_{U_i})$ with password P. By default, PK_{U_i} and $E_P(SK_{U_i})$ are stored in fixed location of U_i's hard disk. Also, P might be shared among other online services of U_i. Therefore, if attacker can steal $E_P(SK_{U_i})$ and P, then she can impersonate U_i.

To protect key pair and password from external attacker, Korean PKI implementation (typically as web browser plugin) includes endpoint protection software (anti-keylogger, firewall, etc.) by default. Additional mitigation suggested by Korean government is to store PK_{U_i} and $E_P(SK_{U_i})$ in removable storage, but it does not increase security. Because of that, Korean government decides to move the storage to USIM card, which provides hardware-based access control by design.

According to Korean patents related to USIM-based PKI service, secure channel exists between smartphone and certificate management server, and communication between smartphone and USIM card is done in plaintext [6]. To access USIM secure storage during key pair installation and cryptographic operation, its password P_{USIM} is used instead of P. Thus, it implies that decryption of $E_P(SK_{U_i})$ is done either in PC or smartphone application. On the other hand, additional vulnerability is introduced by certificate management application.

3.1   System Description

Workflow of Korean USIM-based PKI system consists of installation of existing certificate, and certificate usage. Available installation methods are copying existing certificate, and direct key pair generation on USIM card. Although directly generating key pair on USIM card is the most secure method, it is not feasible for daily usage because current USIM-based PKI is not available on mobile applications, and using separate key pairs for different application is not possible. Therefore, most users will retain their PK_{U_i} and $E_P(SK_{U_i})$ on disk, along with PK_{U_i} and SK_{U_i} installed in USIM card. Figure 1 shows communication process during certificate installation and usage.

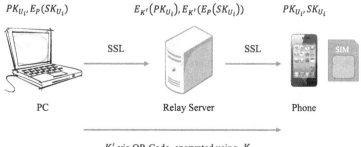

Fig. 1. Key pair installation of Korean USIM-based PKI

On PC side during key pair installation, PC application checks whether $E_P(SK_{U_i})$ belongs to U_i by decrypting it inside the PC. If the key pair is successfully decrypted, additionally encrypted $E_{K'}(PK_{U_i})$ and $E_{K'}(E(SK_{U_i}))$ are sent to relay server via SSL. QR code is generated simultaneously, containing K', address of relay server and session information, encrypted using SEED-CBC with K_{QR}. They are valid for 3 min. Smartphone captures QR code, downloads, decrypts and installs the key pair stored in relay server.

To use certificate stored in USIM card, user select Secure Token in certificate location dialog. Another window asks user's mobile phone number, to send push message and execute certificate management application. The PC application will display list of public keys in USIM card. After selecting certificate, P_{USIM} is typed on PC. Relay server sends encrypted P_{USIM} using SEED-CBC with K_{PIN}, along with cleartext to be signed to mobile phone. If P_{USIM} entered from PC is correct, then the text is signed by SK_{U_i} in USIM card, and sent back to the user. Before performing cryptographic operations, a confirmation dialog is displayed on smartphone by mobile application.

3.2   Threat Model

Memory Hacking on PC. Operating systems provide APIs for accessing other processes' memory region and control execution to use in debuggers. Malware writers, on the other hand, can use the same APIs to access sensitive data of other application. This technique is called memory hacking. To use memory hacking to steal private information, malware needs to be installed inside victim's computer. Numerous bugs of application and user's unawareness of possible malware makes it easy to install the malware.

SSL MitM Attack. Content manipulating proxy like Paros [7] can hijack HTTPS communication. Paros presents faked SSL certificate to the client, which may use different domain name and/or signing authority than the real one. Without prior register of faked CA root certificate, web browsers will display certificate warning by default and refuse to continue operation unless explicitly told to do so. Applications may use certificate pinning to explicitly allow pre-defined certificate, and reject all other certificates. On Android application, certificate validity are checked by default, unless application author explicitly disabled the check.

For navigating bank web pages, security of HTTPS session depends on that of web browser. Modern web browsers have EV certificate (Extended Validation Certificate) feature to present visual indicator of certificate validity. This is still vulnerable when user initially enters HTTP URL first, then redirected to HTTPS. In most cases, web contents are the same even using different protocol, SSLstrip [8] uses that property to change all HTTPS requests to HTTP when user initially used HTTP.

To perform SSL MitM attack, we use rogue AP (Access Point) for Wi-Fi or ARP spoofing and activate web proxy behind the scenes. Users do not know what is happened behind, or are hidden from what is actually going on.

Effect of Android Rooting. Numerous vulnerabilities in mobile operating system allows user or malware to gain root permissions, which is typically blocked in general. With rooted phones, Android security measures are not effective since root user can see everything inside sandbox, deactivate operating system functionalities and mobile vaccine. Application handling sensitive information can check whether the phone is rooted or not. Common methods are checking existence of su binary and root permission management application, vendor-specific warranty bits indicating rooting. Some methods could be bypassed, allowing rooted phone to execute particular application.

3rd-party Malware. Malware can steal private information by collecting user information using Android API, monitoring system logs to check existence of private information, and accessing outside of sandbox on rooted phones. If an application presents its private information using insecure way like printing it inside Android system log, malware can steal that information. Developers can access Android logging facility by `android.util.log` series of API [9], and read the logs using logcat [10] utility or GUI tools from PC. According to Google, it is adviced to remove all logging API calls before releasing the application. Android logging API uses system-wide log buffer to collect all application logs, and logcat application shows combined logs of all running applications. Since logcat is terminal-based application, there are some GUI log management applications on Play Store. Although Google blocked system wide log access for apps since Android 4.1, collecting logs via ADB on PC or rooted device is still possible.

Repackaging. Android applications are written in both Java and native codes. Android Java code is compiled to DEX (Dalvik EXecutable) which could be converted back to Java code using dex2jar [11] and Java decompiler, or smali [12] code (Dalvik assembly) using smali/baksmali combination. Repackaging tool like apktool [13] assists extracting and modifying smali code, creating repackaged APK of application. Repackaged application is visually the same as original one. They are distributed through various channels, and when victim executed particular application, malware injected by attacker is executed.

4 System Analysis

4.1 PC Application

It is easy to write memory hacking application since address of private data is always the same, due to absence of ASLR (Address Space Layout Randomization). By using memory hacking, attacker can obtain user's information including P, PK_{U_i}, $E_P(SK_{U_i})$ and SK_{U_i}. The K_{QR} and IV_{QR} to encrypt K', server address and session information is hard-coded inside application. If attacker knows K_{QR}, she can hijack the session in behalf of victim. If SSL MitM proxy changes relay server's certificate, the application refuses to generate QR code, probably due to usage of certificate pinning or strict certificate check.

4.2 Mobile Application

The application is obfuscated in custom method involving transformation of Dalvik bytecode. Figure 2 shows the method to decode obfuscated application during runtime. Unencrypted bootstrap executes native library to decode obfuscated part before executing the real application. By recollecting memory area using memory map on `/proc/PID/maps`, we can reassemble the decrypted ODEX (Optimized DEX) of application. During Android application execution, Dalvik optimizes functions in device framework before storing application's DEX inside Dalvik cache on memory. This optimized ODEX could be converted back to

DEX file using deodex tools, with framework files of the device where ODEX is generated. Decoded DEX file is not obfuscated; original names of class, method, variable names are untouched.

classes.dex

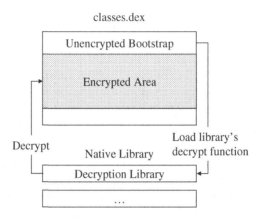

Fig. 2. Obfuscation method of application [1]

During key pair installation, Android application uses SD card for temporary storage of PK_{U_i} and $E_P(SK_{U_i})$. Using application repackaging to retain temporary files, or create race condition to copy key files from SD card before its removal, it is possible to hijack PK_{U_i} and $E_P(SK_{U_i})$. Vulnerable version of application printed out every USIM APDU (Application Protocol Data Unit) used for communication between phone and USIM, to Android system log. We implement small malware to read the logs and extract information from it.

The application also lacks some security measurements, or degraded platform security deliberately. Application integrity is not checked; attacker can distribute malicious repackaged app to steal private information. While the application refuses to run in rooted device, it could be easily circumvented by renaming su binary to other name, and removing root permission management application like SuperSU. The application communicates with relay server via HTTPS channel, whose SSL certificate verification is explicitly turned off. This enables attacker to perform MitM attack on SSL without knowledge to the user. On our experiment with rogue AP, we successfully collect private information inside SSL session.

4.3   USIM Application

To analyze communication between mobile phone and USIM card, we can modify application to print out logs of USIM communication, or use hardware based sniffing device like SIMtrace [14]. There is no unified API for accessing USIM card inside mobile operating system: Apple iOS provides private API (not accessable for general developers), AOSP (Android Open Source Project) and their derivatives do not include API at all. Example of USIM access API implementation in Android is SEEK for Android [15], which is often included in stock ROM of devices. Device manufacturer and mobile network operator may provide their own private API for accessing USIM card and its applications. SIMtrace allows eavesdropping of phone-USIM channel without knowledge about APIs for accessing USIM, and modification of target application.

(a) SIMtrace hardware   (b) Phone connection

Fig. 3. SIMtrace hardware and phone connection

Figure 3a shows SIMtrace device. Original USIM card from mobile phone goes to SIMtrace's USIM card slot (upper right of figure), and mobile phone is connected to SIMtrace using FPCB (Flexible Printed Circuit Board) cable (lower right of figure). By connecting device to computer and using SIMtrace application, we can eavesdrop channel between phone and USIM card. Figure 3b shows SIMtrace connected to Samsung Galaxy S III (SHW-M440S) for demonstration. In this mobile phone, FPCB cable is easy to route since there is no other objects blocking the cable. Different FPCB cable placing is required when USIM slot is underneath battery, or USIM card is connected to phone via tray.

With SIMtrace connected to the phone via FPCB cable and PC via USB, executing `simtrace` application and powering up the phone gives traces of USIM communication in GSMTAP format via local UDP socket. When an application sends command to USIM card, SIMtrace will send the packet containing APDU of particular application. Packets from SIMtrace and USIM communication logs of application were the same, making it easier to trace phone-USIM communication without modification on application or phone firmware.

5 Attack Evaluation

Following attacks were possible in each components:

- PC application: Memory hacking, SSL Hijacking (partially), Circumventing anti-keylogger

- Mobile application: Circumventing rooting check, Log sniffing, SSL Hijacking, No integrity check on message
- USIM application: Unprotected phone-USIM channel.

We implement custom C&C server to collect and display PK_{U_i} and SK_{U_i}, public and private exponents, phone number, P_{USIM}, P of victim. It also provides PK_{U_i} and SK_{U_i} download function, allowing attacker to directly impersonate victim without further processing.

On PC application, we implement memory hacking malware to steal and upload PK_{U_i}, $E_P(SK_{U_i})$, SK_{U_i} and P during key pair installation. Although Paros worked on bank web site, Internet Explorer 11 on Windows 7 displayed certificate warning before actually navigating the site. SSL MitM attack revealed $E_{K_{PIN}}(P_{USIM})$ and cleartext to be signed. Hardcoded K_{PIN} and IV_{PIN} inside application allows attacker to decode P_{USIM}. Cleartext to be signed could be changed in theory, but on our tested bank web site only hash of original message was visible. Anti-keylogger software is ineffective while malware is running with USB keyboard.

On Mobile application, we implement custom Android log stealing malware to steal PK_{U_i}, SK_{U_i} (during key pair installation) and P_{USIM} (all certificate operation). Some phones required workaround to avoid background application termination problem, by using a dummy thread to make application as active. If attacker wants to install key pair on her USIM card, only PK_{U_i} and SK_{U_i} are required. To use key pair on PC, attacker can re-encrypt SK_{U_i} using unrelated P', because Korean PKI implementation on PC expects encrypted SK_{U_i}.

There is no way to find out whether cleartext to be signed comes from legitimate source. Also, person with headset displayed before cryptographic operation do not clearly represent secure user operation. As Alma Whitten et al. suggested [16], the image could be replaced to represent cryptographic operation instead. By hijacking SSL session it is also possible to steal private information in mobile application.

Using SIMtrace, we found that communication channel between USIM and phone is not encrypted and showed the same messages as system log during accessing USIM card. An advanced attacker can create fake signing application from scratch by analyzing how messages are processed.

6   Discussion

During our research, several new implementations of USIM based certificate in Korea emerged. Unlike Estonia where one unified solution is used among all mobile operators, multiple vendors implemented their own solution to mobile network operators. Android application is different from what we have analyzed in previous section, but USIM-phone communication method uses the same telco-specific API and similar USIM APDU structure. If USIM-phone channel is not properly secured, fundamental problem of information leakage will not be solved. Although all services were certified by KISA, the certification is limited to USIM itself, not including applications for service. Current certification process is broken since any vulnerable component in application chain makes whole process vulnerable.

Since fixing problems in higher level like Android and PC application is trivial, and most problem could be remedied by following secure coding guidelines, we more focus on lower level design to survive problems in higher level, for example, rooting of the device and vulnerable applications.

6.1   Mitigation

One mitigation to prevent memory hacking on PC is ASLR (Address Space Layout Randomization), where operating system changes memory layout of binaries for each execution. From attacker's point of view, location of sensitive changes between each execution. Another mitication is anti-debugging techniques like executable packing (e.g. Themida [17]), self-modifying code, code obfuscation. This can slow down the application analysis, but not completely prevent it.

To prevent SSLStrip like attack, HSTS (HTTP Strict Transport Security) [18] uses HTTP header information to tell the browser that it must use HTTPS for next visit. If web browser has HSTS information for particular web site, then it will always use HTTPS even user entered HTTP URL. Attacker still can strip down HSTS header when user visits web site for the first time. To prevent header strip attack, web browser vendors have whitelist of HSTS-enabled sites to force HTTPS.

Application repackaging could be mitigated by integrity check. If integrity check is implemented in Android Java code, attacker still can circumvent it by modifying application to return fake values for integrity checking routine. Implementing sensitive routine like integrity check in native code makes modification and repackaging more difficult. Android obfuscation tools like ProGuard [19] makes application analysis difficult, but not impossible.

Even with these mitigations, running attacker's code on PC or mobile phone is still possible. To solve root cause of problem caused by implementing security operations on PC or mobile platform, dedicated hardware based security is highly recommended.

6.2   Secure User Interface

First of all, sensitive user interface must be implemented using USIM application toolkit, or inside TrustZone container for better protection.

Figure 4 shows how USIM application toolkit is handled inside Android, other mobile platforms have similar structure. Application binary is contained inside USIM card, secured by card operating system. When mobile operating system is booted, USIM card tells whether toolkit menu is available or not. Mobile OS then shows USIM application toolkit "application" to access application inside USIM card. The "application" in mobile OS can not access application binary directly, the only interface is USIM toolkit terminal messages sent via RIL and baseband.

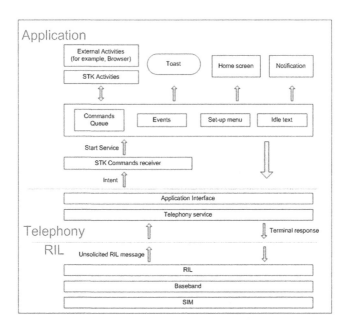

Fig. 4. USIM application toolkit architecture in Android [20]

Android application acts only as wrapper of USIM card's output and input messages. When the application is not tempered, it will only display messages from USIM and pass user's input values to it. USIM toolkit handling application is installed as system application, whose modification requires rooting of the device and may cause unexpected consequences on system operation.

To protect modification of preinstalled system application, we can use Trust-Zone [21] container to isolate application from other applications. TrustZone-based application environment like Samsung Knox [22] is not easily tempered by simple device rooting. Isolating USIM toolkit application will prevent from application modification to disguise and eavesdrop messages from USIM card. By this scenario we can provide secure display opened to application. Input event must be secured too, making no other party except USIM toolkit application can receive or monitor events to reconstruct user input values.

The application must show confirmation message starting from USIM card. If confirmation dialog is displayed by Android application, malware can press OK on the dialog without knowledge of user. If the dialog came from USIM card, then toolkit message must be passed through USIM card to actually press OK, which requires extra step to do this.

6.3 Secure Communication Channel

If communication method of phone and USIM is revealed to external attacker, it is analogous as sending password using HTTP in web application. By using faked certificate application, it can collect necessary information to sign the plaintext on user's behalf, and hacker can use stolen identity to cause damages to user. Moreover, if confirmation steps are only implemented in Android side and USIM lacks any kind of verification, identity theft is more easy. Secure channel starting from USIM card can prevent these from happen by preventing USIM APDU leakage.

Estonian Mobile ID secures communication channel by preshared symmetric key based encryption on SMS [5]. Binary SMS is typically not passed to mobile operating system and directly handled inside radio layer and USIM application of the phone. This provides extra protection layer not provided by Korean USIM-based certificate services, and eliminiates framework hijacking problem by not using USIM communication channel on Android application.

7   Conclusion

To implement secure USIM-based authentication service, only securing certificate itself inside USIM card is not sufficient. There are numerous communication channel around smartphone and USIM card, including application layer protocols, Android application, and USIM to phone channel. Our analysis showed that Korean USIM certificate implementation lacks security measures, some of which is fixable, but some are fundamental problems requiring at least reprogramming of USIM card and changes on service architecture.

USIM card can host secured application with user interface, additional security on mobile phone by using TrustZone can further protect those application from external attackers. USIM application can survive application modification, since card operating system prevents direct access of application binary. We strongly recommend implementing secure user interface inside USIM, instead of Android application. We also recommend extending certification scope of Korean USIM-based certificate to the whole system including user interfaces and communication channels.

References

1. Park, S., Park, S., Yun, I., Kim, D., Kim, Y.: Security analysis of USIM-based certificate service in Korea. In: Conference on Information Security and Cryptography (2014)
2. ASi Sertifitseerimiskeskus, About SK - History. https://www.sk.ee/en/about/history/
3. Vaata Maailma, NutiKaitse 2017. http://www.vaatamaailma.ee/en/nutikaitse
4. KISA, Operational Programs (in Korean). http://www.rootca.or.kr/kor/hsm/hsm.jsp
5. Laud, P., Roos, M.: Formal analysis of the estonian mobile-ID protocol. In: Jøsang, A., Maseng, T., Knapskog, S.J. (eds.) NordSec 2009. LNCS, vol. 5838, pp. 271–286. Springer, Heidelberg (2009)
6. Raonsecure Inc., Digital Signature System Using Mobile Device (in Korean), Patent KR 10–2013-0 065 149, 30 December 2013

7. Paros. http://sourceforge.net/projects/paros/
8. Marlinspike, M.: SSLstrip. http://www.thoughtcrime.org/software/sslstrip/
9. Android Open Source Project, Android Developers: Log. http://developer.android. com/reference/android/util/Log.html
10. Android Open Source Project, Android Developers: logcat. http://developer. android.com/tools/help/logcat.html
11. dex2jar. https://code.google.com/p/dex2jar/
12. smali/baksmali. https://code.google.com/p/smali/
13. apktool. https://code.google.com/p/android-apktool/
14. OsmocomBB Project, SIMtrace. http://bb.osmocom.org/trac/wiki/SIMtrace
15. Secure Element Evaluation Kit for the Android platform. https://code.google.com/ p/seek-for-android/
16. Whitten, A., Tygar, J.D.: Why Johnny can't encrypt: a usability evaluation of PGP 5.0. In: Proceedings of the 8th USENIX Security Symposium, vol. 99, p. 16. McGraw-Hill (1999)
17. Themida. http://www.oreans.com/themida.php
18. Hodges, J., Jackson, C., Barth, A.: HTTP Strict Transport Security (HSTS), RFC 6797 (Proposed Standard), Internet Engineering Task Force, November 2012. http://www.ietf.org/rfc/rfc6797.txt
19. Android Open Source Project, Android Developers: ProGuard. http://developer. android.com/tools/help/proguard.html
20. Android Open Source Project, Android Open Source: SIM Toolkit Application. http://www.kandroid.org/online-pdk/guide/stk.html
21. ARM Inc., TrustZone. http://www.arm.com/products/processors/technologies/ trustzone/index.php
22. Samsung, Samsung KNOX. http://www.samsung.com/global/business/mobile/ platform/mobile-platform/knox/

AMAL: High-Fidelity, Behavior-Based Automated Malware Analysis and Classification

Aziz Mohaisen[1](✉) and Omar Alrawi[2]

[1] Verisign Labs, Reston, VA, USA
amohaisen@verisign.com
[2] Qatar Computing Research Institute, Doha, Qatar

Abstract. This paper introduces AMAL, an operational automated and behavior-based malware analysis and labeling (classification and clustering) system that addresses many limitations and shortcomings of the existing academic and industrial systems. AMAL consists of two subsystems, AutoMal and MaLabel. AutoMal provides tools to collect low granularity behavioral artifacts that characterize malware usage of the file system, memory, network, and registry, and does that by running malware samples in virtualized environments. On the other hand, MaLabel uses those artifacts to create representative features, use them for building classifiers trained by manually-vetted training samples, and use those classifiers to classify malware samples into families similar in behavior. AutoMal also enables unsupervised learning, by implementing multiple clustering algorithms for samples grouping. An evaluation of both AutoMal and MaLabel based on medium-scale (4,000 samples) and large-scale datasets (more than 115,000 samples)—collected and analyzed by AutoMal over 13 months—show AMAL's effectiveness in accurately characterizing, classifying, and grouping malware samples. MaLabel achieves a precision of 99.5 % and recall of 99.6 % for certain families' classification, and more than 98 % of precision and recall for unsupervised clustering. Several benchmarks, costs estimates and measurements highlight and support the merits and features of AMAL.

Keywords: Malware · Classification · Automatic analysis

1 Introduction

Malware classification and clustering is age old problem that many industrial and academic efforts have tackled in the past. There are two common and broad techniques used for malware detection, that are also utilized for classification: signature based [15,23,28] and behavior based [18,19,22,27,30] techniques. Signature based techniques use a common sequence of bytes that appear in the binary code of a malware family to detect and identify malware samples. On the one hand, while signature-based techniques are very fast since they do not require the effort to run the sample to identify it (the whole decision is based on a static scan), their drawbacks is that they are not always accurate, they can be

© Springer International Publishing Switzerland 2015
K.-H. Rhee and J.H. Yi (Eds.): WISA 2014, LNCS 8909, pp. 107–121, 2015.
DOI: 10.1007/978-3-319-15087-1_9

thwarted using obfuscation, and they require a prior knowledge, including a set of known signatures associated with the tested families.

The behavior-based approach uses artifacts the malware creates during execution. While this approach to analysis and classification is more expensive since it requires running the malware sample in order to obtain artifacts and features for behavior characterization, they tend to have higher accuracy in characterizing malware samples due to the availability of several heuristics to map behavior patterns into families. Also, behavior characterization is agnostic to the underlying code and can easily bypass code obfuscation and polymorphism, relying on somewhat easier-to-interpret features.

Several academic studies used behavioral analysis for classification and labeling of malware samples. The first work to do so is by Baily et al. [5], in which it is shown that high-level features of the number of processes, files, registry records, and network events, can be used for characterizing and classifying (multi-class clustering) malware samples. However, the work falls short in many aspects. First, the technique makes use of only high-level features, and misses explicit low-level and implicit features (the authors leave that part for future work). Second, their work also relies on a small number of samples for validation of the technique, and the only source for creating ground truth for those samples was the side channel of antivirus labeling. Third, their technique is limited to one clustering algorithm (hierarchical clustering with the Jaccard index for similarity), and it is unclear how other algorithms perform for the same task. Last, their technique is for clustering, and does not consider two-family classification problems, so it is unclear how the features work with classification.

More recently, Bayer et al. [6] improved on the results in [5] in two ways. First, the authors contributed the use of locality-sensitive hashing (LSH) for memory-efficient clustering. Second, instead of using high-level behavior characteristics, the authors proposed to use low OS-level features based on API-hooking for characterizing malware samples. While effective, the technique has several shortcomings and limitations. First of all, malware samples scan for installed drivers and uninstall or bypass the driver used for kernel logging. More important, rootkits (like TDSS/TDL and ZeroAccess–both families are studied in our evaluation), a popular set of families of malware, are usually installed in the kernel and the kernel logger can be blind to all of their activities [26]. Rieck et al. [22], uses the same API-hooking technique in [6] to collect artifacts and use them for extracting features to characterize malware samples. However, their technique suffers from a low accuracy rates, perhaps due to their choice of features. While they match the highest accuracy we achieve, our lowest accuracy of classification of a malware family is 20 % higher than the lowest accuracy in their system.

In this paper we introduce AMAL, an operational and large-scale behavior-based solution for malware analysis and classification (both binary classification and clustering) that addresses the shortcomings of the previous solutions. To achieve its end goal, AMAL consists of two sub-systems, AutoMal and MaLabel. AutoMal builds on the prior literature in characterizing malware samples by their memory, file system, registry, and network behavior artifacts. Unlike [6],

MaLabel uses low-granularity behavior artifacts that are even capable of characterizing differences between variants of the same malware family. On the other hand, and given the wide-range of functionalities of MaLabel, which includes binary classification and clustering, it incorporate several techniques with several parameters and automatically chooses among the best of them to produce the best results. To do that, and unlike the prior literature, MaLabel relies on analyst-vetted and highly-accurate labels to train classifiers and assist in labeling clusters grouped in unsupervised learning. Finally, the malware analysis and artifacts collection part of AMAL (AutoMal) has been in production since early 2009, and it enabled us to collect tens of millions, analyze several hundreds of thousands, and to manually label several tens of thousands of malware samples—thus collecting in-house intelligence beyond any related work in the literature.

The organization of the rest of this paper is as follows. In Sect. 2, we review the related literature. In Sect. 3 we describe our system in details, including AutoMal, the automatic malware analysis sub-system and MaLabel, the automated malware classification sub-system. In Sect. 4, we evaluate our system. In Sect. 5 we outline some of the future work and concluding remarks.

2 Related Work

There has been plenty of work in the recent literature on the use of machine learning algorithms for classifying malware samples [5,15,20–23]. These works are classified into two categories: signature based and behavior based techniques. Our work belongs to the second category of these works, where we used several behavior characteristics as features to classify the Zeus malware sample. Related to our work is the literature in [18,22,23,30]. In [18], the authors use behavior graphs matching to identify and classify families of malware samples, at high cost of graph operations and generation. In [22,23], the authors follow a similar line of thoughts for extracting features, and use SVM for classifying samples, but fall short in relying on a single algorithm and using AV-generated labels (despite their pitfalls).

To the best of our knowledge, the closest work in the literature to ours is the work in [5,6,22] with the shortcomings highlighted earlier. Related to our use of network features is the line of research on traffic analysis for malware and botnet detection, reported in [10,11,14] and for the particular families of malware that use fast flux, which is reported in [12,17]. Related to our use of the DNS features for malware analysis are the works in [3,4,8]. None of those studies are concerned by behavior-based analysis and classification of malware beyond the use of remotely collected network features for inferring malicious activities and intent. Thus, although they share similarity with our work in purpose, they are different from our work in the utilized techniques.

The use of machine learning techniques to automate classification of behavior of codes and traffic are heavily studied in the literature. The reader can refer to recent surveys in [24,25]. More related work is deferred to the technical report [16].

3   System Design

The ultimate goal of AMAL is to automatically analyze malware samples and classify them into malware families based on their behavior. To that end, AMAL consists of two components, AutoMal and MaLabel. AutoMal is a behavior-based automated malware analysis system that uses memory and file system forensics, network activity logging, and registry monitoring to profile malware samples. AutoMal also summarizes such behavior into artifacts that are easy to interpret and use to characterize and represent individual malware samples at lower level of abstraction.

On the other hand, MaLabel uses the artifacts generated by AutoMal to extract unified representation, in the form of feature vectors, and builds a set of classifiers and clustering mechanisms to group different samples based on their common and distinctive behavior characteristics. For binary classification, AutoMal builds classifiers trained from highly-accurate, manually-inspected, analyst-vetted and labeled malware samples. MaLabel then uses the classifier to accurately classify unlabeled samples into similar groups, and to tell whether a given malware sample is of interest or not. Finally, MaLabel also provides the capability of clustering malware samples based on their behavior into multiple-classes, using hierarchical clustering with several settings to label such clusters. To perform highly accurate labeling, MaLabel uses high-fidelity expert-vetted training labels among other methods. With those overall system design goals and objectives, we now proceed to describe the system flow of both AutoMal and MaLabel.

3.1   System Flow

AutoMal: Behavior-Based Malware Analyzer. AutoMal is an operational system used by many customers, including large financial institutions, AV vendors, and internal users (called analysts). AutoMal is intended for a variety of users and malware types, thus it supports processing prioritization, multiple operating system and format selection, runtime variables and environment adjustment, among other options. The main features of AutoMal are as follows. (1) Sample priority queue: Allows samples to have processing priority based on submission source. (2) Run time variable: Allows submitter to set run time for the sample in the virtual machine (VM) environment. (3) Environment adjustment: Allows submitter to adjust operating system (OS) environment via script interface before running a sample. (4) Multiply formats: Allows submission of various formats like, EXE, DLL, PDF, DOC, XSL, PPT, HTML, and URL. (5) VMware-based: Uses VMware as virtual environment. (6) OS selection: Allows submitter to select operating system for the VM, supports Windows XP, 7, and Vista with various Service Packs (SP). Adding a new OS to AutoMal systems requires very little effort. (7) Lower Privilege: Allows submitter to lower the OS privilege before running a sample. By default, samples run as a privileged user in Windows XP. (8) Reboot option: Allows submitter to reboot the system after a sample is executed to expose other activities of malicious code that might be dormant.

AutoMal is a malware analysis system that comprises of several components, allowing it to scale horizontally for parallel processing of multiple samples at a time. An architectural design consists of a sample submitter, controller, workers (known as virtual machines, or VMs), and back-end indexing and storage component (database). Each component is described in the following:

Samples Submitter. The submitter is responsible for feeding samples to AutoMal. The samples are selected based on their priority in the processing queue. Given that AutoMal has multiple sources of sample input including, customer submissions, internal submissions, and AV vendor samples, prioritization is used. Each of the samples are ranked with different priority with customer submissions having the highest priority followed by the internal submissions and finally the AV vendor feeds. When the system is ideal, AutoMal's controller fetches samples for processing from the process queue, which has the highest priority.

Controller. The controller is the main component of AutoMal and it is responsible for orchestrating the main process of the system. The controller fetches highest priority samples from the queue with the smallest submission time (earliest submitted) and processes them. The processing begins by the sample being copied into an available VM, applying custom settings to the VM, if there are any, and running the sample. The configuration for each VM is applied via a python agent installed on each VM allowing the submitter to modify the VM environment as they see fit. For example if an analyst identifies that a malware sample is not running because it checks a specific registry key for environment artifact to detect the virtual environment, the analyst can submit a script with the sample that will adjust the registry key so the malware sample fails to detect the virtual environment and proceed to infect the system. The agent also detects the type of file being submitted and runs it correctly. For example, if a DLL file is submitted, the agent will install the DLL as a Windows Service and start the service to identify the behavior of the sample. If a URL is submitted, the agent would launch Internet Explorer browser and visit the URL. After the sample is run for the allotted time, the controller pauses the VM and begins artifact collection. The controller runs several tools to collect the following artifacts: (1) File system: files created, modified, and deleted, file content, and file meta data. (2) Registry: registry created, modified, and deleted, registry content, and registry meta data. (3) Network: DNS resolution, outgoing and incoming content and meta data. (4) Volatile Memory: This artifact is only stored for one week to run YARA signatures [2] (details are below) on the memory to identify malware of interest.

The file system, registry, and network artifacts and their semantics are extracted from the VMware Disk (VMDK) [29] and the packet capture (PCAP) file. The artifacts and their semantics are then parsed and stored in the back-end database in the corresponding tables for each artifact. The PCAP files are also stored in the database for record keeping. The VMware machine also saves a copy of the virtual memory to disk when paused. The controller then runs our own YARA signatures on the virtual memory file to match any families that our analysts have identified, and tags them accordingly. The virtual memory files are stored for 1 week on the AutoMal then discarded due to the size of each memory dump. For example, if the malware sample is run in a VM that has 512 MB of RAM then the stored virtual memory file would be 512 MB for that sample plus the aforementioned artifacts. Storing virtual memory files indefinitely does not scale hence we discard them after 1 week.

YARA signatures: YARA signatures are static signatures used to identify and classify malware samples based on a sequence of known bytes in a specific malware family. Our analysts have developed several YARA signatures based on their research and reverse engineering of malware families. Developing these signatures is time consuming because they require reverse engineering several malware samples of a family and then identifying a specific byte sequence that is common among all of them. A YARA signature is composed of 3 sections, meta section, string section, and condition section.

In our system we did not utilize memory signatures as a feature for classification or clustering because not every sample in our system has those artifacts available. We only store the memory artifacts for one week, hence we only have a window of one week that covers a small set of malware processed in AutoMal. If we identify a feature of importance in memory we can modify our system to log those features for future samples and we can add it to our feature set. We currently utilize memory files and YARA signatures to classify samples based on our analysts experience for malware families. We augment this information with our behavior-based classification and clustering for automatic labeling.

Workers. The workers' VMs are functionally independent of the controller, which allows the system to add and remove VMs without affecting the overall operation of the system. The VMs consist of VMDK images that have different versions of OSes with different patch levels. The current system supports Windows XP, Vista, and 7 with various service packs (SP). The VMs also have software such as Microsoft Office, Adobe Reader, and a python agent used to copy and configure the VM by the controller. The software installed on the VMs vary based on OS version. For most samples reported in this paper in Sect. 4, we used VMs with Windows XP SP2 and with several software packages and programs installed, including Microsoft Office 2007, Adobe Acrobat 9.3, Java 6-21, FireFox 3.6, Internet Explorer 6, Python 2.5, 2.6, and VMware Tools. For hardware configuration for the VMs see Table 2 (all software packages are trademarks of their corresponding producers). This choice of OS was necessitated by the fact that infections are reported by customers on that OS. However, in case where samples are known to be associated with a different OS version, the proper OS is chosen with similar software packages.

Backend Storage – Database. The collected artifacts are parsed into a MySQL database [1] by the controller. The database contains several tables like *files*, *registry*, *binaries*, *PCAP* (packet captures), *network*, *HTTP*, *DNS*, and *memory_signature* table. Each of the table contains meta data about the collected artifacts with exception to *PCAP* and *binaries* table. The *binaries* table stores files meta data and content where the *files* table stores meta information about files created, modified, and deleted per sample run. The *files* table contains parsed meta data from the *binaries* table. The *PCAP* table is large in size, and stores the complete raw network capture of the sample during execution which would include any extra files downloaded by the sample. The *HTTP*, *DNS*, and *network* tables store parsed meta data from the *PCAP* table for quick lookups.

MaLabel: Automated Labeling. MaLabel is a classification and clustering system that takes behavior profiles containing artifacts generated by AutoMal, extracts representative features from them, and builds classifiers and clustering algorithms for behavior-based group and labeling of malware samples. Based on the class of algorithm to be used in MaLabel, whether it is binary classification or clustering, the training (if applicable) and testing data into MaLabel is determined by the user. If the data is to be classified, MaLabel trains a model using a verified and labeled data subset and uses unlabeled data for classification. MaLabel allows for choosing among several classification algorithms, including support vector machines (SVM)—with a dozen of settings and optimization options, decision trees, linear regression, and k-nearest-neighbor, among others. MaLabel leaves the final decision of which algorithm to choose to the user based on the classification accuracy and cost (both run-time and memory consumption). MaLabel also has the ability to tune algorithms by using feature and parameter selection (more details are in Sect. 4). Once the user selects the proper algorithm, MaLabel learns the best set of parameters for that algorithm based on the training set, and uses the trained model to output labels of classes for the unlabeled data. Those labels serve as an ultimate results of MaLabel, although they can be used to re-train the classifier for future runs. Using the same features used for classification, MaLabel uses unsupervised clustering algorithms to group malware samples into clusters. MaLabel features a hierarchal clustering algorithm, with several variations and settings for clustering, cutting, and linkage (cf. Sect. 4). Those settings are adjustable by the user. Unlike classification, the clustering portion is unsupervised and does not require a training set to cluster the samples into appropriate clusters. The testing selector component will run hierarchal clustering with several settings to present the user with preliminary cluster sizes and number of clusters created using the different settings. Based on the preliminary results the user can pick which setting fits the data set provided and can proceed to labeling and verification process.

3.2 Features and Their Representation

While the artifacts generated by AutoMal provide a wealth of features, in MaLabel we used only a total of 65 features for classification and clustering. The features are broken down based on the class of artifacts used for generating them into three groups—a listing of the features is shown in Table 1:

Table 1. List of features. Unless otherwise specified, all of the features are counts associated with the named sample.

Class	Features
File system	Created, modified, deleted, file size distribution, unique extensions, count of files under selected and common paths
Registry	Created keys, modified keys, deleted keys, count of keys with certain type
Network	
IP and port	Unique destination IP, counts over certain ports
Connections	TCP, UDP, RAW
Request type	POST, GET, HEAD
Response type	Response codes (200s through 500s)
Size	Request and response distribution
DNS	MX, NS, A records, PTR, SOA, CNAME

File System Features. File system features are derived from file system artifacts created by the malware when run in the virtual environment. We use counts for files created, deleted, and modified. We also use counts for files created in predefined paths like %APPDATA%, %TEMP%, %PROGRAMFILES%, and other common locations. We keep a count for files created with unique extensions. For example if a malware sample creates 4 files on the system, a batch file (.BAT), two executable files (.EXE), and a configuration file (.CFG), we would count 3 for the number of unique extensions. Finally, we use the file size of created files; for that we do not use raw file size but create the distribution of the files' size. We divide the file size range, corresponding to the difference between the size of the largest and smallest files generated by a malware, into multiple ranges. We typically use four ranges, one for each quartile, and create counts for files with size falling into each range or quartile.

Registry Features. The registry features are similar to the file features since we use counts for registries created, modified, and deleted, registry type like REG_SZ, REG_BIN, and REG_DWORD. While our initial intention of using them was exploratory, those features ended up very useful in identifying malware samples, especially when combined with other features (more details are in Sect. 4).

Network Features. The network features make up the majority of our 65 features. The network features have 3 groups. The first group is raw network features, which includes count of unique IP addresses, count of connections established for 18 different port numbers, quartile count of request size, and type of protocol (we limited our attention to three popular protocols, namely the TCP, UDP, RAW). The second group is the HTTP features which include counts for POST, GET, and HEAD request; the distribution of the size of reply packets (using the quartile distribution format explained earlier), and counts for HTTP response codes, namely 200, 300, 400, and 500. The third category includes DNS features like counts for A, PTR, CNAME, and MX record lookups.

4   Evaluation

To evaluate the different algorithms in each application group, we use several accuracy measures to highlight the performance of various algorithms. Those measures are the classical used literature metrics: precision, recall, accuracy, and F-1 score.

4.1   Hardware and Benchmarking

In Table 2, we disclose information about the hardware used in AMAL. While the hardware equipment used in running MaLabel are not fully utilized, the hardware specifications used in AutoMal are important for its performance. For example, memory signatures and file system scans heavily depend on those specifications. For that, the parameters are selected to be large enough to run the samples and the hosting operating system, but not too large to make the analysis part infeasible within the allotted time for each sample. Notice that, and as explained earlier, the operating system used in AutoMal can be adjusted in the initialization before running samples. However, for consistency we use the same OS to generate the artifacts for the different samples.

4.2   Datasets

The dataset used in this work is mainly from AutoMal, and as explained earlier, is fed to the system by internal user and external customers. Internal users are internal analysts of malicious code, and external users of the system are customers, who could be security analysts in corporates (e.g.,

Table 2. Benchmarking of hardware used for the different parts of our system. MaLabel 1 and MaLabel 2 are platforms used for clustering and classification, respectively.

Component	AutoMal VM	MaLabel 1	MaLabel 2
# CPUs	1	1	1
RAM	256MB	120GB	192GB
Hard drive	6GB	200GB	2TB
OS	Win XP*	CentOS 6	CentOS 6

banks, energy companies, etc.), or other antivirus companies who are partners with us (they do not pay fees for our service, but we mutually share samples and malware intelligence). The main dataset used in this study consists of 115, 157 malware samples. The set of samples used in this study is selected as a simple random sample from a larger population of malware samples generated over that period of time. More details on the samples are in [16].

Labeling for Validation: A selected set of families to which those samples belong (with their corresponding labels) are shown in Table 3. The dataset particularly includes 2086 samples that are entirely inspected and verified as Zeus

Table 3. Malware samples and their labels used in the classification training and testing.

Size	%	Family	Description
1,077	0.94	Ramnit	File infector and a Trojan with purpose of stealing financial, personal, and system information
1,090	1.0	Bredolab	Spam and malware distribution bot
1,091	1.0	ZAccess	Rootkit trojan for bitcoin mining, click fraud, and paid install
1,205	1.1	Autorun	Generic detection of autorun functionality in malware
1,336	1.2	Spyeye	Banking trojan for stealing personal and financial information
1,652	1.4	SillyFDC	An autorun worm that spreads via portable devices and capable of downloading other malware
2,086	1.8	Zbot	Banking trojan for stealing personal and financial information
2,422	2.1	TDSS	Rootkit trojan for monetizing resources of infected machines
5,460	4.7	Virut	Polymorphic file infector virus with trojan capability
7,691	6.7	Sality	same as above, with rootkit, trojan, and worm capability
21,047	18.3	Fakealert	Fake antivirus malware with purpose to scam victims
46,157	40.1	Subtotal	
69,000	59.9	Others	Small mal, <1k samples each
115,157	100	Total	

or one of its variants by security analysts, while other labels are either generated using the same method (on a subset of the samples in the family) and the rest of the label makes use of census over returned antivirus detections. For that, we query a popular virus scanning service with 42 scan engines, and pass the MD5 of all samples in the larger dataset to it. We use the detection provided by the scan to create a census on the label of individual samples: if a sample is detected and labeled by a majority of virus scanners of a certain label, we use that label as the ground truth (those labels are shown in Table 3). We note that the Zeus family reported in Table 3 is manually inspected and labeled by internal analysts, and results returned by the antivirus scanners for the MD5s belonging to samples this family either agree with this labeling, or assign generic labels to them, thus establishing that one can rely on this census method for labeling and validation.

4.3 High-Fidelity Malware Classification

We focus on the binary classification problem using the Zeus malware family [9], given its unique ground truth, where every sample in this family is classified and labeled manually by analysts. We then show the evaluation of different algorithms implemented in MaLabel to classify other malware families using the same set of features used in Zeus. In all evaluations we use 10-fold cross validation—a formal definition and settings are provided in [16].

Classification of Analyst-Vetted Samples. MaLabel implements several binary classification algorithms, and is not restricted to a particular classifier. Examples of such algorithms include the support vector machine (SVM), linear regression (LR), classification trees, k-nearest-neighbor (KNN), and the perceptron method—all are formally defined along with their parameters in [16]. We note that KNN is not a binary classifier, so we modified it by providing it with proper (odd) k, then voting is performed over which class a sample belongs to. To understand how different classification algorithms perform on the set of features and malware samples we had, we tested the classification of the malware samples across multiple algorithms and provided several recommendations. For the SVM, and LR, we used several parameters for regularization, loss, and kernel functions (definitions are in [16]).

For this experiment, we selected the same Zeus malware dataset as one class, as we believe that the highly-accurate labeling provides high fidelity on the results of the machine learning algorithms. For the second class we generated a dataset with the same size as Zeus from the total population that excludes ZBot in Table 3. Using 10-fold cross validation, we trained the classifier on part of both datasets using the whole of 65 features, and combined the remaining of each set for testing. We ran the algorithms shown in Table 4 to label the testing set. For the performance of the different algorithms, we use the accuracy, precision, recall, and F-score.

The results are shown in Table 4. First of all, while all algorithms perform fairly well on all measures of performance by achieving a precision and recall above 85 %, we notice that SVM (with polynomial kernel for a degree of 2) performs best, achieving more than 99 % of precision and recall, followed by decision trees, which is slightly lagged by SVM (with linear kernel). Interestingly, and despite being simple and lightweight, the logistic regression model achieves close to 90 % on all performance measures, providing competitive results. While they provide less accuracy than the best performing algorithms, we believe that all of those algorithms can be used as a building block in MaLabel, which can ultimately make use of all classifiers to achieve better results.

As for the cost of running the different algorithms, we notice that the SVM with polynomial kernel is relatively slow, while the decision trees require the most number of features to achieve high accuracy (details are omitted). On the other hand, while the dual SVM provides over 95 % of performance on all measures, it runs relatively quickly. For that, and to demonstrate other aspects in our evaluation, we limit our attention to the dual SVM, where possible. SVM is known for its generalization and resistance to noise [22].

Features Ranking and Selection. We also followed the recent literature [7,8,13] to rank the different features by their high-level category. We ran our classifier on the file system, memory (where available), registry, and network features independently. For the network features, we

Table 4. Results of binary classification using several algorithms in terms of their accuracy, precision, recall, and F-score.

Algorithm	A	P	R	F
SVM Polynomial Kernal	**99.22%**	**98.92%**	**99.53%**	**99.22%**
Classification Trees	99.13%	99.19%	99.06%	99.13%
SVM Linear Kernal	97.93%	98.53%	97.30%	97.92%
SVM Dual (L2R, L2L)	95.64%	96.35%	94.86%	95.60%
Log. Regression (L2R)	89.11%	92.71%	84.90%	88.63%
K-Nearest Neighbor	88.56%	93.29%	83.11%	87.90%
Log. Regression (L1R)	86.98%	84.81%	90.09%	87.37%
Perceptron	86.15%	84.93%	87.89%	86.39%

further ranked the connection type, IP and port, request/response type and size, and DNS as sub-classes of features. From this measurement, we found that while the file system features are the most important for classification—they collectively achieve more than 90 % of precision and recall for classification—the port features are the least important. It was not clear how would the memory feature rank for the entire population of samples, but using them where available, they provide competitive and comparable results to the file system features. Finally, the rest of the features were ranked as network request/response and size, DNS features, then registry features. All features and their rankings are deferred to [16].

4.4 Large Scale Classification

One limitation of the prior evaluation of the classification algorithm is its choice of relatively small datasets that are equal in proportion for training and testing, for both the family of interest and the mixing family. This, however might not be the case in operational contexts, where even a popular family of malware can be as small as 1 % of the total population as shown in Table 3 for several examples. Accordingly, in the following we test how the different classifiers are capable of predicting the label of a given family when the testing set is mixed with a larger set of samples. For that, we use the labeled samples as families of interest, while the rest of the population of samples as the "other" family (they are collectively indicated as one class). We run the experiment with the same settings as before (5 % is saved for training the classifier and the rest is used for testing). Where possible, we use 10-fold cross validation to minimize bias. In the following we summarize the results of seven of interest. The results are in Table 5.

First of all, we notice that although the performance measures are less than those reported for Zeus in Sect. 4.3, we were still able to achieve a performance nearing or above 90 % on all performance measures for some of the malware families. For the worst case, those measures where as low as 80 %. While these measures are competitive compared to the state-of-the-art results in the literature (e.g., the results in [22] were as low as 60 % for some families), understanding the reasons behind false alarms is worth investigation. To understand those reasons, we looked at the samples marked as false alarms and concluded the following reasons behind the degradation in the performance. First, we noticed that many of the labels used for the evaluation that resulted into the final result are not by analysts, but come from the census over antivirus scans—even though a census on a large number of AV scans provides a good accuracy, it is still imperfect. Second, we notice that the class of interest is too small, compared to the total population of samples, and a small error is amplified for that class—notice that this effect is unseen in [22] where classes are more balanced in size (e.g., 1 to 9 ratios versus 1 to 99 ratio in our case). Finally, part of the results is attributed to the relatively similar context of the different families of malware samples, as shown in Table 3, thus in the future we will explore enriching the features to achieve higher accuracy.

Table 5. Binary classification of several malware families.

Family	A	P	R	F
ZAccess	85.9 %	80.7 %	94.3 %	87.0 %
Ramnit	91.0 %	87.1 %	96.3 %	91.5 %
FakeAV	85.0 %	82.5 %	88.8 %	85.6 %
Autorun	87.9 %	85.2 %	91.8 %	88.4 %
TDSS	90.3 %	89.6 %	91.2 %	90.4 %
Bredolab	91.2 %	88.0 %	95.3 %	91.5 %
Virut	86.6 %	85.9 %	87.5 %	86.7 %

Benchmarking and Scalability. We benchmarked our 115,157 samples using several distance calculation algorithms and hierarchal clustering methods with a cut off threshold of 0.70. From this benchmarking, we observe the high variability of time it takes for computing the distance matrix, which is the shared time between all algorithms settings. For example, computing the distance matrix using the Jaccard index (which is the only distance measure used in the literature for this purpose thus far [6]) takes 5820 s (97 min) whereas all other distance measures require between 27.8 and 36.2 min.

5   Conclusion

In this paper we introduced AMAL, the first operational large-scale malware analysis, classification, and clustering system. AMAL is composed of two subsystems, AutoMal and MaLabel. AutoMal runs malware samples in virtualized environments and collects memory, file system, registry, and network artifacts, which are used for creating a rich set of features. Unlike the prior literature, AutoMal combines signature-based techniques with purely behavior-based techniques, thus generating highly-representative features, and use them for both classification and clustering.

References

1. MySQL, May 2013. http://www.mysql.com/
2. Yara Project: a malware identification and classification tool, May 2013. http://bit.ly/3hbs3d
3. Antonakakis, M., Perdisci, R., Dagon, D., Lee, W., Feamster, N.: Building a dynamic reputation system for dns. In: USENIX Security Symposium (2010)
4. Antonakakis, M., Perdisci, R., Lee, W., Vasiloglou II, N., Dagon, D.: Detecting malware domains at the upper dns hierarchy. In: USENIX Security Symposium (2011)
5. Bailey, M., Oberheide, J., Andersen, J., Mao, Z.M., Jahanian, F., Nazario, J.: Automated classification and analysis of internet malware. In: Kruegel, C., Lippmann, R., Clark, A. (eds.) RAID 2007. LNCS, vol. 4637, pp. 178–197. Springer, Heidelberg (2007)
6. Bayer, U., Comparetti, P.M., Hlauschek, C., Krügel, C., Kirda, E.: Scalable, behavior-based malware clustering. In: NDSS (2009)
7. Bilge, L., Balzarotti, D., Robertson, W.K., Kirda, E., Kruegel, C.: Disclosure: detecting botnet command and control servers through large-scale netflow analysis. In: ACSAC (2012)
8. Bilge, L., Kirda, E., Kruegel, C., Balduzzi, M.: Exposure: finding malicious domains using passive dns analysis. In: NDSS (2011)
9. Falliere, N., Chien, E.: Zeus: king of the bots. Symantec Security Response, November 2009. http://bit.ly/3VyFV1
10. Gorecki, C., Freiling, F.C., Kührer, M., Holz, T.: Trumanbox: improving dynamic malware analysis by emulating the internet. In: SSS (2011)
11. Gu, G., Perdisci, R., Zhang, J., Lee, W.: Botminer: clustering analysis of network traffic for protocol- and structure-independent botnet detection. In: USENIX Security Symposium (2008)
12. Holz, T., Gorecki, C., Rieck, K., Freiling, F.C.: Measuring and detecting fast-flux service networks. In: NDSS (2008)
13. Hong, C.-Y., Yu, F., Xie, Y.: Populated ip addresses: classification and applications. In: ACM CCS, pp. 329–340 (2012)
14. Jacob, G., Hund, R., Kruegel, C., Holz, T.: Jackstraws: picking command and control connections from bot traffic. In: USENIX Security Symposium (2011)
15. Kinable, J., Kostakis, O.: Malware classification based on call graph clustering. J. Comput. Virol. **7**(4), 233–245 (2011)
16. Mohaisen, A., Alrawi, O., Larson, M.: Amal: High-fidelity, behavior-based automated malware analysis and classification. Technical report, Verisign Labs (2013)
17. Nazario, J., Holz, T.: As the net churns: fast-flux botnet observations. In: MALWARE, pp. 24–31 (2008)
18. Park, Y., Reeves, D., Mulukutla, V., Sundaravel, B.: Fast malware classification by automated behavioral graph matching. In: CSIIR Workshop. ACM (2010)
19. Perdisci, R., Lee, W., Feamster, N.: Behavioral clustering of http-based malware and signature generation using malicious network traces. In: USENIX NSDI (2010)
20. Provos, N., McNamee, D., Mavrommatis, P., Wang, K., Modadugu, N., et al.: The ghost in the browser analysis of web-based malware. In: USENIX HotBots (2007)
21. Ramilli, M., Bishop, M.: Multi-stage delivery of malware. In: MALWARE (2010)
22. Rieck, K., Holz, T., Willems, C., Düssel, P., Laskov, P.: Learning and classification of malware behavior. In: Zamboni, D. (ed.) DIMVA 2008. LNCS, vol. 5137, pp. 108–125. Springer, Heidelberg (2008)

23. Rieck, K., Trinius, P., Willems, C., Holz, T.: Automatic analysis of malware behavior using machine learning. J. Comput. Secur. **19**(4), 639–668 (2011)
24. Rossow, C., Dietrich, C.J., Grier, C., Kreibich, C., Paxson, V., Pohlmann, N., Bos, H., van Steen, M.: Prudent practices for designing malware experiments: status quo and outlook. In: IEEE Sec. and Privacy (2012)
25. Sommer, R., Paxson, V.: Outside the closed world: on using machine learning for network intrusion detection. In: IEEE Symposium on Security and Privacy (2010)
26. Strackx, R., Piessens, F.: Fides: selectively hardening software application components against kernel-level or process-level malware. In: ACM CCS (2012)
27. Strayer, W.T., Lapsley, D.E., Walsh, R., Livadas, C.: Botnet detection based on network behavior. In: Botnet Detection (2008)
28. Tian, R., Batten, L., Versteeg, S.: Function length as a tool for malware classification. In: IEEE MALWARE (2008)
29. VMWare. Virtual Machine Disk Format (VMDK), May 2013. http://bit.ly/e1zJkZ
30. Zhao, H., Xu, M., Zheng, N., Yao, J., Ho, Q.: Malicious executables classification based on behavioral factor analysis. In: IC4E (2010)

Systematically Breaking Online WYSIWYG Editors

Ashar Javed[(✉)] and Jörg Schwenk

Chair for Network and Data Security Horst Görtz Institute for IT-Security,
Ruhr-University Bochum, Bochum, Germany
{ashar.javed,joerg.schwenk}@rub.de

Abstract. Cross-Site Scripting (XSS) — around fourteen years old vulnerability is still on the rise and a continuous threat to the web applications. Only last year, 150505 defacements (*this is a least, an XSS can do*) have been reported and archived in Zone-H (a cybercrime archive) (http://www.zone-h.org/). The online **WYSIWYG** (**W**hat **Y**ou **S**ee **I**s **W**hat **Y**ou **G**et) or rich-text editors are now a days an essential component of the web applications. They allow users of web applications to edit and enter HTML rich text (i.e., *formatted text, images, links* and *videos* etc.) inside the web browser window. The web applications use **WYSIWYG** editors as a part of comment functionality, private messaging among users of applications, blogs, notes, forums post, spellcheck as-you-type, ticketing feature, and other online services. The XSS in **WYSIWYG** editors is considered more dangerous and exploitable because the user-supplied rich-text contents (may be dangerous) are viewable by other users of web applications.

In this paper, we present a security analysis of twenty (20) popular **WYSIWYG** editors powering thousands of web sites. The analysis includes **WYSIWYG** editors like Enterprise TinyMCE, EditLive, Lithium, Jive, TinyMCE, PHP HTML Editor, markItUp! universal markup jQuery editor, FreeTextBox (popular ASP.NET editor), Froala Editor, elRTE, and CKEditor. At the same time, we also analyze rich-text editors available on very popular sites like Twitter, Yahoo Mail, Amazon, GitHub and Magento and many more. In order to analyze online **WYSIWYG** editors, this paper also present a systematic and **WYSIWYG** editors's specific XSS attack methodology. We apply the XSS attack methodology on online **WYSIWYG** editors and found XSS is all of them. We show XSS bypasses for old and modern browsers. We have responsibly reported our findings to the respective developers of editors and our suggestions have been added. In the end, we also point out some recommendations for the developers of web applications and **WYSIWYG** editors.

1 Introduction

Cross-Site Scripting (XSS) vulnerabilities in modern web applications are now "an epidemic". According to Google Vulnerability Reward Program (GVRP)

© Springer International Publishing Switzerland 2015
K.-H. Rhee and J.H. Yi (Eds.): WISA 2014, LNCS 8909, pp. 122–133, 2015.
DOI: 10.1007/978-3-319-15087-1_10

report of 2013, XSS is at number one as far as valid bug bounty submissions are concerned [1]. According to Google Trends, XSS is googled more often than SQL injection for the first time in history [2]. Recently, an XSS attack has been successfully used for the closure of a very popular web and mobile application i.e., TweetDeck [3]. The XSS issue in TweetDeck was able to affect more than 80,000 users within 96 min [13]. The XSS in **WYSIWYG** editors is considered more dangerous, effective and exploitable because the user-supplied rich-text contents (may be dangerous) are most of the time viewable by other users of the web applications e.g., we found an XSS in **WYSIWYG** editor of Twitter Translation center's forum[1] even in the presence of a Content Security Policy (CSP) [14] (see Sect. 3.1). The CSP is the W3C standard for the mitigation of an XSS attack. In case of an XSS in **WYSIWYG** editor, the attacker does not need to trick user to visit his page.

Fig. 1. A **WYSIWYG** Editor

The online **WYSIWYG** (**W**hat **Y**ou **S**ee **I**s **W**hat **Y**ou **G**et) or rich-text editors (see Fig. 1) are main component of the modern web applications. **WYSI-WYG** editors allow users of web applications to edit and enter HTML-based rich text (i.e., formatted text e.g., **bold**, *italic* and underline, *images*, *links* and *videos* etc.) inside the web browser. The modern web applications use **WYSI-WYG** editors as a part of comment feature, private messaging among users of applications, blogs, wiki, notes, forums post, spellcheck as-you-type, ticketing feature, and other online services. The main purpose of rich-text editors is to provide users of web applications a better editing experience. The third-party **WYSIWYG** editors are normally available in the form of client-side JavaScript library, PHP or ASP based sever-side component and Rails gem.

The online cross-browser **WYSIWYG** are very popular e.g.:

- **Jive** — very popular editor and in use on sites like Amazon, T-Mobile and Thomson-Reuters etc. [5].
- **TinyMCE** — Javascript HTML **WYSIWYG** editor and in use on sites like XBox, Apple, Open Source CMS Joomla and Oracle etc. [6].
- **Lithium** — another popular rich-text editor and in use on sites like Paypal, Skype and Sephora etc. [8].
- **Froala** — jQuery **WYSIWYG** text editor and has been downloaded around 6000 times within two and half months of its launch [9].
- **EditLive** — an advanced **WYSIWYG** editor and 1500 organizations like Verizon, The New York Times and Nissan etc. are using it [11].

---

[1] https://translate.twitter.com.

- **CKEditor** — it has been downloaded 9472723 times and in use in sites like MailChimp, IBM and Terapad etc. [4]. It is formally known as FCKEditor.
- **Markdown** — another popular rich-text editor and in use on sites like Twitter, GitHub and Gitter (a private chat service for GitHub) [12].

This paper presents a study of analyzing 20 popular **WYSIWYG** editors. In order to evaluate **WYSIWYG** editors, we also present a systematic attack methodology (see Sect. 2.2). For testing purpose, we use the demo pages available by **WYSIWYG** editor. All the testing is carried out on the demo pages so that it will not harm any real user of the respective editor (see Sect. 2.1). Further, we also study home-grown **WYSIWYG** editors available on top sites like Yahoo Mail, Twitter and Magento Commerce. During evaluation of our attack methodology, we were able to break all **WYSIWYG** editors (see Sect. 3). We found XSS bypasses for old and modern browsers. We have responsibly reported our findings to the respective projects and our suggestions have been added in **WYSIWYG** editors like TinyMCE, Lithium, Jive and Froala. At the same time, we were awarded bug bounties by companies like Magento Commerce, GitHub and Paypal for finding bugs in their **WYSIWYG** editors and acknowledged by Twitter, Paypal and GitHub on their security hall of fame pages. To the best of our knowledge, this is the first study of analyzing XSS attacks in **WYSIWYG** editors. In the end, we also recommend best practices that **WYSIWYG** editors and web applications may adopt for the mitigation of an XSS attack (see Sect. 4).

This paper makes the following contributions:

- A security analysis of 20 popular **WYSIWYG** editors. The complete list of **WYSIWYG** editors is avaiable in the appendix (see Sect. A in appendix). Further, we also analyze **WYSIWYG** editors of top sites like Paypal, Yahoo, Amazon, Twitter and Magento.
- A systematic and step-wise attack methodology for evaluating **WYSIWYG** editors.
- Our suggestions have been added in top **WYSIWYG** editors like Lithium, Jive, TinyMCE and Froala.
- We also point out best practices that **WYSIWYG** editors and web applications may use in order to minimize the affect of XSS.

2   Methodology

In this section, we describe the testing and attack methodology.

2.1   Testing Methodology

In this section, we briefly describe the testing process. In order to test **WYSIWYG** editors, we use the demo pages made available by the respective developers of **WYSIWYG** editors. The main advantage of testing on demo pages is that it will not harm any user. In case, we found an XSS during testing process, we act responsibly and filled the bug(s) on GitHub or directly report via email. During testing of **WYSIWYG** editors, we identify common injection points (almost all **WYSIWYG** editors support these injection points) that are of an attacker interest e.g., link creation, image and video insertion, description of images, class or id names and styling of contents. In the next section, we will present a respective XSS attack methodology for these injection points.

2.2   Attack Methodology

In this section, we describe the XSS attack methodology for the common injection points identified in previous section. The attack methodology for every injection point is systematic in nature.

Attacking Link Creation Feature: All **WYSIWYG** editors support "`create link`" feature. The "`create link`" functionality corresponds to HTML's anchor tag i.e., `<a>` and its "`href`" attribute. The user-supplied input as a part of "`create link`" in **WYSIWYG** editor lands as a value of "`href`" attribute. The attacker can abuse this functionality with the help of following steps (see Fig. 2) and can execute arbitrary JavaScript in the context of a web application. The step ❶ makes use of JavaScript URI e.g., `javascript:alert(1)` in order to execute JavaScript e.g., we found XSS via JavaScript URI in Froala, EditLive, CNET's **WYSIWYG** editor and Twitter etc. The attacker can also use different types of encoding in JavaScript URI e.g., "`javascript:alert%28 1 %29`" (URL encoded parenthesis) and "`jav&Tab;ascr&Tab;ipt&colon;alert(1)`" (HTML5 entity encoding). In case, **WYSIWYG** editor filters the word "`javascript`", then attacker can use DATA URI based JavaScript execution in step ❷ e.g., "`data: text/html;base64,PHN2Zy9vbmxvYWQ9YWxlcnQoMik+`". We found XSS via DATA URI in Jive because Jive does not allow JavaScript based URI. In step ❸, the attacker can also leverage VbScript based code execution but it is limited to Internet Explorer browser. In last step i.e., step ❹, the attacker can make use of valid URL but as a part of query parameter's value, he uses the following attack string i.e., `"onmouseover="alert(1)` in order to break the URL context. The step ❹ is very useful in case if **WYSIWYG** editors only accept URLs start with "`http(s)`". We found XSS in Amazon's **WYSIWYG** editor with the help of step ❹.

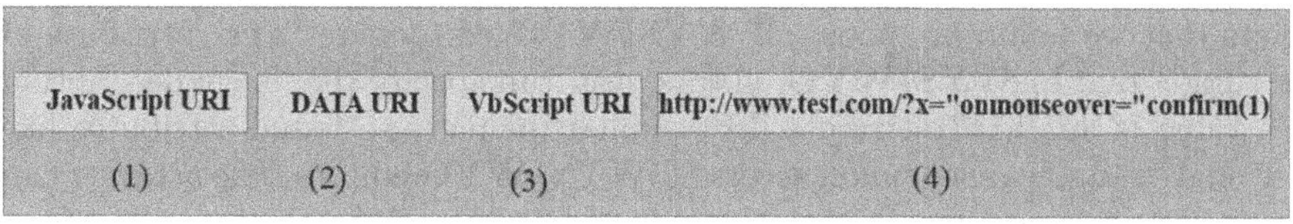

JavaScript URI	DATA URI	VbScript URI	http://www.test.com/?x="onmouseover="confirm(1)
(1)	(2)	(3)	(4)

Fig. 2. Attack Methodology for Link Creation Feature

Attacking Image Insertion Feature: Another common functionality that all **WYSIWYG** editors support is "`Insert/Edit Image`". The "`Insert/Edit`

Image" feature corresponds to HTML's <img> and its "src" attribute. The user-supplied input as a part of "Insert/Edit Image" in **WYSIWYG** editor lands as a value of "src" attribute. The attacker may use the following XSS attack methodology (see Fig. 3) in order to abuse this feature. The step ❶ consists of a valid "jpg" image URL ends in ? and after the question mark "onmouseover="alert(1). In URL, the question mark symbol is legally valid and all browsers respect it while at the same time for the **WYSIWYG** editors, it is also a legit input at this point because their implementations expect input to be a valid URL but then we used hard-coded " symbol and the sole purpose is to break or jump out of the context and execute JavaScript via eventhandler e.g., onmouseover. We found XSS in Amazon's **WYSIWYG** editor with the help of first step. The step ❷ consists of a valid SVG image hosted on free domain for demo purpose. The step ❷ serves two purpose:

1. JavaScript execution via SVG image. We found XSS in GitHub's rich-text markup feature with the help of an SVG image and we were awarded bounty for that. In favor of space restrictions, we refer to the work by Heiderich *et al.* in [15] and it shows how an attacker can leverage SVG images for arbitrary JavaScript code execution.
2. If **WYSIWYG** editors are doing explicit decoding on the server side then JavaScript can be executed because decoding will convert the %22 into hard-coded ", which in turns break the context. We found XSS in Alexa's rich-text tool bar creation feature with the help of this technique.

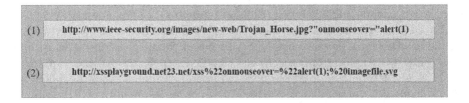

Fig. 3. Attack Methodology for Image Insertion Feature

Attacking "alt", "id" *and* "class" *attributes:* Another common injection points that we found in almost all **WYSIWYG** editors are "alt" attribute of an <img> tag. In **WYSIWYG** editors, user can specify the image description as a value of an "alt" attribute. In a similar manner, we found attributes like "id" and "class" are common across all **WYSIWYG** editors. The attacker can abuse these injection points with the help of following XSS attack methodology (see Fig. 4). The step ❶ consists of attack vector "anytext"onmouseover="alert (1)". It is clear from the attack string that if **WYSIWYG** editors fail to properly sanitize/filter ", then the attack string will jump out from the attribute context and attacker can execute JavaScript. We found XSS in Yahoo Mail's **WYSIWYG** editor with the help of this attack vector. The step ❷ is related to innerHTML based XSS and specific to old Internet Explorer (IE) browser. The old IE browser treats back-tick i.e., (``) as a valid separator for attribute and its value. The back-tick based XSS attack string is very useful in cases where **WYSIWYG** editors properly filter double quotes (") and do not allow to break the context e.g., the following XSS attack vectors would result in an innerHTML based XSS in IE8 browser. `<div class="``onmouseover=alert(1)">`div layer `</div>`, `<a href="#" id="``onmouseover=alert(1)">`click`</a>` and `<img src="x" alt="``onmouseover=alert(1)">` etc. Almost all **WYSIWYG** editors are vulnerable to innerHTML based XSS including Lithium, TinyMCE, Froala and GitHub's **WYSIWYG** editor. For details about innerHTML based XSS, we refer to the recent work by Heiderich *et al.* in [16].

Fig. 4. Attack Methodology for Attributes

Attacking Video Insertion Feature: **WYSIWYG** editors (not all) support "Insert Video" feature. As a part of this feature, **WYSIWYG** editors only allow HTML's `<object>` and/or `<embed>` tag. The attacker can abuse this feature with the help of following example code snippet (see Fig. 5). The code snippet is taken from the Youtube's video sharing via embedded code feature. In the perfectly legit code snippet, we have added "`onmouseover=alert(1)`" in order to fool **WYSIWYG** editors. We found XSS in froala with the help of this trick.

```
<object width="560" height="315" onmouseover=confirm(1)><param name="movie" value="//www.youtube-nocookie.com
/v/KoA7Cpujrus?version=3&amp;hl=en_US"></param><param name="allowFullScreen" value="true"></param><param
name="allowscriptaccess" value="always"></param><embed src="//www.youtube-nocookie.com/v/KoA7Cpujrus?version=3&
amp;hl=en_US" type="application/x-shockwave-flash" width="560" height="315" allowscriptaccess="always"
allowfullscreen="true"></embed></object>
```

Fig. 5. Attack Methodology for Video Insertion Feature

Attacking "Styles": All **WYSIWYG** editors support "styling" of the rich-text contents e.g., user can specify the height, width, color and font properties of the contents. The attacker can easily abuse this feature with the help of CSS expressions [17]. The old versions of Internet Explorer (IE) browsers support JavaScript execution via CSS expressions. The XSS attack vectors may use for this purpose are: "`width:expression(alert(1))`" or "`x:expr/**/ession (alert(1))`". We found XSS in Ebay, Magento, Amazon, TinyMCE and CKEditor's **WYSIWYG** editors with the help of "styles".

3 Evaluation of Attack Methodology

In this section, we discuss the results of evaluating attack methodology on popular **WYSIWYG** editors. We were able to break all **WYSIWYG** editors in one or other common injection points discussed in the previous section. In favor of space restrictions, here we discuss three examples that we consider worth sharing as a part of evaluation.

3.1 XSS in Twitter Translation Forum's WYSIWYG editor

Twitter[2] (Alexa rank #9), a popular social networking web site. Twitter is one the handful of web sites that are using CSP for the mitigation of XSS attacks. Twitter's CSP is available at the following URL http://i.imgur.com/ESkQG9O. jpg. The CSP explicitly tells the browser about trusted resources for images, script, media, and styles etc. Twitter Translation[3] is one of the Twitter's service where community can help in translating Twitter related stuff in different languages. On Twitter Translation forum, we found that it supports rich-text markup feature. The following Fig. 6 shows Twitter's markdown cheat sheet. We found one of the way of specifying links in the forum post is: `[Twitter]` (https://twitter.com) (see area marked in red in Fig. 6). As discussed in previous section (see Sect. 2.2), the attacker can abuse the link creation feature with the help of JavaScript, Data and VbScript URI. By keeping in mind attack methodology related to "`create link`", we input the following: `[Twitter]` (`javascript:alert(1)`). Twitter internally treats the above input in the following manner: `<a href="javascript:alert(1">Twitter</a>`. The JavaScript does not execute because of the missing closing parenthesis in "`alert(1`". The reason we found is: Twitter's **WYSIWYG** editor's syntax is causing problem because internally it treats the closing parenthesis of "`alert(1)`" as "URL ends here" and did not look for the last parenthesis. As a part of next step, we convert the small parenthesis into the respective URL encoded form i.e., (becomes %28 and) becomes %29. The next attack string looks like: `[Twitter]`(`javascript: alert%28 1%29`) and this time it works as expected and internally it looks like: `<a href="javascript:alert%28 1%29">Twitter</a>`. The following Fig. 7 shows JavaScript execution in Twitter's **WYSIWYG** editor.

3.2 XSSes in TinyMCE's WYSIWYG editor

TinyMCE [6] is one of the most popular **WYSIWYG** editor. We found three different XSSes in TinyMCE: one in "`create link`" feature (see Sect. 2.2), one in "`styling`" feature (see Sect. 2.2) and one innerHTML based XSS in "`alt`" attribute (see Sect. 2.2). We filled three different bugs[4] in TinyMCE's bug tracker and now all XSSes have been fixed [7]. The following list items summarizes our findings:

---

[2] https://twitter.com/.

[3] https://translate.twitter.com.

[4] http://www.tinymce.com/develop/bugtracker_view.php?id=6855|6851|6858.

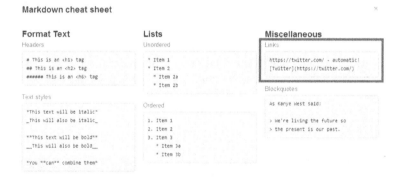

Fig. 6. Markdown Cheat Sheet

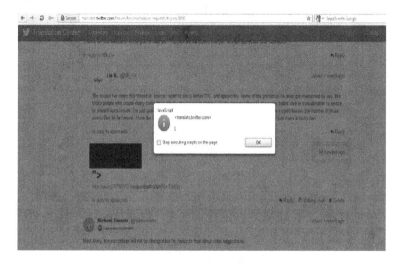

Fig. 7. XSS in Twitter Translation

1. TinyMCE was vulnerable to an XSS in "`create link`" feature with the help of DATA URI i.e., "`data:text/html;base64,PHN2Zy9vbmxvYWQ9YWxlcnQooM ik+`".
2. TinyMCE was vulnerable to an XSS in "`style`" functionality. In order to execute XSS, we used CSS expressions i.e., "`x:expr/**/ession(alert(1))`". TinyMCE's implementation does not allow the word "`expression`" as a part of styles and that's why we used "`expr/**/ession`" i.e., use of multi-lin comments in "`expression`" word and old IE browsers simply ignores it.
3. TinyMCE was also vulnerable to an innerHTML based XSS and the attack vector used for this purpose was: `` ``onmouseover=alert(1). ``

3.3   XSSes in Froala's WYSIWYG editor

Froala — jQuery **WYSIWYG** text editor is also one of the popular and latest rich-text editor [10]. We found XSSes in almost all common injection points identified in Sect. 2.2. A bug[5] has been filled on GitHub and all reported XSS issues have been fixed in the upcoming version. The following list items summarizes our findings:

Fig. 8. XSS in Froala

1. "Create Link" feature was vulnerable to an XSS e.g., "javascript:alert(1)" and "data:text/html;base64,PHN2Zy9vbmxvYWQ9YWxlcnQoMik+ worked.
2. "Insert Image" feature was vulnerable to a trick discussed in previous section (see Sect. 2.2) i.e., attacker can execute JavaScript with the help of following: http://www.ieee-security.org/images/new-web/Trojan_Horse.jpg? "onmouseover="alert(1).
3. "Insert Video" feature was vulnerable to the attack method discussed earlier (see Sect. 2.2). The Fig. 8 shows XSS in Froala via "Insert Video" functionality.
4. "Image Title" feature was vulnerable to an innerHTML based XSS attack method discussed earlier (see Sect. 2.2).

4   Practical and Low Cost Countermeasures

Web applications normally integrate third-party **WYSIWYG** editor(s) in order to give customers of web application a better and rich editing experience. In this section, we discuss low cost, practical and easily deployable countermeasures that web applications may adopt in order to minimize the affect of an XSS in **WYSIWYG** editor(s). Further, we also recommend some suggestions to the developers of **WYSIWYG** editors.

---

[5] https://github.com/froala/wysiwyg-editor/issues/33.

4.1   HttpOnly Cookies

Web applications use cookies in order to maintain a session state between authenticated client and server because of the stateless nature of an HTTP protocol. If
a flag "HttpOnly" is set on a cookie then JavaScript can not read the value of this
cookie and all modern browsers respect this. We recommend web applications'
developers to use "HttpOnly" cookie especially if **WYSIWYG** editor is in use.
In case of an XSS in **WYSIWYG** editor, the attacker can not read the session
cookie of the victim with the help of JavaScript. We found an XSS in Magento's
(an Ebay company) **WYSIWYG** editor and found "PHPSESSID" cookie was not
"HttpOnly" and at the same time site only allows authenticated users to post
on forum. With the help of this XSS in **WYSIWYG** editor, attacker may steal
the session cookie of the forum administrator and hack the forum. The XSS in
Magento's **WYSIWYG** editor is now fixed and the details are available in a
post here[6]. Magento acknowledged our findings and we were awarded thousand
US dollar in the form of bug bounty.

4.2   Iframe's "sandbox"

We recommend developers of the web applications to use <iframe sandbox> in
order to integrate third-party **WYSIWYG** editor. With the help of "sandbox"
attribute, the developers of the web applications can restrict the capabilities of
third-party **WYSIWYG** editor. In case of an XSS in **WYSIWYG** editor, if
"sandbox" attribute is used then attacker can not access the DOM contents
of the main web page or locally stored data on the client side. All mordern
browsers support iframe's "sandbox". For details about <iframe sandbox>,
we refer to [18] for interested readers.

4.3   Content Security Policy

We recommend developers of web applications to retrofit their applications for
CSP [14]. The CSP policy is now a W3C standard for the mitigation of an XSS
attacks. The CSP is based on directives for images, script, media, styles and
iframes etc. The developers of web applications can explicity tell the browser
about the trusted resources. By default, CSP prohibits inlining scripting. In
case of an XSS in **WYSIWYG** editor, if CSP is defined then first browser will
not allow injected, inline script to execute (unless "unsafe-inline" directive
is specified) and second CSP helps in minimizing the affect of an XSS because
attacker can not ex-filtrate sensitive data to his domain.

4.4   Guidelines for Developers of WYSIWYG editors

In this section, we briefly describe some guidelines for **WYSIWYG** editors'
developers.

---

[6] http://www.scribd.com/doc/226925089/Stylish-XSS-in-Magento-When-Style-
helps-you.

– Should force users to input URL or "`create link`" that starts with an
"`http://`" or "`https://`".
– Should not allow SVG images. With the help of an SVG image, attacker may
execute JavaScript.
– Should properly encode potentially dangerous characters in attributes e.g.,
double quotes and back-tick because these characters can help attacker to
break the attribute context and execute JavaScript.
– Should not allow CSS expressions in "`styling`" of the contents.
– Should not allow Flash-based movies because attacker can execute JavaScript
code via Flash file.
– In case, **WYSIWYG** editor allows to upload a file then developers should
validate the file type.

5   Conclusion

In this paper, we analyzed twenty popular **WYSIWYG** editors and found XSS
in all of them. We had presented a systematic XSS attack methodology for
common injection points in **WYSIWYG** editors. We hope that this paper will
raise awareness about the XSS issue in modern feature of an HTML5-based web
applications i.e., rich-text editors.

A   List of WYSIWYG Editors

1. Mercury Editor: The Rails HTML5 WYSIWYG editor (http://jejacks0n.
github.com/mercury)
2. bootstrap-wysihtml5: Simple, beautiful wysiwyg editor (https://github.com/
jhollingworth/bootstrap-wysihtml5)
3. KindEditor (http://kindeditor.org/)
4. PHP HTML Editor (http://phphtmleditor.com/demo/)
5. elRTE — an open-source WYSIWYG HTML-editor (http://elrte.org/)
6. medium-editor (https://github.com/daviferreira/medium-editor)
7. TinyMCE (http://www.tinymce.com/)
8. Lithium (http://www.lithium.com/)
9. Jive (http://www.jivesoftware.com/)
10. Froala (http://editor.froala.com/)
11. CKEditor (http://ckeditor.com/)
12. EditLive (http://ephox.com/editlive)
13. jquery.qeditor (https://github.com/huacnlee/jquery.qeditor)
14. mooeditable (http://cheeaun.github.io/mooeditable/)
15. HTML5 WYSIWYG Editor (https://github.com/bordeux/HTML-5-WYSI
WYG-Editor)
16. markItUp! universal markup jQuery editor (http://markitup.jaysalvat.com/
home/)
17. FreeTextBox HTML Editor (http://www.freetextbox.com/)
18. Markdown (http://daringfireball.net/projects/markdown/)
19. CLEditor (http://premiumsoftware.net/CLEditor/SimpleDemo)
20. Bootstrap Wysihtml5 with Custom Image Insert (https://github.com/rcode5/
image-wysiwyg-sample)

References

1. Google Vulnerability Reward Program Report for year 2013.: https://www.youtube.com/watch?v=oAYjZy1Nuyg
2. Google Trends.: http://www.google.com/trends/explore#q=XSS%2C%20SQL%20Injection&date=today%2012-m&cmpt=q
3. TweetDeck ShutDown.: https://twitter.com/TweetDeck/status/476770732987252736
4. CKEditor.: http://ckeditor.com/about/who-is-using-ckeditor
5. Jive.: http://www.jivesoftware.com/why-jive/customers/#view=list
6. TinyMCE.: http://www.tinymce.com/enterprise/using.php
7. TinyMCE Tracker.: http://www.tinymce.com/develop/bugtracker.php
8. Lithium.: http://www.lithium.com/why-lithium/customer-success/
9. Froala.: https://github.com/stefanneculai/froala-wysiwyg/issues/33#issuecomment-41170451
10. Froala Editor.: http://editor.froala.com/
11. Edit Live.: http://ephox.com/customers
12. Markdown.: http://daringfireball.net/projects/markdown/
13. From "I wonder..." to Exploitable Worm in 96 Minutes.: https://storify.com/pacohope/from-i-wonder-to-exploitable-worm
14. Content Security Policy 1.1.: http://www.w3.org/TR/CSP11/
15. Heiderich, M., Frosch, T., Jensen, M., Thorsten, H.: Security risks of scalable vectors graphics. In: CCS, Crouching Tiger - Hidden Payload (2011)
16. Heiderich, M., Schwenk, J., Frosch, T., Magazinius, J., Yang, E.Z.: mXSS attacks: attacking well-secured web-applications by using innerHTML mutations.. In: CCS (2013)
17. About Dynamic Properties.: http://msdn.microsoft.com/en-us/library/ie/ms537634(v=vs.85).aspx
18. Play safely in sandboxed IFrames.: http://www.html5rocks.com/en/tutorials/security/sandboxed-iframes/

Applied Cryptography

New Integrated Long-Term Glimpse of RC4

Ryoma Ito$^{(\boxtimes)}$ and Atsuko Miyaji

Japan Advanced Institute of Science and Technology,
1-1 Asahidai, Nomi-shi, Ishikawa 923-1292, Japan
{s1310005,miyaji}@jaist.ac.jp

Abstract. RC4, which was designed by Ron Rivest in 1987, is widely used in various applications such as SSL/TLS, WEP, WPA, etc. In 1996, Jenkins discovered correlations between one output keystream and a state location, known as Glimpse Theorem. In 2013, Maitra and Sen Gupta proved Glimpse Theorem and showed correlations between two consecutive output keystreams and a state location, called long-term Glimpse. In this paper, we show a new long-term Glimpse and integrate both the new and the previous long-term Glimpse into a whole.

Keywords: RC4 · Correlation · Long-term Glimpse

1 Introduction

RC4, which was designed by Ron Rivest in 1987, is widely used in various applications such as Secure Socket Layer/Transport Layer Security (SSL/TLS), Wired Equivalent Privacy (WEP) and Wi-fi Protected Access (WPA), etc. Due to its popularity and simplicity, RC4 has become a hot cryptanalysis target since its specification was made public on the internet in 1994. For example, typical attacks on RC4 are distinguishing attack [3,4,10], state recovery attack [1,6,9] and key recovery attack [2,8,11].

In 1996, Jenkins discovered correlations between one output keystream and a state location, which is known as Glimpse Theorem [5]. These correlations have biases with the probability about $\frac{2}{N}$ higher than that of random association $\frac{1}{N}$ using the knowledge of one output keystream. In 2013, Maitra and Sen Gupta presented the complete proof of Glimpse Theorem and showed $S_r[r+1] = N-1$ occurs with the probability about $\frac{2}{N}$ when two consecutive output keystreams Z_r and Z_{r+1} satisfies $Z_{r+1} = Z_r$, where $S_r[r+1]$ is the $r+1$-th location of the state array in the r-th round as usual. They also showed the probability of $S_r[r+1] = N-1$ is further increased to about $\frac{3}{N}$ when $Z_{r+1} = r+2$ as well as $Z_{r+1} = Z_r$ occurs. Here, we call correlation with a probability significantly higher or lower than $\frac{1}{N}$ (the probability of random association) *positive bias* or *negative bias*, respectively. Then, their results of $S_r[r+1] = N-1$ with the probability about $\frac{2}{N}$ correspond to cases with positive biases. Note that Theorem 2 implicitly means that there exists a value of $S_r[r+1]$ with negative bias since $S_r[r+1]$ varies in $[0, N-1]$ when $Z_{r+1} = Z_r$ has happened. We often

© Springer International Publishing Switzerland 2015
K.-H. Rhee and J.H. Yi (Eds.): WISA 2014, LNCS 8909, pp. 137–149, 2015.
DOI: 10.1007/978-3-319-15087-1_11

assume uniform randomness of other certain events to prove bias of a certain event. Therefore, it is important to prove the existence of a value with negative bias explicitly. We also call such a case with negative bias to *dual case* of a positive bias.

In this paper, we first show a dual case of $S_r[r+1] = N-1$, that is $S_r[r+1] = 0$, occurs with the probability about $\frac{1}{N^2}$ when $Z_{r+1} = Z_r$, which will be shown as Theorem 4. Then, Theorem 5 will give each probability of $S_r[r+1] = 0$ when $Z_{r+1} = r + x$ ($\forall x \in [0, N-1]$) as well as $Z_{r+1} = Z_r$ occurs. Furthermore, during our careful observation of the dual case, we also find a new positive bias on $S_r[r+1]$, which will be shown in Theorem 6. Our results show that, giving two consecutive keystreams Z_r and Z_{r+1} satisfying with $Z_{r+1} = Z_r$ and $Z_{r+1} = r + 1 + x$ ($x \in [2, N-1]$), the probability of $S_r[r+1] = N - x$ is about $\frac{2}{N}$, which is significantly higher than random association $\frac{1}{N}$. Note that the previous results are limited to a value of $S_r[r+1] = N-1$, but our results varies $S_r[r+1] \in [0, N-2]$. Furthermore, both our new and the previous results are integrated into long-term Glimpse of $Z_{r+1} = Z_r$ in Theorem 7.

This paper is organized as follows. Section 2 briefly summarizes notation and RC4 algorithms. Section 3 presents the previous works on Glimpse Theorem [5] and long-term Glimpse [7]. Section 4 first discusses positive and negative biases, and shows Theorems 4–7. Section 5 demonstrates experimental simulations. Section 6 concludes this paper.

2 Preliminary

The following notation is used in this paper.

$$K, l : \text{secret key, the length of secret key (bytes)}$$
$$r : \text{number of rounds}$$
$$N : \text{number of arrays in state (typically } N = 256)$$
$$S_r^K \text{ or } S_r : \text{state of KSA or PRGA after the swap in the } r\text{-th round}$$
$$i_r, j_r : \text{indices of } S_r \text{ for the } r\text{-th round}$$
$$Z_r : \text{one output keystream for the } r\text{-th round}$$
$$t_r : \text{index of } Z_r$$

RC4 consists of two algorithms: Key Scheduling Algorithm (KSA) and Pseudo Random Generation Algorithm (PRGA). KSA generates the state S_N^K from a secret key K of l bytes as described in Algorithm 1. Then, the final state S_N^K in KSA becomes the input of PRGA as S_0. Once the state S_0 is computed, PRGA generates one output keystream Z_r of bytes as described in Algorithm 2. The output keystream Z_r will be XORed with a plaintext to generate a ciphertext.

Algorithm 1. KSA
1: **for** $i = 0$ to $N - 1$ **do**
2:    $S_0^K[i] \leftarrow i$
3: **end for**
4: $j \leftarrow 0$
5: **for** $i = 0$ to $N - 1$ **do**
6:    $j \leftarrow j + S_i^K[i] + K[i \mod l]$
7:    Swap($S_i^K[i], S_i^K[j]$)
8: **end for**

Algorithm 2. PRGA
1: $r \leftarrow 0, i_0 \leftarrow 0, j_0 \leftarrow 0$
2: **loop**
3:    $r \leftarrow r + 1, i_r \leftarrow i_{r-1} + 1$
4:    $j_r \leftarrow j_{r-1} + S_{r-1}[i_r]$
5:    Swap($S_{r-1}[i_r], S_{r-1}[j_r]$)
6:    $t_r \leftarrow S_r[i_r] + S_r[j_r]$
7:    **Output:** $Z_r \leftarrow S_r[t_r]$
8: **end loop**

In this paper, we focus on PRGA and investigate correlations between two consecutive output keystreams and a state location. The probability of one location by random association is $\frac{1}{N}$ and uniform randomness of the RC4 stream cipher is assumed if there are no significant biases.

3   Previous Works

In 1996, Jenkins discovered correlations between one output keystream and a state location [5], which is proved as Glimpse Theorem in [7]. Glimpse Theorem is given as follows.

Theorem 1. [7] *After the r-th round of PRGA for $r \geq 1$, we have*

$$\Pr(S_r[j_r] = i_r - Z_r) = \Pr(S_r[i_r] = j_r - Z_r) \approx \tfrac{2}{N}.$$

In 2013, Maitra and Sen Gupta discovered other correlations between two consecutive output keystreams and the $r + 1$-th location of the state array in the r-th round, which is called long-term Glimpse [7]. Long-term Glimpse is given as follows. Note that Theorem 3 is a special case of Theorem 2.

Theorem 2. [7] *After the r-th round of PRGA for $r \geq 1$, we have*

$$\Pr(S_r[r + 1] = N - 1 | Z_{r+1} = Z_r) \approx \tfrac{2}{N}.$$

Theorem 3. [7] *After the r-th round of PRGA for $r \geq 1$, we have*

$$\Pr(S_r[r + 1] = N - 1 | Z_{r+1} = Z_r \wedge Z_{r+1} = r + 2) \approx \tfrac{3}{N}.$$

4   New Results on Long-Term Glimpse

4.1   Observation

Let us investigate the previous results (Theorems 2 and 3) in detail. Here, we call correlation with a probability significantly higher or lower than $\frac{1}{N}$ (the probability of random association) to *positive bias* or *negative bias*, respectively. Theorems 2 and 3 give cases with positive biases. Then, Theorem 2 implicitly means that there exists a value of $S_r[r + 1]$ with negative bias since $S_r[r + 1]$

varies in $[0, N-1]$ even when $Z_{r+1} = Z_r$ has happened. We often assume uniform randomness of other certain events to prove bias of a certain event. Therefore, it is important to prove the existence of a value in $S_r[r+1]$ with negative bias explicitly. We also call such a case with negative bias a *dual case* of a positive bias.

One of our motivation is to find a dual case of Theorem 2, which will be shown as Theorem 4. Then, we will also prove a special case of Theorem 4 in the same way as Theorem 3 to Theorem 2, which will be shown as Theorem 5. Furthermore, during our careful observation of the dual case, we also find a new positive bias on $S_r[r+1]$, which will be shown in Theorem 6. Our new results can integrate long-term Glimpse when $Z_{r+1} = Z_r$. The previous results are limited to the case of $S_r[r+1] = N-1$ when $Z_{r+1} = Z_r$. Our results are not limited to $S_r[r+1] = N-1$ but varies $S_r[r+1] \in [0, N-2]$. Finally, both results can be integrated in Theorem 7.

4.2   New Negative Biases

First, Theorem 4 shows a dual case of Theorem 2 as follows.

Theorem 4. *After the r-th round of PRGA for $r \geq 1$, we have*

$$\Pr(S_r[r+1] = 0 | Z_{r+1} = Z_r) \approx \frac{2}{N^2}\left(1 - \frac{1}{N}\right).$$

Proof. We define main events as follows:

$$A := (S_r[r+1] = 0), B := (Z_{r+1} = Z_r).$$

We first compute $\Pr(B|A)$, and apply Bayes' theorem to prove the claim. Assuming that event A happened, we get

$$j_{r+1} = j_r + S_r[i_{r+1}] = j_r + S_r[r+1] = j_r.$$

Then, $\Pr(B|A)$ is computed in three paths: $j_r = r$ (Path 1), $j_r = r+1$ (Path 2) and $j_r \neq r, r+1$ (Path 3). These paths include all events in order to compute $\Pr(B|A)$. Let $X = S_r[r]$ and $Y = S_r[j_r]$.

Path 1. Figure 1 shows a state transition diagram in Path 1. First, we prove $t_r \neq t_{r+1}$. After the r-th round, $t_r = 2X$ holds since $i_r = j_r = r$. In the next round, $t_{r+1} = X$ holds since $j_{r+1} = j_r = r$ and $i_{r+1} = r+1$. Thus, we get $t_r \neq t_{r+1}$ with probability 1 since $X \neq 0$. Then, if event B occurs, t_{r+1} must be swapped from t_r. This is why $\Pr(\text{Path 1}) = \Pr(B|A \wedge j_r = r)$ is computed in two subpaths: $i_r = 1 \wedge t_{r+1} = 1$ (Path 1-1) and $i_r = 254 \wedge t_{r+1} = 255$ (Path 1-2).

Path 1-1. Figure 2 shows a state transition diagram in Path 1-1. Then, we get event B since $Z_{r+1} = S_{r+1}[1] = 0$ and $Z_r = S_r[2] = 0$. Thus, we can compute the probability of Path 1-1 as follows.

$$\Pr(\text{Path 1-1}) = \Pr(\text{Path 1} \wedge i_r = 1 \wedge t_{r+1} = 1) = 1.$$

Path 1-2. Figure 3 shows a state transition diagram in Path 1-2. Then, we get event B since $Z_{r+1} = S_{r+1}[255] = 255$ and $Z_r = S_r[254] = 255$. Thus, we can compute the probability of Path 1-2 as follows.

$$\Pr(\text{Path 1-2}) = \Pr(\text{Path 1} \wedge i_r = 254 \wedge t_{r+1} = 255) = 1.$$

Therefore, the probability of Path 1 is computed as follows.

$$\Pr(\text{Path 1}) = \Pr(\text{Path 1-1}) \cdot \Pr(i_r = 1 \wedge t_{r+1} = 1)$$
$$+ \Pr(\text{Path 1-2}) \cdot \Pr(i_r = 254 \wedge t_{r+1} = 255)$$
$$\approx 1 \cdot \left(\frac{1}{N} \cdot \frac{1}{N} \right) + 1 \cdot \left(\frac{1}{N} \cdot \frac{1}{N} \right) = \frac{2}{N^2}.$$

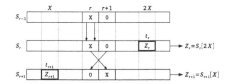

Fig. 1. Path 1

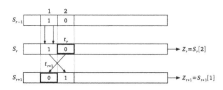

Fig. 2. Path 1-1

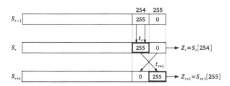

Fig. 3. Path 1-2

Path 2. Figure 4 shows a state transition diagram in Path 2. We get $t_r \neq t_{r+1}$ in the same way as Path 1. Then, event B never occurs because t_{r+1} can not be swapped from t_r. Therefore, the probability of Path 2 is computed as follows.

$$\Pr(\text{Path 2}) = \Pr(B|A \wedge j_r = r + 1) = 0.$$

Path 3. Figure 5 shows a state transition diagram in Path 3. We get $t_r \neq t_{r+1}$ in the same way as Path 1. Then, if event B occurs, t_{r+1} must be swapped from t_r. This is why $\Pr(\text{Path 3}) = \Pr(B|A \wedge j_r \neq r, r + 1)$ is computed in two subpaths: $t_r = j_r \wedge t_{r+1} = r + 1$ (Path 3-1) and $t_r = r + 1 \wedge t_{r+1} = j_{r+1}$ (Path 3-2).

Path 3-1. Figure 6 shows a state transition diagram in Path 3-1. Then, we get event B since $Z_{r+1} = S_{r+1}[r+1] = r+1$ and $Z_r = S_r[j_r] = r+1$. Thus, we can compute the probability of Path 3-1 as follows.

$$\Pr(\text{Path 3-1}) = \Pr(\text{Path 3} \wedge t_r = j_r \wedge t_{r+1} = r+1) = 1.$$

Path 3-2. Figure 7 shows a state transition diagram in Path 3-2. Then, we get event B since $Z_{r+1} = S_{r+1}[j_{r+1}] = 0$ and $Z_r = S_r[r+1] = 0$. Thus, we can compute the probability of Path 3-2 as follows.

$$\Pr(\text{Path 3-2}) = \Pr(\text{Path 3} \wedge t_r = r+1 \wedge t_{r+1} = j_r) = 1.$$

Therefore, the probability of Path 3 is computed as follows.

$$
\begin{aligned}
\Pr(\text{Path 3}) &= \Pr(\text{Path 3-1}) \cdot \Pr(t_r = j_r \wedge t_{r+1} = r+1) \\
&\quad + \Pr(\text{Path 3-2}) \cdot \Pr(t_r = r+1 \wedge t_{r+1} = j_{r+1}) \\
&\approx 1 \cdot \left(\frac{1}{N} \cdot \frac{1}{N}\right) + 1 \cdot \left(\frac{1}{N} \cdot \frac{1}{N}\right) = \frac{2}{N^2}.
\end{aligned}
$$

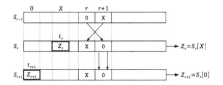

Fig. 4. Path 2

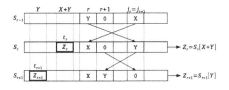

Fig. 5. Path 3

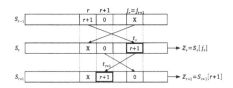

Fig. 6. Path 3-1

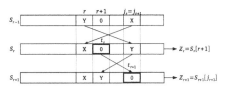

Fig. 7. Path 3-2

From these results, $\Pr(B|A)$ is computed as follows.

$$
\begin{aligned}
\Pr(B|A) &= \Pr(\text{Path 1}) \cdot \Pr(j_r = r) + \Pr(\text{Path 2}) \cdot \Pr(j_r = r+1) \\
&\quad + \Pr(\text{Path 3}) \cdot \Pr(j_r \neq r, r+1) \\
&\approx \frac{2}{N^2} \cdot \frac{1}{N} + 0 \cdot \frac{1}{N} + \frac{2}{N^2} \cdot \left(1 - \frac{2}{N}\right) = \frac{2}{N^2}\left(1 - \frac{1}{N}\right).
\end{aligned}
$$

$\Pr(A|B)$ is computed as follows by applying Bayes' theorem since events A and B occur with the probability of random association $\frac{1}{N}$.

$$\Pr(A|B) = \frac{\Pr(B|A) \cdot \Pr(A)}{\Pr(B)} \approx \frac{\frac{2}{N^2}\left(1 - \frac{1}{N}\right) \cdot \frac{1}{N}}{\frac{1}{N}} = \frac{2}{N^2}\left(1 - \frac{1}{N}\right). \qquad \square$$

Next, Theorem 5 shows a special case of Theorem 4 as follows.

Theorem 5. *After the r-th round of PRGA for $r \geq 1$ and $\forall x \in [0, N-1]$, we have*

$$\Pr(S_r[r+1] = 0 | Z_{r+1} = Z_r \wedge Z_{r+1} = r + x) \approx \begin{cases} \dfrac{1}{N}\left(1 - \dfrac{2}{N^2}\right) & \text{if } x = 1 \\[2mm] \dfrac{2}{N^2}\left(1 - \dfrac{1}{N}\right) & \text{if } x = 255 \\[2mm] \dfrac{1}{N^2}\left(1 - \dfrac{2}{N}\right) & \text{if } x = N - r \\[2mm] & (x \neq 1, 255). \end{cases}$$

Proof. We define main events as follows.

$$A := (S_r[r+1] = 0), B := (Z_{r+1} = Z_r), C := (Z_{r+1} = r + x).$$

$\Pr(A|B \wedge C)$ is difficult to compute because events B and C are not independent. To avoid this problem, we define a new event $B' := (Z_r = r+x)$. Then, $\Pr(A|B \wedge C) = \Pr(A|B' \wedge C)$ since $B \wedge C$ and $B' \wedge C$ are the same event. $\Pr(A|B' \wedge C)$ is decomposed as follows by using Bayes' theorem:

$$\Pr(A|B' \wedge C) = \frac{\Pr(A \wedge B' \wedge C)}{\Pr(B' \wedge C)} = \frac{\Pr(C|B' \wedge A) \cdot \Pr(B'|A) \cdot \Pr(A)}{\Pr(B' \wedge C)}.$$

We first compute $\Pr(C|B' \wedge A)$ in three paths: $j_r = r$ (Path 1), $j_r = r + 1$ (Path 2) and $j_r \neq r, r + 1$ (Path 3). These paths are the same as in Theorem 4, and thus the proof itself is similar to Theorem 4. Let $X = S_r[r]$ and $Y = S_r[j_r]$.

Path 1. Figure 1 shows a state transition diagram in Path 1. Note that $t_r \neq t_{r+1}$ from the discussion of Path 1 in Theorem 4, and that event C is limited to two subpaths: $i_r = 1$ for $r + x = 0$ (Path 1-1) and $t_{r+1} = 255$ for $r + x = 255$ (Path 1-2).

Path 1-1. Figure 2 shows a state transition diagram in Path 1-1. Then, event C holds under event $B' \wedge A$ since $Z_{r+1} = S_{r+1}[1] = 0$ and $Z_r = S_r[2] = 0$. Note that $i_r = 1$ and $r + x = 0$ hold if and only if $x = 255$. Thus, we can compute the probability of Path 1-1 as follows.

$$\Pr(\text{Path 1-1}) = \Pr(\text{Path 1} \wedge i_r = 1) = 1 \text{ if } x = 255.$$

Path 1-2. Figure 3 shows a state transition diagram in Path 1-2. Then, event C holds under event $B' \wedge A$ since $Z_{r+1} = S_{r+1}[255] = 255$ and $Z_r = S_r[254] = 255$. Note that $i_r = 254$ (see Fig. 3) and $r+x = 255$ hold if and only if $x = 1$. Thus, we can compute the probability of Path 1-2 as follows.

$$\Pr(\text{Path 1-2}) = \Pr(\text{Path } 1 \wedge t_{r+1} = 255) = 1 \quad \text{if } x = 1.$$

Therefore, the probability of Path 1 is computed as follows.

$$\Pr(\text{Path 1}) = \begin{cases} \Pr(\text{Path 1-1}) \cdot \Pr(i_r = 1) \approx \dfrac{1}{N} & \text{if } x = 255 \\ \Pr(\text{Path 1-2}) \cdot \Pr(t_{r+1} = 255) \approx \dfrac{1}{N} & \text{if } x = 1 \\ 0 & \text{otherwise.} \end{cases}$$

Path 2. Event C never occurs in Path 2 from the discussion of Path 2 in Theorem 4. Therefore, the probability of Path 2 is computed as follows.

$$\Pr(\text{Path 2}) = \Pr(C|B' \wedge A \wedge j_r = r + 1) = 0.$$

Path 3. Figure 5 shows a state transition diagram in Path 3. Note that $t_r \neq t_{r+1}$ from the discussion of Path 3 in Theorem 4, and that event C is limited to two subpaths: $t_{r+1} = r+1$ for $x = 1$ (Path 3-1) and $t_r = r+1 \wedge t_{r+1} = j_{r+1}$ for $r + x = 0$ (Path 3-2).

Path 3-1. Figure 6 shows a state transition diagram in Path 3-1. Then, event C holds under event $B' \wedge A$ since $Z_{r+1} = S_{r+1}[r + 1] = r + 1$ and $Z_r = S_r[j_r] = r + 1$. Thus, we can compute the probability of Path 3-1 as follows.

$$\Pr(\text{Path3} - 1) = \Pr(\text{Path3} \wedge t_{r+1} = r + 1) = 1 \quad \text{if } x = 1.$$

Path 3-2. Figure 7 shows a state transition diagram in Path 3-2. Then, event C holds under event $B' \wedge A$ since $Z_{r+1} = S_{r+1}[j_{r+1}] = 0$ and $Z_r = S_r[r+1] = 0$. Note that $r+x = 0 \ (\forall r \in [0, N-1])$ means $x = N - r$. Thus, we can compute the probability of Path 3-2 as follows.

$$\Pr(\text{Path 3-2}) = \Pr(\text{Path } 3 \wedge t_r = r + 1 \wedge t_{r+1} = j_{r+1}) = 1.$$

Therefore, the probability of Path 3 is computed as follows.

$$\begin{aligned} \Pr(\text{Path 3}) &= \Pr(\text{Path 3-1}) \cdot \Pr(t_{r+1} = r + 1) \\ &\quad + \Pr(\text{Path 3-2}) \cdot \Pr(t_r = r + 1 \wedge t_{r+1} = j_{r+1}) \\ &\approx \begin{cases} 1 \cdot \dfrac{1}{N} + 1 \cdot \left(\dfrac{1}{N} \cdot \dfrac{1}{N} \right) = \dfrac{1}{N}\left(1 + \dfrac{1}{N}\right) & \text{if } x = 1 \\ 0 \cdot \dfrac{1}{N} + 1 \cdot \left(\dfrac{1}{N} \cdot \dfrac{1}{N} \right) = \dfrac{1}{N^2} & \text{if } x = N - r(x \neq 1). \end{cases} \end{aligned}$$

From these results, $\Pr(C|B' \wedge A)$ is computed as follows.

$$\Pr(C|B' \wedge A) = \Pr(\text{Path 1}) \cdot \Pr(j_r = r) + \Pr(\text{Path 2}) \cdot \Pr(j_r = r+1)$$
$$+ \Pr(\text{Path 3}) \cdot \Pr(j_r \neq r, r+1)$$

$$\approx \begin{cases} \dfrac{1}{N} \cdot \dfrac{1}{N} + \dfrac{1}{N} \cdot \left(1 + \dfrac{1}{N}\right) \cdot \left(1 - \dfrac{2}{N}\right) = \dfrac{1}{N}\left(1 - \dfrac{2}{N^2}\right) & \text{if } x = 1 \\[2ex] \dfrac{1}{N} \cdot \dfrac{1}{N} + \dfrac{1}{N^2} \cdot \left(1 - \dfrac{2}{N}\right) = \dfrac{2}{N^2}\left(1 - \dfrac{1}{N}\right) & \text{if } x = 255 \\[2ex] 0 \cdot \dfrac{1}{N} + \dfrac{1}{N^2} \cdot \left(1 - \dfrac{2}{N}\right) = \dfrac{1}{N^2}\left(1 - \dfrac{2}{N}\right) & \text{if } x = N - r \\[1ex] & (x \neq 1, 255). \end{cases}$$

$\Pr(A|B \wedge C)$ is computed as follows by applying Bayes' theorem since events A, B', C and $B'|A$ occur with the probability of random association $\frac{1}{N}$.

$$\Pr(A|B \wedge C) = \frac{\Pr(C|B' \wedge A) \cdot \Pr(B'|A) \cdot \Pr(A)}{\Pr(B' \wedge C)} \approx \frac{\Pr(C|B' \wedge A) \cdot \frac{1}{N} \cdot \frac{1}{N}}{\frac{1}{N} \cdot \frac{1}{N}}$$

$$= \Pr(C|B' \wedge A) \approx \begin{cases} \dfrac{1}{N}\left(1 - \dfrac{2}{N^2}\right) & \text{if } x = 1 \\[2ex] \dfrac{2}{N^2}\left(1 - \dfrac{1}{N}\right) & \text{if } x = 255 \\[2ex] \dfrac{1}{N^2}\left(1 - \dfrac{2}{N}\right) & \text{if } x = N - r(x \neq 1, 255). \end{cases} \qquad \square$$

4.3   New Positive Biases and Their Integration

Theorem 6 shows a new positive bias on $S_r[r+1]$ as follows.

Theorem 6. *After the r-th round of PRGA for $r \geq 1$ and $\forall x \in [2, N-1]$, we have*

$$\Pr(S_r[r+1] = N - x | Z_{r+1} = Z_r \wedge Z_{r+1} = r+1+x) \approx \frac{2}{N}\left(1 - \frac{1}{N} + \frac{1}{N^2}\right).$$

Proof. We define main events as follows.

$$A := (S_r[r+1] = N - x), B := (Z_{r+1} = Z_r),$$
$$B' := (Z_r = r+1+x), C := (Z_{r+1} = r+1+x).$$

The proof itself is similar to Theorem 5. We first compute $\Pr(C|B' \wedge A)$ in three paths: $j_r = r$ (Path 1), $j_r = r+1$ (Path 2) and $j_r \neq r, r+1$ (Path 3). Let $X = S_r[r]$, $Y = S_r[j_r]$ and $W = S_r[j_{r+1}]$.

Path 1. Both t_r and t_{r+1} are independent since we get $t_r = 2X$ and $t_{r+1} = N - x + W$. Then, event C is limited to three subpaths: $t_{r+1} = r+1$ (Path 1-1), $N - x = r+1+x \wedge t_{r+1} = j_{r+1}$ (Path 1-2) and $t_{r+1} = t_r$ except when

t_r equals either $r+1$ or j_{r+1} (Path 1-3). We can compute the probability of each subpath as follows.

$$\Pr(\text{Path 1-1}) = \Pr(\text{Path } 1 \wedge t_{r+1} = r+1) = 1,$$
$$\Pr(\text{Path 1-2}) = \Pr(\text{Path } 1 \wedge N - x = r+1+x \wedge t_{r+1} = j_{r+1}) = 1,$$
$$\Pr(\text{Path 1-3}) = \Pr(\text{Path } 1 \wedge t_{r+1} = t_r) = 1 - \tfrac{2}{N}.$$

Therefore, the probability of Path 1 is computed as follows.

$$
\begin{aligned}
\Pr(\text{Path 1}) &= \Pr(\text{Path 1-1}) \cdot \Pr(t_{r+1} = r+1) \\
&\quad + \Pr(\text{Path 1-2}) \cdot \Pr(N - x = r+1+x \wedge t_{r+1} = j_{r+1}) \\
&\quad + \Pr(\text{Path 1-3}) \cdot \Pr(t_{r+1} = t_r) \\
&\approx 1 \cdot \frac{1}{N} + 1 \cdot \left(\frac{1}{N} \cdot \frac{1}{N}\right) + \left(1 - \frac{2}{N}\right) \cdot \frac{1}{N} = \frac{1}{N}\left(2 - \frac{1}{N}\right).
\end{aligned}
$$

Path 2. We get $t_r \neq t_{r+1}$ since $t_r = N - x + X$, $t_{r+1} = N - x + W$ and $X \neq W$. Then, event C is limited to two subpaths: $t_{r+1} = r+1$ (Path 2-1) and $N - x = r+1+x \wedge t_{r+1} = j_{r+1}$ (Path 2-2). We can compute the probability of each subpath as follows.

$$\Pr(\text{Path 2-1}) = \Pr(\text{Path } 2 \wedge t_{r+1} = r+1) = 1,$$
$$\Pr(\text{Path 2-2}) = \Pr(\text{Path } 2 \wedge N - x = r+1+x \wedge t_{r+1} = j_{r+1}) = 1.$$

Therefore, the probability of Path 2 is computed as follows.

$$
\begin{aligned}
\Pr(\text{Path 2}) &= \Pr(\text{Path 2-1}) \cdot \Pr(t_{r+1} = r+1) \\
&\quad + \Pr(\text{Path 2-2}) \cdot \Pr(N - x = r+1+x \wedge t_{r+1} = j_{r+1}) \\
&\approx 1 \cdot \frac{1}{N} + 1 \cdot \left(\frac{1}{N} \cdot \frac{1}{N}\right) = \frac{1}{N}\left(1 + \frac{1}{N}\right).
\end{aligned}
$$

Path 3. Both t_r and t_{r+1} are independent since we get $t_r = X + Y$ and $t_{r+1} = N - x + W$. Then, event C is limited to three subpaths: $t_{r+1} = r+1$ (Path 3-1), $N - x = r+1+x \wedge t_{r+1} = j_{r+1}$ (Path 3-2) and $t_{r+1} = t_r$ except when t_r equals either $r+1$ or j_{r+1} (Path 3-3). We can compute the probability of each subpath as follows.

$$\Pr(\text{Path 3-1}) = \Pr(\text{Path } 3 \wedge t_{r+1} = r+1) = 1,$$
$$\Pr(\text{Path 3-2}) = \Pr(\text{Path } 3 \wedge N - x = r+1+x \wedge t_{r+1} = j_{r+1}) = 1,$$
$$\Pr(\text{Path 3-3}) = \Pr(\text{Path } 3 \wedge t_{r+1} = t_r) = 1 - \tfrac{2}{N}.$$

Therefore, the probability of Path 3 is computed as follows.

$$
\begin{aligned}
\Pr(\text{Path 3}) &= \Pr(\text{Path 3-1}) \cdot \Pr(t_{r+1} = r+1) \\
&\quad + \Pr(\text{Path 3-2}) \cdot \Pr(N - x = r+1+x \wedge t_{r+1} = j_{r+1}) \\
&\quad + \Pr(\text{Path 3-3}) \cdot \Pr(t_{r+1} = t_r) \\
&\approx 1 \cdot \frac{1}{N} + 1 \cdot \left(\frac{1}{N} \cdot \frac{1}{N}\right) + \left(1 - \frac{2}{N}\right) \cdot \frac{1}{N} = \frac{1}{N}\left(2 - \frac{1}{N}\right).
\end{aligned}
$$

From these results, $\Pr(C|B' \wedge A)$ is computed as follows.

$$\Pr(C|B' \wedge A) = \Pr(\text{Path 1}) \cdot \Pr(j_r = r) + \Pr(\text{Path 2}) \cdot \Pr(j_r = r + 1)$$
$$+ \Pr(\text{Path 3}) \cdot \Pr(j_r \neq r, r + 1)$$
$$\approx \frac{1}{N}\left(2 - \frac{1}{N}\right) \cdot \frac{1}{N} + \frac{1}{N}\left(1 + \frac{1}{N}\right) \cdot \frac{1}{N} + \frac{1}{N}\left(2 - \frac{1}{N}\right) \cdot \left(1 - \frac{2}{N}\right)$$
$$= \frac{2}{N}\left(1 - \frac{1}{N} + \frac{1}{N^2}\right).$$

As a result, $\Pr(A|B \wedge C)$ is computed as follows.

$$\Pr(A|B \wedge C) \approx \Pr(C|B' \wedge A) \approx \frac{2}{N}\left(1 - \frac{1}{N} + \frac{1}{N^2}\right). \qquad \Box$$

Finally, we can integrate long-term Glimpse on $S_r[r + 1]$ as Theorem 7.

Theorem 7. *After the r-th round of PRGA for $r \geq 1$ and $\forall x \in [0, N - 1]$, we have*

$$\Pr(S_r[r + 1] = N - x | Z_{r+1} = Z_r \wedge \ Z_{r+1} = r + 1 + x)$$
$$\approx \begin{cases} \dfrac{1}{N}\left(1 - \dfrac{2}{N^2}\right) & \text{if } x = 0 \\[2mm] \dfrac{1}{N}\left(3 - \dfrac{6}{N} + \dfrac{2}{N^2}\right) & \text{if } x = 1^{[1]} \\[2mm] \dfrac{2}{N}\left(1 - \dfrac{1}{N} + \dfrac{1}{N^2}\right) & \text{otherwise.} \end{cases}$$

5   Experimental Results

In order to check the accuracy of biases shown in Theorems 4–6, the experiments are executed using 2^{24} randomly chosen keys of 16 bytes and 2^{24} output keystreams for each key, which mean $2^{48}(= N^6)$ trials of RC4. Note that $\mathcal{O}(N^3)$ trials are reported to be sufficient to identify the biases with reliable success probability since each correlation here is of about $\frac{1}{N}$ with respect to a base event of probability $\frac{1}{N}$. Our experimental environment is as follows: Linux machine with 2.6 GHz CPU, 3.8 GiB memory, gcc 4.6.3 compiler and C language. We also evaluate the percentage of relative error ϵ of experimental values compared with theoretical values:

$$\epsilon = \frac{|\text{experimental value} - \text{theoretical value}|}{\text{experimental value}} \times 100(\%).$$

---

[1] The probability of correlation when $x = 1$ can be precisely revised to $\frac{1}{N}(3 - \frac{6}{N} + \frac{2}{N^2})$ from [7] in the same way as our other cases of $x \neq 1$, whose precise proof will be given in the final paper.

Table 1. Comparison between experimental and theoretical values

Results		Experimental value	Theoretical value	ϵ (%)
Theorem 4		0.000030522	0.000030398	0.406
Theorem 5	for $x = 1$	0.003922408	0.003906131	0.415
	for $x = 255$	0.000030683	0.000030398	0.929
	for $x = N - r$ $(x \neq 1, 255)$	0.000015259	0.000015140	0.780
Theorem 6		0.007812333	0.007782102	0.387

Table 1 shows experimental, theoretical values and the percentage of relative errors ϵ, which indicates ϵ is small enough in each case such as $\epsilon \leq 0.929$. Therefore, we have convinced that theoretical values closely reflects the experimental values.

6 Conclusion

In this paper, we have shown dual cases of the previous long-term Glimpse. We have also shown a new long-term Glimpse. We note that the previous long-term Glimpse is limited to $S_r[r + 1] = N - 1$ but that our results varies $S_r[r + 1] \in [0, N - 2]$. As a result, these long-term Glimpse can be integrated to biases of $S_r[r + 1] \in [0, N - 1]$. These new integrated long-term Glimpse could contribute to the improvement of state recovery attack on RC4, which remains an open problem.

References

1. Das, A., Maitra, S., Paul, G., Sarkar, S.: Some combinatorial results towards state recovery attack on RC4. In: Jajodia, S., Mazumdar, C. (eds.) ICISS 2011. LNCS, vol. 7093, pp. 204–214. Springer, Heidelberg (2011)
2. Gupta, S.S., Maitra, S., Paul, G., Sarkar, S.: Proof of empirical RC4 biases and new key correlations. In: Miri, A., Vaudenay, S. (eds.) SAC 2011. LNCS, vol. 7118, pp. 151–168. Springer, Heidelberg (2012)
3. Sen Gupta, S., Maitra, S., Sarkar, S.: (Non-)random sequences from (non-)random permutations - analysis of RC4 stream cipher. J. Cryptol. **27**(1), 67–108 (2014)
4. Isobe, T., Ohigashi, T., Watanabe, Y., Morii, M.: Full plaintext recovery attack on broadcast RC4. In: Moriai, S. (ed.) FSE 2013. LNCS, vol. 8424, pp. 179–202. Springer, Heidelberg (2014)
5. Jenkins, R.J.: ISAAC and RC4 (1996)
6. Knudsen, L.R., Meier, W., Preneel, B., Rijmen, V., Verdoolaege, S.: Analysis methods for (alleged) RC4. In: Ohta, K., Pei, D. (eds.) ASIACRYPT 1998. LNCS, vol. 1514, pp. 327–341. Springer, Heidelberg (1998)
7. Maitra, S., Sen Gupta, S.: New Long-Term *Glimpse* of RC4 Stream Cipher. In: Bagchi, A., Ray, I. (eds.) ICISS 2013. LNCS, vol. 8303, pp. 230–238. Springer, Heidelberg (2013)

8. Maitra, S., Paul, G., Sarkar, S., Lehmann, M., Meier, W.: New results on generalization of roos-type biases and related keystreams of RC4. In: Youssef, A., Nitaj, A., Hassanien, A.E. (eds.) AFRICACRYPT 2013. LNCS, vol. 7918, pp. 222–239. Springer, Heidelberg (2013)
9. Maximov, A., Khovratovich, D.: New state recovery attack on RC4. In: Wagner, D. (ed.) CRYPTO 2008. LNCS, vol. 5157, pp. 297–316. Springer, Heidelberg (2008)
10. Sarkar, S., Sen Gupta, S., Paul, G., Maitra, S.: Proving TLS-attack related open biases of RC4. IACR Cryptology ePrint Archive, 2013:502 (2013)
11. Sepehrdad, P., Vaudenay, S., Vuagnoux, M.: Discovery and exploitation of new biases in RC4. In: Biryukov, A., Gong, G., Stinson, D.R. (eds.) SAC 2010. LNCS, vol. 6544, pp. 74–91. Springer, Heidelberg (2011)

Improved Modular Multiplication
for Optimal Prime Fields

Hwajeong Seo[1], Zhe Liu[2], Yasuyuki Nogami[3], Jongseok Choi[1],
and Howon Kim[1(✉)]

[1] School of Computer Science and Engineering, Pusan National University, San-30,
Jangjeon-Dong, Geumjeong-Gu, Busan 609–735, Republic of Korea
{hwajeong,jschoi85,howonkim}@pusan.ac.kr
[2] Laboratory of Algorithmics, Cryptology and Security (LACS),
University of Luxembourg, 6, Rue R. Coudenhove-Kalergi,
1359 Luxembourg-kirchberg, Luxembourg
zhe.liu@uni.lu
[3] Graduate School of Natural Science and Technology, Okayama University,
3-1-1, Tsushima-naka, Kita, Okayama 700-8530, Japan
yasuyuki.nogami@okayama-u.ac.jp

Abstract. Optimal Prime Fields (OPFs) are considered to be one of
the best choices for lightweight elliptic curve cryptography implementation on resource-constraint embedded processors. In this paper, we
revisit efficient implementation of the modular arithmetic over the special prime fields, and present improved implementation of modular multiplication for OPFs, called Optimal Prime Field Coarsely Integrated
Operand Caching (OPF-CIOC) method. OPF-CIOC method follows the
general idea of (consecutive) operand caching technique, but has been
carefully optimized and redesigned for Montgomery multiplication in
an integrated fashion. We then evaluate the practical performance of
proposed method on representative 8-bit AVR processor. Experimental
results show that the proposed OPF-CIOC method outperforms the previous best known results in ACNS'14 by a factor of 5 %. Furthermore,
our method is implemented in a regular way which helps to reduce the
leakage of side-channel information.

Keywords: Montgomery multiplication · Optimal prime fields · Embedded processors · Public key cryptography · Operand caching · Consecutive operand caching

1 Introduction

Public key cryptography applications including RSA [15], ECC [6] and pairing-
based cryptography [16] are commonly used for secure and robust network

This work was supported by the Industrial Strategic Technology Development Pro-
gram (This work was supported by the ICT R&D program of MSIP/IITP. [10043907,
Development of high performance IoT device and Open Platform with Intelligent
Software]).

K.-H. Rhee and J.H. Yi (Eds.): WISA 2014, LNCS 8909, pp. 150–161, 2015.
DOI: 10.1007/978-3-319-15087-1_12

services. These protocols highly rely on finite field operations. The main difference between real world number and finite field representation is that finite field computations should conduct reduction process once results go beyond the size of target field. Montgomery algorithm [14] is one of the efficient algorithms to perform the modular multiplication and squaring since it replaces expensive division operation with normal multiplication operations. Recently, a variant of Montgomery multiplication on OPFs was introduced in [3]. This method can be seen as a simplified version of Montgomery multiplication on OPFs, which is proposed to enhance the performance of Elliptic Curve Cryptography (ECC) on 8-bit AVR processors. One of the features of OPFs is the low hamming weight, which allows to remove or replace part of multiplication operations with several addition instructions when using Montgomery algorithm to perform modular multiplciation.

In this paper, we present a novel technique for implementing the Montgomery multiplication on OPFs. Instead of adopting the "traditional" multiplication techniques, e.g. operand scanning, product scanning and hybrid scanning multiplication, our work follows the state-of-the-art (consecutive) operand caching and has been finely redesigned for OPF-Montgomery algorithm. For practical performance evaluation, we implemented the proposed methods on 8-bit AVR processors and the performance enhancements are 5 % than previous best known results in ACNS'14 [13]. The remainder of this paper is organized as follows. In Sects. 2 and 3, we recap previous multi-precision multiplication methods and OPF-Montgomery algorithms. In Sect. 4, we present novel OPF-Montgomery multiplication. In Sect. 5, we describe the performance evaluation on 8-bit RISC microprocessors. Finally, Sect. 6 concludes the paper and shows the ideas for future work.

2   Multi-precision Multiplication

Multi-precision multiplication is a crucial operation for modular multiplication. In the past several decades, a large body of research has been attempted to speed up the performance of multiplication on 8-bit processors. The most basic technique is called operand scanning method, which consists of two parts, i.e. the inner and outer loops. In the inner loop, one register holds a digit of an operand and computes the partial product by multiplying all the digits of another operand. While in the outer loop, the index of operand increases by a word-size and then the inner loop is executed. An alternative method is called product scanning method, which computes all partial products in the same column by multiplication and addition [2]. Since each partial product in the column is computed and then accumulated, registers are not needed for intermediate results. The results are stored once, and the stored results are not reloaded since all computations have already been conducted. In CHES'04, the classical hybrid scanning method was proposed which combines both of the advantages of operand scanning and product scanning. Hybrid scanning method employs the product scanning as the outer loop and operand scanning method as the inner loop.

This method reduces the number of load instructions by sharing the operands within one block [5]. In CHES'11, the operand caching (OC) method was introduced [7]. The method follows the product scanning method [2], but it divides the calculation into several row sections. By reordering the sequence of inner and outer row sections, the operands which have been loaded in working registers are reused for the next partial products. A few store instructions are added, but the number of required load instructions is reduced. However, a straightforward implementation of OC method has to reload operands whenever a row is changed, which generates unnecessary overheads. In order to avoid these shortcomings, an advanced version of operand caching named consecutive operand caching (COC) method was introduced at WISA'12 [17]. COC provides a connection point among rows that share the common operands for partial products.

3   Optimal Prime Field Montgomery Algorithm

The Montgomery algorithm was firstly proposed in 1985 [14]. Montgomery algorithm avoids division in modular multiplication and reduction by introducing simple shift operations. Given two integers A and B and the modulus M, in order to compute the product $P = A \cdot B \bmod M$ using Montgomery method, the first step is to convert the operands A and B into Montgomery domain, namely, $A' = A \cdot R \bmod M$ and $B' = B \cdot R \bmod M$. For efficiency, the Montgomery residue R is generally selected as a power of 2 and the constant $M' = -M^{-1} \bmod 2^r$ has to be pre-computed. Montgomery multiplication can be computed in the following three steps: (1) $P = A \cdot B$, (2) $Q = P \cdot M' \bmod 2^r$, (3) $Z = (P + Q \cdot M)/2^r$.

In 2006, a special family of prime fields, named Optimal Prime Fields (OPFs), was proposed by Großschädl in [3]. A typical y-bit OPF prime M can be represented as the form $M = U \cdot 2^k + V$. U and V are relatively small coefficients compared to 2^k, U is normally chosen as 8-, 16-bit which can be stored into one or two registers on 8-bit processor, V has several bits. Character k denotes $y - m \cdot w$ where m is a small integer and $m \cdot w$ is the size of U. The OPFs chosen in [3] set U as 16-bit long integer and V as 1 and is formalized in $M = U \cdot 2^{(y-16)} + 1$. Most of bits of OPF prime are 0 except a few bits in most and least significant words. Some examples of OPF are given in Table 1. Due to low hamming weight

Table 1. OPF prime for 160-, 192-, 224- and 256-bit [3]

160-bit: $52542 \times 2^{144} + 1$
0xCD3E00000000000000000000000000000000000001
192-bit: $55218 \times 2^{176} + 1$
0xD7B200000000000000000000000000000000000000000001
224-bit: $50643 \times 2^{208} + 1$
0xC5D3000000000000000000000000000000000000000000000000000001
256-bit: $37266 \times 2^{240} + 1$
0x9192000000000000000000000000000000000000000000000000000000000001

of optimal prime field, Montgomery multiplication is much simpler than ordinary counterparts. Recently, elliptic curve cryptography implementations over OPFs have been reported, for example, the work in [10] used OPF as the underlying field to evaluate GLV and Montgomery curves on 8-bit AVR processors. Their results show that OPF is efficient yet secure prime field which can be used for lightweight elliptic curve cryptography implementation.

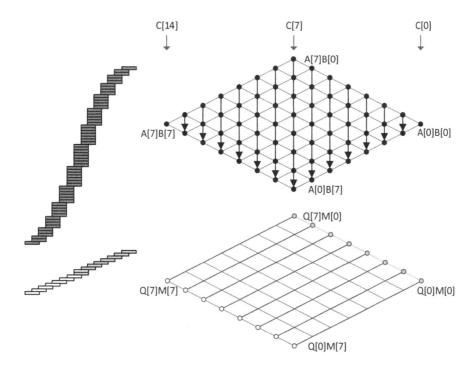

Fig. 1. Separated product scanning method for optimal prime fields

Throughout the paper, we will use the following notations. Let A and B be two operands with a length of y-bit that are represented by multiple-word arrays. Each operand is written as follows: $A = (A[n-1], ..., A[2], A[1], A[0])$ and $B = (B[n-1], ..., B[2], B[1], B[0])$, whereby $n = \lceil y/w \rceil$, and w is the word size. The result of multiplication $C = A \cdot B$ is twice length of A, and represented by $C = (C[2n-1], ..., C[2], C[1], C[0])$. For clarity, we describe the method using a multiplication structure and rhombus forms. The multiplication structure describes order of partial products from top to bottom and each point in rhombus form represents a multiplication $A[i] \cdot B[j]$. The rightmost corner of the rhombus represents the lowest indices $(i, j = 0)$, whereas the leftmost represents corner the highest indices $(i, j = n-1)$. The lowermost side represents result indices $C[k]$, which ranges from the rightmost corner $(k = 0)$ to the leftmost corner $(k = 2n-1)$. To describe Montgomery multiplication, we introduce

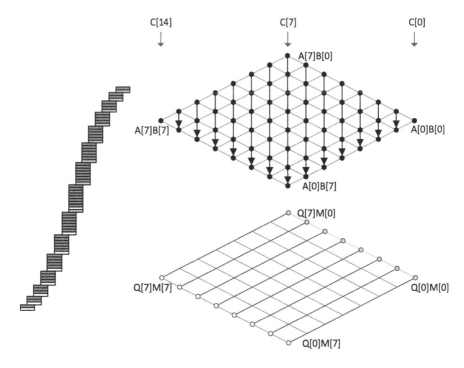

Fig. 2. Finely integrated product scanning method for optimal prime fields

double rhombus forms. Upper rhombus represents multi-precision multiplication and under rhombus represents Montgomery reduction. The under rhombus form has two operands Q and M. Each operand follows same representation we used for multi-precision multiplication. For OPF-Montgomery reduction, we use two colored dots. The yellow dots describe the addition of Q to intermediate results because parameter M has one in the least significant bit which is computable with simple addition operation instead of partial products. In case of white dots, 16-bit partial products on $Q \cdot M$ are updated to intermediate results.

In general, the Montgomery multiplication can be implemented in a separated or integrated fashion according to the computation order. The separated mode performs the reduction process after the entire multiplication as shown in Fig. 1. For example, Separated Product Scanning (SPS) [9,11] firstly conducts multiplication in product-scanning, and then performs the Montgomery reduction. The distinctive strength of SPS is that it requires less registers, since three intermediate registers are sufficient. For this reason, this method is considered to be a good choice when it comes to resource constrained devices where the platform has limited number of registers. The alternative method, Separated Operand Scanning (SOS), calculates the products in an operand scanning way and then reduces the results separately [8]. However, this is not recommended on embedded processors since the OS method needs more memory-access instruction in order to get the intermediate results.

In case of integrated mode, the multiplication and reduction are performed in an interleaved way. This can avoid a number of memory accesses for intermediate results, but it requires many registers to retain a number of parameters including operands, modulus and intermediate results. The Coarsely Integrated Operand Scanning (CIOS) method improves previous SOS method by integrating the multiplication and reduction steps. Instead of computing the multiplication processes separately, multiplication and reduction steps are alternated in every loop. With this technique, we can update intermediate results more efficiently. In CIOS, two inner loops are computed separately and this causes inefficient computation processes. The alternative method, Finely Integrated Operand Scanning (FIOS) integrates the two inner loops of multiplication and reduction and compute the one inner loop. However, operand scanning method is not good choice due to high requirements of registers to retain operands. In order to further improve performance, many works have studied Finely Integrated Product Scanning (FIPS) described in Fig. 2 [1,4,13,19]. The method conducts product scanning multiplication and reduction in integrated form. This method pursues two main benefits. On one hand, the number of required registers is relatively lower than OS because PS does not need many registers for intermediate results. On the other hand, the method does not re-load/store intermediate results so the number of memory access is significantly reduced. However, PS method is not the fastest multiplication method so far. In CHES'11 and WISA'12, OC and COC multiplication methods are released. It shows that there is some space to improve Montgomery multiplication by adopting the OC and COC multiplication methods. In this paper, we challenge to this point and present novel OPF-Montgomery multiplication with OC and COC methods.

4   Optimal Prime Field-Coarsely Integrated Operand Caching (OPF-CIOC)

In this section, we present novel Coarsely Integrated Operand Caching for OPFs (OPF-CIOC). We selected the fastest multiplication methods including operand caching and consecutive operand caching methods for multiplication part. In order to further reduce the number of intermediate results `load` and `store` instructions, we chose the integrated mode. The OC and COC multiplication methods show high performance in ordinary multi-precision multiplication but they consume a number of registers to retain operands. To combine the multiplications on resource constrained devices, we divided multiplication into two parts. First part is only computing multi-precision multiplication by size of $n-m$ where n and m represent size of operand and inverse of modulus (M'). The first part is computed with multiplication methods including OC and COC. The both methods have very similar performance, so we should carefully select the proper method depending on operand parameters. The detailed costs are drawn in Table 2. The result shows that COC method is only slightly faster than OC in case of OPF-256-bit so for the others OC methods are better choice than COC. Secondly, remaining multiplication part is integrated with reduction computations. The size of remaining part is size of inverse of modulus (M'). In the paper,

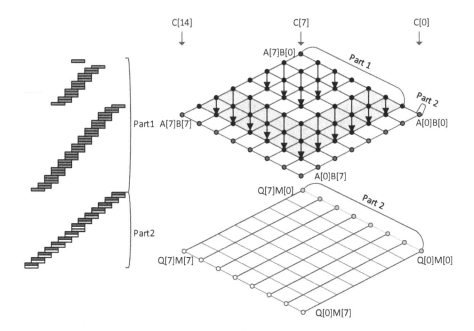

Fig. 3. Coarsely integrated operand caching method for optimal prime fields

we pick OPF-CIOC in Fig. 3 to describe our method, but this is simply applied to OPF-CI(C)OC as described in Fig. 4.

The proposed OPF-CIOC method combines the OC multiplication together with OPF reduction process for Montgomery multiplication as described in Fig. 3. The multiplication is divided into two parts. Part 1 computes ordinary multiplications on $A[i] \cdot B[j]$ where $1 \leq i \leq 7$ and $0 \leq j \leq 6$. The number of row is computed by following the equation $\lceil (n - m)/c \rceil$ where n, m and c are size of operand, inverse of modulus and caching registers. Part 2 is integrating remaining partial products and Montgomery reduction. For the first step, partial products on $A[i] \cdot B[j]$ where $0 \leq i, j \leq 7$ are computed and then operand $Q[k]$ where $0 \leq k \leq 7$ is generated. After then Montgomery reduction described in yellow and white dots are computed with multiplying $M[i]$ by $Q[j]$ where $0 \leq i, j \leq 7$. In particular, the yellow dots are simple addition operations and white dots are 16-bit multiplication operations so it has lower overheads than ordinary Montgomery algorithm. Finally the results are updated to intermediate result and this process is iterated till the end of operands.

In Fig. 5, we give a detailed example of OPF-CIOC in 160-bit operand and 8-bit word sizes but this is readily extended to COC multiplication and other operand and word sizes. The main body is divided into Part 1 and 2. Part 1 conducts multiplication and Part 2 computes remaining multiplications together with reduction process.

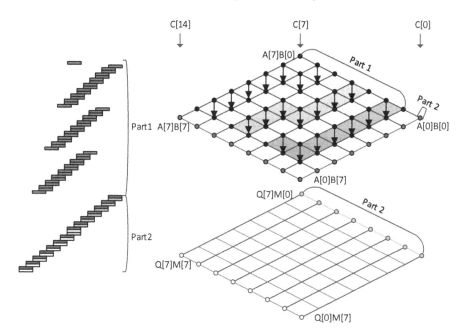

Fig. 4. Coarsely integrated consecutive operand caching method for optimal prime fields

Part 1. The size of operand and inverse of modulus is 160-bit ($n = 20$) and 32-bit ($m = 4$). The length of Part 1 is 128-bit ($160 - 32$, $n - m$) and the number of row is 2 ($\lceil 16/10 \rceil$, $\lceil (n - m)/c \rceil$) where caching registers are 10. These two rows compute partial products on $A[i] \cdot B[j]$ where $4 \leq i \leq 19$ and $0 \leq j \leq 16$ by following operand caching method.

Part 2. The reduction and remaining partial products are integrated in Part 2. The partial products ($A[0 - 3] \cdot B[0 - 3]$ named block 1 is computed and then parameter $Q[0 - 3]$ is obtained by multiplying intermediate results ($C[0 - 3]$) by inverse of modulus (M'). In block 2, the partial products ($Q[0 - 3] \cdot M[0]$) are added to intermediate results ($C[0 - 3]$). Following this order, remaining blocks from 3 to 9 are computed. In block 10, most significant word is multiplied before generate parameter $Q[18 - 19]$. After then in block 11, yellow dots including $M[0] \cdot Q[16 - 19]$ are added to intermediate results. From block 12 to 21, the same process of multiplication and reduction are iterated.

Final Subtraction Without Conditional Statements in OPF. Final subtraction is conducted when final results go beyond size of target prime field. The final subtraction of Montgomery multiplication is computable with conditional branch by checking the carry bit, which is vulnerable to side-channel attacks since the attacker can catch the leakage information based on this conditional

Table 2. Comparison of operand caching and consecutive operand caching in terms of number of memory access

Algorithms	load	store	total
OC 128-bit for OPF 160-bit	50	44	94
OC 160-bit for OPF 192-bit	70	60	130
OC 192-bit for OPF 224-bit	116	84	200
OC 224-bit for OPF 256-bit	152	108	260
COC 128-bit for OPF 160-bit	50	44	94
COC 160-bit for OPF 192-bit	70	60	130
COC 192-bit for OPF 224-bit	118	90	208
COC 224-bit for OPF 256-bit	146	110	256

statement [18]. Our work follows the idea of constant-time Montgomery multiplication which has been presented in [10,11].

5 Result

This section discusses the computation complexity of the proposed OPF-Montgomery multiplications in terms of memory access and real implementations on 8-bit AVR processor.

Memory Access. The number of memory access should be concerned because the operations are extremely expensive on embedded processors. OPF-CIOC consists of two main bodies. The Part 1 conducts multiplication on operand by $n - m$. We adopted (consecutive) operand caching method where the number of load and store instructions is $2(n-m)^2/c$ and $(n-m)^2/c+(n-m)$, respectively. Part 2 conducts integrated multiplication and reduction which needs to load intermediate results by $2 \cdot (n - m)$ and operands A and B by $2n$ for remaining multiplications. For reduction, we load modulus (M) by 16-bit. In case of store instruction, final results are stored by $2n$ times because after reduction process, length of results are reduced from $4n$ to $2n$. Finally total costs of load and store for OPF-CI(C)OC are $2(n - m)^2/c + 4n - 2m$ and $(n - m)^2/c + 3n - m$, respectively.

Evaluation on 8-Bit Platform ATmega128. On an AVR platform, each `mul`, `load` and `store` instruction consumes 2 clock cycles, while other arithmetic and logical operations need 1 clock cycle. Target board runs at a frequency of 7.3728 MHz and program is evaluated using AVR studio 6.0.

In Table 3, performance evaluations of OPF-Montgomery algorithm are described. In ACNS'14, works by [13] adopted FIPS because this method is

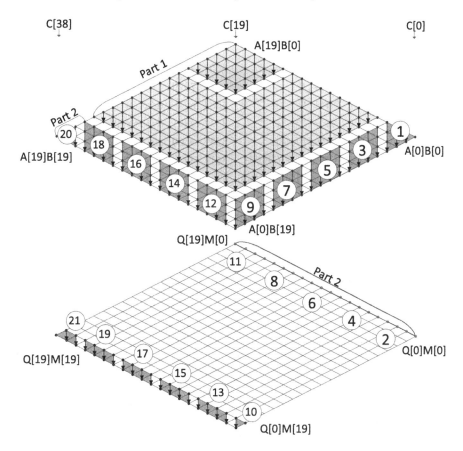

Fig. 5. Coarsely integrated operand caching for optimal prime field in 160-bit

readily integrating the reduction and multiplication and requiring small number of registers. They achieved 3237, 4500, 5971 and 7650 clock cycles for 160-, 192-, 224- and 256-bit OPF-Montgomery multiplications. For comparison, the proposed OPF-CIOC method achieves 3116, 4288, 5650 and 7258 clock cycles. The performance gains are from 3.7 ~ 5 %. The reason to draw high performance enhancement is we adopt the most advanced multiplication for OPF-Montgomery multiplication and finely integrated multiplication and reduction processes. To do this, we divided OC and COC methods into two parts and then integrated second part of multiplication with reduction process. This approach challenges to current OPF-FIPS and breaks the speed records. Furthermore, our method is implemented in a constant-time way and therefore resists against simple power analysis attack.

Table 3. Execution time (in clock cycles) of OPF-montgomery multiplication for different operand lengths on the ATmega128.

Algorithms	160	192	224	256
OPF-FIPS [4]	5239	7070	n/a	n/a
OPF-FIPS [1]	3588	n/a	n/a	n/a
OPF-FIPS [19]	3542	4851	6545	8091
OPF-FIPS [10,13]	3237	4500	5971	7650
This work (OPF-CIOC)	3116	4288	5650	7258
This work (OPF-CICOC)	3116	4288	5668	7250

6   Conclusion and Future Work

In this paper, we presented novel Optimal Prime Field Montgomery multiplication over embedded microprocessors. For high performance enhancements, we integrated previous best known multiplications with OPF reduction process. This is first trial to combine OC and COC with OPF Montgomery reduction. The design is highly exploiting limited number of registers together with high performance gains. In order to measure power of proposed method, we implemented the method on representative 8-bit RISC processor. Finally, we achieved remarkable performance enhancements by 5 % than previous best known results.

A future work based on this work is to evaluate the proposed technique for the modular squaring over OPFs. Furthermore, it would also be interesting to apply the proposed method to enhance the performance of elliptic curve cryptography over OPFs on resource constrained devices, similar as the work [12], which employed COC methods to push the speed limit of NIST curve on 8-bit AVR processors.

References

1. Chu, D., Großschädl, J., Liu, Z., Müller, V., Zhang, Y.: Twisted edwards-form elliptic curve cryptography for 8-bit AVR-based sensor nodes. In: Proceedings of the first ACM workshop on Asia public-key cryptography, pp. 39–44. ACM (2013)
2. Comba, P.G.: Exponentiation cryptosystems on the IBM PC. IBM Syst. J. **29**(4), 526–538 (1990)
3. Großschädl, J., Tinysa: A security architecture for wireless sensor networks. In: Proceedings of the 2006 ACM CoNEXT conference, p. 55. ACM (2006)
4. Großschädl, J., Hudler, M., Koschuch, M., Krüger, M., Szekely, A.: Smart elliptic curve cryptography for smart dust. In: Zhang, X., Qiao, D. (eds.) QShine 2010. LNICST, vol. 74, pp. 623–634. Springer, Heidelberg (2012)
5. Gura, N., Patel, A., Wander, A., Eberle, H., Shantz, S.C.: Comparing elliptic curve cryptography and RSA on 8-bit CPUs. In: Joye, M., Quisquater, J.-J. (eds.) CHES 2004. LNCS, vol. 3156, pp. 119–132. Springer, Heidelberg (2004)
6. Hankerson, D., Vanstone, S., Menezes, A.J.: Guide to Elliptic Curve Cryptography. Springer, New York (2004)

7. Hutter, M., Wenger, E.: Fast multi-precision multiplication for public-key cryptography on embedded microprocessors. In: Preneel, B., Takagi, T. (eds.) CHES 2011. LNCS, vol. 6917, pp. 459–474. Springer, Heidelberg (2011)
8. Koç, Ç.K., Acar, T., Kaliski Jr., B.S.: Analyzing and comparing montgomery multiplication algorithms. Micro IEEE **16**(3), 26–33 (1996)
9. Liu, Z., Großschädl, J., Kizhvatov, I.: Efficient and side-channel resistant RSA implementation for 8-bit AVR microcontrollers. In: Proceedings of the 1st International Workshop on the Security of the Internet of Things (SECIOT 2010) (2010)
10. Liu, Z., Großschädl, J., Wong, D.S.: Low-weight primes for lightweight elliptic curve cryptography on 8-bit AVR processors. In: Lin, D., Xu, S., Yung, M. (eds.) The 9th China international Conference on Information Security and Cryptology–INSCRYPT 2013. LNCS. Springer, New York (2013)
11. Liu, Z., Großschädl, J.: New speed records for montgomery modular multiplication on 8-Bit AVR microcontrollers. In: Pointcheval, D., Vergnaud, D. (eds.) AFRICACRYPT. LNCS, vol. 8469, pp. 215–234. Springer, Heidelberg (2014)
12. Liu, Z., Seo, H., Großschädl, J., Kim, H.: Efficient implementation of NIST-compliant elliptic curve cryptography for sensor nodes. In: Qing, S., Zhou, J., Liu, D. (eds.) ICICS 2013. LNCS, vol. 8233, pp. 302–317. Springer, Heidelberg (2013)
13. Liu, Z., Wenger, E., Großschädl, J.: MoTE-ECC: energy-scalable elliptic curve cryptography for wireless sensor networks. In: Boureanu, I., Owesarski, P., Vaudenay, S. (eds.) ACNS 2014. LNCS, vol. 8479, pp. 361–379. Springer, Heidelberg (2014)
14. Montgomery, P.L.: Modular multiplication without trial division. Math. Comput. **44**(170), 519–521 (1985)
15. Rivest, R.L., Shamir, A., Adleman, L.: A method for obtaining digital signatures and public-key cryptosystems. Commun. ACM **21**(2), 120–126 (1978)
16. Scott, M.: Implementing cryptographic pairings. Lect. Notes Comput. Sci. **4575**, 177 (2007)
17. Seo, H., Kim, H.: Multi-precision multiplication for public-key cryptography on embedded microprocessors. In: Lee, D.H., Yung, M. (eds.) WISA 2012. LNCS, vol. 7690, pp. 55–67. Springer, Heidelberg (2012)
18. Walter, C.D., Thompson, S.: Distinguishing exponent digits by observing modular subtractions. In: Topics in Cryptology CT RSA 2001, pp 192–207. Springer (2001)
19. Zhang, Y., Grossschadl, J.: Efficient prime-field arithmetic for elliptic curve cryptography on wireless sensor nodes. In: IEEE International Conference on Computer Science and Network Technology (ICCSNT), vol. 1, pp. 459–466 (2011)

Network Security

Context Based Smart Access Control
on BYOD Environments

Dongwan Kang$^{(\boxtimes)}$, Joohyung Oh, and Chaetae Im

Korea Internet and Security Agency, Songpa-gu, Seoul, Korea
{lupin428, jhoh, chtim}@kisa.or.kr

Abstract. Recent mobile communication developments and the penetration of smartphones are spurring the increase of the number of smart devices owned by individuals. Mobile devices, because of the multitude of services they provide other than simple communication have become deeply rooted into each individual's life. This development has spread into the work environment spawning a new trend commonly known as BYOD (bring your own device). However, with this trend serious security issues are emerging as a diversity of personal devices with unreliable security are increasingly accessing the typically closed intranets of conventional work environments. Corporations want to improve their productivity by taking advantage of the benefits of BYOD but it is difficult to handle an open BYOD work environment with current security technologies. This study analyzes the characteristics of BYOD environments, current threats to security and required security technologies, and presents a security framework suitable for BYOD environments. The framework presented here can manage a variety of devices despite their disparate operating systems and also control network factors according to the nature of the habits of BYOD users. As it is not based on IP or port-based analysis, which had been primarily used in the past, but on high quality, context information.

Keywords: BYOD · Context · Access control · Security policy · Behavior pattern

1 Introduction

The broad penetration of Internet infrastructure and mobile communication developments has brought huge changes to society. As the number of portable mobile devices like smartphones with their plethora of uses has surged, they have become deeply rooted into the social lives of their users, not merely a means of simple communication. Such a trend has spread into the work environment emerging as BYOD (bring your own device) [1]. BYOD is the concept of workers using their personal devices at work. It refers to the concept and policy of permitting employees to bring their own mobile devices (smartphones, laptops, tablets, etc.) to their workplace and use them to access the internal IT resources of their workplace such as databases and applications. From a corporate perspective, BYOD is expected to provide speed, efficiency and productivity by having work tasks completed more efficiently. In addition, using personal devices eliminates the cost burden of supplying additional devices for work. Therefore, many corporations are mulling whether to adopt BYOD even though many people are already using their personal devices at work without their employer being fully prepared.

© Springer International Publishing Switzerland 2015
K.-H. Rhee and J.H. Yi (Eds.): WISA 2014, LNCS 8909, pp. 165–176, 2015.
DOI: 10.1007/978-3-319-15087-1_13

However, security issues are rising to be a priority concern as diverse personal devices with disparate operating systems and unreliable security are accessing typically closed and conventional intranets of work environments [2]. Current work environments typically operate a static security policy, allocating IPs and verifying MAC (Media Access Control) on PCs. Also, additional agents like PMS (Patch Management System) are installed on PCs used at corporate offices, creating work areas within their control. On the other hand, it is not easy to place smart devices owned by individuals under control as they are highly portable and their managerial cycles are unpredictable. They are frequently replaced and prone to be lost or stolen, making it impossible to predict any change from a managerial perspective. *Symantec Project Honeystick* [4] for example, has proven that accessing the internal infrastructure of a corporation with a lost/stolen personal device happens quite frequently. In fact, 25 % of employees in the US have had their personal devices used at work infected by malicious codes or hacked. Therefore, security is the top priority when considering the introduction of BYOD [3].

It is difficult for security technologies suitable for conventional, closed work environments to proactively address such a change. In particular, the reality is that, in order to protect corporate information, the areas to cover have significantly diversified and increased compared to the past, including changes in ownership of personal devices, establishing a security policy suitable for the deployed network environment (i.e. intranet, mobile), and monitoring personal behavior after access.

This study analyzed BYOD environments depending on user behavior patterns and presents a more comprehensive and flexible security framework. It is not corporations but users, devices and data that are central to any BYOD environment. This study addressed security policies through generalization of the behavior of each object and surrounding factors, which are applied as policy factors. Also, since individual behavior patterns are predictable based on various access environments and personalized device usage patterns, this study presents a security framework that detects loss, theft and malicious access of devices on the back of these patterns, and selectively finds malicious behaviors through multi-level control.

2 BYOD Environments and Security Threats

2.1 BYOD Environments

BYOD (bring your own device) is the concept of using personal devices at work. It refers to the concept and policy of permitting employees to bring their own mobile devices (smartphones, laptops, tablets etc.) to their workplace and use them to access the internal IT resources of their work place such as databases and applications. BYOD implementation entails close scrutiny of the technologies and security measures involved.

The emergence of BYOD has transformed corporate internal infrastructure from being a closed environment to an open one. In other words, employees can now ac-cess work and service servers, which used to exist only in the corporate intranet, via the Internet with their personal smart device. Corporate data, which used to be processed

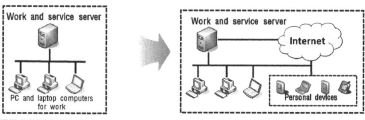

Classification	Enterprise Infrastructures (Closed Environment)	Enterprise Infrastructures (Open Environment)
Company Data	Processing: Devices owned by company, Store: Devices owned by company	Processing: Devices owned by individuals, Store: Devices owned by individuals
Device Ownership/ Management and Leadership	IT division in company	Individual users
Security Policy	User-centric security policy (user authentication)	Device/User-centric Security policy (device and user authentication)

Fig. 1. Change of enterprise workspace

and stored by corporate-owned equipment in a closed environment, can now be processed and stored by individually-owned devices in an open environment. Ownership, administration and control over devices have moved over to individual users from the IT departments of corporations as shown Fig. 1.

According to a *Cisco* survey of over 600 companies in 2012, 95 % had already permitted employees to use their personal smart devices at their workplace and decided that this enhanced employees' productivity. However, the emergence of a new IT environment like BYOD heightens security threats as much as it expands convenience. One of the causes that raise such security threats is the issue of how to control a system comprised of a wide variety of devices operating on a variety of operating systems and running a variety of apps. Currently countless manufacturers are making smart devices with a variety of operating systems. According to a research study conducted by *OpenSignal* in 2012, there were no fewer than 3,997 devices using An-droid, around 70 % of which used operating systems modified by their manufacturers. Problems lie not only in such devices themselves, but also in that important corporate information is leaked due to negligence in controlling the device, and the fact that it is difficult to efficiently control personal devices due to the frequency of their replacement.

There is no doubt that all users including individuals, corporations and institutions need to invest in information security in proportion to the benefit of convenience they bring. According to an IT World survey conducted in 2013 of over 1,192 corporate IT supervisors, it was found that the supervisors emphasized security as the top concern of introducing BYOD.

2.2 Security Threats

In conventional enterprise environments, devices that can access corporate infrastructure are fixed. Through IPs and MACs that are kept static, it is known which devices are currently accessing the corporate network. Also, it is easy to install data control programs in corporate-owned devices if necessary. That is, in conventional enterprise environments, the principal body that accesses the corporate network and the ways to control it are fixed, and it is possible to control them to some extent de-pending on the security policy of the corporation.

However, in a BYOD environment, personal devices of many different kinds access a variety of environments. Mobile devices, typically based either on iOS or An-droid, run on countless, fragmented operating systems and versions customized by their manufacturers. They can access via wired and wireless Internet or mobile networks. Access location can be expanded within local or from abroad, or from inside or outside one's company. Moreover, it is difficult to determine the security level of personal devices being maintained if at all.

Given such circumstances, the largest security threat is information leakage. It is assumable that someone can access corporate infrastructure via a personal device and send confidential corporate information to an external party via the same device. Malicious intent of a user, infection by a malicious code or a stolen/snatched device can cause such a situation.

For the purpose of analysis, security weaknesses that can cause information leaks can be categorized into users, devices and services. Users can be further classified according to the type of identity theft as either an unauthorized user or a user with malicious intent. Devices can be classified into those infected by a malicious code or those stolen/snatched. Identity theft occurring while the user is unawares is one of the most difficult situations for a corporation to control. From the service provider's side that has many access points, web hacking from both inside or outside must be considered.

3 Security Requirements for BYOD Environments and Limitations of Conventional Security Technologies

3.1 Security Requirements for BYOD Environments

BYOD has diversified work patterns that had previously been standardized and rather conventional in nature. However, these changes have brought with them a variety of inherent security weaknesses that can lead to information leakage. In this light, security requirements for enterprise security in BYOD environments were analyzed as follows.

When analyzing security requirements in BYOD environments, a primary consideration can be the security requirements of the principal body. First, users need a stricter and more flexible authentication technology. Unconditional adherence to a stricter authentication is not desirable to corporate productivity. A proper means should be devised factoring in the objects to be protected by each corporation and its level of security. The policy should not be fixed but rather a flexible one that is selectively applicable in many different environments. Second, it should be possible to efficiently control personal devices that tend to be frequently replaced. It is mandatory to track which devices are currently in use, those that have not been in use for a long time, and to register new devices. Third, on the services side, it is required to monitor which user uses which information and with which device. Monitoring users on their information usage should mean being able to not only watch user access but also do high-level monitoring on post-access behaviors, real-time inspection of potential violation of policies, and dynamic control. When it comes to control, in particular, flexible implementation of policies is needed such as applying a higher-grade security level to suspicious areas rather than just blocking access. Moreover, many environment factors and diverse devices in a BYOD environment make it highly likely to incur personalized characteristics such as access time, location and information of choice. Therefore, extracting such behavioral traits and turning them into a pattern can make it easier to analyze abnormal behaviors that are not a violation of policy. That is, it is necessary to ensure:

- automatic controls to respond to user/device changes
- control of personalized behaviors
- operation of security policies suitable to diverse environments
- establishment of high-level, flexible security policies

Factoring in such issues, technological requirements are defined as follows.

Smart Context Mining. In order to identify complex and rapidly changing environment easily, it need meaningful information to administrator. (Access environments of accessing devices/users from network-based and agent-based analysis).

Smart Behavior Insight. In order to analyze a personalized pattern of the various environmental factors, it need a high-level analysis function that able to inference behavior by analyzing the context during pre-admission and post-admission.

Smart Access Control (Context-based Security Policy Administration, Multi-level Dynamic Control). In order to keep as much as possible the availability in a variety of situations, it need flexible and differential management policy according to security level.

3.2   Limitations of Conventional Security Technologies

It is difficult to replace security technologies required by BYOD with conventional ones. Using a personal device at work itself is a new concept, so the closed working environment of the past has inadvertently transformed into an open one. Therefore, conventional static security technologies cannot satisfy security requirements of BYOD environments. The limitations of conventional security technologies are analyzed as follows:

Difficulties in Controlling Devices: Considering the static nature of conventional work environments, identifying a new device attempting to access and register it costs a lot as it incurs a change to the existing fixed structure that is systemized for conventional reception. However, in a BYOD environment, frequent changes in device control occur due to the characteristics of personal devices. This makes it challenging to address such changes.

Inflexible Security Policies (Control by Security Level): Conventional security policies are implemented based on individual, department and assignment criteria. In a BYOD environment, however, users who work on the same assignment within the same department are on different security levels, depending on whether they access from inside the organization or outside, whether they use a smartphone or a laptop, and whether they use an unreliable open wireless LAN or a mobile network. Such factors are crucial in judging the level of security of an accessing device. Still, with conventional security policies, it is challenging to control these diverse factors in a flexible manner.

Monitoring Post-access Behavior: The purpose of monitoring is to identify a behavior that is suspicious or violates policies from the perspective of security. Convention-al monitoring is based on the network, which depends on low-level information like traffic volume of two-way transmission. Given that the transmission format and users' behavioral patterns differ depending on the characteristics of each device, it is necessary to prepare measures for high-level monitoring that take these factors into account.

4 Related Works

As BYOD has become a hot topic of the industry, many security companies have rushed to release solutions. BYOD related solutions typically emphasize control of the devices. Here, control implies many things; it expands controls mostly available in conventional work environments to personal devices (starting with the security of a device to authentication, registration and data input/output). Its ultimate goal is to secure control over personal devices' access to enterprise data, but its approach is different.

First, network-based technology traditionally handles control and authentication of accessing devices at a network level like an NAC (Network Access Control) [5]. Controlling a network can eliminate the dependency of personal devices but has limited control about post admission.

Second, there is device-based control technology such as MDM (Mobile Device Management) [6]. Centralized remote control of a device is enabled by installing a control agent. This can be a fault-proof way for control but installation of a control agent in personal devices may make users uncomfortable. In fact, corporations implement this type of control policy for strict control but challenges remain when distributing such an agent to personal devices. In addition, mobile devices are constantly evolving so it is necessary for corporations to continuously distribute agents to address this, which is not an easy decision to make considering the hefty costs involved.

Lastly, there is hybrid-type control technology that combines both network-based and device-based technologies. This enables corporations to take a more flexible approach depending on their situation. More efficient implementation can be achieved by opting for device-based control on the areas that require strict control, while performing network-based control on areas that need more flexibility. These are the technologies that are in place currently, but it is difficult to address the absence of implementation policies and the needs for higher-level monitoring on behavior.

In point of behavior analysis, a behavior-based NAC model was proposed at [7]. This model is classified into groups according to the roles of each network object as pre-defined. When new object access, each group decides the degree of similarity through group voting, then decision for entry. In addition, after entry, it is examined behaviors of a new object deciding whether or not through group voting by the respective group members. In [8], a method to detect current abnormalities based on network traffic characteristics, such as past packet count, in 3G mobile network environment was proposed. Unlike a wired network, a mobile network displays different traffic characteristics according to such environments as time and day of the week. Therefore, considering time and day of the week elements, this method performs comparative analysis for current behaviors against behavioral patterns of the past under a similar environment.

5   Security Framework in BYOD Environments

A corporation should be able to maintain its required levels of security depending on the roles and objectives of the employees and the value and types of information it owns. Also, it should ensure that its policies to maintain such levels of security are based on a sophisticated system that is manageable in an intuitive and flexible manner while incorporating many complex elements. As such, we propose smart access control for BYOD environments, which defines context based on context.

Unlike conventional methods that rely on such components as TCP/IP or user groups, the proposed method is (1) more intuitive, (2) able to define behaviors and context available to be used as policies, (3) transform user behavior into a pattern, and (4) combine various environment factors to establish effective policies.

Also, it is constructed in a hybrid format, minimizing its dependency on agents and factors in a control framework that links analysis of the network with existing security equipment (Fig. 2).

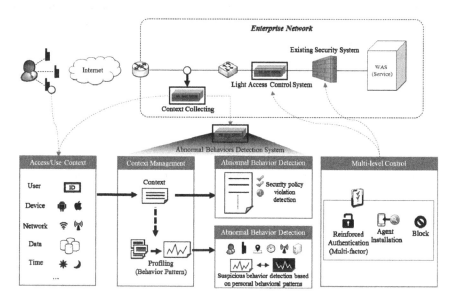

Fig. 2. Proposed BYOD security framework

5.1 Smart Context Mining

Context identifies subjects including users, devices and data, and defines access environment factors like time, location and network. It also includes actions like inquiry, registration, modification and deletion.

Device/User Context: Personal information data such as user identity or group information are objects to be identified. Device information consists of types, operating systems, browsers and installed programs. Usually, this information can be extracted from the User-Agent of HTTP header [9], Geo API [10], and analyzed using device fingerprinting methods like OS fingerprinting [11], browser fingerprinting [12], etc.

Access Environment Context. When, where and via which network a device accesses enterprise network. It does not simply state the time of access but generalizes such information into a meaningful context such as clock-in time and hours worked. Access locations are divided into domestic and overseas. Domestic locations are further divided into inside/outside the company, and GPS information is included when available.

Service Use Context. Objects of access like the URI and database table, and use behavior. Here, access resources are identified by analyzing the URI which includes information of the HTTP header such as the GET and POST. Furthermore, use behavior can be analyzed (inquiry, registration, modification and deletion) by mapping them with database usage on the back end of the WAS.

Context collecting requires various traffic analysis techniques. It basically needs device/OS fingerprinting and an agent that can be installed to collect authentication request/result information from the authentication system and GPS information of devices. However, the agent is not a must in this proposal. Depending on policy, it separately defines context that needs to be collected and requests installation of the agent.

Most contexts are collected in a network but some need analysis on access status. For example, when a user uses two devices at once, context cannot be collected on a device level. Instead, it can be identified whether a user is on multiple devices by controlling the access status activated in the collection system.

5.2 Smart Behavioral Insight

When a user or a device accesses the enterprise network, various environment components are collected through context. Once a certain amount of behaviors are ac-cumulated, a user's set of behaviors can be turned into a pattern. A profile is defined based on the users past behavioral pattern. By managing this profile, one can man-age the history of the user and his/her device.

Context needs to be specified in order to turn behaviors into a pattern. Depending on the characteristics of a corporation or department, behaviors can be generalized based on such components as devices used, access time and access day (i.e. weekday or weekend). Here, it must be configured that a user's behavior maps with one of the context components that are comprised as a discrete set. In this case, user behaviors can be described in a standardized format.

To create a discriminating behavioral pattern, it is important to select components that will comprise a behavior. A behavior has a set of behavioral components. A user has one behavioral component of each behavior. For instance, when Behavior A is "access time", its behavioral components can be set as $\{a_1: AM, a_2: PM\}$ or $\{a_1:0H \sim 6H, a_2:6H \sim 18H, a_3:18H \sim 24H\}$. Then, when a set of behaviors by a user or a device is defined Behavior A = $\{a_1, a_2,..., a_i\}$, Behavior B = $\{b_1, b_2,..., b_j\}$,..., Behavior N = $\{n_1, n_2,..., n_k\}$, the current behavior of a user can be modeled as $\{a_x, b_y, ..., n_z\}$.

User behavior = $\{a_x, b_y, ..., n_z\}$ (A = $\{a_1, a_2, ..., a_i\}$) (Fig. 3).

Personal Behavior Model

Device	Brower	Location	Connection Time	Connection Network	Other Action
Android	IE	Inside	Rush our	Intranet	...
iOS	Chrome	Outside	AM(Work Time)	Wi-Fi	
Windows	Safari	Oversea	PM(Work Time)	Mobile	
etc...	etc...	etc...	etc...	etc...	

Fig. 3. User behavior model

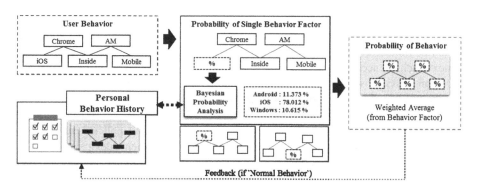

Fig. 4. Possibility analysis of behavior with other factor by bayesian inference

Accumulating information on behaviors can analyze a user's access pattern in each context. Using *Bayesian Inference* [13], its likelihood can be estimated by analyzing how often each context component occurs and which behavioral component is highly likely to occur along with a specific behavioral component Fig. 4. Bayesian Probability theory generally used in SPAM classification based on frequency of a word in relation to word composition of a document [14]. In this study is not to decide a specific behavior pattern as abnormal, but to decide patterns different from the existing to be abnormal. Once the probability of each behavioral component is analyzed, overall probability can be derived by placing weightings on each behavioral component (which factors in work characteristics) and using the weighted average based on this. Weightings can be placed either across the board or per work unit. Discriminating behavioral components can get a higher weighting based on the analysis of the user's past behavioral data. As each individual differs in the way he/she uses a device at work and how much of his/her behavior has been turned into a pattern, weightings can be based on entropy analysis of an individual's behavioral components.

5.3   Context-Based Security Policy Administration

In order to maintain proper security levels per context, it should be possible to recognize a context and apply a dynamic policy accordingly. For instance, an access from a foreign country with a vulnerable Internet environment must go through a certain security app, while an access from a domestic location is only allowed to make inquiry into specific services. Environment components including user identity and device types should be factored in when determining enforcement of security policies.

As such, in a BYOD environment, each given situation should be identified with con-text and policies enforced based on it. A security policy must include at least one context and allow its administrator to configure the range and level of control with flexibility. An administrator-friendly GUI that can visually show the relations of sequence and inclusion is a must as policies need to utilize many components.

Determining which policy to apply can be based on users' access and use cycles. That is, there is a policy for when a device approaches an enterprise network, another one for real-time monitoring of violations after a device is connected, and yet another one for constant monitoring across the board. Also, once connected, the device should be monitored to detect any violation of the policy (that only includes constant context such as accessing user and device), and the operating system of the device within an activated session. A policy that includes changeable context such as location and type of services accessed needs to be continuously monitored for potential violation until the device is disconnected.

As the number of established policies increases, processing policies may hinder performance. This is because there is a policy to be enforced when a device approaches an enterprise network and another one for real-time monitoring after a device is connected. In such a situation, monitoring performance can be improved by structuring policies into a decision tree as policies are comprised of a limited number of context components.

5.4   Multi-level Dynamic Control

When a policy is violated or a suspicious access/use behavior occurs, no benefit of BYOD can be earned from simply cutting them off. Uniform ways of control are bound to lower usability no matter how diverse context-based policies are operated. As such, BYOD maintains continuity of work while keeping more robust authentication methods or stricter control over devices for more precise judgment when detecting a violation of policy or suspicious abnormal behavior. Extreme control such as immediate cut-off should be enforced for mission-critical areas of a corporation. However, a multi-level control policy is required to verify suspicious behaviors or violations of policy. Multi-factor authentication using OTP or installation of an agent to gain control over a device is an example of multi-level control policy. When an access deviates significantly from a user's usual access pattern, a strengthened multi-factor authentication verifies the user one more time before giving permission. A user who is on a business trip to a country with vulnerable security should install an agent in his access device to temporarily raise its level of security as required. In addition, if an unusual volume of information is requested or a scarcely used service is accessed, enforcing extra security controls can keep the level of security of a corporation in a dynamic and flexible manner.

Such control requires real-time collection of context and immediate control measures to detect any violation of policy or suspicious behavior. To ensure actual control, it must be coupled with authentication portals like the captive portal tech-nique or security equipment like NAC and the firewall (web firewall) already in place by corporations. Most couplings can be done through a standardized method like SNMP but also made available using a separate API. Another option is to couple with equipment like an MDM that controls data inside a device.

6 Conclusion

The practice of BYOD has diversified the previously standardized conventional work environment. Such diversification has made it difficult to control security with traditional security equipment. Security threats like information leaks, challenges in managing personal devices, and establishing effective security policies are major challenges hindering the spread of BYOD environments.

Given that users are already using their personal devices at work, however, corporations should utilize them to raise productivity rather than restrict them all. In order to achieve this, developing security technologies is required to analyze and address security threats in BYOD environments. This study defined smart access control as a security technology required for BYOD environments and proposed a security framework that satisfies such a requirement. The proposed security framework for BYOD environments can transform low-level information into an intuitively meaningful context. It also allows corporations to establish context-based, flexible security policies using accessing objects, access environments and use behaviors, and control policies for each level depending on context. In addition, by modeling user's behavioral patterns as a context, it creates profiles for personalized patterns, based on whether it can detect abnormal behaviors that were not previously recognizable, thereby enforcing stricter security policies to enlarge the possibility of behavior-based detection.

Acknowledgments. This work was supported by the ICT R&D program of MSIP/IITP. [10045109, The Development of Context-Awareness based Dynamic Access Control Technology for BYOD, Smartwork Environment].

References

1. IDG Deep Dive: Guide to BYOD Strategy. IDG Korea (2012)
2. Johnson, K.: Mobility/BYOD Security Survey. SANS Institute (2012)
3. Miller, K.W., Voas, J., Hurlburt, G.F.: BYOD: security and privacy considerations. IT Prof. **14**(5), 53–55 (2012)
4. Symantec, Smartphone Honey Stick Project. http://www.symantec.com
5. Inverse, PacketFence. http://www.packetfence.org
6. Henderson, T.: How mobile device management works. IT WORLD (2011)
7. Frias-Martinez, V., Stolfo, S.J., Keromytis, A.D.: Behavior-based network access control: a proof-of-concept. In: Wu, T-C., Lei, C-L., Rijmen, V., Lee, D-T. (eds.) ISC 2008. LNCS, vol. 5222, pp. 175–190. Springer, Heidelberg (2008)
8. D'Alconzo, A.: A distribution-based approach to anomaly detection and application to 3G mobile traffic. In: GLOBECOM, pp. 1–8 (2009)
9. Fielding, R., Gettys, J., Mogul, J., Frystyk, H., Berners-Lee, T.: Hypertext Transfer Protocol-HTTP/1.1, RFC 2068 (1997)
10. W3C: Geolocation API. http://en.wikipedia.org/wiki/W3C_Geolocation_API
11. Nmap: Remote OS Detection. http://nmap.org
12. Kohno, T., Broido, A., Claffy, K.: Remote physical device fingerprinting. IEEE Trans. Dependable Secure Comput. **2**(2), 93–108 (2005)
13. Jose, M.B., Smith, A.F.M.: Bayesian Theory. Wiley, New York (1994)
14. Graham, P.: A Plan for Spam. http://www.paulgraham.com/spam.html

Scalable and Autonomous Mobile Device-Centric Cloud for Secured D2D Sharing

Chao-Lieh Chen[1(⊠)], Shen-Chien Chen[2], Chun-Ruei Chang[1], and Chia-Fei Lin[1]

[1] Department of Electronic Engineering,
National Kaohsiung First University of Science and Technology,
Kaohsiung, Taiwan, R.O.C
{frederic,u0052801,s0140750}@nkfust.edu.tw
[2] Department of Computer Science and Information Engineering,
National Cheng-Kung University, Tainan, Taiwan, R.O.C
xol700@ismp.csie.ncku.edu.tw

Abstract. This study proposes a highly scalable, autonomous, and easy to implement mobile device-centric cloud (MDCC) model for secure device-to-device (D2D) sharing and user-centric services. Users of a certain sociological relation are connected via mobile devices and based on short secret sharing the mobile devices initiate an autonomous and tiny mobile data center with an elected broker. The broker administrates physical network attachments, resource associations, and multimedia service brokering such that quantitative security service level agreements (SLA) in addition to streaming quality SLAs are configured. Content owners or producers in the MDCC immediately share digital contents without uploading to a specific cloud server. Two examples are implemented. The first is video broadcasting and the second is service coverage extension of a DLNA LAN by associating the DLNA gateway with MDCC to securely publish contents outward over the Internet and to get contents from outside the LAN. Both examples show that secure D2D sharing are achieved with high scalability and autonomy while anxiety of security issues of traditional big data centers is relieved.

Keywords: Mobile cloud computing · Device-Centric cloud · User-Centric service · Device-to-Device sharing · Information security

1 Introduction

Traditional content sharing is through big data centers – upload then share. However, security issues arise because a user always has no idea what would happen to the uploaded content and the big data centers give no warranty. The security issues include privileged user access, regulatory compliance, data location, data segregation, recovery, and investigative support, as mentioned in [1–3]. The primary cause of these anxieties is because the contents to be shared are totally out of management from the producer since these contents were uploaded. However, this is the basic nature of

© Springer International Publishing Switzerland 2015
K.-H. Rhee and J.H. Yi (Eds.): WISA 2014, LNCS 8909, pp. 177–189, 2015.
DOI: 10.1007/978-3-319-15087-1_14

traditional cloud computing – resources are virtualized and allocation of resources is always transparent. Proposed in [4] is a security sharing framework with parameter (n, k) such that quantitative service level agreement (SLA) for security in cloud storage service can be customized. However, neither mobility nor social network-based peer sharing among mobile devices were supported in [4]. The mobile-centric computing model, People as a Service (PeaaS), proposed in [5] is able to generate and keep sociological profiles of users such that these profiles can be securely provided to third parties. Users are aware of access control of these profiles for contributing to collective sociological information. However, we still need a cloud computing architecture based on mobile devices to achieve social network defined quantitative SLA.

In this paper we propose and implement a mobile device-centric cloud (MDCC) computing architecture which provides a tradeoff between security and service offloading. In this model, devices are contents producers, service providers, and consumers at the same time. When sharing with friends, such as streaming a video to an individual or a group of users, a mobile device acts as contents producer and service provider. Thus, the user providing service can configure the access right, compliance setting, data distribution, and logging of the contents to be shared. To maintain a certain level of resource transparency, autonomous and scalability are the primary concerns. After the configuration, the system management and control are then transparent. When acting a consumer such as receiving video streams, a user remains to be not necessarily aware of resources status. For example, CPU and memory usage, network topology, and bandwidth allocation are remained transparent to the consumers.

Different from traditional peer to peer (P2P) sharing, the proposed MDCC model provides not only sharing of files but also sharing of IT resources. Furthermore, the grouping of the cloud devices is based on a specific social relation, which can be instantly created and conducted. For example, a group of friends in a coffee shop nearby a famous scenic spot are to share their video and photos taken a few minutes ago and to share in multimedia contents of people who are still strolling outside. The D2D sharing does not need a specific server. The attending devices group together becoming a temporary tiny cloud to provide and to acquire services. It is not necessary to connect to the Internet if the requested services are available in the tiny MDCC. A broker among the attending devices is elected to monitor resources status and to connect to the Internet if necessary. The autonomously and dynamically grouped MDCC is also different from those cloudlets that use a proximate small data centers for users to subscribe in [6–8].

Device-to-device (D2D) sharing is still a new research field and hence the security issues are still not much addressed yet. Security of mobile device-centric cloud computing is still an open research challenge [9]. In this paper, the proposed model compromises resource virtualization and security. People with this model see what's going on while do not have to know how and where the service be retrieved. Thus, the security anxieties of traditional cloud computing are relieved by the following advantages:

- Social network-privileged user access: the authorization and authentication are configured by user who produced the contents since the MDCC is created based on social network profiles. Furthermore, adopting (n, k) security sharing, security is also parameterized into levels.

- Reliability against mobility: the mobility in traditional mobile cloud computing usually refers to that clients are mobile. In MDCC, a device has multiple roles. Therefore, with (n,k) secret sharing, member device detachment does not cause service failure if number of available shares is greater than the threshold k.
- Regulatory compliance: the proposed architecture is dedicated to portable devices which use the same implemented APP. The APP invokes the broker election procedure and then broker regulate the attending devices.
- Data location: The users publishing contents for sharing are aware of physical location of the cloud, e.g. the coffee shop nearby certain scenic spots.
- Recovery: a user is responsible for maintaining their contents while recovery is not an issue for D2D sharing.
- Investigative support: all requests and task assignments are logged. These logs can be used for later analysis for detection of free-riding or attacking of malware. Accounting is also achievable by analyzing the log.

This paper is organized as follows. Section 2 gives the system architecture including broker's internal queuing structure and essential subsystems. Section 3 depicts the messaging protocols including broker election, MDCC grouping, service request forwarding and execution. In Sect. 4, exemplar implementations of the MDCC are conducted to see the effectiveness on D2D sharing. Evaluations and open security issues of the MDCC are discussed in Sect. 5. Finally, we give conclusion in Sect. 6.

2 System Architecture

The MDCC system includes large amount of resources in user devices. We assume each user's resource list including IT resource status, lists of digital contents, and personal information is protected by the (n, k) secret sharing scheme. At the very first stage, n proximate users (initiators) of a sociological relation present resource lists for initiating a MDCC group analog to clubs or fans groups in Facebook. Every resource list has a respective security level defined by (n, k) and is encrypted with a password key (PWK). The aggregation of the resource lists from members is called the MDCC profile. The initiators possess enough number of secrets (PWKs) to maintain administration of the MDCC. On the management aspect, to adapt to the dynamics such as dynamic joining and leaving the system domain caused by user mobility, or device failure, we exploit adaptive brokering mechanism to tackle these uncertain dynamics of the mobile ad hoc network. Furthermore, MDCC is scalable due to the joining protocol of each new member is common to all the other devices in the MDCC. Here, we present the components in the MDCC before we present the protocols in Sect. 3.

2.1 Member Devices

The member devices are facilitated with Web servers such that digital contents are indexed with URL addresses. For devices in a DLNA LAN, we publish content list in the Web server of the DNLA gateway. Thus, the DLNA gateway becomes a member devices and it also forward requests to the broker such that other devices also share contents with DLNA devices. A member attaches to a group after successful authentication by the broker and presents his resource lists to associate with the MDCC. For each resource list protected by the (n, k) secret sharing, all other member device stores a key split and data split distributed from the broker. A resource list is available if the number of splits distributed in members is greater than the threshold k. That is, the number of devices is greater than k. Thus, reliability of accessing MDCC resources is quantitatively measurable according to events of user leaving and physical connection failure.

2.2   Broker

An MDCC is managed by a broker administrating network connectivity, member association, request processing, content searching, and task assignment. As shown in Fig. 1, a MDCC broker is either dynamically elected among initiators according to the resources status or chosen from a trusted server. The MDCC is similar to the small data center proposed in [6, 7], owned by a smaller business unit such as a coffee shop or a clinic. However, what different from [6, 7] is that an MDCC is autonomously grouped by user devices which also share resources with others. The broker optionally connects to the Internet. In the proposed architecture, contents and computational resources in each device are virtualized.

2.3   Broker Internal Architecture

As shown in Fig. 2, the internal architecture comprises queues of requests and tasks, a feedback control loop and logging units. A feedback control loop further comprises three subsystems including Cloud Inspection Subsystem (CIS), Cloud Control Subsystem (CCS), and Cloud Execution Subsystem (CES) which are analog to observer, controller, and plant respectively in a classic feedback control system. The respective functions of CIS, CCS and CES are described as follows.

(1)   **CIS — Cloud Inspection Subsystem.** A CIS subsystem receives state updates sourced from local virtual machines (VMs) and member devices. As an observer, it filters system states including member devices' remaining IT resources and multimedia contents distribution. Then, it retrieves and updates MDCC profile. Thus, the CIS database becomes distributed. The CIS writes the observed

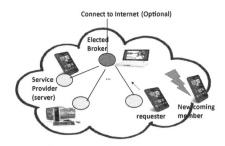

Fig. 1. MDCC network topology.

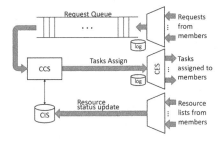

Fig. 2. Broker internal architecture.

information to the CIS database for CCS's reference on performing management and control. The digital content list is indexed with URL contents. For the statuses of remaining IT resources, the CIS aggregate them in percentages in the total inside MDCC respectively according to each member device's respective CPU ability, memory/storage size, available bandwidths, and battery energy.

(2) **CCS — Cloud Control Subsystem.** The broker's CCS determines distribution of new MDCC splits to members on CIS accomplishing update of a resource list. The CCS also locates splits for recovering a resource list. Then, the CCS checks the request with its CIS database to see which devices are able to serve a requesting member. If the requested service is available, the serving member devices are assigned with tasks to provision the requested service. Otherwise, the request is dropped. The simplest assigned tasks for sharing multimedia contents are web services indexed by URL addresses of the contents. Having a URL address replied from the broker, the requester invokes multimedia streaming service. The CCS checks with CIS's monitoring about availability of computational resources for streaming. Thus, for the pure streaming case, service provider's IT resources are shared to the requester (consumer) by the MDCC brokering scheme. Simple SLA such as streaming and video qualities are included in a multimedia streaming request.

(3) **CES — Cloud Execution Subsystem.** The CES is an actuator of the control loop in Fig. 2. The main mission of the CES submission is to receive CCS's controls and task assignments, then either invokes local VMs or forwards the task assignments to members. It makes members transparent to the CCS as if it is the single plant of the CCS controller. Actually, it regards local VMs its members. The task execution results and state updates from members are filtered by the CIS for database refreshment. Since it is CES executing tasks rather than the CCS, the CCS is able to process next request queued in the "Request Queue" in Fig. 2 without waiting for the end of current job execution.

3 Protocol Design

In this section, we depict messaging protocols for MDCC network virtualization. The virtualization is accomplished by summarizing IT resources and multimedia contents in XML lists to update the broker's CIS database when the member devices are associating with the group. The CIS is the primary reference for CCS's resource allocation to assign service tasks corresponding to a request.

3.1 Broker Election

Before grouping members, the broker is selected. The broker selection has two ways. In the first way, as Fig. 3(a), the broker is selected by an existing proximate server which chooses the device of highest score as the cloudlet broker according to the sorted IT resource status updates. The second way, as Fig. 3(b), is via election that all the user devices broadcast their resource states and each one performs the same scoring as in the first way. Both ways are securely performed since message exchanges of states (j, l_k)

are PWK-encrypted. The score evaluation can be multi-concerned. In this paper, the scoring results in electing the most computational ability (CPU power and memory size) as the cloudlet broker. Other selection algorithms can also be chosen for optimizations of different metrics. On selected, the broker which is also a user device, invoke its CCS to grant the admissions of attachment and associate requests and it control CES to form a device-centric cloud. In case there is a broker leaving or failure occurrence, the broker election is reinitialized. A malicious device cannot be elected as the broker since it cannot have enough secrets to pretend one of the initiators. That is, a later broker is elected only from the MDCC initiators.

3.2 Member Attachment

The admission of network attachment is the first phase of member grouping before member associations. A member device requests attachment for physical network connection. The attachment is conducted by the broker. The broker assigns port number for each requesting device. A device use the port for later authentication purpose. Being authenticated, a requesting device can then request for association with the MDCC.

3.3 Device Association

After physical network attachment, user configure resources' security levels and access rights quantitatively using thresholds (n, k) for sharing with others. The device information is then collected in XML format for broker's reference. In addition to device information, a device ID can optionally comprises GPS coordinate, network port, and IP fields for future authentication, authorization, and accounting (AAA) purposes. When associating with a group, shown in Fig. 3, the member device j issues association request "Associate req. state(j, l_k)" for uploading resource lists l_k of security level k. The device j presents its ID and PWKs for the lists to the broker. The broker partitions each list into n splits along with n key splits of the PWK respectively and then it distributes the split pairs to all members including itself. The CIS database records location of each split while the CCS maintain the records. A device j updates its resource list using the request "Associate req. state(j, l_k)" occasionally on update event, on demand of the broker, or periodically. In this paper, we adopt event-driven updates for digital contents.

3.4 Service Request and Execution

A user inputs service request containing a keyword of a media for content searching. As shown in Fig. 3(c), the request is encrypted by PWK of a resource list and sent to the broker for searching keyword in that list. When the request is received and decrypted, the broker CCS module searches the keyword in the CIS database that records the MDCC profile share locations. In this paper, the digital content indexing methods are not studied since we are focusing MDCC cloud computing. On successful locating the requested media content, the URL of the content is encrypted using the PWK of the resource list and sent to the requesting device. The URL includes port and ID of the server. The serving device is selected by the broker to provide the service. We noticed that only MDCC profile is distributed in member devices while the digital contents are not. An owner or producer of contents does not have to launch large amount of data transfers for uploading contents. Therefore, the content sharing based on MDCC saves energy especially in a mobile wireless environment.

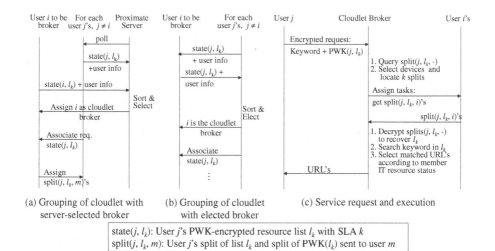

(a) Grouping of cloudlet with server-selected broker

(b) Grouping of cloudlet with elected broker

(c) Service request and execution

state(j, l_k): User j's PWK-encrypted resource list l_k with SLA k
split(j, l_k, m): User j's split of list l_k and split of PWK(l_k) sent to user m

Fig. 3. MDCC protocols.

4 System Implementation and Examples

4.1 Virtualization

We implement an exemplar MDCC where the user devices include cellular phones, tablets, laptops, and desktops. The cloudlets are grouped by user end devices. A MDCC link could comprise more than one physical network hops while each hop could be connected by WiFi, 3G, or wired Ethernet. Handhelds and tablets are embedded with Android operating systems while desktops are facilitated with Windows systems. Each device is further installed with a Java virtual machine (JVM), Web server, and SQL/SQL-lite database system. A Windows system can comprise multiple virtual machines (VMs) in addition to the JVM. The primary programming language is Java for implementing CCS, CES, the broker queuing architecture (Fig. 2), and the network virtualization connecting virtual machines. A SQL server plays as the CIS subsystem and all devices are embedded with web servers for publishing digital contents through the MDCC. Except JVM, all the VMs are managed by the Oracle Virtual Box manager [10]. Similar to the platform Xen Cloud Platform [11], the manager is domain 0 managing VMs identified as domain 1 to n and all the domains dwell in a desktop Windows physical machine (PM). Each Android system has only one VM, the JVM. Each VM, JVM or not, acts as either a broker or a member.

4.2   System Operations

As shown in Fig. 4, we implement four system primary operations include network attachment, member association, request forwarding, and service execution. The network attachment is based on the network virtualization where VM machines are connected. With the initial network connection, each VM member broadcasts its resource list in XML format to elect the broker. Then, the admitted VM members use the ports respectively assigned by the broker to synchronize the broker's CIS SQL database with their own. This finishes the member association. Then, users issue requests by entering keyword and optional media quality in the Android GUI. A streaming request is wrapped with source VM ID (IP, port, GPS coordinate), timeout, keyword, and quality. Using keyword and quality to constitute the query, the broker returns the URLs of the content to the requesting VM on successfully retrieving the resource splits, recovering the resource list, and locating the server VM with available IT resource. Otherwise, the broker returns an unavailable notification after timeout specification.

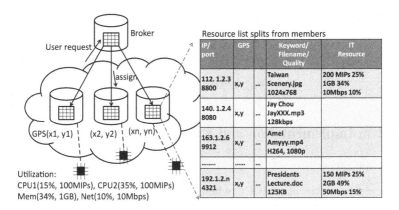

Fig. 4. Aggregation of resource list splits comprises keywords and IT resource states in a broker's CIS database.

4.3   Examples

We illustrate three examples demonstrating that the proposed MDCC architecture possesses dynamic task offloading ability using member resources such that existing security techniques are easily applied.

Example (1) Video multicasting. The virtualization enables different type of devices sharing multimedia contents via different physical network connections in real-time. The physical environment is shown in Table 1 where we can see different network interfaces are used. Phone 1 is elected as the broker. Since only phone 2 has the video, it is assigned as the multicasting server. Users turn in a specific broadcasting channel or enter their requests forwarded to the broker, the broker and server then provide the URL of the requested video to all the requesting devices if query of CIS database succeeded. Via Java service API, the access of the video is automatically started while the streaming task at the server side is in background. Note that the energy consumption of the server would be high if the number of clients becomes large. Once the number of clients exceeds a threshold, the broker assigns relaying task to one of the current clients to forward its video packets to later incoming clients. Thus, the multicast streaming task is offloaded. Shown in Fig. 5 is a handheld device elected as a broker logging the system operation while the serving handheld is performing the multicasting task.

Table 1. Devices participating the MDCC of Example 1.

Device	Laptop 1	Laptop 2	Phone 1	Phone 2	Tablet
Network IF	Ethernet	WiFi	3G	WiFi	WiFi
Media File	none	none	none	Video.mp4	none
PM OS	Windows XP	Windows 7	Android	Android	Android
VM	JVM	JVM	JVM	JVM	JVM

Fig. 5. In a video multicasting case, a broker is logging system operation and different types of clients are playing the same video through different physical networks.

Table 2. Devices participating MDCC of Example 2.

Device	Desktop PC	Phone 1	Phone 2 (DLNA gateway)
Network IF	Ethernet	3G	WiFi
Media files	none	Video2.mp4	jay1.mp4, jay2.mp4
PM OS	Windows XP	Android	Android
VM	JVM	JVM	JVM
Location	Kaohsiung (KH)	Taipei (TP)	Taipei (TP)

Example (2) Enabling DLNA/UPnP sharing over WAN. Traditionally, DLNA/ UPnP functions are available only inside the LAN where the DLNA device is deployed. The proposed MDCC enables accesses of DLNA/UPnP resources over the

Internet. The videos outside the LAN are also accessible to the DLNA devices. Table 2 lists the devices used in this example. We configure the DLNA gateway as a member device which is embedded with a Web server such that each multimedia file in the LAN is publishable via the Web server. We use a desktop PC as the broker in which the CIS database is updated by the DLNA gateway and a 3G handheld device (Phone 1). To show the network virtualization, the desktop PC is deployed in the KH City while the DLNA LAN and the handheld device are in the TP City. These two cities are apart from each other about 360 KM. The results that the DLNA LAN shares video with the Internet are shown as Fig. 6(a)–(e), which are respectively resource list update in XML format received by the broker, parsing result of the XML at the broker, logging the query response at the broker, responded URLs that match the request keyword "jay", and the video stream decoded at the client side (phone1). For the device sharing its video with the DLNA LAN, the request destined to the DLNA gateway is forwarded to the broker. Then, on succeeded query, the URL of the video file in the 3G phone is responded via the DLNA gateway to the requesting device. The results appear the same as Fig. 6 except the video and IT resources contents are different. The treatments to these two sharing directions are the same and this reveals that resources are virtualized no matter where they are.

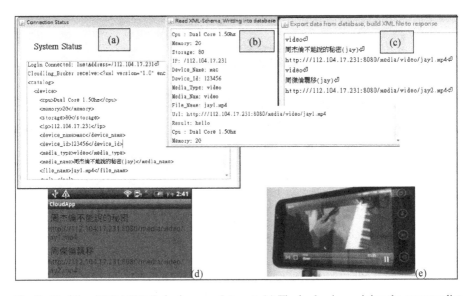

Fig. 6. Enabling DLNA/UPnP sharing over Internet: (a) The broker is receiving the resource list (XML) from the DLNA gateway. (b) The parsing result of the resource list saying "hello" to admit the DLNA gateway to join the MDCC. (c) Log of the successful query at the broker. (d) Replied URL results on successful query of "jay." (e) Video displayed on the requesting device.

5 Evaluations and Discussions

5.1 Scalability and Autonomy

From the above examples, we conclude that a MDCC is scalable since a broker can group as many member devices as possible and the members are of different types including single device, VM, and even a LAN (DLNA). The video sharing is also scalable if the multicasting were relayed via some of the MDCC members. The autonomous advantage comes from that the management is performed by the broker which is elected among the mobile devices. The authentication of network attachment and resource association are conducted by the broker in MDCC. In the future, the authorization such as the conditional access of the media files can be configured by each device and the configuration becomes part of XML resource list. The accounting is also possible according to the statistics of IT resource usage and size of media files shared in the sharing.

5.2 Complexity

The management complexity comes from partition of each resource list state(j, l_k) into n splits split(j, l_k, m), encryption and decryption of splits, and distribute the splits. For an MDCC with n members (include broker itself) each of which has average l lists, there are $n^2 l$ splits to distribute to n members. Since every resource list has much smaller data size than multimedia files, the energy consumption and latency caused by management overhead will not greater than that caused by uploading multimedia files to a traditional cloud center. The broker undertakes most of the administration tasks. Energy-aware broker election and grouping methodology will be developed for fairness and better energy utilization.

5.3 Open Security Issues in MDCC

The common security anxiety of subscribed users of a big data center is that unseen of how the shared contents are configured with access right, how and where they are kept, whether and how the recovery procedure is provided, and how the access history is logged. The anxiety mainly comes from that the contents are no longer under control of users since they are uploaded to the big data center. The MDCC provides compromise between the resource virtualization and security. Users remain control of data to be shared with since they are produced. Thus, existing security techniques are available to secure the MDCC computing with the compromised virtualization. Specifically, the following security techniques are available for the MDCC:

- Fake and harmful files: Users becomes publishers in MDCC just similar to that APP developers are publishers [12]. The published contents could be malicious executables. The simplest solution is to prohibit sharing of executables. This is common seen in many email systems that do not allow executable files being attachments.
- DDoS attack: Large amount of requests from distributed users will slow down the performance of MDCC and wastes energy. In the broker, incoming request

sampling time and quota limit by number of requests during the sampling time interval provide a solution. Furthermore, the MDCC disassociates and detaches those devices that frequent exceed the quota limit according to a threshold of the frequency.

- Broker substitution and DOS attack from a virus-infected broker: A virus-infected initiator device could win the broker position in the election. Then, it keeps assigning tasks to some specific devices to wastes their IT resources and energy. A broker evaluation scheme performed by the members, similar to the method proposed in [13], can be applied to exclude the malicious broker device and then restart the MDCC grouping procedure.

There are still many open security issues for MDCC such as avoiding free riding, completeness of AAA, digital right management, and protection from malicious Web server with fishing, URL redirection, malicious java script injection, etc. This paper does not intent to solve all the security problems from which mobile computing also suffer. However, we do implement the MDCC that turns the use of traditional security techniques more possible.

6   Conclusion

We have proposed the mobile device-centric cloud (MDCC) computing which enables secured device-to-device (D2D) sharing. Different from traditional P2P that requires a specific server, the MDCC is autonomously grouped and members are dynamically associated. The MDCC is also different from those cloudlets which use a small data center. Devices autonomously elect a broker. The broker administrates physical network attachments and resources virtualization through the association protocols before regulating the secured service brokering. Two examples, video multicasting and enabling DLNA/UPnP sharing over Internet shows that MDCC easily offloads streaming tasks to/ from member devices and it breaks through traditional sharing fashion - upload before share. The MDCC relieves the anxiety of security when sharing contents through big data centers. There are still open security issues for MDCC such as free riding, completeness of AAA, digital right management, etc. In the future, development of robust security techniques and quantitative analysis of MDCC are to be continued.

References

1. Kandukuri, B.R., Paturi, R. V, and Rakshit, A.: Cloud security issues. In: IEEE International Conference on Services Computing (2009)
2. Jensen, M., Schwenk, J., Gruschka, N., and Iacono, L.L.: On technical security issues in cloud computing. In: IEEE International Conference on Cloud Computing (2009)
3. Brodkin, J.: Gartner: seven cloud-computing security risks. http://www.networkworld.com/news/2008/070208-cloud.html
4. Huang, Y.-T.: An SLA-aware data dispersion method for short-secret-sharing cloud storage system. Thesis of Master Degree, Computer Science and Information Engineering, National Cheng-Kung University Taiwan (2013)

5. Guillen, J., Miranda, J., et al.: People as a service: a mobile-centric model for providing collective sociological profiles. IEEE Softw. **31**, 48–53 (2014)

6. Mahadev, S., Paramvir, B., et al.: The case for VM-based cloudlets in mobile computing. IEEE Pervasive Comput. **8**, 14–23 (2009)

7. Mahadev, S.: Mobile computing: the next decade. In: 1st ACM Workshop on Mobile Cloud Computing & Services: Social Networks and Beyond, pp. 1–6, ISBN: 978-1-4503-0155-8, New York (2010)

8. Mikko, R., Tommi, M., et al.: Mobile content as a service a blueprint for a vendor-neutral cloud of mobile devices. IEEE Softw. **29**, 28–32 (2012)

9. Raj, M., Di Francesco, M., Das, S.K.: Secure Mobile Cloud Computing. In: Das, S., Kant, K., Zhang, N. (eds.) Handbook on Securing Cyber-Physical Critical Infrastructure, pp. 411–429. Elsevier, Waltham (2012)

10. Oracle, VirtualBox Documentation. http://www.oracle.com/technetwork/server-storage/virtualbox/documentation/index.html

11. Xen Project, Xen Cloud Platform. http://www.xen.org/products/cloudxen.html

12. Qing, L., Clark, G.: Mobile security: a look ahead. IEEE Secur. Priv. **11**, 78–81 (2013)

13. Su, W.-T., Chang, K.-M., Kuo, Y.-H.: eHIP: an energy-efficient hybrid intrusion prohibition system for cluster-based wireless sensor networks. Comput. Netw. **51**(4), 1151–1168 (2007)

SecaaS Framework and Architecture: A Design of Dynamic Packet Control

Ngoc-Tu Chau, Minh-Duong Nguyen, Seungwook Jung,
and Souhwan Jung[⊠]

School of Electronic Engineering, Soongsil University, Seoul, Korea
{chaungoctu,nguyenminhduong,seungwookj,souhwanjung}@ssu.ac.kr

Abstract. This paper introduces SecaaS framework, a solution that allows security vendors to move their business into the cloud. By doing so, it is possible for tenants of SecaaS framework to freely choose between various security products depending on their own business requirements. OpenFlow protocol is applied in our framework to control the data paths of tenants and forward those data to a chaining of subscribed services before going out to the Internet. This paper also proposes the Open-Flow Dynamic Packet Control (ODPC) system for optimizing network stability and performance of our system when a new service is added or existing service is removed. ODPC system, which works as an application, will calculate the cost of delay for data paths inside of our network and set-up the path that guarantees the minimum delay for each tenant. The contribution of this paper includes the solution to solve the vendor locked-in limitation in others' SecaaS architecture. Moreover, this architecture is also considered as a solution for small scale security vendors to move their products into the cloud. In this paper, the proof-of-concept for SecaaS framework is also presented through demonstration. Furthermore, the ODPC system is considered as one of our efforts in order to improve the network performance in our system.

1 Introduction

One of the emerging trends in the cloud computing is the transfer of security services onto the clouds, a virtualized environment. Until now, researchers and cloud vendors have been searching for the suitable and innovative security solution for applying into their own systems [1,2]. For example, in October 2008, one of Juniper Networks companies, named Altor Networks Inc., has introduced Altor Virtual Firewall (Altor VF) 1.0, a security solution for virtual data center and clouds [3]. Altor VF is actually a software security application running on the virtualized environment that provides enforced security policies for virtual machines. CryptZone introduced AppGate Security Server, a secure role and policy-based access system, to protect virtual and physical IT assets with inbuilt firewall [4]. In 2010, Brock M. and Goscinski A. have presented a logical design of Cloud Security Framework that provides cloud infrastructure protection, security of communication and storage as well as tenants' authentication

© Springer International Publishing Switzerland 2015
K.-H. Rhee and J.H. Yi (Eds.): WISA 2014, LNCS 8909, pp. 190–201, 2015.
DOI: 10.1007/978-3-319-15087-1_15

and authorization [5]. However, those solutions are facing the vendor locked-in problem. Because of that problem, customers do not have enough flexibly security options to build their own security strategy.

Moreover, with the expeditious development of cloud computing, it is possible for large vendors like Altor Networks or McAfee to invest on SecaaS technologies and solutions to move their products into the cloud. In the other size, small size security vendors stuck with their owns products due to limitation of budget.

In order to solve the above problems, SecaaS framework is designed to enables small sizes security vendors to migrate their security products into the cloud. The availability of multiple security products that are provided by different vendors allows customers of SecaaS to make their own security plan based on their business budget.

For supporting services chaining (service-to-service) mechanism, SecaaS framework was designed with Software Defined Networking (SDN) technologies [6,7]. SDN provides the separation between control planes and data planes in the network. With the help of SDN, SecaaS framework can control data path and forward those data to a chaining of subscribed services before going out to the Internet.

Although data path can be consolidate setup, the performance of SecaaS framework can not be optimized due to the fact that the processing capacity of security services are fluctuating over time. In addition, the change of the whole SecaaS network topology (like adding new service, removal of existing services, services live migration) could cause degradation in network performance. In order to improve performance problem, this paper also introduces OpenFlow Dynamic Packet Control (ODPC) System, an application which calculates network delay and modifies data path of tenants based on the calculation to guarantee minimum process delay of data flows.

The paper is organized as follows. The second section will present the design of SecaaS Framework as well as how service chaining mechanism can be achieved in SecaaS framework. The next section will introduce ODPC and explain how ODPC system with designed algorithm can optimize SecaaS Framework. The implementation of SecaaS framework is presented on following section. Last section will summary our work and the direction of our future work.

2 Design of Secaas Framework Architecture

2.1 Design Motivation

Until now, most widely known of SecaaS is the providing of a secure access system that protects assets of companies and users on the clouds. For example, in [5], authors provide a Cloud Security Framework (CSF) for authorizing accesses to cloud services or in [8], McAfee provides security suites that is called "Total Protection" to support Network Data Leak Prevention (DLP), Host DLP, Endpoint Encryption for PC and others security offerings.

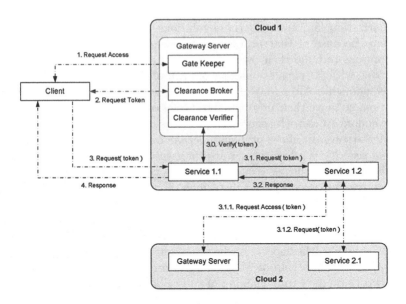

Fig. 1. Cloud security framework

SecaaS framework, unlike other solutions, provides different model by helping security vendors to leverage their systems to cloud-based. Figures 1 and 2 illustrate the model for CSF and Secaas Framework:

As illustrated in Fig. 2, SecaaS ecosystem enables security vendors to migrate their products to the cloud. Each product will become a security node inside SecaaS framework. The collection of security nodes will form a network inside SecaaS framework. With that design, SecaaS framework has different characteristics than others business models. Table 1 shows different characteristic between SecaaS Framework and others models:

Table 1. Comparison between Secaas Framework and Other models

Characteristics	Secaas Framework	Others
Vendors	Multiple	Single
Services	Multiple	Multiple
Security service deployment location	Network node	Network edge
Security Strategy	Various options	Single option

The main difference between SecaaS framework and other models is the ability to provide multiple security services, in which each service belongs to a different vendor. Moreover, unlike other design, in which on-transmit packets were inspected at the network edge, SecaaS framework inspects packets in each network node. With this feature, tenants can choose different security services that

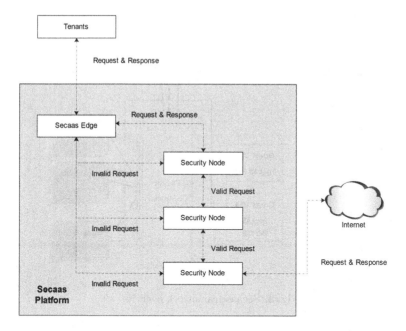

Fig. 2. Secaas framework

belong to different vendors. Tenants of SecaaS framework can combine various options to plan their own security strategy. For example, a company can choose DLP service of vendor A and web filter service of vendor B in the Engineer Department, and choose DLP service of vendor C combined with mail filter function of vendor D in their Accounting Department.

2.2   Software Architecture and Design

The overview of SecaaS architecture is illustrated in Fig. 3. In that figure, tenants can register their accounts with subscribed security services through web interface of SecaaS framework. SecaaS framework will store tenants information into its database and provides tenant with unique ID and password for log-in into VPN gateway. Inside of SecaaS framework are collections of security services that were registered by service providers. A data packet of a tenant will be forwarded to his subscribed services and go out to the Internet if it is filtered as valid.

SecaaS framework is divided into three layer: Infrastructure layer, Operations Support System (OSS), and Business Support System (BSS). Infrastructure includes functions related to SecaaS framework's infrastructure like routing control, cloud platform management. OSS provides functions that related to resources of framework. BSS consists of business-related functions like account management, billing, service management, and others.

SecaaS framework includes three administrator roles: Platform Administrator, SSP Administrator and Tenant Administrator. Each security provider

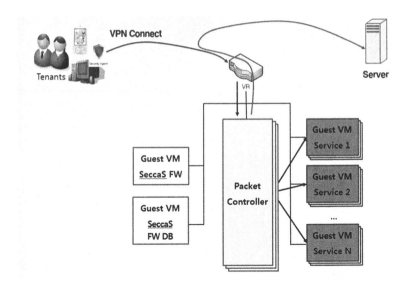

Fig. 3. Secaas framework overview

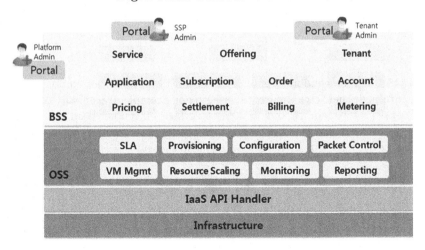

Fig. 4. Secaas framework software architecture

can register their own account in SecaaS framework, those accounts are called Security Service Provider (SSP) administrator account. With SSP administrator account, security provider can upload their products into SecaaS Framework. Tenant Administrator can also be registered in SecaaS Framework. Tenant Administrator account can create tenant accounts and subscribes those accounts with security services. Platform administrators responsible for account management, services management, billing, metering and other platform management tasks.

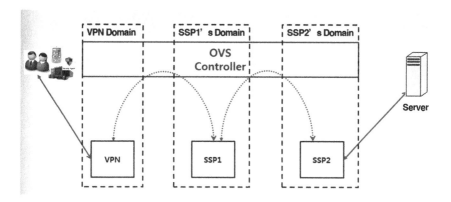

Fig. 5. Path registration

2.3   Secaas Framework Service Chaining Mechanism

Section 2 of this paper has shown the new model called SecaaS framework that offers multiple services provided by multiple vendors. This chapter will explain how packet control can be achieved in SecaaS framework.

Nowadays, Software Defined Networking (SDN) has become the one of the most prominent topics for discussion [9,10]. SDN architectures were made in order to decouple the network control and forwarding functions. Until now, there are many SDN solutions and protocols have been proposed, one of those proposal is OpenFlow protocol [11–13]. In order to provide data path control and packet forwarding functions in Secaas Framework, OpenFlow protocol is applied. Figure 5 illustrates how packet control can be applied into Secaas. With OpenFlow controller installed inside of Secaas framework, the data path will be updated every time a tenants subscribe or unsubscribe to a service.

Basically, after the registration of data path is finished, no future update will be made to the Flow Controller. However, any change in security node can affect the tenants' data flow. Subscription or unsubscription to a service in the framework can also lead to reducing of network performance. Figures 6 and 7 show the data flow that originated by a tenant who subscribed some security services. It can be easily seen that in Fig. 7, after changing the service, the flow controller has changed the services order. As a result, the path of data flow might be twisted back and forth among hosts. In this situation, it is not easy to decide if the data path should be in the order {SN1 to SN4 to SN3} or {SN1 to SN3 to SN4}.

In order to determine the optimized data path for tenant's packet, a solution is needed.

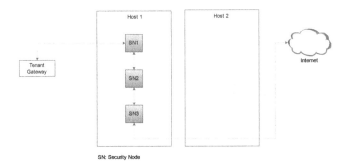

Fig. 6. Original services

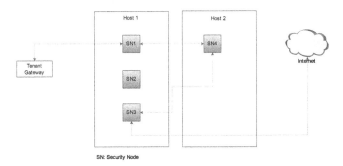

Fig. 7. Service changed

3   OpenFlow Dynamic Packet Control

In order to solve the data path optimization problem, we propose the Open-Flow Dynamic Packet Control (ODPC) system that implements our algorithm to check and optimize data path for SecaaS framework model.

Basically, ODPC is an application that works with OpenFlow controller and calculates delay value for all security nodes. The delay value consists of processing delay and travelling cost between two security nodes.

Assume that we have n nodes in Secaas Framework (including the gateway node). A tenant that chooses k − 1 services will have total of $\frac{k*(k-1)}{2}$ possible paths. Each possible path will have delay value w_i. So that for SecaaS framework, we have the $W = \{W_1, W_2, ... W_{\frac{k*(k-1)}{2}}\}$.

The Fig. 8 illustrates SecaaS framework with k = 7:

The delay value between source security node i and destination security node j can be calculated by the following equation:

$$W_i j = P_i j + T_i j$$

Where $P_i j$ is the processing delay of security node j and $T_i j$ is the travelling cost to go from node i to node j. Both metrics can be calculated inside controller.

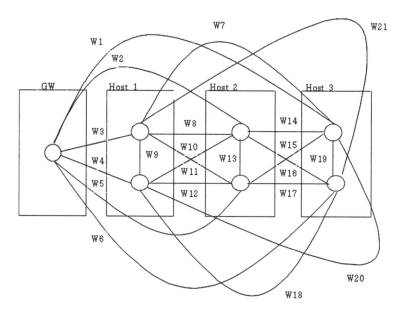

Fig. 8. Sample network with k = 7 and packets are generated from Gateway (GW)

Based on the delay value, we can choose the destination based on the following procedure:

Data: Weight collections ($W = \{W_1, W_2, ...W_{\frac{k*(k-1)}{2}}\}$)
Result: Ordered list of travelled node
initialization blank list of output;
while *Size of W is not equals 0* **do**
    Find minimum weight m in W;
    Add minimum weight m into output list;
    Remove m from W;
end

Based on the output, we can set the path to the Flow Table in controller.

4 Demonstration of SecaaS Framework

In order to prove the possibility of SecaaS Framework, we have setup a cloud architecture with the following specification:

1. Hypervisors: 3 Xenserver Citrix, each with 3 network interfaces (Two for cloud communications, and one connecting with OpenFlow's domain). Each of Xenserver deployed 1 Squids transparent proxy servers, each blocks a different websites. One of those xenservers deploy VPN virtual machine, which acts as tenant gateway.
2. Cloud Management: 1 Cloudstack server with 2 network interfaces (One for private network communications, one for public network)

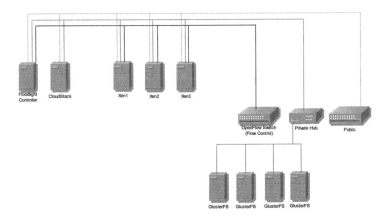

Fig. 9. Implementation architecture of SecaaS Framework

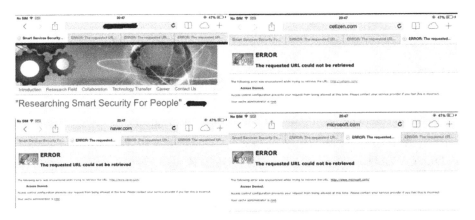

Fig. 10. Tenant browsing result

3. OpenFlow Controller Server: 1 Floodlight server with 3 network interfaces (One for private network communications, one for public network, One for OpenFlow's domain)
4. Storage Servers: 4 GlusterFS servers with 1 network interface for private network communications)

The full demonstration of SecaaS Framework architecture is presented in Fig. 9.

In order to test the possibility of our system, we created a tenant who chooses all services. This tenant connected to VPN through iPad. It is also noted that it is possible for tenants to connect to our VPN through other devices (like laptop, PC, or mobile phones) that run on Android or Windows operating system.

We connect to the website in the following order: One unblocked website and 3 blocked websites. Figure 10 shows the result of a tenant browsing websites.

The demonstration result shows the possibility of SecaaS framework that can provide multiple services for tenants.

5   Discussion of the Solution

Most of the cloud environment now consider SDN-based packet control in the following situation:

1. Firewall/Access control list [14]
2. Network Configuration
3. Routing [15,16]
4. High Availability, Load Balancing [17].

As in our framework, we use SDN to solve the service chaining problem. In our framework, services within the same host are considered as same distance because theirs communications belong to the same host, which is done by memory mapping in the host itself without data control by OpenFlow switch. So the distance metric is only considerable only when tenant chooses a list of services that belong to different hosts.

A data path decision algorithm is applied with a modification version of Dijkstra routing algorithm, a simple and well known algorithm for ensuring routing performance. Unlike Dijkstra algorithm that only makes routing decision based only on node distance, SecaaS framework needs both distance and processing delay of services for making routing decision. Because of that reason, we create a weight value, which is the combination between processing delay and travelling delay. The routing order for a tenant depends on the size of subscribed service delay, which guarantees the minimum delay for a request.

The performance degradation point of SecaaS framework is the calculation of processing delay. The time for updating routing table is the factor to be considered. If we choose to periodically calculate all routing table, the small calculation period could lead to network congestion, and the large calculation period could lead to inefficiency of data flow. In this paper, we decide to calculate the routing decision only in the following conditions:

1. Tenants update their subscribed services (including the case when new tenant added into the framework)
2. A service is added or removed from framework.

Delay calculation and routing decision are applied to all tenants each time those conditions occur to prevent congestion and to ensure that all tenants share equal framework resources.

6   Summary and Future Work

Secaas Framework is one of the interesting approaches that can help small size security providers to migrate their product into clouds. The result in "Sect. 4:

Demonstration of SecaaS Framework" has proved the feasibility of our framework. However, similar to other's incubating ideas, SecaaS Framework is still suffering from various weak points as well as security and performance consideration points. It is obvious that optimization should be considered in order to keep the framework effective. This paper contributes with the solution to solve the vendor locked-in limitation in others' SecaaS architecture. SecaaS framework also introduces security service chaining with mechanism and demonstration, which provide new research directions for SecaaS. Furthermore, ODPC system is considered as one of our efforts in order to improve the network performance in our system. In our future research, the implementations of the whole system and detail performance analysis in different scenarios as well as performance improvement plan will be implemented to make SecaaS framework more stable and effective.

Acknowledgments. This work was supported by the IT R&D program of ACT under the MOTIE/KEIT. [10045904, The development of Fundamental Technology for Security as a Service(SecaaS) Framework under cloud computing environment and the implementation of 1Gbps mobile data loss prevention(DLP) service based on the SecaaS Framework.]

This research was supported by the MSIP(Ministry of Science, ICT&Future Planning), Korea, under the ITRC(Information Technology Research Center) support program (NIPA-2014-H0301-14-1010) supervised by the NIPA(National IT Industry Promotion Agency).

References

1. Senk, C.: Adoption of security as a service. J. Internet Serv. Appl. **4**, 11 (2013)
2. Mohammed, H., Hanady, A.: SECaaS: security as a service for cloud-based applications. In: Proceedings of the Second Kuwait Conference on e-Services and e-Systems, vol. 8 (2011)
3. Juniper Networks, Securing Virtual Server Environments with Juniper Networks and Altor Networks, White Paper, Oct 2009
4. Cryptzone: Securing SAP/ERP with the AppGate Unified Access Solution, White Paper 2009
5. Brock, M., Goscinski, A.: Toward a framework for cloud security. In: Hsu, C.-H., Yang, L.T., Park, J.H., Yeo, S.-S. (eds.) ICA3PP 2010, Part I. LNCS, vol. 6082, pp. 254–263. Springer, Heidelberg (2010)
6. Open Networking Foundation: Software-Defined Networking: The New Norm for Networks, ONF White Paper 2013
7. McKeown, N., et al.: OpenFlow: Enabling innovation in campus networks. ACM SIGCOMM Commun. Rev. **38**(2), 69–74 (2009)
8. Shackleford D.: SANS Review: McAfee's Total Protection for Data, A SANS Whitepaper 2009
9. Feamster, N., et al.: The road to SDN. Mag. Queue Large-Scale Implementations 11(12) (2009)
10. Feamster, N., et al.: The case for separating routing from routers. In: Proceedings of the ACM SIGCOMM Workshop on Future Directions in Network Architecture, pp. 5–12 (2014)

11. Tennenhouse, D.L., et al.: A survey of active network research. IEEE Commun. **35**(1), 80 (1997)
12. van der Merwe, J.E., et al.: The tempest: a practical framework for network programmability. IEEE Network **12**(3), 20–28 (1997)
13. IETF ForCES Group: IETF ForCES (Forwarding and Control Element Separation) (2001)
14. Dennis, G., Ivan, P., Ruslan, S.: toward network access control with software-defined networking. In: INTERNET 2013, June 2013
15. Gautam, K., Saurabh, K.S.: Demystifying routing services in software-defined networking. In: White paper (2013)
16. Rothenberg, C.E., et al.: Revisiting routing control platforms with the eyes and muscles of software-defined networking. In: Proceedings of the First Workshop on Hot Topics in Software Defined Networks, pp. 13–183 (2013)
17. Dan, W., Hani, J.: Cementing high availability in OpenFLow with RuleBricks. In: Proceedings of the First Workshop on Hot Topics in Software Defined Networks, pp. 139–144 (2013)

Name Server Switching: Anomaly Signatures, Usage, Clustering, and Prediction

Aziz Mohaisen[1]([✉]), Mansurul Bhuiyan[2], and Yannis Labrou[1]

[1] Verisign Labs, Reston, VA, USA
amohaisen@verisign.com
[2] Indiana University—Purdue University, Indianapolis, IN, USA

Abstract. There exists a significant number of domains that have frequently switched their name servers for several reasons. In this work, we delved into the analysis of name-server switching behavior and presented a novel identifier called "NS-Switching Footprint" (NSSF) that can be used to cluster domains, enabling us to detect domains with suspicious behavior. We also designed a model that represents a time series, which could be used to predict the number of name servers that a domain will interact with. We performed the experiments with the dataset that captured all `.com` and `.net` zone changing transactions (i.e., adding or deleting name servers for domains) from March 28 to June 27, 2013.

1 Introduction

The Domain Name System (DNS) is an essential component in the operation of the Internet. While domain names are easy to remember by human, Internet Protocol (IP) addresses are numerical labels for identifying network entities on the Internet. The process of finding an IP address associated with a domain name is called the DNS name resolution, and is the first step required for navigating on the Internet. For example, a user entering "http://www.verisign.com" in the browser would be unaware of complexities and procedures performed in translating the domain name `verisign.com` into the IP address (`69.58.181.89`) for the Verisign web server. The resolution process is recursive in nature, meaning that a request for an IP address of `verisign.com` will propagate to the authoritative name server through intermediaries until a resolution happens successful by reaching such authoritative name server. Figure 1 illustrates the process of DNS resolution for an example of `abc.com`.

In the DNS ecosystem, the life cycle of a domain starts with its registration under a top level domain (TLD; such as `.com`, `.net`, etc.). TLDs are maintained by registries, and as part of the registration process a domain name is paired with a name server, which serves as the gate keeper of the domain name. Name servers, specially the authoritative ones, are a significant entity of a domain's operation as they will tell users where to look for the domain. A domain name may have one or more name servers to resolve it.

While it is natural to expect a one-to-one mapping of a domain name to a name server, it is often desirable to maintain multiple name servers for a domain

© Springer International Publishing Switzerland 2015
K.-H. Rhee and J.H. Yi (Eds.): WISA 2014, LNCS 8909, pp. 202–215, 2015.
DOI: 10.1007/978-3-319-15087-1_16

name to facilitate reliability, availability, tolerance to failure, and geographical diversity, among other desirable performance metrics and features. For example, when multiple name servers are associated with one domain name, they will enable connectivity to the domain name by other users even when some of the name servers fail. Additionally, having multiple name servers can enable load balancing [1]: a DNS resolver aware of multiple requests for the same domain name will be able to intelligently distribute the incoming requests to individual servers, and to provide different translation for the same domain name, thus serving the contents of the resolved domain from arbitrarily many servers in a uniform fashion at fairly well-balanced loads. The same idea of load balancing when couple with the geographical location of the requesting users can be further utilized to enable geographical diversity: the requests for a domain name can be resolved to an IP address that is located closer to the user, based on the user's location. An example of a technology that utilizes DNS for enabling geographical diversity is the content distribution network (CDN) [2], which have seen a great adoption in delivering content to users more reliably and efficiently. To that end, using multiple name servers can improve reliability, scalability, and utility in IP networks.

Although multiple name servers can be associated with the same domain, this association does not imply any form of dynamics. The set of multiple name servers is usually assigned to a domain name at the registration time of the domain name, and an update of those name servers happens less often once the domain name is set up and operated. Natural causes for updating the name servers associated with the domain name can include transferring between service providers, retiring hardware used as the name server, among others, which all are naturally less frequent and hard to observe in a short term.

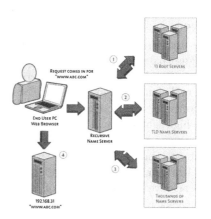

Fig. 1. DNS Resolution of abc.com

It is however noted that there exists a nontrivial number of domain names that perform frequent updates to their name servers, even by switching among name servers that belong to multiple service providers. Such transactions might not be reasonable in many situations because they demand interference with the existing DNS services. Accordingly, several studies in the literature were set out to understand this phenomenon and its implications. In [3], the author interprets name servers switching as a hiding mechanism of a domain's intended usage, and shows that domains with such behavior tend to display unsavory behavior, including the hosting of malware, pornography, and the sales of unauthorized pharmaceuticals drugs, among other illicit activities. In [4], researchers used the number of name servers of a domain within a period of time as a feature to develop a classifier for detecting malicious domain names. In [5], researchers developed an inference system to build proactive blacklist of domains where they used the name servers information of exiting blacklisted domains. They showed that future blacklisted domains tend to follow the same trend on name servers selection.

All of the prior work has looked at the aggregate feature of association between domain names and name servers to infer a better understanding of the use of domain names. A limiting aspect in the prior literature is that nobody had access to a continuous stream of data representing the dynamics of association between name servers and domain names over time. To this end, while motivated by the prior work in [3–5], we look deeper into the subject. Our unique position on the topic is facilitated by a unique data-point: we have considered not only the total number of name servers used by a domain or how much switching has happened within a period of time but also the evolution of the name servers associated with a domain name. For example, we looked at the changes in the number of name servers associated with a domain name: in a time slot t how many name servers are added to the pool of servers associated with a given domain name, and in time $t + 1$ how many name servers got deleted. We also try to understand how the sequence of addition and detection of name servers associated with a domain name proceeds over time.

We use this name server evolution of a domain to build an identifier called "NS-Switching-Footprint" (NSSF). Following [5], we hypothesize that NSSF can be used as a vital artifact to characterize domain names' intended usage. We argue that such an artifact can be used as a building block in a security system that associates the name servers to potentially check whether a domain name is malicious or benign. The NSSF is not only a feature that can be used to determine if a domain name is malicious or not, but can be further extended to highlight many intended uses of domain names, like advertising, traffic redirection, search engine optimization, etc. Our design of NSSF is intended to be robust, and is not limited to exact footprint matches. Rather, we use a partial match that makes comparison on various substrings within the fingerprint to achieve the same goal of understanding the intended characterization and usage of a domain name. To show the feasibility of NSSF, we experimentally analyzed the relationship between the characteristics of domains and NSSF and observed that domains of similar types (e.g., malicious domains and advertisement) tend to have similar footprints.

Building on preliminary findings on the power of NSSF, we also developed a prediction model that can estimate how many name servers a domain might interact with in the future given historical interactions. The prediction model serves two purposes. First, it enables us to identify a complete NSSF (within the certainty guarantees of the prediction model) for interactions that did not happen yet. Second, it enables us to probabilistically identify intended uses for domain names, using the predicted NSSF, before the intended use happen. This latter feature would enable proactive actions to be done in case, for example, of intended misuse of a domain name. Experimental results of the proposed prediction model unveil its power and potential use.

Contributions. First, we introduced the NSSF, a feature for characterizing the use of domain names based on the dynamics of association between the domain name and their name servers. Experimental results on .com and .net zone files show that the proposed feature is capable of capturing the intended use of various domain names. Second, we proposed a method for clustering domain names based on their NSSF structures, which captures their usages with applications to anomalies. Third, we examined the power of an-off-the-shelf method for predicting the NSSF.

Organization. The background is in Sect. 2, the proposed method for characterizing domain names by their name server switching patterns is proposed in Sect. 3. The observations on the proposed method for understanding domain name servers are in Sect. 4. Clustering of domain names using their NSSFs is presented in Sect. 5. A model for predicting NSSF is proposed in Sect. 6. The related work is in Sect. 7, and concluding remarks are in Sect. 8.

2   Background

In this section we will introduce preliminaries required for understanding the rest of the paper. First we elaborate on the interactions between domain names and name servers, and their book-keeping, while emphasizing on the terminology in that field. Then, we elaborate on time series data analysis used for predicting the intended use of domains.

2.1   Domain and Name Server Interaction

The domain name ecosystem consists of three entities: a registry, registrar, and registrant. The registrant is the entity that has the right to use the domain name. The registry is the organization responsible for maintaining a database of information about domain names and their name server mapping (that database is also called "registry"). Each TLD is associated with a registry, like VeriSign, which maintains such information about the TLD. Registrants and the registry are separated by a registrar, an entity that reserves domain names on behalf of registrants.

When a registrant wants to register a domain, one of the ICANN (Internet Corporation for Assigned Names and Numbers) accredited registrars of the registrant's choice creates a lease document with the consent of the relevant TLD registry (i.e., Verisign for .com and .net) for the intended use period. Upon the activation of the domain, the registry stores the DNS information of the domain in the corresponding DNS *zone file*. In the the zone file, all the authoritative name-servers of a domain are listed. In this work, we only considered .net and .com domains which in fact constitute almost 50 % of all domains [6]. Any action that results in the addition or deletion of a domain name, name server, or the association of a name server with a domain name is called a *transaction* and is logged into the zone file. Atomically, there are three types of transactions: *add*, *update* and *delete* that are considered zone-impacting transactions. Actions that use those transactions are propagated in the zone file.

2.2   Time Series Data Analysis and Forecast

Time series analysis is a well-established field in statistics which provides systematic approaches to model data with time correlations. We focus in this paper on the (discrete) time domain approach as it is typically more appropriate for dealing with (possibly) non-stationary, shorter time series with a focus on predicting future values [7]. As we alluded to earlier, and discussed at length later, the problem of predicting the number of name-servers of a domain given the history of interactions can be modeled as a time series prediction problem. To this end, we specifically focus on the multiplicative models, represented by a systematic class called autoregressive integrated moving average (ARIMA) models [8]. These models assume that the observed data results from products of factors involving differential operators responding to a white noise input. The ARIMA model is a generalization of the more widely used autoregressive moving average models (ARMA), which found many applications in statistical process control [9], financial forecasting [10], biomedical dynamics modeling [11], and web traffic modeling and forecasting [12]. In this study, we focused on using the standard ARIMA [8] model for time series name-server prediction. Let X_t be a time series, where y is an integer index and X_t is a real number for t. The ARIMA model is defined as $Y_t = (1 - L)^d X_t$, where Y_t is the predicted variable, L is the lag operator (or backshift; defined as an operator on the time series to produce the previous element), and d is a multiplicity factor. For more details on the model and its operation, see [8]. Other techniques from the literature that we use as tools are *hierarchical clustering* methods. For a review of the technique and the different parameters in a similar context, see [13].

3   Proposed Measure of Switching Behavior

In this section we turn our attention to explaining the method used for characterizing the behavior of a domain name using name server switching.

3.1   Name Server Switching

To characterize the dynamics of name servers associated with domain names, we consider a discretizing process of the time domain. Let w be a window of events defined as a succession of at least one *add* operation followed by at least one *delete* operation followed by at least one *add* operation. Let a transition be defined as the set-theoretic difference of the set of name servers of a window (NSw) and the set of name servers of the previous window (NSw'). A name server switching occurs when the transition set is non-empty (i.e., NSw\NSw' $\neq \phi$). The intuition is that by ignoring individual successive additions and deletions of name servers, and instead focusing on aggregate changes, we will capture significant changes in the state of a domain's NS providers.

Example. The above definition of switching is explained by a simple toy example shown in Fig. 2, and discussed as follows.

In Fig. 2(a) and (c) there is only 1 window but in Fig. 2(b) there are 2 windows, which can be manually vetted. At the end of each window we decide whether a switching of name server occurs or not. In Fig. 2(a), the first two *add* operations cause the domain "a.com" to have two name servers. Then following two *delete* operations of the previously added name server cause domain "a.com" to have no name servers

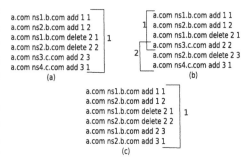

Fig. 2. A toy example of the NS-Switching

associated with it, but the last two *add* operations make the domain "a.com" associated with two new name servers than before, thus we consider this scenario as switching of name serves. At the end of the first window in Fig. 2(a), the domain "a.com" has two servers.

In Fig. 2(b), we can see that there are two windows. At the end of the first window, the domain "a.com" has two name servers where one is a new name server ("ns3.c.com") added to the previously allocated name servers in the set of "a.com" by the end of the first two *add* operations—hence one switching of name server is recorded. Then at the end of the second window, domain "a.com" has two name servers where one ("ns4.c.com") is new to what "a.com" had at the end of the first window, and hence the second switching name server is observed. Finally, in Fig. 2(c), we only have one window. At the end of the window, domain "a.com" has two domains which are the same as it had at the beginning of the window, and hence no switching of name server is observed or recorded.

Since the concept of name servers switching is now made clear, we move on to the description of the name server switching footprint, which is the main feature used for identifying the use of domain names in the rest of the paper.

3.2 NSSF: Name Server Switching Footprint

The NSSF is a domain name's unique identifier for characterizing the pattern of name servers switching over time. In Fig. 3, we present the pseudo code for building the NSSF for a domain. In the footprint, we incorporate the number of name servers added or deleted along with the time period of these operations. Since we have a fixed number of time units of data (at the level of days)—in which name zone impacting transactions are observed and recorded, we set the length of each time period to one day. According to the algorithm in Fig. 3, given a domain, the corresponding NSSF is generated as a string representing the number of additions, followed by the number of deletions of the name servers associated with the domain name, followed by a time index. Figure 4 illustrates a simple example on NSSF building.

input = domain d
output = Footprint of d
T = Total time period = 90
Build_NSSF(domain d):
1. **for** d exists in t time period where
   $t \in (1, T)$:
2. NSSF = concate(NSSF,
   concate(#ofAdded-NS(d),
      #ofDeleted-NS(d) , t,sep="_"), sep=":")

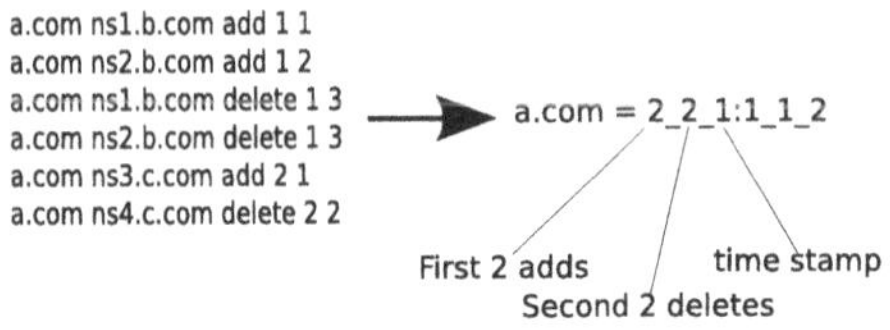

```
a.com ns1.b.com add 1 1
a.com ns2.b.com add 1 2
a.com ns1.b.com delete 1 3                a.com = 2_2_1:1_1_2
a.com ns2.b.com delete 1 3
a.com ns3.c.com add 2 1
a.com ns4.c.com delete 2 2
```

First 2 adds   time stamp
Second 2 deletes

Fig. 3. Footprint Building Algorithm   **Fig. 4.** NS-Switch Footprint(NSSF)

4   Experiments Observations

Next, we use the NSSF to detect anomalies in the domain name usages based on name server interactions. We rely in our study on a large corpus of name zone alerts associated with the registry of .com and .net which are operated by VeriSign.

Dataset. The dataset used in this study belongs to the registry operation of the com and net TLDs operated by VeriSign. As outlined in Sect. 2, upon the activation of a domain name the registry stores the DNS information of the domain in the corresponding DNS *zone file*. Verisign, as the registry of the com and net TLDs, has created the method called Domain Name Zone Alerts (DNZA) to capture all zone impacting transactions in a specific format in a special extension file called .rzu (rapid zone update). While the format and extension create a platform of such information to interested parties (for data usability), they capture an interesting aspect relevant to our study: the DNZA maintains an order of the transactions as they happen in reality, and log them in the format.

Using the DNZA files generated for the com and net TLDs, and for a given domain name, we can extract a completely ordered set of events that impact the zone file since the creation of the domain name until its retirement. For its operations, and at any point in time, VeriSign maintains DNZA files for the past 90 days, and makes it available for interested parties (through data agreements in place). We used this dataset during the 90 days covering the period between March 28, 2013 to June 27, 2013 in this study.

We only considered the domains that are registered within these 90 days since they are likely to be of interest and revealed their intended usages within that period of time. For that same period, we had

Table 1. Statistics of DNZA dataset

# of transactions	Avg transactions/day	# of domains	# of Name servers
31,586,839	350,964	7.9 mil	480K

approximately 31 million transactions, averaging about 350 thousand transactions per day, with 7.9 million unique domain names, and about 480 thousand unique name servers. These statistics are summarized, more precisely, in Table 1.

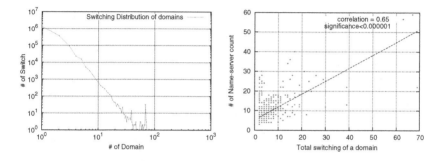

Fig. 5. (a) Log-log plot of switching. (b) Scatter plot of switching of all domain

Analysis of Name Server Switching. In the following, we first analyze the basic name server switching characteristics of domain names added to the zone of `.com` and `.net` in the 90 days covered by the data in this study. We ran our algorithm to compute the total number of switching of name servers for each domain in the DNZA dataset based on the definition in Sect. 3.1. We notice that 25 % of all domains performed at least one NS switching. Figure 5(a) shows the switching distribution of domains, where the distribution exhibits a power law characteristic. Figure 5(b) shows the total number of switching versus the number of unique name servers of a domain name.

We also fitted a straight line to capture and demonstrated the positive correlation between the number of name servers and the count of overall switching associated with a domain. We also observed that most of the domains with a higher switching count tend to exhibit unusual behaviors and types as discussed in Sect. 1.

Table 2 shows some of the major findings by highlighting some examples of such domain names. For example, we see that "`amazingweb007.com`" is an adult dating website which does not follow mainstream dating website concepts; "`teknotigr.com`" is an empty

Table 2. Top 5 switching domains

domain	Switchings	Type
`amazingweb007.com`	164	Adult Dating
`teknotigr.com`	151	Empty Blog
`climate13.com`	148	Fake Conference
`zqbifen8.com`	84	Advertisement
`dxsmalvn.com`	81	Page Not found

blog that has a lot of NS activity; "`climate13.com`" is a fake conference website mentioned in "`scamwarners.com`"; and "`dxsmalvn.com`" was not loaded in the browser. All of the above are *only examples* of those domain names with an unfavorable behavior, which were spotted by using the name server switching as a side channel information.

5   Domain Clustering

One limitation of the findings so far is that a highly supervised process is needed to make use of the triggers made by the NSSF signature, and to identify the intended usage of domain names. While a great part of this process can be automated (e.g., by automatic crawling, analysis, etc.), for every domain name with a number of switchings, a manual vetting might be necessary to facilitate this process and ensure a high accuracy.

To this end, and in search for alternatives to this seemingly costly process, in the following we look at trading the cost for less supervision. In this section, we present in detail an experimental analysis of domain clustering based on the NSSF as the main feature. Initially, we cluster domains based on the exact matching of a footprint, then we introduce a more robust clustering method based on the n-grams created from the NSSF. The intuition for using this process of clustering is that one may have labels for a certain number of domain names, indicating their usage, and would want to extrapolate those labels for the rest of unlabeled domains. To that end, groups of domain names based on their NSSF similarity would greatly facilitate this operation. Next, we discuss the clustering approach to the problem with various settings.

5.1   Cluster Domains by Exact Footprint Matching

Given the strict definition of the NSSF, one would think that it is unlikely for two domain names to have the same footprint using the whole NSSF as a signature over the entire period of 90 days where domain names are observed in this study. However, to motivate for a partial footprint, we first tried this extreme scenario: we clustered domain names based on the exact match of their total footprint. To do that, we have followed the following steps. First, we computed the NSSF of

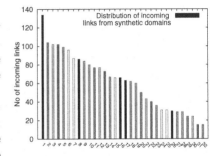

Fig. 6. Distribution of incoming links

each domain name from the DNZA files, as described in Fig. 3. Then, using a simple counting, we grouped the domain names by the exact match of the footprint.

To manually vet the resulting clustering, we selected clusters with at least 10 domain names, with footprints of length greater than five. Using those settings, we ended up with 2604 domains in 84 clusters with the median and maximum sizes of 23 and 99, respectively. After analyzing these clusters, we identified two special types of groups of domains: take over domains and domains that work collaboratively to increase the page rank of third party domains. Informally speaking, take over domain names are domains with registrations that expired and registered by another registrant in the hope of attracting traffic and utilizing it based on the previous usage of the domain name. We found 31 takeover domains in 2 clusters of size 18 and 13 with NSSF of length 40. All of these domains used DNS providers that have the service of domain parking to generate revenue. By examining their WHOIS information, we found that all of these domains are owned by the same entity.

In the second case, and by statically analyzing the content of the web sites for the identified domain names, we found a set of domains that maintain links (referral urls) to the target domains to increase their page rank. After analyzing the contents hosted on these domains, we found that all of these domains are synthetically generated; we also found 343 domains that work together to increase the page rank of 32 third party domains, where all of them are owned by one entity and maintain a similar pattern of NS switching. In Fig. 6, we show the distribution of incoming links from 343 domain to the 32 third party domains.

Note that, while those experiments are mainly manual, they are easy to automate using off-the-shelf tools and in-house datasets. As a registry of the studied TLDs, VeriSign also runs operations of crawling certain level of contents of those TLDs, and identify their usage by analyzing such contents. Also, information such as WHOIS contents, while are not totally under the control of the registry, are easy to obtain automatically to identify associations between domain names based on that additional dimension. To this end, findings in the work can be easily automated operationally.

5.2   The n-Gram Based Clustering

The exact matching outlined above is promising in identifying certain groups of domain names based on the whole NSSF, however the major drawback of the technique is that it will not capture associations between domains which have partial similarities. To work around this drawback, we consider clustering domains based on n-grams, defined as the reoccurring substrings within the footprint. The main challenging part of this clustering model is in identifying the n-gram given a domain name's footprint. Particularly, defining the proper distance metrics and measures is a significant challenge given the special nature of the NSSF. These distance measures will be used to cluster domains using any off-the-shelf clustering algorithm. In this experiment, we adopt the agglomerative hierarchical clustering. In the following sections, first we introduce two n-gram based distance metrics and two heuristics on building n-grams from the footprints.

n-gram based distance metric. After building n-grams from a footprint, we want to compute a pairwise distance measure between domains. We use two metrics suitable for that purpose: (I) Tribased_Dist [14] and (II) Keselj [15] distance

$$Tribased\_Dist(x, y) = 1 - \frac{1}{1 + |tri(x)| + |tri(y)| - 2 * |tri(x) \cap tri(y)|}$$

$$Keselj\_dist(x, y) = \frac{1}{|tri(x)| + |tri(y)|} \sum_{w \in tri(x) \cap tri(y)} \left(\frac{f_x(w) - f_y(w)}{f_x(w) + f_y(w)} \right)^2$$

Now we explain two heuristics for identifying the n-grams from a footprint.

Heuristic I. Suppose that a domain "abc.com" has footprint 2_0_1 : 0_2_2 : 4_3_3 which we denote as $NSSF_{abc.com}$ (this footprint can be read as domain "abc.com" adds 2 name servers at time 1, deletes both of the name servers at time 2, and adds 4 then delete 3 name servers at time 3). To build the n-gram, we first split the $NSSF_{abc.com}$ across time and consider each part of the footprint as an item of a set from which we will construct the n-gram. $NSSF_{abc.com}$ spans over 3 time-stamps, so if we split the footprint across time, we get a set of three items $\{2\_0\_1, 0\_2\_2, 4\_3\_3\}$. We then apply the n-gram construction method over the set. In all of our experiments, we set $n = 3$.

Heuristic II. In heuristic II, we relax the rules of splitting the footprint. We split the footprint based on events (add, delete) and time. For footprint $2\_0\_1 : 0\_2\_2 : 4\_3\_3$, we gather the added name server event which construct a set $\{2, 0, 4\}$. The same thing is done for deletion of name servers as well as the time-stamps, and build a set $\{0, 2, 3\}$ and $\{1, 2, 3\}$ respectively. We then construct 3 n-grams from these sets. Each of these n-grams will compute a distance measure (Tribased or Keselj) for a domain pair and final distance is taken by averaging these distances.

Empirical evaluation. To empirically evaluate the performance of both of the heuristics described above, we select a dataset of $7,830$ domains with footprint length 6 and higher. Then we compute a pairwise distance metric as mentioned in Sect. 5.2 between a domain pair and analyze the distribution of the measure. Figures are omitted for the lack of space. We observe that the distribution of the keselj distance using heuristic I as described in Sect. 5.2 is very skewed. Such skewness has an impact on the clustering by producing a smaller number of large size clusters and large number of small size clusters. On the other hand, we notice that heuristic-II reduces the skewness, with a similar insight on the resulting cluster size.

Next, we performed a hierarchical (with complete linkage; defined as $d(A, B) = \max_{a \in A, b \in B} d(a, b)$) clustering algorithm with an appropriate threshold k on pairwise distance. Setting the threshold affects the way clusters are formed: this means that the algorithm will cluster two domains if the distance between them is less than k. A threshold $k = 0.4$ is empirically found to be appropriate in our dataset. Table 3 shows basic statistics of cluster analysis for both the trigram and keselj distance metric while using heuristic-II. Table 4, shows the quantile summary on the size of the top 50 clusters.

Table 3. Cluster statistics of the result when using heuristic-II.

# domains	# clusters	Avg size	# dom (top-50)
7,830	1893	4.1	5631
7,830	1774	4.4	5763

Table 4. Quantile summary of the top 50 clusters NSSF and heuristic-II.

Distance	min	25%	50%	75%	max
Trigram	8	12	19	50	3536
Keselj	8	11	19	54	3535

Clusters vetting. To analyze the identity of the resulting clustering by understanding the use of the domain names, we again selected the top 50 clusters in size and obtained the registration information of those domain names. We extracted the registration information for the domain name (registrant and registrar) from the whois database. We found that all domain names within each cluster belong to the same registrant, and are registered via the same registrar. For legal reasons, we could not present further details on the registrants, however Table 5 shows the quantile distribution of the percentage of domains that belong to the same owner in a cluster.

Table 5. Quantile summary (%) of domains hosted by a same owner per heuristic-II.

Median	min	25%	50%	75%	max
60	2.83	22.01	58.05	99.50	100

Table 6. Quantile summary (%) of domains hosted by the same service per heuristic-II.

Median	min	25%	50%	75%	max
50	11.11	28.57	59.35	100	100

Finally, we performed a similar analysis with host information to check whether domain names that were grouped within the same cluster also were hosted on the same host, or using the same hosting providers. Our analysis shows that it is almost always the case that such domains would be hosted using the same hosting infrastructure. For legal reasons, we could not name those individual domains and their hosting providers, however general statistics on the quartile distribution of the percentage of domain names hosted by the same hosting provider residing in the same cluster are shown in Table 6.

6 Prediction Model

Given the value of the NSSF as discussed above, we looked further into the predictability of this feature. As discussed in Sect. 1, there are many interesting applications that can be built on such predictability. The final interesting aspect that we examined is the power of an off-the-shelf prediction algorithm in predicting the NSSF. For that, we built a time series based prediction model to estimate the number of name servers that a domain will interact with, given the history of interaction of the respective domain.

We used Autoregressive Integrated Moving Average (ARIMA) [8] model for prediction. In this model, instead of time, we consider ordered events to build the time series data (i.e., the index used in the

Table 7. Prediction accuracy for top domains

Domain	True value	Predicted value	MSE
amazingweb007.com	2 , 2	2.47 , 2.23	0.136
teknotigr	2 , 1	2.4 , 1.3	0.125
climate13.com	2 , 2	2.35 , 2.15	0.072

NSSF is used as for the time series). We trained the model with populated data series and predicted the number of interactive name server for future events. To validate our model, we omitted the data points for the last 2 events, predicted them, and computed the errors using the mean sum of squares (MSE; defined as $1/n \sum_{i=1}^{n}(a_i - b_i)^2$). Table 7, presents prediction results for the top three switching domains in Table 2. By rounding the predicted values, we can marginalize the error resulting from the prediction, and achieve a high accuracy of the results.

7   Related Work

To the best of our knowledge, there is no prior work in the literature that looked at the dynamics of associations between name servers and domain names at the level of granularity we use in this work to understand domain names' usage. However, there are several works in the literature on using aggregates of the name servers as a feature for identifying the intended use of domain names, as pointed out earlier. For example, the work in [3–5], identifies the number of name servers associated with a domain name over a period of time as a feature for extrapolating the label of malicious or benign and show that this feature is very effective.

Timeseries are used in the literature, in the context of intrusion detection systems, to character and process intrusion alerts at an aggregate level [16,17]. Other security applications of time series have found in detection of distributed of denial services [18,19], and authentication [20], among others.

The use of machine learning techniques in security, including clustering, is not new. There has been a large body of work in the matter, summarized in [21] and [13].

8   Conclusion

We analyzed the name server switching patterns for domains to potentially use this information for security applications. We used the evolution of name servers to build an identifier for domains that can be used to group domains of similar behavior. We clustered domains based on footprint and observed that the majority of domains in a cluster have the same owner and are hosted by the same provider. We have also presented a time series analysis to estimate number of name servers that a domain will interact with.

References

1. Salchow, K.: Load balancing 101: Nuts and bolts. White Paper, F5 Networks Inc. (2007)
2. Nygren, E., Sitaraman, R.K., Sun, J.: The akamai network: a platform for high-performance internet applications. SIGOPS Oper. Syst. Rev. **44**(3), 2–19 (2010)
3. Snoke, T.: Watching domains that changes dns servers frequently. CERT/CC Blog (2013)
4. He, Y., Zhong, Z., Krasser, S., Tang, Y.: Mining dns for malicious domain registrations. In: CollaborateCom (2010)
5. Felegyhazi, M., Kreibich, C., Paxson, V.: On the potential of proactive domain blacklisting. In: LEET (2010)
6. Lardinois, F.: More than 250m domain names have now been registered, almost half are .com and .net, April 2013. http://tcrn.ch/1i3G0Fh
7. Shumway, R., Stofer, D.: Time Series Analysis and Its Applications. Springer, New York (2000)

8. Box, G., Jenkins, G.: Time Series Analysis: Forecasting and Control. Holden-Day, San Francisco (1970)

9. Alwan, L.C., Roberts, H.V.: Time-series modeling for statistical process control. J. Bus. Econ. Stat. **6**, 87–95 (1988)

10. Porter, S.: Hudak: an application of the seasonal fractionally differenced model to the monetary aggregates. J. Am. Stat. Assoc. **85**, 338–344 (1990)

11. Shumway, R., Stoffer, D.: Dynamic linear models with switching. J. Am. Stat. Assoc. **86**(415), 763–769 (1991)

12. Chrysostome Bolot, J., Hoschka, P.: Performance engineering of the world wide web: application to dimensioning and cache design. Comput. Netw. **28**, 1397–1405 (1996)

13. Mohaisen, A., Alrawi, O.: Amal: highfidelity, behavior-based automated malware analysis and classification. Technical report, Verisign Labs (2013)

14. Lin, D.: An information-theoretic definition of similarity. In: ICML (1998)

15. Miao, Y., Kešelj, V., Milios, E.: Document clustering using character n-grams: a comparative evaluation with term-based and word-based clustering. In: CIKM (2005)

16. Viinikka, J., Debar, H., Mé, L., Lehikoinen, A., Tarvainen, M.: Processing intrusion detection alert aggregates with time series modeling. Inf. Fusion **10**, 312–324 (2009)

17. Axelsson, S.: Intrusion detection systems: a survey and taxonomy. Technical report, BTH (2000)

18. Cabrera, J.B., Lewis, L., Qin, X., Lee, W., Prasanth, R.K., Ravichandran, B., Mehra, R.K.: Proactive detection of distributed denial of service attacks using mib traffic variables-a feasibility study. In: IEEE IM (2001)

19. Liu, H., Kim, M.S.: Real-time detection of stealthy ddos attacks using time-series decomposition. In: IEEE ICC (2010)

20. Mayrhofer, R., Gellersen, H.-W.: Shake well before use: authentication based on accelerometer data. In: LaMarca, A., Langheinrich, M., Truong, K.N. (eds.) Pervasive 2007. LNCS, vol. 4480, pp. 144–161. Springer, Heidelberg (2007)

21. Sommer, R., Paxson, V.: Outside the closed world: on using machine learning for network intrusion detection. In: IEEE Security and Privacy, pp. 305–316 (2010)

A Trustless Broker Based Protocol to Discover Friends in Proximity-Based Mobile Social Networks

Fizza Abbas, Ubaidullah Rajput, Rasheed Hussain, Hasoo Eun,
and Heekuck Oh$^{(\boxtimes)}$

Department of Computer Science and Engineering, Hanyang University,
Seoul, South Korea
fizza_alvi85@yahoo.com, hkok@hanyang.ac.kr

Abstract. Due to the rapid growth of online social networking and mobile devices, proximity based mobile social networks (PMSN) are gaining increasing popularity. PMSN refers to the social interaction among physically proximate mobile users where they directly communicate through Bluetooth/Wi-Fi. In PMSN, while making friends, users match their profiles in accordance with their interests. In this regard, preserving a user's privacy is crucial during profile matching. Users use their profiles for matching. An attacker in user's near proximity can learn these profiles' values. This poses significant threat to a user's privacy. In this regard, we propose a protocol to preserve user's sensitive information. During discovery of friends in our protocol we use a broker that is an intermediate entity between interacting mobile users. Our protocol does not require trustworthy broker and hence no valuable information is given to broker that can cause a privacy threat. For secure computations paillier encryption has been used in our protocol. Furthermore, we implement and analyze our protocol to show its acceptable computational and communication cost.

Keywords: Proximity based mobile social network · Broker · Interests · Paillier encryption

1 Introduction

With the explosion of mobile devices, mobile social networks (MSNs) are becoming an intimate part of our lives. People use Facebook, Twitter, Hi5 and other online social networks (OSNs) to find their old college friends, to find job according to their skills, salary and level of experience [1]. MSN is the combination of mobile computing and social networks. MSN not only enables people to use their existing online social networks (OSNs) anywhere and anytime, but also introduce numerous mobility-oriented applications. These applications include services which help mobile user to search friends having same interests or attributes by using matchmaking mechanism through which users share their common

© Springer International Publishing Switzerland 2015
K.-H. Rhee and J.H. Yi (Eds.): WISA 2014, LNCS 8909, pp. 216–227, 2015.
DOI: 10.1007/978-3-319-15087-1_17

interests. Matchmaking applications are very popular nowadays. Among them, an important service is to make new social connections/friends within one's physical proximity based on matching of their personal profiles. Proximity-based mobile social networking (PMSN) refers to the social interaction among physically proximate mobile users. In contrast to traditional web-based online social networking, PMSN can enable more tangible face-to-face social interactions in public places such as universities, subways, gardens, shopping malls and hospitals. Social serendipity [3], SmokeScreen [4], Mobiclique [5] and E-SmallTalker [8] etc. are MSN applications that match one with nearby people for dating or friend-making based on their common interests. There are many useful ways where matchmaking can help users to improve themselves, for example in their social life, in finding people with common hobbies and even in health issues. To preserve a user's privacy, matchmaking needs to address a few issues. During the matchmaking phase a user needs to show their interests to other user so that their common interests can be matched. However, there are various scenarios in which a user may not want to disclose her interests to other user unless she is sure that other user has same interests. Consider a scenario where a patient in a hospital may wish to find someone with same disease or symptoms she is suffering, but on the other hand, she does not want to reveal her disease to anyone who does not has that disease. This kind of scenarios make matchmaking a challenge for the privacy concerned users. In PMSN, match-making mechanisms also have another criterion according to mobile user location. This criterion is based on a user's location so that on successful matchmaking people can meet with each other and share their experience with respect to their matched attributes. Due to the described above threats, users are putting themselves at risk both offline (e.g. stalking) and online (e.g. identity theft). Therefore, following concerns should be resolved [2].

- The privacy protection of users is related to both their profiles and their profile matching results.
- Protection from malicious users who are curious about the personal information of others.
- Protection from neighbors in mobile environment who may eavesdrop, store, and correlate their personal information.
- The Internet keeps a permanent record of the online conversation which can be tracked.

This paper proposes a privacy preserving protocol for profile matchmaking in PMSN. Our protocol blindly computes the intersection set of the attributes of participants with the help of an additive homomorphic scheme known as Paillier encryption. Moreover, we have introduced the concept of a trustless broker which is an intermediate entity in our protocol and in case of compromise no valuable information will be revealed to the attacker. The reminder of the paper is organized as follow. Section 2 gives related work. Section 3 includes preliminaries. Section 4 provides proposed protocol. In Sect. 5 performance evaluation is discuss. Section 6 provides conclusion and future work.

2   Related Work

Realizing the potential benefits brought by the PMSNs, recent research efforts have been put on to improve the effectiveness and efficiency of the secure and privacy preserved profile matchmaking computation among the PMSN user. This section highlights these protocols and techniques proposed by different authors and also present their limitations.

2.1   Centralized Approach

The protocols which follow the centralized approach rely on some trusted third party (TTP). For example Social Serendipity [3] approach relies on server containing users' profiles along with matchmaking preferences. The profiles are similar to those stored in other social software programs such as LinkedIn and Match.com. Smoke screen [4] replaces trusted server with a service provider plus an opaque identifier to protect real identities. It also introduces a broker that knows matching result. These approaches have limitations, for example, not all users are willing to report their sensitive personal information such as interest and Geo-location to a central server. Looptmix [6] and Gatsby [7] are some other approaches in which a server tracks users' location, saves information into its database and then performs matchmaking. But a central server can have the risk of being compromised.

2.2   Distributed Approach

In distributed approach user broadcast their information like in MobiClique [5], in which users download information from Facebook to their device and broadcast it to any nearby Bluetooth device and then performs matchmaking between the receiver and owner by sharing profile information. The drawback in these approaches is the absence of an arbitrator in case of a malicious activity by a user and also burden of computing intersection on user's device.

2.3   Private Set Intersection (PSI) Protocols

Matchmaking protocol can also be described as private cardinality of set intersection (PCSI) problem or private set intersection (PSI) problem [9,10]. Private set intersection (PSI) deals with the finding of common objects. The term emerged from set theory where intersection operation is used to find common elements in two sets. Private cardinality of set intersection (PCSI) only provides the number of matched elements. Many authors uses Commutative encryption based protocol to solve PSI and PCSI problems [11]. Commutative encryption states that $Ek_1 (Ek_2 (m)) = Ek_2 (Ek_1 (m'))$. That means if m is encrypted with a secret key and again encrypted by another key then changing the order will not have any effect on the result. Either of the users will know that $m = m'$ only when $Ek_1 (Ek_2 (m)) = Ek_2 (Ek_1 (m'))$, but none of them could know the information of second party outside of the intersection because of lack of necessary key information. However, mostly commutative encryption primitives are all deterministic, which means they provide weaker security guarantees. In [11], authors uses commutative encryption and TTP but only in setup phase for certifying users' interest. The protocol is based on asymmetric key cryptography. However, this protocol can only be used to find a friend, without considering the best one who has the largest number of mutual interests with initiator. Wang et al. proposed a protocol [12] which is a further enhancement of [11] work. In their work, an initiator can find the best match among the candidates, and only exchange attributes intersection set with the best match, while other users only know the size of the attributes intersection set mutually. This protocol prevents against semi-honest attacks and malicious attacks. But this approach only utilizes Bluetooth technology. Also, there is a verification server (VS) which is used to certify a user's identity and also certify the interests a user have. But due to the use of commutative encryption it inherent the drawbacks of deterministic encryption, because the number of users interests comprises a finite set hence multiple run of the protocol may leak information about different queries.

2.4   Paillier Encryption Based Protocol

In [13–15] authors used paillier encryption for secure communication. Previous approaches are mostly based on coarse grained approach. To get more better result authors proposed fine grained approaches using paillier encryption. These approaches use paillier encryption computation on mobile device which can be costly.

At the end of literature survey we conclude that the distributed protocol prove too costly for mobile devices because all computations are on mobile device. While centralized approaches rely heavily trust on the "trusted" server assumption. The approaches presented [11,12] use commutative encryption which is computationally not much feasible. In this regard, we propose a protocol which uses a broker which securely and blindly computes intersection of users' interests. The protocol is also secure against semi-honest users as well as the man-in-middle attacks. Moreover, the protocol utilizes a non-deterministic encryption technique to prevent the server use brute force attack on limited number of interested to find their equivalent encryption. This make our broker trust less entity in Protocol.

3   Preliminaries

This section describes adversary model, assumptions, cryptographic tool and system model.

3.1   Adversary Model

In this paper, we focus on the users that want to perform matchmaking in a region or proximity without disclosing their personal information. These are the users with mobile devices. Our adversary model considers semi-honest users. These are those users which follow the protocol but are curious to learn about other user's interests. For example consider a scenario in which two parties are running a matchmaking protocol then one of them can try to learn other's interests while not revealing his interests fully or showing only a subset of his interests. Our protocol prevents user to collude. We also consider the scenario when users can collude with each other. However we do not consider the collusion among users and server.

3.2 Assumptions

In our protocol we assume that when a user is connected with the broker, then the broker will not learn her location. We can encounter it with the help of Orbot [17] which is free proxy software available at Google play for android devices. Any phone using Orbot can surf the web anonymously. Orbot uses Tor to use Internet securely by encrypting the internet traffic. It hides the IP address by bouncing through different computers over the Internet. A user installs an Orbot supported web browser such as Orweb [17] and then can access broker for anonymous communication.

3.3 Paillier Encryption

A Probabilistic Cryptosystem is a Public Key Cryptosystem [18]. In probabilistic encryption, the encryption results are probabilistic instead of deterministic. The same plaintext may map to two different ciphertexts at two different probabilistic encryption processes:

$$C_1 = E_k(M), C_2 = E_k(M), C_3 = E_k(M), ..., C_n = E_k(M)$$

The Paillier Cryptosystem provides significant facilities to guarantee the security of the designed protocols. Our approach rely uses Paillier cryptosystem that is s an additive homomorphic cryptosystem; this means that, given only the public-key and the encryption of m_1 and m_2, one can compute the encryption of $m_1 + m_2$. It is suitable for our scenario and semantically secure for sufficiently large N and g which are of 1024 and 160 bits. Under this assumption:

- a public key$<N, g>$ is of 1184 bits.
- a ciphertext is of 2048 bits.
- a Paillier encryption needs two 1024-bit exponentiations
  $c = g^m . r^n \ mod \ n^2$
- one 2048-bit multiplication, and a Paillier decryption costs essentially one 2048-bit exponentiation $m = L(c^{\lambda(n)}) \ mod \ n^2) \mu \ mod \ n$ where
  $\lambda = [(p-1)(q-1)]$
  $n = p.q$
  $g = $ non zero integer in $\mathbb{Z}_{n^2}$
  $r = $ random number
  $L(.) = $ Car Michael's Theorem

3.4   System Model

Our proposed system comprises of three participants: Initiator, Broker and Users in a region. Fig. 1 depicts the overall system components

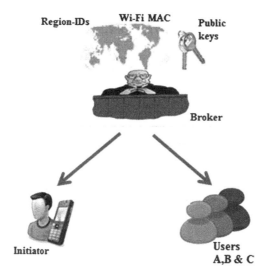

Fig. 1. System model

1. **Initiator:** An initialer starts the protocol and send request to broker to find users in his proximity.
2. **Broker:** Broker keeps a database (DB) for each user and his corresponding region. It has the ability to find which of the users are in the same region. It also holds the public key and MAC address of the Wi-Fi module of user's device. This is necessary because in case of malicious activity broker can block the device for taking part further in protocol. We assume that this information cannot be altered by a user. To support our assumption we argue this restriction can easily be made during the implementation of the protocol.

Table 1. Sample DB of broker

User Pseudonym	Public Key	Region-ID	WI-FI Mac address
A	16UwLL9Ris	20ABC2	00-15-E9-2B-99-3C
B	QfPqBUvKof	30AGF8	00-18-C1-4A-88-5B
C	HmBQ7wMtj	25HD1	00-21-D3-8C-52-6B
-	-	-	-
-	-	-	-

Such that, a client side application, installed on a user device can get its MAC address and send it to broker. In Table 1, a sample DB is illustrated.

3. **Users in a region:** In our approach users are divided in regions based on their proximity. Each region has a unique Region-ID. Regions can be made large enough to blur the exact location of users. In the proposed approach we divide the geographic space of the world into cloaking regions. This concept is similar to our previous work in [16] as shown in Fig. 2.

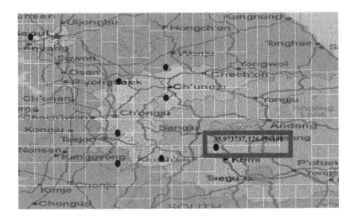

Fig. 2. An illustration of the concept of regions [16]

Note that each user has a light-weight client side application as discussed earlier that has the ability to send Region-ID to Broker, generate public keys and also encrypt a user's interests/attributes. This application also sends the Wi-Fi MAC address of the user's device to the broker. The application is light weight and can be easily handled by today's smart phones' hardware. Furthermore this application does not need to do paillier computations that can be costly to perform on mobile device. In our protocol the broker performs this computation.

4   Proposed Protocol

This section describe our proposed protocol. In our protocol each user is identified by using his paillier public key and his device by Wi-Fi MAC. At the time of registration, the client side application generates a paillier public private key pair. Besides this the client side application calculates the current region id of the user with respect to its longitude and latitude coordinates acquired by GPS and sends the Region-ID to the broker.

In our protocol, when an initiator initiates the protocol request, the broker finds her Region-ID from its database and locates other users in that region. For the sake of the simplicity we are assuming that broker finds three users

Table 2. Notations

Notation	Explanations
I	Initiator
A, B, C	Users
$I_1, I_2,...,I_n$	Initiator's interests
$A_1, A_2,...,A_n$	A's interests
$B_1, B_2,...,B_n$	B's interests
$C_1, C_2,...,C_n$	C's interests

Table 3. Number of interests

Serial Number	Interest Name	Value
1	sports	1
2	TV	0
3	reading	0
-	-	-
-	-	-
30	Movies	1

in the same region as initiator. Table 2 represents the notations we are using in our protocol for initiator and users. Note that the client side application presents each user with a similar interface where interests are shown with their corresponding positions which forms a vector as shown in Table 3. If a user selects one attribute as his interest then the client side application assigns a value of 1 to the corresponding position otherwise 0. This will form a vector comprises of 1 and 0 value. The vector will be look like v = {1, 0, 0,...,1}.

4.1   Working of Proposed Protocol

Following is the working mechanism of the proposed protocol. First initiator requests to start the protocol. She first sends the request (REQ) to initiate the protocol to the broker along with her interests wrapped in paillier encryption public key $(I_1)_{PK_I}$, $(I_2)_{PK_I}$,...., $(I_n)_{PKI}$. It is to be noted that these values are simply the encryption of integer 1 or 0. The broker then finds the users in the corresponding region and finds A,B and C (as per our assumption). It then sends public keys of A,B and C to I while sends RTS (Request To Send) to A, B and C for their interests in their public keys. Users A, B and C encrypt the interests in their respective public keys and send to broker. It should be noted that the client side application write these encrypted values in a serialize manner on a file. (This will be explained more in the implementation). Meanwhile I also encrypt her interests in A, B and C's public keys and sends them to broker. Now broker have interest of I and each of A, B and C. Broker calculates the

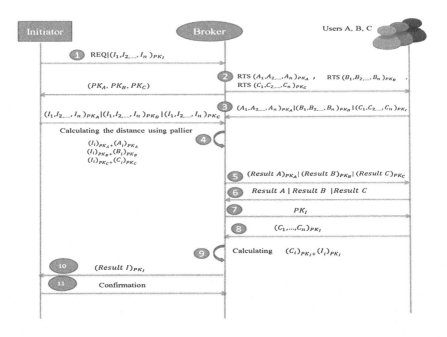

Fig. 3. Proposed protocol

sum using homomorphic properties of paillier encryption system for each of the encrypted values of I with each encrypted attribute of users. The Fig. 3 explains working of our proposed protocol.

Broker then reshuffles the results and sends this back to each user. The purpose of reshuffling is to prevent a user knowing in advance which attributes have been matched, thus the users with low number of matches (and hence later be discarded) will not be able to know the interests of I. It should be noted that if two users have same interests then their resultant value will be 2 (as they have same attribute (same integer values)) or a negative 1 or 0 (in case of a mismatch in corresponding attribute). Upon receiving the values, users will decrypt and discard the values of 0 and 1, and then adds the 2's. Hence the user with the highest sum is closest to I in term of matching interests. All the users will send their sums to the broker.

Let us suppose that the results were 10, 8 and 12 for users A, B and C respectively (having matched 5, 4 and 6 of their interests). The broker will select C because it has the highest matching attributes. Now it will start to confirm this result by providing C with the public key of I. C will encrypt his interests in I's public key and sends this back to broker. Note that broker already have I's interests in her public key which I gave to broker in the start. Broker will now again calculates the difference and sends this to I. I will decrypt it and sends the results back to broker that it is indeed a score of 12 and broker will notify both parties that they can proceed to be friends.

5   Performance Evaluation

This section includes analysis of proposed protocol and implementation.

5.1   Analysis of Proposed Protocol

In our proposed protocol we consider semi-honest users. We use a broker as intermediate party but consider it as trustless entity. In case broker compromises no valuable information can be revealed to an attacker. In fact the attacker only gets region-ID and public keys and Wi-Fi MAC address which are of no use of him. Furthermore, the broker blindly computes the intersection of users' interests and due to non-deterministic nature of paillier it cannot find any interest value by launching a brute force attack. In our proposed protocol there is little computational overhead on user's mobile device due to encryption/decryption. This overhead is kind of a trade off because we are not trusting broker to let our interest know. Also the broker chooses candidate users randomly in region which prevents an attacker from performing Sybil attacks. Protocol performs paillier arithmetic computations on broker. Our implementation also shows less communication overhead for attribute exchanging between broker and users and our results show that a server is quite efficient to perform arithmetic on encrypted values.

5.2   Implementation

We implemented the client side application with the help of a Java extension for Android, in Android Enabled Eclipse environment, named as Android Developers Tools (ADT). The application saves encryptions for each interest serially on a .ser format for storing BigIntegers. The .ser file is then compressed yielding

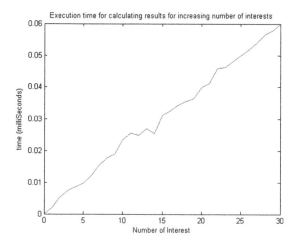

Fig. 4. Execution time for calculating results for increasing number of interests

a size of 1.5 KB for 30 encrypted attribute values. This compressed .ser file is then transferred to the broker and broker also uses the same file format and compression to sending back the results.

We took results of our implementation with respect to execution time on a server and the data which is being transferred to and from server to mobile devices. Our test bench comprises of an Intel i7 machine with 4 GB RAM acting as broker. Fig. 4 shows the execution time for calculating results for increasing number of interests from 5 to 30. It shows a linear increase in computation time from 0.00 to 0.06 of a milliseconds. The file containing 30 encrypted interests is taking around 1.5 KB.

6   Conclusion and Future work

Privacy preserving profile match making is an important issue in PMSN. Calculation of intersection sets with the help of a centralized trusted server is not an efficient solution while decentralized approaches have their own drawbacks like absence of an arbitrator in case of deviation of protocol by a user. They also suffer with the computational burden on users' mobile devices. After analyzing various approaches we propose an efficient solution which utilizes a broker who does not need to be trusted. Not only this solution takes benefit from the advantages of a centralized server like using computational power of the server but also it prevents a user's device from computationally expensive cryptographic arithmetic operations. The broker blindly calculates the users interests. Our results show that our scheme is not only efficient with respect to running time but also have lower communications overheads with respect to number of encrypted attributes exchanging between users and the broker. In future we try to enhance the protocol by reducing the computational and communication overhead.

References

1. Beach, A., Gartrell, M., Han, R.: Solutions to security and privacy issues in mobile social networking. In: IEEE International Conference on Computational Science and Engineering, pp. 1036–1042 (2009)
2. Kayastha, N., Niyato, D., Wang, P., Hossain, E.: Applications, architectures, and protocol design issues for mobile social networks: a survey. Proc. IEEE **99**, 2130–2158 (2011)
3. Eagle, N., Pentland, A.: Social serendipity: mobilizing social software. IEEE J. Pervasive Comput. **4**, 28–34 (2005)
4. Cox, L.P., Dalton, A., Marupadi, V.: SmokeScreen: flexible privacy control for presence-sharing. In: ACM 5th International Conference on Mobile Systems, Applications and Services, pp. 233–245 (2007)
5. Pietilainen, A.K., Oliver, E., LeBrun, J., Varghese, G., Diot, C.: Mobiclique: middleware for mobile social networking. In: 2nd ACM Workshop on Online Social Networks (WOSN), pp. 49–54 (2009)
6. Looptmix. http://www.looptmix.com
7. Gatsby. http://meetgatsby.com

8. Yang, Z., Zhang, B., Dai, J., Champion, A., Xaun, D., Li, D.: E-SmallTalker: a distributed mobile system for social networking in physical proximity. In: IEEE International Conference on Distributed Computer System, pp. 468–477 (2010)

9. Freedman, M.J., Nissim, K., Pinkas, B.: Efficient private matching and set intersection. In: Cachin, C., Camenisch, J.L. (eds.) EUROCRYPT 2004. LNCS, vol. 3027, pp. 1–19. Springer, Heidelberg (2004)

10. Agrawal, R., Evfimievski, A., Srikant, R.: Information sharing across private databases. In: ACM International Conference on Management of Data (SIGMOD), pp. 86–97 (2003)

11. Xie, Q., Hengartner, U.: Privacy-preserving matchmaking for mobile social networking secure against malicious users. In: IEEE 9th International Conference on Trust, Security and Privacy in Computing and Communications, pp. 252–259 (2011)

12. Wang, Y., Zhang, T., Li, H., Peng, J.: Efficient privacy preserving matchmaking for mobile social networking against malicious users. In: IEEE 11th International Conference on Trust, Security and Privacy in Computing and Communications, pp. 610–615 (2012)

13. Zhang, L., Li, X.Y., Liu, Y.: Message in a sealed bottle: privacy preserving friending in social networks. In: IEEE 33rd International Conference on Distributed Computing Systems (ICDCS), pp. 327–336 (2013)

14. Zhang, R., Zhang, Y., Sun, J., Yan, G.: Fine-grained private matching for proximity-based mobile social networking. In: IEEE INFOCOM, pp. 1969–1977 (2012)

15. Zhang, R., Zhang, Y., Sun, J., Yan, G.: Privacy-preserving profile matching for proximity-based mobile social networking. IEEE J. Sel. Areas Commun. **31**, 656–668 (2013)

16. Fizza, A., Rasheed, H., Junggab, S., Heekuck, O.: Privacy preserving cloud-based computing platform (PPCCP) for using location based services. In: 6th IEEE/ACM International Conference on Utility and Cloud Computing (UCC), pp. 60–66 (2013)

17. Torproject. https://www.torproject.org/docs/android.html.en

18. Zhang, F., Zhao, G., Xing, T.: Privacy-preserving distributed k-nearest neighbor mining on horizontally partitioned multi-party data. In: Huang, R., Yang, Q., Pei, J., Gama, J., Meng, X., Li, X. (eds.) ADMA 2009. LNCS, vol. 5678, pp. 755–762. Springer, Heidelberg (2009)

Cryptography

Shared and Searchable Encrypted Data for Semi-trusted Servers with Controllable Sharing Property

Minkyu Joo and Pil Joong Lee[⊠]

Department of Electrical Engineering, POSTECH, Pohang, Republic of Korea
{mkjoo,pjl}@postech.ac.kr

Abstract. To support encrypted data sharing and searching between multiple users in the remote data storage server, in 2011, Dong et al. proposed a scheme for data encryption with keyword search in multi-user (all-user) settings. The scheme allows all authorized users to share their encrypted data. The encrypted data can be searched using keyword search method by all users. The keyword search method makes the server find the encrypted data containing encrypted keywords without decrypting them, so information of both the data and the keywords is not exposed to the server. However, the scheme only considered a scenario sharing all stored data with users, and did not consider a case for storing private data in the server. In this work, we modify the Dong et al.'s scheme to propose a scheme that a user can select his private data when he wants to share them with all users in the system.

Keywords: Searchable encryption · Re-encryption

1 Introduction

As the amount of digital data increases, people want to outsource their data to a remote data storage server (semi-trusted server). However, in this case, the contents of the stored data could be exposed to the server. Thus, data confidentiality is one of the important requirements. A typical solution is that a data owner encrypts data using his secret key. However, in this solution, the server cannot search specific data because the contents of the encrypted data are not seen to the server. Therefore, the user must download all encrypted data.

To solve this problem, searchable encryption schemes in single-user setting have been proposed [1, 5]. These schemes allow users to search encrypted data based on keywords with maintaining the confidentiality of both the data and the keywords.

This research was supported in part by the MSIP (Ministry of Science, ICT and Future Planning), Korea, under the "IT Consilience Creative Program" (NIPA-2014-H0201-14-1001) supervised by the NIPA (National IT Industry Promotion Agency) and in part by the MSIP (Ministry of Science, ICT and Future Planning), Korea, under the ITRC (Information Technology Research Center) support program (NIPA-2014-H0301-14-1004) supervised by the NIPA (National IT Industry Promotion Agency).

© Springer International Publishing Switzerland 2015
K.-H. Rhee and J.H. Yi (Eds.): WISA 2014, LNCS 8909, pp. 231–243, 2015.
DOI: 10.1007/978-3-319-15087-1_18

Song et al. proposed a scheme that the entities who have a shared secret key can store encrypted data with encrypted keywords, and search the encrypted data using the encrypted keywords [5]. In Boneh et al.'s scheme [1], people who know a user's public key can encrypt and store data with keywords for the user, and only the user holding the corresponding private key can generate a trapdoor for specific keywords to search the encrypted data.

Nowadays, many practical remote data storage service provide a functionality which allows all authorized users in a group to share their data, and search the data. A single-user setting searchable encryption is not appropriate to be applied to this situation. If we uses a single-user setting searchable encryption in this case, we have to encrypt the same data n times where n is the number of users in the system. A common approach to solve this problem is that all authorized user share the same secret key which is used to store and search data. However, in this case if the system revokes the rights of a user to exploit the system, the system must generate a new secret key and transmit it to all users except the user to be revoked. Therefore, the revocation process is very inefficient in terms of computation and communication costs.

Considering them, a scheme for data encryption with keyword search in multi-user (all-user) settings is proposed [4]. The scheme allows any authorized users to share their data with all users and search all data stored by all users. In [4], semi-trusted proxy server is used for storing and searching each user's data without leaking any information about the data to the server. The trusted key management server (fully trusted entity) generates both user side keys and the corresponding server side keys. To store data with keywords, a user encrypts both the data and the keywords using the user side keys, and sends the result to the proxy server. The proxy server then re-encrypts the given ciphertexts with the corresponding server side key. To search data for a keyword, any user in the system generates a trapdoor for the keyword, and sends it to the proxy server. Then, the proxy server searches the encrypted data using the trapdoor. If the proxy server finds the encrypted data that the user wants, the proxy server pre-decrypts the data with the server side keys corresponding to the user who generated the trapdoor. Then, the user decrypts the pre-decrypted data with his keys to obtain plaintext of the data. When a user executes the above operations, he only uses the user side keys only known to him. Because of this, the scheme can revoke a specific user's key without affecting other user's key. Therefore, the scheme can provide revocation process with lower cost than that of the above common approach which is sharing the same secret key with all users.

However, in [4], the scheme only considered a scenario sharing all stored data with users, and did not consider a case for storing private data in the server. In this paper, we focus on a scenario where a user stores his private data and the user can share his specific private data with all users at any time he wants. This scenario is more practical than that of the Dong et al.'s scheme because many people have private data and sometimes they want to share their specific data with all users. We can use the Dong et al.'s scheme to satisfy our scenario in two ways. First trivial solution uses an additional private storage space such as a hard disk. At first, a user stores his data in private data storage. When he wants to share the data, he searches his data which are stored in private data storage, and stores it in shared data storage. However, the first trivial solution requires an additional private data storage and the user needs to store data two times in total when he shares his data. Second trivial solution uses the proxy server as both the private data storage and the shared data storage. Before a user stores data to the proxy server, the user encrypts the data using a symmetric encryption scheme with his secret key which is different from the user's private key in the Dong et al.'s scheme. The user then uses Dong et al.'s scheme to store the encrypted data. Namely, in second trivial solution, a message of Dong et al.'s scheme is the encrypted data. Other users cannot see the contents of the data because the data are encrypted with the keys only known to the user who stored the data. However, the second trivial solution is inefficient in terms of communication and computation cost.

In this paper, we modify the Dong et al.'s scheme to satisfy our scenario in the above. In the proposed scheme, a user in the system can privately encrypt both data and keywords and store them in the proxy server. Also, the user can search his private data based on the keyword search method with preserving confidentiality of the data and the keywords against the proxy server. Only a user who privately stored the data can generate a trapdoor to search his data. Additionally, if the user wants to share his private data with all users in the system, the user generates a *Re-enc-key* for the data and the keywords. On receiving the *Re-enc-key*, the proxy server converts the private data and the private keywords to shared data and shared keywords. Lastly, all users can generate a trapdoor to search shared data. Compared with the first trivial solution using the Dong et al.'s scheme to satisfy our scenario, the proposed scheme does not need an additional private data storage. Although the first trivial solution has to store data two times (one storing the data in private data storage, one storing the data in shared data storage), the proposed scheme only stores the data one time in shared data storage. In the second trivial solution, one decryption of the data and one storing the data are required to share the data. However, in the proposed scheme, one efficient *Re-enc-key* generation and one re-encryption are required. If we generate *Re-enc-key* efficiently, the proposed scheme is more efficient in terms of communication and computation than that of the second trivial solution.

2 Preliminary

2.1 Security Definition

In this section, we describe security notions and security definitions that were proposed in [2–4].

Definition 1 (DDH assumption). We say that the DDH problem is hard if for any probabilistic polynomial time adversary A, the probability

$$\left| \Pr\left[A\left(G, q, g, g^{\alpha}, g^{\beta}, g^{\alpha\beta}\right) = 1 \right] - \Pr[A\left(G, q, g, g^{\alpha}, g^{\beta}, g^{\gamma}\right) = 1] \right|$$

is negligible in the security parameter $|q|$, where q is an order of a cyclic group G, g is a generator of G, and α, β, γ are random elements of Z_q.

References [2–4] introduced the concept of non-adaptive indistinguishability security. At first, we define some important notions based on [2–4]. D is the total documents in the system, containing the sequences of data D_j and keywords $w(D_j)$

(i.e. $D = (D_j, w(D_j)$ for $1 \leq j \leq n$, where n is the total number of the stored documents in the system). $id(D)$ is the identifier of data such as memory location. q is a query and $R_q(w)$ is the results of a query for the keyword w (i.e. $R_q(w) = \{i, id(D)\}$). A history H_t is an interaction between a user and the proxy server over t queries on total documents D. (i.e. $H_t = \{D, q_1, \ldots, q_t\}$). A view $V(H_t)$ is the information that the adversary can obtain from the history H_t. (i.e. $V(H_t) = \{id(D_1), \ldots, id(D_n), E_P(D_1), \ldots, E_P(D_n), KE_P(w(D_1)), \ldots, KE_P(w(D_n)), E_{RE}(D_1), \ldots, E_{RE}(D_l), KE_{RE}(w(D_1)), \ldots KE_{RE}(w(D_l)), q_1, \ldots, q_t\}$ where E_P is the private data encryption, KE_P is the private keyword encryption, E_{RE} is the data re-encryption for sharing, KE_{RE} is the keyword re-encryption for sharing, n is the total number of stored data, and l is the total number of shared data). A trace is all the information the adversary can obtain. (i.e. $Tr(H_t) = \{id(D_1), \ldots, id(D_n), |E_P(D_1)|, \ldots, |E_P(D_n)|, |KE_P(w(D_1))|, \ldots, |KE_P(w(D_n))|, |E_{RE}(D_1)|, \ldots, |E_{RE}(D_l)|, |KE_{RE}(w(D_1))|, \ldots, |KE_{RE}(w(D_l))|, R_q(w_1), \ldots, R_q(w_t), \Pi\}$ where Π is the search pattern over the history). The non-adaptive indistinguishability security means in the scheme the adversary cannot obtain any additional information except the information which the adversary can obtain from the traces. In other words, the scheme only leaks the information of the traces to the adversary. The basic concepts of the non-adaptive indistinguishability security is that the adversary is hard to distinguish between two non-adaptive query histories which have the same traces. The same traces means initial information is the same. Namely, if the adversary cannot obtain additional information beyond view of histories from an interaction between a user and the proxy server, the adversary cannot distinguish between the non-adaptive query histories. Then the scheme is non-adaptively indistinguishable.

Definition 2. (Non-adaptive indistinguishability against an honest but curious server). A multi-user searchable data encryption scheme is secure in the sense of non-adaptive indistinguishable against an semi-trusted server (honest but curious server) if for all query t, for all PPT adversaries A, the probability

$$\Pr[b' = b \mid (params, msk) \leftarrow Init(1^k), (k_u, k_s) \leftarrow Keygen(msk, u),$$
$$(H_{t0}, H_{t1}) \leftarrow A(k_s),$$
$$b \leftarrow \{0, 1\},$$
$$b' \leftarrow A(k_s, V_{k_u}(H_{tb}))]$$

is negligibly close to 1/2 in the security parameter k where k_u is the user side keys for every users and k_s is the corresponding sever side keys for every users.

3 The Proposed Scheme

3.1 Entities

- **The Trusted Key Management Server:** We consider the trusted key management server as fully trusted entity. The trusted key management server allows a user to join our system by generating user side keys and the proxy server side keys.

When the trusted key management server makes a decision to revoke the rights of a user to exploit the system, it requests the proxy server to delete the proxy server side keys for the user.

- **The Proxy Server:** We consider the proxy server as semi-trusted entity. The proxy server can be called honest but curious server. The proxy server correctly executes the algorithm, but it wants to obtain the information of both stored data and keywords. The proxy server can search encrypted data using a trapdoor for a keyword. In case that the result of the search is private data of the user, the proxy server sends it to the user without any operation. If the result is shared data, the proxy server pre-decrypts the encrypted data with proxy server side keys corresponding to the user who generated the trapdoor. After the decryption of the proxy server, the user can obtain plaintext by decrypting the pre-decrypted data with his private keys. Although the proxy server decrypts the encrypted data with the keys, the encrypted data is not decrypted completely, so the plaintext of the encrypted data is not exposed to the proxy server.
- **Users:** A user privately encrypts both data and keywords with his own keys, and stores them. The user can generate a trapdoor for a keyword to search the data containing the keyword over his privately stored data. A proper trapdoor cannot be generated by users who did not encrypt and store the data and the keyword. Whenever the user wants to share the private data and the private keyword, the user generates *Re-enc-keys* for the data and the keywords and sends them to the proxy server. The proxy server use *Re-enc-key* to re-encrypt both the privately encrypted data and the privately encrypted keywords, then they will be converted to both the shared data and the shared keywords. All users of the system can generate a trapdoor to search the shared data, and can decrypt the data.

3.2   Construction

Let m be a message, w be a keyword to be stored, $\underline{w}$ be a keyword that a user wants to find, $\underline{c_{m1}}''$ be a part of encrypted data that a user wants to share, and $\underline{c_{w1}}''$ be a part of encrypted keyword that a user wants to share. A message m could be data itself or a symmetric key which is used to encrypt data with hybrid encryption. In our scheme, we assume the message m is the data itself.

Setup

The trusted key management server runs $Init(1^k)$ to generate system parameters and its private keys. If user i wants to use our proposed scheme, the trusted key management server uses its private keys to run $Keygen(x, s, i)$ which generates user side keys and the proxy server keys for user i.

$Init(1^k)$: *Run by the trusted key management server.*

- Given the security parameter 1^k, determine q, g, k', k'', and l where q is the order of the group G, g is a generator of G, k' is the key size for a pseudorandom function F, k'' is the output length for a hash function H, and l is the input length for the pseudorandom function F. Define the pseudorandom function $F: \{0,1\}^{k'} \times \{0,1\}^l \to \{0,1\}^l$ and the hash function $H: \{0,1\}^* \to \{0,1\}^{k''}$.

- Choose a random element s for the key of the pseudorandom function F and another random element $x \in Z_q$, and compute $h = g^x$.
- Output public parameters $params = (G, g, q, h, F, H)$ and secret keys $msk = (x, s)$.

Keygen(x, s, i): Run by the trusted key management server.

- Choose random elements $x_{i_1}, x_{i_{11}}$, and $x_{i_{12}} \in Z_q$.
- Compute $x_{i_2} = x - x_{i_1} \bmod q$ and $x_{i_{13}} = x_{i_1} - (x_{i_{11}} + x_{i_{12}}) \bmod q$.
- Transmit $(x_{i_{11}}, x_{i_{12}}, x_{i_{13}}, s)$ securely to user i and $(x_{i_2}, x_{i_{12}})$ securely to the proxy server.

Private Data and Keyword Encryption

User i who obtained the user side keys runs *P-Keygen(i)* to generate a secret key for pseudorandom function F. User i can encrypt his private data m and keyword w_j by running *P-Data-Enc$(x_{i_{11}}, m)$* and *P-Keyword-Enc$(x_{i_{11}}, s, s_i, w_j)$* for $1 \leq j \leq n$ where n is the number of the keywords for data m, then transmits them to the proxy server.

P-Keygen(i): Run by user i.

- Choose a random element s_i for the key of the pseudorandom function F

P-Data-Enc$(x_{i_{11}}, m)$: Run by user i.

- Choose a random element $r_m \in Z_q$, and compute $c_{m1}'' = g^{r_m}$ and $c_{m2}'' = g^{r_m x_{i_{11}}} m$.
- Output $c_i''(m) = (c_{m1}'', c_{m2}'')$.

P-Keyword-Enc$(x_{i_{11}}, S, S_i, w)$: Run by user i.

- Choose a random element $r_w \in Z_q$, and compute $\sigma_w = Fs(w)$ and $\sigma_w' = Fs_i(w)$.
- Compute $c_{w1}'' = g^{r_w + \sigma_w}$, $c_{w2}'' = g^{r_w x_{i_{11}} + x_{i_{11}} \sigma_w + x_{i_{11}} \sigma_w'}$, $c_{w3}'' = H(g^{r_w x_{i_{11}} + x_{i_{11}} \sigma_w})$, and $c_{w4}'' = H(h^{r_w})$.
- Output $c_i''(w) = (c_{w1}'', c_{w2}'', c_{w3}'', c_{w4}'')$.

Private Keyword Search Method and Private Data Decryption

When user i wants to search data containing keyword $\underline{w}$, he runs *P-Trapdoor$(x_{i_{11}}, x_{i_{12}}, s_i, \underline{w})$* to generate a trapdoor for keyword $\underline{w}$ and transmits it to the proxy server. On receiving the trapdoor, the proxy server runs *P-Search$(i, T_{pi}(\underline{w}), E(D_i), x_{i_{12}})$* and transmits the output to user i, User i then can obtain the data m by running *P-Data-Dec$(x_{i_{11}}, c_i''(m))$*.

P-Trapdoor$(x_{i_{11}}, x_{i_{12}}, s_i, \underline{w})$: Run by user i.

- Choose a random element $r_{pt} \in Z_q$ and compute $\sigma_{\underline{w}}' = Fs_i(\underline{w})$.
- Compute $t_{p1} = g^{r_{pt}}$ and $t_{p2} = g^{r_{pt} x_{i_{12}} + x_{i_{11}} \sigma_{\underline{w}}'}$.
- Output $T_{pi}(\underline{w}) = (t_{p1}, t_{p2})$.

P-Search$(i, T_{pi}(\underline{w}), E(D_i), x_{i_{12}})$: Run by the proxy server.

- Compute $T_p = t_{p2} \cdot (t_{p1})^{-x_{i_{12}}}$.
  - $t_{p2} \cdot (t_{p1})^{-x_{i_{12}}} = g^{r_{pt} x_{i_{12}} + x_{i_{11}} \sigma_{\underline{w}}'} \cdot (g^{r_{pt}})^{-x_{i_{12}}} = g^{x_{i_{11}} \sigma_{\underline{w}}'} = T_p$.

- For each $(c_i''(m), c_i''(w)) \in E(D_i)$ where D_i is all documents of user i containing the sequences of data D and keywords $w(D)$, verify the equation $H(c_{w2}'' \cdot T_p^{-1}) = c_{w3}''$.
  - $c_{w2}'' \cdot T_p^{-1} = g^{r_w x_{i_{11}} + x_{i_{11}} \sigma_w + x_{i_{11}} \sigma_w'} \cdot (g^{x_{i_{11}} \sigma_{\underline{w}}'})^{-1}$. If $\sigma_w' = \sigma_{\underline{w}}'$, $H(c_{w2}'' \cdot T_p^{-1})$
    $= H(g^{r_w x_{i_{11}} \sigma_w}) = c_{w3}''$.

- If the above equation holds, transmit $(c_i''(m), c_{w1}'')$ to user i.

  P-Data-Dec$(x_{i_{11}}, c_i''(m))$: *Run by user i.*

- Compute $m = c_{m2}'' \cdot (c_{m1}'')^{-x_{i_{11}}}$.
  - $c_{m2}'' \cdot (c_{m1}'')^{-x_{i_{11}}} = g^{r_m x_{i_{11}}} m \cdot (g^{r_m})^{-x_{i_{11}}} = m$.

Data and Keyword Re-encryption for Sharing

If user i wants to share his private data m and keyword w with all users, he runs *Re-Enc-Keygen*$(w, c_{m1}'', c_{w1}'', x_{i_{11}}, x_{i_{12}}, x_{i_{13}})$ to obtain *Re-enc-key*, and transmits *Re-enc-key* and the trapdoor for keyword w to the proxy server (If the proxy server stored the trapdoor, it is unnecessary to transmit it to the proxy server again). If the user wants to generate *Re-enc-key* efficiently, he can generate $k_{data\text{-}re}(w)$ as $(c_{\underline{m1}}'')^{(x_{i_{12}} + x_{i_{13}})}$ and $k_{keyword\text{-}re}(w)$ as $(c_{\underline{w1}}'')^{(x_{i_{12}} + x_{i_{13}})}$. Since this *Re-enc-key* does not reveal any information, it will not decrease the security of the proposed scheme. On receiving *Re-enc-key* and the trapdoor, the proxy server runs *Re-Enc*$(i, k_{re}(w), T_{pi}(w), E(D_i), x_{i_{12}}, x_{i_2})$ to share data m and keyword w with all users.

  Data-Re-Enc-Keygen$(c_{\underline{m1}}'', x_{i_{12}}, x_{i_{13}})$: *Run by user i.*

- Choose a random element $r_{re} \in Z_q$.
- Set $k_1 = c_{\underline{m1}}''$, $k_2 = g^{r_{re}}$, and compute $k_3 = g^{r_{re} x_{i_{12}}} (c_{\underline{m1}}'')^{(x_{i_{12}} + x_{i_{13}})}$.
- Output $k_{data\text{-}re}(w) = (k_1, k_2, k_3)$.

  Keyword-Re-Enc-Keygen$(c_{\underline{w1}}'', x_{i_{12}}, x_{i_{13}})$: *Run by user i.*

- Choose a random element $r_{re}' \in Z_q$.
- Set $k_4 = c_{\underline{w1}}''$, $k_5 = g^{r_{re}'}$, and compute $k_6 = g^{r_{re}' x_{i_{12}}} (c_{\underline{w1}}'')^{(x_{i_{12}} + x_{i_{13}})}$.
- Output $k_{keyword\text{-}re}(w) = (k_4, k_5, k_6)$.

  Re-Enc-Keygen$(w, c_{\underline{m1}}'', c_{\underline{w1}}'', x_{i_{11}}, x_{i_{12}}, x_{i_{13}})$: *Run by user i.*

- Run *P-Trapdoor*$(x_{i_{11}}, x_{i_{12}}, s_i, w)$, *Data-Re-Enc-Keygen*$(c_{\underline{m1}}'', x_{i_{12}}, x_{i_{13}})$, and *Keyword-Re-Enc-Keygen*$(c_{\underline{w1}}'', x_{i_{12}}, x_{i_{13}})$.
- Outputs *Re-enc-key* $k_{re}(w) = (k_{data\text{-}re}(w), k_{keyword\text{-}re}(w))$ and $T_{pi}(w)$.

  Data-Re-Enc$(i, k_{data-re}(w), c_i''(m), x_{i_{12}}, x_{i_2})$: *Run by the proxy server.*

- Set $c_{w1}' = c_{w1}''$ and compute $c_{m2}' = c_{m2}'' \cdot (k_2)^{-x_{i_{12}}} \cdot k_3 \cdot (c_{m1}'')^{x_{i_2}}$.
  - $c_{m2}' = c_{m2}'' \cdot (k_2)^{-x_{i_{12}}} \cdot k_3 \cdot (c_{m1}'')^{x_{i_2}} = g^{r_m x_{i_{11}}} m \cdot g^{-r_{re} x_{i_{12}}} \cdot g^{r_{re} x_{i_{12}} + r_m (x_{i_{12}} + x_{i_{13}})}$.
    $g^{r_m x_{i_2}} = m g^{r_m (x_{i_{11}} + x_{i_{12}} + x_{i_{13}})} \cdot g^{r_m x_{i_2}} = g^{r_m (x_{i_1} + x_{i_2})} m = g^{r_m x} m$.
- Output $c_i'(m) = (c_{m1}', c_{m2}')$.

Keyword-Re-Enc$(i, k_{keyword-re}(w), c_i''(w), x_{i_{12}}, x_{i_2}, Tp)$: Run by the proxy server.

- Set $c_{w1}' = c_{w1}''$ and $c_{w3}' = c_{w4}''$, and compute $c_{w2}' = c_{w2}'' \cdot (k_5)^{-x_{i_{12}}} \cdot k_6 \cdot (c_{w1}'')^{x_{i_2}} \cdot T_p^{-1}$.

  • $c_{w2}' = c_{w2}'' \cdot (k_5)^{-x_{i_{12}}} \cdot k_6 \cdot (c_{w1}'')^{x_{i_2}} \cdot T_p^{-1} = g^{r_w x_{i_{11}} + x_{i_{11}} \sigma_w + x_{i_{11}} \sigma_w'} \cdot g^{-r_{re}' x_{i_{12}}} \cdot$
  $g^{r_{re}' x_{i_{12}}} (g^{r_w + \sigma_w})^{(x_{i_{12}} + x_{i_{13}})} \cdot (g^{r_w + \sigma_w})^{x_{i_2}} \cdot g^{-x_{i_{11}} \sigma_w'}$
  $= (g^{r_w + \sigma_w})^{(x_{i_{11}} + x_{i_{12}} + x_{i_{13}})} \cdot (g^{r_w + \sigma_w})^{x_{i_2}} = (g^{r_w + \sigma_w})^{(x_{i_1} + x_{i_2})} = (g^{r_w + \sigma_w})^x = h^{r_w} g^{x \sigma_w}.$

- Output $c_i'(w) = (c_{w1}', c_{w2}', c_{w3}')$.

Re-Enc$(i, k_{re}(w), T_{pi}(w), E(\mathbf{D}_i), x_{i12}, x_{i2})$: Run by the proxy server.

- Compute $T_p = t_{p2} \cdot (t_{p1})^{-x_{i_{12}}}$.

  • $t_{p2} \cdot (t_{p1})^{-x_{i_{12}}} = g^{r_{pt} x_{i_{12}} + x_{i_{11}} \sigma_w'} \cdot (g^{r_{pt}})^{-x_{i_{12}}} = g^{x_{i_{11}} \sigma_w'} = T_p$

- For each $(c_i''(m), c_i''(w)) \in E(\mathbf{D}_i)$ where $\mathbf{D}_i$ is all documents of user i containing the sequences of data D and keywords $w(D)$, find $(c_i''(m), c_i''(w))$ which holds the equation $c_{m1}'' = k_1$ and $c_{w1}'' = k_4$.

- Run *Data-Re-Enc$(i, k_{data-re}(w), c_i''(m), x_{i12}, x_{i2})$* to obtain $c_i'(m) = (c_{m1}', c_{m2}')$.

- Run *Keyword-Re-Enc$(i, k_{keyword-re}(w), c_i''w, x_{i12}, x_{i2}, T_p)$* to obtain $c_i'(w) = (c_{w1}', c_{w2}', c_{w3}')$.

- Store $c_i'(m) = (c_{m1}', c_{m2}')$ and $c_i'(w) = (c_{w1}', c_{w2}', c_{w3}')$.

Multi-user Keyword Search Method and Shared Data Decryption

Any user who wants to search for shared data containing keyword $\underline{w}$ run *M-Trapdoor$(x_{i_1}, s, \underline{w})$*. If the proxy server receives the output of the algorithm, the proxy server runs *M-Search$(i, T_{mi}(\underline{w}), E(\mathbf{D}_m), x_{i_2})$* and transmits the outputs to the user who transmitted the trapdoor for keyword $\underline{w}$. The user can obtain the data m by running *M-Data-Dec$(x_{i_1}, c_i(m))$*.

M-Trapdoor$(x_{i_1}, s, \underline{w})$: Run by user i.

- Choose a random element $r_{mt} \in Z_q$ and compute $\sigma_{\underline{w}} = Fs(\underline{w})$.
- Compute $t_{m1} = g^{r_{mt} - \sigma_{\underline{w}}}$ and $t_{m2} = h^{r_{mt}} g^{-x_{i_1} r_{mt}} g^{x_{i_1} \sigma_{\underline{w}}}$.

  • $t_{m2} = h^{r_{mt}} g^{-x_{i_1} r_{mt}} g^{x_{i_1} \sigma_{\underline{w}}} = g^{x_{i_2} r_{mt}} g^{x_{i_1} \sigma_{\underline{w}}}$.

- Output $T_{mi}(\underline{w}) = (t_{m1}, t_{m2})$.

M-Search$(i, T_{mi}(\underline{w}), E(\mathbf{D}_m), x_{i_2})$: Run by the proxy server.

- Compute $T_m = t_{m2} \cdot (t_{m1})^{-x_{i_2}}$.

  • $t_{m2} \cdot (t_{m1})^{-x_{i_2}} = g^{r_{mt} x_{i_2} + x_{i_1} \sigma_{\underline{w}}} \cdot g^{-r_{mt} x_{i_2} + x_{i_2} \sigma_{\underline{w}}} = g^{(x_{i_1} + x_{i_2}) \sigma_{\underline{w}}} = g^{x \sigma_{\underline{w}}} = T_m$.

- For each $(c_i'(m), c_i'(w)) \in E(\mathbf{D}_m)$ where $\mathbf{D}_m$ is all shared documents containing the sequences of data D and keywords $w(D)$, verify the equation $H(c_{w2}' \cdot T_m^{-1}) = c_{w3}'$.

  • $c_{w2}' \cdot T_m^{-1} = h^{r_w} g^{x \sigma_w} \cdot g^{-x \sigma_{\underline{w}}}$. If $\sigma_w' = \sigma_{\underline{w}}'$, $H(c_{w2}' \cdot T_m^{-1}) = H(h^{r_w}) = c_{w3}'$.

- If the above equation holds, set $c_{m1} = c_{m1}'$ and compute $c_{m2} = c_{m2}' \cdot (c_{m1}')^{-x_{i_2}}$.

  • $c_{m2} = c_{m2}' \cdot (c_{m1}')^{-x_{i_2}} = g^{r_m x} m \cdot g^{-r_m x_{i_2}} = g^{r_m x_{i_1}} m$.

- Transmit $c_i(m) = (c_{m1}, c_{m2})$ to user i.

M-Data-Dec$(x_{i_1}, c_i(m))$: *Run by user i.*

- Compute $m = c_{m2} \cdot (c_{m1})^{-x_{i_1}}$.
  - $c_{m2} \cdot (c_{m1})^{-x_{i_1}} = g^{r_m x_{i_1}} m \cdot (g^{r_m})^{-x_{i_1}} = m$.

Revocation

When the trusted key management server wants to revoke the rights of user i to use the scheme, the trusted key management server makes the proxy server run *Revoke(i)*.
    Revoke(i): *Run by the proxy server.*

- Delete the proxy server key $(x_{i_2}, x_{i_{12}})$ for user i.

3.3   Security Analysis

In this section, we analyze the security of the proposed scheme based on [3, 4].

Theorem 1. If the DDH problem is hard, then in the proposed scheme the private data encryption and the data re-encryption for sharing are indistinguishable under chosen-plaintext attack *(IND-CPA)* secure against the proxy server. That is, for any PPT adversary A, the probability

$$Succ^A_{data}(k) = \Pr[b' = b \mid (params, msk) \leftarrow Init(1^k), (k_u, k_s) \leftarrow Keygen(msk, u),$$
$$(m_0, m_1) \leftarrow A^{P\text{-}Data\text{-}Enc(k_u, \cdot)}(k_s),$$
$$b \leftarrow \{0, 1\},$$
$$c_i''(m_b) = P\text{-}Data\text{-}Enc(x_{i11}, m_b),$$
$$b' \leftarrow A^{P\text{-}Data\text{-}Enc(k_u, \cdot)}(k_s, c_i''(m_b))]$$

is negligibly close to 1/2 in the security parameter k where k_u is the user side keys for every users and k_s is the corresponding sever side keys for every users.

Proof. A PPT adversary A' uses A as subroutine to challenge the DDH problem.
- **Setup:** The input of A' is G, q, g, g_1, g_2, g_3 where $g_1 = g^\alpha$, $g_2 = g^\beta$, $g_3 = g^{\alpha\beta}$ or g^γ, and α, β, γ are random elements of Z_q. A' chooses H, F, s, and a random element r_1 for $h = g^{r_1}$. It then transmits (G, g, q, h, F, H) to A. For each user $i \in u$ where u is all users, A' chooses random elements $x_{i_2}, x_{i_{12}}, x_{i_{13}} \in Z_q$ and computes $g^{x_{i11}} = g_1 \cdot g^{-x_{i_{12}} -x_{i_{13}} -x_{i_2}}$. A' transmits $(i, x_{i_2}, x_{i_{12}})$ to A and keeps $(i, x_{i_2}, x_{i_{12}}, x_{i_{13}}, g^{x_{i11}})$.
- **Query:** At any time, A sends m to A' to access the private data encryption oracle, A' chooses a random element $r_2 \in Z_q$ and transmits $(g^{r_2}, g^{r_2 x_{i11}} m)$ to A. Whenever A transmits $\underline{c_{m1}}''$ to A', A' computes data re-encryption key $k_1 = \underline{c_{m1}}''$, $k_2 = g^{r_3}$, and $k_3 = g^{r_3 x_{i_{12}}} (c_{m1}'')^{(x_{i_{12}} + x_{i_{13}})}$ where r_3 is a random element of Z_q, then sends $k_{data\text{-}re}(w) = (k_1, k_2, k_3)$ to A.
- **Challenge:** A outputs m_0 and m_1, then A' chooses a random bit b and transmits $(g_2, g_3 g_2^{-x_{i_{12}} -x_{i_{13}} -x_{i_2}} m_b)$ to A. Also, A' computes $k_1' = g_2, k_2' = g^{r_4}$, and $k_3' = g^{r_4 x_{i_{12}}} (g_2)^{(x_{i_{12}} + x_{i_{13}})}$ where r_4 is a random element of Z_q, then sends $k_{data\text{-}re}'(w) = (k_1', k_2', k_3')$ to A.

– **Output:** A outputs b', A' verifies $b = b'$. If the equation holds, A' outputs 1, otherwise outputs 0.

We can consider two cases depending on the value of g_3.

- **Case 1.** $g_3 = g^\gamma$, in this case $\left(g_2, g_3 g_2^{-x_{i_{12}} - x_{i_{13}} - x_{i_2}} m_b\right) = \left(g^\beta, g^{\gamma - \beta\left(x_{i_{12}} + x_{i_{13}} + x_{i_2}\right)} m_b\right)$. If $\left(g^\beta, g^{\gamma - \beta\left(x_{i_{12}} + x_{i_{13}} + x_{i_2}\right)} m_b\right)$ is re-encrypted for sharing, then $\left(g^\beta, g^{\gamma - \beta\left(x_{i_{12}} + x_{i_{13}} + x_{i_2}\right)} g^{\beta x_{i_{12}} + x_{i_{13}} + x_{i_2}} m_b\right) = \left(g^\beta, g^\gamma m_b\right)$. Because γ is a random element, A cannot obtain meaningful information to distinguish m_0 and m_1 from above equation. Therefore, the output of A is exactly random value. Then, the probability $\Pr[A'(G, q, g, g^\alpha, g^\beta, g^\gamma) = 1]$ is 1/2.
- **Case 2.** $g_3 = g^{\alpha\beta}$, in this case $\left(g_2, g_3 g_2^{-x_{i_{12}} - x_{i_{13}} - x_{i_2}} m_b\right) = \left(g^\beta, g^{\beta\left(\alpha - x_{i_{12}} - x_{i_{13}} - x_{i_2}\right)} m_b\right) = \left(g^\beta, g^{\beta x_{i_{11}}} m_b\right)$. This is a kind of the ciphertexts encrypted under the private data encryption (*P-Data-Enc*). If $\left(g^\beta, g^{\beta\left(\alpha - x_{i_{12}} - x_{i_{13}} - x_{i_2}\right)} m_b\right)$ is re-encrypted for sharing, then $\left(g^\beta, g^{\beta\left(\alpha - x_{i_{12}} - x_{i_{13}} - x_{i_2}\right)} g^{\beta\left(x_{i_{12}} + x_{i_{13}} + x_{i_2}\right)} m_b\right) = \left(g^\beta, g^{\beta\alpha} m_b\right)$. This is a kind of the ciphertexts encrypted under the data re-encryption for sharing (*Data-Re-Enc*). Then, the probability $\Pr\left[A'\left(G, q, g, g^\alpha, g^\beta, g^{\alpha\beta}\right) = 1\right]$ is $Succ_{data}^A(k)$.

If DDH problem is hard, $\left|\Pr\left[A'\left(G, q, g, g^\alpha, g^\beta, g^{\alpha\beta}\right) = 1\right] - \Pr[A'(G, q, g, g^\alpha, g^\beta, g^\gamma) = 1]\right|$ is negligible, then $\left|Succ_{data}^A(k) - 1/2\right|$ is negligible.

Therefore, $Succ_{data}^A(k)$ is negligibly close to 1/2. $\qquad\square$

Theorem 2. If the DDH problem is hard, then in the proposed scheme the private keyword encryption and the keyword re-encryption for sharing are indistinguishable under chosen-plaintext attack (*IND-CPA*) secure against the proxy server. That is, for any PPT adversary A, the probability

$$Succ_{keyword}^A(k) = \Pr[b' = b \mid (params, msk) \leftarrow Init(1^k), (k_u, k_s) \leftarrow Keygen(msk, u),$$
$$(w_0, w_1) \leftarrow A^{P\text{-}Keyword\text{-}Enc(k_u, \cdot)}(k_s),$$
$$b \leftarrow \{0, 1\},$$
$$c_i''(w_b) = P\text{-}Keyword\text{-}Enc(x_{i_{11}}, w_b),$$
$$b' \leftarrow A^{P\text{-}Keyword\text{-}Enc(k_u, \cdot)}(k_s, c_i''(w_b))]$$

is negligibly close to 1/2 in the security parameter k where k_u is the user side keys for every users and k_s is the corresponding sever side keys for every users.

Proof. A PPT adversary A' uses A as subroutine to challenge the DDH problem.
– **Setup:** The input of A' is G, q, g, g_1, g_2, g_3 where $g_1 = g^\alpha$, $g_2 = g^\beta$, $g_3 = g^{\alpha\beta}$ or g^γ, and α, β, γ are random elements of Z_q. A' chooses H, F, s, s_i, and sets $h = g_1$. It then transmits (G, g, q, h, F, H) to A. For each user $i \in u$ where u is all users, A' chooses random elements $x_{i_2}, x_{i_{12}}, x_{i_{13}} \in Z_q$ and computes $g^{x_{i_{11}}} = h \cdot g^{-x_{i_{12}} - x_{i_{13}} - x_{i_2}}$. A' transmits $(i, x_{i_2}, x_{i_{12}})$ to A and keeps $(i, x_{i_2}, x_{i_{12}}, x_{i_{13}}, g^{x_{i_{11}}})$.

- **Query:** At any time, A sends w to A' to access the private keyword encryption oracle, A' chooses a random element $r_1 \in Z_q$, and computes $\sigma_w = Fs(w), \sigma_w' = Fs_i(w)$, $c_{w1}'' = g^{r1+\sigma w}$, $c_{w2}'' = g^{r_1 x_{i_{11}} + x_{i_{11}} \sigma_w + x_{i_{11}} \sigma_w'}$, $c_{w3}'' = H(g^{r_1 x_{i_{11}} + x_{i_{11}} \sigma_w})$, and $c_{w4}'' = H(h^{r_1})$. It then transmits $c_i''(w) = (c_{w1}'', c_{w2}'', c_{w3}'', c_{w4}'')$ to A. Also, whenever A transmits $\underline{c_{w1}}''$ to A', A' computes keyword re-encryption key $k_4 = \underline{c_{w1}}'', k_5 = g^{r_2}$, and $k_6 = g^{r_2 x_{i_{12}}} (\underline{c_{w1}}'')^{(x_{i_{12}} + x_{i_{13}})}$ where r_2 is a random element of Z_q, then sends $k_{keyword\text{-}re}(w) = (k_4, k_5, k_6)$.
- **Challenge:** A outputs w_0 and w_1, then A' chooses a random bit b and computes $\sigma_{w_b} = Fs(w_b), \sigma_{w_b}' = Fs_i(w_b), c_{w_b1}'' = g_2 g^{\sigma_{w_b}}$, $c_{w_b2}'' = g_3 g_2^{-x_{i_{12}} - x_{i_{13}} - x_{i_2}} g^{x_{i_{11}} \sigma_{w_b} + x_{i_{11}} \sigma_{w_b}'}$, $c_{w_b3}'' = H(g_2^{x_{i_{11}}} g^{x_{i_{11}} \sigma_{w_b}})$, and $c_{w_b4}'' = H(g_3)$. It then transmits $c_i''(w_b) = (c_{w_b1}'', c_{w_b2}'', c_{w_b3}'', c_{w_b4}'')$ to A. Also, A' computes $k_4' = c_{w_b1}'', k_5' = g^{r_3}$, and $k_6' = g^{r_3 x_{i_{12}}} (c_{w_b1}'')^{(x_{i_{12}} + x_{i_{13}})}$ where r_3 is a random element of Z_q, then sends $k_{keyword-re}'(w) = (k_4', k_5', k_6')$ to A.
- **Output:** A outputs b', A' verifies $b = b'$. If the equation holds, A' outputs 1, otherwise outputs 0.

We can consider two cases depending on the value of g_3.

- **Case 1.** $g_3 = g^\gamma$, in this case $c_i''(w_b) = (c_{w_b1}'', c_{w_b2}'', c_{w_b3}'', c_{w_b4}'') = (g^{\beta + \sigma_{wb}}, g^{\gamma - \beta(x_{i_{12}} + x_{i_{13}} + x_{i_2})} g^{x_{i_{11}} \sigma_{w_b} + x_{i_{11}} \sigma_{w_b}'}, H(g^{\beta x_{i_{11}} + x_{i_{11}} \sigma_{w_b}}), H(g^\gamma))$. If $(g^{\beta + \sigma_{wb}}, g^{\gamma - \beta(x_{i_{12}} + x_{i_{13}} + x_{i_2})} g^{x_{i_{11}} \sigma_{w_b} + x_{i_{11}} \sigma_{w_b}'}, H(g^{\beta x_{i_{11}} + x_{i_{11}} \sigma_{w_b}}), H(g^\gamma))$ is re-encrypted for sharing, then
  $(g^{\beta + \sigma_{wb}}, g^{\gamma - \beta(x_{i_{12}} + x_{i_{13}} + x_{i_2})} g^{x_{i_{11}} \sigma_{w_b}} g^{(\beta + \sigma_{wb})(x_{i_{12}} + x_{i_{13}} + x_{i_2})}, H(g^\gamma)) = (g^{\beta + \sigma_{wb}}, g^{\gamma + \alpha \sigma_{wb}}, H(g^\gamma))$.
  Because γ is a random element, A cannot obtain meaningful information to distinguish w_0 and w_1 from above equation. Therefore, the output of A is exactly random value. Then, the probability $\Pr[A'(G, q, g, g^\alpha, g^\beta, g^\gamma) = 1]$ is 1/2.
- **Case 2.** $g_3 = g^{\alpha\beta}$ in this case $c_i''(w_b) = (c_{w_b1}'', c_{w_b2}'', c_{w_b3}'', c_{w_b4}'') = (g^{\beta + \sigma_{wb}}, g^{\beta x_{i_{11}} + x_{i_{11}} \sigma_{w_b} + x_{i_{11}} \sigma_{w_b}'}, H(g^{i_{11}} + x_{i_{11}} \sigma_{w_b}), H(g^{\alpha\beta}))$. This is a kind of the ciphertexts encrypted under the private keyword encryption ($P\text{-}Keyword\text{-}Enc$). If $(g^{\beta + \sigma_{wb}}, g^{\beta x_{i_{11}} + x_{i_{11}} \sigma_{w_b} + x_{i_{11}} \sigma w_b'}, H(g^{\beta x_{i_{11}} + x_{i_{11}} \sigma_{w_b}}), H(g^{\alpha\beta}))$ is re-encrypted for sharing, then $(g^{\beta + \sigma_{wb}}, g^{\alpha\beta + \alpha \sigma_{wb}}, H(g^{\alpha\beta}))$. This is a kind of the ciphertexts encrypted under the keyword re-encryption for sharing ($Keyword\text{-}Re\text{-}Enc$). Then, the probability $\Pr[A'(G, q, g, g^\alpha, g^\beta, g^{\alpha\beta}) = 1]$ is $Succ_{keyword}^A(k)$.

If DDH problem is hard, $|\Pr[A'(G, q, g, g^\alpha, g^\beta, g^{\alpha\beta}) = 1] - \Pr[A'(G, q, g, g^\alpha, g^\beta, g^\gamma) = 1]|$ is negligible, then $\left| Succ_{keyword}^A(k) - 1/2 \right|$ is negligible.

Therefore, $Succ_{keyword}^A(k)$ is negligibly close to 1/2.   □

Theorem 3. *If the DDH problem is hard, then the proposed scheme is a non-adaptive indistinguishable secure multi-user searchable encryption scheme.*

Proof. We will compare each component of the view.

- **Data identifiers** $id(D_1)$, ..., $id(D_n)$: As the traces of the histories are the same (i.e. $Tr(H_{t0}) = Tr(H_{t1})$), the adversary cannot distinguish the data identifiers.
- **Ciphertexts of the private data encryption and the data re-encryption for sharing** $E_P(D_1)$, ..., $E_P(D_n)$, $E_{RE}(D_1)$, ..., $E_{RE}(D_l)$: By **Theorem 1**, the adversary cannot distinguish the ciphertexts.
- **Ciphertexts of the private keyword encryption and the keyword re-encryption for sharing** $KE_P(w(D_1))$, ..., $KE_P(w(D_n))$, $KE_{RE}(w(D_1))$, ..., $KE_{RE}(w(D_l))$: By **Theorem 2**, the adversary cannot distinguish the ciphertexts.
- **Queries** q_1, ..., q_t : As the traces of the histories are the same (i.e. $Tr(H_{t0}) = Tr(H_{t1})$), the query pattern is the same.
  - A private trapdoor query is $T_{pi}(\underline{w}) = (t_{p1}, t_{p2}) = \left(g^{r_{pt}}, g^{r_{pt} x_{i_{12}} + x_{i_{11}} \sigma_w'}\right)$. Because r_{pt} is a random element and σ_w' is pseudorandom number, the adversary cannot distinguish between the private trapdoor queries.
  - A multi-user trapdoor query is $T_{mi}(\underline{w}) = (t_{m1}, t_{m2}) = (g^{r_{mt} - \sigma_w}, h^{r_{mt}} g^{-x_{i_1} r_{mt}} g^{x_{i_1} \sigma_w}) = (g^{r_{mt} - \sigma_w}, g^{x_{i_2} r_{mt}} g^{x_{i_1} \sigma_w})$. Because r_{mt} is a random element and σ_w is pseudorandom number, the adversary cannot distinguish between the multi-user trapdoor queries.   □

4   Discussion and Conclusion

The proposed scheme is also vulnerable to collusion attack shown in [4], which means that the secret keys of the trusted key management server can be easily computed if one of the authorized users colludes with the proxy server. One of the authorized users sends his private keys $(x_{i_{11}}, x_{i_{12}}, x_{i_{13}}, s)$ to the proxy server, then the proxy server computes $x = x_{i_{11}} + x_{i_{12}} + x_{i_{13}} + x_{i_2}$ using the proxy server secret keys $(x_{i_2}, x_{i_{12}})$. The proxy server can easily obtain the secret keys of the trusted key management server $msk = (x, s)$. If the proxy server has msk, he can decrypt all stored shared data. Dong et al. said the design of fully collusion-resistant scheme is open problem and introduced some possible solutions in practice to prevent the problem in [4]. The privately stored data are secure under the collusion attack.

In this work, we modify Dong et al.'s scheme to propose a scheme that a user can selectively share his specific private data. In the proposed scheme, a user in the system can privately encrypt both data and keywords and store them in the proxy server. Also, the user can search his private data based on the keyword search method with preserving confidentiality of the data and the keywords against the proxy server. Only a user who privately stored the data can generate a trapdoor to search his data. Additionally, the user can share his specific private data at any time he wants. Lastly, all users can generate a trapdoor to search shared data.

References

1. Boneh, D., Di Crescenzo, G., Ostrovsky, R., Persiano, G.: Public key encryption with keyword search. In: Cachin, C., Camenisch, J.L. (eds.) EUROCRYPT 2004. LNCS, vol. 3027, pp. 506–522. Springer, Heidelberg (2004)
2. Curtmola, R., Garay, J., Kamara, S., Ostrovsky, R.: Searchable symmetric encryption: improved definitions and efficient constructions. In: Juels, A., Wright, R., De Capitani di Vimercati, S. (eds.) ACM Conference on Computer and Communications Security (CCS 2006), pp. 79–88. ACM, New York (2006)
3. Dong, C., Russello, G., Dulay, N.: Shared and searchable encrypted data for untrusted servers. In: Atluri, V. (ed.) DAS 2008. LNCS, vol. 5094, pp. 127–143. Springer, Heidelberg (2008)
4. Dong, C., Russello, G., Dulay, N.: Shared and searchable encrypted data for untrusted servers. J. Comput. Secur. **19**(3), 367–397 (2011)
5. Song, D., Wagner, D., Perrig, A.: Practical techniques for searching on encrypted data. In: IEEE Symposium on Research in Security and Privacy, pp. 44–55. IEEE Computer Society, Los Alamitos (2000)

Fair Multi-signature

Pairat Thorncharoensri$^{(\boxtimes)}$, Willy Susilo, and Yi Mu

School of Computer Science and Software Engineering,
Centre for Computer and Information Security, University of Wollongong,
Wollongong, Australia
pt78@uowmail.edu.au, {wsusilo,ymu}@uow.edu.au

Abstract. Numerous signature schemes have been proposed in the literature. One of the major applications of digital signature is the notion of multi-signature, that enables many co-signers to authorize a document on their behalf. Nevertheless, the major impediment in this notion relies on the need to have *all* signers to behave in accordance to the protocol correctly. If one of the signers does not release his signature, then all of the other signers will be disadvantaged while the malicious signer can obtain a valid multi-signature on behalf of the others with his own knowledge on his partial signature. In this paper, we aim to bridge this gap by proposing the notion of *fair multi-signatures*. In our notion, when there is any dishonest signer in the group, then the honest signers will not be disadvantaged. Furthermore, if the signing protocol is incomplete, nobody will be able to produce a valid signature on behalf of the group. However, if the protocol completes, then each signer can output a signature on the agreed message. Our notion provides one step ahead in terms of the adoption of multi-signature in practice.

Keywords: Fairness · Multi signatures

1 Introduction

A multi-signature (MS) scheme allows a group of n parties, who engage in an interactive protocol, to generate a joint signature on their choices of message m. Multi-signature schemes provide several advantages over the standard signature scheme. First, the size of a multi-signature is constant and short, which is comparable to a standard signature. Second, the verification algorithm is as efficient as a standard signature. Nevertheless, multi-signatures enable multiple parties to co-sign a document that they have agreed. This has offered many practical applications, such as contract signing.

When all the parties behave correctly, i.e. following the protocol, then multi-signatures can be invoked securely. Nevertheless, if there exists a malicious signer in the group, who eventually refused to release his/her signature after receiving the others', then multi-signature schemes will no longer be *fair* to the honest users. In this situation, the honest users cannot obtain the valid multi-signature, while the malicious user can enjoy the valid multi-signature after adding his/her

© Springer International Publishing Switzerland 2015
K.-H. Rhee and J.H. Yi (Eds.): WISA 2014, LNCS 8909, pp. 244–256, 2015.
DOI: 10.1007/978-3-319-15087-1_19

partial signature to the partial multi-signatures provided by the honest signers. To illustrate this situation, let us consider the following scenario. Alice, Bob and Claire would like to jointly sign an agreement. Bob and Claire work in accordance to the multi-signature scheme to produce their partial signatures, and release them. However, after Alice obtains the necessary information to output the signature on the agreement, Alice refuses to send her information which Bob and Clair need to complete the protocol and output the multi-signature on the agreement. Hence, the multi-signature becomes unfair to Bob and Claire, who have engaged in the protocol honestly.

Our Contributions: In this paper, we introduce the notion of fair multi-signature (FMS) schemes to solve the above problem. In our notion, nobody will be able to produce a valid signature until all signers produce their partial signatures correctly. We describe the model of the FMS scheme and its security notions to capture the integrity of a message, and the non-repudiation of the signers. We also present a generic construction scheme of FMS schemes which are proven to be secure in our security model.

Previous Works: A multi-signature scheme is an algorithm for a group of n signers working together to produce a (constant size and/or short) signature on the same message. Since its invention in 1983 by Itakura and Nakamura [5], many schemes have been proposed [2,7,9–11].

An aggregated signature scheme is a variant of multi-signature scheme which was firstly introduced by Boneh, Gentry, Lynn, and Shacham (BGLS in short) [3]. In their work, the verifiable encrypted signature based on aggregated signature was introduced. The idea is similar to the aggregated signature by adding a simulated signature into an original signature. In 2004, Lysyanskaya, Micali, Reyzin and Shacham [8] proposed a sequential aggregated signature scheme based on RSA cryptosystem. Later in Eurocrypt 2006, Lu, Ostrovsky, Sahai, Shacham and Waters (LOSSW in short) [6] proposed a new sequential aggregated signature scheme and a new verifiable encrypted signature. Their schemes are efficient and provably secure in the standard model and their completed proofs can be found in [7].

A fair exchange protocol [1,4] is provided for two parties to fairly exchange their items so that no one can gain any advantage in the process. A fair exchange can be realized simply by introducing an online trusted third party who acts as a mediator: earth party sends the item to the trusted third party, who upon verifying the correctness of both items, forwards each item to the other party. It seems that a fair exchange protocol together with a multi-signature protocol can be used to exchange a multi-signature in a fair way. Nevertheless, in practice, the above combination scheme is meaningless since there will be always one honest party who could not completed the protocol and obtain a multi-signature. This is a drawback of the above approach.

Paper Organization: The rest of the paper is organized as follows. In the next Section, we will review some preliminaries that will be used throughout this paper. The definition of FMS and its security notations will be described in

Sect. 3. In the Sect. 4, we present a generic construction of FMS scheme from verifiable encrypted signature scheme based on aggregate signature and provide its instantiation in Sect. 6. Then, in the Sect. 5, we describe the proof of the security of generic construction. Finally, we conclude the paper.

2   Notation

For the sake of consistency, the following notations will be used throughout the paper. Let PPT denote a probabilistic polynomial-time algorithm. When a PPT algorithm F privately accesses and executes another PPT algorithm E, we denote it by $F^{E(.)}(.)$. We denote by $poly(.)$ a deterministic polynomial function. For all polynomials $poly(k)$ and for all sufficiently large k, if $q \leq poly(1^k)$ then we say that q is polynomial-time in k. We say that a function $f : \mathbb{N} \to \mathbb{R}$ is *negligible* if, for all constant $c > 0$ and for all sufficiently large n, $f(n) < \frac{1}{n^c}$. Denote by $l \xleftarrow{\$} L$ the operation of picking l at random from a (finite) set L. A collision of a function $h(.)$ refers to the case when there is a message pair m, n of distinct points in its message space such that $h(m) = h(n)$. We denote by $||$ the concatenation of two strings (or integers). Let $\mathbb{G}_1$ and $\mathbb{G}_2$ be cyclic multiplicative groups generated by g_1 and g_2, respectively. The order of both generators is a prime p. Let $\hat{e} : \mathbb{G}_1 \times \mathbb{G}_2 \to \mathbb{G}_T$ be a bilinear mapping from $\mathbb{G}_1$ and $\mathbb{G}_2$ to $\mathbb{G}_T$.

3   Notion of Fair Multi-signature Schemes (FMS)

It is assumed that all parties, who need to use his/her public-private key in this scheme, comply with a registration protocol with a certificate of authority to obtain certificates on their public key prior to the communication with others. Let $\mathcal{LS}$ be a list of all of the signers' public keys such that $\mathcal{LS} = \{pk_{S_i}\}$ where i is an index of the signer and pk_{S_i} is a public key of the i-signer. Let n be the total number of signer involved in the signature. Let TP denote a semi-trusted third party who is not included in the list of signer $\mathcal{LS}$ and TP is assumed to be trusted for some certain level. We give a definition of fair multi-signature scheme as outlined below.

Definition 1. *A fair multi-signature scheme Σ is an 7-tuple.*

$$\Sigma = (Setup, TKeyGen, SKeyGen, Sign, Verify)$$

such that

System Parameters Generation (Setup): Setup is a PPT algorithm that, on input a security parameter K, outputs the system parameters param.
TP Key Generator (TKeyGen): TKeyGen is a PPT algorithm that, on input the system parameters param*, outputs strings (sk_{TP}, pk_{TP}) where they denote a secret key and a public key of semi-trusted third party, respectively. That is $\{pk_{TP}, sk_{TP}\} \leftarrow TKeyGen(\mathsf{param})$.*

Signer Key Generator (SKeyGen): SKeyGen is a PPT algorithm that, on input the system parameters param, outputs strings (sk_{S_i}, pk_{S_i}) where they denote a secret key and a public key of the ith signer, respectively. That is $\{pk_{S_i}, sk_{S_i}\} \leftarrow SKeyGen(\text{param})$.

Signature Signing (Sign): Sign is an interactive protocol involving a group of signer and a semi-trusted third party. Let us denote by $\sigma \leftarrow Sign.\langle S_1(sk_{S_1}), ..., S_n(sk_{S_n}), TP(sk_{TP})\rangle (\mathcal{LS}, pk_{TP}, M, \text{param})$ a signing protocol Sign that involves a group of signer and a semi-trusted third party and outputs a signature σ, where M is an input message, param is the system parameters and $\mathcal{LS}$ is a list of signer's public key involving in the signing process.

Signature Verification (Verify): On input the list of signer's public key $\mathcal{LS}$, a message M, the system parameters param and a signature σ, $\Sigma.Verify$ outputs a verification decision $d \in \{Accept, Reject\}$. That is $d \leftarrow \Sigma.Verify$ $(M, \sigma, \mathcal{LS}, \text{param})$.

3.1 Unforgeability

In this paper, when we discuss the unforgeability property, it means that the security against existential unforgeability under an adaptive chosen message and chosen public key attack. Intuitively, the unforgeability property of FMS schemes is provided that, with the corporation of n − 1 corrupted signers and the corrupted TP, an adversary should not be able to forge the multi-signature without interacting with an honest signer, where n is a total number of signers signing on the message. Here, our definition of the unforgeability is to provide an assurance that one with access to a key generation oracle, a signing oracle and a verification oracle, and with the entire set of signer public parameters $pk_{S_1}, ..., pk_{S_n}$ and the knowledge of the n − 1-signer secret keys $sk_{S_1}, ..., sk_{S_{n-1}}$ and a TP secret key sk_{TP}, should be unable to produce a multi-signature on a new message even with the capability of arbitrarily choosing the n − 1-signer secret keys, a TP secret key and message M as inputs. The following game describes the existential unforgeability of the FMS scheme. Let $CM\text{-}CPK\text{-}A$ be the adaptively chosen message, chosen public key and insider corruption attack and let $EUF\text{-}FMS$ be the existential unforgeability of the FMS scheme. We denote by $\mathcal{A}_{EUF\text{-}FMS}^{CM\text{-}CPK\text{-}A}$ the adaptively chosen message, chosen public key, and insider corruption adversary. We also denote by $\mathcal{F}$ the simulator.

First, let $\mathcal{PS}$ be an algorithm that maintains the list of public-private key pair, where $\mathcal{PS} \leftarrow \mathcal{PS}(pk_I, sk_I)$ is the recording operation that keeps pk_I and sk_I in the list and $sk_I \leftarrow \mathcal{PS}(pk_I)$ is the retrieving operation that takes pk_I as input and outputs sk_I. $\mathcal{QS}$ is defined an algorithm that maintains the list of queried public-private key pair and works in the same way as $\mathcal{P} + \mathcal{S}$. Then, we define the signer's public key generation oracle $\mathcal{SPO}$, the signer's private key generation oracle $\mathcal{SKO}$, the semi-trusted third party's private key generation oracle $\mathcal{TKO}$, the interactive signing oracle $\mathcal{SSO}$, and the random oracle $\mathcal{HO}$ as in the Fig. 1. In fact, $\mathcal{SKO}$ is not required since the adversary can generate a pair of public and private keys using $SKeyGen$ directly. However, due to the registered key model, the adversary also needs to register their the public and

Oracle $\mathcal{SPO}$:	Oracle $\mathcal{SSO}(S_1, ..., S_n, TP)$
If $I = S$ then	$\sigma \leftarrow Sign.\langle S_1(sk_{S_1}), ..., S_n(sk_{S_n}),$
$\quad (pk_{S_i}, sk_{S_i}) \leftarrow SKeyGen(\text{param})$	$\quad TP(sk_{TP})\rangle(M, pk_{TP}, \mathcal{LS})$
ElseIf $I = TP$ then	Return σ
$\quad (pk_{TP}, sk_{TP}) \leftarrow TKeyGen(\text{param})$	Oracle $\mathcal{HO}(str)$:
$\mathcal{PS} \leftarrow \mathcal{PS}(pk_I, sk_I)$	$m \leftarrow H(str)$
Return pk_I	Return m
Oracle $\mathcal{TKO}(pk_{TP})$:	Oracle $\mathcal{SKO}(pk_{S_i})$:
$sk_{TP} \leftarrow \mathcal{PS}(pk_{TP})$	$sk_{S_i} \leftarrow \mathcal{PS}(pk_{S_i})$
$\mathcal{QS} \leftarrow \mathcal{QS}(pk_{TP}, sk_{TP})$	$\mathcal{QS} \leftarrow \mathcal{QS}(pk_{S_i}, sk_{S_i})$
Return sk_{TP}	Return sk_{S_i}

Fig. 1. Oracles for adversary attacking unforgeability of FMS scheme

private key prior to the signing protocol. Hence, it is smoother in the simulating process and easier to understand by assuming that the adversary obtains a pair of public and private keys by using $\mathcal{SKO}$ in which we can skip the process of public key registration. Let $\mathcal{LS}^*$ be a list of all of the signers' public keys that at least one signer public key pk_{S_i*} that has never been queried for its private key sk_{S_i*}. Let $M*$ be a message that has never been queried for a signature σ^*. The experiment in Fig. 2 shows the existential unforgeability of the FMS scheme. The success probability function such that $\mathcal{A}_{EUF\text{-}FMS}^{CM\text{-}CPK\text{-}A}$ wins the above game is defined as $\mathcal{Succ}_{EUF\text{-}FMS}^{CM\text{-}CPK\text{-}A}(.)$.

$\text{Expt}^{\mathcal{A}_{EFC\text{-}FMS}^{CM\text{-}CPK\text{-}A}}(k)$	$\mathcal{A}$ wins the above game if:
$\quad \text{param} \leftarrow \text{Setup}(1^k)$	1. $pk_{S_i*} \in \mathcal{LS}^*$; $sk_{S_i*} \notin \mathcal{QS}$.
$\quad (\perp, st) \leftarrow \mathcal{A}^{\mathcal{SSO}(.), \mathcal{SPO}(.), \mathcal{SKO}(.), \mathcal{HO}(.)}(\text{param})$	2. $sk_{TP*} \notin \mathcal{QS}$.
$\quad (\perp, \sigma^*) \leftarrow A(\mathcal{LS}^*, pk_{TP_*}, M^*, st)$	3. Accept $\leftarrow \Sigma.Verify(M^*, \sigma^*, \mathcal{LS}^*)$.
$\quad \text{return } \sigma^*$	

Fig. 2. The experiment of unforgeability game

Definition 2. *The FMS scheme is said to be $(t, q_H, q_{SP}, q_{SS}, q_{SK}, \epsilon)$-secure existentially unforgeable under an adaptive chosen message, chosen public key and insider corruption attack if there is no PPT adversary $\mathcal{A}_{EUF\text{-}FMS}^{CM\text{-}CPK\text{-}A}$ such that the success probability $\mathcal{Succ}_{EUF\text{-}FMS}^{CM\text{-}CPK\text{-}A}(k) = \epsilon$ is negligible in k, where $\mathcal{A}_{EUF\text{-}FMS}^{CM\text{-}CPK\text{-}A}$ runs in time at most t, makes at most q_H, q_{SP}, q_{SS}, and q_{SK} queries to the random oracles, $\mathcal{SPO}$ oracle, $\mathcal{SSO}$ oracle and $\mathcal{SKO}$ oracle, respectively.*

3.2 Fairness

Intuitively, the definition of fairness has two sub-properties. First, completeness, if the signing protocol is completed and the semi-trusted third party is not compromised, then every signer in $\mathcal{LS}$ should output the same multi-signature. Second, soundness, if the signing protocol is uncompleted or interrupted and the semi-trusted third party is not compromised, then no one should be able to output a multi-signature corresponding to the list $\mathcal{LS}$ and a message M. However, fairness with completeness is straightforward and its meaning is the same as the completeness of FMS scheme. Hence, we will only cater for the fairness with soundness. The following game describes the existential fairness with soundness of the FMS scheme. We denote by $EFS\text{-}FMS$ the existential fairness with soundness of the FMS scheme. Let $\mathcal{A}_{EFS\text{-}FMS}^{CM\text{-}CPK\text{-}A}$ be the adaptively chosen message, chosen public key, and insider corruption adversary. Let $\mathcal{F}$ be a simulator of the existential fairness with soundness game. The interactive signing oracle $\mathcal{SSO}$, the random oracle $\mathcal{HO}$, the signer's public key generation oracle $\mathcal{SPO}$ and the signer's private key generation oracle $\mathcal{SKO}$ are defined as same as in the Sect. 3.1. Note that $\mathcal{LS}^*$ is a list of all of the signers' public keys, including the honest signer's public key pk_{S_i*}.

Given a choice of messages M and an access to the above oracles, $\mathcal{A}$ arbitrarily makes queries to the oracles. At the end of these queries, $\mathcal{F}$, who plays a role of the honest signer $pk_{S_i}^*$, interacts with $\mathcal{A}$ who plays a role of corrupted signers. We assume that $\mathcal{A}$ outputs a forged multi-signature σ^* on a message M^* with respect to $\mathcal{LS}^*, pk_{TA}$. $\mathcal{A}$ wins the above game if the private key of the honest signer $pk_{S_i}^*$ in $\mathcal{LS}^*$ is not known to $\mathcal{A}$ and $\mathcal{F}$(as a signer S_i^*) did not fully completed the signing protocol with $\mathcal{A}$ and TP. Note that "not fully completed the interaction" means that $\mathcal{F}$ communicated only with signers in the $\mathcal{LS}^*$ but not with TP and, hence, neither $\mathcal{F}$ nor signers in the $\mathcal{LS}^*$ should be able to output a multi-signature σ^*. The success probability function such that $\mathcal{A}_{EFS\text{-}FMS}^{CM\text{-}CPK\text{-}A}$ wins the above game is defined as $\mathcal{S}ucc_{EFS\text{-}FMS}^{CM\text{-}CPK\text{-}A}(.)$.

Definition 3. *The FMS scheme is said to be $(t, q_H, q_{SP}, q_{SS}, q_{SK}, \epsilon)$-secure existentially fairness with soundness under an adaptive chosen message, chosen public key and insider corruption attack if there is no PPT adversary $\mathcal{A}_{EFS\text{-}FMS}^{CM\text{-}CPK\text{-}A}$ such that the success probability $Succ_{EFS\text{-}FMS}^{CM\text{-}CPK\text{-}A}(k) = \epsilon$ is negligible in k, where $\mathcal{A}_{EFS\text{-}FMS}^{CM\text{-}CPK\text{-}A}$ runs in time at most t, makes at most q_H, q_{SP}, q_{SS}, and q_{SK} queries to the random oracles, $\mathcal{SPO}$ oracle, $\mathcal{SSO}$ oracle and $\mathcal{SKO}$ oracle, respectively.*

3.3   Semi-Trustiness

Intuitively, the definition of semi-trustiness is to prevent an adversary, who acts as a semi-trusted third party, from outputting the multi-signature after interacting with the signing protocol that involves the honest signers. To simplify this matter, we say that an adversary, corrupted with the semi-trusted third party, arbitrarily interacts with honest signers and breaks the semi-trustiness of FMS scheme if the adversary outputs a multi-signature σ^* on a new message M^* after completing the interaction with the arbitrarily chosen honest signers. Let us denote by $CM\text{-}CPK\text{-}A$ the adaptively chosen message, chosen public key attack and denote by $EST\text{-}FMS$ the existential semi-trustiness of the FMS scheme. Let $\mathcal{A}_{EST\text{-}FMS}^{CM\text{-}CPK\text{-}A}$ be the adaptively chosen message, chosen public key, and insider corruption adversary. Let $\mathcal{F}$ be a simulator of the existential semi-trustiness game. The interactive signing oracle $\mathcal{SSO}$, the random oracle $\mathcal{HO}$, the signer's public key generation oracle $\mathcal{SPO}$ and the signer's private key generation oracle $\mathcal{SKO}$ are defined as same as in the Sect. 3.1. The following game describes the existential semi-trustiness of the FMS scheme.

$$
\begin{array}{|l|}
\hline
\text{Expt}^{\mathcal{A}^{CM\text{-}CPK\text{-}A}_{EST\text{-}FMS}}(k):\\
\quad \text{param} \leftarrow \text{Setup}(1^k)\\
\quad (\perp, st) \leftarrow \mathcal{A}^{\mathcal{SSO},\mathcal{SPO},\mathcal{SKO},\mathcal{HO}}(\text{param})\\
\quad (\perp, \sigma) \leftarrow Sign.\langle S_1(sk_{S_1}),...,S_n(sk_{S_n}),\\
\quad\quad A(sk_{TP})\rangle(\mathcal{LS}, pk_{TP}, M)\\
\quad \text{return } \sigma\\
\hline
\mathcal{A} \text{ wins the above game if}\\
\quad 1.\ sk_{S_1},...,sk_{S_n} \notin \mathcal{QS}\\
\quad 2.\ \text{Accept} \leftarrow \Sigma.Verify(M, \sigma, \mathcal{LS})\\
\hline
\end{array}
$$

The success probability function such that $\mathcal{A}^{CM\text{-}CPK\text{-}A}_{EST\text{-}FMS}$ wins the above game is defined as $Succ^{CM\text{-}CPK\text{-}A}_{EST\text{-}FMS}(.)$.

Definition 4. *The FMS scheme is said to be $(t,q_H,q_{SP},q_{SS},q_{SK},\epsilon)$-secure existentially semi-trustiness under an adaptive chosen message, chosen public key attack if there is no PPT adversary $\mathcal{A}^{CM\text{-}CPK\text{-}A}_{EST\text{-}FMS}$ such that the success probability $Succ^{CM\text{-}CPK\text{-}A}_{EST\text{-}FMS}(k) = \epsilon$ is negligible in k, where $\mathcal{A}^{CM\text{-}CPK\text{-}A}_{EST\text{-}FMS}$ runs in time at most t, makes at most q_H, q_{SP}, q_{SS}, and q_{SK} queries to the random oracles, $\mathcal{SPO}$ oracle, $\mathcal{SSO}$ oracle and $\mathcal{SKO}$ oracle, respectively.*

4   Generic Construction for FMS Scheme

In this section, we present a generic construction for FMS scheme. Before describing our generic construction, in the following subsection, we will discuss the aggregated signature and the verifiable encrypted signature which are constructed from an aggregated signature. Then, we will proceed with the generic construction of FMS.

4.1   Verifiable Encrypted Signature Scheme from Aggregate Signature

There are two existing well-known verifiable encrypted signatures (VES) which are constructed from aggregate signatures. The first scheme [3] is constructed from BLS signature and the second scheme [6] is constructed from Waters signature scheme [13]. From the above two schemes, we adopt their VES model and describe it as follows.

System Parameters Generation ($VES.Setup$): *Setup* is a PPT algorithm that, on input a security parameter $\mathcal{K}$, outputs the system parameters param.

Key Generator (*VES.KeyGen*): *KeyGen* is a PPT algorithm that, on input the system parameters param, outputs strings (sk, pk) where they denote a secret key and a public key, respectively. That is $\{pk, sk\} \leftarrow KeyGen(\text{param})$. Note that we assume that the key generator algorithm for a signer is same as the key generator algorithm for adjudicator. Even VES requires these algorithms to be different, there are only a trivial adjustment.

Signature Signing (*VES.Sign*): On input the system parameters param, the ith signer's secret key sk_{S_i}, the signer's public key pk_{S_i} and a message M, *Sign* outputs signer's signature σ. That is $\sigma \leftarrow Sign(\text{param}, M, sk_{S_i}, pk_{S_i})$.

Signature Verification (*VES.Verify*): On input the system parameters param, the ith signer's public key pk_{S_i}, a message M and a signature σ, *Verify* outputs a verification decision $d \in \{Accept, Reject\}$. That is $d \leftarrow Verify(\text{param}, M, \sigma, pk_{S_i})$.

Verifiable Encryption (*VES.Enc*): On input the system parameters param, the adjudicator's public key pk_{AD} and a signature σ, *Enc* outputs a verifiable encrypted signature δ. That is $\delta \leftarrow Enc(\text{param}, \sigma, pk_{AD})$.

Verifiable Encrypted Signature's Verification (*VES.EVF*): On input the system parameters param, the adjudicator's public key pk_{AD}, the ith signer's public key pk_{S_i}, a message M and a verifiable encrypted signature δ, *EVF* outputs a verification decision $d \in \{Accept, Reject\}$. That is $d \leftarrow EVF$ (param, $M, \delta, pk_{AD}, pk_{S_i}$).

Verifiable Encrypted Signature's Adjudication (*VES.ADJ*): On input the system parameters param, the adjudicator's public key pk_{AD}, the adjudicator's secret key sk_{AD}, the ith signer's public key pk_{S_i}, a verifiable encrypted signature δ and a message M, *ADJ* outputs a signature σ. That is $\sigma \leftarrow ADJ(\text{param}, M, \delta, sk_{AD}, pk_{AD}, pk_{S_i})$.

Note that signatures from *VES.Sign* can be aggregated since the verifiable encryption signature scheme is based on the aggregate signature scheme.

4.2 Aggregate Signature Scheme

We describe an aggregate signature scheme as follows.

Setup (*AS.Setup*) **and Key Generator** (*AS.KeyGen*): *AS.Setup* and *AS. KeyGen* are same as *VES.Setup* and *VES.KeyGen* in VES scheme, respectively.

Sign (*AS.Sign*) **and Verify** (*AS.Verify*): *AS.Sign* and *AS.Verify* are same as *VES.Sign* and *VES.Verify* in VES scheme, respectively.

Aggregation (*AS.Aggregate*): On input the system parameters param, signatures $\sigma_{S_1}, ..., \sigma_{S_n}$ and a message M, *AVerify* outputs an aggregate signature δ. That is $\delta \leftarrow Aggregate(\text{param}, M, \sigma_{S_1}, ..., \sigma_{S_n})$.

Aggregate Signature Verification (*AS.AVerify*): On input the system parameters param, signers' public keys $pk_{S_1}, ..., pk_{S_n}$, a message M and an aggregate signature δ, *AVerify* outputs a verification decision $d \in \{Accept, Reject\}$. That is $d \leftarrow AVerify(\text{param}, M, \delta, pk_{S_1}, ..., pk_{S_n})$.

4.3   Generic Construction Scheme

In this section, we present our generic construction scheme. The main idea is to achieve fairness by a composition of verifiably encrypted signature (VES) that is constructed from aggregate signatures. The outer one is verified by the public key of the semi-trusted third party while the inner one is verified by a publicly shared key except the semi-trusted third party who acts as a signature distributor. Hence, once the signatures are exchanged, a multi-signature can be easily constructed by relying on the aggregation function of the aggregated signature scheme. It is also easy to verify the signature by using the verification function of the aggregated signature scheme. The scheme works as follows.

$\Sigma.Setup$: On input a security parameter $\mathcal{K}$, $Setup$ runs $VES.Setup$ and returns param.

$\Sigma.TKeyGen$: On input a system parameters param, a semi-trusted third party TP randomly generates a private key sk_{TP} and a public key pk_{TP} as follows: run $VES.KeyGen$ and output (sk_{TP}, pk_{TP}) as a secret key and public key of the semi-trusted third party, respectively.

$\Sigma.SKeyGen$: Similar to $TKeyGen$, $SKeyGen$ runs $VES.KeyGen$ to get (sk_{S_i}, pk_{S_i}) as a secret key and public key of the signer, respectively.

$\Sigma.Sign$: Assume that the communication between parties is secure. Given a message M, a list of signer $\mathcal{LS} = \{pk_{S_1}, ..., pk_{S_n}\}$ and a secret key sk_{S_i} of the ith signer, where $i \in \{1, ..., n\}$, processes the $Sign$ protocol as follows:

Round 1: All signers work together and run $VES.KeyGen$ to generate (sk_R, pk_R) as a shared random secret key and a shared random public key, respectively. In this round, any secured encryption scheme can be use to construct the shared random secret key and subsequently the shared random public key.

Round 2: On input $sk_R, pk_R, sk_{S_i}, pk_{S_i}, pk_{TP}$, the ith signer computes as follows: First, generate a signature $\varpi_i = VES.Sign(\text{param}, M, sk_{S_i}, pk_{S_i})$. Second, using $VES.Enc$ to encrypt ϖ_i with pk_R such that $\vartheta_i = VES.Enc$ $(\text{param}, \varpi_i, pk_R)$. Let $\vartheta_i = (\vartheta_i', \vartheta_i'')$ where ϑ_i' is the random related component and ϑ_i' is the encrypted signature component. Next, $VES.Enc$ to encrypt ϑ_i with pk_{TP} such that $\bar{\delta}_i = VES.Enc(\text{param}, \vartheta_i', pk_{TP})$. Finally, gather all components $\delta_i = (\bar{\delta}_i, \vartheta_i'')$. S_i then sends $\Upsilon_i = (\delta_i, pk_R)$ to TP.

Round 3: upon receiving the $\Upsilon_1, ..., \Upsilon_n$, TP first checks whether pk_R in $\Upsilon_1, ..., \Upsilon_n$ are the same. Next, check whether $\forall i \in \{1, ..., n\}$:

$$VES.EVF(\text{param}, M, \Upsilon_i, pk_{TP}, pk_{S_i}) \overset{?}{=} Accept$$

and let $\lambda_i = VES.ADJ(\text{param}, \delta_i, M, sk_{TP}, pk_{TP}, pk_{S_i})$. Then check whether

$$VES.EVF(\text{param}, M, \lambda_i, pk_R, pk_{S_i}) \overset{?}{=} Accept.$$

Finally, if the above holds then TP outputs a vector $\bar{\lambda} = \{\lambda_1, ..., \lambda_n\}$ and sends to all signers.

Extract the multi-signature: each signer computes $\forall i \in \{1, ..., n\} : \sigma_i = VES.$ $ADJ(\text{param}, \lambda_i, sk_R)$. The multi-signature on message M is $\Theta := AS.$ $Aggregate(\sigma_1, ..., \sigma_n)$.

$\Sigma.Verify$: Given $\mathcal{LS} = \{pk_{S_1}, ..., pk_{S_n}\}, \Theta$ and a message M, a verifier V runs $AS.AVerify(\text{param}, M, \Theta, pk_{S_1}, ..., pk_{S_n})$. If $AS.AVerify$ outputs $Accept$ then accept the signature. Otherwise, reject.

5   Security Analysis for the Generic Construction Scheme

5.1   Unforgeability

Theorem 1. *Our fair multi-signature scheme is existentially unforgeable under an adaptive chosen message, chosen public key attack and insider corruption if the verifiable encrypted signature scheme is secure against existential forgery.*

Due to the page limitation, please find the proof for Theorem 1 in the full version of this paper [12].

5.2   Fairness

Theorem 2. *Our fair multi-signature scheme is existentially fairness with soundness secure an adaptive chosen message, chosen public key attack and insider corruption if the verifiable encrypted signature scheme is secure against existential forgery.*

Due to the page limitation, please find the proof for Theorem 2 in the full version of this paper [12].

5.3   Semi-Trustiness

Theorem 3. *Our fairness multi-signature scheme is existentially semi-trustiness secure an adaptive chosen message and chosen public key attack if the verifiable encrypted signature is secure against extraction defined in [3].*

Due to the page limitation, please find the proof for Theorem 3 in the full version of this paper [12].

6   Instantiation of Signatures

6.1   LOSSW's Verifiably Encrypted Signatures

Lu, Ostrovsky, Sahai, Shacham and Waters [6] proposed a verifiably encrypted signature (VES) scheme based on aggregate signature in the standard model. We present their VES scheme as a 7-triple (*Setup, KeyGen, Sign, Verify, Enc, EVF, ADJ*). We elaborate the LOSSW's verifiably encrypted signature scheme as follows:

Setup: *Setup* sets param $= (p, \hat{e}, g \in \mathbb{G}_1, u_0, u_1, ..., u_k, \psi : \mathbb{G}_1 \rightarrow \mathbb{G}_2, H : \{0,1\}^* \rightarrow \{0,1\}^k, \hat{e} : \mathbb{G}_1 \times \mathbb{G}_2 \rightarrow \mathbb{G}_T)$ be a system parameter.

KeyGen: On input a system parameter param, *KeyGen* choose a random secret key $x, y \in \mathbb{Z}_p$. Then, for signer, *KeyGen* returns $pk_{S_i} = \mathbf{X} = \hat{e}(g, g)^x$ and $sk_{S_i} = x$ as the public key and a private key of the signer, respectively. For adjudicator, *KeyGen* returns $pk_{AD} = Y = g^y$ and $sk_{AD} = y$ as the public key and a private key of the signer, respectively.

Sign: Given a message M as a bit string $(m_1, ..., m_k) \in \{0,1\}^k$, pk_{S_i} and sk_{S_i}, S randomly chooses $r \in \mathbb{Z}_p$ and computes $\sigma = (\theta_1 = g^x u_0 \prod_{i=1}^k u_i^{m_i}, \theta_2 = g^r)$ as a signature on message M.

Verify: Given pk_{S_i}, σ and a message M, a verifier V checks whether $\hat{e}(\theta_1, g)$ $\hat{e}(\theta_2, u_0 \prod_{i=1}^k u_i^{m_i})^{-1} \stackrel{?}{=} \mathbf{X}$ holds or not. If not, then it outputs reject. Otherwise, it outputs accept.

Enc: Given a signature σ on message M, *Enc* chooses a random integer $r \in \mathbb{Z}_p$ and computes $E_1 = \theta_1 \cdot Y^r$; $E_2 = \theta_2$; $E_3 = g^r$. Then, compute a verifiably encrypted signature $\delta = (E_1, E_2, E_3)$.

EVF: Given pk_{S_i}, pk_{AD}, δ and a message M, a verifier V checks whether $\hat{e}(E_1, g) \cdot \hat{e}(E_2, u_0 \prod_{i=1}^k u_i^{m_i})^{-1} \cdot \hat{e}(E_3, Y)^{-1} \stackrel{?}{=} \mathbf{X}$ holds or not. If not, then it outputs reject. Otherwise, it outputs accept.

ADJ: Given a message sk_{AD} and δ, S computes $\sigma = (\theta_1 = E_1 \cdot E_3^{-y}, \theta_2 = E_2)$ as a signature on message M.

6.2 LOSSW Instantiation

In this section, we present the instantiation of our generic construction scheme in the standard model. The scheme works as follows:

$\Sigma.Setup$: $\Sigma.Setup$ works as the LOSSW $VES.Setup$.

$\Sigma.TKeyGen$: $\Sigma.TKeyGen$ works as the LOSSW $VES.KeyGen$. Let $sk_{TP} = y, pk_{TP} = Y = g_1^y$ be a secret key and public key of the semi-trusted third party, respectively.

$\Sigma.SKeyGen$: Run the LOSSW $VES.KeyGen$ to get $sk_{S_i} = x, pk_{S_i} = \mathbf{X} = \hat{e}(g, g)^x$ as a secret key and public key of the signer, respectively.

$\Sigma.Sign$: Assume that the communication between parties is secure. Given a message M, a list of signer $\mathcal{LS} = \{pk_{S_1}, ..., pk_{S_n}\}$ and a secret key sk_{S_i} of the ith signer, where $i \in \{1, ..., n\}$, processes the *Sign* protocol as follows:

- Round 1: Each signer randomly selects γ_i and exchange with each other. Each signer generates $sk_R = \gamma = \prod_{i=1}^n \gamma_i, pk_R = R = g_1^\gamma$ as a shared random secret key and a shared random public key, respectively.
- Round 2: On input $sk_R, pk_R, sk_{S_i}, pk_{S_i}, pk_{TP}$, the ith signer first randomly selects r, r_1, r_2 and computes a signature $\varpi_i = (\theta_{1,i} = g^{x_i} u_0 \prod_{i=1}^k u_i^{m_i}, \theta_{2,i} = g^r)$. Then, encrypt ϖ_i with pk_R such that $\vartheta_i = (E_1' = \theta_1 \cdot R^{r_1}, E_2' = \theta_2, E_3' = g^{r_1})$. Subsequently, putting aside the random component in the previous encryption(E_3'), S_i encrypts ϑ_i with pk_{TP}

such that $\bar{\delta}_i = (E_1'' = E_1' \cdot Y^{r_2}, E_2'' = E_2' = \theta_2, E_3'' = g^{r_2})$. Finally, $\delta_i = (E_{1,\,i} = E_1'', E_{2,\,i} = E_2'', E_{3,\,i} = E_3', E_{4,\,i} = E_3'')$. S_i then sends $\Upsilon_i = (\delta_i, pk_R)$ to TP.

- Round 3: upon receiving the $\Upsilon_1, ..., \Upsilon_n$, TP first check whether pk_R in $\Upsilon_1, ..., \Upsilon_n$ are the same. Next, check whether $\forall i \in \{1, ..., n\}$: $\hat{e}(E_{1,\,i}, g) \cdot \hat{e}(E_{2,\,i}, u_0 \prod_{j=1}^{k} u_j^{m_j})^{-1} \cdot \hat{e}(E_{3,\,i}, R)^{-1} \cdot \hat{e}(E_{4,\,i}, Y)^{-1} \stackrel{?}{=} \mathbf{X}_i$ and let $\lambda_i = (K_{1,\,i} = E_{1,\,i} \cdot E_{4,\,i}^{-y}, K_{2,\,i} = E_{2,\,i}, K_{3,\,i} = E_{3,\,i})$ Then check whether $\hat{e}(K_{1,\,i}, g) \cdot \hat{e}(K_{2,\,i}, u_0 \prod_{j=1}^{k} u_i^{m_j})^{-1} \cdot \hat{e}(K_{3,\,i}, R)^{-1} \stackrel{?}{=} \mathbf{X}_i$ hold or not. Finally, if the above holds then TP outputs a vector $\bar{\lambda} = \{\lambda_1, ..., \lambda_n\}$ and sends to all signers.
- Extract the multi-signature: each signer computes $\forall i \in \{1, ..., n\}$: $\sigma_i = (\theta_i = K_{1,\,i} \cdot K_{3,\,i}^{-\gamma}, \phi_i = K_{2,\,i})$ Finally, each signer computes a multi-signature on message M which is $\Theta = (\theta = \prod_{i=1}^{n} \theta_i, \phi = \prod_{i=1}^{n} \phi_i)$.

$\Sigma.Verify$: Given $\mathcal{LS} = \{pk_{S_1}, ..., pk_{S_n}\}$, Θ and a message M, a verifier V checks whether $\hat{e}(\theta, g) \cdot \hat{e}(\theta, u_0 \prod_{j=1}^{k} u_j^{m_j})^{-1} \stackrel{?}{=} \prod_{j=1}^{n} \mathbf{X}_j$ holds or not. If the equation holds, then accept the signature. Otherwise, reject.

7 Conclusion

We introduced the notion of fair multi-signature (FMS) schemes to capture the need for fairness of the authenticity of the message produced by senders (signers) in multi-signature schemes. Our FMS notion bridges the gap between theory and practice, by enabling all honest signers to be assured with the fairness of the scheme. We proceeded with a generic construction of FMS schemes from VES, together with its instantiation that is secure in the standard model. Moreover, our current progressing work are transforming fair multi-signatures to optimistic fair multi-signatures and construct efficient schemes for both fair multi-signature and optimistic fair multi-signature.

References

1. Bao, F., Deng, R.H., Mao, W.: Efficient and practical fair exchange protocols with off-line ttp. In: IEEE Symposium on Security and Privacy, pp. 77–85. IEEE Computer Society (1998)
2. Bellare, M., Neven, G.: Multi-signatures in the plain public-key model and a general forking lemma. In: Juels, A., Wright, R.N., di Vimercati, S.D.C. (eds.) ACM Conference on Computer and Communications Security, pp. 390–399. ACM (2006)
3. Boneh, D., Gentry, C., Lynn, B., Shacham, H.: Aggregate and verifiably encrypted signatures from bilinear maps. In: Biham, E. (ed.) EUROCRYPT 2003. LNCS, vol. 2656, pp. 416–432. Springer, Heidelberg (2003)
4. Cleve, R.: Limits on the security of coin flips when half the processors are faulty (extended abstract). In: Hartmanis, J. (ed.) STOC, pp. 364–369. ACM (1986)

5. Itakura, K., Nakamura, K.: A public key cryptosystem suitable for digital multisignatures. NEC Res. Dev. **71**, 1–8 (1983)

6. Lu, S., Ostrovsky, R., Sahai, A., Shacham, H., Waters, B.: Sequential aggregate signatures and multisignatures without random oracles. In: Vaudenay, S. (ed.) EUROCRYPT 2006. LNCS, vol. 4004, pp. 465–485. Springer, Heidelberg (2006)

7. Lu, S., Ostrovsky, R., Sahai, A., Shacham, H., Waters, B.: Sequential aggregate signatures, multisignatures, and verifiably encrypted signatures without random oracles. J. Cryptology **26**(2), 340–373 (2013)

8. Lysyanskaya, A., Micali, S., Reyzin, L., Shacham, H.: Sequential aggregate signatures from trapdoor permutations. In: Cachin, C., Camenisch, J.L. (eds.) EUROCRYPT 2004. LNCS, vol. 3027, pp. 74–90. Springer, Heidelberg (2004)

9. Micali, S., Ohta, K., Reyzin, L.: Accountable-subgroup multisignatures: extended abstract. In: ACM Conference on Computer and Communications Security, pp. 245–254 (2001)

10. Okamoto, T.: A digital multisignature schema using bijective public-key cryptosystems. ACM Trans. Comput. Syst. **6**(4), 432–441 (1988)

11. Ristenpart, T., Yilek, S.: The power of proofs-of-possession: securing multiparty signatures against rogue-key attacks. In: Naor, M. (ed.) EUROCRYPT 2007. LNCS, vol. 4515, pp. 228–245. Springer, Heidelberg (2007)

12. Thorncharoensri, P., Susilo, W., Mu, Y.: Fair multi-signature. In: Rhee, K.-H., Yi, J.H. (eds) WISA 2014, LNCS 8909, pp. 244–256. Springer, Heidelberg (2015)

13. Waters, B.: Efficient identity-based encryption without random oracles. In: Cramer, R. (ed.) EUROCRYPT 2005. LNCS, vol. 3494, pp. 114–127. Springer, Heidelberg (2005)

An Efficient Variant
of Boneh-Gentry-Hamburg's Identity-Based
Encryption Without Pairing

Ibrahim Elashry$^{(\boxtimes)}$, Yi Mu, and Willy Susilo

Centre for Computer and Information Security Research School of Computer Science
and Software Engineering, University of Wollongong, Wollongong, Australia
ifeae231@uowmail.edu.au, {ymu,wsusilo}@uow.edu.au

Abstract. Boneh, Gentry and Hamburg presented an encryption
system known as BasicIBE without incorporating pairings. This system has short ciphertext size but this comes at the cost of less time-
efficient encryption/decryption algorithms in which their processing time
increases drastically with the message length. Moreover, the private key
size is l elements in $\mathbb{Z}_N$, where N is a Blum integer and l is the message
length. In this paper, we optimize this system in two steps. First, we
decrease the private key length from l elements in $\mathbb{Z}_N$ to only one element. Second, we present two efficient variants of the BasicIBE in terms
of ciphertext length and encryption/decryption speed. The ciphertext is
as short as the BasicIBE, but with more time-efficient algorithms which
do not depend on the message length. The proposed system is very time
efficient compared to other IBE systems and it is as secure as the BasicIBE system.

Keywords: Identity-based encryption · Quadratic residuosity assumption · IND-ID-CPA

1 Introduction

In 1985, Shamir [12] presented the notion of identity-based encryption (IBE) in
which the user's identity represents his public key and consequently, no public
key certificate is required. Shamir successfully managed to design an identity-
based signature based on the RSA algorithm but he was unable to design an
IBE because sharing an RSA modulus between different users makes RSA insecure [12]. The design of a provable secure IBE remained an open problem for
sixteen years until Boneh and Franklin [4] proposed a provably secure IBE in
the random oracle model based on bilinear maps. Subsequently, there has been
a rapid development in IBE based on bilinear maps, such as [2,3,10,13].

However, all the previously mentioned IBEs are based on pairing operations.
According to MIRACL benchmarks, a 512-bit Tate pairing takes 20 ms while a
1024-bit prime modular exponentiation takes 8.80 ms. The pairing computations
are expensive compared to normal operations. The costly pairing computation

© Springer International Publishing Switzerland 2015
K.-H. Rhee and J.H. Yi (Eds.): WISA 2014, LNCS 8909, pp. 257–268, 2015.
DOI: 10.1007/978-3-319-15087-1_20

limits it from being used in wide applications, specially when time and power consumptions are a major concern such as in limited wireless sensor networks. Hence, the seek for a scheme that does not rely on pairings is desirable.

Another approach to design IBEs is based on the quadratic residuosity (QR) assumption. The first IBE based on this approach is due to Cocks [6]. This system is IND-ID-CPA secure in the random oracle model. It is time-efficient compared to pairing-based IBEs, but it produces a long ciphertext of two elements in $\mathbb{Z}_N$ for every bit in the message.

The design of efficient IBEs without pairings was an open problem until Boneh, Gentry and Hamburg [5] presented two space-efficient systems (BasicIBE and AnonIBE) in which the ciphertext is reduced from $2l$ elements to only one element in $\mathbb{Z}_N$. As in Cocks' IBE, the security of BasicIBE is based on the QR assumption in the random oracle model. Although the concrete instantiation of BasicIBE is highly space-efficient, this comes at the cost of less time-efficient encryption/decryption algorithms. To encrypt an l-bit message, BasicIBE solves $l+1$ equations in the form $Rx^2 + Sy^2 \equiv 1 \pmod{N}$ for known values of R, S and N [5]. Solving such an equation requires a 'solubility certificate' and obtaining these certificates requires the generation of primes [6–8]. The obtained certificates can be used to solve $Rx^2 + Sy^2 \equiv 1 \pmod{N}$ efficiently using the Cremona-Rusin algorithm [8]. The prime generation is a time-consuming process and it is the bottleneck in the BGH systems. Moreover, the decryption key is l elements in $\mathbb{Z}_N$ because the identity ID is hashed to a different value to encrypt each bit. AnonIBE is based on BasicIBE and it is Anon-IND-ID-CPA secure in the standard model under the interactive quadratic residuosity (IQR) assumption [5]. Moreover, the ciphertext length is reduced to one element in $\mathbb{Z}_N$ plus $l + 1$ bits.

Jhanwar and Barua [11] made some significant observations on the BGH systems (for solving equations in the form $Rx^2 + Sy^2 \equiv 1 \pmod{N}$) and proposed a trade-off system that reduces the private key length but increases the ciphertext length. They found that by knowing the value of $S \pmod{N}$, one can find a random solution to the equation $Rx^2 + Sy^2 \equiv 1 \pmod{N}$ using only one inversion in $\mathbb{Z}_N$. The sender solves only $2\sqrt{l}$ equations in the form $Rx^2 + Sy^2 \equiv 1 \pmod{N}$ using only $2\sqrt{l}$ inversions in $\mathbb{Z}_N$ and thus, no prime generation is required. This increases the encryption/decryption speed dramatically. The private key is only one element in $\mathbb{Z}_N$. However, this system produces a large ciphertext of $2\sqrt{l}$ elements in $\mathbb{Z}_N$.

Our Contribution. In this paper, we first present some definitions and review Basic IBE. After that, we optimise BasicIBE in two steps. First, we prove that hashing the identity ID to a different value to encrypt each bit is as secure as hashing the identity once to encrypt the whole message and therefore, the private key length is reduced to one element in $\mathbb{Z}_N$. Then, we present a variant of BasicIBE (V-BasicIBE) which is both time- and space- efficient. Moreover, we prove that V-BasicIBE is as secure as BasicIBE. Although the proposed variant has the same ciphertext length as BasicIBE, it only solves two equations in the form $Rx^2 + Sy^2 \equiv 1 \pmod{N}$ regardless of the message length. We also present another version of V-BasicIBE with a time-space trade-off. For V-BasicIBE, with only the cost of one more element in $\mathbb{Z}_N$, the sender can find a solution to $Rx^2 + Sy^2 \equiv 1 \pmod{N}$ using only one inversion in $\mathbb{Z}_N$ and the receiver does not have to solve any of these equations. The proposed variant is time- and power-efficient compared to other IBE systems. It does not use expensive-computational operations such as pairing like Boneh-Boyen or Boneh-Franklin IBEs [2,4] or even a prime modular exponentiation such as RSA. Table 1 compares all systems in this paper, where V2-BasicIBE is the proposed systems with the trade-off applied. In this table, the symbol m represents prime modular exponentiation while e and p represents pairing operation and prime generation respectively. l represents the message length. The symbols G and G_T represents an element in two groups G and G_T such that $e : G \times G \to G_T$.

Table 1. Comparison between various IBEs and the proposed IBEs

	Expensive mathematical operations	Ciphertext length
Cock's	0	$2l(\log N)$
The BasicIBE	$(l+1)p$	$\log N + 2l$
The AnonIBE	$(2l+1)p$	$\log N + l + 1$
V-BasicIBE	$2p$	$\log_2 N + 2l$
V2-BasicIBE	0	$2\log_2 N + 2l$
Jhanwar-Barua	0	$2\sqrt{l}\log N + 2l$
Boneh-Boyen	$e+3m$	G_T+2G
Boneh-Franklin	e	$G+l$

2 Definitions

2.1 IND-ID-CPA

The IND-ID-CPA security model of an IBE is described as a game between an adversary $\mathcal{A}$ and a challenger $\mathcal{C}$ [4,12]. This game is as follows:

- Setup(λ): $\mathcal{C}$ generates the public parameters (PP) and sends them to $\mathcal{A}$ and keeps the master secret (MSK) to himself.
- Query Phase: In this phase, $\mathcal{A}$ sends private key queries to $\mathcal{C}$ for identities ID_s of his choice. These queries are adaptive based on previous queries.
- Challenge: Satisfied with private key queries, $\mathcal{A}$ sends to $\mathcal{C}$ two messages m_1 and m_2 for an identity ID^*. $\mathcal{C}$ tosses a coin $b \in [0,1]$ randomly and encrypts m_b using ID^*. Note that ID^* must not be queried in the query phase.
- Guess: $\mathcal{A}$ outputs $\bar{b} \in [0,1]$. $\mathcal{A}$ wins the game if $b = \bar{b}$.

The advantage of $\mathcal{A}$ to attack a system ξ and win this game is:

$$IBEAdv_{\mathcal{A},\xi}(\lambda) = |pr[\bar{b} = b] - \tfrac{1}{2}|.$$

If $\mathcal{A}$ submits two pairs of (ID_0, m_0) and (ID_1, m_1) in the challenge phase, then this game is called the ANON-IND-ID-CPA security model. The advantage of the adversary winning this game is the same as above.

2.2 QR Assumption and Jacobi Symbols

For a positive integer N, define the following set:

$$J(N) = [a \in \mathbb{Z}_N : \left(\frac{a}{N}\right) = 1],$$

where $\left(\frac{a}{N}\right)$ is the Jacobi symbol of a w.r.t N [5]. The Quadratic Residue set $QR(N)$ is defined as follows

$$QR(N) = [a \in \mathbb{Z}_N : gcd(a, N) = 1 \wedge x^2 \equiv a \pmod{N} \text{ has a solution}].$$

Definition 1. *Quadratic Residuosity Assumption: Let RSAgen(λ) be a probabilistic polynomial time (PPT) algorithm. This algorithm generates two equal size primes p, q. The QR assumption holds for RSAgen if it cannot distinguish between the following two distributions for all PPT algorithms $\mathcal{A}$ [5].*

$$P_{QR}(\lambda) : (N, V)(p, q) \leftarrow RSAgen(\lambda), N = pq, V \in_R QR(N),$$

$$P_{NQR}(\lambda) : (N, V)(p, q) \leftarrow RSAgen(\lambda), N = pq, V \in_R J(N) \setminus QR(N).$$

In other words, the advantage of $\mathcal{A}$ against QR assumption $QRAdv_{\mathcal{A}, RSAgen(\lambda)} =$

$$|\Pr[(N, V) \leftarrow P_{QR}(\lambda) : \mathcal{A}(N, V) = 1]| - |\Pr[(N, V) \leftarrow P_{NQR}(\lambda) : \mathcal{A}(N, V) = 1]|$$

is negligible. i.e. $\mathcal{A}$ cannot distinguish between elements in $J(N) \setminus QR(N)$ and elements in $QR(N)$.

3   Review of the BasicIBE System [5]

BasicIBE encrypts an l-bit message m using a square $S \equiv s^2 \pmod{N}$ where $s \in_R \mathbb{Z}_N$, the user's identity ID and a pair of Jacobi symbols for each bit. It first hashes ID to different values $H(ID, i) = u^a R_i = r_i^2$ where $a \in \{0, 1\}$, $u \in J(N) \setminus QR(N)$ and i is the bit index. Then it solves the equations $R_i x_i^2 + S y_i^2 \equiv 1 \pmod{N}$ and $u R_i \overline{x}_i^2 + S \overline{y}_i^2 \equiv 1 \pmod{N}$ to get $(x_i, y_i, \overline{x}_i, \overline{y}_i)$. The ciphertext is $(S, c, \overline{c})$ where $c \leftarrow [c_1, c_2, c_3, ..., c_l]$, $c_i = m \cdot \left(\frac{2 + 2y_i s}{N}\right)$ and $\overline{c} \leftarrow [\overline{c}_1, \overline{c}_2, \overline{c}_3, ..., \overline{c}_l]$, $\overline{c}_i = m \cdot \left(\frac{2 + 2\overline{y}_i s}{N}\right)$. To decrypt, one needs to know the square-root of R_i or $u R_i$. If $R_i = r_i^2$, the message is $m_i = c_i \cdot \left(\frac{1 + x_i r_i}{N}\right)$ and if $u R_i = r_i^2$, the message is $m_i = \overline{c}_i \cdot \left(\frac{1 + \overline{x}_i r_i}{N}\right)$.

4 Optimization of BasicIBE

4.1 Optimization of the Private Key Length

As shown above, the BasicIBE system hashes the identity ID to different values $H(ID, i) = u^a R_i = r_i^2, a \in \{0, 1\}$. This has a negative impact on the system. First, the private key length is larger than the message by a factor of $\mathbb{Z}_N$ which consumes bandwidth and memory. Second, the Private Key Generator (PKG) must generate n private keys of l elements in $\mathbb{Z}_N$ where n is the number of users in the whole system. This overloads the PKG. Third, this not suitable for encrypting variable messages length.

In this section, we prove that hashing the identity ID to different values $R_i = H(ID, i)$ does not have a positive impact on the security of BasicIBE. Solving the equations $Rx_i^2 + Sy_i^2 \equiv 1 \pmod{N}$ is exactly equivalent to solving the equations $R_i x_i^2 + Sy_i^2 \equiv 1 \pmod{N}$. Consequently, there is no need for generating a long private key of l elements in $\mathbb{Z}_{\mathbb{N}}$.

Theorem 1. *Hashing the identity ID to a different value to encrypt each bit is as secure as hashing the identity once to encrypt the whole message.*

Proof. Jhanwar and Barua [1] showed that there is $N - 1$ solutions for the equation $Rx^2 + Sy^2 \equiv 1 \pmod{N}$ if $S, R \in QR(N)$. The solution (x, y) for that equation is in the form:

$$\left(\frac{-2st}{R + St^2}, \frac{R - St^2}{s(R + St^2)} \right)$$

for some $t \in \mathbb{Z}_N^*$ such that $R + St^2 \in \mathbb{Z}_N^*$.

$$Rx_i^2 + Sy_i^2 = R\left(\frac{-2st}{R + St^2} \right)^2 + Sy_i^2 = \left(\frac{4SR}{(R + St^2)^2} \right) t^2 + Sy_i^2 = R_i \bar{x}_i^2 + Sy_i^2$$

$$\text{where } R_i = t^2 \text{ and } \bar{x}_i = \frac{-2sr}{R + St^2}.$$

Since t is random in $\mathbb{Z}_N^*$, R_i looks mathematically random exactly as $R_i = H(ID, i)$. □

4.2 V-BasicIBE

In this section, we explain how to implement a variant of BasicIBE (V-BasicIBE) that is both time and space efficient. Like any other IBE, V-BasicIBE consists of four algorithms; Setup, KeyGen, Encrypt and Decrypt.

- Setup(λ): Using RSAgen(λ), generate (p,q), calculate the modulus $N \leftarrow pq$, choose $u \in J(N) \setminus QR(N)$, and choose a hash function $H : ID \rightarrow J(N)$. The public parameters PP are $[N, u, H]$. The master secret MSK parameters are p, q and a secret key K for a pseudorandom function $F_K : ID \rightarrow [0, 1, 2, 3]$.

- KeyGen(MSK, ID, l): Calculate $R \leftarrow H(ID) \in J(N)$ and $w \leftarrow F_K(ID) \in \{0, 1, 2, 3\}$. Choose $a \in \{0, 1\}$ such that $u^a R \in QR(N)$. Let $[z_0, z_1, z_2, z_3]$ be the four square roots of $u^a R \in \mathbb{Z}_N$, then $r \leftarrow z_w$.
- Encrypt(id, m): To encrypt a message $m \in \{-1, 1\}^l$, V-BasicIBE calculates $[x_i, y_i, \overline{x}_i, \overline{y}_i]$, $i \in [0, l-1]$ such that these variables satisfy the following equations:

$$[x_i, y_i] \leftarrow Rx_i^2 + S^j y_i^2 \equiv 1 \pmod{N} , \ [\overline{x}_i, \overline{y}_i] \leftarrow uR\overline{x}_i^2 + S^j \overline{y}_i^2 \equiv 1 \pmod{N}$$

for an odd number $j = 2i + 1$. To solve these equations, we review a product formula presented by Boneh, Gentry and Hamburg [5].

Lemma 1. *For $i = 1, 2$ let (x_i, y_i) be a solution to $R_i x^2 + Sy^2 \equiv 1 \pmod{N}$. Then (x_3, y_3) is a solution to*

$$R_1 R_2 x^2 + Sy^2 \equiv 1 \pmod{N},$$

where $x_3 = \frac{x_1 x_2}{Sy_1 y_2 + 1}$ and $y_3 = \frac{y_1 + y_2}{Sy_1 y_2 + 1}$.

Proof. By directly substituting the values of x_3 and y_3 in the equation $R_1 R_2 x^2 + Sy^2 \equiv 1 \pmod{N}$.

Jhanwar and Barua [11] presented a variant of Lemma 1 to implement their system. This lemma states that:

Lemma 2. *For $i = 1, 2$ let (x_i, y_i) be a solution to $Rx^2 + S_i y^2 \equiv 1 \pmod{N}$. Then (x_3, y_3) is a solution to*

$$Rx^2 + S_1 S_2 y^2 \equiv 1 \pmod{N},$$

where $x_3 = \frac{x_1 + x_2}{Rx_1 x_2 + 1}$ and $y_3 = \frac{y_1 y_2}{Rx_1 x_2 + 1}$

Proof. Same as Lemma 1.

To solve these equations, BasicIBE calculates $[x_0, y_0]$ and then uses Lemma 2 to find $[x_i, y_i]$ as follows.

$$\hat{x} = \frac{2x_0}{Rx_0^2 + 1}, \ \hat{y} = \frac{y_0^2}{Rx_0^2 + 1}, \ x_i = \frac{\hat{x} + x_{i-1}}{R\hat{x}x_{i-1} + 1}, \ y_i = \frac{\hat{y}y_{i-1}}{R\hat{x}x_{i-1} + 1},$$

where $[\hat{x}, \hat{y}]$ is a solution to $R\hat{x}^2 + S^2\hat{y}^2 \equiv 1 \pmod{N}$. Similarly, $[\overline{x}_i, \overline{y}_i]$ are generated as shown above.

The message $m \leftarrow [m_0, m_1, ..., m_{l-1}]$ is encrypted using the following formula:

$$c_i \leftarrow m_i \cdot \left(\frac{2y_i s^j + 2}{N}\right) , \ \overline{c}_i \leftarrow m_i \cdot \left(\frac{2\overline{y}_i s^j + 2}{N}\right).$$

The ciphertext is $C \leftarrow (S, c, \overline{c})$.

– Decrypt(C, r): The message can be retrieved from the ciphertext as follows.

$$m_i \leftarrow c_i \cdot \left(\frac{x_i r + 1}{N} \right) \quad \text{if } r^2 = R \quad \text{and} \quad m_i \leftarrow \bar{c}_i \cdot \left(\frac{\bar{x}_i r + 1}{N} \right) \quad \text{if } r^2 = uR.$$

Correctness: As in [5], it is easy to prove that:

$$(x_i r + 1) \cdot (2y_i s^j + 2) = 2x_i r y_i s^j + 2x_i r + 2y_i s^j + 2 + (Rx_i^2 + S^j y_i^2 - 1)$$
$$= (x_i r + y_i s^j + 1)^2,$$
$$\left(\frac{x_i r + 1}{N} \right) \cdot \left(\frac{2y_i s^j + 2}{N} \right) = 1, \quad \left(\frac{x_i r + 1}{N} \right) = \left(\frac{2y_i s^j + 2}{N} \right).$$

4.3   V-BasicIBE Security

Theorem 2. *Suppose the quadratic residuosity assumption holds for RSAgen and F is a secure PRF. Then the proposed V-BasicIBE is IND-ID-CPA secure based on the QR assumption when H is modelled as a random oracle. In particular, suppose $\mathcal{A}$ is an efficient IND-ID-CPA adversary, then there exist efficient algorithms B_1, B_2 whose running time is the same as that of $\mathcal{A}$ such that:*

$$IBEAdv_{\mathcal{A}, V-BasicIBE}(\lambda) \leq 2QRAdv_{B_2, RSAgen}(\lambda) + PRFAdv_{B_1, F}(\lambda).$$

We first introduce Lemma 3 [5].

Lemma 3. *Let $N = pq$ be an RSA modulus, $S_i, R \in J(N)$. Then*

– *1-When $R \in J(N) \setminus QR(N)$, $S_i \in QR(N)$, the Jacobi symbols $\left(\frac{g(s_i)}{N} \right)$ for any function g are uniformly distributed in $\{\pm 1\}$, where s_i is a random variable uniformly chosen among the four square roots of S_i modulo N and $g(s_i)g(-s_i) R \in QR(N)$ for all the four values of s_i.*
– *2-When $S_i \in J(N) \setminus QR(N)$, $R \in QR(N)$, the Jacobi symbols $\left(\frac{f(r)}{N} \right)$ for any function f are uniformly distributed in $\{\pm 1\}$, where r is a random variable uniformly chosen among the four square roots of R modulo N and $f(r)f(-r) S_i \in QR(N)$ for all the four values of r.*
– *3-When $S_i, R \in QR(N)$, the Jacobi symbols $\left(\frac{g(s_i)}{N} \right)$ and $\left(\frac{f(r)}{N} \right)$ are constant, i.e. the same for all four values of r and s_i.*

Proof. Let $s_i, \bar{s}_i$ be the four square roots of $S_i \in QR(N)$ such that $\bar{s}_i = s_i$ (mod p) and $\bar{s}_i = -s_i$ (mod q), then the four square roots of S_i are $\{\pm\bar{s}_i, \pm s_i\}$. We can assume the same for $R \in QR(N)$ and the four square roots are $\{\pm\bar{r}, \pm r\}$, where $\bar{r} = r$ (mod p) and $\bar{r} = -r$ (mod q).

Case 1

$$\left(\frac{g(s)g(-s)R}{N}\right) = \left(\frac{g(s)g(-s)R}{p}\right) = \left(\frac{g(s)g(-s)R}{q}\right) = 1.$$

$$\left(\frac{R}{p}\right) = \left(\frac{R}{q}\right) = -1,$$

$$\left(\frac{g(s)g(-s)}{p}\right) = \left(\frac{g(s)g(-s)}{q}\right) = -1,$$

$$\left(\frac{g(s)}{p}\right) = -\left(\frac{g(-s)}{p}\right) \quad and \quad \left(\frac{g(s)}{q}\right) = -\left(\frac{g(-s)}{q}\right),$$

$$\left(\frac{g(s)}{N}\right) = \left(\frac{g(-s)}{N}\right).$$

$$\left(\frac{g(\bar{s})}{p}\right) = \left(\frac{g(s)}{p}\right).$$

$$\left(\frac{g(\bar{s})}{q}\right) = \left(\frac{g(-s)}{q}\right) = -\left(\frac{g(s)}{q}\right),$$

$$\left(\frac{g(\bar{s})}{p}\right)\left(\frac{g(\bar{s})}{q}\right) = -\left(\frac{g(s)}{p}\right)\left(\frac{g(s)}{q}\right),$$

$$\left(\frac{g(\bar{s})}{N}\right) = -\left(\frac{g(s)}{N}\right),$$

$$\left(\frac{g(\bar{s})}{N}\right) = \left(\frac{g(-\bar{s})}{N}\right) = -\left(\frac{g(s)}{N}\right) = -\left(\frac{g(-s)}{N}\right).$$

That means that among the four Jacobi symbols $\left(\frac{g(\bar{a})}{N}\right)$, $\left(\frac{g(-\bar{a})}{N}\right)$, $\left(\frac{g(a)}{N}\right)$, $\left(\frac{g(-a)}{N}\right)$ two are $+1$ and two are -1. Case 2 and Case 3 can be proven similarly to Case 1.

- **Security Proof.** We define a sequence of games and let W_i represents the winning of the i_{th} game by the adversary $\mathcal{A}$. These games are defined as follows.
  - **Game-0.** This game is the usual adversarial game.
  - **Game-1.** This game replaces the PRF F with a truly random function.
  - **Game-2.** This game explains how to simulate the hash function H.
  - **Game-3.** This game sets $u \in QR(N)$.
  - **Game-4.** This game explains how to respond to an encryption query from $\mathcal{A}$.
  - **Game-5.** This game sets $R \in J(N) \setminus QR(N)$.
  - **Game-6.** This game sets $S_i = s_i^2$ for each bit.
  - **Game-7** replaces the message m with a random number z.
- Game-0. This is the usual adversarial game for defining the IND-ID-CPA security of IBE protocols. The challenger picks the random oracle $H : ID \rightarrow$

$J(N)$ at random from the set of all such functions in the *Setup* algorithm and allows $\mathcal{A}$ to query H at arbitrary points. Thus, we have

$$\left| \Pr[W_0] - \frac{1}{2} \right| = IBEAdv_{\mathcal{A}, V-BasicIBE}(\lambda).$$

- Game-1. This is the same as Game-0, with the following change. In *Setup* algorithm, instead of using a PRF F to respond to $\mathcal{A}$'s private key queries, we use a truly random function $f : ID \rightarrow \{0, 1, 2, 3\}$. If F is a secure PRF, $\mathcal{A}$ will not notice the difference between Game-0 and Game-1. In particular, there exists an algorithm B_1 (whose running time is about the same as that of $\mathcal{A}$) such that

$$|\Pr[W_1] - \Pr[W_0]| = PRFAdv_{B_1, F}(\lambda).$$

- Game-2. (N, u, H) are the public parameters PP given to $\mathcal{A}$ in the previous game where u is uniform in $J(N) \setminus QR(N)$ and the random oracle H is a random function $H : ID \rightarrow J(N)$. We make the following change in the random oracle H in this game. The challenger responds to a query to $H(ID)$ by picking $a \in_R \{0, 1\}$ and $v \in_R \mathbb{Z}_N$ and setting $H(ID) = u^a v^2$. Thus the challenger implements a random function $H : ID \rightarrow J(N)$ as in the previous game. The challenger responds to a private key query as follows.

  Suppose $R = H(ID) = u^a v^2$ for some $a \in_R \{0, 1\}$ and $v \in_R \mathbb{Z}_N$. The challenger responds to a private key query for ID by setting either $R^{\frac{1}{2}} = v$ (when $a = 0$) or $(uR)^{\frac{1}{2}} = uv$ (when $a = 1$). Since v is uniform in $\mathbb{Z}_N$ this will produce a square root of R or uR which is also uniform among the four square roots, as in the previous game. Thus, $\mathcal{A}$'s views in Game-1 and Game-2 are identical and therefore,
$$|\Pr[W_1] = \Pr[W_2]|.$$

- Game-3. In this game, the challenger chooses u uniformly in $QR(N)$ instead of $J(N) \setminus QR(N)$. Since this is the only change between Game-2 and Game-3, $\mathcal{A}$ will not notice the difference assuming that the QR assumption holds for RSAgen. In particular, there exists an algorithm B_2 (whose running time is about the same as that of $\mathcal{A}$) such that:

$$|\Pr[W_3] - \Pr[W_2]| = QRAdv_{B_2, RSAgen}(\lambda).$$

- Game-4. We describe below in detail how, in this game, the challenger responds to an encryption query from $\mathcal{A}$.
  - He chooses $R \in QR(N)$ and sets $H(ID) = R$. (*)
  - He chooses $s \in_R \mathbb{Z}_N$ and computes $S^j = s^{2j}$ for an odd value j.
  - He sets $c \leftarrow Encrypt(PP, ID, m_b)$.
  - He sends (S, c) to $\mathcal{A}$.
- Game-5. In this game, we make a change in the challenge phase. We replace the line (*) in Game-4 with the following:
  - He chooses $R \in J(N) \setminus QR(N)$ and sets $H(ID) = R$.

Since the only difference between Game-5 and Game-4 is that $R \in J(N) \setminus QR(N)$ in Game-5 instead of $R \in QR(N)$ in Game-4, $\mathcal{A}$ will not notice the difference assuming that the QR assumption holds for RSAgen. In particular, there exists an algorithm B_2 (whose running time is about the same as that of $\mathcal{A}$) such that:

$$|\Pr[W_5] - \Pr[W_4]| = QRAdv_{B_2, RSAgen}(\lambda).$$

- Game-6: In this game, we encrypt the message by choosing $s_i \in \mathbb{Z}_N$ independently and randomly for each bit. In other words, we replace the Jacobi symbols $\left(\frac{2y_i s^j + 2}{N}\right)$ and $\left(\frac{2\overline{y}_i s^j + 2}{N}\right)$ with the Jacobi symbols $\left(\frac{2y_i s_i + 2}{N}\right)$ and $\left(\frac{2\overline{y}_i s_i + 2}{N}\right)$ respectively i.e. $c_i = m_i \cdot \left(\frac{2y_i s_i + 2}{N}\right)$ and $\overline{c}_i = m_i \cdot \left(\frac{2\overline{y}_i s_i + 2}{N}\right)$. To prove that Game-6 is indistinguishable from Game-5, we present the following Theorem.

Theorem 3. *The distribution of the Jacobi symbols* $\left(\frac{2y_i s^j + 2}{N}\right)$ *is indistinguishable from the distribution the Jacobi symbols* $\left(\frac{2y_i s_i + 2}{N}\right)$.

The proof of this theorem is based on the work of Damgard [9]. He proved that the Jacobi sequences are indistinguishable from random. i.e. if an adversary knows the value of $\left(\frac{a}{N}\right)$, it is a hard problem to find $\left(\frac{a+1}{N}\right)$ for an unknown value a. Although the values of a and $a+1$ are highly correlated and dependent, that does not mean that their Jacobi symbols are correlated. We now present a formal proof for the above theorem.

Proof. Damgard proved that the following is a hard problem [9].

Lemma 4. *Let J be the Jacobi sequence modulo N with a starting point a and length $P(k)$, for a security parameter k and polynomial P. Given J, find* $\left(\frac{a+P(k)+1}{N}\right)$.

This means that, knowing $\left(\frac{a}{N}\right), \left(\frac{a+1}{N}\right), \left(\frac{a+2}{N}\right), ..., \left(\frac{a+a_1}{N}\right), ..., \left(\frac{a+a_2}{N}\right), ...,$ $\left(\frac{a+P}{N}\right)$, it is a hard problem to find $\left(\frac{a+P+1}{N}\right)$.

We first choose a and P such that $a + P + 1 = 2y_i s^j + 2$, then we can write the above sequence in two different forms:

$$\left(\frac{a}{N}\right), \left(\frac{a+1}{N}\right), \left(\frac{a+2}{N}\right), ..., \left(\frac{2y_{i_1} s^{j_1} + 2}{N}\right), ..., \left(\frac{2y_{i_2} s^{j_2} + 2}{N}\right), ..., \left(\frac{a+P}{N}\right)$$

where $a_1 = 2y_{i_1} s^{j_1} + 2 - a$, $a_2 = 2y_{i_2} s^{j_2} + 2 - a$, and $j_1 < j_2 < j$.

$$\left(\frac{a}{N}\right), \left(\frac{a+1}{N}\right), \left(\frac{a+2}{N}\right), ..., \left(\frac{2y_{i_1} s_{j_1} + 2}{N}\right), ..., \left(\frac{2y_{i_2} s_{j_2} + 2}{N}\right), ..., \left(\frac{a+P}{N}\right)$$

where $a_1 = 2y_{i_1} s_{j_1} + 2 - a$, $a_2 = 2y_{i_2} s_{j_2} + 2 - a$.

Since $\mathbb{Z}_N$ is an additive group, the values of a_1, a_2 and P exist in both sequences for any value y or s which means that both sequences represent the Damgard hard problem. Moreover, guessing the Jacobi symbol $\left(\frac{2y_i s^j + 2}{N}\right)$

from the sequence $\left(\frac{2y_i s + 2}{N}\right)$, $\left(\frac{2y_i s^2 + 2}{N}\right), ..., \left(\frac{2y_i s^{j-1} + 2}{N}\right)$ is as hard as guessing the same Jacobi symbol from the sequence $\left(\frac{2y_i s_1 + 2}{N}\right), \left(\frac{2y_i s_2 + 2}{N}\right), ..., \left(\frac{2y_i s_j + 2}{N}\right)$. The same holds for $\left(\frac{2\overline{y}_i s^j + 2}{N}\right)$ and $\left(\frac{2\overline{y}_i s_i + 2}{N}\right)$. □

Based on Theorem 3, $\mathcal{A}$ will not be able to distinguish between Game-5 and Game-6. i.e.

$$| \Pr[W_6] = \Pr[W_5]|.$$

- Game-7: In this game, we replace the message $m^{(b)}$ by a random string $z \in_R$ $\{-1, 1\}^l$ i.e., $c_i = z_i \cdot \left(\frac{2y_i s_i + 2}{N}\right)$ and $\overline{c}_i = z_i \cdot \left(\frac{2\overline{y}_i s_i + 2}{N}\right)$. We first prove that $(2y_i s_i + 2)(-2y_i s_i + 2)R \in QR(N)$.

Proof. Let $g(s_i) = (2y_i s_i + 2)$, then we have

$$g(s_i)g(-s_i)R = 4(y_i s_i + 1)(-y_i s_i + 1)R,$$
$$g(s_i)g(-s_i)R = 4(1 - (y_i s_i)^2)R,$$
$$g(s_i)g(-s_i)R = 4(Rx_i^2)R = (2Rx_i)^2 \in QR(N).$$

Similarly, we can prove that $(2\overline{y}_i s_i + 2)(-2\overline{y}_i s_i + 2)uR \in QR(N)$.

Since $s_i \in QR(N)$, $R \in J(N) \setminus QR(N)$, $(2y_i s_i + 2)(-2y_i s_i + 2)R \in QR(N)$ and $(2\overline{y}_i s_i + 2)(-2\overline{y}_i s_i + 2)uR \in QR(N)$ then Case 1 in Lemma 3 can be applied and the distribution of the Jacobi symbols $\left(\frac{2y_i s_i + 2}{N}\right)$ and $\left(\frac{2\overline{y}_i s_i + 2}{N}\right)$ are random in $\{\pm 1\}$. Thus, $\mathcal{A}$ will not be able to distinguish between Game-6 and Game-7. i.e.

$$| \Pr[W_7] = \Pr[W_6]|.$$

- Clearly in Game-7 we have

$$| \Pr[W_7] = \frac{1}{2}|.$$

Combining all the previous equations proves theorem.

5 Space-Time Tradeoff

In this section, we present a trade-off between the time and the ciphertext length of the proposed systems. For V-BasicIBE, instead of sending S along with c and $\overline{c}$ as the full ciphertext C, the sender sends $C = (x_0, \overline{x}_0, c, \overline{c})$. Thus, he can solve $Rx^2 + Sy^2 \equiv 1 \pmod{N}$ using only one inversion in $\mathbb{Z}_N$. This results in high encryption speed. In the decryption, the receiver does not have to solve any equations and he can generate x_i or $\overline{x}_i$ (based on if $r^2 = R$ or uR) using Lemma 2. This, of course, comes at the cost of sending one more element in $\mathbb{Z}_N$.

6 Conclusion

This paper proposed a variant of BasicIBE. The proposed variant is more efficient (in terms of computation time) than previous IBE systems. We also proved that the proposed variant has the same security level as the BasicIBE system. Moreover, the proposed systems have only one element in the $\mathbb{Z}_N$ private key instead of l elements in $\mathbb{Z}_N$ as in BasicIBE. We also produced a time-space trade-off variant that is both time- and space-efficient.

References

1. Barua, R., Jhanwar, M.: On the number of solutions of the equation $Rx^2 + Sy^2 = 1 \bmod N$. Sankhya A Math. Stat. Probab. **72**, 226–236 (2010). doi:10.1007/s13171-010-0010-9
2. Boneh, D., Boyen, X.: Efficient selective-ID secure identity-based encryption without random oracles. In: Cachin, C., Camenisch, J.L. (eds.) EUROCRYPT 2004. LNCS, vol. 3027, pp. 223–238. Springer, Heidelberg (2004)
3. Boneh, D., Boyen, X.: Secure identity based encryption without random oracles. In: Franklin, M. (ed.) CRYPTO 2004. LNCS, vol. 3152, pp. 443–459. Springer, Heidelberg (2004)
4. Boneh, D., Franklin, M.: Identity-based encryption from the weil pairing. In: Kilian, J. (ed.) CRYPTO 2001. LNCS, vol. 2139, p. 213. Springer, Heidelberg (2001)
5. Boneh, D., Gentry, C., Hamburg, M.: Space-efficient identity based encryption without pairings. In: Proceedings of the 48th Annual IEEE Symposium on Foundations of Computer Science, FOCS '07, pages 647–657. IEEE Computer Society, Washington, DC, USA (2007)
6. Cocks, C.: An identity based encryption scheme based on quadratic residues. In: Honary, B. (ed.) Cryptography and Coding 2001. LNCS, vol. 2260, pp. 360–363. Springer, Heidelberg (2001)
7. Cohen, H.: A Course in Computational Algebraic Number Theory. Springer, New York (1993)
8. Cremona, J.E., Rusin, D.: Efficient solution of rational conics. Math. Comput. **72**(243), 1417–1441 (2003)
9. Damgård, I.B.: On the randomness of legendre and jacobi sequences. In: Goldwasser, S. (ed.) CRYPTO 1988. LNCS, vol. 403, pp. 163–172. Springer, Heidelberg (1990)
10. Gentry, C.: Practical identity-based encryption without random oracles. In: Vaudenay, S. (ed.) EUROCRYPT 2006. LNCS, vol. 4004, pp. 445–464. Springer, Heidelberg (2006)
11. Jhanwar, M.P., Barua, R.: A variant of Boneh-Gentry-Hamburg's pairing-free identity based encryption scheme. In: Yung, M., Liu, P., Lin, D. (eds.) Inscrypt 2008. LNCS, vol. 5487, pp. 314–331. Springer, Heidelberg (2009)
12. Shamir, A.: Identity-based cryptosystems and signature schemes. In: Blakely, G.R., Chaum, D. (eds.) CRYPTO 1984. LNCS, vol. 196, pp. 47–53. Springer, Heidelberg (1985)
13. Waters, B.: Efficient identity-based encryption without random oracles. In: Cramer, R. (ed.) EUROCRYPT 2005. LNCS, vol. 3494, pp. 114–127. Springer, Heidelberg (2005)

Joint Signature and Encryption in the Presence of Continual Leakage

Fei Tang[1,2,3]($\boxtimes$) and Hongda Li[1,2]

[1] State Key Laboratory of Information Security, Institute of Information Engineering of Chinese Academy of Sciences, Beijing, China
tangfei127@163.com
[2] Data Assurance and Communication Security Research Center of Chinese Academy of Sciences, Beijing, China
lihongda@iie.ac.cn
[3] University of Chinese Academy of Sciences, Beijing, China

Abstract. The goal of leakage-resilient cryptography is to build schemes secure even if the secrets are partially leaked to the adversary. As far as we know, most existing leakage-resilient cryptographic schemes are studied in the setting of single secret, e.g., signing key of signature scheme, decryption key of encryption scheme. In this paper, we study the case of double secrets, i.e., the notion of a joint signature and encryption in the presence of continual leakage, for the first time. Following the terminology of [2], we refer to this primitive as leakage-resilient signcryption. In particular, we give two instantiations of such signcryption scheme based on existing leakage resilient signature and encryption schemes.

Keywords: Digital signatures · Public-key encryption · Continual leakage

1 Introduction

Signcryption. Digital signatures and public-key encryption schemes are two of the most fundamental and well studied cryptographic primitives for providing authenticity and confidentiality, respectively. In the beginning, they have been viewed as important but distinct basic building blocks of various cryptosystems, and have been designed and analyzed separately. But for most real-word applications, we need both confidentiality and authenticity at the same time. Based on this consideration, Zheng [25] studied the notion of a joint signature and encryption with the primary goal of reaching greater efficiency than when carrying out the signature and encryption operations separately. Whereafter, An, Dodis, and Rabin [2] argued that efficiency is not the only one concern, albeit it is important, when designing a secure joint signature and encryption. They used

This research is supported by the National Natural Science Foundation of China (Grant No. 60970139) and the Strategic Priority Program of Chinese Academy of Sciences (Grant No. XDA06010702).

K.-H. Rhee and J.H. Yi (Eds.): WISA 2014, LNCS 8909, pp. 269–280, 2015.
DOI: 10.1007/978-3-319-15087-1_21

the term "signcryption" to refer to a "joint signature and encryption" for any scheme achieving both authenticity and confidentiality in the public key setting. Following [2], we also use the term "signcryption" for any scheme have properties of confidentiality and authenticity but irrespective of its performance.

Security for signcryption. An, Dodis, and Rabin [2] studied the security for the signcryption schemes in the two-user setting and analyzed its security that are constructed by generically composing signature and encryption schemes. Depending on the adversary's knowledge of the keys, they gave two definitions for security of signcryption depending on whether the adversary is an "outsider" (i.e., a third party who only knows the public information) or "insider" (i.e., a legal user of the network, either the sender of the receiver, or someone that knows the secret key of either the sender or the receiver). Correspondingly, they called them "outsider security" and "insider security". We may note that the inside adversary is more powerful than the outside adversary, and hence the notion of insider security is stronger than the notion of the outsider security. In this paper, we define the security of the signcryption scheme in the model of insider security. Baek, Steinfeld, and Zheng [10] then studied the security of signcryption scheme in the multi-user setting. The definitions of the two-user and multi-user settings will be given in Sect. 3. In addition, Boyen [8] studied the security for the signcryption schemes in the identity-based setting that will not be considered in this paper.

Black-box assumption vs. *reality.* The formal security proofs (for cryptographic schemes) traditionally treat the scheme as a "black box", meaning that an adversary is able to access in a relatively limited fashion. For example, in the model (of outside adversary) of signcryption schemes, an adversary is given the public keys, then allowed to query the challenger for valid ciphertexts (or decrypt ciphertext) on some messages of its choice, but is unable to obtain any other information about the secret key or any state information used during ciphertext generation or decryption. That is, in the black-box model, we assume that the honest users' secret information is completely hidden to the adversary. However, for most real-word applications, on the other hand, an adversary may be able to recover a significant amount of leakage information not captured by the standard security models. Examples include information leaked by various of side-channel attacks, e.g., power consumption [16], fault attacks [5], and timing attacks [3]. Therefore, when the traditional proof encounters real-world attacks, the security of the signcryption schemes is problematic.

Leakage-resilient cryptography. In order to modeling the security with information leakage for cryptographic schemes, in the past few years cryptographers have made tremendous progress, and in constructing leakage-resilient cryptosystems secure even in case such leakage occurs. A cryptographic scheme is said to be leakage-resilient if its security could be proved in the presence of information leakage. To modeling the behavior that the adversary exploits partial information about the secret state from the physical device, we define an additional oracle, named leakage oracle, besides the ordinary oracles which can be accessed by the adversary in the setting of black-box model. Then the adversary can query the leakage oracle on input a computable function $f : \{0,1\}^* \to \{0,1\}^\lambda$ (where the f is called a leakage function and λ is the leakage parameter), and finally the adversary is returned back a value that the leakage function acts on the secret states.

Leakage model. We may note that if the leakage function f outputs the secret state or key totally (e.g., f is an identity function $f(\mathsf{sk}) = \mathsf{sk}$), then the adversary can do everything that the honest user can do. Therefore, we should specify the domain and range of the leakage function with some appropriate and reasonable ways. A different way defines a different leakage model, here we present three kinds of them which will be used in this paper.

- Only computation leaks information model [19]: The leakage is assumed that only occurs on the values which have accessed during current computation. Hence, the domain of the leakage function is defined on the active part of the secret state.
- Bounded leakage model: The size of the overall amount of the leakage is bounded on a pre-fixed value λ, e.g., the allowed leakage is less than half of the size of the secret key.
- Continual leakage model: The size of the overall amount of the leakage can be unbounded.

Obviously, in order to resist the continual leakage attacks, the secret key should be refreshed every once in a while (while its public key should be remain fixed). In the continual leakage model, the amount of the leakage is bounded only in between any two successive key refreshes.

Leakage-resilient signature and encryption schemes. In the past few years, many leakage-resilient signature and encryption schemes have been proposed, e.g., PKE [17,21], IBE [11,24], and signatures [9,13–15,18,20,22]. More specifically, in [17], Kiltz and Pietrzak used the technique of blinding (i.e., the secret key is split into two parts which will be blinded when invoking them) to construct a leakage-resilient ElGamal encryption in the continual leakage model. A main advantage of their scheme is that its efficiency is close to that of non leakage-resilient pairing-based ElGamal scheme. Kiltz et al. [17] proved that their scheme is leakage-resilient in the generic group model. They considered the model of IND-CCA1 in the presence of continual leakage, i.e., the scheme remains IND-CCA1 secure even if with every decryption query the adversary can learn a bounded amount (almost half of the bits of the secret key) of arbitrary state information about the computation. Then, Galindo and Vivek [15] used Kiltz et al.'s technique to construct a leakage-resilient signature scheme based on Boneh-Boyen IBE scheme [4]. After that, Tang et al. [22] also used this technique to construct two more efficient leakage-resilient signature schemes based on Boneh-Lynn-Shacham (BLS) signature [7] and Waters signature [23] schemes, respectively. Following [17]'s results, all of these three signature schemes (one of [15] and two of [22]) allow for continual leakage and can tolerate leakage of almost half of the size of the secret key at every new signature invocation.

Our results. As far as we know, most existing leakage-resilient cryptographic schemes are studied in the setting of single secret, e.g., singing key of signature scheme, decryption key of encryption scheme. That is, there is only one party (of the communication) has secret which will be partially leaked to the adversary. In this paper, we consider the case of double secrets, i.e., the notion of a "joint signature and encryption" in the presence of continual leakage, for the first time. Following the terminology of [2], we refer to this primitive as leakage-resilient signcryption. First, this paper provides a formal treatment of signcryption in the presence of continual leakage. Second, we give two secure instantiations based on Kiltz et al.'s [17] leakage-resilient PKE and Tang et al.'s [22] leakage-resilient signature (that one based on the BLS signature) schemes. In [2], An et al. showed that, in the black-box model, "encrypt-then-sign", "sign-then-encrypt", and "commit-then-encrypt-and-sign" methods, when modeled properly, are secure composition methods in the public key setting. Following [2], we use the "sign-then-encrypt" method to construct leakage-resilient signcryption schemes.

2 Definitions of Signcryption

A signcryption scheme involves two parties, a sender and a receiver. In order to send messages with a confidential and authentic way, the sender signs and encrypts the message using his secret key and the receiver's public key, respectively. For convenience of description, we fix the sender and receiver to Alice and Bob, respectively.

2.1 Syntax

A signcryption scheme Π consists of the following six algorithms:

- Setup is a PPT algorithm takes as input a security parameter k, then outputs the system's global parameters params which will be used in all of the following algorithms and we omit this implicit description from now on. We write it params $\leftarrow$ Setup(1^k).
- KeyGen is a PPT algorithm takes as input the security parameter k, then outputs user Alice's signing key sk_A and verification key pk_A, Bob's decryption key sk_B and encryption key pk_B. We write it $(sk_A, pk_A, sk_B, pk_B) \leftarrow$ KeyGen(1^k)[1].
- Sig is a PPT algorithm, Alice takes as input (sk_A, m) to produce a signature Σ. We write it $\Sigma \leftarrow$ Sig(sk_A, m).
- Enc is a PPT algorithm, Alice takes as input (pk_A, pk_B, m, Σ) to produce a ciphertext Δ. We write it $\Delta \leftarrow$ Enc(pk_A, pk_B, m, Σ).

---

[1] In our definition, each user has a single key pair (sk, pk) which can be used for both signing and decryption, in some other definitions, e.g., [2], the signing and decryption keys may be generated by different key-generation algorithms.

- Dec is a deterministic algorithm, Bob takes as input (sk_B, Δ) to recover (m, Σ). We write it $(\mathsf{pk}_A, m, \Sigma) \leftarrow \mathsf{Dec}(\mathsf{sk}_B, \Delta)$.
- Ver is a deterministic algorithm, Bob takes as input $(\mathsf{pk}_A, m, \Sigma)$ to verify the validity of the signature, if it is valid then outputs 1 (accept m). Otherwise, outputs 0 (reject m). We write it $1/0 \leftarrow \mathsf{Ver}(\mathsf{pk}_A, m, \Sigma)$.

The definition of the signcryption scheme, in many other papers (e.g., [2,25]), the Sig and Enc algorithms are merged as a single "Signcryption" algorithm, and the Dec and Ver algorithms are merged as a single "Unsigncryption" algorithm. We adopt the approach of [8,12] that the signcryption scheme defined as above supports a separation is conducive to the analysis of the security. However, we should note that Sig and Enc are not two independent algorithms, the output of these two algorithms is a signcryption ciphertext. When we need describe them as a single algorithm, we write it Sig&Enc (Signcryption). Similarly we denote Dec&Ver (Unsigncryption) as the merged algorithm of the Dec and Ver algorithms, in some cases, the outputs of the algorithm Dec&Ver (Unsigncryption) denoted by the signature $(\mathsf{pk}_A, m, \Sigma)$ which can be verified by anyone.

Correctness. For correctness, we require that for all security parameter k, all message m, and keys $(\mathsf{sk}_A, \mathsf{pk}_A, \mathsf{sk}_B, \mathsf{pk}_B) \leftarrow \mathsf{KeyGen}(1^k)$, we have

$$\Pr[\mathsf{Ver}(\mathsf{pk}_A, \mathsf{Dec}(\mathsf{sk}_B, \mathsf{Sig\&Enc}(\mathsf{sk}_A, \mathsf{pk}_B, m))) = 1] = 1.$$

2.2 Stateful Signcryption

The general signcryption schemes obviously cannot tolerate leakage directly, e.g., the adversary learns the signing key sk_A or decryption key sk_B bit by bit and finally recover the whole sk_A or sk_B. The reason that the adversary can do like this is that the signing key or decryption key always been used directly. One method to avoid this problem is that blinding the signing key or decryption key such that the blinded keys have the same functionality as the original ones. However, if we always use the single blinded signing or decryption key, the adversary finally also can obtain them and recover the original secret key. Hence, we need to refresh the blinded keys every once in a while and thus the adversary cannot collect enough leakage information to recover it. Kiltz and Pietrzak [17] used this method to construct a leakage-resilient ElGamal encryption scheme. They split users' secret key into two parts which are stored in two memories, then the decryption algorithm is divided into corresponding two phases, and the input/output behaviors of the two memories will exactly the same as the real decryption key. Subsequently, Galindo et al. [15] and Tang et al. [22] used this technique to construct three efficient leakage-resilient signature schemes. Similarly, we call the signcryption scheme is stateful if its signing key or decryption key (or both) will be refreshed before (or after) each signing or decryption algorithm invocation while the corresponding public keys remain fixed.

Formally, the signing key sk_A is split into two initial states A_0 and A_0' in the beginning. Then the signing algorithm consists of a sequence of two phases

$\mathsf{Sig} = (\mathsf{Sig}_{Pha1}, \mathsf{Sig}_{Pha2})$. The i-th invocation of signature (with key (A_{i-1}, A'_{i-1})) is computed as:

$$(A_i, w_i) \leftarrow \mathsf{Sig}_{Pha1}(A_{i-1}, m_i); (A'_i, \Sigma_i) \leftarrow \mathsf{Sig}_{Pha2}(A'_{i-1}, w_i), \qquad (1)$$

where the parameter w_i is some state information passed from Sig_{Pha1} to Sig_{Pha2}. After this round of signature, the signing key will be updated to (A_i, A'_i). Similarly, the decryption key sk_B also will be split into two parts which are stored in two memories, then the decryption algorithm also be divided into corresponding two phases, $\mathsf{Dec} = (\mathsf{Dec}_{Pha1}, \mathsf{Dec}_{Pha2})$. The i-th invocation of decryption (with key (B_{i-1}, B'_{i-1})) is computed as:

$$(B_i, v_i) \leftarrow \mathsf{Dec}_{Pha1}(B_{i-1}, \Delta_i); (B'_i, (m_i, \Sigma_i)) \leftarrow \mathsf{Dec}_{Pha2}(B'_{i-1}, v_i), \qquad (2)$$

where v_i is some state information passed from Dec_{Pha1} to Dec_{Pha2}. After this round of decryption, the decryption key will be updated to (B_i, B'_i). Both of the signing and decryption keys will not be accessed in the encryption and verification algorithms, hence there is no leakage during the invocation of these two algorithms (in the only computation leaks information model).

3   Security Notions for Leakage-Resilient Signcryption

In this section, we define the security notions for signcryption schemes in the presence of continual leakage. The security of the signcryption scheme could be divided into outsider and insider security forms [2]. Informally the outsider is a third party except that the sender Alice and receiver Bob, and the insider is a legal user of the system (i.e., the sender or the receiver themselves or some who knows either the sender's signing key or the receiver's decryption key). The insider security is a quite strong notion which is considered in this paper.

We now define the leakage for the signcryption scheme. As shown in the Introduction, the leakage is modeled as some computable functions chosen by the adversary, the domain and range of the functions are depend on the leakage model. In this paper, we consider the continual leakage model, hence the amount of the leakage is assumed to be bounded in between any two successive key updated and the total amount of the leakage is unbounded. We also consider the only computation leaks model, hence we always assume that the used keys can be erasure securely and the internal state that the adversary can exploit is that only accessed during an invocation. Because the internal state of the four algorithms, Sig_{Pha1}, Sig_{Pha2}, Dec_{Pha1}, and Dec_{Pha2} are different, we define four groups of leakage functions e_i, f_i, g_i, and h_i, respectively. Though, of course, if the signing (resp. decryption) algorithm can be run with a secure way means that no adversary can launch side-channel attack to the device of signing (resp. decryption) program, then we have no need to split the signing (resp. decryption) algorithm into two parts. Without loss of generality, we treat the case of both keys leak information.

We say that a signcryption scheme is leakage-resilient (LRSC) if it has the following two properties: unforgeability and confidentiality, in the presence of leakage.

3.1 Unforgeability in the Presence of Leakage

This notion guarantees that the receiver can be convinced that a valid signcryption ciphertext from a purported sender. This notion is defined by the model of existential unforgeability under adaptive chosen message and leakage attacks (EU-CMLA). This model is defined by the following experiment $\mathbf{Exp}_{\Pi,\mathcal{A}}^{eu-cmla}(k)$ played by a EU-CMLA adversary $\mathcal{A}$ and a challenger.

1. **Initial:** The challenger runs params $\leftarrow$ Setup(1^k) and ($\mathsf{sk}_A, \mathsf{pk}_A, \mathsf{sk}_B, \mathsf{pk}_B$) $\leftarrow$ KeyGen(1^k), then gives (params, $\mathsf{pk}_A, \mathsf{pk}_B, \mathsf{sk}_B$) to the adversary.
2. **Queries:** The challenger is probed by the adversary who makes the following queries.
   - Sig&Enc oracle: The adversary submits a message m and an arbitrary receiver's public key pk_R to the challenger. The challenger runs algorithm Sig&Enc($\mathsf{sk}_A, \mathsf{pk}_R, m$) and gives the resulting Δ to the adversary.
   - Leakage oracle: The adversary submits two leakage functions e_i and f_i to the challenger. The challenger retrieves the state information sta_{e_i} and sta_{f_i}, which has involved in the corresponding execution, and computes $\Lambda = e_i(\mathsf{sta}_{e_i})$ and $\Lambda' = f_i(\mathsf{sta}_{f_i})$, then gives the resulting Λ, Λ' to the adversary.
3. **Output:** Finally, the adversary outputs a forgery Δ^*.

We say that the adversary wins this experiment if: (1) Δ^* is a valid signcryption ciphertext under the sender Alice and receiver Bob and (2) the adversary did not query the Sig&Enc oracle for (m^*, pk_B), where m^* is the embedded message of the signcryption ciphertext Δ^*. The advantage of the adversary is defined as $\mathbf{Adv}_{\Pi,\mathcal{A}}^{eu-cmla}(k) = \Pr[\mathcal{A} \text{ wins}]$.

In the above experiment, the insider adversary is given the receiver's secret key sk_B, and hence he has no need to query the Dec&Ver oracle and leakage oracle on the Dec algorithm. In addition, the above experiment defined in the multi-user setting. In the two-user setting, the adversary is only allowed to query the Sig&Enc oracle on input (m, pk_B) (i.e., $\mathsf{pk}_R = \mathsf{pk}_B$).

Definition 1. A signcryption scheme Π is EU-CMLA secure if no PPT adversary can win the above experiment with non-negligible advantage.

3.2 Confidentiality in the Presence of Leakage

Message confidentiality provides the guarantee that any adversary (other than the appointed receiver) cannot obtain any information about the signcrypted message even if the adversary obtains some leakage information about the decryption key of the legal receiver. We define the notion of indistinguishability under chosen ciphertext and leakage attacks (IND-CCLA1). This notion is formalized by the following experiment $\mathbf{Exp}_{\Pi,\mathcal{A}}^{ind-ccla1}(k)$ which is played by an IND-CCLA1 adversary $\mathcal{A}$ and a challenger.

1. **Initial:** The challenger runs params $\leftarrow$ Setup(1^k) and $(\mathsf{sk}_A, \mathsf{pk}_A, \mathsf{sk}_B, \mathsf{pk}_B) \leftarrow$ KeyGen(1^k), then gives (params, $\mathsf{pk}_A, \mathsf{pk}_B, \mathsf{sk}_A$) to the adversary.
2. **Queries:** The challenger is probed by the adversary who makes the following queries.
   - Dec&Ver oracle: The adversary submits a ciphertext Δ and an arbitrary sender's public key pk_S to the challenger. The challenger runs Dec&Ver(sk_B, pk_S, Δ) and then gives the result to the adversary.
   - Leakage oracle: The adversary submits two leakage functions g_i and h_i to the challenger. The challenger retrieves the state information sta_{g_i} and sta_{h_i}, which has involved in the corresponding execution, and computes $\Theta = g_i(\mathsf{sta}_{g_i})$ and $\Theta' = h_i(\mathsf{sta}_{h_i})$, then gives the resulting Θ, Θ' to the adversary.
3. **Challenge:** The adversary outputs a pair of equal-length messages (m_0, m_1). The challenger first chooses a random bit b, then runs Sig&Enc($\mathsf{sk}_A, \mathsf{pk}_B, m_b$) to generate a challenge signcryption ciphertext Δ^*. Next, it gives Δ^* to the adversary.
4. **Output:** Finally, the adversary outputs a bit b'.

We say that the adversary wins this experiment if $b' = b$. The advantage of the adversary is defined as $\mathbf{Adv}_{\Pi,\mathcal{A}}^{ind-ccla1}(k) = |\Pr[b' = b] - \frac{1}{2}|$.

In the above experiment, the insider adversary is given the sender's secret key sk_A, and hence he has no need to query the Sig&Enc oracle and leakage oracle on the Sig algorithm. In addition, the above experiment defined in the multi-user setting. In the two-user setting, the adversary is only allowed to query the Dec&Ver oracle on input (Δ, pk_A) (i.e., $\mathsf{pk}_S = \mathsf{pk}_A$).

Definition 2. A signcryption scheme Π is IND-CCLA1 secure if no PPT adversary can win the above experiment with non-negligible advantage.

4   Instantiations

In this section, we give two instantiations of signcryption schemes which can tolerant continual leakage. Our constructions are based on bilinear groups. Let $\mathbb{G}$ and $\mathbb{G}_T$ be two multiplicative cyclic groups with a same prime order p. Let g be an arbitrary generator of the group $\mathbb{G}$. We say that $\mathsf{e} : \mathbb{G} \times \mathbb{G} \to \mathbb{G}_T$ is an admissible bilinear mapping if it satisfies the following three properties:

- *Bilinearity:* $\forall a, b \in \mathbb{Z}_p, \mathsf{e}(g^a, g^b) = \mathsf{e}(g, g)^{ab}$.
- *Non-degeneracy:* $\mathsf{e}(g, g) \neq 1$.
- *Computability:* $\forall a, b \in \mathbb{Z}_p$, there exists efficient algorithm to compute $\mathsf{e}(g^a, g^b)$.

We assume that BilGen(1^k) is a PPT algorithm takes as input a security parameter k to generate parameters $(\mathbb{G}, \mathbb{G}_T, p, g, \mathsf{e})$ to satisfy the above properties.

4.1   An LRSC Scheme Using Sign-then-Encrypt Method

As shown by An et al. [2], a EU-CMA adversary can easily replace the encryption with its own encryption albeit this attack does not break the security of *existential* unforgeability. (Please refer to [2] for details.) To avoid such attack, we use An et al.'s idea that binding together the signature and encryption used in the signcryption with the public key of the sender, i.e., $C \leftarrow \mathsf{Enc}(\mathsf{pk}_B, (m||\Sigma||\mathsf{pk}_A))$.

Construction. We adopt Kiltz and Pietrzak's leakage-resilient PKE scheme [17], denoted by $\mathcal{E}_{\mathsf{KP}}$, and Tang, Li, Niu, and Liang's leakage-resilient signature scheme [22], denoted by $\mathcal{S}_{\mathsf{TLNL}}$, as the building blocks to construct a leakage-resilient signcryption scheme as follows.

- $\mathsf{Setup}(1^k)$: The global parameters are $\mathsf{params} = (\mathbb{G}, \mathbb{G}_T, p, g, \mathsf{e}, H)$, where $(\mathbb{G}, \mathbb{G}_T, p, g, \mathsf{e}) \leftarrow \mathsf{BilGen}(1^k)$, and $H : \{0,1\}^* \rightarrow \mathbb{G}$ is a hash function.
- $\mathsf{KeyGen}(1^k)$: Alice first chooses a random number $x \leftarrow \mathbb{Z}_p$, then computes $X = g^x \in \mathbb{G}$ and $X_T = \mathsf{e}(X, g) = \mathsf{e}(g, g)^x$. She also chooses a random number $a_0 \leftarrow \mathbb{Z}_p$ and sets $(A_0, A_0') = (g^{a_0}, g^{x-a_0})$. Her public key and initial state of secret key are $\mathsf{pk}_A = X_T$ and $\mathsf{sk}_{A_0} = (A_0, A_0')$, respectively. Similarly, Bob's public key and initial state of secret key are $\mathsf{pk}_B = Y_T$ and $\mathsf{sk}_{B_0} = (B_0, B_0')$, respectively, where $B_0 = g^{b_0}, B_0' = g^{y-b_0}$ and $Y_T = \mathsf{e}(Y, g) = \mathsf{e}(g^y, g)$.
- $\mathsf{Sig}(\mathsf{sk}_{A_{i-1}}, m)$: Alice's secrets are stored into two memories $\mathcal{M}_{A_1}$ and $\mathcal{M}_{A_2}$. Therefore, the signing algorithm should be sequential processed as the following two phases:
  1. *Phase 1 (A_{i-1}, m)*: In the first phase, Alice takes as input A_{i-1} and m, where the i is the state information indicates that the i-th invocation of the signature. She first chooses a random integer $a_i \leftarrow \mathbb{Z}_p$ to blind her secret key, i.e., $A_i = A_{i-1}g^{a_i}$. Then she chooses another random number $s \leftarrow \mathbb{Z}_p$ and computes $S = g^s$ and $\sigma' = A_i H(m)^s$. Finally, the memory $\mathcal{M}_{A_1}$ passes state information $w_i = (a_i, S, \sigma')$ to the next memory.
  2. *Phase 2 (A_{i-1}', w_i)*: After receiving w_i from the last memory, the memory $\mathcal{M}_{A_2}$ does as follows: it first computes $A_i' = A_{i-1}'g^{-a_i}$ and $\sigma = A_i'\sigma'$. Then, it outputs the signature $\Sigma = (S, \sigma)$.
- $\mathsf{Enc}(\mathsf{pk}_A, \mathsf{pk}_B, m, \Sigma)$: After the signature Σ is generated, Alice runs the encryption algorithm on inputs $\mathsf{pk}_A, \mathsf{pk}_B, m$, and Σ. She first chooses a random number $r \leftarrow \mathbb{Z}_p$ and computes $R = g^r$. Then she computes $c = Y_T^r \oplus (m||\Sigma||X_T),^2$ and sets $C = (R, c)$. Finally, she outputs the ciphertext $\Delta := C$.
- $\mathsf{Dec}(\mathsf{sk}_{B_{i-1}}, \Delta)$: Bob's secrets are stored into two memories $\mathcal{M}_{B_1}$ and $\mathcal{M}_{B_2}$. Therefore, the decryption algorithm should be sequential processed as the following two phases:
  1. *Phase 1 (B_{i-1}, Δ)*: In the first phase, Bob takes as input B_{i-1} and Δ, where the i is the state information indicates that the i-th invocation of the decryption. He first chooses a random number $b_i \leftarrow \mathbb{Z}_p$ to blind his secret key, i.e., $B_i = B_{i-1}g^{b_i}$. Then the memory $\mathcal{M}_{B_1}$ computes $K' = \mathsf{e}(B_i, R)$, and passes the state information $v_i = (b_i, K')$ to the next memory.

---

[2] Here, we need a public hash or encoding function to map Y_T^r to a bit string whose length is same as the bit representation of $(m||\Sigma||X_T)$. Then, the same function will be used in the decryption algorithm.

2. *Phase 2* (B'_{i-1}, v_i): After receiving v_i from the last memory, the memory $\mathcal{M}_{B_2}$ does as follows: it first computes $B'_i = B'_{i-1} g^{-b_i}$, $K'' = \mathsf{e}(B'_i, R)$, and $K = K'K''$. Finally, it computes and outputs $(m||\Sigma||X_T) = K \oplus c$.

- $\mathsf{Ver}(\mathsf{pk}_A, m, \Sigma)$: After the message and signature are recovered, Bob verifies its validity as follows: he first parses Σ as (S, σ) and check whether $\frac{\mathsf{e}(\sigma, g)}{\mathsf{e}(H(m), S)} \overset{?}{=} X_T$. Output 1 if it holds; else output 0 and reject the message.

Security. The security of the above signcryption scheme Π is rely on the security of the underlying signature scheme $\mathcal{S}_{\mathsf{TLNL}}$ and encryption scheme $\mathcal{E}_{\mathsf{KP}}$. Due to the limitation of space, the proofs of the following two theorems will be given in the full version of this paper.

Theorem 1. *The signcryption scheme Π is EU-CMLA secure with respect to the Definition 1 in the multi-user setting. The advantage of a q-query adversary who gets at most λ bits of leakage of the signing key per each invocation of Sig_{Pha1} or Sig_{Pha2} and all bits of the decryption key is $O(\frac{q^2}{p} 2^{2\lambda})$.*

Theorem 2. *The signcryption scheme Π is IND-CCLA1 secure with respect to the Definition 2 in the multi-user setting. The advantage of a q-query adversary who gets at most λ bits of leakage of the decryption key per each invocation of Dec_{Pha1} or Dec_{Pha2} and all bits of the signing key is $O(\frac{q^3}{p} 2^{2\lambda+1})$.*

4.2   An LRSC Scheme Using a Single Random Number

We now give a variant scheme which, denoted by Π^*, is slightly modified from the scheme Π. In Π, the random numbers used in the Sig and Enc algorithms are different. In Π^*, however, we use a single random number for the Sig and Enc algorithms. This approach actually has been used repeatedly to construct signcryption schemes, e.g., [1,6,12].

Construction. $\Pi^* = (\mathsf{Setup}^*, \mathsf{KeyGen}^*, \mathsf{Sig}^*, \mathsf{Enc}^*, \mathsf{Dec}^*, \mathsf{Ver}^*)$, where Setup^*, KeyGen^*, Dec^*, and Ver^* algorithms are same as the Setup, KeyGen, Dec, and Ver algorithms of the scheme Π, respectively. For the Sig^* and Enc^* algorithms, other than the scheme Π in which choosing the random number independently (i.e., s for the signing algorithm and r for the encryption algorithm), we use a single random number s for the both algorithms.

In the encryption execution, Alice needs to compute $c = Y_T^s \oplus (m||\Sigma||X_T)$, and hence the random number s should be passed from Sig^*_{Pha1} to Enc^* (note that the random number s only used in Sig^*_{Pha1} but not Sig^*_{Pha2}). Therefore, if we run the Enc^* algorithm in the second memory $\mathcal{M}_{A_2}$, then the random number s should be transmitted from $\mathcal{M}_{A_1}$ to $\mathcal{M}_{A_2}$. To avoid that the single randomness s may be leaked twice in Alice's two memories (it also may be leaked in the channel from $\mathcal{M}_{A_1}$ to $\mathcal{M}_{A_2}$), we put these two algorithms Sig^*_{Pha1} and Enc^* in Alice's first memory $\mathcal{M}_{A_1}$, and the Sig^*_{Pha2} algorithm is putted in Alice's second memory $\mathcal{M}_{A_2}$. Therefore, to generate a signcryption ciphertext, $\mathcal{M}_1$ first runs Sig^*_{Pha1} to generate partial signature σ', then passes the state information

$w_i = (a_i, \sigma')$ to the memory $\mathcal{M}_2$. After receiving w_i, $\mathcal{M}_2$ runs Sig^*_{Pha2} to generate σ and returns it to $\mathcal{M}_{A_1}$. Next, $\mathcal{M}_{A_1}$ integrates a full signature $\Sigma = (S, \sigma)$ and runs the Enc^* algorithm, i.e., $c = Y_T^s \oplus (m||\Sigma||X_T)$. Finally, it outputs the signcryption ciphertext $\Delta = (S, c)$. Here, we should note that such allocation strategy does not change the input-output behaviors of the scheme Π^*.

Security. We give the following theorems that the security of Π^* in the two-user setting. Due to the limitation of space, the proofs of the following theorems will be given in the full version of this paper.

Theorem 3. The signcryption scheme Π^* is EU-CMLA secure with respect to the Definition 1 in the two-user setting. The advantage of a q-query adversary who gets at most λ bits of leakage of the signing key per each invocation of Sig^*_{Pha1} or Sig^*_{Pha2} and all bits of the decryption key is $O(\frac{q^2}{p} 2^{2\lambda})$.

Theorem 4. The signcryption scheme Π^* is IND-CCLA1 secure with respect to the Definition 2 in the two-user setting. The advantage of a q-query adversary who gets at most λ bits of leakage of the decryption key per each invocation of Dec^*_{Pha1} or Dec^*_{Pha2} and all bits of the signing key is $O(\frac{q^3}{p} 2^{2\lambda+1})$.

Acknowledgement. The authors would like to thank anonymous reviewers for their helpful comments and suggestions.

References

1. Arriaga, A., Barbosa, M., Farshim, P.: On the joint security of signature and encryption schemes under randomness reuse: efficiency and security amplification. In: Bao, F., Samarati, P., Zhou, J. (eds.) ACNS 2012. LNCS, vol. 7341, pp. 206–223. Springer, Heidelberg (2012)
2. An, J.H., Dodis, Y., Rabin, T.: On the security of joint signature and encryption. In: Knudsen, L.R. (ed.) EUROCRYPT 2002. LNCS, vol. 2332, pp. 83–107. Springer, Heidelberg (2002)
3. Boneh, D., Brumley, D.: Remote timing attacks are practical. Comput. Netw. **48**(5), 701–716 (2005)
4. Boneh, D., Boyen, X.: Efficient selective-ID secure identity-based encryption without random oracles. In: Cachin, C., Camenisch, J.L. (eds.) EUROCRYPT 2004. LNCS, vol. 3027, pp. 223–238. Springer, Heidelberg (2004)
5. Biham, E., Carmeli, Y., Shamir, A.: Bug attacks. In: Wagner, D. (ed.) CRYPTO 2008. LNCS, vol. 5157, pp. 221–240. Springer, Heidelberg (2008)
6. Barreto, P.S.L.M., Libert, B., McCullagh, N., Quisquater, J.-J.: Efficient and provably-secure identity-based signatures and signcryption from bilinear maps. In: Roy, B. (ed.) ASIACRYPT 2005. LNCS, vol. 3788, pp. 515–532. Springer, Heidelberg (2005)
7. Boneh, D., Lynn, B., Shacham, H.: Short signatures from the weil pairing. In: Boyd, C. (ed.) ASIACRYPT 2001. LNCS, vol. 2248, pp. 514–532. Springer, Heidelberg (2001)
8. Boyen, X.: Multipurpose identity-based signcryption. In: Boneh, D. (ed.) CRYPTO 2003. LNCS, vol. 2729, pp. 383–399. Springer, Heidelberg (2003)

9. Boyle, E., Segev, G., Wichs, D.: Fully leakage-resilient signatures. In: Paterson, K.G. (ed.) EUROCRYPT 2011. LNCS, vol. 6632, pp. 89–108. Springer, Heidelberg (2011)

10. Baek, J., Steinfeld, R., Zheng, Y.: Formal proofs for the security of signcryption. In: Naccache, D., Paillier, P. (eds.) PKC 2002. LNCS, vol. 2274, pp. 80–98. Springer, Heidelberg (2002)

11. Chow, S.S.M., Dodis, Y., Rouselakis, Y., Waters, B.: Practical leakage-resilient identity-based encryption from simple assumptions. In: CCS'10, pp. 152–161. ACM (2010)

12. Chen, L., Malone-Lee, J.: Improved identity-based signcryption. In: Vaudenay, S. (ed.) PKC 2005. LNCS, vol. 3386, pp. 362–379. Springer, Heidelberg (2005)

13. Faust, S., Hazay, C., Nielsen, J.B., Nordholt, P.S., Zottarel, A.: Signature schemes secure against hard-to-invert leakage. In: Wang, X., Sako, K. (eds.) ASIACRYPT 2012. LNCS, vol. 7658, pp. 98–115. Springer, Heidelberg (2012)

14. Faust, S., Kiltz, E., Pietrzak, K., Rothblum, G.N.: Leakage-resilient signatures. In: Micciancio, D. (ed.) TCC 2010. LNCS, vol. 5978, pp. 343–360. Springer, Heidelberg (2010)

15. Galindo, D., Vivek, S.: A practical leakage-resilient signature scheme in the generic group model. In: Knudsen, L.R., Wu, H. (eds.) SAC 2012. LNCS, vol. 7707, pp. 50–65. Springer, Heidelberg (2013)

16. Kocher, P.C., Jaffe, J., Jun, B.: Differential power analysis. In: Wiener, M. (ed.) CRYPTO 1999. LNCS, vol. 1666, pp. 388–397. Springer, Heidelberg (1999)

17. Kiltz, E., Pietrzak, K.: Leakage resilient ElGamal encryption. In: Abe, M. (ed.) ASIACRYPT 2010. LNCS, vol. 6477, pp. 595–612. Springer, Heidelberg (2010)

18. Katz, J., Vaikuntanathan, V.: Signature schemes with bounded leakage resilience. In: Matsui, M. (ed.) ASIACRYPT 2009. LNCS, vol. 5912, pp. 703–720. Springer, Heidelberg (2009)

19. Micali, S., Reyzin, L.: Physically observable cryptography. In: Naor, M. (ed.) TCC 2004. LNCS, vol. 2951, pp. 278–296. Springer, Heidelberg (2004)

20. Malkin, T., Teranishi, I., Vahlis, Y., Yung, M.: Signatures resilient to continual leakage on memory and computation. In: Ishai, Y. (ed.) TCC 2011. LNCS, vol. 6597, pp. 89–106. Springer, Heidelberg (2011)

21. Naor, M., Segev, G.: Public-key cryptosystems resilient to key leakage. In: Halevi, S. (ed.) CRYPTO 2009. LNCS, vol. 5677, pp. 18–35. Springer, Heidelberg (2009)

22. Tang, F., Li, H., Niu, Q., Liang, B.: Efficient leakage-resilient signature schemes in the generic bilinear group model. In: Huang, X., Zhou, J. (eds.) ISPEC 2014. LNCS, vol. 8434, pp. 418–432. Springer, Heidelberg (2014)

23. Waters, B.: Efficient identity-based encryption without random oracles. In: Cramer, R. (ed.) EUROCRYPT 2005. LNCS, vol. 3494, pp. 114–127. Springer, Heidelberg (2005)

24. Yuen, T.H., Chow, S.S.M., Zhang, Y., Yiu, S.M.: Identity-based encryption resilient to continual auxiliary leakage. In: Pointcheval, D., Johansson, T. (eds.) EUROCRYPT 2012. LNCS, vol. 7237, pp. 117–134. Springer, Heidelberg (2012)

25. Zheng, Y.: Digital signcryption or how to achieve cost(signature & encryption) << cost(signature) + cost(encryption). In: Kaliski Jr., B.S. (ed.) CRYPTO '97. LNCS, vol. 1294, pp. 165–179. Springer, Heidelberg (1997)

Hardware Security

Wireless Key Exchange Using Frequency Impairments

Jörn Müller-Quade and Antonio Sobreira de Almeida$^{(\boxtimes)}$

Karlsruhe Institute of Technology, Institute of Theoretical Informatics,
Am Fasanengarten 5, 76131 Karlsruhe, Germany
{mueller-quade,almeida}@kit.edu

Abstract. Security methods have traditionally been deployed in the upper layers of the protocol stack. Therefore, the properties of the physical layer, like the wireless channel, have remained unexplored for authentication and confidentiality purposes. Some methods to expand the security mechanisms to lower levels have been suggested and thoroughly analyzed. The usage of the wireless channel for the development of key exchange protocols is based on two main properties: reciprocity and multipath propagation on fading channels. Several methods on how to extract and generate common secrecy using these properties have already been proposed. However, some security drawbacks have also been identified. In this paper, we propose to increase the security of these techniques by additionally utilizing hardware-related properties, namely the impairments in the transceivers' local oscillators. The validation of this technique is performed in an experimental setup using the USRP/GNU Radio software-defined radio platform.

Keywords: Confidentiality · Physical layer · Reciprocity · Fading · Frequency · Impairments · Local oscillator

1 Introduction

Cryptography is an essential pillar in the architecture of modern communication systems. Symmetric encryption can be achieved when both communicating parties share some kind of secret - the *secret key*. This implies that these parties must somehow previously exchange this key. The challenge of key distribution in the public channel can be addressed using public key cryptography techniques. As a result, hybrid systems were developed, combining public key techniques for the key exchange (as RSA or Elliptic Curve Cryptography) with private cryptography methods (e.g., AES) for the encryption and decryption of the transmitted messages. Nevertheless, public key cryptography methods strongly rely on computational assumptions (like the factoring problem in the RSA cryptosystem) and usually require a big amount of time and energy consuming calculations, making it not often suitable for mobile communications, where such resources are limited.

© Springer International Publishing Switzerland 2015
K.-H. Rhee and J.H. Yi (Eds.): WISA 2014, LNCS 8909, pp. 283–294, 2015.
DOI: 10.1007/978-3-319-15087-1_22

Wireless key exchange is a solution for the problem of key exchange relying on no computational assumptions. The key extraction is simply performed from the physical structure of the environment where the wireless transmission takes place. The *common randomness* is originated by sounding the common channel between both legitimate parties. Hereby, a probing signal is sent through the channel. This signal will be scattered and reflected in several objects in the surrounding environment. As a result, a receiver antenna will receive a superposition of several echoes corresponding to different reflections. This technique is based on two properties of the wireless channel: *reciprocity* and *multipath interference*. On the one hand, reciprocity ensures that both legitimate parties will receive a similar wave from the bidirectional successive channel sounding process. Different methods have been proposed to transform the analog probing received signal into a binary key. On the other hand, assuming that the environment is *complex enough*, multipath interference guarantees secrecy.

Being located far enough from both parties, an adversary will receive strongly decorrelated signals from the signals both legitimate parties receive ([MTM+08]). This is a consequence of the different reflection paths that the waves reaching the adversary have to travel. These methods aim to be reliable, efficient and to generate a key having as much entropy as possible. They are suited for key extraction and key agreement in wireless and mobile settings, such as wireless sensor networks. We propose to explore the properties of some hardware components, namely the local oscillators of the transceivers, as an additional source of randomness shared by the legitimate parties. This is done without affecting the overall system symmetry. Consequently, reciprocity will still hold, allowing key extraction. The method has still the advantage of being more resistant to known side-channel attacks on reciprocity-based wireless key exchange, due to the fact that those hardware properties are also unpredictable for an adversary.

In Sect. 2, we shortly describe some previous results about the wireless key exchange protocol and its different implementations. We will present the concepts necessary for understanding reciprocity-based key exchange using symmetry in the channel in Sect. 3 and explain how we can extend this symmetry to the hardware, using the example of a direct-conversion receiver. We then introduce our key extraction method in Sect. 4. In Sect. 5, we describe in detail our implementation of the protocol and we validate our method with the results obtained in several indoor environments. Our work is concluded in Sect. 6.

2   Previous Work

Cryptographic algorithms have traditionally been implemented in the upper levels of the protocol stack. Lower levels seemed not to offer any properties that could be employed for security purposes. In recent years, a few authors have been proposing methods for exploring the lower levels of the stack, namely the *physical layer*, for improving the security of the overall system, as described in [BB11]. Several approaches for security on this layer have been proposed by different authors. Some other information-theoretic solutions have been introduced, like the ones based on *reciprocity*, such as [HHY95] or [HSHC96]. More recent works discuss a few security problems in the protocol given that the environment is not complex enough. A *side-channel attack* [DLMQdA10] on wireless key exchange implementations has also been described. An attack against this protocol in presented in [ESWM12]. In [AHT+05] and [SHOK04], reciprocity-based key exchange is combined with techniques using ESPAR antennas in order to improve the security by introducing a new variable that the adversary cannot predict - the controlled beam-forming of these antenas. A few practical setups performing this protocol have been implemented. In all of them, the authors present different *key extractors* for generating the key from the received signal, given that some *non-reciprocities* (like different hardware employed or additive noise) strongly influence the final result ([MTM+08]). Hence, most of the recent research focus on finding stable and efficient key quantizers that deal with these impairments ([CPK10] and [PJC+13]). Moreover, other authors pondered the possibility of using device-dependent data, i.e. information that depends on the transmitter hardware, for the purpose of transmitter authentification. In Brik et al. [BBGO08], this property is referred to as *radiometric identity* or radio-frequency (RF) fingerprinting.

3   The Key Exchange Protocol

3.1   Channel

It is usual to describe mathematically the radio channels through their impulse response. $h_{AB}(t)$ represents the impulse response of the multipath fading channel between Alice and Bob in a time-invariant channel (during the short time period of the protocol execution), while $h_{BA}(t)$ the impulse response of the channel in the opposite direction. Because of reciprocity, we can state that $h_{BA}(t) = h_{AB}(t)$, which means that the channel characteristics are approximately the same in both directions, within the coherence time for fading channels (which is around 2.5 ms, according to [TV05]). Hershey et al. [HHY95] proposed to use this common characteristic in order to generate a secret key between Alice and Bob, as this signal corresponds to the signature of the channel between these parties. Because of the spatial decorrelation of signals in a fading channel, the channel responses $h_{AE}(t)$ and $h_{BE}(t)$ that Eve receives are uncorrelated to $h_{AB}(t)$ and $h_{BA}(t)$, respectively. This guarantees the secrecy of the key. In [MTM+08], and [CPK10], some practical implementations of this protocol have been described in detail.

However, the measured values might be influenced by several impairments, like additive noise, differences in hardware [CPK10], interference, manufacturing conditions and the fact that the channel is not sounded in both directions at the same time [PJC+13]. This can affect the channel state information and induce "asymmetries" in the system. Consequently, *information reconciliation* should be performed at the end of the protocol, in order to ensure that both parties possess the same key.

Some issues related to synchronization are also addressed in [CPK10]. This protocol only accounts for passive attackers. This means that it is assumed that Eve is not able to jam the probing signals. Eve is supposed to be sufficiently separated (at least a few wavelengths) from Bob.

Now let $s_A(t) = A\cos(2\pi f_A t)$ be the channel probing carrier signal sent by Alice. Bob receives the signal

$$r_B(t) = \sum_{i=1}^{n} \rho_i s_A(t - \tau_i) = A\sum_{i=1}^{n} \rho_i \cos(2\pi f_A(t - \tau_i)), \tag{1}$$

which is the sum of n attenuated and delayed replicas of the original wave of amplitude A, $s_A(t)$, corresponding to the different signal components arriving to Bob throught n different paths. ρ_i and τ_i are the attenuation coefficients and delays for each path, respectively.

3.2   Direct-Conversion Receivers

One important type of common receivers are the so-called *direct-conversion receivers*. This is the kind of receivers often used by the *software-defined radio* community. It is an example of a simple receiver, where only one conversion stage is employed. Nevertheless, our observations are still valid for the multi-conversion case. Unlike superheterodyne receivers, a direct-conversion receiver (DCR) uses no intermediary frequency for performing the demodulation. It uses instead a local oscillator with a similar frequency to that of the carrier signal. A simplified diagram of a DCR can be seen in Fig. 1.

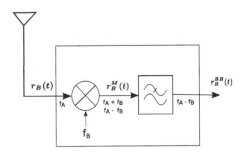

Fig. 1. Direct-conversion receiver (simplified) at Bob.

The received signal $r_B(t)$ (Eq. 1) will then be downconverted in the mixer with local oscillator with frequency f_B and phase φ_B. The resulting signal is therefore

$$r_B^M(t) = A\sum_{i=1}^{n} \rho_i \cos(2\pi f_A(t - \tau_i)) \cos(2\pi f_B t + \varphi_B) \tag{2}$$

Applying well-known trigonometric identities to (2), we obtain

$$r_B^M(t) = \sum_{i=1}^{n} C_i[\cos(2\pi(f_A - f_B)t + \phi_i) +$$
$$+ \underbrace{\cos(2\pi(f_A + f_B)t + \phi_i)}_{\text{filtered out}}], \tag{3}$$

where C_i are amplitude coefficients depending on A, ρ_i and τ_i, and ϕ_i phases depending on τ_i and φ_B.

As we can see from Eq. 2, due to the mixing of different frequencies, new signal components with frequencies $f_A - f_B$ and $f_A + f_B$ are created in this process. Therefore, a filtering stage is applied in order to filter out the signal's higher frequency components. This process removes the $f_A + f_B$ component. Applying a low-pass filter to $r_B^M(t)$, we then obtain the baseband signal

$$r_B^{BB}(t) = \sum_{i=1}^{n} C_i \cos(2\pi(\underbrace{f_A - f_B}_{\delta f})t + \phi_i) \tag{4}$$

This means that the DCR-receiver outputs a signal whose amplitude is basically defined by the channel characteristics and whose frequency, δf, is exclusively due to the sender and receiver local oscillators' frequencies. Combining these two factors, we propose the protocol described next.

3.3 Protocol

In real-world applications, the transceivers' local oscillators inherently contain unavoidable errors, i.e., small unpredictable variations of the oscillation frequency. As an example, an absolute error of 500 kHz in an oscillation frequency of 2.4 GHz accounts for a relative error of 0.02 %. A totally accurate oscillation frequency is therefore unattainable. Actually, when Alice intends to tune her local oscillator to a certain frequency f_{c_j}, the device gets tuned for $f_{c_j} \pm \epsilon_A$, where ϵ_A is the inherent frequency error depending on manufacturing conditions, temperature, and other uncontrollable variables. The same happens with Bob, whose device gets tuned for $f_{c_j} \pm \epsilon_B$. The difference in the actual tuned frequencies, $\delta f = |\epsilon_A - \epsilon_B|$, will be responsible for the creation of a new signal baseband component of frequency δf, as explained in Sect. 3.2. Our measurements show that the values of δf are smaller than the predictable coherence bandwidth for this type of environments for line-of-sight (LOS) positions, whose values for the band 2.4 GHz can reach 250 MHz [Jan92]. Therefore, the received sounding signals will not be affected by the slight difference of the sounding signals frequencies.

Taking this into consideration, we developed the following protocol:

1. Alice tunes her local oscillator to the value f_{c_j}. Consequently, a carrier wave with frequency $f_{c_j} \pm \epsilon_A$ is generated and used for *sounding the channel*.
2. Using a packet transmission, *sync signal*, Alice signalizes Bob that she already started sending a signal with a theoretical frequency f_{c_j}.

3. Bob saves the incoming signal during a certain period of time, Δt, tuning his local oscillator for the same frequency value $f_{c_j} \pm \epsilon_B$.
4. Bob informs Alice that she can already stop sending the analog probing signal and Alice interrupts the transmission of the wave. A signal with frequency $\delta f = |\epsilon_A - \epsilon_B|$ is generated.
5. Alice and Bob exchange their roles and perform the previous steps accordingly.
6. Repeat this procedure F times for other frequency values $f_{c_j}, j = 2, ..., F$.

4   Key Extraction

In this Section, a novel method for generating the key extracted from the surrounding environment is described in detail.

Basically, all *key extractors* consist of two components:

1. Features Extraction block (filter): selects and processes some selected features of the incoming signal.
2. Quantizer: transforms the signal coming out of the filter into a binary sequence.

Most experimental studies on this subject use the time variation of the signals' RSSI (*Received Signal Strength Indicator*) values as input of the quantization block. The values are then processed in such a way that the system disparities are minimized and the entropy rate of the secret keys maximized ([MTM+08, CPK10], and [PJC+13]).

We consider the baseband signal demodulated by the transceiver in iteration j, represented as $r_j^{BB}(t)$. As explained before, we do not restrict ourselves to the amplitude values, but we also consider the effect of the frequency of this signal as a new source of common entropy. Keeping this in mind, a simple Features Extraction block is developed. For each iteration j of the protocol, each party computes the output of this block as:

$$q(j) = \underbrace{\frac{1}{N} \sum_{k=1}^{N} |X_k|}_{\text{fading}} \cdot \underbrace{\frac{1}{M-1} \sum_{l=1}^{M-1} |Z_{l+1} - Z_l|}_{\text{local oscillators}}, \tag{5}$$

where X_k are the local maxima and minima, and Z_l the zero crossings, respectively, of the signal $r_j^{BB}(t)$, as depicted in Fig. 2. This equation corresponds to the *product of the averages* of the main features: the amplitude (contained in the values X_k) and the frequency (translated in the values Z_l, being the interval between two zero crossings approximately half of the period of the wave). The *averaging* process tends to minimize the influence of the measurements' associated noise.

This technique is quite efficient since the number of performed calculations needed for the key generation is small: for each sent frequency, one just needs to calculate the peaks and the zero crossings of the signal. This is not hard to implement either in software or hardware.

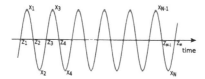

Fig. 2. Baseband Signal with local extrema and zero crossings.

The *key extractor* (Eq. 5) combines the signal strength and frequency offset together through multiplication. Therefore the signal strength values are scaled non-linearly in the Features Extraction block: a higher frequency (closer *zero-crossings*) leads to a smaller combined value. However, the output of this block is quantized uniformly, which means that an increasing number of signal strength values are quantized to the same bit sequence. This reduces the entropy of the generated key. In order to cope with this problem, we propose the usage of non-linear quantization methods for further work.

5 Implementation

In this Section, our experimental efforts to measure the feasibility of our technique are described. A testbed was designed and the results analyzed.

5.1 Channel

In order to experimentally validate this protocol, we conducted a series of experiments in different positions at a static indoor environment. The experiments were performed during an inactivity time period at our Institute.

5.2 Equipment

We used one USRP1 device per party as a transceiver frontend for generating the probing signals and measuring the corresponding echoes. Each USRP1 device was equipped with RFX2400 daughterboards. They provide a good performance in the 2.4–2.483 GHz band and have 50 mW of output power. Our implementation uses the GNU RADIO platform [gnu] installed in similar laptops running Linux-OpenSUSE distributions for the interaction with the transceivers. Synchronization was performed by sending and receiving packets through the 802.11 Ethernet cards installed in the laptops.

We collected data for each carrier frequency $f_{c_j}, j = 1, ..., F$ of the protocol presented in Sect. 3.3. 4096 points were saved for each received wave. In order to avoid any interferences between the *sounding signal* sent by the USRP1 and the *sync signal* around 2.4 GHz being sent by the laptop's ethernet cards (Fig. 3b), the starting *sounding carrier* frequency was chosen to be higher than 2.4 GHz, namely $f_{c_1} = 2.43$ GHz. The sounding frequencies were separated by $\Delta f = 1$ MHz, until reaching the value of 2.473 GHz, which corresponds to $F = 44$ probing bands. These values lie within the 2.4 GHz ISM band.

The signal traces were saved in the laptop and later transfered to a PC, where the analysis and processing steps of the *key extractor* described in Sect. 4 were performed offline using MATLAB®. Each USRP receiver measures an in-phase (or real) component (I) and a quadrature (Q) component for each received signal $R^{BB}(t)$, say $R^{BB}(t) = R_I^{BB}(t) + \jmath R_Q^{BB}(t)$. As input of our signal transformation block, we considered only the in-phase component of the signal, i.e., $r^{BB}(t) = R_I^{BB}(t) = \text{Re}(R^{BB}(t))$, since the quadrature component brings no further information about the channel.

5.3   Measurements

In order to investigate the feasibility of our method, we tested at long distances, namely at the long corridor at our Institute. For this group of experiments, two transceiver platforms (a set of USRP, laptop and antenna) are placed constantly at positions X (Alice) and Y (Bob), whereas the platform (Eve) is subsequentially placed at positions $Z = a, b, c, ..., k$ (see Fig. 3a and b). Each position Z defines a topological *layout*. We performed five complete runs of the protocol for each *layout*.

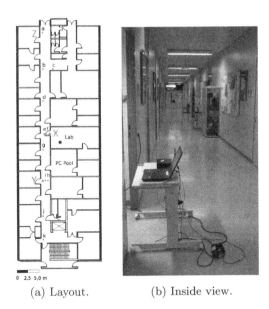

(a) Layout.   (b) Inside view.

Fig. 3. Corridor.

This procedure is repeated for each one of the layouts $Z = a, ..., k$.

5.4   Results and Discussion

As figure of merit for the quality of our method, we defined the key agreement rate (KAR) as the ratio of the Hamming-Distance, HD, between the generated keys at Alice, k_A and Bob, k_B, and the length of the keys, $L = |k_A| = |k_B|$. Mathematically, $KAR = HD(k_A, k_B)/L$. Table 1 shows the average KAR for the experiment. For all layouts, the KAR values for the *Alice-Bob* channel are more than 85 %, which numerically confirms the reciprocity property. The KAR values for the eavesdropper's channels (channels *Alice-Eve* and *Bob-Eve*) are clearly smaller than the KAR values for the *Alice-Bob* channel. For most cases, Eve's KAR values are around 50 %, which numerically validates the multipath property. Further work is needed to explain the few exceptions, like for $Z = d$.

Table 1. KAR (%) values for all layouts.

Layout/Parties	A-B	E-A	E-B	Layout/Parties	A-B	E-A	E-B
a	85.8	43.5	47.0	g	92.0	43.5	26.4
b	93.2	59.8	47.4	h	90.6	42.9	50.2
c	91.5	47.7	46.8	i	87.6	53.9	37.3
d	93.8	51.5	79.1	j	91.5	40.0	33.9
e	90.3	44.0	53.7	k	94.4	42.7	59.8
f	88.0	49.5	54.2				

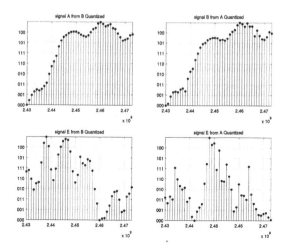

Fig. 4. Key extractor output for layout $Z = a$.

The obtained plots from the output of the *key extractor* (we plot, as an example, the output for layouts $Z = a$ and $Z = g$ in Figs. 4 and 5) validate the reciprocity and multipath properties of the wireless channels, as well as the effect of the local oscillators. Using visual inspection, we consistently observed that both signals received by Alice and Bob (upper plots) are identical, whereas those received by Eve seem to be quite different (column-by-column comparison).

Comparing the quantizer output for layouts $Z = a$ and $Z = g$, one can see that the channel is quite static, since the signals received by Alice and Bob practically don't change with the time. On the other hand, Eve's position changed from position a to position g. This becomes clear when comparing Eve's quantizer's output for both layouts (downner plots of Figs. 4 and 5).

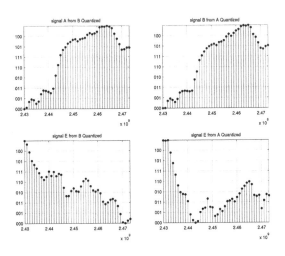

Fig. 5. Key extractor output for layout $Z = g$.

Moreover, the quantization method accounts for the difference of scale resulting from impairments like different transmitted and received gains set at the amplifiers, since the amplitude of the output of the *Features Extraction block* is divided in equal parts during the quantization process.

However, we acknowledge that more entropy in the key would be desirable. This correponds to more *abrupt transitions* in the quantizers' profiles. As mentioned in Sect. 4, this could be achieved by employing a different kind of *quantizer*, namely some kind of non-linear quantizer.

6   Conclusions

The usage of the physical layer properties for the key agreement problem has lately been a fast growing research topic in wireless security. Some implementations aiming to extract a key from common randomness have been proposed.

The shared randomness is contained in the common wireless channel between both legitimate parties.

The current focus of research in this area has been to maximize the bit generation rate and to cope with impairments in the transceiver and asymmetries in the channel. The eventuality of a too simple environment, providing low entropy, or even the existence of side-channel attacks on this protocol has been mostly neglected. We extend the source of randomness to a certain type of unavoidable imparities in the transmitter and receiver hardware. In this work, we leverage the differences in the oscillation frequency of the local oscillators in order to enhance the security of the wireless key exchange method. We demonstrate how the spurious signals usually created by mixing signals with different frequencies can be used in order to augment the security of the key exchange system based on Rayleigh fading, in the presence of a passive attacker.

We established the validity of our method in certain kind of transceivers and we evaluate its feasibility for real-world applications with a proper implementation in a testbed. Our experimental results evidence that this method seems to be a robust technique for secret key generation, at least in indoor environments, as the key agreement ratio indicates. This conclusion is also supported by the quantizers' output profile. The experiments suggest that the oscillation imparities act in the same way as the ESPAR antennas. In this case, the adversary is not able to find the beam-forming characteristic of the antennas. Similarly, in our technique for key generation, the adversary is unable to predict the frequency of the received waves resulting from the unavoidable differences in the legitimate parties' local oscillators. By taking this into account, we introduce another source of entropy when generating the key.

One advantage of extending the source of randomness to the hardware components lies in the fact that known side-channels attacks against this protocol will be hardened. The environment might be too simple or an adversary might be able of collecting reradiation from the antennas; however, as long as Eve doesn't know to which frequency she should tune her receiver, the received signals by Alice and Bob are, by itself, no longer enough for her to reconstruct the baseband signal. In order to launch an attack on this method, Eve additionally needs to measure very precisely (i.e., with an error $\epsilon \approx 0$) Alice and Bob's frequencies, which substantially increases the overall difficulty of guessing the secret key. Due to the deployment of a linear quantizer in our experiments, we limited the generated entropy. Therefore, the usage of non-linear quantizers should be a topic for further work.

Another advantage of our method resides in the fact that it is easy to implement, both in software and hardware. This means that such a system can be directly implemented in off-the-shelf equipment.

References

[AHT+05] Aono, T., Higuchi, K., Taromaru, M., Ohira, T., Sasaoka, H.: Wireless secret key generation exploiting the reactance-domain scalar response of multipath fading channels : RSSI interleaving scheme. In: The European Conference on Wireless Technology, pp. 173–176, October 2005

[BB11] Bloch, M., Barros, J.: Physical-Layer Security: From Information Theory to Security Engineering. Cambridge University Press, Cambridge (2011)

[BBGO08] Brik, V., Banerjee, S., Gruteser, M., Oh, S.: Wireless device identification with radiometric signatures. In: Garcia-Luna-Aceves, et al. [GLASS08], pp. 116–127

[CPK10] Croft, J.: Patwari, N., Kasera, S.K.: Robust uncorrelated bit extraction methodologies for wireless sensors. In: IPSN, pp. 70–81 (2010)

[DLMQdA10] Döttling, N., Lazich, D., Müller-Quade, J., de Almeida, A.S.: Vulnerabilities of wireless key exchange based on channel reciprocity. In: Chung, Y., Yung, M. (eds.) WISA 2010. LNCS, vol. 6513, pp. 206–220. Springer, Heidelberg (2011)

[ESWM12] Eberz, S., Strohmeier, M., Wilhelm, M., Martinovic, I.: A practical man-in-the-middle attack on signal-based key generation protocols. In: Foresti, S., Yung, M., Martinelli, F. (eds.) ESORICS 2012. LNCS, vol. 7459, pp. 235–252. Springer, Heidelberg (2012)

[GLASS08] Garcia-Luna-Aceves, J.J., Sivakumar, R., Steenkiste, P. (eds.) Proceedings of the 14th Annual International Conference on Mobile Computing and Networking, MOBICOM 2008, San Francisco, California, USA, 14–19 September 2008. ACM (2008)

[gnu] http://www.gnuradio.org

[HHY95] Hershey, J.E., Hassan, A.A., Yarlagadda, R.: Unconventional cryptographic keying variable management. IEEE Trans. Commun. **43**, 3–6 (1995)

[HSHC96] Hassan, A.A., Stark, W.E., Hershey, J.E., Chennakeshu, S.: Cryptographic key agreement for mobile radio. Digital Sig. Process. **6**, 207–212 (1996)

[Jan92] Janssen, G.J.: Short range propagation measurements at 2.4, 4.5 and 11.5 GHz in indoor and outdoor environments, May 1992

[MTM+08] Mathur, S., Trappe, W., Mandayam, N.B., Ye, C., Reznik, A.: Radio-telepathy: extracting a secret key from an unauthenticated wireless channel. In: Garcia-Luna-Aceves, et al. [GLASS08], pp. 128–139

[PJC+13] Premnath, S.N., Jana, S., Croft, J., Lakshmane Gowda, P., Clark, M., Kasera, S.K., Patwari, N., Krishnamurthy, S.V.: Secret key extraction from wireless signal strength in real environments. IEEE Trans. Mob. Comput. **12**(5), 917–930 (2013)

[SHOK04] Sun, C., Hirata, A., Ohira, T., Karmakar, N.C.: Fast beamforming of electronically steerable parasitic array radiator antennas: theory and experiment. In: IEEE Transactions on Antennas and Propagation, pp. 1819–1832, July 2004

[TV05] Tse, D., Viswanath, P.: Fundamentals of Wireless Communication. Cambridge University Press, Cambridge (2005)

Exploiting the Potential of GPUs for Modular Multiplication in ECC

Fangyu Zheng[1,2,3], Wuqiong Pan[1,2(✉)], Jingqiang Lin[1,2], Jiwu Jing[1,2], and Yuan Zhao[1,2,3]

[1] Data Assurance and Communication Security Research Center, CAS, Beijing, China
[2] State Key Laboratory of Information Security, Institute of Information Engineering, CAS, Beijing, China
wqpan@is.ac.cn
[3] University of Chinese Academy of Sciences, Beijing, China
{fyzheng,linjq,jing,zhaoyuan12}@is.ac.cn

Abstract. In traditional multiple precision large integer multiplication algorithm, the required number of additions approximates the number of multiplications needed. In some platforms, the great number of add instructions will occupy about half of computing latency in the overall implementation. In this paper, we propose a multiplication algorithm using separated multiply-add-with-carry instruction supported by NVIDIA GPUs. In the algorithm, we reorder the computational sequence, in which nearly all additions and carry flags handling can be combined with the multiplication instructions. The number of add instructions needed decreases from $O(n^2)$ in prevailing schoolbook algorithm to $O(n)$. Our resulting 256-bit modular multiplication and modular square over Mersenne prime respectively achieve 3.3837 billion and 5.9928 billion operations per second and reach 96 % of GPU hardware limitation. An elliptic curve point multiplication implementation using our algorithm achieves 43.6 % speedup compared to the existing fastest work.

Keywords: GPU · CUDA · Modular multiplication · ECC

1 Introduction

Asymmetrical cryptography is the core of modern Internet security. Widely used secure communication protocols in financial industry and e-commerce, rely on secure key exchange and digital signature algorithms such as the ECC [13,15] and RSA [20] algorithms. Unfortunately, great number of large integer modular multiplications seriously affects the performance of the algorithms, and becomes the bottleneck that restricts its wider application. To offload the costs, many researchers resort to graphics processing units (GPUs).

F. Zheng—This work was partially supported by the National 973 Program of China under award No. 2013CB338001 and the Strategic Priority Research Program of Chinese Academy of Sciences under Grant XDA06010702.

K.-H. Rhee and J.H. Yi (Eds.): WISA 2014, LNCS 8909, pp. 295–306, 2015.
DOI: 10.1007/978-3-319-15087-1_23

Many previous papers report performance benchmark results to demonstrate that the GPU architecture can already be used as an asymmetric cryptography workhorse, such as RSA [9,11,16,22], and ECC [1,4–6,8,22]. References [4,5,9,22] pioneered implementation of modular multiplication on CUDA. Bernstein et al. [5] implemented an 280-bit modular multiplication with single precision floating point (SPF) instructions, in which several threads compute an modular multiplication. In their follow-up work [4], they turned into integer instructions and employed single thread to handle an entire multiplication without the overhead of thread synchronization. Giorgi et al. [9] proposed a C++ library (PACE) to support modular arithmetic on an NVIDIA 9800GX2 GPU, in which the Montgomery representation of large integers is used to perform modular multiplication using the Finely Integrated Operand Scanning (FIOS) [14]. Antão et al. [1,2] used RNS (Reside Number System) to implement modular multiplication. In latest work [19], Pu et al. employed several threads to handle one multiplication with parallel RNS-based [3] computing model. The implementations above are based on generic modulus. In 2012 Bos et al. [6] accomplished modular multiplication over NIST P-224 modulus. His optimization focuses on elliptic curve point multiplication and only uses schoolbook modular multiplication algorithm [10], which is not suitable for GPUs. In this paper, we aim to fully exploit the potential of GPU for the implementation of the large integer modular multiplication over Mersenne prime [21].

Our contribution is to make full use of CUDA-featured separated multiply-add-with-carry instruction to avoid most of the add instructions and make the algorithm procedure more suitable for CUDA hardware framework. Using this instruction, we integrate nearly all additions in multiply-add instructions and very few carry flags need to be handled using extra instruction. The number of add instructions needed decreases from $O(n^2)$ in prevailing schoolbook algorithm to $O(n)$.

Directed at NVIDIA GeForce GTX Titan, a 2688-CUDA-core GPU, our resulting modular multiplication and modular square respectively reach 3.3837 billion and 5.9928 billion operations per second, reaching nearly 96 % of the GPU's limitation. For better evaluation, we also implement an elliptic curve point multiplication implementation using our algorithm which reaches 391,595 operations per second.

The paper is organized as follows. Section 2 presents the overview of NVIDIA GPU and its multiplication instruction. Section 3 describes our proposed algorithm in detail. Section 4 analyses performance of proposed algorithm and compares it with previous work. Section 5 concludes the paper.

2   Background

2.1   CUDA GPUs and Its Multiplication Instruction

Our target platform GTX Titan is a GK-110 GPU, which contains 14 streaming multiprocessors (SM). 32 threads (grouped as a *warp*) can concurrently run in a clock. Following the SIMT (Single Instruction Multiple Threads) architecture, each GPU thread runs one instance of the kernel function. A warp may be preempted when it is stalled due to memory access delay, and the scheduler may switch the runtime context to another available warp. Multiple warps of threads are usually assigned to one SM for better utilization of the pipeline of each SM. These warps are called one *block* [18].

Multiplication instruction of NVIDIA GPU has a unique feature: when calculating the 32-bit × 32-bit multiplication, the whole 64-bit product cannot be obtained using one instruction, but requires 2 independent instructions: one is for lower-32-bit half, the other for upper-32-bit half. Although the whole multiplication (`mul.wide`) is provided which is used in [12,17], it is a virtual instruction but not the native instruction, which will be broken into 2 instructions (`mul.lo.` and `mul.hi`) when running on the GPUs.

Ten work patterns of multiplication (or multiply-add) instruction are supported by NVIDIA GPUs. Among them, the separated multiply-add-with-carry instruction $s =$ `madc.cc{.lo,.hi}`(a, b, c) can multiply 32-bit integer a and b, extract lower or upper half of the 64-bit product, and add a third value c with CF (carry flag) bit in the condition code register (CC). The 32-bit result and the carry that it produces will be respectively written to s and the CF bit in CC [18].

3   Proposed Algorithm Description

3.1   Large Integer Multiplication Algorithm

Traditional large integer multiplication algorithm is introduced in *Guide to Elliptic Curve Cryptography* [10]. Bos et al. [6] used this algorithm to accomplish modular multiplication. However, this algorithm is not well supported in CUDA due to its separated multiplication instruction. Through experiment, we found that, when compiling, $2(m-1)(n-1)$ add instructions are needed, whose number approximates the number of multiply instructions.

Based on this observation, we make attempt to minimize the number of add instructions. As mentioned in Sect. 2.1, CUDA platform supports separated multiply-add-with-carry instruction. Taking advantage of this character, we propose a brand new algorithm. In the proposed algorithm, the computational sequence is carefully scheduled to utilize separated multiply-add-with-carry instructions and reduce extra handling of carry flags. We take 5-word × 5-word multiplication for example to demonstrate the overall computational sequence, which is shown in Fig. 1, where $A[0:4] = \sum_{i=0}^{4} a_i 2^{ri}$ and $B[0:4] = \sum_{i=0}^{4} b_i 2^{ri}$ are the multiplicands, $C[0:9] = \sum_{i=0}^{9} c_i 2^{ri}$ is the product, r stands for word length.

The upper part of Fig. 1 indicates the adjusted computational sequence. We accumulate each row into the product $C[0:9]$ from the top to the bottom. For convenience, we color each row by white or gray. The white rows contain only the lower-half instructions, while, the gray rows include only the upper-half.

The lower part of Fig. 1 takes the last 2 rows to demonstrate the detailed step of the accumulation. In each row, from left to right, we accumulate the

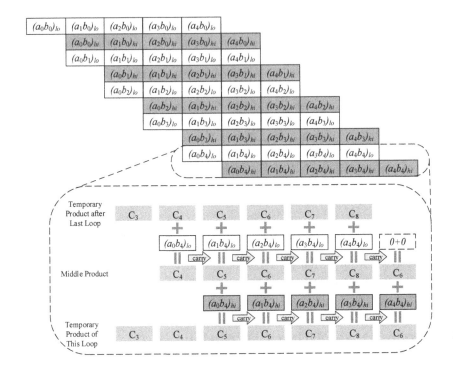

Fig. 1. $5 - word \times 5 - word$ multiplication structure using proposed algorithm

half product into $C[0:9]$. Firstly, we accumulate the white row. Using instruction `madc.cc`, each cell in the white row accumulates its lower half product into the corresponding word of $C[0:9]$, also accumulates the CF bit that previous instruction produces (except the first instruction), then writes back its carry to CF bit. The CF bit that the last instruction produces needs to be stored using add-with-carry instruction `addc(0,0)`. The accumulation for the gray row is similar, but we do not need to handle the CF bit that the last instruction produces because it will not produce carry. Note that there are n white rows totally. Among them, the 0th white row need no temporary variable, because its last instruction adds zero thus will not produce carry. Therefore, $2mn$ multiplication and $(n-1)$ add instructions are needed in total. Detail is shown in Algorithm 1.

3.2   Large Integer Square Algorithm

Compared with multiplication, square operation has a natural advantage: some sub-products can be reused. Equation below shows this advantage in detail, which takes $(A[0:n-1])^2$ for example, where $A[0:n-1] = \sum_{i=0}^{n-1} a_i 2^{ri}$.

Algorithm 1. Proposed Multiplication Algorithm(r bits per word)

Input:

m-word-length Multiplicand, $A[0:m-1] = \sum_{i=0}^{m-1} a_i 2^{ri}$;

n-word-length Multiplier, $B[0:n-1] = \sum_{i=0}^{n-1} b_i 2^{ri}$;

$m > n$

Output:

(m+n)-word-length Product, $C[0:m+n-1] = A[0:m-1] \times B[0:n-1] = \sum_{i=0}^{m+n-1} c_i 2^{ri}$;

1:   $C[0:m+n-1] = 0$
2: **for** $i = 0$ *to* $n-1$ **do**
3:    **for** $j = 0$ *to* $m-1$ **do**
4:     set CF $= 0$
5:     $c_{i+j} = \mathtt{madc.cc.lo}(a_j, b_i, c_{i+j})$
6:    **end for**
7:    **if** $i \neq 0$ **then**
8:     $c_{i+n} = \mathtt{addc}(0,0)$
9:    **end if**
10:   set CF $= 0$
11:   **for** $j = 0$ *to* $m-1$ **do**
12:    $c_{i+j+1} = \mathtt{madc.cc.hi}(a_j, b_i, c_{i+j+1})$
13:   **end for**
14: **end for**
15: **return** $C[0:m+n-1]$;

$$
\begin{aligned}
(A[0:n-1])^2 &= \sum_{0 \leq i < j \leq n-1} [2^{r(i+j)}(a_i \times a_j)_{lo} + 2^{r(i+j+1)}(a_i \times a_j)_{hi}] \\
&+ \sum_{0 \leq i \leq n-1} [2^{2ri}(a_i^2)_{lo} + 2^{r(2i+1)}(a_i^2)_{hi}] \\
&+ \sum_{0 \leq j < i \leq n-1} [2^{r(i+j)}(a_i \times a_j)_{lo} + 2^{r(i+j+1)}(a_i \times a_j)_{hi}] \\
&= 2 \sum_{0 \leq i < j \leq n-1} [2^{r(i+j)}(a_i \times a_j)_{lo} + 2^{r(i+j+1)}(a_i \times a_j)_{hi}] \\
&+ \sum_{0 \leq i \leq n-1} [2^{2ri}(a_i^2)_{lo} + 2^{r(2i+1)}(a_i^2)_{hi}]
\end{aligned}
$$

In this way, only $(\frac{n(n-1)}{2} + n) \times 2 = n^2 + n$ multiplications are needed.

For convenience, we take 5-word square operation for example. Firstly, we calculate $\sum_{0 \leq i < j \leq n-1}^{n} [2^{r(i+j)}(a_i \times a_j)_{lo} + 2^{r(i+j+1)}(a_i \times a_j)_{hi}]$. In upper part of Fig. 2, the 2 white pieces are corresponding to it. We choose the upper separated piece to calculate. Before calculation, we carry out a transformation for it. As demonstrated in the middle part of Fig. 2, we "flatten" it into the new structure. In this structure, we can accumulate each row into the product from the top to the bottom, which is similar with the operation in previous section. And in each row, we accumulate the product from left to right.

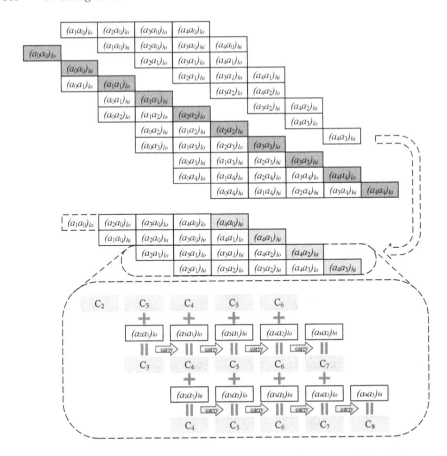

Fig. 2. $5 - word \times 5 - word$ square structure using proposed algorithm

The lower part of Fig. 2 takes the last 2 rows to demonstrate the detailed step of the accumulation. Using instruction madc.cc, each cell in the row accumulates its lower or upper half product into the corresponding word of $C[0:9]$, also accumulates the CF bit that previous instruction produces (except the first instruction), then writes back its carry to CF bit. CF bit that the last instruction produces needs no extra handling, because that if the last instruction of each row is upper-word multiply-add instruction, it will not produce carry. It can be proved as below.

Proof. Assuming a, b is 32-bit integer, their upper half product is at most $2^{32} - 2$, because

$$(a \times b)_{hi} \leq \lfloor \frac{(2^{32} - 1) \times (2^{32} - 1)}{2^{32}} \rfloor = 2^{32} - 2 \qquad (1)$$

We take a row as a unit to employ mathematical induction.

(1) Obviously, the last instruction of row 0 will not produce carry, because it adds with zero.

(2) Assume the last instruction of row $k - 1$ does not produce carry. Thus it affects only the $(n + k - 1)$-th or lower word of the product. In this way, the $(n + k)$-th or higher word of temporary product remains zero. As to row k, the second-last instruction may produce carry to the $(n + k)$-th. According to equation (1), after executing its last instruction, the $(n+k)$-th word of temporary product is less than or equal to $(2^{32} - 2) + 1 = 2^{32} - 1$. It implies that it will not produce carry, either.

In this way, we prove that when every last instruction of the row is the upper-half multiply-add instruction, it will not produce carry. As shown in Fig. 2, every last instruction of the row meets this requirement. Thus, we do not need to handle the CF bit that the last instruction produces.

Secondly, we need to double the temporary product. Since temporary product is $(2n - 2)$ words (from 1th to $(2n - 2)$-th word), we need $(2n - 1)$ add instructions to double it (extra one add instruction is used for storing CF the last add instruction produces).

Thirdly, we add the gray piece, which is corresponding to $\sum_{0\leq i\leq n-1}^{n}[2^{2ri}(a_i^2)_{lo}+ 2^{r(2i+1)}(a_i^2)_{hi}]$. Like what we did before, gray piece can also be flattened into one row similarly. Using the instruction `madc.cc`, no add instruction is needed.

Therefore, in total, (n^2+n) multiply and $(2n-1)$ add instructions are needed. There is a slight difference between situations when n is odd or even. Detail is shown in Algorithm 2.

4   Implementation and Performance Evaluation

4.1   Comparison between Traditional and Proposed Algorithm

In theory, our proposed algorithm needs only $O(n)$ add instructions, while the traditional one needs $O(n^2)$. However, in practice, we should take other factors into consideration.

In CUDA GPU, integer add and multiplication instruction use different computing units, which allows the 2 kinds of instructions to execute parallelly. Due to multi-thread feature of GPU, when some threads occupy the multiplier, others can use the adder. Thus, in some situations, the decrease of add instruction may not lead to significant performance promotion.

To measure how the number of add instructions affects the overall performance, we conduct an experiment. A function which contains 128 multiply-add instructions (that 256-bit multiplication needs) with several add instructions appending is constructed for evaluation. To ignore other overheads, we run 10,000 loops of the test function, in which uses result in the loop as a new operand for the next loop. In this experiment, 14×1024 threads are used to fully occupy the computing resource. Varying the number of add instructions, we record its latency. The experimental data shows in Fig. 3.

We can see from Fig. 3, when the number of add instructions is less than 128, the performance changes slightly. After reaching the threshold 128, the latency starts to correlate positively with the number of add instructions. From this

---

Algorithm 2. Proposed Square Algorithm(r bits per word)

Input:
    n-word-length Multiplicand, $A[0:n-1] = \sum_{i=0}^{n-1} a_i 2^{ri}$;

Output:
    $2n$-word-length $C[0:2n-1] = A[0:n-1]^2 = \sum_{i=0}^{2n-1} c_i 2^{ri}$;

1: $C[0:2n-1] = 0$,set CF=0
2: **for** $i = 0$ *to* $\lceil \frac{n}{2} \rceil - 2$ **do**
3:    **for** $j = i+1$ *to* $n-i-2$ **do**
4:       $c_{i+j} = \texttt{madc.cc.lo}(a_j, a_i, c_{i+j})$
5:    **end for**
6:    **for** $k = 0$ *to* i **do**
7:       $c_{n+2k-1} = \texttt{madc.cc.lo}(a_{n-1-i+k}, a_{i+k}, c_{n+2k-1})$
         $c_{n+2k} = \texttt{madc.cc.hi}(a_{n-1-i+k}, a_{i+k}, c_{n+2k})$
8:    **end for**
9:    set CF=0
10:   **for** $j = i+1$ *to* $n-i-2$ **do**
11:      $c_{i+j+1} = \texttt{madc.cc.hi}(a_j, a_i, c_{i+j+1})$
12:   **end for**
13:   **for** $k = 0$ *to* i **do**
14:      $c_{n+2k} = \texttt{madc.cc.lo}(a_{n-1-i+k}, a_{i+k+1}, c_{n+2k})$
        $c_{n+2k+1} = \texttt{madc.cc.hi}(a_{n-1-i+k}, a_{i+k+1}, c_{n+2k+1})$
15:   **end for**
16: **end for**
17: **if** n is even **then**
18:   set CF $= 0$
19:   **for** $k = 0$ *to* $\frac{n}{2} - 1$ **do**
20:      $c_{n+2k-1} = \texttt{madc.cc.lo}(a_{n/2+k}, a_{n/2+k-1}, c_{n+2k-1})$
        $c_{n+2k} = \texttt{madc.cc.hi}(a_{n/2+k}, a_{n/2+k-1}, c_{n+2k})$
21:   **end for**
22: **end if**
23: set CF=0
24: **for** $i = 1$ *to* $2n-1$ **do**
25:    $c_i = \texttt{addc}(c_i, c_i)$
26: **end for**
27: set CF=0
28: **for** $i = 0$ *to* $n-1$ **do**
29:    $c_{2i} = \texttt{madc.cc.lo}(a_i, a_i, c_{2i})$
      $c_{2i+1} = \texttt{madc.cc.hi}(a_i, a_i, c_{2i+1})$
30: **end for**
31: **return** $C[0:2n-1]$;

---

phenomenon, we can speculate that the traditional and proposed multiplication algorithms will perform the same. Because the number of add instructions does not reach the threshold in both algorithms.

However, our optimization is not useless. We choose $P = 2^{256} - 2^{224} - 2^{96} + 2^{64} - 1$ as modulus, which is used in *Chinese Public Key Cryptographic Algorithm SM2 Based on Elliptic Curves* [7]. As a Mersenne prime, fast reduction

method can be applied to conduct modular reduction based on the work by
[21]. Through optimizing, a 256-bit modular reduction over P consumes about
110 add instructions in total. Due to the great decrease of add instructions,
when cooperating with modular reduction, our proposed modular multiplication
algorithm is still on the "flat" line, while, traditional modular multiplication
algorithm has surpassed the threshold, whose latency increases by nearly 20 %.

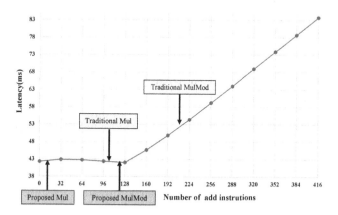

Fig. 3. Latency of 10,000 loops of test function (128 multiplication instructions with
varying number of add instructions appending)

Our performance evaluation comparison proves the speculation well, which
is shown in Table 1.

Table 1. Comparison between the traditional algorithm and the proposed algorithm
(GeForce GTX Titan, 14×1024 threads)

		Traditional	Proposed
256-bit multiplication	Throughput (10^9/s)	3.3939	3.4121
	Latency (µs)	4.2241	4.2015
256-bit modular multiplication	Throughput (10^9/s)	2.8853	3.3837
	Latency (µs)	4.9687	4.2368
256-bit square	Throughput (10^9/s)	5.6436	6.0011
	Latency (µs)	2.5402	2.3889
256-bit modular square	Throughput (10^9/s)	5.1661	5.9928
	Latency (µs)	2.7750	2.3922

4.2   Related Work Comparison

In this section, we compare our resulting implementation with previous work [2,4,6,9,19]. For fair comparison, we firstly evaluate the CUDA platform of each work.

It is difficult to evaluate performance of each CUDA platform since they are constructed in different architectures. Note that [2,4,6,9,19] and ours are all based on integer arithmetic. Therefore, we can measure their performance depending mainly on integer processing capability as shown in the former part of Table 2. The parameters in Table 2 origin from [23], but the integer processing power is not given directly, we calculate them by SM Number, processing power of each SM and Shader Clock. Note that 9800GX2, GTX 285 and GTX 295 support only 24-bit multiply instruction, while, the other platforms support 32-bit multiply instruction. Hence, we adjust their integer multiply processing capability by a correction parameter $(\frac{24}{32})^2$. The overall integer processing capability *Int Capability* is graded by how many operations including a multiplication (or multiply-add) and an add instruction can be accomplished in a second.

Since the results of modular multiplication are not given in some papers, we also implement a simple elliptic curve point multiplication using our algorithm for evaluation. In overall structure, we use single thread to execute one elliptical curve point multiplication. Except for the modular multiplication, we do not take special optimization for it.

For better comparison, we scale the modular multiplication performance of each implementation using the Eq. 2:

$$MulMod(scaled) = MulMod \times \frac{370.7}{Int\ Capability} \times (\frac{Bits}{256})^2 \times (1 + isModulusGeneric) \quad (2)$$

The scaled point multiplication performance *Curve(scaled)* is defined similarly. The latter part of Table 2 shows the corresponding numerical results.

From Table 2, we can see that our algorithm makes great improvement compared with previous implementations. We gain over 3 times performance of the next fastest implementation [4]. Our point multiplication implementation also outperforms others by a considerable margin. We achieve 43.6 % performance promotion of the existing fastest implementation [6].

Additionally, we measure the hardware limiting performance for 256-bit modular multiplication. In modular multiplication, the number of multiplication instructions is the bottleneck of the performance, which cannot be reduced. From Table 2, we can see that the throughput of the 32-bit multiplication instruction reaches 448.6×10^9/s in GTX Titan. 256-bit modular multiplication costs $(\frac{256}{32})^2 \times 2 = 128$ instructions, thus the upper bound of modular multiplication performance is $\frac{448.6}{128} = 3.5047 \times 10^9$/s. Similarly evaluated, the upper bound of the modular square performance is $\frac{448.6}{72} = 6.2306 \times 10^9$/s. Respectively, our modular multiplication and square algorithm reach $\frac{3.3837}{3.5047} = 96.5\%$ and $\frac{5.9928}{6.2306} = 96.2\%$ of the GPU hardware limitation.

Table 2. Throughput and latency of operations per second

	Giorgi et al.[9]	Antão et al.[2]	Bernstein et al.[4]	Bos et al.[6]	Pu et al.[19]	Ours
Bits	256-bit	224-bit	210-bit	224-bit	224-bit	256-bit
isModulusGeneric	Yes	Yes	Yes	No	Yes	No
CUDA platform	9800GX2	GTX 285	GTX 295	GTX 580	GTX 680	GTX Titan
SM Number	32	30	60	16	8	14
Shader Clock(GHz)	1.500	1.476	1.242	1.544	1.006	0.993
Int Mul/SM(/Clock)	8	8	8	16	32	32
Int Add/SM(/Clock)	10	10	10	32	160	160
Int Mul(G/s)	216	199	335	395	257	448.6
Int Add(G/s)	480	443	791	745	1288	2224
Int Capability(G/s)	149.0	137.3	235.3	258.1	226.4	370.7
MulMod $(10^6/s)$	12.34	-	481	-	219	3383.7
MulMod(scaled) $(10^6/s)$	61.40	-	1019	-	549	3383.7
SqrMod $(10^6/s)$	-	-	-	-	-	5992.8
Curve(/s)	1,620	9,827	-	290,535	47,000	391,595
Curve(scaled)(/s)	8,061	40,627	-	272,681	117,839	391,595

5   Summary

In this paper, we propose and implement a new modular multiplication algorithm for ECC implementation in CUDA, aiming to minimize the number of add instructions and develop the full potential of GPU. In our proposed multiplication algorithm, the number of add instructions needed decreases from $O(n^2)$ in prevailing schoolbook algorithm to $O(n)$. Our resulting modular multiplication and modular square respectively reach 3.3837 billion and 5.9928 billion operations per second, reaching over 96 % of GPU hardware limitation. And a simple elliptic curve point multiplication using our algorithm is implemented at speed of 391,595 per second, which achieves 43.6 % speedup compared to the existing fastest work.

References

1. Antão, S., Bajard, J.C., Sousa, L.: Elliptic curve point multiplication on GPUs. In: IEEE International Conference on Application-specific Systems Architectures and Processors (ASAP), pp. 192–199 (2010)
2. Antão, S., Bajard, J.C., Sousa, L.: RNS-Based elliptic curve point multiplication for massive parallel architectures. Comput. J. **55**(5), 629–647 (2012)
3. Bajard, J.C., Didier, L.S., Kornerup, P.: Modular multiplication and base extensions in residue number systems. In: Proceedings of the 15th IEEE Symposium on Computer Arithmetic, pp. 59–65 (2001)

4. Bernstein, D.J., Chen, H.C., Chen, M.S., Cheng, C.M., Hsiao, C.H., Lange, T., Lin, Z.C., Yang, B.Y.: The billion-mulmod-per-second PC. In: Workshop Record of SHARCS, vol. 9, pp. 131–144 (2009)

5. Bernstein, D.J., Chen, T.-R., Cheng, C.-M., Lange, T., Yang, B.-Y.: ECM on graphics cards. In: Joux, A. (ed.) EUROCRYPT 2009. LNCS, vol. 5479, pp. 483–501. Springer, Heidelberg (2009)

6. Bos, J.W.: Low-latency elliptic curve scalar multiplication. Int. J Parallel Prog. **40**(5), 532–550 (2012)

7. Chinese Commercial Cryptography Administration Office: public key cryptographic algorithm SM2 based on elliptic curves (in Chinese) (2013). http://www.oscca.gov.cn/UpFile/2010122214822692.pdf

8. Cohen, A.E., Parhi, K.K.: GPU accelerated elliptic curve cryptography in GF (2^m). In: IEEE International Midwest Symposium on Circuits and Systems (MWSCAS), pp. 57–60 (2010)

9. Giorgi, P., Izard, T., Tisserand, A., et al.: Comparison of modular arithmetic algorithms on GPUs. In: ParCo'09: International Conference on Parallel Computing (2009)

10. Hankerson, D., Vanstone, S., Menezes, A.J.: Guide to Elliptic Curve Cryptography. Springer, New York (2004)

11. Harrison, O., Waldron, J.: Efficient acceleration of asymmetric cryptography on graphics hardware. In: Preneel, B. (ed.) AFRICACRYPT 2009. LNCS, vol. 5580, pp. 350–367. Springer, Heidelberg (2009)

12. Henry, R., Goldberg, I.: Solving discrete logarithms in smooth-order groups with CUDA. In: Workshop Record of SHARCS, pp. 101–118. Citeseer (2012)

13. Koblitz, N.: Elliptic curve cryptosystems. Math. Comput. **48**(177), 203–209 (1987)

14. Koç, Ç.K., Acar, T., Kaliski Jr, B.S.: Analyzing and comparing montgomery multiplication algorithms. Micro IEEE **16**(3), 26–33 (1996)

15. Miller, V.S.: Use of elliptic curves in cryptography. In: Williams, H.C. (ed.) CRYPTO 1985. LNCS, vol. 218, pp. 417–426. Springer, Heidelberg (1986)

16. Moss, A., Page, D., Smart, N.P.: Toward acceleration of RSA using 3D graphics hardware. In: Galbraith, S.D. (ed.) Cryptography and Coding 2007. LNCS, vol. 4887, pp. 364–383. Springer, Heidelberg (2007)

17. Neves, S., Araujo, F.: On the performance of GPU public-key cryptography. In: IEEE International Conference on Application-Specific Systems, Architectures and Processors (ASAP), pp. 133–140 (2011)

18. NVIDIA: CUDA Toolkit Documentation v6.0 (2014). http://docs.nvidia.com/cuda/index.html#axzz39iNG9lqx

19. Pu, S., Liu, J.-C.: EAGL: an elliptic curve arithmetic GPU-based library for bilinear pairing. In: Cao, Z., Zhang, F. (eds.) Pairing 2013. LNCS, vol. 8365, pp. 1–19. Springer, Heidelberg (2014)

20. Rivest, R.L., Shamir, A., Adleman, L.: A method for obtaining digital signatures and public-key cryptosystems. Commun. ACM **21**(2), 120–126 (1978)

21. Solinas, J.A.: Generalized mersenne numbers. Citeseer, Bielefeld (1999)

22. Szerwinski, R., Güneysu, T.: Exploiting the power of GPUs for asymmetric cryptography. In: Oswald, E., Rohatgi, P. (eds.) CHES 2008. LNCS, vol. 5154, pp. 79–99. Springer, Heidelberg (2008)

23. Wikipedia: Wikipedia: list of NVIDIA graphics processing units (2014). http://en.wikipedia.org/wiki/Comparison_of_NVIDIA_Graphics_Processing_Units

The Unified Hardware Design
for GCM and SGCM

Yeoncheol Lee, Hwajeong Seo, and Howon Kim[✉]

School of Computer Science and Engineering, Pusan National University,
San-30, Jangjeon-dong, Geumjeong-gu, Busan 609–735, Republic of Korea
{lycshotgunl,hwajeong,howonkim}@pusan.ac.kr

Abstract. Authenticated Encryption (AE) schemes are an important security tool. Especially, GCM has been widely adopted on account of its performance and efficiency and used widely. As GCM has some weaknesses, SGCM has been proposed in 2011 and both AE schemes sometimes are used in the same system or hardware architecture. In this paper, we present the novel unified hardware for GCM and SGCM. Both modes are readily integrated into single architecture with little modification. The main contributions are three folded. Firstly, we unified GCM and SGCM using dual field adder. Secondly, we improved the previous dual field multiplier to fit our architecture. Our dual field multiplier just needs half cycles of referred one. For quantitative analysis, we calculate areas except for LEA core and add areas of AES which was used by each of previous works. We expect to achieve 29 % or 35 % less size than previous one. Lastly, we applied LEA instead of AES for the compact hardware implementation. Our unified hardware for GCM and SGCM is implemented within 16,133 GE and achieves 0.5 Gbps on 500 Mhz. Our unified hardware using LEA has 48 % less size than the one using AES.

Keywords: Unified GCM and SGCM · Hardware · Dual field multiplier · Block cipher

1 Introduction

Message authentication schemes are an important security tool. Especially, Authenticated Encryption (AE) scheme is a symmetric-key mechanism by which a plain-text is a transformed into a cipher-text with MAC code. It is a block cipher mode of operation which provides authenticity, confidentiality, integrity at once. New other Authenticated Encryption schemes have been development and proposed until now. Six different authenticated encryption modes (GCM, CCM, CWC, OCB, and EAX) have been standardized in ISO/IEC until 2009. From among these, GCM has been widely adopted on account of its performance

This work was supported by the ICT R&D program of MSIP/IITP. [10043907, Development of high performance IoT device and Open Platform with Intelligent Software].

K.-H. Rhee and J.H. Yi (Eds.): WISA 2014, LNCS 8909, pp. 307–320, 2015.
DOI: 10.1007/978-3-319-15087-1_24

and efficiency. GCM is included in NASA Suite B cryptography and [10, 23] show that it is used in IETF IPsec standards. we also confirm that it is one of mode of operations in SSH in [6]. Besides, GCM mode is used in various parts like ANSI Fibre Channel Security Protocols (FC-SP), IEEE 802.1 AE (MACsec), Ethernet security, IEEE 02.11ad known as WiGig, and TLS 1.2. [15].

But GCM has a weakness once it is employed with a short authentication tag [3]. The weakness is to raise the probability of successful forgery significantly and attacker can know the authentication key if they are able to create successful forgeries. So, SGCM has been proposed as a variant of the GCM mode overcoming it's weaknesses in 2011 [14]. SGCM uses prime field $GF(p)$ known as Sophie Germain prime, instead of the binary field $GF(2^{128})$. Thus, It is time for GCM and SGCM to use in the same period and we feel the necessity of making the design of unified hardware for GCM and SGCM.

Many previous GCM implementations are proposed until now and two types of designs which is sequential and parallel exist. GCM architecture in [12] implemented with Mastrovito multiplier and we changed S-box among LUT (Look-up Table) S-box or composite S-box. Yang et al. [25] employed two AES core. Iterative AES is used for generating H for the finite field multiplication and the other one is pipelined AES for encryption. Designs in [12,25] is sequential but both areas is above 100,000 GE using fully pipelined AES which is all of the round steps are pipelined. GCM Hardware implementations in the following have areas under 100,00 GE. We find two kind of implementations in [16]. The first is the sequential implementation completely and the second is the implementation using 4 parallel AES and one multiplier. Both designs in this paper use 4-stage pipelined loop and composite field $GF(((2^2)^2)^2)$. Lastly, GCM architectures in [19,24] have single encryption and simple loop. Areas of them achieved smaller size than previous ones and this implementations are suitable to compare with our implementation. In the case of SGCM, it is proposed in 2011 but studies about implementation of SGCM in hardware have not been proposed briskly. In addition, there are no papers about unifying both GCM and SGCM.

In this situation, we have proposed the compact implementation of the unified hardware for GCM and SGCM. We have three main contributions. Firstly, GCM and SGCM have similar architecture. Thus, we unified GCM and SGCM using dual field multiplier. Secondly, we improved dual field multiplier proposed in [4] to fit our architecture. Our dual field multiplier just needs half cycles of referred one. For quantitative analysis, we calculate areas except for LEA core and add Areas of AES which was used by each of previous works. we expect to achieve 29 % less size than [19] and 35 % less size than [24]. Lastly, we applied LEA instead of AES for the compact hardware implementation. Our implementation of the unified hardware for GCM and SGCM features size of 16,133 GE, 500 Mhz frequency, and 0.5 Gbps throughput. LEA-Unified[d] has 48 % less size than AES-Unified[c].

For describing this, the paper is structured as follows. In Sect. 2, we explain related works such as GCM, SGCM, Dual Field multiplier, and LEA. In Sect. 3, we introduce our architecture and design of unified hardware for GCM and

SGCM, and our Dual Field Multiplier in detail. In Sect. 4, we analyzed the results obtained by our design and compare it to other previous ones. Conclusions are described in Sect. 5.

2   Related Works

2.1   Galois/Counter Mode GCM

An authenticated encryption (AE) symmetric scheme provides both encryption and authentication using a single key, and is often more efficient and easy to employ than using two separate encryption and authentication schemes (e.g. AES-CTR with HMAC). The Galois/Counter Mode (GCM) is an AE scheme which is built upon a block cipher, usually AES [9,23]. It was standardized by NIST and is used in IPSec, SSH and TLS. For each message block, GCM encrypts it using the underlying block cipher in CTR mode and xors the ciphertext into an accumulator, which is then multiplied in F2128 by a key-dependent constant. After processing the last block, this accumulator is used to generate the authentication tag.

GCM has four input strings: secret key K, an initial vector IV (96 bits), authenticated data A, and plaintext P. We use n and u for indicating the total number of bits in the plaintext is $(n-1) \cdot 128 + u$, where $1 \leq u \leq 128$. the plaintext, ciphertext, and authenticated data is donated as: $(P_1, P_2, ..., P_{n-1}, P_n^*)$, $(C_1, C_2, ..., C_{n-1}, C_n^*)$, and $(A_1, A_2, ..., A_{n-1}, A_n^*)$, where the number of bits in C_n^* is u and the total number of bits in A is $(m-1) \cdot 128 + v$ and $1 \leq v \leq 128$. Each final bock of P_n^* and C_n^* is filled with zeros when it is shorter than 128 bits. The authenticated encryption operation is defined as follow equations:

$$
\begin{aligned}
H &= E(K, 0^{128}) \\
Y_0 &= \begin{cases} IV||0^{31}1 & if \; len(IV) = 96, \\ GHASH(H, , IV) & otherwise, \end{cases} \\
Y_i &= Y_{i-1} + 1 & for \; i = 1, ..., n \\
C_i &= P_i \oplus E(K, Y_i) & for \; i = 1, ..., n-1 \\
C_n^* &= P_i^* \oplus MSB_u(E(K, Y_n)) \\
T &= MSB_t(GHASH(K, A, C)) \oplus E(K, Y_0)
\end{aligned}
\tag{1}
$$

The GHASH function defined over the $GF(2^{128})$ is operated for tag creation. When GHASH(H, A, C) = X_{m+n+1} and variables X_i for $i = 0, ..., m+n+1$, GHASH is defined as follow:

$$
X_i = \begin{cases}
0 & for \; i = 0 \\
(X_{i-1} \oplus A_i) \cdot H & for \; i = 0, ..., m-1 \\
(X_{m-1} \oplus (A_m^*||0^{128-v}))) \cdot H & for \; i = m \\
(X_{i-1} \oplus C_i) \cdot H & for \; i = m+1, ..., m+n+1 \\
(X_{m+n-1} \oplus (C_m^*||0^{128-u}))) \cdot H & for \; i = m+n \\
(X_{m+n-1} \oplus (len(A)||len(C))) \cdot H & for \; i = m+n+1
\end{cases}
\tag{2}
$$

2.2 The Sophie Germain Counter Mode SGCM [14]

Sophie Germain Counter Mode (SGCM) is an authenticated encryption mode of operation, to be used with 128-bit block ciphers such as AES. SGCM is a variant of the NIST standardized Galois/Counter Mode (GCM) which has been found to be susceptible to weak key/short cycle forgery attacks. The GCM attacks are made possible by its extremely smooth-order multiplicative group which splits into 512 subgroups. Whereas Instead of GCM's $GF(2^{128})$, SGCM uses $GF(p)$ with

$$p = 2^{128} + 12451 = 340282366920938463463374607431768223907. \qquad (3)$$

Here $\frac{p-1}{2}$ is also a prime. SGCM is intended for those who want a concrete largely technically compatible alternative to GCM. All aspect of SGCM except for using $GF(p)$ instead of $GF(2^{128})$ are equivalent to GCM. Let the input of sequences X_i and $H = E(K, 0^{128}) + 2$ is defined. When staring encryption, we iterate for $i = 1, ..., n$ as follow:

$$Y_i = (Y_{i-1} + X_i) \cdot H \; mod \; p. \qquad (4)$$

The results of SGHASH(H, X) should be equal to 2^{128} or larger and we may require more than 128-bits width blocks. But the final iteration block of SGHASH(H, X) is truncated $mod \; 2^{128}$. In this paper, we SGHASH is donated as GHASH because we designed unified both SGHASH and GHASH using dual field multiplier. As below, we show the example of SGCM in little-endian fashion:

$$\begin{aligned}
X = \lfloor 2^{126}\pi \rfloor &= 267257146016241686964920093290467695825 \\
X &= D11CDC808B62C6C434C26821A2DA0FC9 \\
Y = \lfloor 2^{126}e \rfloor &= 231245843636555084287727758960834198769 \\
Y &= F13C3D272056DCAF9A4ABBA25854F8AD \\
Z = XY \; mod \; p &= 92057282056638797466523895082203571 0352 \\
Z &= 90E1BD2C9607A36319D9D9AE6D964145
\end{aligned}$$

2.3 Dual Field Adder and Multiplier

Because operation time of the multiplication in finite fields $GF(p)$ or $GF(2^m)$ are the most time consuming operations in cryptographic applications such as GCM/SGCM, elliptic curve cryptography, RSA, Diffie-Hellman key exchange algorithm, Digital Signature Standard, the design of multiplication units that provides efficient and fast execution in both $GF(p)$ and $GF(2^m)$ is of interest for cryptographic applications. Papers such as [4,20–22] are proposed for Dual Field Multiplier in hardware. There are two types of Dual Field Multiplier, which is using the Montgomery algorithm or Bit-Serial Multiplier. Montgomery algorithm is proper to use continuously the multiplication like in elliptic curve cryptography, as needing a conversion overhead, but not suitable for GCM or SGCM which demand frequently conversion from Montgomery numbers to real numbers. So, we employ the Bit-Serial Multiplier to unify GCM and SGCM.

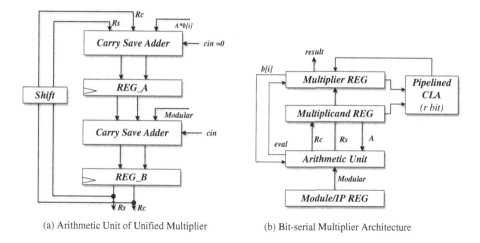

(a) Arithmetic Unit of Unified Multiplier   (b) Bit-serial Multiplier Architecture

Fig. 1. Architecture of Dual Field Multiplier in [4]

We refer to [4] and thus we introduce it in this section. Figure 1 (a) indicates the multiplication unit proposed in [4]. Two Carry Save Adders have to be operated with $(n + 1)$-bit precision. The *sum* output R_S and the *carry* output R_C of the adders are loaded to each registers REG_A and REG_B. One of two CSA (*Carry Save Adder*) generates a partial-product and the other makes a subtraction for the modular operation. The subtraction is performed by adding the two's complement, which is indicated as the input *Modular*. So, addition and subtraction are essentially the same operation. According to the MSB-first iterative algorithm, B has left shift at every clock cycles and $b[i]$ which is a output of the MSB-bit of B also changes at every clocks. The addition of the partial product $A * b[i]$ is implemented at the top of Fig. 1. The output of first CSA is saved to REG_A and used to evaluate the multiple of the modulus to be subtracted at the second CSA. The evaluation is to select the *Modular* among the one value of $0 * M$, $1 * M$, or $2 * M$. At the next clock, the second CSA subtract *Moduler* from R_S and R_C and the result of the second CSA is saved to REG_B. As next processing is starting, the output of the REG_B is shifted in module *Shift*. If an extra subtraction is demanded, the outputs R_S and R_C of the second CSA are fed back to the first CSA without a left-shift. If no extra subtraction is needed, the processing of the multiplier bit is finished. The outputs of the second CSA are fed back to the inputs of the first CSA with a 1-bit hard-wired left-shift.

After the least significant bit B[0] has been processed, result (R_S, R_C) is saved to $Multiplier\_REG$ and $Multiplicand\_REG$ in Fig. 1 (b). Next the redundant result should be changed into the non-redundant value. It is done by r-bit *Pipelined CLA* (*Carry − Lookahead Adder*) and it takes $\lceil n/r \rceil$ clock cycles. The result of *Pipelined CLA* is loaded to $Multiplier\_REG$ again. The difference $GF(2^m)$ to $GF(p)$ in Dual Field Multiplier just is decided by the addition operation and whether Carry is used or not. The signal *eval* decide to perform the extra subtraction. Whenever $eval$ is 1, $Multiplier\ REG$ stop the shift and Arithmetic Unit operates subtraction until $eval = 0$. We improved Dual Field Multiplier proposed in [4] and describe it as the following section.

2.4   LEA [5]

LEA is a block cipher with 128-bit block. Key size is 128-bit, 192-bit, and 256-bit. LEA also has each of the number of rounds: 24 rounds of 128-bit key, 28 rounds of 192-bit key, and 32 rounds of 256-bit key. Just using LEA having the 128-bit of the key for GCM and SGCM, we explain on only LEA having 128-bit key length in the this section.

Notations. As we use notations in this section, We specify notations following as:

- P: 128-bit plaintext, consisting of 32-bit words $P = (P[0], P[1], P[2], P[3])$.
- C: 128-bit ciphertext, consisting of 32-bit words $C = (C[0], C[1], C[2], C[3])$.
- K: Master key. It is a concatenation of 32-bit words. $K = (K[0], K[1], K[2], K[3])$.
- X_i: 128-bit intermediate value (an input of i-th round in the encryption function,
    consisting of 32-bit words $X_i = (X_i[0], X_i[1], X_i[2], X_i[3])$.
- RK: Concatenation of all round keys, defined by
    $RK_i = (RK_i[0],\ RK_i[1], RK_i[2], RK_i[3], RK_i[4], RK_i[5])$.
- $x \oplus y$: Exclusive OR of 32 bit strings x and y.
- $x + y$: Addition modulo 2 power of 32 of 32 bit strings x and y.
- r: The number of rounds. ($r = 24$ when using 128 bit block).
- $ROL_i(x)$: The i-bit left rotation on a 32-bit value x.
- $ROR_i(x)$: The i-bit right rotation on a 32-bit value x.

Key Schedule. LEA use constants for key schedule, which is specified as:

$$\delta[0] = 0xc3efe9db, \qquad \delta[1] = 0x44626b02,$$
$$\delta[2] = 0x79e27c8a, \qquad \delta[3] = 0x78df30ec,$$
$$\delta[4] = 0x715ea49e, \qquad \delta[5] = 0xc785da0a,$$
$$\delta[6] = 0xe04ef22a, \qquad \delta[7] = 0xe5c40957.$$

128-bit LEA employs only four constants. Others are used for 192- and 256-bit LEA. Constants are XORed $T[i]$ for $0 \leq i \leq 3$ in the key schedule. The fully key scheduling for making round keys is defined as:

$$T[0] \leftarrow ROL_1(T[0] + ROL_i(\delta[imod4])),$$
$$T[1] \leftarrow ROL_3(T[1] + ROL_{i+1}(\delta[imod4])),$$
$$T[2] \leftarrow ROL_6(T[2] + ROL_{i+2}(\delta[imod4])),$$
$$T[3] \leftarrow ROL_{11}(T[3] + ROL_{i+3}(\delta[imod4])),$$
$$RK_i \leftarrow (T[0], T[1], T[2], T[1], T[3], T[1]).$$

Next, we made the LEA key schedule module for a hardware implementation. Master key $K = (K[0], K[1], K[2], K[3])$ is a concatenation of 32-bit words. Let set $T_0[i] = K[i]$ for $0 \leq i \leq 3$ in initialization. Round key RK_i are produced by using T_i for $0 \leq i \leq 24$.

Encryption Process. The encryption procedure sets the $X_0[i] = P[i]$ for $0 \leq i \leq 3$ in initialization. During the 24 rounds, encryption process is processed by using the round key RK_i, called as Iterating Rounds. It is defined as:

$$X_{i+1}[0] \leftarrow ROL_9((Xi[0] \oplus RK_i[0]) + (Xi[1] \oplus RK_i[1])),$$
$$X_{i+1}[1] \leftarrow ROR_5((Xi[1] \oplus RK_i[2]) + (Xi[2] \oplus RK_i[3])),$$
$$X_{i+1}[2] \leftarrow ROR_3((Xi[2] \oplus RK_i[4]) + (Xi[3] \oplus RK_i[5])),$$
$$X_{i+1}[3] \leftarrow X_i[0].$$

Also, Finalization is accomplished at the last round, which defined as:

$$C[0] \leftarrow Xr[0], C[1] \leftarrow Xr[1], C[2] \leftarrow Xr[2], C[3] \leftarrow Xr[3].$$

3 Proposed Methods

3.1 The Architecture of the Unified Hardware for GCM and SGCM

I/O Interface. We designs the module $Wrapper$ as I/O interface for communication between our unified hardware and the outside world. We show $Wrapper$ in Fig. 2. It has the similar access way like dual port RAM memory seemingly but actually has registers used for inputs of the unified hardware for GCM and SGCM. If the signal wr is one, 32-bit width data from $Data\_in$ is saved into registers depend on $addr$ which specifies location and address to read or write to. Otherwise, if wr us zero, we can read data from $Data\_out$ pointed by $addr$. $Wrapper$ also has 128-bit width data-path between I/O interface and our unified hardware for GCM and SGM, which supplies data such as IV, Key, $MESSAGE\_IN$, $MESSAGE\_OUT$, and MAC.

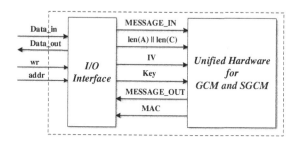

Fig. 2. Wrapper for I/O interface of Unified GCM and SGCM

Unified Hardware for GCM and SGCM. Figure 3 shows our architecture of the unified hardware for GCM and SGCM. We concentrated on making designs for size-optimization. The module $Counter$ changes the input of $Encryption$ each loop of GCM or SGCM. IV (Initial vector) is supplied from I/O and $Counter$ is increases whenever the previous block is processed. 128-bit ($IV^{96} \parallel Counter^{32}$) are used as the input of the $Encryption$ module. $Encryption$ is core of the block cipher module and we employed two kinds of block cipher algorithms: AES or LEA. We selected LEA block cipher for the core of the block cipher to apply unified GCM and SGCM method, named as LEA-Unified. We also designed unified GCM and SGCM using AES which is named as AES-Unified. When we designed LEA-Unified, we used LEA using 32-bit width operations referred in [7]. In case of using AES for unified hardware, we summarize our implementation of AES in the next section.

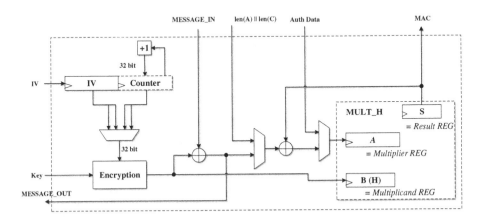

Fig. 3. Our Architecture of the Unified Hardware for GCM and SGCM

$MULT\_H$ is the GHASH function to generate the authentication code. In Fig. 3, the register A, S, and $B(H)$ represent *Multiplier REG*, *Result REG*, and *Multiplicand REG*, respectively. $MULT\_H$ receives the output of the module *Encryption* and save the register A, then it implements the multiplication using dual field multiplier. Finally, the complete authentication code is placed into the register S after all of blocks are processed. In the next section, we describe our Dual Field Multiplier which is the most important arithmetic module for the unified hardware.

3.2 Proposed Dual Field Multiplier

GCM and SGCM have the similar architecture except for the multiplier. Dual Field Multiplier is a important part in our unified hardware for GCM and SGCM. We present novel dual field multiplier in Fig. 4. Our Dual Field Multiplier have half cycles of the design in [4]. The multiplier in [4] saves results of first *Carry Save Adder* (top of the Fig. 1) to REG_A firstly. At the next cycle, REG_A is not used and just REG_B saves results of second *Carry Save Adder* (bottom of the Fig. 1). REG_A and REG_B are employed alternately. In contrast, proposed Dual Field Multiplier employs REG_A and REG_B simultaneously. Our Dual Field Multiplier deal with $A * b[i]$ according to the input of registers *Multiplier REG* which has even or odd bit. When REG_A handles odd bit of *Multiplier REG*, REG_B saves results of second *Carry Save Adder*

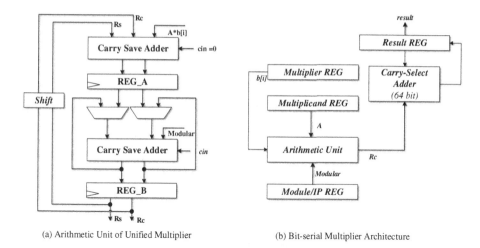

(a) Arithmetic Unit of Unified Multiplier   (b) Bit-serial Multiplier Architecture

Fig. 4. Proposed Dual Field Multiplier

that received even bit result form the REG_A at previous clock. When REG_A handles even bit of *Multiplier REG*, REG_B saves results of odd bit from second *Carry Save Adder*.

In Fig. 5, we further explore the proposed method. Figure 5 (a) describes transitions of both registers: REG_A and REG_B in [4] and Fig. 5 (b) indicates transitions of both registers in our Dual Field Multiplier. It expresses process of $A * B$ and clock cycles (time) is increased toward the under. Boxes about REG_A and REG_B show how to transfer the value is saved to both registers by the time. In Fig. 5 (a), when REG_A saves results of $A * b[i]$ and REG_B don't load results of reduction. So, It needs two clock cycles for processing each of $A * b[i]$. But, in Fig. 5 (b), REG_A and REG_B load values simultaneously. If REG_A deals with $A * b[i]$ where i is odd, REG_B saves results of reduction.

Because REG_A keeps sum of $A * b[i]$ where i is odd and REG_B has sum of it where i is even after processing last $A * b[i]$, we need to add the output of Reg_A and the output of REG_B by using *Carry Select Adder*(64 bit). For this last reduction, they used pipelined *Carry Lookahead Adder* in [4], but we considered *Carry Select Adder*(64 bit) because it makes more high frequency

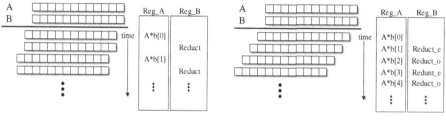

(a) Register Transition of the Reference   (b) Register Transition of the Proposed Method

Fig. 5. Register Transition Diagram for Multiplication

than one using CLA. Thus, our Dual Field Multiplier just needs half cycles of Dual Field Multiplier in [4].

4   Evaluation

In this section, we analyzed and evaluated the results obtained by our designs. All implementations of our designs reported in this paper were described using Verilog HDL and verified by ModelSim 5.6f. Then, we synthesized implementations in ASIC. We employed Synopsys Design Compiler ver. B-2008.09-SP5 in ASIC. In particular, Our RTL level designs of the unified hardware architecture used the TSMC 0.13 μm single-poly five-metal CMOS process library for the synthesis to ASIC.

4.1   Consideration of the Encryption Core

We discuss encryption module for size-optimization in the proposed hardware architecture in this section. Previous works mainly concerns on high performance in terms of speed by adopting pipeline and parallel techniques. But we aimed at size-optimization and considered the block cipher LEA for the core of the unified hardware for GCM and SGCM. We compare LEA to AES in Table 1. LEA has strong points in approximately 5,000 GE, whose frequency is 500 Mhz and which is higher than AES implementations, because LEA consists of only ARX operations for 32 bit words and can achieve these operations with low hardware resources and short critical path. By contrast, AES has high throughput when implementing as large areas.

Table 1. ASIC Synthesis Results of AES and LEA core

Architecture	Size (GE)	Maximum frequency (MHz)	Throughput (Gbps)	Process (μm)
References				
[8]	66,000	200.00	2.33	0.18
[1]	49,300	200.00	2.33	0.18
[17]	5,398	131.24	0.31	0.13
[17]	6,292	137.55	0.40	0.13
[11]	2,400	–	0.06	0.13
[2]	3,400	80.00	–	0.35
[18]	5,400	13.00	0.31	0.11
[13]	7,000	30.00	0.07	0.60
Our designs				
LEA	4,142	500.00	0.53	0.13
AES	18,949	200.00	2.33	0.13

As seeing another side, we used the dual field multiplier whose 128×1 multiplier is implemented 128 times as bit-serial method. Because it takes 128 clock cycles, we should fit this clock cycles when the encryption module is running for size-optimization. When we compare with AES and LEA having under 128 clock cycles, LEA having 96 clock cycles and 2.33 Gbps is faster than previous AESs. We can confirm it easily in Table 1. We can also see our non-pipelined AES implementation in the table. Our AES is needed to compare our unified hardware to previous GCMs in the following section and is used for calculation areas of unified hardware using AES instead of LEA.

4.2 Comparison of Areas

We designed the unified hardware for GCM and SGCM using the dual field multiplier and our designs should be evaluated by using GE (Gate Element) of the architecture. But the previous work trying to unify GCM and SGCM is not existent and research of the SGCM hardware implementation also is not at all. So, we evaluate proposed hardware implementation only using previous GCM architectures.

We researched other previous GCM implementations and summarized them in the Table 2. We found two designs including sequential and parallel. Comparing our results to enormous parallel designs is pointless because our implementation is for size-optimization and ours size is smaller than surveyed parallel implementations as much as it is meaningless. So, we just considered sequential GCM and size-optimized implementations and ones having areas under 100,000 GE.

In Table 2, GCM architecture in [12] implemented with Mastrovito multiplier and changed S-box among LUT (top of the cell) S-box or composite S-box (bottom of the cell). Yang et al. [25] have two AES core. Iterative AES is used for generating H for the finite field multiplication and the other one is pipelined AES for encryption. Designs in [12,25] is sequential but both areas is above 100,000 GE using fully pipelined AES which is all of the round steps are pipelined. GCM Hardware implementations in the following have areas under 100,00 GE and are comparable with ours implementation. We find two kind of implementations in [16]. The first is the sequential implementation completely (top of the cell) and the second is the implementation using 4 parallel AES and one multiplier (bottom of the cell). Both designs in this paper use 4-stage pipelined loop and composite field $GF(((2^2)^2)^2)$. Lastly, GCM architectures in [19,24] have single encryption and simple loop. Areas of them achieved smaller size than previous ones and this implementations are suitable to compare with our implementation.

To compare areas of the unified hardware for GCM and SGCM with areas of the GCM, we calculate areas except for LEA core and add Areas of AES which was used in each of previous works. It is for more accurate comparison by applying each of referred AESs in our unified architecture and is indicated as AES-Unified[b]. We can easily assure that all of AES-Unified[b] is smaller than areas of each of GCM architectures. References [12,16,25] are classified as sequential implementations but used pipelined loop heavily. So, difference of areas between ours and these is great and quantitative analysis is meaningless. Comparing proposed results to [19,24], if we implement the unified hardware design in both references, we expect to achieve 29 % less size than [19] and 35 % less size than [24]. Because it is just comparison between ours and GCM sizes not areas of GCM with SGCM, difference between proposed results and adding areas of the GCM reference and SGCM became bigger.

Table 2. GCM ASIC Synthesis Results Summary

Architecture	Size (GE)	Maximum frequency (MHz)	AES[a] (GE)	AES-unified[b] (GE)	Process (μm)
References					
a. [12]	245,062	286.00	100,000	111,991	0.13
	177,103	222.00	100,000	111,991	
b. [25]	463,328	271.00	287,184	299,175	0.18
c. [16]	73,104	200.00	15,127	27,118	0.13
	96,241	200.00	15,127	27,118	
d. [19]	34,466	200.00	12,454	24,445	0.13
e. [24]	40,335	500.00	14,050	26,241	0.13
Our designs					
AES-Unified[c]	30,940	200.00	–		0.13
LEA-Unified[d]	16,133	500.00	–		0.13

[a]Areas of AES used in each of references
[b]AES-Unified[b] = (LEA-Unified[d] − Areas of LEA) + AES[a]
[c]AES-Unified[c] = (LEA-Unified[d] − Areas of LEA) + (our AES in Table 1)
[d]The proposed design of unified hardware for GCM and SGCM

Lastly, when we employed LEA instead of AES, areas of the unified hardware for GCM and SGCM is more decreased. LEA-Unified[d] has 48 % less size than AES-Unified[c]. Though excepting for AES-Unified[c] and comparing LEA-Unified[d] to each of AES-Unified[b] column, we can understand Using LEA in our architecture instead of AES has more efficient size. LEA-Unified[d] features size of 16,133 GE, 500 Mhz frequency, and 0.5 Gbps throughput.

5   Conclusion

In this paper, we proposed the compact implementation of the unified hardware for GCM and SGCM. We have three main contributions. Firstly, GCM and SGCM have similar architecture. Thus, we unified GCM and SGCM using dual field multiplier. Secondly, we improved dual field adder proposed in [4] to fit our architecture. Our dual field adder just needs half cycles of referred one. For quantitative analysis, we calculate areas except for LEA core and add Areas of AES which was used by each of previous works. we expect to achieve 29 % less size than [19] and 35 % less size than [24]. Lastly, we applied LEA instead of AES for the compact hardware implementation. Our unified hardware for GCM and SGCM is implemented within 16,133 GE and achieves 0.5 Gbps on 500 Mhz. Our unified hardware using LEA has 48 % less size than the one using AES.

References

1. AMPHION. Cs5265/75 aes simplex encryption/decryption cores, Dec 2013. http:// www.chipdig.com/datasheets/parts/datasheet/554/CS5265-pdf.php
2. Feldhofer, M., Wolkerstorfer, J., Rijmen, V.: Aes implementation on a grain of sand. IEE Proc. Inf. Secur. **152**(1), 13–20 (2005)
3. Ferguson, N.: Authnetication weaknesses in gcm. Comments submitted to NIST Modes of Operation Process (2005)
4. Großschädl, J.: A bit-serial unified multiplier architecture for finite fields gf (p) and gf (2m). In: Koç, Ç.K., Paar, C. (eds.) CHES 2001, pp. 202–219. Springer, New York (2001)
5. Hong, D., Lee, J.-K., Kim, D.-C., Kwon, D., Ryu, K.H., Lee, D.-G.: Lea: A 128-bit block cipher for fast encryption on common processors. In: Kim, Y., Lee, H., Perrig, A. (eds.) Information Security Applications, pp. 3–27. Springer, New York (2014)
6. Igoe, K., Solinas, J.: Aes galois counter mode for the secure shell transport layer protocol. Technical report, RFC 5647, August 2009
7. Lee, D., Kim, D.-C., Kwon, D., Kim, H.: Efficient hardware implementation of the lightweight block encryption algorithm lea. Sensors **14**(1), 975–994 (2014)
8. O. L. P. Ltd., OL_aes aes core family, Dec 2013. http://www.ocean-logic.com/pub/ OL_AES.pdf
9. McGrew, D., Viega, J.: The galois/counter mode of operation (gcm). Submission to NIST (2004). http://csrc.nist.gov/CryptoToolkit/modes/proposedmodes/gcm/ gcm-spec.pdf
10. McGrew, D., Viega, J.: The use of galois message authentication code (gmac) in ipsec esp and ah. Technical report, RFC 4543, May 2006
11. Moradi, A., Poschmann, A., Ling, S., Paar, C., Wang, H.: Pushing the limits: a very compact and a threshold implementation of AES. In: Paterson, K.G. (ed.) EUROCRYPT 2011. LNCS, vol. 6632, pp. 69–88. Springer, Heidelberg (2011)
12. Patel, P.: Parallel multiplier designs for the galois/counter mode of operation (2008)
13. Pramstaller, N., Mangard, S., Dominikus, S., Wolkerstorfer, J.: Efficient AES implementations on ASICs and FPGAs. In: Dobbertin, H., Rijmen, V., Sowa, A. (eds.) AES 2005. LNCS, vol. 3373, pp. 98–112. Springer, Heidelberg (2005)
14. Saarinen, M.-J.O.: Sgcm: the sophie germain counter mode. IACR Cryptology ePrint Archive 2011:326 (2011)
15. Salowey, J., Choudhury, A., McGrew, D.: Aes galois counter mode (gcm) cipher suites for tls. Technical report, RFC 5288 (Proposed Standard) (2008)
16. Satoh, A.: High-speed hardware architectures for authenticated encryption mode gcm. In: Proceedings of 2006 IEEE International Symposium on Circuits and Systems, 2006. ISCAS 2006, 4 pp., IEEE (2006)
17. Satoh, A., Morioka, S.: Hardware-focused performance comparison for the standard block ciphers AES, Camellia, and Triple-DES. In: Boyd, C., Mao, W. (eds.) ISC 2003. LNCS, vol. 2851, pp. 252–266. Springer, Heidelberg (2003)

18. Satoh, A., Morioka, S., Takano, K., Munetoh, S.: A compact rijndael hardware architecture with S-Box optimization. In: Boyd, C. (ed.) ASIACRYPT 2001. LNCS, vol. 2248, pp. 239–254. Springer, Heidelberg (2001)
19. Satoh, A., Sugawara, T., Aoki, T.: High-performance hardware architectures for galois counter mode. IEEE Trans. Comput. **58**(7), 917–930 (2009)
20. Sava, E., Tenca, A.F., Koç, Ç.K.: A scalable and unified multiplier architecture for finite fields $GF(p)$ and tex2html_wrap_inline111. In: Paar, C., Koç, Ç.K. (eds.) CHES 2000. LNCS, vol. 1965, pp. 277–292. Springer, Heidelberg (2000)
21. Tenca, A.F., Koç, Ç.K.: A scalable architecture for modular multiplication based on montgomery's algorithm. IEEE Trans. Comput. **52**(9), 1215–1221 (2003)
22. Tenca, A.F., Savas, E., Koç, C.: A design framework for scalable and unified multipliers in gf (p) and gf (2m). Int. J. Comput. Res. **13**(1), 68–83 (2004)
23. Viega, J., McGrew, D.A.: The use of galois/counter mode (gcm) in ipsec encapsulating security payload (esp) (2005)
24. Wang, S.: An architecture for the AES-GCM security standard. Ph.D. thesis, University of Waterloo (2006)
25. Yang, B., Mishra, S., Karri, R.: A high speed architecture for galois/counter mode of operation (gcm). IACR Cryptology ePrint Archive, 2005:146 (2005)

Successful Profiling Attacks with Different Measurement Environments for Each Phase

Yongdae Kim[✉]

The Attached Institute of Electronics and Telecommunications Research Institute,
P.O.Box 1, Yuseong, Daejeon 305-600, Korea
kimyd@ensec.re.kr

Abstract. Power analysis attacks have received a great deal of attention, because they can be carried out easily than conventional cryptanalysis. Profiling attacks are one of the most efficient attacks among power analysis attacks. However, profiling attacks have the limitation of using the same experimental environment for both the profiling and attacking phases. If two sets of power traces are obtained from different setups, then the attack may not be feasible. We propose a new method to overcome this limitation with different measurement environments using multivariate regression analysis. Our results show that the proposed method can successfully retrieve a secret key using two different types of power traces. Moreover, the success rate is higher than for non-profiling attacks, i.e., Correlation Power Analysis (CPA).

Keywords: Power analysis attack · Profiling attack · Multivariate regression analysis · Advanced Encryption Standard (AES)

1 Introduction

Kocher et al. introduced the first power analysis attack in 1999. Since then, various types of attacks have been proposed. Among them, the so-called 'profiling attack' is the most efficient method [1]. Profiling attacks, involve an adversary deploying prior leakage information obtained with a reference module, that has the identical physical characteristics as the target module. Profiling attacks have existed for years and come in many forms, e.g. template attacks [2], stochastic model attacks [3], and multivariate regression analysis attacks [4].

Several researchers have studied the performance and effectiveness of profiling attacks [5–9]. However, all of the prior research assumes that an adversary will utilize the exact same measurement environment in both the profiling and attacking phases. Profiling attacks use a set of captured traces in the profiling phase when an attack is performed. Therefore, to retain the physical features of the traces, the adversary deploys the same measurement setup in both phases. In other words, if an adversary deploys two different measurement setups for each phase, the physical characteristics of the measured traces obtained from each phase will be widely dissimilar. Therefore, a naive approach to profiling attacks may not be feasible.

© Springer International Publishing Switzerland 2015
K.-H. Rhee and J.H. Yi (Eds.): WISA 2014, LNCS 8909, pp. 321–330, 2015.
DOI: 10.1007/978-3-319-15087-1_25

Elaabid et al. showed that the template attacks almost have same success rate even though they used two different acquisition campaign for each phase [10]. In addition, Choudary et al. introduced very interesting experimental results using 4 different devices and 5 different types of traces (4 types of traces are obtained from each devices, 1 type of traces is captured from same device, but different date) [11]. In [10, 11], they argue that they utilized different acqution campaigns, the major different parameters for each measurement are VCC for target device, acqution date, and resistor. However, the most of other parameters are fixed for measurement yet. Mainly, they used a same acquisition board which have an exact same measurement mechanism. In this paper, we utilized totally different measurement environments for each phase. We propose a method to resolve the limitation to acquitision environments. In this paper, we demonstrate concrete results using two sets of power traces.

Our proposed method is examined through the Advanced Encryption Standard (AES) implementation on an 8-bit Atmel AVR microcontroller. From the results, the proposed method is robust against these types of the measurement environments. In this study, we utilized two different commercial measurement tools, Differential Power Analysis (DPA) Workstation from Cryptographic Research, and Inspector from Riscure. We deployed two different tools for each phase and still, we successfully retrieved the secret AES key in the attacking phase. We also show results for non-profiling attacks, i.e., Correlation Power Analysis (CPA) [12], and the typical multivariate regression attack using same types of traces for comparison purposes.

2   Profiling Attacks

2.1   Discussion

Various types of attack have been introduced to date, e.g., CPA [12], Mutual Information Analysis (MIA) [13], Template Attack [2], etc. These power analysis attacks can be divided into two classes: (i) attacks without a reference module (non-profiling attacks), and (ii) attacks with a reference module (profiling attacks). The reference module is identical to the target module, and is fully controllable by the adversary. For example, the adversary is able to modify the secret key in the reference module and run the encryption (or decryption) process as he can with any plaintext (or ciphertext) value. Profiling attack adversaries exploit not only power traces directly measured from the target module, that non-profiling attack adversaries do, but also exploit power traces from the reference module with known plaintext (or ciphertext) and a secret key. Therefore, profiling attacks, can retrieve a secret key from inside a module with a smaller amount of information (fewer power traces) than typical non-profiling attacks.

Profiling attacks consist of two phases: (i) the profiling phase, and (ii) the attacking phase. In the first phase, an adversary captures power traces from a reference module, and determines the physical characteristics for the next phase. In the attacking phase, the adversary measures the power traces from a target module to reveal a secret key.

However, if the two sets of power traces obtained from each phase have different physical characteristics, it is difficult to apply the profiling attacks, because the prior information (e.g. mean and covariance of power traces in the template attack) obtained from the profiling phase is not similar to the physical characteristics of the measured power traces from the target module. Therefore, profiling attacks assumed that an adversary is able to use the reference module. However, even if the reference module is deployed, if different measurement environments are used for each phase, the physical characteristics will also be varied. Actually, all previous profiling attack research is assumed to use exactly the same measurement environment for both phases. We propose a new method using a multivariate regression attack to overcome this limitation to measurement setups. We have shown, for the first time to the best of our knowledge, a concrete experimental results using two different sets of power traces for each phase in the profiling attacks. However, other profiling attacks (i.e., template attacks and stochastic model attacks) are not feasible if an adversary deploys different types of traces. Therefore, we do not show results for other types of profiling attacks in this paper. Next, we describe multivariate regression attacks.

2.2   Multivariate Regression Attacks

Multivariate regression attacks are robust against selection of *interesting points*, which are time instants containing data-dependent variations, and efficient for modeling in the profiling phase with fewer power traces than other profiling attacks [4]. This type of attack has two phases as follows.

Profiling Phase. First, the hypothetical power consumption, h_i (given by the i-th input) is the response variable in the multivariate regression model. Normally, h_i is equivalent to the hamming weight (or distance) value seen in many cases. The CPA result provides the k interesting points, $\boldsymbol{p} = (p_1, p_2, \cdots, p_k)$, and each point is sorted in descending order of the CPA correlation coefficient value. The explanatory variables are selected as follows:

$$w_{i,p_1}, w_{i,p_2}, \cdots, w_{i,p_k}. \tag{1}$$

In this phase, the multivariate regression model is built as,

$$\hat{s}_i = \hat{\beta}_0 + \sum_{n \in \boldsymbol{p}} \hat{\beta}_n w_{i,n}, \tag{2}$$

where $\hat{s}_i, \hat{\beta}$ are represented by the fitted value of the hamming weight (or distance) and the estimator of coefficients, respectively.

Attacking Phase. In this phase, an adversary deploys the regression model, Eq. 2 to estimate the hamming weight (or distance) value using measured traces from the target module. Then, it finds the highest correlation value between the estimated value and calculated hamming weight (or distance) value, i.e., s_{i,k_j}, for each key candidates, k_j as follows:

$$k_{ck} = \underset{k_j \in k^*}{\operatorname{argmax}} \, corr(\hat{s}_i, s_{i,k_j}), \tag{3}$$

where $corr(a, b)$ is the correlation coefficient between a and b.

3   Experimental Method

In this section, we explain in detail, how we utilize the multivariate regression attack in two different measurement environments. First, we briefly describe the two commercial tools that we used in this study. Those tools have different measurement mechanism for power consumption.

3.1   Commercial Tools

There are several tools used to examine cryptographic modules against side-channel attacks. In this paper, we used the following two commercial tools.

DPA Workstation. The DPA Workstation from Cryptographic Research is the pioneering testing tool for side-channel attacks [14]. The DPA Workstation consists of hardware and software. The hardware includes a workstation, high-speed Peripheral Component Interconnect (PCI) data acquisition hardware, a digital oscilloscope and a smart card test fixture to measure power consumption or Electromagnetic (EM) emanation from a smart card. The main board for measurement is isolated from the communication board by an optical cable to the reduce noise effect. Users are required to write a script to operate the DPA Workstation. The script may include encryption and data acquisition commands for the digital oscilloscope.

Inspector SCA. Riscure developed Inspector Side-Channel Attack (SCA) as a side-channel test platform [15]. This tool provides a smart card reader (Power Tracer) with measurement points, a trigger signal generator, and accompanying software (Inspector) to control the Power Tracer and analyze captured traces. Moreover, they provide additional optional equipment such as an EM probe XYZ-station and a CleanWave to remove carrier wave noise from contactless smart cards, current probes, etc. Inspector is based on JAVA; therefore, users may write and compile the code to extend its usage. In addition to Inspector's source code, an open API, hardware SDK, and an integrated development environment are provided. Power Tracer is a hardware tool with a smart card insert, trigger generation module, and many other detailed configurations modules (e.g., card voltage, delay, clock frequency) that are controlled by Inspector.

3.2   Method

We implemented the AES on a smart card based on an 8-bit AVR microcontroller as the reference and the target modules. We measured 400 power traces both from DPA Workstation and Inspector SCA. The sampling rate of two sets of traces may differ from each other, due to a different digital oscilloscope parameter. Therefore, all traces are resampled at a constant frequency rate, to maintain the equivalent sampling rate. We merely calculate the average value of multiple points, and make one point as follows:

$$w'_i = \sum_{j=T\times(i-1)+1}^{T\times i} \frac{w_j}{T}, \qquad (4)$$

where $w_j(w_i')$, T represents power traces at j-th (i-th) time instants and a parameter for resampling, respectively. For example, if the original traces are captured at 200 MHz, then T will be 50 in order to resample traces at 4 MHz.

Even if we set the exact same parameter on the digital oscilloscope for capturing, the two sets of traces captured from the tools will have different physical characteristics, because they include different shunt resistors, circuit boards noise characteristics, electronic components, etc. Therefore, we need to normalize the different scales to a common scale as follows:

$$w_i' = \sum_{i=1}^{P} \frac{w_i - \mu_w}{\sigma_w}, \tag{5}$$

where P, μ_w, and σ_w represents the total number of sample points, average value of traces, and standard deviation value of traces, respectively.

Once all preprocessing has finished, we determine the *interesting points* in power traces with a data-dependent order for each measurement environment. There are alternative methods for deciding the order of points, and this remains an open problem. However, in this paper, we do not discuss the detailed method used for point selection.

Next, we describe the detail of the setup. We set the same master key and the interesting points for all cases. The first round of AES encryption was our target; therefore we adjusted the range of the oscilloscope and captured power traces to include the first round encryption.

Case 1. We utilized 400 power traces captured from DPA Workstation for the profiling phase, and deployed Inspector to capture another 400 traces for the attacking phase.

Case 2. On the contrary, we used the same number of traces from Inspector and DPA Workstation for the profiling and the attacking phase, respectively.

Case 3. For comparison, we carried out typical profiling attacks. In this case, we used the DPA Workstation for both phases.

Case 4. The Inspector SCA is deployed for both phase.

4   Results

Figure 1 shows the measured traces for both tools after resampling and normalization. Figure 1 shows that, both traces Y-axis (the magnitude in Eq. 5) show almost the same range (between -4 and 4), because we normalized the scales for both traces.

At first, we explain why the template attack is not feasible of our measurements. In the attacking phase of template attack, an adversary find out which template (i.e. mean, m and covariance, C obtained in profiling phase) is well matched with power trace, $w = (w_1, \cdots, w_W)$. It is conducted by calculating probability density function of multivariate normal distribution as follows:

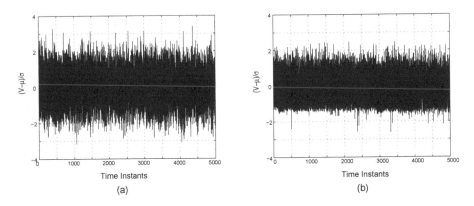

Fig. 1. Measured trace from (a) DPA Workstation, and (b) Inspector SCA

$$p(\boldsymbol{w}; (\boldsymbol{m}, \boldsymbol{C})_h) = \frac{exp\left(-\frac{1}{2}(\boldsymbol{w} - \boldsymbol{m})^T \boldsymbol{C}^{-1}(\boldsymbol{w} - \boldsymbol{m})\right)}{\sqrt{(2\pi)^W det(\boldsymbol{C})}}, \qquad (6)$$

where $det(\boldsymbol{C})$, $\boldsymbol{q}^T$ and h denote the determinant of $\boldsymbol{C}$, the transpose of vector $\boldsymbol{q}$ and the hamming weight (or distance) value. Therefore, an adversary find the hamming weight (or distance) value by finding the highest probability when the power trace $\boldsymbol{w}$ is given in attacking phase. The value can be used to retrive a secret key finally. If any of templates is not matched, the probability is extremely low.

We used 3 sets of traces: (i) DPA WS (Profiling) and (ii) DPA WS (Attack) is traces from DPA Workstation in profiling phase and attacking phase. (iii) Inspector (Attack) is traces from Inspector SCA in attacking phase. In Fig. 2 represents mean and variance of traces (we use the main diagonal of covariance

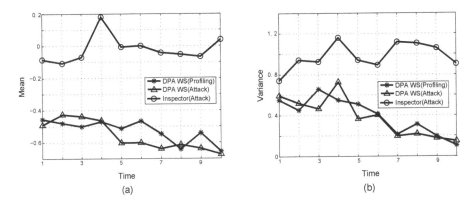

Fig. 2. Mean and variance of traces obtained different acquisition campaign (a) Mean, and (b) Variance

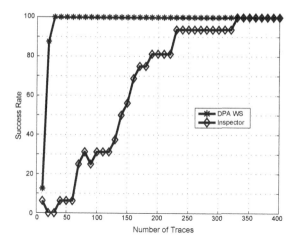

Fig. 3. CPA result

for a reason of visualization) on 10 interesting points, and the corresponding hamming weight value is 3. As shown in the figure, (i) and (ii) traces are very similar in mean and variance, however (i) and (iii) traces are widely different forms. However, in [10,11], the main differences of each trace from different acquision campaigns is a constant offset, so it is relatively easy to compensate it to apply template attack. The probabilities (Eq. 6) are 0.8158 and 1.0054×10^{-8} using (i)–(ii) and (i)–(iii) pairs, respectively. Therefore, it is hard to apply template attack by just adjusting the offset using our experimental environments.

Figure 3 presents the result of a non-profiling attacks, i.e., CPA, for the sake of comparison. The y-axis represents the percentage of success rate calculated as follows:

$$SuccessRate_i = \frac{N_i^{ck}}{16} \times 100, \tag{7}$$

where N_i^{ck} denotes the number of correctly estimated keys using i traces. For example, $SuccessRate_{120} = 100$ means that 16 subkeys of AES were correctly retrieved using 120 traces. The minimum number of traces to have 100 % success rate is defined as Measurements To Disclosure (MTD) as an evaluation criteria for performance of attacks in this paper. Our results confirmed that the MTD of CPA by using DPA Workstation and Inspector is 30 and 340, respectively. We assumed that the Signal-to-Noise Ratio (SNR) of traces using DPA Workstation was higher than those using Inspector.[1]

Figure 4 uses the traces from Fig. 1 to show the results for all cases. This confirmed that the profiling attack was successfully conducted, even though two different measurement environments were used. The performance of attacks for

---

[1] We do not represent DPA Workstation is better than Inspector SCA. Because the SNR can be very varied depends on target device, environmental settings, etc. Therefore, SNR of traces from Inspector SCA can be higher in some case.

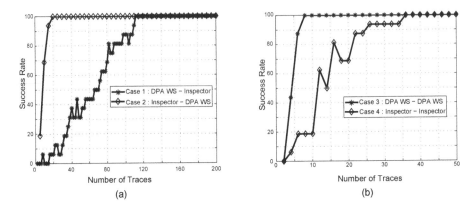

Fig. 4. Success rate (a) Case 1, 2, and (b) Case 3, 4

cases 1 and 2 are obviously lower than those for cases 3 and 4. However, this is the first concrete result that an adversary can utilize different types of traces for the profiling and attacking phases and still successfully retrieve a secret key.

Next, we investigated the effectiveness of the order of interesting points. First, we determined the interesting points in descending order of the correlation, as we described in the previous section. However, sometimes, it is impractical to order the points. Therefore, we examined how much the order of the points affects the performance of the attacks. We randomly selected the index of the interesting points first. In addition, we expected that if we determined the points in reverse order (ascending order), this would have had a negative effect on the results. Therefore, we also determined the reverse order of the interesting points for comparison. Figure 5 show the success rates using the different orderings of the interesting points. Figure 5(a) shows, as we expected, the MTD was the lowest when the reverse order of points was used. In addition, we saw the intermediate

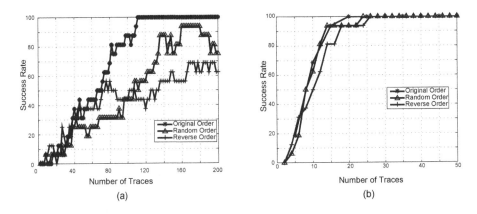

Fig. 5. Success rate using different order of the points (a) Case 1, and (b) Case 2

performance when random order was used in case 1. However, Fig. 5(b) shows that it was almost the same performance despite using different ordering of the points in case 2. We think that the order of points has a small influence on the performance of attacks if the SNR of traces is relatively high.

Finally, Table 1 presents the MTD of all the case including CPA. We define the improvement as follows for comparison with the non-profiling attack (CPA).

$$Improvement_c(\%) = \frac{M_{CPA} - M_c}{MTD_{CPA}} \times 100, \tag{8}$$

where c and M_{CPA} represents case number and the MTD using CPA. Our results showed that the profiling attacks still performed better that the CPA, in spite of using different sets of power traces.

Table 1. The MTD and improvement of all experimental results

Experiment	Tool	MTD	Improvement (%)
CPA	DPA WS	30	-
CPA	Inspector	340	-
Case 1	DPA WS - Inspector	115	66.2
Case 2	Inspector - DPA WS	20	33.3
Case 3	DPA WS - DPA WS	8	73.3
Case 4	Inspector - Inspector	36	89.4

5   Conclusion

A method to apply profiling attacks using two different sets of power traces captured by different tools, and concrete results were presented in this paper. Conventionally, power traces are obtained using the same measurement environment in both the profiling and attacking phases of a profiling attack, because two sets of power traces should have exactly the same physical characteristics. However, this assumption is unnecessary with the proposed method. For the first time, we have shown that our method can successfully extract all AES keys despite using two different measurement setups. Our method is more practical than others in many cases. Moreover, we have additional types of measurement setups and several cryptographic modules. Therefore, our future research will concern developing a framework to integrate the power traces from all different tools.

References

1. Standaert, F.-X., Gierlichs, B., Verbauwhede, I.: Partition *vs.* comparison side-channel distinguishers: an empirical evaluation of statistical tests for univariate side-channel attacks against two unprotected CMOS devices. In: Lee, P.J., Cheon, J.H. (eds.) ICISC 2008. LNCS, vol. 5461, pp. 253–267. Springer, Heidelberg (2009)

2. Chari, S., Rao, J., Rohatgi, P.: Template attacks. In: International Workshop on Cryptographic Hardware and Embedded Systems (CHES), pp. 13–28 (2002)
3. Schindler, W., Lemke, K., Paar, C.: A stochastic model for differential side channel cryptanalysis. In: Rao, J.R., Sunar, B. (eds.) CHES 2005. LNCS, vol. 3659, pp. 30–46. Springer, Heidelberg (2005)
4. Sugawara, T., Homma, N., Aoki, T., Satoh, A.: Profiling attack using multivariate regression analysis. IEICE Electron. Expr. **7**, 1139–1144 (2010)
5. Standaert, F.-X., Archambeau, C.: Using subspace-based template attacks to compare and combine power and electromagnetic information leakages. In: Oswald, E., Rohatgi, P. (eds.) CHES 2008. LNCS, vol. 5154, pp. 411–425. Springer, Heidelberg (2008)
6. Archambeau, C., Peeters, E., Standaert, F.-X., Quisquater, J.-J.: Template attacks in principal subspaces. In: Goubin, L., Matsui, M. (eds.) CHES 2006. LNCS, vol. 4249, pp. 1–14. Springer, Heidelberg (2006)
7. Rechberger, C., Oswald, E.: Practical template attacks. In: Lim, C.H., Yung, M. (eds.) WISA 2004. LNCS, vol. 3325, pp. 440–456. Springer, Heidelberg (2005)
8. Kim, Y., Homma, N., Aoki, T., Choi, H.: Security evaluation of cryptographic modules against profiling attacks. In: Kwon, T., Lee, M.-K., Kwon, D. (eds.) ICISC 2012. LNCS, vol. 7839, pp. 383–394. Springer, Heidelberg (2013)
9. Gierlichs, B., Lemke-Rust, K., Paar, C.: Templates vs. stochastic methods. In: Goubin, L., Matsui, M. (eds.) CHES 2006. LNCS, vol. 4249, pp. 15–29. Springer, Heidelberg (2006)
10. Abdelaziz, E.M., Sylvain, G.: Portability of templates. J. Cryptographic Eng. **2**, 63–74 (2012)
11. Choudary, O., Kuhn, M.G.: Template attacks on different devices. In: Prouff, E. (ed.) COSADE 2014. LNCS, vol. 8622, pp. 179–198. Springer, Heidelberg (2014)
12. Brier, E., Clavier, C., Olivier, F.: Correlation power analysis with a leakage model. In: Joye, M., Quisquater, J.-J. (eds.) CHES 2004. LNCS, vol. 3156, pp. 16–29. Springer, Heidelberg (2004)
13. Gierlichs, B., Batina, L., Tuyls, P., Preneel, B.: Mutual information analysis: a generic side-channel distinguisher. In: Oswald, E., Rohatgi, P. (eds.) CHES 2008. LNCS, vol. 5154, pp. 426–442. Springer, Heidelberg (2008)
14. Cryptographic Research, DPA Workstation. http://www.cryptography.com/technology/dpa-workstation.html
15. Riscure, Inspector SCA. https://www.riscure.com/security-tools/inspector-sca/

Function Masking: A New Countermeasure Against Side Channel Attack

Taesung Kim[1,3], Sungjun Ahn[2], Seungkwang Lee[1], and Dooho Choi[1,2(✉)]

[1] Electronics and Telecommunications Research Institute, Daejeon, South Korea
{taesung,skwang,dhchoi}@etri.re.kr
[2] Korea University of Science and Technology, Daejeon, South Korea
asj503@ust.ac.kr
[3] Korea Advanced Institute of Science and Technology, Daejeon, South Korea
ruthere@kaist.ac.kr

Abstract. Masking schemes have been developed to implement secure cryptographic algorithms against Side Channel Analysis(SCA) attacks. Technically, the first-order masking method is vulnerable to the second order Differential Power Analysis(2ODPA) attacks, but the current solutions against 2ODPA are expensive to implement. Moreover, worse performance will be shown if the cryptographic algorithms include boolean and arithmetic operations. In this paper, we propose a new masking scheme to resist SCA attacks, which is called the Function Masking. Function Masking method conceals functions instead of data in the algorithms and makes it resistant to attacks as much as 2ODPA. We apply our masking scheme to the HIGHT algorithm. The encryption of function masked HIGHT takes only 1.79 times more than one of the original algorithm, even though it needs 25 kbytes to store lookup tables in memory.

Keywords: Side channel attack · Countermeasure · Second-order masking

1 Introduction

A lot of researches have been published about various methods to secure implementations of different kinds of cryptographic algorithms, after Kocher *et al.* [11] introduced Simple Power Analysis(SPA) and Differential Power Analysis(DPA), types of power analysis. SCA attacks are physical attacks to find out secure data by using Side Channel Information such as power consumption, electromagnetic wave, timing, and so on during the execution. The attacks are based on the statistical dependency between the intermediate values and leaked information. It means that it is possible for adversaries to determine the entire secret key related to the intermediate values.

It is very common to randomize the sensitive variables by masking techniques when a countermeasure is used to protect implementations of block ciphers against SCA. One or several random values are added to the secret data during the execution of cryptographic algorithms, which means that every intermediate

© Springer International Publishing Switzerland 2015
K.-H. Rhee and J.H. Yi (Eds.): WISA 2014, LNCS 8909, pp. 331–342, 2015.
DOI: 10.1007/978-3-319-15087-1_26

value is independent of any secret variable. But, the first-order masking method is vulnerable to a second-order SCA. The second-order masking schemes should be considered to resist the attacks, but decrease performance.

Some cryptographic algorithms use the boolean and arithmetic operations to make the security. To counteract the SCA attacks, it is necessary to convert back and forth between the boolean masking and the arithmetic masking. Thus, Goubin *et al.* [3] has suggested a secure method to convert between masks, which is only applicable to the first-order masking. However, it is shown that it is impossible to apply the Goubin's method to the second-order masking schemes [4]. Vadnala *et al.* [4] has proposed masking conversion for the second-order masking, but it requires 1027 times more operations to convert 8-bit size of masks. It is not possible to use it on embedded devices.

In this paper, we suggest a new countermeasure method which randomizes all the intermediate values of cryptographic algorithms. We call it a function masking. Our scheme makes lookup tables which randomly convert all the functions and operations in the algorithms with encoding and decoding(we call it linear and non-linear function masks). The algorithms are reconstructed by using these lookup tables. Actually, this method is similar to white-box cryptography because of encoded lookup tables. However, our method dynamically inputs the round keys while white-box cryptography includes the round keys in lookup tables. Thus, it is possible to change the round keys depending on the environments and the attackers cannot predict all the intermediate values during the execution of cryptographic algorithms. We show the security of the function masking, apply it to HIGHT algorithm, and compare with second order masking.

The remainder of this paper is organized as follows. Section 2 describes the existing countermeasures of SCA and HIGHT cryptography algorithm which we applied the function masking. In Sect. 3, we introduce the concept of function masking and explain the implementation method of HIGHT algorithm to apply function masking. We show the security and performance analysis in Sect. 4. Finally, in Sect. 5, we offer the conclusion.

2   Related Work

2.1   Countermeasures Against Side Channel Attacks

To the best of our knowledge, the most widely used technique protecting against DPA is to mask key-dependent intermediate data by random values. This is called masking. For a key-dependent intermediate byte x and a random mask m, masking requires a function $f(x, m) = x \cdot m$, where $\cdot$ is defined as bitwise XOR(boolean masking), modulo addition (additive masking) or multiplication (multiplicative masking).

$$y \oplus m' = \mathbf{MaskedSbox}(x \oplus m \oplus k)$$
$$m, m' : \text{random values(mask)}, y = \mathbf{Sbox}(x \oplus k)$$

However, using only one mask which is called a first-order masking is vulnerable to a second-order DPA.

$$y_1 \oplus m' = \mathbf{MaskedSbox}(x_1 \oplus m \oplus k_1), y_1 = \mathbf{Sbox}(x_1 \oplus k_1)$$
$$y_2 \oplus m' = \mathbf{MaskedSbox}(x_2 \oplus m \oplus k_2), y_2 = \mathbf{Sbox}(x_2 \oplus k_2) \qquad (1)$$

$$y_1 \oplus m' \oplus y_2 \oplus m' = y_1 \oplus y_2 = \mathbf{Sbox}(x_1 \oplus k_1) \oplus \mathbf{Sbox}(x_2 \oplus k_2) \qquad (2)$$

To be specific, Eqs. (1) and (2) show that an attacker can obtain a non-masked result value of XORing two S-box outputs by XORing two masked S-box outputs. This is due to the fact that m' is canceled out by the XOR operation. A second-order DPA is therefore started by making two target points of a power trace as one point using subtractions or multiplications. The next step is to mount DPA based on a hypothetical value computed by XORing two S-box outputs [2].

Protection of second-order DPA requires more than two masks, and all intermediate values have to be masked through out the execution of the algorithm. Especially, each of input and output bytes of S-box must use different masks. For this reason, a masked AES implementation requires 16 masked S-boxes. As a result, a high-order masking of AES gives rise to an efficient implementation of S-boxes. Unfortunately, Table 1 shows that implementing a high-order masking scheme affects the performance of AES. To be more precise, the countermeasures are 150–300 times slower than a straightforward implementation. This might be an intolerable performance for a practical solution. HIGHT algorithms, which we will apply function masking, includes both boolean and arithmetic operations. To properly apply data masking, it is required to use a secure boolean-from/to-arithmetic mask conversion without exposing non-masked intermediate values against a second-order DPA. Goubin proposed secure mask conversion which can hide sensitive intermediate in convert process [3]. However, this conversion can only resist for first-order DPA. Vadnala et al. [4] proposed new conversion method which can work for second-order DPA. This method as shown in Algorithm 1 requires $4 \times 2^k + 3$ operations for conversion of a k-bit mask. An arithmetic-to-boolean conversion also requires the similar number of operations. It must be a critical overhead when it is applied to all mask conversions.

Table 1. Performance of the high-order masking scheme in AES

Method	Cycles	RAM(bytes)	ROM(bytes)
Unprotected implementation			
No masking [7]	2×10^3	32	1150
Provably Secure second-order SCA resistant implementation			
[5]	675.4×10^3	0	768
[6]	265.5×10^3	0	816

Algorithm 1. Boolean to arithmetic conversion of 2nd order

Input: Boolean share: $x_1 = x \oplus x_2 \oplus x_3, x_2, x_3$
Output: Arithmetic share: $A_1 = (x - A_2) - A_3, A_2, A_3$
 1: Randomly generate n-bit numbers r, A_2, A_3
 2: $r' \leftarrow (r \oplus x_2) \oplus x_3$
 3: **for** $a = 0$ to $2^n - 1$ **do**
 4:      $a' \leftarrow a \oplus r'$
 5:      $T[a'] \leftarrow ((x_1 \oplus a) - A_2) - A_3$
 6: **end for**
 7: $A_1 = T[r]$ **return** A_1, A_2, A_3

2.2 HIGHT Algorithm

The HIGHT(HIGh security and light weigHT) [8] is a symmetric cipher which encrypts and decrypts data with a 64-bit block cipher using a key of size 128 bits. It provides light-weight and low-powered hardware implementation for ubiquitous computing devices. We will briefly introduce the algorithm of HIGHT. The 64-bit plaintext and ciphertext are denoted by concatenations of 8 bytes such as $P = P_7\|P_6\|P_5\|P_4\|P_3\|P_2\|P_1\|P_0$ and $C = C_7\|C_6\|C_5\|C_4\|C_3\|C_2\|C_1\|C_0$. Round functions are consisted of several mathematical operations: $\boxplus$ addition mod 2^8, $\boxminus$ subtraction mod 2^8, $\oplus$ XOR, and $\lll r$ r-bit left rotation. The encryption of HIGHT algorithm is totally made up of initial transformation, round function, final transformation, and key schedule. It is described in detail below.

Algorithm 2. HIGHT encryption

Input: $P = P_7\|P_6\|P_5\|P_4\|P_3\|P_2\|P_1\|P_0$
Output: $C = C_7\|C_6\|C_5\|C_4\|C_3\|C_2\|C_1\|C_0$
   $X_{0,i} = P_i \ for \ i = 1,3,5,7$
   $X_{0,0} = P_0 \boxplus WK_0$
   $X_{0,2} = P_2 \oplus WK_1$
   $X_{0,4} = P_4 \boxplus WK_2$
   $X_{0,6} = P_6 \oplus WK_3$
   for $i = 0$ to 31 **do**
       $X_{i+1,1} = X_{i,0}; \ X_{i+1,3} = X_{i,2}; \ X_{i+1,5} = X_{i,4}; \ X_{i+1,7} = X_{i,6}$
           $X_{i+1,0} = X_{i,7} \oplus (F_0(X_{i,6}) \boxplus SK_{4i+3})$
           $X_{i+1,2} = X_{i,1} \boxplus (F_1(X_{i,0}) \oplus SK_{4i+2})$
           $X_{i+1,4} = X_{i,3} \oplus (F_0(X_{i,2}) \boxplus SK_{4i+1})$
           $X_{i+1,6} = X_{i,5} \boxplus (F_1(X_{i,4}) \oplus SK_{4i})$
   end for
   $C_0 = X_{32,1} \boxplus WK_4; \ C_1 = X_{32,2}$
   $C_2 = X_{32,3} \oplus WK_5; \ C_3 = X_{32,4}$
   $C_4 = X_{32,5} \oplus WK_6; \ C_5 = X_{32,6}$
   $C_6 = X_{32,7} \boxplus WK_7; \ C_7 = X_{32,0}$

$WK_{0 \leq i \leq 7}$ means whitening key and $SK_{0 \leq i \leq 127}$ is subkey. Round function uses functions F_0 and F_1:

$$F_0 = (x \lll 1) \oplus (x \lll 2) \oplus (x \lll 7)$$
$$F_1 = (x \lll 3) \oplus (x \lll 4) \oplus (x \lll 6)$$

The decryption process is similar to the encryption of HIGHT.

3   Function Masking for Symmetric Cryptography Algorithm

3.1   Function Masking

Our function masking is inspired by a white-box implementation [9] of block ciphers. Protection of a key-customized encryption function E_k in a white-box implementation is replaced by $E'_k = G \cdot E_k \cdot F^{-1}$, where F and G are input and output encoding, respectively. Being chosen randomly without reference to k, the use of G and F unlikely weakens the ordinary black-box security of E_k. However, one of the serious problems of this solution is the large size of the lookup tables. Our motivation in this matter is that an attacker in a gray-box model is not fully privileged to access the lookup table. For this reason, we try to generate a dynamic-key lookup table which takes both a key and an operand as an input. To be specific, it can be represented by

$$E(k, x) = G(E(k, F^{-1}(x)))$$

where x is an operand to be involved with k.

By generating a lookup table for $E(k, x)$, we can significantly reduce the total size of the lookup table than a white-box implementation because the table can be shared throughout all rounds. Also, this yields an additional advantage over a white-box lookup table: it can support dynamic key applications. In other words, this method can be also used when a secret key is updated from time to time like in the case of a session key. A potential problem is how to design the lookup table within practical size because a key is added to an input to the table. In the following, we explain how to apply function masking to HIGHT in such an efficient way.

3.2   Applying Function Masking to HIGHT Algorithm

Function Masking Method
Encoding & Decoding. It is required to conceal all of the intermediate values. The function masking method uses non-linear, linear encoding and random masking. Chow *et al.* [9] has suggested input and output encodings to protect a table. An encoding is a bijection. Encodings are networked with input and output of tables. If a table T is prevented with chosen bijections G,H

$$T' = H \circ T \circ G^{-1}$$

G is the input encoding and H is the output encoding. In case of two tables for lookup operations, it is expressed in a networked fashion. For example, tables T_1 and T_2 are protected with encodings as follows.

$$T'_2 \circ T'_1 = (H \circ T_2 \circ G^{-1}) \circ (G \circ T_1 \circ H^{-1}) = H \circ T_2 \circ T_1 \circ H^{-1}$$

Encodings make all lookup tables to obfuscate in Function Masking method. Furthermore, linear functions L and M are used to achieve diffusion for security, defined by Shannon [12]. There is also random mask to conceal 2×4-bit output values. Random mask is used to encode the modular addition in round.

4-bit non-linear function mask G, H, G^{-1}, H^{-1}: $\{0,1\}^4 \rightarrow \{0,1\}^4$
8-bit linear function mask L, M, L^{-1}, M^{-1}: $\{0,1\}^8 \rightarrow \{0,1\}^8$
8-bit random mask $C_1, C_2 (0 \leq C_1 \leq 255, \ 0 \leq C_2 \leq 255)$

Several types of lookup tables (See Figs. 1, 2 and 3) could be generated with above masks.

Reduction of Lookup Table Size. The modular addition and XOR operation result in a value with two operands. If two input values are 8-bit, it can be shown that all of the $2^{16} (= 65536)$ possible output values produce distinct lookup tables. However, it is too much big to store in memory sometimes. To overcome this problem, it could be transformed into $2 \times 2^{12} (= 8192)$ lookup tables. Then, it could significantly reduce the size of lookup tables. At first, an 8-bit operand and a high 4-bit of another operand will become input values of the first lookup table. An 8-bit output of the first table and a low 4-bit of another operand produce an 8-bit result value of the modular addition or XOR operation by using the second table. For example, the XOR operation of two 8-bit operands can be computed with type III-1 and III-2 tables. There are also two tables of type IV-1 and IV-2 for the modular addition.

Applying Function Masking to HIGHT Algorithm. The Function Masking method is applied to the HIGHT algorithm. It is required to make 12 lookup tables of 5 types for HIGHT algorithm.

Initial Transformation downsizing the size of lookup tables is applied to the modular addition and XOR with 2×8-bit input. P_0 and P_1 are encoded by a type I-2 table. In the case of P_0, the encoded value is added with Whitening Key by using two tables of type IV-1 and IV-2 tables. Then $X_{0,0}$ is obtained after changing the mask from type I-4 table. The intermediate value $X_{0,1}$ is the encoded value of P_1. Moreover, P_2 and P_3 are encoded by type I-1 table. The encoded value of P_2 is XORed with Whitening Key by using two tables of type III-1 and III-2 tables. Thus, a table lookup of type I-3 yields the intermediate value $X_{0,2}$. The intermediate value $X_{0,3}$ is the encoded value of P_3. P_4, P_5 and P_6, P_7 are the same process as above lookup operations P_0, P_1 and P_2, P_3 respectively.

Round Transformation. Let's take a close look at the first two 8-bit values of the round inputs shown in Fig. 4. Subkey is protected by encoding through type

I-1 table. Type II-1 and III-2 tables operate functions F and XOR. A high 4-bit of the encoded subkey and the 8-bit value $X_{i-1,0}$ are the input value of the type II-1 table. Thus, The output and a low 4-bit of the encoded subkey go into the type III-2 table. And the 8-bit value of $X_{i-1,1}$ and a high 4-bit of the XORed value make the 8-bit output by using a type IV-1 table. The intermediate value $X_{i,2}$ is obtained by a type IV-2 table with the central output and a low 4-bit of the XORed value. $X_{i-1,0}$ becomes $X_{i,1}$ just as it is.

The next process is similar to the previous process but the modular addition and XOR operation are out of order. A type I-2 table encodes a subkey to conceal. A high 4-bit of the encoded subkey and the 8-bit value $X_{i-1,2}$ are the input of a type II-2 table. The result and a low 4-bit of the encoded subkey calculate the modular addition by the type IV-2 table. After computing the modular addition by lookup operations, the output is divided into 2×4-bit values. Thus, the high 4-bit output and the value $X_{i-1,3}$ are the input of a type III-1 table. The 8-bit outcome value of the type III-1 table and the low 4-bit output make the intermediate value $X_{i,4}$. $X_{i,3}$ is gained by the $X_{i-1,2}$. The rest of process is the same as before. $X_{i,5}, X_{i,6}$ could be output of $X_{i-1,4}, X_{i-1,5}$ by the same process of the first one. The later process makes $X_{i,7}, X_{i,0}$ with input of $X_{i-1,6},$ $X_{i-1,7}$. Lastly all of the output values are rearranged by a left cyclic shift.

Final Transformation. It is easy to look into the final transformation since it is similar to the initial transformation. The value $X_{32,0}$ is added with a Whitening Key by using lookup tables, type IV-1 and IV-2 tables. A first byte C_0 of ciphertext is obtained after decoding table of a type V-1. C_1 is the output of the type V-1 from the intermediate value $X_{32,1}$. The value $X_{32,2}$ XOR with a Whitening key by using lookup tables of type III-1 and III-2. C_3 is obtained by a type V-2 table with an input value $X_{32,3}$. C_4, C_5 and C_6, C_7 are derived from $X_{32,4}, X_{32,5}$ and $X_{32,6}, X_{32,7}$ by the same process of $X_{32,0}, X_{32,1}$ and $X_{32,2}, X_{32,3}$ respectively.

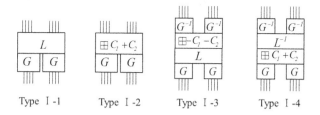

Fig. 1. Tables of Type I

4   Security and Performance Analysis

4.1   Security Analysis

To demonstrate the security of the proposed method against side channel attack, we mainly show that a masked intermediate value is independent from a

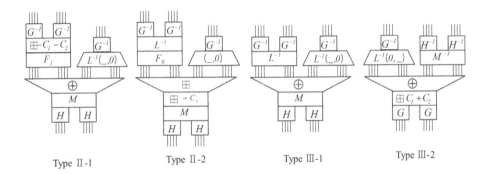

Fig. 2. Tables of Type II and Type III

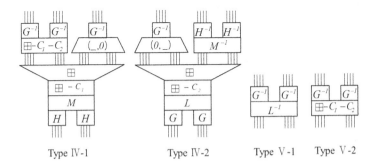

Fig. 3. Tables of Type IV and Type V

non-masked value. To do so, we first compare each bit of a masked and a non-masked intermediate values using the proposed and the original HIGHT implementations, respectively. The target intermediate value to be compared is X_2(third byte, see Algorithm 2) in the first round output because it is affected by the first byte of the first round key. The main step of single-bit DPA is to compute a differential trace after dividing power traces into two sets according the value of a target bit. The protection of DPA can be then justified if two bits of the non-masked and the masked X_2 at each bit position are different with probability 1/2. For the verification, we have performed encryption for 10,000,000 different plaintexts using the two HIGHT implementations, and also compared each bit of the masked and the non-masked values of X_2. As a result, Table 2 shows that they are different with a nearly 1/2 probability for every bit position. This property prevents a DPA attacker from constructing the correct sets of power traces and thus DPA is unlikely to work when using function masking.

In the case of CPA(correlation power analysis), an attacker computes a correlation value between the Hamming weights of a hypothetical value and the power consumption [13]. This is due to the fact that the power consumption of a micro-controller at a given point is known to be proportional or inversely proportional to the Hamming weight of a processed data. To demonstrate the

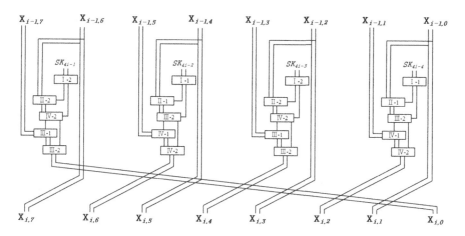

Fig. 4. Round transformation

Table 2. Probability of different bit between function masking and no masking intermediate

Bit position	1	2	3	4	5	6	7	8
Probability	49.99 %	50.00 %	50.01 %	50.00 %	50.01 %	49.97 %	50.00 %	49.99 %

protection of CPA, we show that the Hamming weights of a masked and a non-masked values of X_2 are independent from each other. Let HW_α denote the set of plaintexts that lead to the Hamming weight α of the non-masked value of X_2. Then, we have $\alpha \in [0, 8]$ because there are nine possible Hamming weights for an 8-bit value. We have performed encryption for 10,000,000 random plaintexts using the original HIGHT implementation and divided the plaintexts into HW_α, where $\alpha \in [0, 8]$. The next step is to show that the plaintexts in HW_α lead to well-distributed Hamming weights of X_2 in our implementation. For this purpose, we have repeated encryption on our proposed implementation for each set of plaintexts in HW_α, where $\alpha \in [0, 8]$. If the Hamming weights of the masked values of X_2 are uniformly distributed, they will show the probabilities for the Hamming weights of an 8-bit value shown in Table 3. For $\alpha \in [0,8]$, our experimental result shown in Table 4 gives us that the plaintexts in HW_α cause the Hamming weights of X_2 to be almost uniformly distributed in our implementation. This means that a masked and a non-masked values are not correlated to each other with overwhelming probability. We can therefore conclude that our function masking can also protect against CPA.

4.2   Performance Analysis

In this section, we compared the performance of the data masking and function masking. There is no secure implementation of HIGHT with second-order masking so far. Thus, it was tried to estimate the approximate overhead by calculating

Table 3. Probability distribution for the Hamming weight of a uniformly distributed 8-bit value [10]

HW	0	1	2	3	4	5	6	7	8
Prob	0.004	0.031	0.109	0.219	0.273	0.219	0.109	0.031	0.004

Table 4. Probability distribution for the Hamming weight of a function masked value

HW_α \ Masked HW	0	1	2	3	4	5	6	7	8
HW_0	0.0038	0.0307	0.1062	0.2201	0.2773	0.2196	0.1073	0.0313	0.0038
HW_1	0.0038	0.0311	0.1100	0.2189	0.2730	0.2197	0.1093	0.0303	0.0039
HW_2	0.0040	0.0312	0.1092	0.2185	0.2738	0.2190	0.1092	0.0312	0.0039
HW_3	0.0039	0.0312	0.1097	0.2189	0.2730	0.2186	0.1095	0.0313	0.0038
HW_4	0.0040	0.0312	0.1094	0.2186	0.2736	0.2189	0.1092	0.0312	0.0039
HW_5	0.0039	0.0312	0.1091	0.2188	0.2736	0.2189	0.1094	0.0312	0.0039
HW_6	0.0039	0.0312	0.1090	0.2191	0.2735	0.2189	0.1093	0.0312	0.0039
HW_7	0.0038	0.0311	0.1089	0.2183	0.2746	0.2187	0.1088	0.0317	0.0039
HW_8	0.0040	0.0314	0.1097	0.2150	0.2744	0.2189	0.1121	0.0306	0.0039

the number of operations required additional. Conversion of boolean and arithmetic mask is needed 10 times for one round function, when an implementation is used converting algorithm of [4]. Initial and final transformation are required two times mask conversion.

If data masking is applied at the beginning and end of 4 round, namely 8 rounds, initial and final transformation, the required operations of mask conversion are 86,268($((8 \times 10) + (2 \times 2)) \times 1027$) because one mask conversion needs 1,027 additional operations. In the case of no masking HIGHT, 392 operations are required because initial and final transformation need 4 operations in each and one round needs 12 operations where the HIGHT is composed of 32 rounds. Thus, it can be estimated that data masking version is over 200 times slower than the straightforward version. Even this is optimistic estimate excluding random number creation for mask conversion.

HIGHT applied function masking requires 16 times table lookup for initial transformation, 20 times for final transformation and 20 times for each round. For 8 rounds masking, table lookup will be 196 times. Since rest of unmasked 24 rounds require 288 operations, total operations for function masking are 484 times. Although this means function masking is 1.2 times slower than original HIGHT, actual runtime should be slower than the expectation because memory operation takes longer than ALU operation in CPU.

We implemented the function masked HIGHT in C language using a Intel core i7. Table 5 shows that lookup tables are around 25 Kbytes and it takes 1.79 times longer than original HIGHT.

Table 5. Lookup table size and time complexity of function masked HIGHT

Size of lookup tables			Time complexity	
Type I	4 tables	4×256	HIGHT (no masking)	754 cycles
Type II	2 tables	2×4096		
Type III	2 tables	2×4096	HIGHT (function masking)	1351 cycles
Type IV	2 tables	2×4096		
Type V	2 tables	2×256		
Total	26,112 bytes (25.5 kbytes)		Ratio	1.79 times

5   Conclusion

Prior works have documented the masking methods against the standard DPA attack. However, The masking method is vulnerable to the high-order DPA attacks since the attacks use correlation coefficient between two points or more. To resist the high-order attack, the high-order masking schemes have been proposed but it is not easy to implement in reality because of bad performance. In this study, it is possible to implement our function masking scheme which needs only a little overhead in reality. Thus, our scheme takes only 1.79 times more than the original HIGHT algorithm, but spends almost 200 times less than the second-order masking method. It means that it is possible to implement the masked HIGHT algorithm on the microprocessor against SCA by using 25 KB memory.

In the future, we should consider about the reduction of table size. The efficiency and security of the masked HIGHT should be verified by applying the function masking to the standard cryptographic algorithms, AES or ARIA. We expect that it is possible to compare with the high-order masked AES since many researches of high-order masking AES have been published. And it will be confirmed on the small processor devices as well as PC with different environments.

Acknowledgment. This work was supported by the K-SCARF project, the ICT R&D program of ETRI(Research on Key Leakage Analysis and Response Technologies).

References

1. Oswald, E., Mangard, S., Herbst, C., Tillich, S.: Practical second-order DPA attacks for masked smart card implementations of block ciphers. In: Pointcheval, D. (ed.) CT-RSA 2006. LNCS, vol. 3860, pp. 192–207. Springer, Heidelberg (2006)
2. Schramm, K., Paar, C.: Higher order masking of the AES. In: Pointcheval, D. (ed.) CT-RSA 2006. LNCS, vol. 3860, pp. 208–225. Springer, Heidelberg (2006)
3. Goubin, L.: A sound method for switching between boolean and arithmetic masking. In: Koç, Ç.K., Naccache, D., Paar, C. (eds.) CHES 2001. LNCS, vol. 2162, p. 3. Springer, Heidelberg (2001)

4. Vadnala, P.K., Großschädl, J.: Algorithms for switching between boolean and arithmetic masking of second order. In: Gierlichs, B., Guilley, S., Mukhopadhyay, D. (eds.) SPACE 2013. LNCS, vol. 8204, pp. 95–110. Springer, Heidelberg (2013)

5. Rivain, M., Prouff, E.: Provably secure higher-order masking of AES. In: Mangard, S., Standaert, F.-X. (eds.) CHES 2010. LNCS, vol. 6225, pp. 413–427. Springer, Heidelberg (2010)

6. Kim, H., Hong, S., Lim, J.: A fast and provably secure higher-order masking of AES S-box. In: Preneel, B., Takagi, T. (eds.) CHES 2011. LNCS, vol. 6917, pp. 95–107. Springer, Heidelberg (2011)

7. Fumaroli, G., Martinelli, A., Prouff, E., Rivain, M.: Affine masking against higher-order side channel analysis. In: Biryukov, A., Gong, G., Stinson, D.R. (eds.) SAC 2010. LNCS, vol. 6544, pp. 262–280. Springer, Heidelberg (2011)

8. Hong, D., Sung, J., Hong, S.H., Lim, J.-I., Lee, S.-J., Koo, B.-S., Lee, C.-H., Chang, D., Lee, J., Jeong, K., Kim, H., Kim, J.-S., Chee, S.: HIGHT: A new block cipher suitable for low-resource device. In: Goubin, L., Matsui, M. (eds.) CHES 2006. LNCS, vol. 4249, pp. 46–59. Springer, Heidelberg (2006)

9. Chow, S., Eisen, P., Johnson, H., Van Oorschot, P.C.: White-box cryptography and an AES implementation. In: Nyberg, K., Heys, H. (eds.) Selected Areas in Cryptography. LNCS, vol. 2595, pp. 250–270. Springer, Heidelberg (2003)

10. Mangard, S., Oswald, E., Popp, T.: Power analysis attacks: revealing the secrets of smart cards, vol. 31. Springer, Heidelberg (2008)

11. Kocher, P., Jaffe, J., Jun, B.: Differential power analysis. In: Wiener, M. (ed.) CRYPTO' 99. LNCS, vol. 1666, pp. 388–397. Springer, Heidelberg (1999)

12. Shannon, C.E.: Communication theory of secrecy systems. Bell Syst. Tech. J $28(4)$, 656–715 (1949)

13. Brier, E., Clavier, C., Olivier, F.: Correlation power analysis with a leakage model. In: Joye, M., Quisquater, J.-J. (eds.) CHES 2004. LNCS, vol. 3156, pp. 16–29. Springer, Heidelberg (2004)

Critical Infrastructure Security
and Policy

Multivariate Statistic Approach to Field Specifications of Binary Protocols in SCADA System

Seungoh Choi[✉], Yeop Chang, Jeong-Han Yun, and Woonyon Kim

The Attached Institute of ETRI, P.O. Box 1, Yuseong, Daejeon 305-600, Korea
{sochoi, ranivris, dolgam, wnkim}@ensec.re.kr

Abstract. In recent years, there has been an increasing interest in security of Industrial Control System (ICS) to figure out vulnerabilities in Supervisory Control and Data Acquisition (SCADA) system. One of the popular methods to find vulnerabilities is fuzzing, which is test of pushing data to the target for more secure operations. However, it is necessary to have in-depth knowledge of protocol specification as long as we want to utilize fuzzing in both intelligent and time-efficient manner. Although extensive research has been carried out on protocol specification, most studies in this field have focused on plain text protocol such as typically Hyper Text Transport Protocol (HTTP). In this paper, we have proposed multivariate statistic approach to binary protocols in SCADA system in order to obtain information of field specification. Then, we showed that informative results with field specification from our approach.

Keywords: Security · Reverse engineering · Binary protocol · SCADA

1 Introduction

Supervisory Control and Data Acquisition (SCADA) system is an Industrial Control System (ICS) designed to facilitate the control of devices and acquire information in a centralized manner. To effectively operate SCADA system, protocol over communication channel is essential. Recently, the uses of protocols have been steadily extended to include communication with components such as sensors, actuators, and programmable logic controllers (PLCs), etc.

As the operational environment for SCADA was recently switched from local to remote, a new threat to security has arisen. According to ICS-CERT, which deals with ICS security, not only have vulnerabilities related to ICS been steadily reported, but also the number of cyber incidents involving ICS has rapidly increased [1]. ICS-CERT also warned that some control systems can be directly accessed via remote access due to the conjunction point between the closed network and the Internet [2]. Moreover, the trend of communication using control devices has changed from serial to TCP/IP. Therefore, the threat to SCADA is receiving critical attention.

From the perspective of mitigating the threat, 'fuzzing', which takes all combinations of data as input is one good method of detecting vulnerabilities. However, information on the protocol should be provided somehow prior to undertaking fuzzing in an intelligent manner. Namely, it is an ineffective and time-consuming task due to a

© Springer International Publishing Switzerland 2015
K.-H. Rhee and J.H. Yi (Eds.): WISA 2014, LNCS 8909, pp. 345–357, 2015.
DOI: 10.1007/978-3-319-15087-1_27

lack of knowledge. Furthermore, most protocols operating in SCADA system are not published publicly, making it a major problem to acquire in-depth knowledge of a target.

In its current state, research on the extraction of protocol information has been largely restricted to different areas of research than SCADA system. Almost all of the research focuses on the plain text protocol, which is a human-readable like Hyper Text Transport Protocol (HTTP), SIP (Session Initiation Protocol), and SMTP (Simple Mail Transfer Protocol) [3–16].

Despite all of these efforts, it is essentially inadequate for application to a communication protocol in ICS environment. Basically, industrial communication protocols are mostly binary protocols rather than plain text protocols. A binary protocol is intended to be machine-readable in order to provide fast interpretation. Thus, different approach is needed to reflect on binary information in contrast to plain text protocols.

In this paper, we attempt to show how binary protocol can be successfully analyzed. First, we collect a binary stream over the communication channels of DF1 and Modbus, which are widely used in SCADA systems. After that, we apply our multivariate statistic composed of variance and Shannon entropy to DF1 and Modbus. Based on the results obtained from our methods, we finally provide a template including a structure of field and specifications as well. It is expected that our approach could contribute to the application of security such as smart fuzzing and obfuscation in an early stage.

The rest of the paper is organized as follows. Section 2 presents the general background to communication protocols in SCADA. We then explain the motivation for conducting a multivariate statistic approach and its application in Sect. 3. In Sect. 4, we analyze results obtained from the proposed approach. Section 5 presents limitations and future work related to this study. Finally, we conclude in Sect. 6.

2 Background

2.1 DF1 [17]

DF1 protocol is an industrial protocol developed by Allen-Bradley for controlling their products including PLCs. DF1 protocol consists of two layers, data link layer for transferring data over physical link (DH, DH+, and DH485) and application layer for sending commands and command specific data. ASCII control characters, for example DLE (10 h), STX (02 h), and ETX (03 h) are used in DF1 protocols. Following Fig. 1 describes DF1 protocol structures of fields and Table 1 shows its function.

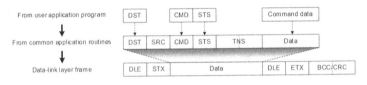

Fig. 1. Structure of field among layers in DF1

Table 1. Functions of field among layers in DF1

Layer	Field	Length (byte)	Function
Data-link	DLE	1	Indicates beginning of message
	STX	1	
	DLE	1	Indicates end of message
	ETX	1	
	BCC/ CRC	2	Checks integrity of data from application layer
Application	DST	1	Address of receiver
	SRC	1	Address of sender
	CMD	1	Performs operation for a desired command
	STS	1	Status of received message
	TNS	2	Verifies transaction and redundant message
	Data	Varies	Information related to CMD

2.2 Modbus [18]

Modbus developed by Modicon is a protocol designed to locally or remotely control and manage PLCs in supervisory control and data acquisition (SCADA) systems. Basically, Modbus is easy to implement because of simple structure of protocol. In addition, Modbus can operate in various communication environments. Available types of support for environments include serial communications such as RS-232, RS-422, and RS-485 as well as TCP/IP over LAN based on Ethernet. According to the environment, Modbus can be classified into various versions including Modbus Serial, Modbus Plus, and Modbus over TCP/IP. All versions of Modbus have layered architecture. In particular, all of the layers (except the application layer) are transparently used without any changes. Figure 2 shows how the structure of field is composed at the application layer in the case of Modbus over TCP/IP. In comparison with the ADU (Application Data Unit) in the Modbus Serial frame, the Modbus frame with TCP/IP transmission takes the function code and data, which are not modified, for the PDU (Protocol Data Unit). Table 2 shows the functions of field in the Modbus frame with TCP/IP. From the perspective of transmission, the RTU (Remote Terminal Unit) and ASCII (American Standard Code for Information Interchange) are supported in Modbus.

3 Multivariate Statistic Approach

3.1 Motivation of Methods

Prior to determining which statistical methods to use, we reasoned out methods based on simple observation of the value among each packet in respect of the communication protocol in SCADA system. Figure 3 shows the results obtained from the preliminary observation of values at each byte position in two different protocols, DF1(Type C) and

Table 2. Functions of field at application layer in Modubs over TCP/IP

Field	Length (byte)	Function
Transaction identifier	2	Transaction pairing along the same TCP connection
Protocol identifier	2	Presenting Modbus services
Length	2	A byte count of the remaining fields
Unit identifier	1	Identifying a remote server located on a non TCP/IP network (for serial bridging)
Function code	1	Providing pre-defined operation
Data	Varies	Including data as requested

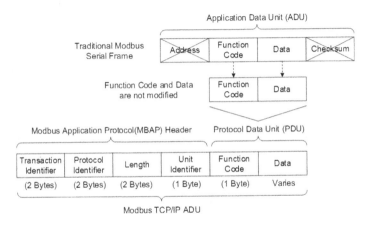

Fig. 2. Structure of field at application layer in Modbus over TCP/IP

Modbus(Type G) represented in Table 5. Taken together, these results suggest that there is an association between distributions of value. In Fig. 3 (a), we cannot distinguish each value of the packet at the first to sixth byte positions because all values at the same position overlap completely. In the case of eighth byte position, almost all of the values are evenly distributed and scattered. This situation is substantially the same as that for Modbus shown in Fig. 3 (b).

The reason why the situation happened is that each field is responsible for its own roles complied rules of protocol. Thus, for the next step, we investigated several common elements between DF1 and Modbus as well as observing the trend of values for the elements as shown in Table 3 based on collected data represented in Table 5.

From views upon the observation, we adopted the multivariate statistic approach, which we applied to both variance and Shannon entropy so that we could separate the conjunct field regardless of the protocol. Shannon entropy is appropriate for the occurrence of different values. Our approach is explained more specifically in the next section.

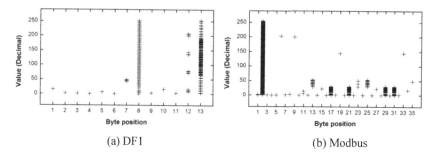

(a) DF1   (b) Modbus

Fig. 3. Value in each byte position for communication protocol in SCADA system

Table 3. Charateristic of valid value for each element

Elements	Range of values	Frequency of values	Occurrence of different values
Address	Wide	High	Low
Function code	Narrow	High	Low
Transaction identifier	Wide	Low	High
Checksum	Wide	Mid	High
Data	Wide+	High	High

3.2   Alignment

When network traffic is collected on a communication channel, it is naturally sorted as a time-series. In this paper, we need to rearrange the collection of traffic to obtain better results. Put simply, the first method of alignment concerns the size of the packet. If the packets are the same size, then there is a high probability that these packets will have same the structure of field. Moreover, there is no interference in each packet. That is, each field cannot be vertically mixed up in the same position.

Second, *Needleman-Wunsch* algorithm, which reorders the sequence of value by searching for a common value at different locations, can be applied for rearrangement [19]. It has been noted that *Needleman-Wunsch* algorithm is effective only if the packets include a delimiter (separator). As a result, we first applied *Needleman-Wunsch* algorithm. If it is impossible to align using the algorithm due to unused separator in the first step, we secondly rearrange packets by the size of packets.

3.3   Variance

Variance generally indicates how far numbers are scattered from the basis of the mean (expected value). According to the definition of variance, the closer numbers are to the mean and to each other, the smaller the variance is and vice versa. Therefore, the range and frequency of values can be fairly represented by variance. In accordance with Table 3, the identifier of transaction sequentially increases so that it tends to show a discrete uniform distribution, and we can obtain its variance defined as Eq. (2), where n is 2 to the power of bit size.

$$var(X) = \frac{1}{n}\sum_{k=1}^{n} k^2 - (n+1)/2 = (n^2 - 1)/12 \qquad (1)$$

Variance is 5461.25 if the transaction identifier uses a single byte and if all values from 0 to 255 are present with equal frequency. On the other hand, variance is intuitively 0 in the case of a fixed value like the separator when all the values are the same. However, the variance is not enough to clearly divide a packet into several fields because it cannot measure how many different values there are. As a result, we must additionally adopt Shannon entropy.

3.4 Shannon Entropy

Shannon entropy was first introduced in an article including on information theory written by C. E. Shannon [20]. In this article, Shannon entropy, which is a measure of uncertainty, can be denoted by $H(X)$ with a set of probabilities as expressed in Eq. (2)

$$H(X) = -\sum_{i=1}^{n} P(x_i) \log_b P(x_i) \qquad (2)$$

Shannon entropy is a suitable method for dealing with diversity of value as mentioned in the previous section. For Shannon entropy in case of bit information, the base of the logarithm uses 2 derived as Eq. (3), where n is 2 to the power of the bit size m like the number of cases for generating valid value within the bit space m and $P(x_i)$ is the probability of occurrence of the value x_i.

$$H(X) = \sum_{i=1}^{n} P(x_i) \log_2 P(x_i), n = 2^m \qquad (3)$$

Regarding the previous problem for variance, we can bring forward a case as shown in Table 4. In the case of variance, they cannot be separated since the difference between variances is not big enough if these two cases are found in consecutive fields. In contrast to variance, Shannon entropy can easily distinguish between cases since uniform case is nearly seven times bigger than the skew case.

Table 4. Comparison of statistics between uniform and skew case

Case	Value										Variance	Shannon entropy
	1st	2nd	3rd	4th	5th	6th	7th	8th	9th	10th		
Uniform	1	2	3	4	5	6	7	8	9	10	8.25	≈3.3219
Skew	1	1	1	1	1	1	1	1	1	10	7.29	≈0.4690

3.5   Multivariate Statistic Approach

To apply multivariate statistic approach, Shannon entropy is paired with variance for coordinate of multivariate statistic. We then put all the pairs as coordinate value on the plane composed of variance and Shannon entropy. To distinguish the pairs, we define degree of division (θ), which stands for the ratio of the interval to statistics. The interval can be calculated with multiplying θ by a difference between minimum and maximum value of each statistics. Thus, the smaller θ makes the more regions in the plane. Based on the regions, the pairs can be separated. Additionally, we can combine the pairs with rule as follows: First, the pairs should be located in the same area; Second, the pairs should be adjacent byte position.

4   Analysis of Results

To capture a bit stream over the communication channel, we composed an environment for DF1 and Modbus. In the case of DF1, we made a link on MicroLogix1100 for the PLC and an engineering tool for RSLogix 500 using a serial port (RS-232). Also, WAGO 750-741 was used for Modbus over TCP/IP with the Ethernet port (RJ-45). Based on this environment, we then collected the bit stream over each channels for DF1 and Modbus. Table 5 shows in brief the network data that we gathered. It should be noted that all the response messages were the same for protected typed logical read with three addresses. Therefore, we excluded those messages from our analysis. In addition, we ignored a part of the TCP/IP header in Modbus due to out of scope. We can also define 'granularity of block' for an in-depth analysis. The granularity can be either a byte or a bit. In this paper, we defined the granularity as a byte.

Table 5. Summary of network data

Protocol	Type	Command	Size (byte)	Num. of pkt.
DF1	A	Protected typed file read	19	245
	B	Response for protected typed file read	24	245
	C	Diagnostic status	13	246
	D	Response for diagnostic status	37	245
	E	Protected typed logical read with three address	18	58
Modbus	F	Read holding register	12	538
	G	Response for read holding register	209	538

4.1   Results of DF1

In the step of aligning for traffic of DF1, we found a common value using *Needleman-Wunsch* algorithm, so the network data did not need to be organized by size.

Figure 4 provided the statistics with variance and Shannon entropy at the byte position. It was apparent from this figure that strong evidence of a fixed value (i.e., the reserved value for the separator) was found when both variance and Shannon entropy were zero at the first, second, thirty-fourth, and thirty-fifth positions. If both statistics were near zero or low enough, it indicated that few values were frequently found so that the values involved in the field act as identifiers of address.

Interestingly, conflicting statistics were observed at the ninth position. This was because that few values, which were far, repeatedly appeared as seen in the example of the skew case. This situation was strongly correlated with function code or command which were repetitive and monotonous.

At the eighth, thirty-sixth, and thirty-seventh positions, both sets of statistics were remarkably higher than the others. For this, the candidates for those locations were transaction and checksum because the value of transaction was supposed to be sequentially increased and checksum had to be randomly generated.

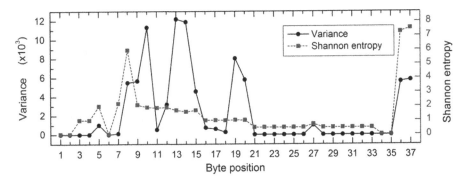

Fig. 4. Variance and Shannon entropy at byte position for DF1

For a straightforward view of the field characteristic, we turned next to the experimental evidence on multivariate statistic. Figure 5 shows the results of field specification by our multivariate statistic approach. As shown in Fig. 5, we could figure out the distribution of values on the axis of variance and Shannon entropy.

First of all, we divided the data into several fields by splitting the XY plane in Fig. 5 based on multivariate statistic. Table 6 shows that the detected field in the data-link layer varying degree of division (θ) for DF1. We found that correctly detected field for all types at data-link layer was higher than about 77 % by multivariate statistic where θ was 0.05.

Second, we also counted how many fields in the application layer were detected even though we did not know a specification of fields in the application layer unlike the data-link layer. Regarding the case of A, C, and E, we excluded a result due to the absence of data from application layer. In the case of types B and D, which were response messages, the greatest number of detected fields was found when θ was 0.05 as shown in Table 7. When we looked through the captured streams of B and D in detail, we identified that the both are two kinds of template for response message referred to detected field.

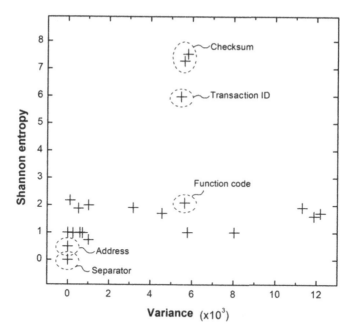

Fig. 5. Multivariate statistic approach for DF1

Table 6. Comparison of correctly detected field in the data-link layer varying θ

Type	Actual num. of field	Num. of correctly detected field		
		$\theta = 0.05$	$\theta = 0.1$	$\theta = 0.2$
A	12	10	10	8
B	7	6	6	4
C	8	6	6	4
D	7	6	6	4
E	13	10	10	8

Table 7. Comparison of detected filed in application layer varying θ

Type	Num. of detected field		
	$\theta = 0.05$	$\theta = 0.1$	$\theta = 0.2$
B	9	8	8
D	12	9	9

Figure 6 presents the template of field specification from which we selectively took two types of message due to constrains on space. The shaded areas in the box represent the correctly detected field. However, we did not apply shade to field in the application layer due to unknown format.

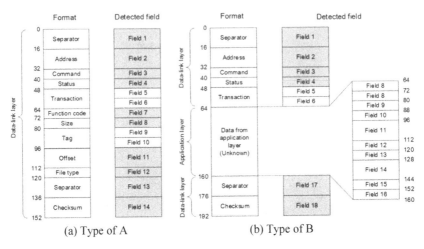

(a) Type of A   (b) Type of B

Fig. 6. Comparison of DF1 message format derived by multivariate statistic where $\theta = 0.05$

4.2 Results of Modbus Over TCP/IP

In the case of network data from Modbus over TCP/IP, the separator could not be identified, so all the data had to be sorted by size. After the process of alignment, we obtained the variance and Shannon entropy for each data size data as shown in Fig. 7.

For request of reading holding register represented by Fig. 7 (a), variance and Shannon entropy, except for the first and second positions, were 0, which means that one kind of value appeared repeatedly. This was similarly observed in Fig. 7 (b) as long as the byte position was lower than eight (i.e., the size of the application header of Modbus over TCP/IP and the function code in the protocol data unit). Notably, it seems that the second position could be the transaction identifier or checksum because variance and Shannon entropy were extremely high.

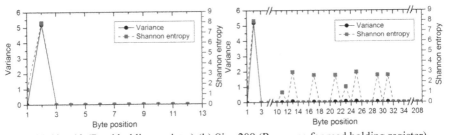

(a) Size 13 (Read holding register) (b) Size 209 (Response for read holding register)

Fig. 7. Variance and Shannon entropy at byte position for Modbus

Figure 8 shows all the values for request and response for reading holding register on the axis of variance and Shannon entropy. As shown in the figure, the symbol of request was placed on three points and the symbol of response was located in three different points because the value was mainly 0.

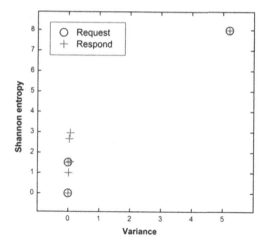

Fig. 8. Multivariate statistic approach for Modbus

For this reason, we obtained the same number of detected fields in the area of the header just before the seventh byte in types F and G, where θ was 0.05, 0.1, and 0.2, respectively. Contrary to the application header, we found that the pattern of values at the seventeenth, twenty-first, twenty-ninth, and thirty-first positions in the application data were fully identical. Therefore, it could be useful information to construct template of Modbus over TCP/IP based on the results obtained from the collection of data.

5   Future Work

This research is an early stage for application as mentioned. For this reason, we showed DF1 and Modbus without sufficient data. For example, few fields can be identified for Modbus over TCP/IP unlike DF1. Therefore, the collection of more diverse data under various situations would help us to establish a greater degree of accuracy on this matter. Additionally, most of the communication protocols used in SCADA systems are proprietary, i.e., they are closed protocols. Thus, it faced with application for security. For our future work, we will carry out a multivariate statistic approach to fuzzing and obfuscation in order to overcome a lack of knowledge.

6   Conclusion

In this paper, we have proposed a multivariate statistic approach based on the observation of the binary protocol, DF1 and Modbus over TCP/IP. The multivariate statistic approach considered distribution not only frequency of values but also the diversity of values at each position, thereby helping us correctly identify fields. By analyzing variance and Shannon entropy which are simple and complementary methods, we could show that informative results with field specification are provided. The multivariate statistic approach is in an early stage to extract specification of the binary protocol, making it necessary to research additional methods. In addition, the results tend to depend upon diversity of the collected data. By compensating for these limitations, we expected that it can help a stage move from dummy fuzzing to smart fuzzing, as well as obfuscation as preparing template by multivariate statistic.

References

1. National Cybersecurity and Communications Integration Center: ICS-CERT Year in Review (2013)
2. National Cybersecurity and Communications Integration Center: NCCIC/ICS-CERT Monitor for January-April (2014)
3. Wondracek, G., Comparetti, P.M., Kruegel, C., Kirda, E., Anna, S.S.S.: Automatic network protocol analysis. In: NDSS, pp. 1–14 (2008)
4. Ming-Ming, X., Shun-zheng, Y., Yu, W.: Automatic network protocol automaton extraction. In: Third International Conference on Network and System Security, 2009. NSS 2009, pp. 336–343 (2009)
5. Gorbunov, S., Rosenbloom, A.: Autofuzz: Automated network protocol fuzzing framework. IJCSNS **10**, 239 (2010)
6. Lin, Z., Jiang, X., Xu, D., Zhang, X.: Automatic protocol format reverse engineering through context-aware monitored execution. In: NDSS, pp. 1–15 (2008)
7. Caballero, J., Song, D.: Automatic protocol reverse-engineering: message format extraction and field semantics inference. Comput. Netw. **57**, 451–474 (2013)
8. Pang, R., Paxson, V., Sommer, R., Peterson, L.: binpac: a yacc for writing application protocol parsers. In: Proceedings of the 6th ACM SIGCOMM Conference on Internet Measurement, pp. 289–300. ACM, Rio de Janeriro, Brazil (2006)
9. DeYoung, M.E.: Dynamic protocol reverse engineering: a grammatical inference approach. In: DTIC Document (2008)
10. Beddoe, M.A.: Network protocol analysis using bioinformatics algorithms (2004)
11. Caballero, J., Yin, H., Liang, Z., Song, D.: Polyglot: automatic extraction of protocol message format using dynamic binary analysis. In: Proceedings of the 14th ACM Conference on Computer and Communications Security, pp. 317–329. ACM, Alexandria, Virginia, USA (2007)
12. Comparetti, P.M., Wondracek, G., Kruegel, C., Kirda, E.: Prospex: protocol specification extraction. In: Proceedings of the 2009 30th IEEE Symposium on Security and Privacy, pp. 110–125. IEEE Computer Society (2009)
13. Yongjun, H., Hui, S., Xiaobing, X.: Protocol reverse engineering based on DynamoRIO. In: International Conference on Information and Multimedia Technology, 2009. ICIMT 2009, pp. 310–314 (2009)
14. Wang, Z., Jiang, X., Cui, W., Wang, X., Grace, M.: ReFormat: automatic reverse engineering of encrypted messages. In: Backes, M., Ning, P. (eds.) Proceedings of the 14th European Conference on Research in Computer Security. Lecture Notes in Computer Science, pp. 200–215. Springer, Saint-Malo, France (2009)
15. Antunes, J., Neves, N., Verissimo, P.: Reverse engineering of protocols from network traces. In: 2011 18th Working Conference on Reverse Engineering (WCRE), pp. 169–178. IEEE (2011)
16. Shevertalov, M., Mancoridis, S.: A reverse engineering tool for extracting protocols of networked applications. In: 14th Working Conference on Reverse Engineering 2007. WCRE 2007, pp. 229–238 (2007)

17. Allen-Bradley: DF1 protocol and command set reference manual. http://literature.
    rockwellautomation.com/idc/groups/literature/documents/rm/1770-m516_-en-p.pdf)
18. Modbus: Modbus application protocol specification V1.1b3. http://www.modbus.org/docs/
    Modbus_Application_Protocol_V1_1b3.pdf)
19. Needleman, S.B., Wunsch, C.D.: A general method applicable to the search for similarities
    in the amino acid sequence of two proteins. J. Mol. Biol. **48**, 443–453 (1970)
20. Shannon, C.E.: A mathematical theory of communication. Bell Syst. Tech. J. **27**, 379–423
    (1948)

Packet Loss Consideration for Burst-Based Anomaly Detection in SCADA Network

Kyoung-Ho Kim[(⊠)], Jeong-Han Yun, Yeop Chang,
and Woonyon Kim

The Attached Institute of ETRI, P.O.Box 1, Yuseong, Daejeon 305-600, Korea
{lovekgh,dolgam,ranivris,wnkim}@ensec.re.kr

Abstract. ICS (Industrial Control System) is a computer-controlled system that monitors and controls distributed field devices for power grid, water treatment and other industrial areas. Because ICS components fulfill their own roles, the network traffic of ICS has obvious regular patterns. These patterns can be used effectively in monitoring ICS network and detecting signs of cyber-attacks. In our previous work, we proposed a burst-based anomaly detection method for DNP3 protocol using the regularity of ICS network traffic. Traffic monitoring method such as switch mirroring causes many problems; packet duplication, packet out-of-order, and packet loss. The problems cause many false alarms. Furthermore, it is hard to decide whether the alarms caused by lost packets are true or false. In this paper, we apply our burst-based approach to TCP protocol in SCADA network and propose a method to manage monitoring problems for burst-based anomaly detection.

Keywords: Industrial control system · SCADA · ICS · Traffic analysis · Whitelist

1 Introduction

ICS (Industrial control system) is computer-controlled system that monitors and controls distributed field devices. It is also known as SCADA, DCS, or Process Control System. We can easily find ICSs in various areas such as electricity, chemical industry, water treatment, manufacturing and so on. They are closely related with our convenience and safety.

Although almost ICSs have proven to be highly vulnerable to cyber-attack, vendors and utilities haven't considered cyber security with deep insight. If a malicious attacker breaks into ICSs and controls them in his own way, critical accidents such as black-out or plant explosion may occur. For example, a train signaling system on the east coast of the US was shut down due to infection of Sobig.F worm [5], while nuclear centrifuges in Iran were destroyed by Stuxnet, which reprograms an original ICS's control logic into an evil control logic [6]. Nowadays cyber threat to ICSs have become very real and the encountered problems urgently need to be resolved.

Until now, cyber security for ICS has focused on the connection link into SCADA network from outside with Firewall, IDS and so on. These security techniques are suitable for protect against external cyber threats, but they have limits on detection of

© Springer International Publishing Switzerland 2015
K.-H. Rhee and J.H. Yi (Eds.): WISA 2014, LNCS 8909, pp. 358–369, 2015.
DOI: 10.1007/978-3-319-15087-1_28

internal threats such as malware infection by thumb drive, attacks by an insider or penetration from field devices. Therefore, monitoring internal traffic in ICS has become becoming significant issue.

We gathered and analyzed the internal network traffic of various control systems currently in operation. After scrutinzing the traffic, we concluded ICS traffic has some charateristic features. First, only fixed nodes work in the network. Any new nodes don't appear or disappear unexpectely. Next, control devices communicate with other specific devices because they only perform their functions in the control system. Additionally, one of the most interesting features which we identified is groups of packets were repeated in the control system traffic. Each of repeated pattern is composed of several packets of the same direction and same size. Figure 1 shows clearly this characteristic of SCADAtraffic. We concluded this pattern of packets called as a burst [8] could be used to detect anomalies ICS effectively [1] on the DNP3 protocol [9] which is widely used in SCADA system.

Based on the characteristic, we developed a monitoring system for the ICS, which we named it SNOW (SCADA Network Observatory with Whitelist). We define the whitelist as the communication list (server IP, server Port, protocol, client IP) and its repetitive communication pattern as the burst type. SNOW's main functions consist in extracting whitelist from network traffic and monitoring ICS traffic. SNOW generates alarms whenever it detects any violations incompatible with whitelists. During SNOW's field test with burst type, we found that SNOW generated far more false alarms than we expected. The main reasons for the false alarms are as follows.

- Packet loss
- Packet retransmission
- Out-of-order packet

The above problems are unavoidable issues for monitoring systems especially in when using port mirroring [4]. These monitoring problems induce *dirty bursts* (rightmost burst in Fig. 1) which make it hard to generate right whitelists needless to say about matching incoming packets with whitelists. Therefore, we enhanced our whitelist generating and monitoring mechanisms with considerations of the monitoring problems.

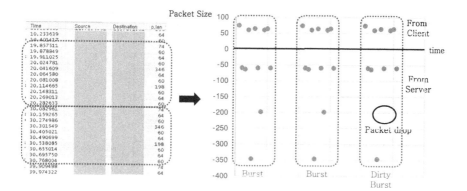

Fig. 1. Characteristic of ICS network traffic

In this paper, we describe how to build whitelist based on burst types and analyzes traffic using the whitelist. After investigating errors including packet loss, we propose an enhanced method to handle dirty burst caused by such errors. Finally we prove the improvement of our method with real ICS network traffic using TCP protocol.

2 Background

2.1 Burst-Based Network Whitelisting in SCADA System

Previous studies observed that the control system networks have different behavior characteristic compared to IT networks [1–3]. For their mission critical goals, every control system node performs its role at a predefined time except under special circumstances, such as unexpected emergencies or manual operations. So some statistical patterns could be found in control networks traffic. These approaches [10] are worthy of consideration, but the approach requires lots of computational power during building learning model and couldn't avoid high false positive. So Yun [1] suggested an alternative whitelist model based on the observation that groups of packets were repeated in ICS communication. Such a packet group is called as a burst which is gathered with a short inter-arrival time [7, 8].

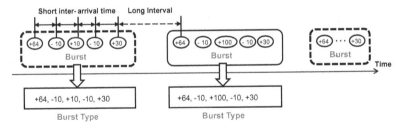

Fig. 2. Concepts of Burst and Burst Type

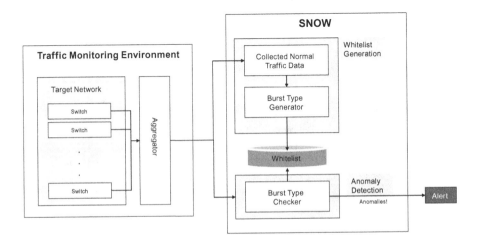

Fig. 3. SNOW system outline based on burst type

Burst type can be defined as a list of signed number in Fig. 2 to express bursts. Each number means size of each packet. Plus sign means the packet was sent from client to server and minus sign is vice versa.

On our experimental basis, we decide that employing burst type is appropriate for a 4-tuple (Server IP, Server Port, protoccol, Client IP) when less than 10 burst types are extracted in normal communication of the 4-tuple. Figure 3 simply depicts the system outline of SNOW.

2.2   Consideration on Packet Capture

There are two typical ways of collecting network traffic, namely network tap and port mirroring. A network tap is a device that is located in-line in a communication line and duplicates every packet transmitted in the communication line to other devices, such as a network traffic capture system or a traffic analyzer. Usually one network tap is required for one communication line monitoring. Port mirroring as a common feature of network switches is used to copy transmitted traffic from monitored ports to a mirrored port for the purpose of monitoring or diagnosing. For port mirroring, we need simple efforts at configuration and one network cable per mirrored port. But the performance and availability of a network switch must be checked because performance degradation by port mirroring has a negative effect on its main function, packet switching.

SNOW is designed to analyze all internal traffic, so port mirroring is an appropriate way of monitoring ICS traffic. Although we adopted a superb network switch compared to real traffic rates, we faced several problems such as out-of-order packets, packet retransmissions and packet loss. These problems lead to undesirable consequences when building and using the whitelist specially about using burst type. For instance, SNOW will extract the wrong burst type and generate false alerts whenever a packet loss occurs.

3   Captured Data Analysis

3.1   Data Description

We collected control network traffic from five different sites in operation. the network switch's mirroring function was used to collecting network traffic. If there are several switches, we merged mirrored traffic via an aggregator tap. Table 1 describes the captured traffic data. We will focus on only TCP traffic in the later part of this paper. But, burst-based anomaly detection can be applied to other protocols such as UDP, ICMP, and ARP. We cannot reveal site names and detail information for security reasons.

3.2   TCP Traffic Exception Analysis

After analyzing the captured traffic, we categorized the errors as retransmission and lost packet as shown in Table 2.

Table 1. Dataset descriptions

Site	Period (days)	Size (Total)	Mbps (avg)	Size (TCP)	No. of TCP Packets	No. of IPs
1	10	400.5 GB	3.8	271.8 GB	746,109,381	136
2	7.2	38.8 GB	0.5	18.6 GB	332,170,501	29
3	9.7	212.5 GB	2.1	62.1 GB	1,107,967,125	49
4	8.1	432.4 GB	5.1	427.9 GB	7,615,649,340	43
5	12.0	197.0 GB	1.6	36.4 GB	654,074,353	53

Table 2. Retransmissions and lost packets in dataset (TCP)

Site	Retransmission	Lost packets	Sum
1	3,419,988	551,694	3,971,682 (0.532 %)
2	9,273,813	4,446	9,279,259 (2.794 %)
3	335,013	2,019	337,032 (0.030 %)
4	183,891	14,055	197,946 (0.003 %)
5	328,781	130,828	459,609 (0.070 %)

Table 3. Our-of-order packets in dataset (TCP)

	Site 1	Site 2	Site 3	Site 4	Site 5
Out-of-order Packets	112,237	3	44	40	969

The reason of each error in network monitoring is judged;

- (Fast) Retransmission: low-performance of network nodes
- Lost packet: low-performance of network switch

One regularity between errors was found after examining them minutely. i.e. repetition of 'packet loss' error and 'packet retransmission' error. The cause of this recursive emergion is a 'out-of-order packets' in network monitoring. When $n + 1$th packet enters the monitoring device earlier than nth packet, the traffic analyzer draws a hasty conclusion, namely 'lost packet' was occured. Next, when nth packet enters the monitored device, the device judges that the packet has been retransmitted because nth packet was regarded as a previously sent (but missed) packet. Out-of-order packets were easily found in all captured network traffic and the count of out-of-order errors is in Table 3. SNOW may regard the out-of-order packets in burst as difference burst type. So these errors must be managed.

4 Packet Loss Consideration

SNOW provides two main functions for detecting anomaly based on burst type.

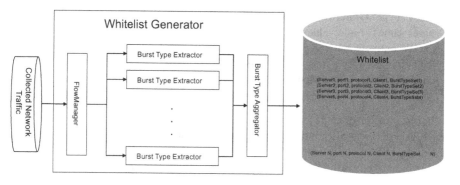

Fig. 4. Whitelist generation of SNOW

```
Func: BurstTypeExtractor( serverIP, serverPort, protocol, clientIP, clientPort)
packetList = [ ]    // empty list
burstTypeSet = { }  // empty set
timeInterval = 2    // 2 second is default time threshold for burst division

WHILE(isEmpty(packetList))
    p = Current Packet in packetList
    IF packetList!= [ ]   AND   p.time - packetList.tail.time > timeInterval :
        burstType = ExtractBurstType( packetList, serverIP )
        IF burstType exists:   burstTypeSet.add(burstType)
        packetList = [ ]
    packetList.attach(p)

    //Process for Last Burst
    IF packetList != [ ]
            AND   End Time of TrafficData - packetList.tail.time > timeInterval:
        burstType = ExtractBurstType( packetList, serverIP )
        IF burstType exists :   burstTypeSet.add(burstType)

Func: ExtractBurstType( packetList, serverIP )
burstType = [ ]
FOR i=0, i< packetList.length, i++
    p = packetList[i]
    IF p.srcIP==serverIP:   burstType.attach( p.packet_size )
    ELSE:                   burstType.attach( -p.packet_size )
RETURN burstType
```

Fig. 5. Func: BurstTypeExtractor

- **Burst Type Generation:** SNOW divides network traffic into each flow which shares same 5-tuple values (Server IP, Server Port, Client IP, Client Port, Protocol). SNOW extracts burst type candidate appeared repetitively in each flow. Finally SNOW aggregates burst types and produce whitelist.
- **Anomaly Detection based on Burst Type:** SNOW monitors network traffic and judges each flow violates whitelist including burst type or not in real time

In our prior research [1], we presumed that every packet arrived at the monitoring device in order. But after intricate analysis, we found captured traffic has some errors such as 'out-of-order sequence', 'packet retransmission', and 'packet loss'. So here we propose improved methods that cover the errors that occur in traffic collecting.

4.1   Improving Burst Type Extraction for Whitelist Generator

Figure 4 shows how SNOW builds whiltelist briefly. First FlowManager splits network traffic into each flow based on 5-tuple. Burst type extrator finds repeated pattern of packets in each flow and extracts burst type candidates. Next, Burst type aggregator merges burst types of 5-tuples which share 4-tuple.

We present a simplified algorithm for burst type extraction in Fig. 5 without considering errors in the mirrored traffic. The original algorithm reads packets sequentially, so the monitoring problems cause the insertion of abnormal burst types into the whitelist.

```
Func: NewExtractBurstType( packetList, serverIP )
burstType = [ ]
packetList = sortBySequence(packetList)
IF duplicated packet in packetList : delete packet
IF lost packet in packetList : RETRUN NO_TYPE
ELSE:
    firstServerSequenceNumber = 0
    firstClientSequenceNumber = 0
    WHILE(isEmpty(packetList))
        p = Current Packet in packetList
        IF p.srcIP==serverIP:
            IF firstServerSequenceNumber==0:  firstServerSequenceNumber = p.seq
                burstType.attach((p.packet_size, p.seq - firstServerSequenceNumber)
        ELSE:
            IF firstClientSequenceNumber==0:  firstClientSequenceNumber = p.seq
                burstType.attach((-p.packet_size, p.seq - firstClientSequenceNumber)
    RETURN burstType
```

Fig. 6. Func: NewExtractBurstType

Packet out-of-order and packet retransmission can be easily solved by reordering packets by sequence number. However, if there are lost packets in a burst, we cannot verify whether it is a real burst type. Therefore, if a packet is lost in a burst, the burst type must not be added to the whitelist.

Figure 6 shows our improved algorithm, named **NewExtractBurstType**, to consider the monitoring problems for burst type extraction. **NewExtractBurstType** reorders packets based on sequence numbers. The reordering corrects packet out-of-order and detects packet duplication and packet loss. If there is no lost packet in a burst, **NewExtractBurstType** adds its burst type to the whitelist.

In **NewExtractBurstType**, we add *normalized sequence numbers* to the format of burst type. The information is used to consider lost packets during burst type comparison for whitelist rule match.

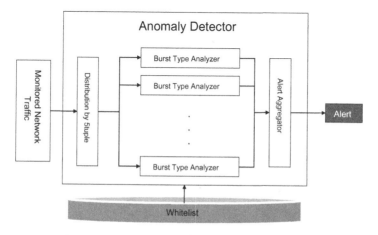

Fig. 7. Burst-based anomaly detection of SNOW

```
Func: BurstTypeAnalyzer( serverIP, serverPort, protocol, clientIP, clientPort)

burstType = [ ]         // empty list
lastPacketTime = -1
timeInterval = 2        // 2 second is default time threshold for burst division

WHILE(isEmpty(packetList))
    p = Current Packet in packetList
    IF lastPacketTime != -1 AND  p.time - lastPacketTime > timeInterval:
        IF burstType    NOT IN  Whitelist(serverIP, serverPort, protocol, clientIP):
        Send ALERT
    IF p.srcIP==serverIP:    burstType.attach( p.packet_size )
    ELSE: burstType.attach( -p.packet_size )
```

Fig. 8. Func: BurstTypeAnalyzer

```
Func: NewBurstTypeAnalyzer( serverIP, serverPort, protocol, clientIP,
clientPort)

burstType = [ ]        // empty list
lastPacketTime = -1
timeInterval = 2    // 2 second is default time threshold for burst division

WHILE(isEmpty(packetList))
    p = Current Packet in packetList
    IF lastPacketTime!=-1 AND p.time-lastPacketTime > timeInterval:
        result = check( burstType, Whitelist(serverIP, serverPort,
protocol, clientIP) )
        IF result == ALL_MATCH:
            NO_ALERT
        ELIF result == lost packet:
            Send LOW_ALERT (number of lost packet)
        ELSE:
            Send HIGH_ALERT
    IF p.srcIP==serverIP:
        burstType.insertion_without_dup( (p.packet_size, p.seq) )
    ELSE:
        burstType. insertion_without_dup( (-p.packet_size, p.seq) )
```

Fig. 9. Func: NewBurstTypeAnalyzer

4.2 Improving Burst Type Comparison for Anomaly Detector

To detect anomalies usign burst types, SNOW divides the bursts of each 5-tuple and checks whether the burst types of all the bursts are included in the whitelist of its related 4-tuple. This process is simply depicted in Fig. 7. Although its actual implementation is more complicated, the details of implementation are omitted in this paper.

In Fig. 7, **BurstTypeAnalyzer** is the function to detect anomaly of a 5-tuple. **BurstTypeAnalyzer** extracts burst types and checks whether they are included in whitelist of the 4-tuple that is related to the 5-tuple. Because **BurstTypeAnalyzer** does not consider monitoring problems, packet duplication or packet loss can cause abnormal burst types although the original bursts has permitted burst types. Figure 8 is the pseudo code of **BurstTypeAnalyzer**.

Pseudo code of the improved version, **NewBurstTypeAnalyzer**, is Fig. 9. Similar with **NewExtractBurstType**, **NewBurstTypeAnalyzer** uses packet reordering. Packet reordering solves packet duplication and packet out-of-order but also detects packet loss. Using sequence number information in burst types, we can check the possibility whether the burst can have a burst type in whitelist if the lost packet has proper packet size.

Figure 10 shows examples of the generation of alerts considering a lost packet. Candidates are burst types with a lost packet. Regardless the lost packet, candidate1

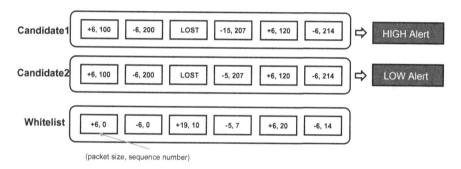

Fig. 10. Example: alert generation considering lost packets

cannot match any burst type in whitelist. But, Candidate2 is possible to have a burst type in whitelist following the lost packet. Therefore **NewBurstTypeAnalyzer** distinguishes the degrees of alert among the candidates.

5   Experiment

In this chapter, we verified improvement made when we applied the proposed method to the collected network traffic from 5 different sites.

Table 4 shows number of bursts that are extracted from all of the collected network traffic. The notable point here is the ratio of dirty bursts is greater than the ratio of error packets in Table 2. This tendency shows that the negative effect of the error packets will be amplified when we build the whitelist.

In Table 5, when we apply burst-based anomaly detection to 4-tuples using under 10 burst types, average 40 % of 4-tuples are included in the *watch list* which is 4-tuple list that uses under 10 burst types during normal communication. Using our improved whitelist generator, we can add several 4-tuples into the watch list.

Table 4. Dirty bursts in the collected traffic data

	Site 1	Site 2	Site 3	Site 4	Site 5
No. of Bursts	109,415,045	19,970,822	14,840,869	52,350,721	42,180,622
No. of Dirty Bursts	2,038,697	1,746,473	70,666	55,781	89,061
Ratio of Dirty bursts (%)	1.86	8.75	0.48	0.11	0.21

In our experiment, the watch list is stable when we extract burst types from 7 days network traffic. There are no false alarms except that are caused by dirty bursts. Our improved burst type checker eliminates the false alarms caused by packet retransmission and out-of-order. In addition, our improved method distinguishes bursts including packet loss or not. Packet loss cannot convince that the bursts including packet loss are abnormal bursts in real traffic. Different alert level can help to analyze anomaly detection result based on burst types.

Table 5. Watch list (4-tuples) and False alarms caused by dirty bursts

	Site 1	Site 2	Site 3	Site 4	Site 5
Total 4-tuples	23,045	317	168	219,983	4,481
4-tuples using under 10 burst types (*with dirty burst*)	18,367 (79.7 %)	151 (47.6 %)	46 (27.4 %)	76,325 (34.7 %)	1,999 (44.6 %)
4-tuples using under 10 burst types (*without dirty bursts*)	18,386 (79.8 %)	157 (49.5 %)	50 (29.8 %)	76,338 (34.8 %)	2,006 (44.8 %)
No. of false alarms caused by dirty bursts	165	169	21	135	107
No. of false alarms caused by dirty bursts including packet loss	37	0	2	130	83

6 Conclusion

Cyber threats to ICS are increasing persistently. Only with conventional security solutions, it is not enough to protect ICS. Therefore research and development for ICS specialized security solutions are urgently needed. We recognized ICSs are originally vulnerable because of its characteristic. Especially, difficulties in installation of security agents into non-general purpose computers and poor patch management due to network separation are a major cause of these vulnerabilities. Therefore, we need a security solution which monitors internal network traffics without agent installation and attack signature updates.

After analyzing ICS traffic, we judged using a burst type as a whitelist is effective for detecting initial sign of cyber-attacks. However, during a field test, we found not a few false alarms generated by problems such as packet loss which may occur in monitoring process. To solve these problems, we proposed a method for whitelist generation and anomaly detection based on burst types. Consequently, we proved our burst-based anomaly detection in ICS networks is very useful.

References

1. Yun, J.H., Jeon, S.H., Kim, K.H., Kim, W.N.: Burst-based anomaly detection on the DNP3 protocol. Int. J. Control Autom. **6**(2), 313–324 (2013)
2. Barbosa, R.R., Sadre, R., Pras, A.: Difficulties in modeling SCADA traffic: a comparative analysis. In: Taft, N., Ricciato, F. (eds.) PAM 2012. LNCS, vol. 7192, pp. 126–135. Springer, Heidelberg (2012)
3. Barbosa, R.R., Sadre, R., Pras, A.: Flow whitelisting in SCADA networks. Int. J. Crit. Infrastruct. Prot. **6**(3), 150–158 (2013)
4. Zhang, J., Moore, A.: Traffic Trace Artifacts due to Monitoring Via Port Mirroring. In: E2EMON, pp. 1–8 (2007)
5. Virus Disrupts Train Signal. http://www.cbsnews.com/news/virus-disrupts-train-signals
6. Falliere, N., Murchu, L.O., Chien, E.: W32. stuxnet dossier. White paper, Symantec Corp., Security Response (2011)

7. Lan, K., Heidemann, J.: A measurement study of correlations of internet flow characteristics. Comput. Netw. **50**(1), 46–62 (2006)
8. Shakkottai, S., Brownlee, N., claffy, kc.: A study of burstiness in TCP flows. In: Dovrolis, C. (ed.) PAM 2005. LNCS, vol. 3431, pp. 13–26. Springer, Heidelberg (2005)
9. Clarke, G., Reynders, D.: Practical modern SCADA protocols: DNP3, 60870.5 and related systems. Newnes (2004)
10. Yoon, M.K., Ciocarlie, G.F.: Communication pattern monitoring: improving the utility of anomaly detection for industrial control systems. In: NDSS Workshop on Security of Emerging Networking Technologies (SENT 2014) (2014)

Defining Security Primitives for Eliciting Flexible Attack Scenarios Through CAPEC Analysis

Ji-Yeon Kim[1] and Hyung-Jong Kim[2(✉)]

[1] Department of Electrical and Computer Engineering,
Carnegie Mellon University, Pittsburgh, USA
kimjy@andrew.cmu.edu
[2] Department of Information Security, Seoul Women's University,
Seoul, Republic of Korea
hkim@swu.ac.kr

Abstract. Cyber-security refers to all approaches to protect cyberspace against cyber-attacks. In order to identify vulnerabilities and develop countermeasures against cyber-attacks, we should be able to reenact both cyber-attacks and defenses. Simulations can be useful for the reenactment by overcoming its limitations including high risk and cost. However, it is difficult to model a variety cyber-attacks making use of pre-developed simulation models, because there is a lack of theoretical basis for modeling cyber-security simulations. In addition, because most simulation models are developed according to their own simulation purposes, it is very difficult to use them as primitives for modeling of new behaviors of cyber-attacks. In this paper, we propose a method for defining behavior primitives for developing flexible attack scenarios by combining the primitives considering flows of cyber-attacks and defenses. We also develop the scenario as simulation models and the models can be executed on the discrete event simulation system. To elicit a new scenario all modeler need to do is to choose primitives from pools and combine them considering simulation purposes and security issues. To extract the possible primitive behaviors, we have analyzed and abstracted all attack patterns of CAPEC (Common Attack Pattern Enumeration and Classification) database.

Keywords: Cyber-security · Cyber-attack · Modeling and simulation · CAPEC (Common Attack Pattern Enumeration and Classification)

1 Introduction

Cyber-security covers a wide range of security domains, such as network security, application security, information security, and so on. This means that there are many types of resources to be protected. It also means that cyber-attacks can be occurred using various attack methods that are based on the characteristics of the target resources and their vulnerabilities. Therefore, in order to study cyber-security more thoroughly, it would be helpful to reenact various forms of cyber-attacks and countermeasures to see if the countermeasures are effective for defending against the cyber-attacks or not.

© Springer International Publishing Switzerland 2015
K.-H. Rhee and J.H. Yi (Eds.): WISA 2014, LNCS 8909, pp. 370–382, 2015.
DOI: 10.1007/978-3-319-15087-1_29

However, there are still inevitable the risks and high cost of reenacting cyber-attacks in the real systems [1]. One alternative to solve the issue is a modeling and simulation. A simulation is a process that involves designing and experimenting with models of real systems or processes [2, 3]. It enables dangerous or expensive experiments to be conducted in virtual environments [4, 5]. Accordingly, we can reenact cyber-attacks in virtual environments by using the simulation. In the domain of cyber-security, however, there is a lack of theoretical basis for modeling a wide range of cyber-security problems. Most of previous studies on cyber-security simulations have addressed network attack simulations, such as a worm simulation and a distributed denial of service (DDoS) simulation. However, most of the studies have designed simulation models according to their own experiment environment and scenarios based on the modelers' knowledge. Because those are already developed with the abstractions considering each simulation purpose and security issue, it is difficult to observe primitive behaviors of cyber-attacks. As a result, we thought that it is very hard to make use of the previously existing models for new goals. If we have a pool of attack and defense primitives for developing attack scenarios, it will be effective and flexible for developing new scenarios under the new security goals and issues.

In this work, we propose a new way of defining attack and defense primitives for the flexible attack scenario development. We analyzed and abstracted the content of CAPEC [6] database (version 2.2) to consider all kinds of attacks and defenses. A part of the behavior primitives of attacks and defenses is shown in Appendix. To develop the new attack scenario, all modeler have to do is to choose primitives and sequence them considering the goal and effect of the scenario. Moreover, our primitives and scenarios are not just conceptual things but executable under the discrete event simulation environment. In this paper, we suggest a method for developing an attack scenario model considering components of discrete event simulation models. We also develop example scenario models of attack patterns of CAPEC in order to explain our method. In addition, we describe a process for transforming a scenario model into a discrete event simulation model considering a simulation purpose as a case study. We model our simulation model based on the discrete event system specification (DEVS) formalism, and execute the model using DEVSJAVA [7], a simulation library for DEVS models. This case study shows the contribution of our proposing method of defining primitives eliciting scenarios by simulation results.

The remainder of this paper is organized as follows. Section 2 identifies related works including previous modeling studies of a cyber-security domain and CAPEC analysis. Section 3 elicits components of a scenario model, and the example models are developed in Sect. 4. In Sect. 5, we model and simulate a worm attack as a case study. Finally, the conclusion is presented in Sect. 6.

2   Related Works

2.1   Previous Modeling Studies of Cyber-Security Domain

The most representative modeling method in the cyber-security domain is the attack tree [8], which models a process to achieve a final attack goal by representing detailed purposes or attacks with combinations of the AND/OR relations. A defense tree [9] represents methods designed to defend against attacks by adding lists of the methods to each node of the attack tree. However, even though the attack tree and a defense tree can help efficiently design a simulation scenario, it is not appropriate to develop a simulation model because these are process-centered modeling methods. For the simulation, we should be able to trace state variables that are changed by the process. Accordingly, in order to develop a cyber-security simulation model, a modeling method for representing state variables of attackers and targets is required.

2.2   Analysis of Cyber-Security Characteristics Through CAPEC Analysis

In order to simulate cyber-security problems, we need to understand the common characteristics of cyber-attacks and defenses in advance and develop a modeling method to represent them. In this section, we extract those characteristics by analyzing CAPEC. CAPEC, which is supported and managed from U.S. Department of Home-land Security and MITRE, defines 400 types of attacks [6]. Some other studies have been conducted to define and classify various computer and network cyber-attacks. Reference [10] defines 24 types of attacks including Trojan horses, viruses, and worms, Ref. [11] defines three types of attacks, including corruption, leakage, and denial, and Ref. [12] classifies attacks into secrecy-confidentiality, accuracy-integrity-authenticity and availability. In addition, Ref. [13] classifies eight types of attacks using an empirical classification method. However, because the purpose of those studies is to define the types of attacks, they do not provide information about attack methods and procedures to be needed for various cyber-security simulations. In comparison, CAPEC provides detailed information including purposes, methods, execution flow, targets, exploiting vulnerabilities, and countermeasures. Thus, we can collect the information needed to model cyber-attacks and defenses by analyzing the CAPEC.

The CAPEC defines 10 types of attack methods including injection, modification of resources, and so on. Because most attack patterns consist of more than one attack method, we have to develop a cyber-attack scenario by combining them. In addition, we need to consider detailed behaviors of each method. For example, a man-in-the-middle attack (CAPEC-ID 94) utilizes three methods, such as spoofing, analysis, and modification of resource, to exploit data between a server and client. However, according to the CAPEC information about the attack execution flow, behaviors of intercepting, modifying, and transmitting data can be executed to implement these methods. Thus, these behaviors must be reflected in an attacker model in a cyber-security simulation.

By analyzing the CAPEC, we extracted two characteristics of cyber-attacks: (1) An attack may consist of more than one attack behavior to achieve the final attack purpose. (2) The execution result of each behavior affects the attack flow. In addition, defense methods can also be modeled with combinations of multiple defense behaviors. In order to simulate a variety of cyber-attacks, accordingly, we extracted all of possible behaviors of cyber-attacks and defenses by analyzing the CAPEC.

3 Elicitation of Components of a Scenario Model

In this section, we elicits components of a scenario model by taking into account attack flows and requirements of a discrete event simulation model. Figure 1 shows an example of a cyber-attack scenario modeled using the attack tree, a representative method of attack modeling. As the figure shows, to achieve the final goal A, both goal A1 (which can be achieved using a successful attack behavior 1) and goal A2 (which can be achieved using successful attack behaviors 2 and 3) should be achieved.

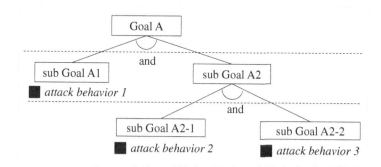

Fig. 1. An example of modeling a cyber-attack scenario using an attack tree

To develop a simulation model with this scenario model, we must take into account the following additional considerations:

(1) **Consideration 1 - Source and destination of a cyber-attack behavior**
The source and destination information explains which element executes a behavior and which element is targeted by the behavior. The scenario in Fig. 1 can be modeled into various types of models. In this work, we explain with three examples of models as shown in Fig. 2. Figure 2(a) shows that one attacker executes all the behaviors, and Figs. 2(b) and (c) show an attacker using other elements of cyberspace to execute an attack. Figures 2(b) and (c) differ in the number of behaviors that the attackers execute.

(2) **Consideration 2 - Sequence of cyber-attack behaviors**
If the event that all the cyber-attack behaviors in Fig. 1 succeed, the flow and result of the attack could differ, depending on characteristics of the attack. We define three types of these characteristics, as shown in Fig. 3.

(a) Type 1 - a cyber-attack that does not allow each attack behavior to fail (Fig. 3(a))

- This type of cyber-attack is terminated when one of the attack behaviors fail, causing the cyber-attack to fail.
- For example, in worm attacks if a host installs patches against the worm, the host cannot progress to the next step because the host removes the worm or its vulnerabilities.
- As a countermeasure, it is possible to defend against this type of attack by developing one of the defense behaviors.

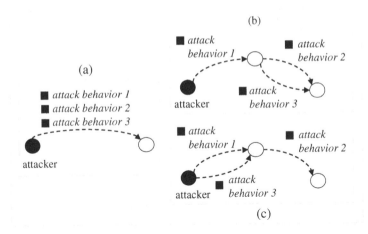

Fig. 2. Example cases of modeling a cyber-attack process using different source and destination elements

(b) Type 2 - a cyber-attack that allows each attack behavior to fail and requires successive successes of all the behaviors (Fig. 3(b))

- If one of the attack behaviors fails, an attacker executes the first behavior again.
- For example, in leveraging time-of-check and time-of-use race condition attacks (CAPEC-29), an attacker injects a command to modify a resource between the times an application checks and requests a resource. Accordingly, attack behaviors such as command injection, resource checking, and resource request should be successively executed.
- As a countermeasure, it is possible to defend against this type of attack by developing one of the defense behaviors.

(c) Type 3 - a cyber-attack that allows each attack behavior to fail and requires sequential successes of all the behaviors (Fig. 3(c))

- An attacker repeats a failed attack behavior so that the attack can progress to the next step.
- For example, in advanced persistent threat (APT) attacks, a variety of attacks are attempted simply to achieve specific step even though the step fails.
- Defense behaviors against all of the attack behaviors should be developed to defend against this type of a cyber-attack.

(3) **Consideration 3 - Processing time of cyber-attack behaviors**

In discrete event simulations, the processing time is a key element for scheduling input/output events. Figure 4 shows the concept of modeling processing time. In Fig. 4, t1, t2, and t3 denote the processing time for attack behavior 1, 2, and 3, respectively. In addition, tL and tN denote the last and next event times. The next event time tN is scheduled according to a result of each behavior. If attack behavior 3 fails, the tN is scheduled by adding the time of t1, t2, or t3 according to the next type of behavior that is scheduled.

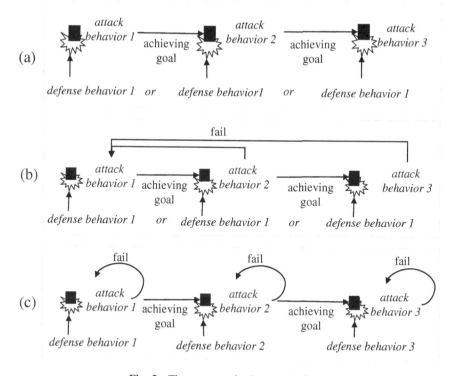

Fig. 3. Three types of cyber-attack flows

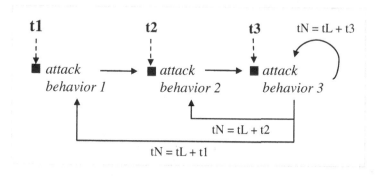

Fig. 4. Time scheduling considering the processing time of the next attack behavior

Considerations such as the source/destination, sequence, and processing time of the attack behaviors can also be used to defend against these behaviors. If a defense behavior has been executed between two attack behaviors, the simulation's flow and next event time will differ, depending to the result of the defense behavior and the processing time of the next behavior. Based on these considerations, the scenario model should be able to represent the following information.

- **source element(element-type)** – unique name of an element that executes attack or defense behaviors (the types of elements of cyberspace)
- **attack/defense behavior** – the types of attack or defense behaviors executed by a source element; a behavior represents a state of a discrete event simulation model
- **destination element(element-type)** – unique name of an element targeted from an attack or defense behavior (the types of elements of cyberspace)
- **processing time** – the time for an attack or defense behavior that is executed by a source element
- **return state** – the next behavior that is scheduled to execute after the failure of attack or defense behavior
- **output** – transmitted data from a source element to a destination element

We will list above information in sequence for the representation of the scenario model as follows:

<source element(element-type), attack/defense behavior, destination element(element-type), processing time, return state, output>

4   Modeling of a Scenario Model

We develop example scenario models of cyber-attacks focusing on the key behaviors described in CAPEC. The models can, however, be designed differently, according to the modelers' decisions regarding the implementation level of attacks.

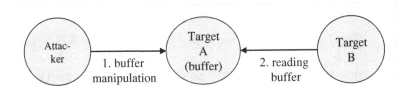

Fig. 5. A buffer attack process (CAPEC-123)

Figure 5 shows a buffer attack process (CAPEC-123).

The following is an example scenario developed by listing derived information in Sect. 3.

Step 1. <Attacker(process), manipulate, buffer, 10, manipulate, none>

Step 2. <Target(process), read, buffer, 5, read, none>

We can model this scenario into the scenario model based on a discrete event simulation model as shown in Fig. 6. In the figure, s_0 means an initial state.

Regarding state variables that require that we observe the changes of the model, we can elicit both default attributes of a process (element-type) and user attributes elicited by modeler. For example, a process has several default attributes, such as PID (process ID), name, creation time, parent PID, child PID, and so on. As user attributes, we can elicit security statuses, such as whether the process manipulates a target buffer with malicious intent, whether the process has vulnerabilities, and whether the process has already been damaged.

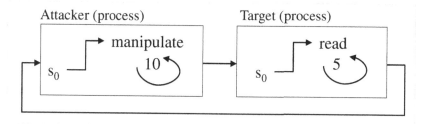

Fig. 6. A structure and state diagram of a scenario model of a buffer attack

For the second example, Fig. 7 shows the attack process of a man-in-the-middle attack (CAPEC-94).

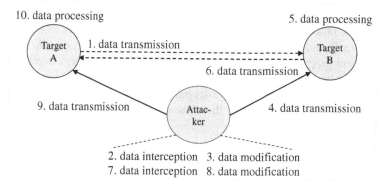

Fig. 7. The process of a man-in-the-middle attack (CAPEC-94)

We develop the following example scenario for a man-in-the-middle attack:

Step 1. <Target A(System), transmit, Target B, 10, transmit, data>
Step 2. <Attacker(System), intercept, data, 20, intercept, none>
Step 3. <Attacker(System), modify, data, 15, modify, none>
Step 4. <Attacker(System), transmit, Target B, 10, transmit, data>
Step 5. <Target B(System), process, data, 15, process, none>
Step 6. <Target B(System), transmit, Target A, 10, transmit, data>
Step 7. <Attacker(System), intercept, data, 20, intercept, none>
Step 8. <Attacker(System), modify, data, 15, modify, none>
Step 9. <Attacker(System), transmit, Target A, 10, transmit, data>
Step 10. <Target A(System), process, data, 15, process, none>

Figure 8 shows a developed scenario model using above scenarios. To observe changes in Target A, Target B, and Attacker, the default attributes of a system (element-type), such as host name, IP address, MAC address, memory, CPU, and OS, and the user attributes regarding vulnerabilities and patching can be set.

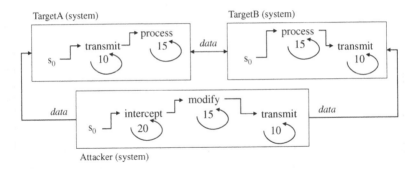

Fig. 8. A structure and state diagrams of a scenario model of a man-in-the-middle attack

5   Case Study

We describe a process for modeling a scenario model of a worm attack and transforming it into a simulation model according to the simulation purpose. With regard to a general worm propagation, a host performs three functions: worm execution, scanning the other hosts, and worm transmission. Listed below are scenarios developed on the basis of the proposed method. All hosts have the same process, but their targets are different. '#' denotes any host ID in the network. We develop the scenario model as shown in Fig. 9.

Step 1. <Host#(System), execute, worm, 5, execute, none>
Step 2. <Host#(System), scan, Host#, 20, scan, none>
Step 3. <Host#(System), transmit, Host#, 10, transmit, worm>

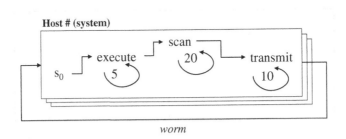

Fig. 9. Structure and state diagram of hosts in a worm simulation

We develop a scenario that observes the state of each host. This scenario can be useful to simulate numerous previous studies, because they usually observe the state of a host to find infected host. We can create this simulation model considering a state relation between the scenario model and the simulation model, as shown in Table 1.

Table 1. Relation between a scenario model and a simulation model

Types of model	States		
Scenario model	execute	scan	transmit
Simulation model	vulnerable	infected	

Figure 10(a) shows the states of the scenario model during simulation. There are 100 hosts in the network, and we set the rate of invulnerable hosts from 20 to 30 percent. In addition, the initial state of each host is set to 'normal.' Over time, the number of behaviors classified as 'normal' decreases while those classified as 'scan' and 'transmit' increase as a result of the worm propagation. In the figure, the number of 'scan' behaviors is greater than that of 'transmit' because infected hosts are repeatedly scanning until they discover a vulnerable host. The number of 'execute' is very low because 'execute' is performed only once when a vulnerable host is infected with worms. Figure 10(b) compares the scenario model with the simulation model. In the figure, the number of infected hosts increases with the 'scan' behaviors because all vulnerable hosts can be discovered and infected by scanning until the simulation ends.

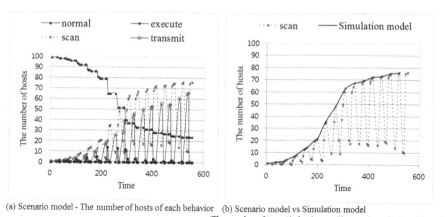

(a) Scenario model - The number of hosts of each behavior   (b) Scenario model vs Simulation model
(The number of 'scan' behaviors vs The number of infected hosts)

Fig. 10. Simulation results of a scenario model and a simulation model

6 Conclusion

In order to simulate a variety of problems of cyber-security domain, we have developed a method for eliciting new attacks that can be modeled into various simulation models according to modelers' purposes or security issues. By considering characteristics of cyber-attack flows and requirements of a discrete event simulation model, we have elicited components of a scenario model, such as elements of source and destination, behaviors of cyber-attacks and defenses, processing time, return state and output. In order to extract possible behavior primitives, we have analyzed CAPEC that defines

400 types of attacks. By sequencing the extracted primitives, we can make flexible scenarios of cyber-attacks and defenses. We have developed scenario models of a buffer attack and a man-in-the-middle attack through CAPEC analysis in order to describe a process of our scenario modeling. As a case study, we have developed a scenario model of a worm attack, and then modeled a simulation model considering a specific simulation purpose of the worm simulation. We then have simulated and analyzed the model to verify the model's design and execution. Through the simulation, we can see that the developed worm scenario model can be executed as a primitive model of the worm simulation. In addition, it can be useful for developing various simulation models according to security purposes.

As future work, we need to continuously update the primitives from CAPEC, because new behaviors of cyber-attacks and defenses are being developed. In addition, we will develop building blocks of cyber-security simulations using our scenario model so that modelers enable to simulate various cyber-attacks by making use of pre-developed building blocks. This study is expected to provide an environment for researching countermeasures, which include security techniques and policies, in a secure, inexpensive, and convenient manner by simulating them in the virtual environment.

Acknowledgement. This research was supported by Basic Science Research Program through the National Research Foundation of Korea (NRF) funded by the Ministry of Education (NRF-2013R1A1A2062654).

Appendix. Extraction of Behaviors of Cyber-attacks and Defenses through CAPEC Analysis (Examples)

ID	Category : Data leakage attacks (ID: 118) cyber-attack behaviors	defense behaviors
31	sniff / steal / guess / decode / analyze / modify / replace	generate / validate
157	monitor / read	obfuscate / hide / customize
259	load / setup / capture	encrypt / detect
463	decrypt / produce	verify

ID	Category : Resource Depletion (ID: 119) cyber-attack behaviors	defense behaviors
82	create / send	check
99	execute / consume / determine	validate
147	record / explore / analyze / send	monitor / disable

ID	Category : Injection (ID: 152) cyber-attack behaviors	defense behaviors
6	record / create / detect / inject	audit / limit
7	research / determine / add / inject / debug / extract / exploit	filter / validate
23	inject	scan / execute / validate
41	create / inject / send	monitor / validate / filter
66	survey / inject / add	search / alert / validate
91	explore / identify / upload / inject / record	monitor / encode / validate
101	send / gain / execute / find / view / execute	encode / cert / monitor / create
193	load / execute / use / record / explore / analyze / inject / develop	validate

(Continued)

Category : Abuse of Functionality (ID: 210)		
ID	cyber-attack behaviors	defense behaviors
12	authenticate / change	encrypt
37	extract / monitor / remove / identify / decode	-
141	intercept / modify / send / modify	send / listen / disable
169	footprint / probe / explore / identify / gather	shut down / change / encrypt
213	access / explore	execute /validate / configure
215	send / modify	obfuscate / hide / cusomize
Category : Probabilistic Techniques (ID: 223)		
ID	cyber-attack behaviors	defense behaviors
39	capture / examine / disassemble / decompile / modify / injection / modify / debug	generate / validate
49	enter / determine	update
61	create / load	detect / alert / record / disconnect / regenerate
62	debug / analyze / sniff / create / send / click	check / authenticate
102	sniff / monitor / capture / insert	modify / detect
467	create / induce / send / tick / click	logout
Category : Exploitation of Privilege/Trust (ID: 232)		
ID	cyber-attack behaviors	defense behaviors
1	capture / record / execute / access / survey	deny
69	find / inject / execute / write	patch / scan / check / monitor / validate
237	analyze / explore / call	obfuscate / update

References

1. Cohen, F.: Simulating cyber attacks, defences, and consequences. Comput. Secur. **18**(6), 479–518 (1999)
2. Kelton, W.D., Law, A.M.: Simulation Modeling and Analysis, 3rd edn. McGraw Hill, Boston (2000)
3. Guizani, M., et al.: Network Modeling and Simulation: A Practical Perspective. Wiley. com (2010)
4. Nicol, D.M.: Modeling and simulation in security evaluation. IEEE Secur. Priv. **3**(5), 71–74 (2005)
5. Saunders, J.H.: The Case for Modeling and Simulation of Information Security. Computer Security Institute Conference (2001). http://www.johnsaunders.com/papers/securitysimulation. htm. Accessed 5 June 2014
6. MITRE. Common Attack Pattern Enumeration and Classification. http://capec.mitre.org. Accessed 5 June 2014
7. Zeigler, B.P., Sarjoughian, H.: Introduction to DEVS modeling & simulation with JAVA™: Developing component-based simulation models. Arizona State University (2003)
8. Schneier, B.: Attack trees. Dr. Dobb's J. **24**(12), 21–29 (1999)
9. Bistarelli, S., Fioravanti, F., Peretti, P.: Defense trees for economic evaluation of security investments. In: The First International Conference on Availability, Reliability and Security, ARES 2006. IEEE (2006)
10. Icove, D., Seger, K., VonStorch, W.: Computer Crime: A Crimefighter's Handbook. O'Reilly & Associates, Sebastopol (1995)

11. Cohen, F.B.: Protection and Security on the Information Superhighway. Wiley, New York (1995)
12. Russell, D., Gangemi, G.T.: Computer Security Basics. O'Reilly, Sebastopol (1991)
13. Neumann, P.G., Parker, D.B.: A summary of computer misuse techniques. In: Proceedings of the 12th National Computer Security Conference (1989)
14. Zeigler, B.P., Praehofer, H., Kim, T.G.: Theory of Modeling and Simulation, 2nd edn. Academic Press, San Diego (2000)
15. Kuhl, M.E., et al.: Cyber attack modeling and simulation for network security analysis. In: Proceedings of the 39th Conference on Winter Simulation: 40 years! The best is yet to come. IEEE Press (2007)
16. Du, P., Nakao, A.: OverCourt: DDoS mitigation through credit-based traffic segregation and path migration. Comput. Commun. **33**(18), 2164–2175 (2010)
17. Ingalls, R.G.: Introduction to simulation. In: Proceedings of the 40th Conference on Winter Simulation. Winter Simulation Conference (2008)
18. Whitley, J.N., et al.: Attribution of attack trees. Comput. Electr. Eng. **37**(4), 624–628 (2011)

Advanced Security Assessment for Control Effectiveness

Youngin You$^{(\boxtimes)}$, Sangkyo Oh, and Kyungho Lee

Center for Information Security Technologies (CIST),
Korea University, Seoul, Korea
{crenius,darkapple,kevinlee}@korea.ac.kr

Abstract. Initially, the field only dealt with sensitive security information. However, as operations on cyber space increases, the need for security in internet also increased. Thus, areas that requires security assessment also increased. But, to date, a security evaluation for each area is performed partially. Since security assessment does not reflect the characteristics of each area, the correct security level is difficult to determine. Therefore, new security indicator is required for the effective and efficient management. In this paper, we provide an advanced security assessment using edited indicators and common indicators.

Keywords: ISMS · Security assessment · Security index

1 Introduction

Most of the organization's business today are performed online. Therefore, to prevent security incidents worldwide, organizations and companies introduced information security management system [6]. This management process is divided into several parts. Among them, the security assessment is the most important part of the management process. In general, security assessment conducted is based on the control items in ISO 27000 series and NIST SP 800 series. These items were used after tuning the control items. Using the above items, organization can check whether items are performed or not. It is common method in Identifying security control status by applying control items [1]. However, the subject of a security assessment is very diverse organization such as general industry or critical infrastructure etc [4]. The Arithmetic formula mentioned above does not reflect the characteristics of each field. Thus, this study suggests a security evaluation method that reflects the characteristics of each following industries (Fig. 1).

This management consists of common indicators and specific indicators. Common indicator mentioned above is Arithmetic method. The purpose of this approach is to grasp the overall security status of organizations. Edited indicators are to reflect the characteristics of the institution such as organizational size, top management support, and industry type [5]. For example smaller organizations suffer from a lack of human and financial resources. The reason why the smaller organizations often implement their information security in an optimal way is due to insufficient managerial and technical skills or the lack of funds to acquire such skills. This fact can lead smaller

© Springer International Publishing Switzerland 2015
K.-H. Rhee and J.H. Yi (Eds.): WISA 2014, LNCS 8909, pp. 383–393, 2015.
DOI: 10.1007/978-3-319-15087-1_30

Fig. 1. Advanced security assessment method

organizations to attaining fewer benefits compared to larger organizations. This is why indicator based on the model is needed [6].

It is based on the relevant laws or regulations of each field and the characteristics of each field. Advanced security index and direction of security management is derived using these two indicators.

This paper introduces an advanced security assessment methodology and conduct the simulation to target the infrastructure of South Korea to show the effectiveness.

2   Assessment Methods

This section will introduce Arithmetic, C.B.I[1] and Weighted Arithmetic formula. These formula are used for security assessment. Each assessment formula is used for different purpose. This table shows measured value and purpose (Table 1).

Table 1. Goal of each assessment

Category	Technique	Measurement	Goal
Commonly used	Arithmetic formula	Average value using equal weighting factor	Security control fulfillment
Newly Suggested	C.B.I	Value using weighting mode according to classification, such as M (Mandatory), SR (Strongly Recommended), R (Recommended)	Observance of the relevant regulations
	Weighted Arithmetic formula	Value using weighting mode according to correlation coefficient of domain	Properties of each field

Explaining the method for measuring must proceeded before describing a specific formula. Basically, assessment is performed with a checklist. Checklist is composed of four choices composed of Yes, N/A[2], No and Partial. Each response shows different level of security and graded with score. Details are shown in the table below [1, 3] (Fig. 2 and Table 2).

---

[1] C.B.I: Classification by Business Impact.

[2] N/A: Not Applicable.

Table 2. Grade score of responses

Answer	Score	Description
Yes	1	Fulfill with reference and documents
N/A	-	Unrelated
No	0	No reference or document, Non-compliance
Partial	0.5	Partial reference or document, Incomplete compliance

Domain	Contents
D.8	Maintenance
D.8.2	Remote maintenance
Description of controls	◑In order to restore service and control system operations needed in the event of an emergency or crisis, there is a need for access to diagnostic services and remote maintenance immediately. If you do not have a security level for accessing diagnostic services and remote maintenance, it is necessary to adopt a suitable alternative control.

Details Code	Questions	Answer area						
		Control status(√)				Answer basis	Evidence	Location of evidence
		Yes	N/A	No	Partial			
D.8.2.6	Remote operation is complete, to terminate the network connection with the sessions of all, it has been confirmed this?	√					Guidelines for security management of power generation control system	
		Cycle						
		Once a year						
		Opinion						

Fig. 2. Example of work sheet

The evaluation sheet below, answers to each items classified as Yes, No, Partial and N/A.

2.1 Arithmetic Formula for Understanding Overall Security Control Fulfillment

This formula use average of the response result to got a value. The values are calculated by dividing sum of response result score by the number of controls. At this moment, the response result 'N/A' is excepted. The formula of the arithmetic is shown as below.

$$\text{Arithmetic Score} = \frac{The\ sum\ of\ all\ the\ scores\ of\ controls(exceptN/A)}{The\ number\ of\ all\ items - The\ number\ answered\ N/A}$$

This value range is from 0 to 1. It uses equal weighting factor for all of the controls. This value is used for understanding current state of security control fulfillment.

2.2   Classification by Business Impact for Observance of the Relevant Regulation

This formula is used for classification of controls. The importance of each domain is applied considering the related law or the environment of the targeted facility. This process is done in order to assess the each domain in depth.

At first, all of the controls are classified by level of importance such as M(Mandatory), SR(Strongly Recommended), and R(Recommended). The control that can lead to critical problem when violated is categorized as mandatory item. The control that effect organization but unrelated with the law is categorized as strongly recommended items. Controls that have insignificant impact to organization is categorized as recommended items.

If the Domain includes non-fulfilling mandatory items, it will receive a zero score. Then if the domain is checked 'No' or 'Partial' on mandatory items, it will get a score of zero.

$$M(Mandatory) = \frac{The\ sum\ of\ scores\ of\ Mandatory items}{The\ number\ of\ all\ Mandatory\ items}$$

$$(\text{If existing answer 'No' or Partial, then } M = 0)$$

$$SR(Strongly\ Recommended) = \frac{The\ sum\ of\ scores\ of\ Strongly\ Recommened\ items}{The\ number\ of\ all\ Strongly\ Recommended\ items}$$

$$R(Recommended) = \frac{The\ sum\ of\ scores\ of\ Recommended}{The\ number\ of\ all\ Recomended\ items}$$

You are able to calculate the total score of each domains using M, SR and R score. Weighting is assigned by the importance of the item. The weight value is applied on three criteria. In the equation, the M corresponds to c, SR corresponds to a and R corresponds to b. Variable a, b, c is in decimal point which sums to 1. The formula is as in the following.

$$\text{Domain Score} = M \cdot (a \cdot SR + b \cdot R + c)$$

$$(a + b + c = 1)$$

For example, if Mandatory is 0.7, SR is 0.2 and R is 0.1, the domain score calculation formula.

$$\text{Domain Score} = M \cdot [(0.2) \cdot SR + (0.1) \cdot R + (0.7)]$$

$$(a + b + c = 1)$$

The total score is calculated by average of all of the domain score.

$$M/SR/R\ Score = \frac{The\ Sum\ of\ scores\ of\ domains}{The\ number\ of\ all\ domain}$$

This method is able to notify the observance of the relevant regulations.

2.3   Weighted Arithmetic Formula Considering Each Field's Characteristics

Facilities damage rate can vary from less critical to critical according to the fulfillment of each controlled domain. In this method, technique applies influential aspect to each domain. This allows formula to apply high points to a domain with high influence that leads to higher contribution. For the lower influential domain, it applies lower point in the influential rate that lead to lower contribution. Through this technique, facilities can differentiate the domains in the importance rate so that they can reflect important domain and apply it in their security assessment.

This formula calculates the score similar to Arithmetic. If you check 'Yes' on the choice, you will receive 1 point, 0 point for 'No', 0.5 point for 'Partial' and 'N/A' is excepted. Domain score is sum of the choices. Then, we can figure out correlation coefficient of domain (Recommend the use of SPSS). Correlation coefficient means the effect of the domain on the whole domain. This value range is from 0 to 1. We can get a weight value from correlation coefficient.

$$\text{Weighted Domain Score}_i = \frac{Coefficient\ of\ correlation_i}{\sum Coefficient\ of\ correlation} \times \text{Domain Score}_i$$

Weighted arithmetic score is generated by weighted domain.

$$\text{Weighted Arithmetic Score} = \sum Weighted\,Domain\,Score_i$$

2.4   Decision Making Process and Method to Derive Security Index

All of the formula above are used in decision-making of efficient security management. The process of deriving the direction of security management is as follow (Fig. 3).

Fig. 3. Decision-making process

First, the security control state is measured. Next, calculate the Arithmetic, Weighted Arithmetic, C.B.I values respectively. Then, we will be able to figure out Security Index using each formula.

The Security Index formula is shown below.

$$\text{Security Index} = (a \cdot \text{Arithmetic}) \times (b \cdot \text{Weighted Arithmetic}) \times (c \cdot \text{C.B.I})$$
$$(0 \leq \text{Security Index} \leq 1, \ a + b + c = 1)$$

The total sum of weight is 1, and it can be adjusted according to the purpose. Then results are compared calculated values. Then, characteristic of the field is derived in according to each formula. Through integrating all derived characteristics, it is able to present directions for security investment.

3 Simulation

In this study, a simulation was conducted to target the infrastructure of South Korea. The assessment targeted the 15 thermal power generation facilities.

Control items are based on the security guidelines of ICS Appendix of NIST SP800-53 for evaluation that reflects the characteristics of the ICS information system. It consists of 186 items and 17 domains. [2, 4] Each domain type, derive ratio of Mandatory, Strongly Recommended, Recommended items and calculates weight of each domain. The calculated values of each domain are as follows. Classification of M/SR/R refers to the criteria of the National Intelligence Service, the energy-related laws and regulations of South Korea (Table 3).

Table 3. Domains weight and catagorization with M/SR/R

	M	SR	R	Weight
D.1 Access Control	20	19	8	0.664
D.2 Audit and Accountability	3	9	3	0.610
D.3 Security Assessment and Authorization	2	7	1	0.653
D.4 Configuration Management	3	2	0	0.464
D.5 Contingency Planning	6	3	0	0.664
D.6 Identification and Authentication	4	2	0	0.545
D.7 Incident Response	3	3	0	0.579
D.8 Maintenance	4	4	1	0.614
D.9 Media Protection	7	3	1	0.633
D.10 Physical and Environmental Protection	9	5	1	0.485
D.11 Planning	0	3	0	0.621
D.12 Personal Security	2	0	0	0.599
D.13 Risk Assessment	1	6	0	0.627
D.14 System and Services Acquisition	3	0	1	0.666
D.15 System and Communications Protection	8	4	9	0.451
D.16 System and Information Integrity	3	4	4	0.660
D.17 Awareness and Training	1	1	3	0.501

By calculating each score of the Weighted Arithmetic and C.B.I based on the table above, it can be compared with the Arithmetic.

3.1   Comparison Between the Arithmetic and C.B.I

Based on the calculated score, we can compare C.B.I and Arithmetic. Difference between the C.B.I score and Arithmetic score shows the following data.

- Arithmetic > C.B.I: Security control is conducted properly as a whole. However, this state did not conduct the Mandatory item.
- Arithmetic < C.B.I: Fulfillment of Mandatory and Strongly Recommended in good condition (Fig. 4).

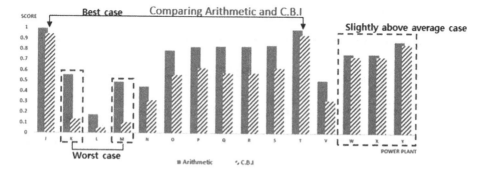

Fig. 4. Comparison graph of Arithmetic and C.B.I

The result is an overall score drop. This means that there is no power plant that conducts all Mandatory items. The large difference in the score indicates that fulfillment of Mandatory item is unsatisfactory.

In the case of 'K' power plant, the difference is shows the largest number of 0 point domain. This means that, unlike shown in the Arithmetic score, fulfillment ratio of Mandatory item is very low. Therefore, it is possible to determine that 'K' power plant have a big threat in practice. Overall trend in the score difference is as follow (Table 4).

Table 4. Trend of difference between scores by Mandatory items

Difference between scores	Facility	Amount of domains that received 0 point
High(0.42)	'K' power plant	10
Low(0.02)	'W' power plant	3
Average amount domains that received 0 point		5.23

Overall, fulfilment of the Mandatory item is incomplete state in five or more domains. Domain of the top four has high frequency of 0 points is as follow (Table 5).

Table 5. Domain of the top four has high frequency of 0 points

Domain	Domain name	Not Fulfil Mandatory detailed item
D.1	Access Control	Access control policies and procedures
		Separation of Duties
		Least Privilege
		Unsuccessful Login Attempts
		Remote Access
		Wireless Access
		Access Control for Mobile Devices
D.6	Identification and Authentication	Identification and Authentication (Organizational Users)
		Device Identification and Authentication
		Identifier Management
		Cryptographic Module Authentication
D.10	Physical and Environmental Protection	Physical Access Control
		Fire Protection
		Prevent flooding
D.15	System and Communications Protection	Application Partitioning
		Transmission Integrity
		Transmission Confidentiality
		Cryptographic Key Establishment and Management
		Collaborative Computing Devices

With reference to the above items in order to prevent the occurrence of the deadly threat for each facility, security investment priority must be performed.

3.2   Comparison Between the Arithmetic and Weighted Arithmetic

Based on the calculated score, this paper compared Weighted Arithmetic and Arithmetic. This means that difference between the Weighted Arithmetic score and Arithmetic score is as follows.

- Arithmetic > Weighted Arithmetic: Security control is conducted properly as a whole. But, it is a state in which the important item of the corresponding field were not conducted.
- Arithmetic < Weighted Arithmetic: Fulfillment of the important item of the corresponding field in good condition.

Difference between calculate score of Arithmetic and Weighted Arithmetic is as follow (Fig. 5).

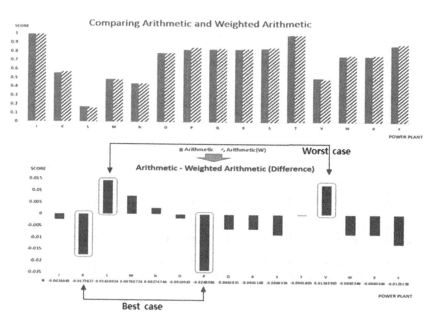

Fig. 5. Comparison graph of Arithmetic and Weighted Arithmetic

'K' and 'P' is the power plant with largest score rise. This indicates that 'P' and 'K' power plant is investing their fund in the security area affectively according to the characteristics of the thermal power generation sector. On the other hand, in 'L' and 'V' power plant, it showed the large drop in the score. 'V' and 'L' power plant indicate that it does not reflect well the characteristics of thermal field. The above facilities need security investment as following direction. Weighted Arithmetic reflects the domain influence to other domains. This means does not mean that there is no increase in a simple score rise. When investment is applies at the domain of high specific area, there is a synergistic effect of the security control proceeds substantially in other domains.

Therefore, a high degree of contribution to an increase in security overall effect security investment is showed. It is necessary to concentrate investment in domain of the top four.

- D.1 Access Control
- D.5 Contingency Planning

– D.14 System and Services Acquisition
– D.16 System and Information Integrity.

3.3   Summary of Simulation

Integrating above results is possible to decision-making on security investments. 'L' power plant for example, need to take complementary measures from M/SR/R and Weighted Arithmetic standpoint. First, if the domain is showed on both formula, it is the first to be considered. Then, it is possible by calculating the Weight of Domains and Mandatory ratio of C.B.I, to determine the priority of investment as follows.

1. D.1 Access Control
2. D.10 Physical and Environmental Protection
3. D.5 Contingency Planning
4. D.15 System and Communications Protection
5. D.6 Identification and Authentication
6. D.14 System and Services Acquisition
7. D.16 System and Information Integrity.

This accuracy and depth is less when compared with Risk Analysis. However, this will take least cost, simplified and assessed in rapid rate when applied to all institutions. Thus, it is possible to effectively invest in security.

4   Process of Using Advanced Security Assessment

A.S.A can be used in following process (Fig. 6).

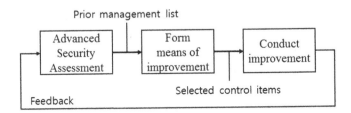

Fig. 6. Process of using Advanced Security Assessment

Prior management list is deducted after performing Advanced Security Assessment through Arithmetic, C.B.I and Weighted Arithmetic. With the result of Advanced Security Assessment, organization will make the means to improve the security status of the domain based on the priority. Among the control items that is positioned in high priority domain, organization will consider their security investment capacity to select the control item. Then, improvement will be conducted based on the selected control item. After the improvement, organization will once again perform Advanced Security Assessment. In the process of performing Advanced Security Assessment, C.B.I will be edited and weight is recalculated. This paper suggest that effective and efficient security management is possible when Advanced Security Assessment is applied in the cycle.

5 Conclusion

As simulated above, each formula is able to support the decision making for security measure. We must deal with mandatory item first in the C.B.I. If we do not take a security measure of mandatory item, the facility will face critical problem. After that, we take a measure of strongly recommended item and recommended item in sequence. Also, we are able to cut low weighted domain out the priority of measurement and can deal with high weighted domain first. If the high weighted domain is improved, we will be able to take the measure of the low weighted domain. This way, facilities will improve the effect of security investment.

Although the risk analysis is precise, in reality, it is almost impossible to analyze risk of all the organizations periodically. However, utilizing this formula makes it possible to make assessment per year or half-year. And through assessment, it is also possible to set directions of security management.

Advanced security assessment is able to compensate the weakness of existing fragmentary security assessment. And it is able to present the whole view of security status based on industrial character.

Furthermore, this assessment not only applicable to thermal power station but also whole of energy industry and critical infrastructure.

Acknowledgement. This research was supported by the MSIP(Ministry of Science, ICT and Future Planning), Korea, under the ITRC(Information Technology Research Center) support program (NIPA-2014-H0301-14-1004) supervised by the NIPA(National IT Industry Promotion Agency).

References

1. International Organization for Standardization, ISO 27001 (2013)
2. National Institute of Standards and Technology, NIST Special Publication 800-53 (2009)
3. National Institute of Standards and Technology, NIST Special Publication 800-55 (2007)
4. Weiss, J.: Industrial control system (ICS) cyber security for water and wastewater systems. In: Clark, R.M., Hakim, S. (eds.) Securing Water and Wastewater Systems. Protecting Critical Infrastructure, vol. 2, pp. 87–105. Springer, New York (2014)
5. Chang, S.E., Ho, C.B.: Organizational factors to the effectiveness of implementing information security management. Ind. Manage. Data Syst. **106**(3), 345–361 (2006)
6. Kankanhalli, A., et al.: An integrative study of information systems security effectiveness. Int. J. Inf. Manage. **23**(2), 139–154 (2003)

Study on the Effectiveness of the Security Countermeasures Against Spear Phishing

Misun Song, JunSeok Seo, and Kyungho Lee[✉]

Center for Information Security Technologies, Korea University, Seoul, Korea
{misun1535,js_seo,kevinlee}@korea.ac.kr

Abstract. The presentation entitled ICS Spear Phishing, held at the 2013 edition of Digital Bond's Supervisory Control and Data Acquisition (SCADA) Security Scientific Symposium (S4) demonstrated that an attacker could employ a spear phishing attack to obtain rights to the accounts of the Industrial Control System (ICS) administrators or technicians. Motivated by this announcement, this paper analyzes the definition, principle, and problem of spear phishing, which is a social engineering attack. Furthermore, the need for countermeasures to the attack was presented. Attacks with spear phishing are gradually increased, but the existing system used in many organizations (e.g. e-mail filtering system) cannot follow the trend utilized by most attackers. Also, organizations have yet to establish adequate countermeasures, much less any standards for the countermeasures, to the problem of spear phishing. There is an urgent need to accomplish these objectives because the attack is gradually evolving. In summary, this paper advocates the awareness of the spear phishing threat and the implementation of countermeasures such as security education or simulation. In addition, it suggests on how to carry out the simulation effectively and how to quantify the gathered data.

Keywords: Phishing · Social engineering · Policy · Simulation

1 Introduction

Spear phishing, named after a fishing method, refers to an attack used to steal the personal information of a specific target such as a senior government executive or a military officer.

This new type of phishing (spear phishing) has appeared as the damage caused by preexisting phishing attacks increased. The defining characteristic of spear phishing is that the attack is targeted on specific purpose. So the attackers can obtain information in advance from posts on a user's blog or his LinkedIn and Facebook pages. Utilizing this data, an attacker can send an e-mail containing information relevant to the target, as well as a payload in the form of a file or URL link. If the target opens or downloads the file, or clicks on the URL, the attackers can obtain personal or financial information on the target.

Spear phishing poses a serious threat to corporations owing to the possibility of access to trade secrets and other classified information. This issue was underscored by the ICS Spear Phishing announcement made at the 2013 edition of Digital Bond's

© Springer International Publishing Switzerland 2015
K.-H. Rhee and J.H. Yi (Eds.): WISA 2014, LNCS 8909, pp. 394–404, 2015.
DOI: 10.1007/978-3-319-15087-1_31

SCADA Security Scientific Symposium (S4) [1, 13]. The data presented indicates that a quarter of the ICS asset owners who participated in the spear-phishing mail test clicked the link. If they did not have an updated security patch, the attacker could obtain access rights to their system. Moreover, according to the 2013 news report, spear phishing is a social issue owing to the estimated significant damage produced by the attack. Reference [2] Based on an analysis of the Phishing Activity Trends Report 2013 (Table 1, Fig. 1), the percentage of spear phishing attempts increased from 35 % to 73 %. In addition, the attacks initiated on sites that do not utilize port 80 have increased steadily (Table 1, Fig. 2) [3–6].

In spite of these problems, corporations have yet to establish any security policy or standard operating procedures.

Table 1. Phishing Activity Trends Report 2013 (1st quarter-3rd quarter), Phishing Activity Trends Report 2012 (4th quarter) [3–6].

(UNIT: %)	January	February	March	April	May	June
Contain some form of target name in URL	50.03	50.75	55.89	50.92	57.45	51.52
No hostname; only IP address	1.84	1.92	5.24	4.57	5.23	5.26
Percentage of sites not using port 80	1.36	2.33	0.64	0.38	0.45	0.80
	July	August	September	October	November	December
Contain some form of target name in URL	35.24	73.51	56.22	60.31	54.23	53.59
No hostname; only IP address	0.15	3.20	1.73	1.63	1.87	1.93
Percentage of sites not using port 80	0.04	0.32	0.86	0.30	0.24	1.04

2 Concepts, Model, and/or Methodology

Even though they are not legally obligated to do so, several organizations perform simulations to assess their defense against malicious mail. The common procedures employed during the simulations are as follows. First, all members of an organization receive a malicious mail without any advance notice. Second, if a member clicks on the malicious URL or downloads the attached file, a warning mail should be sent to him (or her). As illustrated in Fig. 3, in spear phishing, the target is decided in advance. Since the adversary researches the environment of the target beforehand, the probability of a successful attack is high. Furthermore, because it is difficult to capture the adversary, the best method for an e-mail account owner to avoid the attack is to be careful and with cautious.

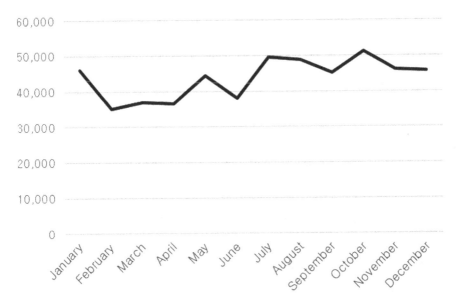

Fig. 1. Number of unique phishing websites detected [3–6]

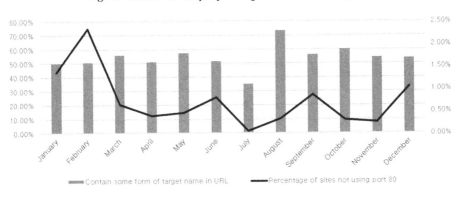

Contain some form of target name in URL   Percentage of sites not using port 80

Fig. 2. Target name in URL and percentage of sites not using port 80 [3–6]

Thus, it is crucial to introduce some policy with consideration of phishing attack's characteristic as described in Fig. 4 which shows policy making processes.

In this paper, the author tries to design simulation score system model after analyzing the principle of spear phishing attacks to overcome limitation of existing e-mail filtering system. After performing the simulation score system modeling, classify the people who read the e-mail, downloaded the file, and reported the e-mail. Based on the compiled data, utilize the statistics to provide additional security education and enhance security regulations [12].

In addition, privileged members such as the database server administrator should construct a virtual environment to minimize the damage to an organization's assets in the case of infection by malicious e-mails. Furthermore, monitoring technologies such as intrusion detection systems (IDS) and intrusion prevention systems (IPS) should be employed for the initial detection of these attacks [16].

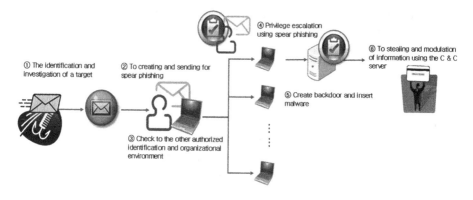

Steps of spear phishing attacks

Fig. 3. Spear Phishing attack scenarios [11]

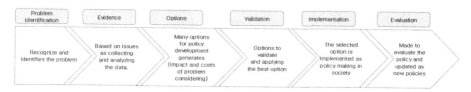

Fig. 4. Policy making processes

3 Experiments, Simulation, and/or Analysis

According to the analysis of Trend Micro, trusted and frequently utilized filename extensions such as .RTF, .XLS, and .ZIP are commonly employed in spear phishing attacks (Fig. 5). In addition, the attacker frequently changes the URL leading to the malicious sites [14, 15, 17].

Therefore, policies concerning the simulations, including their timing, target and period, must be mandated prior to any further attacks (Fig. 6).

The simulation timing is determined in advance to be once a quarter or at a specific date.

If a simulation is performed regularly, it should be conducted four times a year, and if the simulation score does not at least match a standard score, the frequent simulation is carried out. In this scenario, the simulation time is performed at a particular date such as a personnel change time, evaluation time, year-end adjustment period, the budget cleanup time, payday of month, and the date of previous occurrence of a distributed denial of service (DDoS) attack. If an e-mail simulation is to be performed at a specific date, it should be similar to the actual attack.

If a simulation is performed regularly, that process should be conducted at the corporate level. If, however, a simulation is performed frequently, the targets of evolution will be the issued team and the other team members will be randomly chosen.

For example, during a personnel change, the targets of evolution are the human resources team and the randomly chosen members belong to another team such as the administrating department, planning department, or sales department. The various members should occupy diverse roles.

The proportion of the chosen members should differ according to the size of the organization. If a corporation employs more than 1000 employees, the proportion of the other department members should be 10 % of all employees. In the case of 300 to 1,000 employees (mid-sized organization), the proportion of the other department members chosen should be 7 % of all employees. For a small to mid-sized organization of 20 to 300 employees, the proportion of other department members chosen should be 5 % of all employees. A small business, with fewer than 10 employees, should chose 3 % of all employees from the other department members. The proportion of the randomly chosen members should be based on the numbers given above, but can be adjusted within a 1 % margin.

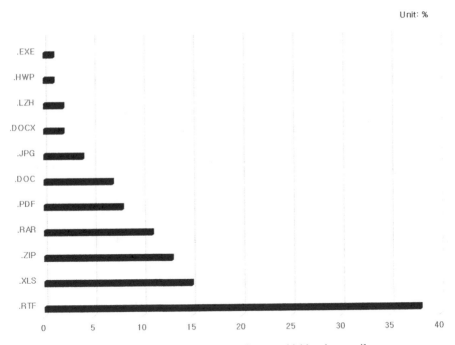

Fig. 5. Top attached file types of spear-phishing in e-mail

Finally, if the simulation is performed regularly, it should be implemented and completed within a week from having written the e-mails to having collected the contents. On Day 1, e-mails are written and sent to the members; then, the data from the simulation e-mails are collected from Day 2 until the morning of Day 5. On Day 5, the gathered data are compiled to obtain the statistics encompassing categories such as the number of people who downloaded the file, clicked the link, and ran the file in the e-mail. Once the statistics have been reported, the simulation ends.

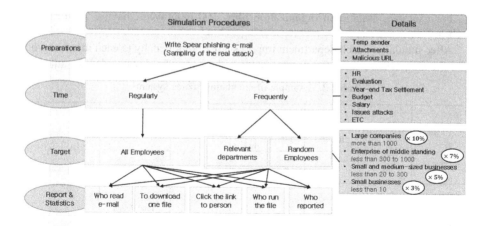

Fig. 6. Simulation procedures and standards

However, an organization performs different types of operations, and it may be the case that the simulation constitutes another considerable task. If the regular simulation is the main simulation, and the result of the statistical calculation does not exceed the standard infection rates, the frequent simulation can be omitted. On the other hand, if the infection rates are higher than the infection rates of other organizations, the frequent simulation can be performed. Thus, this scoring procedure, which could be mandated by policy, incentivizes or penalizes an organization based on its performance.

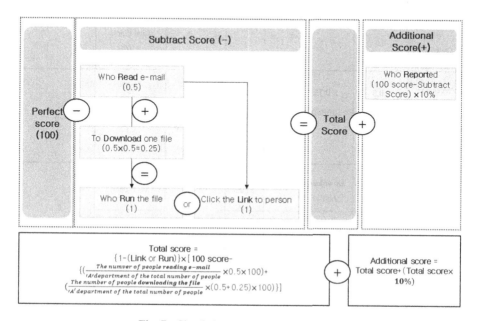

Fig. 7. Simulation score system modeling

For example, assume an organization hires 100 employees, having 20 members each in five departments.

After simulation, each department imposes a 0.5 point penalty to each member who read the mail, a 0.5 + 0.5 * 0.5 point penalty to the ones who downloaded the attached

Table 2. Example of simulation scores system

Actions	Read Mail	Download the file	Run file	Click on the link		Mail report	
Number of people	6	4	0	0	Total Scores	10	'A' department's end scores
Percentage of (Penalty/ Additional)	0.5	0.75	1	1		Total Points ×10%	
Percentage of (Penalty/ Additional) Scores	$\frac{6}{20} \times 0.5$ $\times 100\,Points$ $= 15$	$\frac{4}{20} \times 0.75$ $\times 100\,Points$ $= 15$	0×1 $= 0$	0×1 $= 0$	100-15- 15×(1- 0)=70	70×0.1=7	70+7=77
Actions	Read Mail	Download the file	Run file	Click on the link		Mail report	
Number of people	5	4	1	0	Total Scores	10	'B' department's End scores
Percentage of (Penalty/ Additional)	0.5	0.75	1	1		Total Points ×10%	
Percentage of (Penalty/ Additional) Scores	$\frac{5}{20} \times 0.5$ $\times 100\,Points$ $= 12.5$	$\frac{4}{20} \times 0.75$ $\times 100\,Points$ $= 15$	1×1 $= 1$	0×1 $= 0$	100-12.5- 15×(1-1)=0	0×0.1=0	0
Actions	Read Mail	Download the file	Run file	Click on the link		Mail report	
Number of people	4	2	0	0	Total Scores	14	'C' department's End scores
Percentage of (Penalty/ Additional)	0.5	0.75	1	1		Total Points ×10%	

(Continued)

Table 2. (*Continued*)

	Read Mail	Download the file	Run file	Click on the link	Total Scores	Mail report	End scores
Percentage of (Penalty/ Additional) Scores	$\frac{4}{20}\times0.5$ $\times100\,Points$ $=10$	$\frac{2}{20}\times0.75$ $\times100\,Points$ $=7.5$	0×1 $=0$	0×1 $=0$	$100-10-7.5\times(1-0)=82.5$	$82.5\times0.1=8.25$	$82.5+8.25=90.75$
Actions	Read Mail	Download the file	Run file	Click on the link	Total Scores	Mail report	'D' department's End scores
Number of people	10	4	0	1	Total Scores	5	'D' department's End scores
Percentage of (Penalty/ Additional)	0.5	0.75	1	1		Total Points ×10%	
Percentage of (Penalty/ Additional) Scores	$\frac{10}{20}\times0.5$ $\times100\,Points$ $=25$	$\frac{4}{20}\times0.75$ $\times100\,Points$ $=15$	0×1 $=0$	1×1 $=1$	$100-25-15\times(1-1)=0$	$0\times0.1=0$	0
Actions	Read Mail	Download the file	Run file	Click on the link		Mail report	'E' department's End scores
Number of people	2	3	0	0	Total Scores	15	'E' department's End scores
Percentage of (Penalty/ Additional)	0.5	0.75	1	1		Total Points ×10%	
Percentage of (Penalty/ Additional) Scores	$\frac{2}{20}\times0.5$ $\times100\,Points$ $=5$	$\frac{3}{20}\times0.75$ $\times100\,Points$ $=11.25$	0×1 $=0$	0×1 $=0$	$100-5-11.25\times(1-0)=83.75$	$83.75\times0.1=8.37$ 5	$83.75+8.375=92.125$
The average scores of five departments	$\frac{77+0+90.75+0+92.125}{5}=51.975$				The department of Average Below		'B', 'D'

file, a 1 point penalty to the ones who clicked the link, or who executed the attached file. The penalty points are then deducted from 100 (the standard number of points) and added to the product of the number that members who reported the spam mail and

Table 3. Example of the Simulation results belonging to the department with below average results

Actions	Read Mail	Download the file	Run file	Click on the link	Total Scores	Mail report	'B' department of end scores
Number of people	3	3	0	0		18	
Percentage of (Penalty/ Additional)	0.5	0.75	1	1		Total Scores ×10%	
Percentage of (Penalty/ Additional) Scores	$\frac{3}{20} \times 0.5$ $\times 100\ Scores$ $= 7.5$	$\frac{3}{20} \times 0.75$ $\times 100\ Scores$ $= 75$	0×1 $= 0$	0×1 $= 0$	100-7.5- 7.5×(1- 0)=85	85×0.1=8.5	85+8.5=93.5
Total number of people on the frequent simulation	the number of people of department 'B' + {(The number of people in entire organization the number of people of department 'B') × 0.05} = 20 + 4 = 24						

10 % (0.1) (Fig. 7, Table 2). The departments whose total number falls below the average should be instructed to simulate frequently until the score is above average (Table 3).

Table 2 describes an example of executing the regular test on an organization which consists of 5 departments (each department has 20 members). The average score of this organization is 51.975, and department B and D's scores are under the average. Therefore, these two departments should be the subject for occasion test.

Table 3 is an example of executing the occasion test for department B.

Before testing, testers have to consider the different objective scores for each organization, since the methods used in the spear phishing attack differ by the characteristic, size, security level of target organization. This objective score means the minimum level of security that organization should maintain.

First, the level of security for target organization is calculated by conducting simulation score system suggested in this paper. And then target organization decides the objective goal that needs to be maintained to counter phishing attacks.

With accumulating the data by conducting tests for several years, analyzing the level of security by departments would be easier. Additionally, an organization can determine the criteria for regular test to prevent spear phishing attacks if it is possible to get data from other organizations. The method suggested in this paper is quite useful when it comes to organizing budget on security and education to prevent future spear phishing attacks.

4 Conclusions

On the surface this paper contains information on the definition, attack principle, problem, and severity of spear phishing attack appear to be well-recognized. However, no security countermeasures to spear phishing have been established and users are left with the suggestion that they should read emails carefully.

The customary method is not sufficient to counteract the spear phishing attack. (E-mail filtering system etc.) Therefore, the author suggests utilizing existing e-mail filtering system used by organization as the effective countermeasure against the spear phishing attack. It took the form of a policy that mandated a simulation that mimicked the real-world environment as closely as possible. Detailed information pertaining to the spear phishing attack, such as collection procedures of data, timing, and target was prepared, and the damage caused by spear phishing was presented numerically. These figures were utilized to determine security awareness and educational status, as well as to provide a means to frequently update these measures.

The proposed simulation is the best policy to counteract the spear phishing attack, from large to small organizations. It is the authors' belief that mandatory enforcement of the proposed simulation will prove to be the most effective method of preventing the attack within the shortest time frame. Future work will involve considering how the proposed simulation procedure will be mandated by policy.

Acknowledgements. This work was supported by the IT R&D program of MSIP/KEIT [010041560, A development of anomaly detection and a multi-layered response technology to protect an intranet of a control system for the availability of pipeline facilities].

References

1. McDowell, M.: Avoiding Social Engineering and Phishing Attacks. United States Computer Emergency Readiness Team (2013). http://www.us-cert.gov/ncas/tips/st04-014. Accessed 06 February 2013
2. http://news.heraldcorp.com/view.php?ud=20131230000115&md=20140102004031_AT. Accessed 30 December 2013
3. Anti-Phishing Working Group (APWG) (2013) Phishing Activity Trends Report, 1st Quarter 2013. http://docs.apwg.org/reports/apwg_trends_report_q1_2013.pdf. Accessed 23 July 2013
4. Anti-Phishing Working Group (APWG) (2013) Phishing Activity Trends Report, 2nd Quarter 2013 (2013). http://docs.apwg.org/reports/apwg_trends_report_q2_2013.pdf. Accessed 5 November 2013
5. Anti-Phishing Working Group (APWG) (2013) Phishing Activity Trends Report, 3rd Quarter 2013 (2013). http://docs.apwg.org/reports/apwg_trends_report_q3_2013.pdf. Accessed 10 February 2013

6. Anti-Phishing Working Group (APWG) (2012) Phishing Activity Trends Report, 4th Quarter 2012 (2012). http://docs.apwg.org/reports/apwg_trends_report_Q4_2012.pdf. Accessed 24 April 2013

7. http://www.asiatoday.co.kr/news/view.asp?seq=907299. Accessed 11 December 2013

8. http://www.social-engineer.org/. Accessed 2014

9. https://efraudprevention.net/home/assets/img/spear_phishing.jpg. Accessed 2014

10. http://iconixtruemark.wordpress.com/2011/06/. Accessed 30 June 2011

11. Schackleford, D.: The APT is Dead. Long Live the SST! WordPress Blog (2011). http://daveshackleford.com/?m=201103. Accessed 21 March 2011

12. Choi, K.-H., Lee, D.H.: A study on strengthening security awareness programs based on an RFID access control system for inside information leakage prevention. Multimedia Tools Appl. (2013). Doi:10.1007/s11042-013-1727-y. http://link.springer.com/article/10.1007%2Fs11042-013-1727-y

13. http://www.digitalbond.com/blog/2013/01/30/s4x13-video-ics-spear-phishing/. Accessed 30 January 2013

14. http://www.plixer.com/blog/advanced-persistent-threats-2/internet-threat-defense-solution-part-2/. Accessed 16 February 2013

15. http://securityaffairs.co/wordpress/8390/malware/fireeye-advanced-threat-report-the-inadequacy-of-the-defense.html. Accessed 4 September 2012

16. Kim, Y.-H., Park, W.H.: A study on cyber threat prediction based on intrusion detection event for APT attack detection. Multimedia Tools Appl. (2012). Doi:10.1007/s11042-012-1275-x. http://link.springer.com/article/10.1007/s11042-012-1275-x

17. Townsend, K.: Spear-phishing is the single biggest threat to cyber security today. WordPress Blog (2012). http://kevtownsend.wordpress.com/2012/12/07/spear-phishing-is-the-single-biggest-threat-to-cyber-security-today/. Accessed 7 December 2014

Author Index